AGENTS OF MANIFEST DESTINY

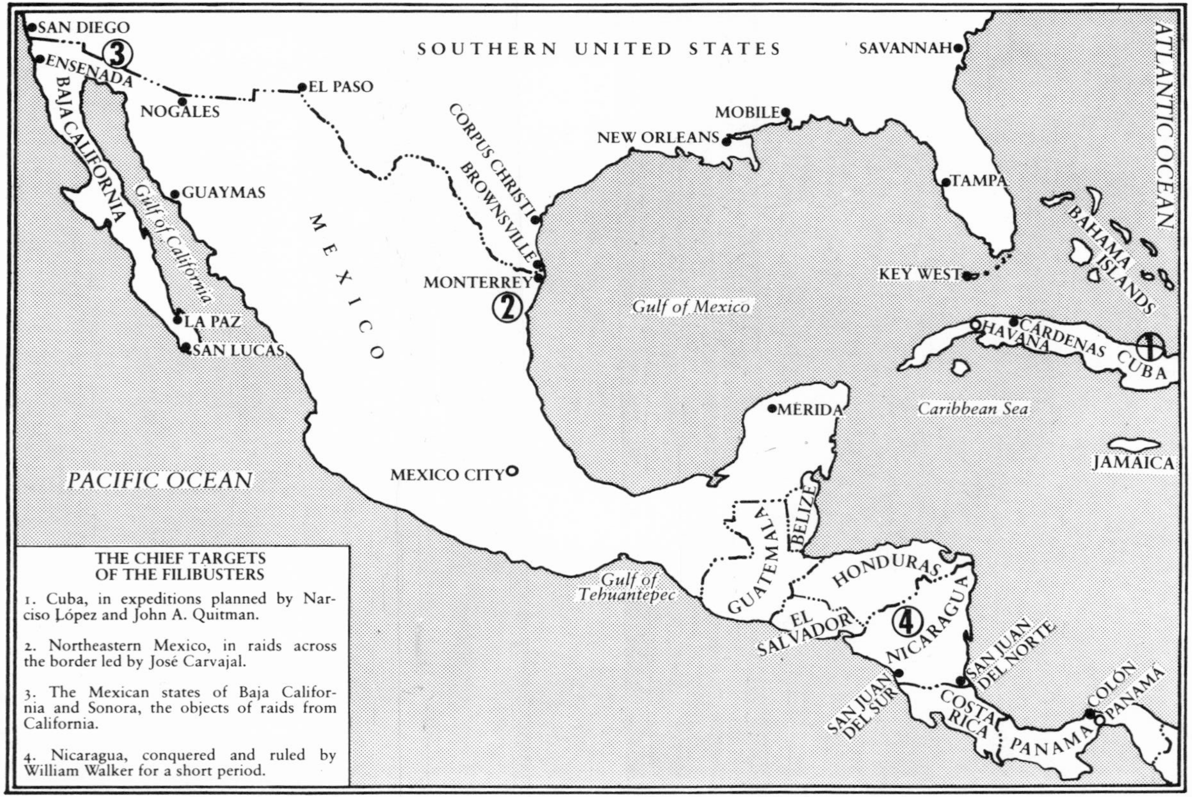

THE CHIEF TARGETS
OF THE FILIBUSTERS

1. Cuba, in expeditions planned by Narciso López and John A. Quitman.

2. Northeastern Mexico, in raids across the border led by José Carvajal.

3. The Mexican states of Baja California and Sonora, the objects of raids from California.

4. Nicaragua, conquered and ruled by William Walker for a short period.

Agents of Manifest Destiny

THE LIVES AND TIMES OF THE FILIBUSTERS

by
Charles H. Brown

THE UNIVERSITY OF NORTH CAROLINA PRESS
CHAPEL HILL

Manufactured in the United States of America
ISBN 0-8078-1361-3
Library of Congress Catalog Card Number 79-383

Library of Congress Cataloging in Publication Data

Brown, Charles Henry, 1910–
Agents of manifest destiny.

Bibliography: p.
Includes index.
1. United States—Territorial expansion. 2. Messianism, American. 3. Filibusters. 4. Militarism—United States—History. 5. United States—History—1849–1877. I. Title.
E415.7.B77 973 79-383
ISBN 0-8078-1361-3

Contents

Figures

Maps

Credits for Figures

Harper's New Monthly Magazine 6 (Dec. 1852), picture signed Lossing-Barritt, figs. 9, 10, 11

Harper's Weekly 1(Mar. 28, 1857), figs. 29, 30; 1 (May 16, 1857), figs. 25, 26; 1 (May 23, 1857), figs. 6, 15, 23

Leslie's Weekly 1 (Dec. 22, 1855), fig. 24; 4 (June 27, 1857), fig. 27; 4 (July 11, 1857), fig. 28

Library of Congress, figs. 1, 2, 3, 4, 5, 8, 12, 16, 17, 18, 31

New-York Historical Society, fig. 7

Maurice Soulié, *The Wolf Cub: The Great Adventure of Count Gaston Raousset-Boulbon in California and Sonora, 1850–1854* (Indianapolis: The Bobbs-Merrill Company, Inc., 1927), figs. 13, 14

E. G. Squire, *Nicaragua, Its People, Scenery, Monuments, Resources, Condition, and Proposed Canal* (New York, 1860), drawings by J. W. Orr, figs. 19, 20, 21, 22

U.S. Signal Corps photo no. 111-B-4407 (Brady Collection), National Archives, fig. 32

AGENTS OF MANIFEST DESTINY

PROLOGUE

The Prototypal Filibusters

In 1806 two attractive men, one a Venezuelan and cashiered officer in the army of Spain who for years had lived in exile, and one a discredited American politician boasting of martial honors won in the Revolution, led military expeditions from the United States against Spanish territory to establish independent states with themselves at the head. Both projects were planned by imaginative intriguers, both were daring in concept, both attracted enthusiastic adherents, and both ended disastrously.

These men—Francisco de Miranda and Aaron Burr—were the first filibusters, a term not to be applied, however, to such adventurers taking part in forays against friendly nations to foment revolution or capture the government until the 1850s. Miranda and Burr were the prototypes of expeditionists at midcentury, the heyday of filibusterism, when no year passed without raids being set afoot against Latin-American countries. Miranda was the foreigner, driven out of his own country and seeking to return with an army recruited in the United States to set himself up in power, and Burr, the unsuccessful and discontented native seeking glory and wealth in depredations upon neighboring states.

Miranda arrived in New York from London in November 1805 to obtain support for an expedition against Venezuela after having devoted two decades to that purpose in England and Europe.[1] Born at Caracas on March 28, 1750, he joined the royal military service and rose to the rank of lieutenant colonel. In Spain he was found guilty of engaging in contraband trade but escaped from prison and fled to the United States in 1783. Such was his charm that he made friends wherever he went. Bearing a grievance against Spain and proclaiming his love of liberty, he was listened to with rapt attention when he expressed the hope that the Spanish colonies could win their freedom as the new republic had won hers. He impressed his hearers—George Washington, Alexander Hamilton, Thomas Paine, John Adams—with his knowledge of the military aspects of the Revolution. Adams wrote that it was the general opinion the visitor "knew more of every campaign, siege, battle, and skirmish that had ever occurred in the whole war, than any officer of our army, or any statesman in our councils."

Late in 1784 Miranda sailed for Europe on a trip that was to last more than twenty years, during which he became involved in British plots to revolutionize the Spanish colonies, met the crowned heads, leading statesmen, and military chiefs of countries he visited on a grand tour, and took part in the French Revolution, his name appearing on the Arc de Triomphe as one of its heroes.

At one period, 1798–1800, he carried on while in London an intrigue with Rufus King, the U.S. minister, and Alexander Hamilton, then practicing law in New York, when it seemed possible that England and the United States would cooperate in revolutionizing Spanish America, the English supplying the naval force and the Americans the land force. The Federalists favored Britain after France and Spain developed close connections following the Treaty of Basel in 1795. When France interfered with American shipping and refused to receive the American minister, there were demands in the United States for war and Washington was recalled as commander in chief with Hamilton as second in command. Hamilton's military ambitions blazed up, and he wrote King that he hoped the Venezuelan enterprise would be mainly an American one. "The command in this case," he said, assuming that the elderly Washington would be only a figurehead, "would very naturally fall upon me, and I hope that I should disappoint no favorable anticipation."[2] The scheme collapsed after the Federalists lost the election of 1800 and the United States settled her differences with France when England shifted her diplomacy to win Spain to her side against Napoleon.

Miranda, now convinced that he would receive no support in London, turned to the United States. Shortly after reaching

New York, he sought the help of King, who explained that an expedition could not be set afoot without the countenance of the government. On King's advice, Miranda went to Washington and presented his ideas to President Jefferson and Secretary of State Madison. They, if not willing to help him, seemed at least to be sympathetic to his aim. On Miranda's return to New York he hinted that the government secretly supported his expedition and he was able to persuade 200 adventurers to sail with him in a small trading vessel, the *Leander*, on February 2, 1806.

At Santo Domingo Miranda added a few more men and two schooners to his force. He expected Venezuelans to spring to arms in his support when, after thirty-five years' absence, he returned to his native land and sounded the tocsin for revolution. Toward the last of April, approaching the coast near Porto Cabello, he was driven off by Spanish warships and the schooners were captured. Miranda fled to Barbados, where he obtained aid from Admiral Alexander Cochrane, commander of the British West Indian station, for another attempt. On August 2, under a British convoy, he landed near Coro and took possession of the town from the unarmed inhabitants. Inaugurating a practice followed by later filibusters, he issued proclamations declaring he was there to liberate the people and calling upon them to join his army. As was to be the experience of his successors, he found that the liberated ones regarded him as a pirate and refused to enlist under his banner. After less than two weeks his position became so dangerous that he withdrew to the island of Aruba and then to Trinidad, where late in September the expedition landed and the members dispersed.*

Meanwhile, in New York the two men most prominent among his supporters, Colonel William S. Smith, surveyor of the port,

*The failure of this expedition did not end Miranda's efforts to free Venezuela. Returning to England, he continued to be indefatigable in plotting to secure independence. After Napoleon's invasion of Spain in 1808 inspired her American colonies to revolt, Miranda sailed to Venezuela in 1810 and the next year was a leader in the issuance of a declaration of independence. He served as generalissimo of the republican forces until forced to capitulate in 1812, an act that has been clouded by charges that he was a traitor who delivered the country to the royalists for gold and for his own safety. His last years were spent in dungeons in Venezuela, Puerto Rico, and Spain. He died in 1816.

and Samuel Ogden, owner of the *Leander*, were prosecuted for violating the Neutrality Act of 1794, passed by Congress after the Citizen Genêt affair in which the French minister had sought to send forth privateers from American ports to attack British shipping. The act made it illegal to fit out an armed expedition against foreign nations from American soil. Smith and Ogden, in their defense, maintained that the expedition had been begun with the knowledge of the government and sought, unsuccessfully, to subpoena the secretary of state and other officials as witnesses. Despite convincing evidence against them, the jury found the two men not guilty.

The fate of the sixty men on the schooners whom Miranda had abandoned and permitted to be captured was the same that befell many later filibusters. Tried for piracy, they were convicted; ten were sentenced to death and the others from eight to ten years' imprisonment.[3] In 1808 the thirty-six surviving Americans petitioned the House of Representatives to obtain their release, declaring they had been entrapped into Miranda's service by assurances that they were employed in the service of the United States and under the authority of the government. Since the Jefferson administration was smarting under the revelations brought out in the trial of Smith and Ogden, the Republicans defeated a resolution asking the president to attempt to obtain their release.* The argument of the Republicans was that because the prisoners had voluntarily expatriated themselves they could not claim assistance from the U.S. government.[4]

While Miranda was suffering his reverses in the Caribbean, Aaron Burr was entering into the last stage of a complicated scheme to invade Mexico and recover fortunes lost when his political career ended with the killing of Alexander Hamilton in their duel at Weehawken, New Jersey, in 1804. President Jefferson effected the defeat of Burr's enterprise, developed with many permutations

*So strongly did Jefferson resent the charge of collaboration with Miranda that in 1809, after leaving office, he wrote the Spanish minister to Washington: "I solemnly, and on my personal truth and honor, declare to you that this was entirely without foundation, and that there was neither cooperation nor connivance in our part." Quoted in Edwin Erle Sparks, ed., "Diary and Letters of Henry Ingersoll, Prisoner at Carthegena, 1806–1809."

over a two-year period. Jefferson issued a proclamation on November 27, 1806, which declared that conspirators were "fitting out and arming vessels in the western waters" and "deceiving and seducing honest and well-meaning citizens" to engage in "criminal enterprises" of organizing a military expedition against "the dominions of Spain," that is, against Mexico. During the past year the president had received reports of plots engaged in by Burr so daring as to their conception and so immoral as to their execution that he had not believed them. Burr's arrest and trial for treason followed.[5]

Burr seems to have conceived his plot during a decline in his political fortunes in 1804. Running for governor of New York as an independent Republican and expecting the vote of many in the declining Federalist party who would have voted for him to defeat the candidate of the Jeffersonites, Burr lost after a scurrilous campaign waged against him by Hamilton. Burr therefore was receptive when General James Wilkinson, commander of U.S. forces in the Mississippi Valley, visited him clandestinely in May and regaled him with prospects of leading Western settlers in a project to seize Mexican territory and establish a new nation. They had become friends as young officers in the Quebec expedition in the Revolution and now, disappointed in their prospects, had two things in common: an overweening ambition for wealth and power and no scruples as to how these were to be obtained.

After the Revolution, Wilkinson became a trader in Kentucky. On a visit to New Orleans he persuaded the Spanish governor, Rodríguez Esteban Miró, that he could induce Western settlers of the United States to place themselves "under the protection or vassalage of his Catholic Majesty." He became a secret subject of Spain and was put on the government payroll, being identified as agent No. 13 in official documents. His efforts to detach the Western territories made no headway, and he entered the armed forces of the United States, rising to the command of troops in the Mississippi Valley while maintaining his undercover relations with Spain. After Jefferson's purchase of Louisiana, Wilkinson became one of the president's chief informants about the region, of which little was known; but, with a fine hand for double-dealing, he continued as an advisor to Spain in the disputes over East and West Florida and the boundaries of the newly acquired territory.

Burr, making Philadelphia his headquarters after the duel with Hamilton, cast about for means to finance the scheme he had discussed with Wilkinson and saw a possibility for help from England through her minister to the United States, Anthony Merry. He made an extraordinary proposal to him which Merry presented to his government early in August: "I have just received an offer from Mr. Burr, the actual Vice-President of the United States . . . to lend his assistance to his Majesty's government in any manner in which they may think fit to employ him, particularly in endeavoring to effect a separation of the western part of the United States from that which lies between the Atlantic and the mountains, in its whole extent."

While waiting for a reply from London, Burr made a trip to East Florida to survey the prospects there, discussed his scheme with confidants in Washington, and presided over the Senate during the closing weeks of the session of Congress. In the spring of 1805 he made a trip to the West to lay the groundwork for the disunion scheme. "In New-York I am to be disfranchised," he wrote a friend, "and in New Jersey hanged. Having substantial objections to both, I shall not for the present, hazard either, but seek another country."

During the trip Burr, who was popular in the West, was entertained by notables along the way, including Andrew Jackson in Nashville, and he revealed his plans discreetly to some he believed would enter into his scheme. When he returned to Washington in the fall, he found the country aroused over his trip. The secret was out, bared by the Philadelphia *Gazette of the United States*, a Federalist newspaper. "How long will it be," the paper asked, "before we shall hear of Colonel Burr being at the head of a revolutionary party on the Western waters? Is it a fact that Colonel Burr has formed a plan to engage the adventurous and enterprising young men from the Atlantic States to Louisiana? Is it one of the inducements that an immediate convention will be called from the States bordering on the Ohio and Mississippi to form a separate government? . . . How soon will the forts and magazines and all the military posts at New Orleans and on the Mississippi be in the hands of Colonel Burr's revolutionary party? How soon will Colonel Burr engage in the reduction of Mexico by granting liberty to its inhabitants, and seizing on its treasures, aided by British ships and forces?"

The British Foreign Office was not interested in the disunion scheme, and by December Burr had given up hope of financing his project in that quarter. He then in an unlikely volte-face turned to another source—Spain. Later filibusters seldom permitted common sense to interfere with their projects, and Burr was typical in this respect in hatching his new plot. He sent one of his cohorts, Jonathan Dayton, former U.S. senator from New Jersey, to the Spanish minister, Carlos Martínez de Yrujo, seeking money for divulging details of the scheme. As it was already being bruited about, Yrujo put him off with vague promises. With no cash immediately forthcoming, Dayton returned with a new proposition that, preposterous though it was, had its attractions because Jefferson was on the verge of asking Congress for a declaration of war against Spain for alleged encroachments on territory obtained in the Louisiana Purchase. The proposal was that Burr would introduce in Washington armed men who at a signal from him would seize the president and other high officials, capture the arsenal, and proclaim himself head of the government. If the capital could not be held, Burr would seize ships at the navy yard, sail to New Orleans, and establish the independence of Louisiana and the West. Even though Yrujo thought that such a projected coup was "almost insane," he believed that if it were undertaken it would cause enough embarrassment to the administration to justify giving Dayton $1,500 and promising additional money when he heard from his government, which, as it turned out, refused to supply the funds.

These failures did not discourage Burr, and by the summer of 1806 new developments seemed to offer a way to implement his plans. Late in 1805 Spanish troops had crossed the Sabine River, which Jefferson held to be the western boundary of the Louisiana Purchase, there had been military skirmishes, and in March the president had sent an ominous message to Congress dealing with the troubled situation. If war with Spain broke out, Burr reasoned, conditions would arise in which he could easily enlist Westerners to attack the Spaniards in Mexico; and in New Orleans was his co-conspirator Wilkinson in command of U.S.

military forces. On July 29 Burr sent Wilkinson a letter in cipher giving him instructions. He had obtained funds, he wrote, to commence operations; Eastern detachments of expeditionists would rendezvous on the Ohio River on November 1 preparatory to sailing to Natchez, where Wilkinson was to join them; British naval protection would be provided on the Mississippi River; and the people of Mexico were prepared to receive the Americans. "The gods invite us to glory and fortune," Burr proclaimed; "it remains to be seen whether we deserve the boon."

Jefferson had received varying reports of the mysterious undertaking. Among his informants was Joseph H. Daveiss, U.S. attorney for Kentucky, a Federalist, who wrote him in January warning of a widespread Western plot against the Union, and followed this with other letters hinting of Wilkinson's relations with Spain and expressing deep suspicion of Burr's Western journey. Making unsupported charges—some of them as staggering as one that Attorney General John Breckinridge was a part of the scheme—the letters did not provide sufficient cause for action. The president became seriously concerned over the plot late in the summer when he received letters from other correspondents which said Burr was engaged in a military expedition against Mexico and which spoke of a scheme to detach the Western country from the Union. The president could not denounce the conspiracy, however, for it appeared that Wilkinson, whom he had appointed governor of Louisiana Territory, violating his principle that military and civilian position must be kept separate, was involved.

Jefferson became free to act in November when he received letters from Wilkinson exposing Burr's plot. As long as the two conspirators remained allies, the president had not dared to do anything that would compel his remote military commander to go over to Spain or to combine with Burr in a war of their own, possibly directed against the government of the United States. Wilkinson's betrayal of his associate seemed to guarantee his loyalty. The president accordingly laid the information received from Wilkinson before his cabinet, and it was determined to issue a proclamation denouncing the expedition and to dispatch orders to officials to arrest assemblages of armed men preparing to descend the Ohio River.

Burr had left Philadelphia, "never to return," as he had written Wilkinson, for Pittsburgh the first week in August. There he made arrangements for receiving his Eastern forces and continued on down the Ohio to complete plans with a man whom he had on his first trip to the West won over to his scheme, Harman Blennerhassett, for constructing boats and obtaining supplies. Blennerhassett, a wealthy Irishman, had come to the United States in 1796 and established himself on an island in the Ohio River opposite Parkersburg, building a mansion and astonishing the settlers with the luxury in which he lived. The testimony of no one involved in Burr's schemes could be trusted because of his deviousness, but Blennerhassett believed that the plan was this: Wilkinson would use force to expel the Spaniards who had occupied U.S. soil east of the Sabine, and thus precipitate an undeclared war; the people of Mississippi and Louisiana Territories were disaffected and a group known as the Mexican Association was ready to revolt and seize the territorial governments; and with navigation of the Mississippi River threatened, the West, led by Burr, would separate from the Union.

Leaving Blennerhassett to his task of building boats and gathering supplies, Burr continued on to Kentucky and Tennessee to obtain additional recruits and transportation. At Frankfort, in October, he provided a plausible cover for the forces he was gathering by making a down payment on a tract of land obtained from Spain in 1795 along the Washita River by a Hollander, the Baron de Bastrop, for settlement by Europeans. Bastrop had sold his grant, and one of the buyers was a Kentuckian, Charles Lynch. If Burr's expedition were challenged by the U.S. government, it could be presented as a legitimate colonization scheme.

By now the countryside from Pittsburgh to New Orleans was abuzz with rumors of the Burr expedition, and attempts were made to stop it. In Kentucky, Jefferson's informant Daveiss sought to have him indicted, but the grand jury refused to issue a true bill. In Ohio an agent of Jefferson sent out from Washington informed the governor of the plot, and the militia was ordered to seize the boats and supplies assembled by Blennerhassett. Before it could raid the island, however, Blennerhassett had departed in the night with forty or fifty men in a half-dozen boats. The governor of Kentucky sent troops against expeditionists gathered at Jeffersonville across the river from Louisville, but by the time they arrived

Burr's followers had also sailed down the river. Meanwhile, Burr, in Nashville, where earlier he had commissioned Andrew Jackson to build boats and obtain recruits for an expedition against the Spaniards in case of war over the border dispute, found his friend distrustful of the project because of the rumors of a conspiracy to break up the Union. Unaware of the developments up the river, Burr descended the Cumberland River to rendezvous with Blennerhassett on the Mississippi. They joined forces on December 27, the assembled expedition consisting of only ten boats and fewer than a hundred men.

Just what Burr expected to accomplish with this small force is not known—probably nothing, but he had crossed the Rubicon and could only continue on. At Bayou Pierre, 30 miles above Natchez, Burr learned about January 10, 1807, that Wilkinson had betrayed him, that Jefferson had issued his proclamation, and that the governor of Mississippi Territory had ordered his arrest. He surrendered to authorities with the story that he had planned no stroke against the Union but intended only to attack Spanish territory. Since the people of the Mississippi were sympathetic to such an ambition, he was fêted at banquets and balls pending the presentation of the case against him to a grand jury. Its report, issued on February 4, was a complete exoneration.

But Burr's peril was not past, for Wilkinson, who had established a military dictatorship in New Orleans, had sent agents to arrest him. His only safety, Burr decided, was in flight. With a single companion as a guide, Chester Ashley, who had been a follower of Philip Nolan in raids across the Texas border a half-dozen years before to obtain wild horses to sell in New Orleans, he disappeared. He was next heard of two weeks later in Alabama. Asking for directions at a house on the night of February 18, Burr, though disguised "in a shabby suit of homespun with an old white hat flapped over his face," was recognized and arrested the next day by troops summoned from Fort Stoddert. A long and wearing journey overland to Richmond to face trial for treason followed. Burr was acquitted after Chief Justice John Marshall instructed the jury that "war could not be levied without the employment and exhibition of force," and no evidence of this had been offered in the trial.

As with filibusters who followed him, Burr, instead of being disheartened by the defeat of his plans, was as eager as ever to carry on with them. Blennerhassett, visiting him in prison at Richmond, reported him "as busy in speculations on reorganizing his projects for action as if he had never suffered the least interruption" and expected "that in six months our schemes could be all remounted." After his release, under widespread opprobrium as an unconvicted traitor, Burr went to London to obtain support for a conquest of Mexico. Failing there, he pursued his schemes in Paris. After four years he returned to his own country to spend the remainder of his life, his conspiratorial talents being devoted to obtaining money from others to maintain his opulent style of living and avoiding his creditors.

If Burr's scheme had been a more open one directed only at seizing the territory of Spain, he might have succeeded, for taking possession of the Floridas and Texas was a popular theme with expansionists. Jefferson maintained, without much substance, that West Florida was included in the Louisiana Purchase and he had demanded East Florida as compensation for spoliation claims against Spain resulting from attacks on American shipping since the beginning of the European wars. Jefferson's view was that the United States was not inviolable to European aggressions as long as the Floridas belonged to a transoceanic power. He considered Cuba an extension of Florida that belonged within the defense perimeter of the United States. When Napoleon invaded Spain in 1808 and put his brother Joseph on the throne and her New World provinces one by one took this as the occasion for declaring their independence, Jefferson adopted a doctrine that was to be upheld by his successors in regard to Cuba and Mexico. So long as they remained under the dominion of Spain, the United States would be content but would be unwilling to see them pass under the dominion of a stronger power, France or England. Burr had been mistaken in his objective and ahead of his time. The adjacent borderlands, where only feeble Spanish authority existed, were the objects of later adventurers who often had the tacit approval if not the connivance of the government.

The first area to succumb was the Baton Rouge area of West

Florida. President Madison encouraged the inhabitants of East and West Florida—most of them lured there by land grants from Spain in a program of populating the region—when the right moment should come. In West Florida it came in September 1810 when settlers captured the fort at Baton Rouge and proclaimed an independent state. A month later Madison issued a proclamation authorizing military occupation as part of Orleans Territory. His action was indorsed by Congress in secret session in January 1811 in a resolution that proposed to extend the area of rule to East Florida as well should local authority consent or a foreign power attempt to occupy it.[6]

The engulfment of East Florida took a little longer. After the War of 1812 the region became a problem because of raids by hostile Seminole Indians from across the border. President Monroe sent General Andrew Jackson in 1817 across the frontier to chastize the Indians. Jackson exceeded his orders and took military control of all East Florida, executing in passing two British nationals he accused of sheltering Indians. There was outrage over this in Washington, but the president refused to censure Jackson, instead issuing an ultimatum to Spain: Spain must either control Florida or cede it to the United States. A settlement was reached in 1819 when Spain renounced her claims to the Floridas and the United States renounced hers to Texas and the two countries agreed on the long-disputed boundaries of the Louisiana Purchase.[7]

The annexation of West Florida had been made possible by emigrants who had settled in the territory and that of East Florida by a small imperialistic war. The third adjacent Spanish area, Texas, took much longer to obtain, and the process of assimilation was more complicated. Texas was the object of several military expeditions mounted in the United States in the ten years following the revolution in Mexico in 1810 to obtain independence. The first was organized by José Bernardo Maximiliano Gutiérrez de Lara, who came to the United States in 1811 to obtain aid and found Secretary of State James Monroe sympathetic to his plan of establishing a republican government in Texas and using Texas as a base for warring against the Royalists in Mexico. Assisted by American adventurers in Louisiana, his chief associate being a former U.S. army officer, Augustus W. Magee, Gutiérrez entered

Texas from the border town of Natchitoches, Louisiana, in 1812. The revolution was successful for a year or two, but the Mexican leaders were defeated by Royalists in 1813, the American expeditionists fleeing to Louisiana.

In the years that followed, new expeditions were planned, set afoot, and frustrated in one way or another. The last of significance in this period during which Mexico sought her freedom from Spain took place from 1819 to 1821. Citizens of Natchez, Mississippi, angry over the treaty with Spain that set the western border of the Louisiana Purchase at the Sabine River, subscribed $500,000 for a campaign to conquer Texas. Soldiers were recruited with the promise of a league of Texas land, and James Long, a surgeon in the War of 1812, was appointed commander. Entering Texas without opposition in June 1819, the expeditionists declared the independence of the province and formed a provisional government. By September, however, Spanish forces had been sent to repel the invaders and succeeded in driving them out of the country. In the next year Long joined forces with a Mexican revolutionist, José Félix Trespalacios, to return to Texas in an attack by sea against the coast. After landing at Point Bolivar in Galveston Bay in April 1820, the expedition was divided when Trespalacios went to Mexico to spread the revolution and Long remained behind to set up the government of what he proclaimed the Republic of Texas. He was forced in September 1821 to surrender to Royalist forces and was arrested. In the meantime Spain had recognized the independence of Mexico and a republic had been established. Taken to Mexico City, Long might have expected to be given his liberty; instead he was shot by a prison guard, accidentally it was said, but his friends maintained that Trespalacios, appointed governor of Texas, had given the order.

In the end it was the colonizer and not the military adventurer who brought Texas into the Union, beginning with Moses Austin, who in 1812 obtained a grant of land from the new nation of Mexico for settlement by 200 American families. The Mexican government adopted a policy of inviting emigration, and subsequent *empresarios*, as they were called, brought in additional settlers to occupy land obtained by charter. Thousands of people in the United States were lured by this opportunity to get cheap land.* Ultimately the settlers were successful in breaking away from Mexico and establishing the Republic of Texas.[8]

The spirit of filibusterism was quiescent for more than two decades until it was revived in the 1840s when visions of national grandeur and purpose were conjured up by the Fifty-four Forty or Fight demands for Oregon and the agitation for annexation of Texas climaxed by the Mexican War, which brought New Mexico and California into the Union. The national goals were summed up in the magic phrase, "Manifest Destiny."

The phrase was coined in 1845 by a magazine and newspaper editor, John L. O'Sullivan, although the basic idea had often been expressed since the Revolution: it was "the will of Heaven" that the colonies would separate from England; "Nature designs" that Canada should be a part of the United States or it was "what the Deity intended for us"; the new republic was "destined" to spread over the entire northern part of the continent; "the manifest indications of nature" were for the United States to possess adjoining territory of Spain; it was "written in the book of fate" that the American republic must stretch her limits; the nation was "destined to manifest to mankind the excellence of divine principles"; Oregon was a part of the domain "which Providence has put under our charge."[9] O'Sullivan, with an eye to national glory, joined the terms "manifest" and "destiny" into one phrase in articles in 1845 when, urging annexation of Texas, he wrote of "our manifest destiny to overspread the continent allotted by Providence" and upheld the American claim to Oregon as being "by the right of our manifest destiny to overspread and to possess the whole of the continent."[10]

The histories of a nation do not always portray past times as they appeared to those who lived through them. In retrospect, the 1850s in the United States seem to have been dominated to the exclusion of other matters by the developing crisis between the North and South over the abolition of slavery and its extension into new territories leading up to the most traumatic experience in the life of the nation, the Civil War. It did not seem so to those

* In the United States the public lands sold for $1.25 an acre and could not be bought on credit, a policy adopted to prevent speculation, but in Texas land could be obtained at a price of 12½ cents an acre.

who lived then. Reading their newspapers day by day, following the debates in Congress, and listening to the speeches of their politicians, they were aware of other issues and aroused to passionate partisanship. It was the period when the spirit of national expansion became most rampant. Successive Democratic presidents—James K. Polk, Franklin Pierce, and James Buchanan—though maintaining a position of rectitude, were in the forefront of the movement, devoting their diplomacy to obtaining Cuba and additional territory from Mexico by purchase and securing by treaty canal and transit rights across the isthmus linking North and South America at several points—Tehuantepec in Mexico, Panama, and Nicaragua. Other expansionists, sometimes working with the presidents and sometimes against them, were a mixed lot. They included financial magnates—George Law and Cornelius Vanderbilt were among the most prominent—and merchants and traders interested in the possibility of wresting fortunes from the backward countries of Latin America; Southern politicians and plantation owners desirous of extending the area of slavery and dominating Congress by bringing new slave states into the Union; secessionists hoping to set up a slave empire forming a great circle encompassing Mexico, the southern regions of the United States, Cuba, and other islands in the West Indies; and missionaries committed to carrying American ideals of freedom and justice to oppressed peoples elsewhere.

The actual leaders of the expeditions were like the prototypal Miranda and Burr—exiles such as Narciso López of Cuba and Juan José Flores of Ecuador and seekers of glory and fortune such as John A. Quitman of Mississippi and William Walker of California. The rank-and-file at first consisted principally of ex-soldiers from the Mexican War armies but soon other types felt the lure: young men eager for adventure, older men with no money to buy land in this country attracted by the offer of free grants in other countries, men unable to find jobs, disappointed seekers of gold in California, loafers and saloon habitués out for plunder, criminals fleeing the law, and European immigrants arriving as penniless strangers at the Atlantic and Gulf ports.

Early in the 1850s the individual member or leader of the expeditions became known as *filibuster*, a term borrowed from the Spanish *filibustero*, (from the Dutch *vrijbuiter*, i.e., *free booty*) employed to designate the pirates, buccaneers, or freebooters raiding the royal colonies of Spain in the New World in the sixteenth century, and the activity in which he was engaged was called filibusterism.[11] Spanish and Latin-American officials denouncing the expeditions almost invariably spoke of these raiders as pirates. Leading filibusters did not like the appellation. William Walker, the best known of them, wrote in answer to his critics of what "you ignorantly call 'Filibusterism,'" and one of his associates, Charles W. Doubleday, resented the epithet, which he said was used by the British to bring discredit on a movement that "bade fair to destroy their timehonored privilege of dominating the affairs of the West India Islands and Central America" and that was "echoed by the antislavery party in the United States."[12]

The 1850s were an exciting period when the self-appointed agents of Manifest Destiny, the filibusters, often deceived by vainglorious and self-seeking foreign revolutionists, carried on elaborate intrigues to organize their expeditions, resorted to ruses to escape the vigilance of officials directed to prevent their departure, landed on foreign soil with only a few armed men to conquer a country, and fought against defending forces, invariably losing sooner rather than later, only to return to the United States to try again—and again and again. But the filibuster movement was a part of larger affairs, the issue of slavery dividing the nation, the rivalry for commercial supremacy with other countries, enforcement of the Monroe Doctrine against encroachments by European powers in the New World, and the assertion by the United States of what a newspaper called its title to "national glory, national greatness."[13]

PART ONE

The Pearl of the Antilles

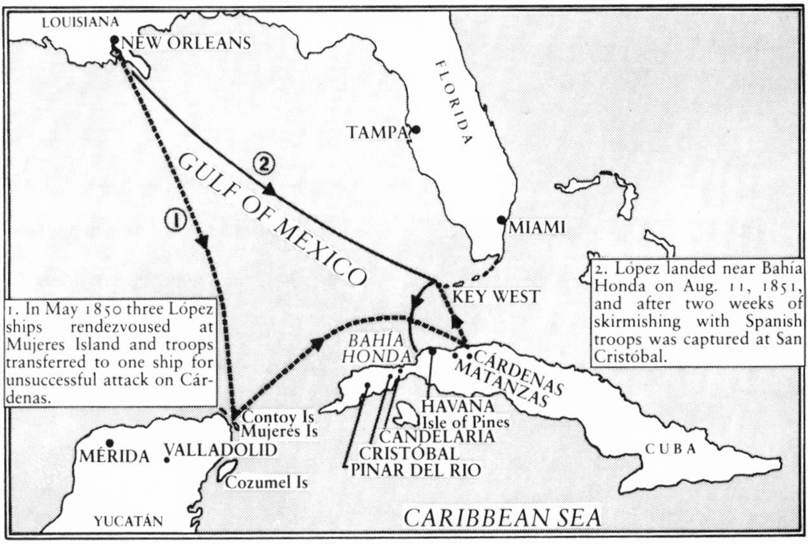

Narciso López's expeditions to Cuba

CHAPTER ONE

The Whetted Appetite for Territory

President James K. Polk on May 10, 1848, almost two years to the day after Congress declared war against Mexico and a month after the Senate ratified a peace treaty drafted at the village of Guadalupe Hidalgo, recorded in his diary the appearance of two visitors upon the heels of a large number of persons he had seen in the morning. They were the Democratic senator from Illinois, Stephen A. Douglas, and the New York journalist and magazine editor, John L. O'Sullivan. Although by completing the annexation of Texas, settling the Oregon boundary dispute with England, and claiming New Mexico and Upper California as war reparations Polk had doubled the land area of the country, he was attracted by a proposal of his two visitors for further expansion. "Their business with me was to urge that I would take early measures with a view to the purchase of the Island of Cuba from Spain," Polk related. "I heard their views, but deemed it prudent to express no opinion on the subject. Mr. O'Sullivan read to me and left with me a paper embodying his views in favour of the measure." But in the privacy of his diary Polk wrote: "Though I expressed no opinion to them I am decidedly in favour of purchasing Cuba & making it one of the States of the Union."[1]

Almost three weeks later, on May 30 at the Tuesday meeting of his cabinet, Polk introduced the question of whether to make an offer to Spain for Cuba. Only two members were strongly in favor. Secretary of the Treasury Robert J. Walker, who had opposed the Guadalupe Hidalgo treaty because he thought all of Mexico should be annexed, advocated purchase, saying he was willing to pay $100 million dollars for the island. Secretary of the Navy John Y. Mason concurred. Postmaster General Cave Johnson did not seem to approve, objecting to incorporating the Spanish population of Cuba into the Union. Secretary of State James Buchanan thought Cuba should be acquired but not at this time because of possible adverse effects for Democrats in the coming presidential election, in which he hoped to be the party candidate. The view of one cabinet member, Secretary of War William L. Marcy, was not given as he was out of the city, but he later supported Buchanan's objection. Polk's twice-a-week cabinet meetings were not democratic proceedings where the majority ruled. He asked the members for their views, heard them, often without comment, and then announced his decision. In this instance he had already made up his mind, and he expressed his "strong conviction that the effort should be made without delay," instructing Buchanan to have a definite proposal to present at the cabinet meeting on Saturday.[2]

If Cuba could be bought, Polk would fulfill a desire of American expansionists that had existed since at least the administration of Thomas Jefferson, who considered the island a necessary appendage of the United States. In 1822 fears were aroused when it appeared that France, in invading Spain to restore Ferdinand VII to the throne, might take possession, or that Spain might cede the island to England in payment of a debt. The control of Cuba was one of the concerns of President Monroe when he formulated his famous doctrine, set forth in his annual message to Congress in December 1823, that the United States would consider dangerous to its peace and safety any attempt of European powers to colonize or extend their system to any point in the Western Hemisphere.

John Quincy Adams had ably summed up the importance of Cuba to the United States:

> Cuba, almost in sight of our shores, from a multitude of considerations has become an object of transcendent importance to the political and commercial interests of our Union. Its commanding position, with reference to the Gulf of Mexico, and the West India seas; the character of its population; its situation midway between our Southern Coast, and the Island of St. Domingo; its safe and capacious harbor of Havana fronting a long line of our shores destitute of the same advantage; the nature of its productions, and its wants furnishing the supplies and needing the returns of a commerce immensely profitable, and mutually beneficial, give it an importance in the sum of our national interests with which that of

no other foreign territory can be compared, and little inferior to that which binds the different members of this Union together.[3]

Three days did not allow much time for deciding on a way to approach Spain in what must be a delicate negotiation if she were not to reject out of hand a proposal that she dispossess herself of "the ever-faithful isle," as she looked upon Cuba, the only one of her New World colonies that had never revolted, and it was not until June 9 that a procedure could be determined and instructions drawn up for the American minister in Madrid.

In the meantime Polk had met twice with O'Sullivan, who revealed to him "confidentially" a plot of wealthy Cuban planters to revolt against Spain and seek annexation to the United States. O'Sullivan, delighting in intrigue, said that an agent of the planters was in Baltimore to obtain American help and that he would confer with him and report back to the president because if the agent came to Washington "his movements would be observed." O'Sullivan also told the president that a "distinguished" general of the army now in Mexico had promised the Cuban conspirators to resign his commission and land an expedition of discharged soldiers on the island to help in the struggle for independence. Polk replied that if the United States obtained Cuba it must be by "amicable purchase" and that as president he could not countenance aiding Spain's rebellious subjects.[4]

The cabinet, including Buchanan who, able quickly to modify his views when expedient, now "heartily approved" of purchasing Cuba, developed an elaborate protocol for approaching Spain. Regarding the matter as being "profoundly confidential," to be confined to the cabinet alone, Polk noted in his diary that he would not even reveal it to O'Sullivan, "who first suggested to me the idea of purchasing Cuba, and who takes such interest in the subject."[5]

But if O'Sullivan was not to be let in on a secret, he had kept one from Polk: his idea of buying Cuba had been submitted first not to the president but more than a year before to his secretary of state, and the two had often discussed the matter. O'Sullivan had not been alone, however, in clandestine projects to annex the island to the United States. Other expansionists had been busy developing their own schemes, and on the island advocates of separation from Spain, mostly wealthy planters and merchants, had been conniving with Mexican War generals to land an army of ex-soldiers to capture the government.

When John L. O'Sullivan approached Polk with his Cuban project, he was known chiefly as a publicist for the Democratic party and as editor of *The United States Magazine and Democratic Review* with its odd marriage of partisan politics and literature. In the first years of the magazine O'Sullivan was content to urge Manifest Destiny in high-sounding declarations, but in 1847 and during the decade that followed he was an artful intriguer and activist who was involved, sometimes clandestinely and sometimes publicly, in efforts to annex Cuba. He was one of the busiest of the conspirators, soldiers of fortune, liberators, and manipulators who plotted to organize armed bands to send to the island to stir up revolts and seize the government, who urged such plots on presidents, cabinet members, and members of Congress, and who operated in the chancelleries of Europe to achieve their goals of territorial aggrandizement and the spread of liberty.

O'Sullivan may almost be said to have inherited his filibustering spirit. His father, John T. O'Sullivan, a ship's captain, had taken part in the expedition of Francisco de Miranda to Venezuela in 1807 and was one of the sixty Americans captured. He had been imprisoned at Carthegena but succeeded in making his escape. He continued in his occupation as a ship's captain and for brief periods served as U.S. consular agent in various places. His son was born in November 1813 on a British man-of-war in the harbor of Gibraltar, where his parents—his father was then consul in the Barbary States—had been given refuge when the plague broke out in North Africa. The boy attended a military school in France and the Westminster School in London, where he won a medal for proficiency in Greek. Upon the death of the father, the family came to the United States. John entered Columbia College in New York in 1828 and received a degree in 1831; but, of a scholarly bent, he continued his studies at the same time he read for the law, earning an advanced degree in 1834.[6]

In two years of law practice O'Sullivan found the profession of attorney so dull that he joined with a brother-in-law, S. D. Langtree, who had been an editor of the *Knickerbocker Magazine*, in establishing a publication that would combine their common interest in literature and politics. The first number of *The United States Magazine and Democratic Review* was issued in Washington in October 1837, but in 1841 the editors moved the magazine to New York. O'Sullivan later recalled that in starting the magazine he and his partner were "both very young, very sanguine, and very democratic." These traits as well as some less attractive ones are borne out in a description by Julian Hawthorne, son of Nathaniel Hawthorne, a frequent contributor and personal friend: "He was always full of grand and world-embracing schemes, which seemed to him, and which he made appear to others, vastly practicable and alluring, but which invariably miscarried by reason of some oversight which escaped notice for the very reason it was so fundamental."[7] As a literary editor, O'Sullivan obtained such writers as Bryant, Poe, Longfellow, and Whittier as contributors, and as a political editor supported the Democratic party of Jefferson and Jackson. He belonged to the party's antislavery and reform wing in New York, known as Barnburners, but his enthusiasm for expansionism, Manifest Destiny, led him to ally himself more and more with Southern slaveholders with their designs on Texas and Spanish possessions for the extension of the institution than with the Northern free-soilers.

O'Sullivan first broached the idea of annexing Cuba to Buchanan in January 1847. Aside from his dreams of glory for the nation, he had a personal interest in the island because of the marriage of a sister to Cristóbal Madan y Madan, a leader in the Havana Club, an organization of wealthy Creoles seeking to join the United States for economic reasons. To support the annexationist program, Madan had organized an agency, the Cuban Council, in New York City.

Later in the year O'Sullivan went to Havana to form a plot with Madan and his fellow Creoles to foment an uprising to make the island independent. In a memorandum to Buchanan on July 6, 1847, O'Sullivan promised the support of financial and commercial leaders on the island: "I speak on the authority of some of the most wealthy and influential of them, when I say that for the Island to pay a hundred or a hundred and fifty millions of dollars, even with their present means, would be a great relief from their present burthens, under the Spanish colonial yoke." Although in

1846 the Wilmot Proviso, a rider to an appropriation bill declaring that slavery would not be permitted in any territories obtained from Mexico, had stirred a debate that divided the nation, O'Sullivan in proposing the purchase of Cuba skirted the issue raised by saying annexation "would involve no extension of slavery." This was true in a way as slavery already existed on the island. In his view, annexation would prove to be so financially attractive and strategically important that it "would be no less popular at the commercial North and East and the grain-growing West, than at the South." He urged immediate action to take advantage of the surge of national pride over victory in the war, although it had not yet been won, and declared that annexation, combined with the acquisitions from Mexico, "would stamp out the term of the administration which should effect it, as one of the great epochs, not only of our country, but of the commercial history of the world."[8]

During his visit to Havana, O'Sullivan met another American who was to become one of the leaders of the movement to bring Cuba into the Union during the Polk administration, Moses Y. Beach, editor of New York's popular penny paper, the *Sun*, returning from Mexico where he had operated as a secret agent under instructions from the president.[9]

Beach in 1846 had conceived the idea of going to Mexico to be first on the scene in case of peace to obtain canal rights across the Isthmus of Tehuantepec, rights held by a British group, and banking privileges in the capital. He called on Buchanan in November to explain his plans, and the secretary of state introduced him to the president. The interview made such slight impression on Polk that he did not mention it in his diary, but he agreed with Buchanan that Beach might provide valuable information and even exert an influence on Mexican leaders to obtain peace through his friendship with General Juan Nepomucemo Almonte, minister to the United States when Texas was annexed.[10] The secretive Polk, following his penchant for dispatching agents abroad to promote his dubious projects, had Buchanan instruct Beach to send the government confidential reports through military channels. Buchanan, himself sometimes guilty of a lack of candor, cautioned Beach against giving "the slightest intimation to any person . . . that you are an agent of this government" and warned him in dealing with officials to be "upon your guard against their wily diplomacy."[11]

In one of his reports to Buchanan, Beach wrote that in Mexico City, to which he had traveled on a British passport obtained at Havana, he had quickly established good relations with leading government officials and friends of General Santa Anna. Polk already had another agent in Mexico, Nicholas Trist, sent as a commissioner to negotiate a peace treaty. Although Beach had not been given any diplomatic powers, a letter from him that Buchanan showed Polk on April 14 indicated that Beach rather than Trist might succeed in inducing Mexican leaders to enter into peace talks. "It is clearly to be inferred from his letter that he will make a treaty with them if he can," Polk noted in his diary. "Should he do so, and it is a good one, I will waive his authority to make it, and submit it to the Senate for ratification. It will make a good joke if he should assume the authority and take the whole country by surprise & make a Treaty."[12]

Beach soon found that the desire for peace was not so strong as he had first thought, both parties—the friends of Santa Anna and his enemies—wishing to continue the war because they thought capitulation would lose them the support of the people. But Beach found the clergy to be against the war because Santa Anna was extorting contributions from the church. Beach promised the bishops the support of the United States if they would lead an organized resistance against the government. "They consented," he reported to Buchanan, "and at the moment of General Scott's debarcation at Vera Cruz they made a most important diversion in his favor by raising the standard of civil war. . . . This occupied five thousand men and all the arms, munitions of war, and means of the government in the city of Mexico for twenty-three days; effectually preventing them from assisting Vera Cruz. . . ." Beach's part in this was suspected by Santa Anna, who had spies follow his movements. He managed to escape by avoiding the main roads in a flight in a carriage to the coast even though a reward of $1,000 had been offered for him dead or alive. He reached Havana while O'Sullivan and Madan were plotting an uprising that would make the island independent.

Although O'Sullivan and Beach agreed on the feasibility of purchasing Cuba, they differed on the method of winning Polk over to the project. O'Sullivan thought they should work indirectly through the secretary of state, and he cast himself in a chief role as the president's confidential emissary to conduct negotiations with Spain. Beach believed the better way would be for him to campaign for annexation in the *Sun* to create a favorable public opinion for action by Polk. He published articles about the island, its people, and its resources and on July 23, 1847, outlined a purchase plan in an editorial headed "Cuba under the Flag of the United States." "Cuba is in the market for sale," the editorial said, "and we are authorized by parties eminently able to fulfill what they propose, to say that if the United States will offer the Spanish government one hundred millions of dollars Cuba is ours, and that with one week's notice, the whole amount will be raised and paid over by the inhabitants of the island." The editorial did not receive much support. *Niles' Weekly Register*, with the acqusition of New Mexico and California in mind, commented that "the appetite for new territory would seem but to increase with its indulgence"; and in New Orleans, years before a center for filibustering in Texas, the *Bee* described the plan "as rickety and jointless and languid an abortion as was ever spawned from the sickly brains of progressive democracy."[13]

While Nicholas Trist was conducting peace negotiations that sought to add New Mexico and California to the American Union and O'Sullivan and Beach were engaged in their underhand machinations to obtain Cuba, the eyes of the nation were turned briefly to another area for annexation—Yucatán, which had declared her independence of Mexico and remained neutral in the war. In the fall of 1847 Yucatán sent an eloquent representative to Washington, Justo Sierra O'Reilly. In February 1848 he protested to Buchanan a peace treaty in which Yucatán was ignored, one that would leave her open "to the fury of the Mandarines of Mexico" because of her neutrality or one that did not leave her "at liberty, to seek for admission, as a free and sovereign state, into the vast confederacy of the United States." But the real fears of the Yucatecans, as later letters to Buchanan revealed, were of the Mayas, who had risen up against the white population at the instigation, Sierra said, of the British who, by a "series of abuses & robberies," had established a colony at Belize on the coast. In several letters he importuned Buchanan for arms and troops to aid a country "suffering all the horrors of a war of extermination, brought against it by barbarous Indians," climaxed by one on March 25 offering "dominion and sovereignty of the Country, to the Nation, which will assume the charge of saving it."[14]

Polk's diary reveals that he did not take much interest in Yucatán's problems or in acquiring a region he still regarded as belonging to Mexico, only reluctantly acceding to the opinion of the cabinet that arms be dispatched for defense; but he became concerned when he heard that European powers had been invited to intervene. He told the cabinet that "we could never agree to see Yucatán pass into the hands of a foreign monarchy. . . and that sooner than this should take place the U.S. should afford the aid & protection asked." He believed, however, this could be done only by the authority of Congress and prepared a message that set forth the situation.[15] Acquisition of the cape, which with Florida made two arms embracing the Gulf of Mexico, by a European power, he said, would violate the Monroe Doctrine and, pointing out the strategic importance of the peninsula, he added: Yucatán "is situate in the Gulf of Mexico . . . and from its vicinity to Cuba, to the cape of Florida, to New Orleans, and indeed to our whole southwestern coast, it would be dangerous to our peace and security if it should become a colony of any European nation."

The Senate Committee on Foreign Relations reported a bill authorizing the president to take temporary military occupation of Yucatán to assist in suppressing the "Indian savages" but denying any intention of permanent occupation. This provoked a debate that went far beyond the question of Yucatán and one in which the possession of Cuba figured prominently. It also contained hints of problems that were to arise in the future, particularly in England's recent action in seizing the Nicaraguan port of San Juan del Norte and renaming it Greytown on the specious grounds of claiming a protectorate over the Mosquito Indians who occupied a strip along the coast.

Senator Edward A. Hannegan, chairman of the Committee on Foreign Relations, mentioning the occupation of San Juan, warned that if England took Yucatán she would soon afterward take Cuba. Senator Jefferson Davis argued that the Gulf of Mexico was "a basin of water belonging to the United States," declaring of

Yucatán and Cuba: "Whenever the question arises whether the United States shall seize these gates of entrance from the south and east, or allow them to pass into the possession of any maritime Power, I am ready, for one, to declare that my step will be forward, and that the cape of Yucatán and the island of Cuba must be ours." Senator Lewis Cass on May 10, twelve days before winning the Democratic nomination for the presidency, echoed Davis in declaring that the Gulf of Mexico "must be practically an American lake" and urged the purchase of Cuba. There were frequent avowals by senators that they would go to war to prevent Cuba's passing out of the hands of Spain into those of another European nation.[16]

Polk mentioned the debate several times in his diary but only once expressed an opinion after reporting that Walker favored ultimate annexation of Yucatán and that Buchanan opposed it. "I concurred with Mr. Walker," the president wrote, "rather than see it fall into the hands of England."[17] The question of what to do about Yucatán ceased to be an active one when news was received of the signing of a peace treaty between the whites and the Mayas. The cessation of hostilities, however, did not last long, and that winter a military expedition was recruited in Mississippi and Louisiana from among discharged Mexican War soldiers to go to Yucatán to fight the Mayas.

It was not exactly a coincidence that John L. O'Sullivan called on President Polk shortly after noon on May 10, the day that Cass spoke out in favor of buying Cuba, to present his plan for the purchase. He obviously, after being put off for a year by vague excuses, could no longer trust Buchanan to be an advocate; and the debate on Yucatán, which revealed such strong sentiment for obtaining Cuba, seemed to indicate that now was the time to approach the president.

With approval by the Mexican Senate of the Treaty of Guadalupe Hidalgo clearing the way for another excursion in territorial acquisition and the cabinet agreed that Cuba should be the object, Buchanan on June 17, 1848, drafted elaborate instructions to the American minister to Spain, Romulus Saunders, to follow in the complicated plot outlined for broaching the question of purchase to Spain. In presenting the scheme to Saunders, Buchanan stressed the danger of acquisition by Great Britain, now pursuing a policy of extending "her dominion over the most important commercial positions of the globe." "Tempted by the weakness and disunion of the Central American States," he wrote, "and acting under the mask of a protector to the King and Kingdom of the Mosquitos,—a miserable, degraded and paltry tribe of Indians,—she is endeavoring to acquire permanent possession of the entire coast of the Caribbean Sea from Cape Honduras to Escuda de Veragua." He believed that England had a "more plausible pretext" for acquiring Cuba because of the debt owed her by Spain.

Next, Buchanan explained the commercial and strategic reasons why ownership of Cuba was desirable for the United States and then outlined the procedures Saunders was to follow in making the offer. The first overtures were to be made in a "confidential conversation" with the Spanish minister for foreign affairs, because to put anything in writing might "produce an absolute refusal" that would embarrass further negotiations. Saunders might begin by referring to the probability of a revolution on the island and convince him of the friendship of the United States toward Spain by reading him dispatches instructing the American consul in Havana to have nothing to do with the rebels and the commanding general in Mexico to prevent embarkation of discharged soldiers at Vera Cruz on an expedition to take part in an uprising. "You may then touch delicately upon the danger that Spain may lose Cuba by a revolution in the Island," Buchanan continued, "or that it may be wrested from her by Great Britain . . . to pay the Spanish debt due to the British Bond-holders. You might assure him, that whilst this Government is entirely satisfied that Cuba shall remain under the dominion of Spain, we should, in any event, resist its acquisition by any other nation. And, finally, you might inform him, that under all these circumstances, the president had arrived at the conclusion that Spain might be willing to transfer the Island to the United States for a fair and full consideration."[18]

Alas for the carefully outlined script written by Buchanan—the *dramatis personae* failed to play the roles he had cast them for. The American minister by background and character had no qualifications for carrying out a sensitive diplomatic mission. Saunders had filled a number of political offices in his native state, North Carolina, and had served several terms in Congress. Strongly partisan, he was also quarrelsome, and had won from John Quincy Adams the aspersive characterization: "There is not a more cankered or venomous reptile in the country."[19] He was given the Madrid post chiefly because at the Democratic national convention of 1844 he had moved the two-thirds rule that prevented Martin Van Buren from getting the presidential nomination and made Polk a dark-horse winner. Knowing no language except English, and "even this he sometimes murders," Buchanan complained later,[20] Saunders found it difficult to conduct diplomacy with practiced officials by the hints and innuendoes outlined for him.

If Saunders was not up to the role for which he was cast, the officials with whom he dealt—General Ramón María Narvaez, minister of war and the president of the govering council, and Pedro J. Pidal, minister of foreign affairs—would not deliver the lines expected of them. They appreciated the disclosures made about revolutionary plots in Cuba, but made only ambiguous replies to his hints that Spain might be willing to give up the island. Moreover, Saunders' attempted wily maneuverings did not remain a secret. The *New York Herald* published a letter on October 20 from its Madrid correspondent, widely reprinted in Europe, that attacked Saunders' ineptitude. The paper sarcastically observed that if Saunders had as much knowledge of good manners and diplomacy as he had of tar, turpentine, and chewing tobacco, he could buy Cuba in less than two months. Although Spanish officials told Saunders they did not blame him for the report, which they found embarrassing, their attitude toward him became even cooler than it had been before. Writing Buchanan about the *Herald* article, Saunders was forced to the unhappy admission that the Spanish "regard Cuba as their most precious gem and nothing short of extreme necessity will ever induce them to part with it."

When the Whigs won the November presidential election and Spanish officials realized they would no longer have to deal with the expansionist Democrats, they ceased to be even diplomatically polite to Saunders. In a last effort to find out if any terms, however liberal, would induce Spain to cede the island, he received the reply from Pidal in December "that it was more than any Minister dare, to entertain any such proposition; that he believed such to be the feeling of the country, that sooner than see the Island transferred to *any power*, they would prefer seeing it sunk in the Ocean."[21]

The Senate bill for military occupation of Yucatán to save the whites from the Mayas had been dropped without a vote upon word that a truce had been effected. But the war was not over, and in less than a week Justo Sierra O'Reilly again appealed to Buchanan for aid. On the day the armistice was arranged, he wrote, it was "treacherously violated" and the Indians "rushed forth again in their career of extermination and destruction."[22] Buchanan did not reply, and Sierra left Washington in June. His departure indicated that he had interpreted American public opinion correctly: the nation, with the war with Mexico about to wind up through the Treaty of Guadalupe Hidalgo, was not for the moment interested in further military incursions except for a few Manifest Destiny diehards.

Sierra's letters to Buchanan had been moving—sometimes hysterical—appeals that portrayed the suffering of his people in vivid terms, but he had not confined his correspondence to the secretary of state. He also had written letters to the newspapers, noting in his diary that "the press in this country has a decisive influence in all matters affecting public affairs" and that he had tried to make it favorable toward him "in the matter of aid and resources" sought from the government. One unexpected result was the receipt, as early as April 1848, of letters from persons offering to organize volunteer regiments and groups of colonists to go to Yucatán. Later, during the Senate debate on the Yucatán bill, he began to see that the offers had possibilities. "In order that Yucatán shall be saved," he wrote, "it is not enough that an expedition from the United States shall go there temporarily; it is necessary that the means of gaining a permanent white population be devised."[23]

When Sierra returned to Yucatán he proposed to Governor Miguel Barbachano that recruits to aid in the fight against the Indians be sought from among the discharged soldiers of the American army. Contacts were made with two young officers in the Thirteenth Regiment of Infantry, First Lieutenant Joseph A. White and Second Lieutenant David G. Wilds, who were commissioned to enlist men in the Yucatecan service. Privates were to be paid $8 a month, receive a suit of clothes every three months, and at the expiration of their term of service be given 320 acres of land.[24] The pay was not much incentive for men who had farms or jobs to go back to, but seemed attractive to thousands turned loose at the southern ports, many of them penniless and with no other prospects. White signed up several hundred—the number has been estimated as between 500 and 700—for the adventure in Yucatán.

Details of Colonel White's expedition (he had promoted himself two grades in rank from the one he held in the American army) are scarce, the chief sources being contemporary newspapers and they give no extensive accounts. The expedition sailed from New Orleans in December and landed on the north coast at Sisal (later called Progreso), the port for the capital city of Mérida about 35 miles inland. The fullest account of their adventures appeared in the *New Orleans Delta* of March 14, 1849, in a letter to the paper written by G. H. Tobin, first a lieutenant and then a captain in White's forces.[25] Like the letters of later filibusters, Tobin's is written in a jocose vein by a man who had a rough sense of humor that delighted in practical jokes and that permitted him to endure hardships and face death in an off-hand, satirical way.

On the march from Sisal to Mérida, Tobin noted the depredations of the Mayas, who had destroyed villages and farms. "During our stay," Tobin related, "a feast day occurred, and we had a good opportunity of seeing the Yucateco belles. They drove during the evening in their volantes, round and round the Corso (their promenade), and made a graceful display until after dusk. Many of them are as fair as the whitest northern ladies, and all elegantly and tastefully dressed." He was less impressed by the "peones," the women being "short, dumpy and very square-built," looking "at first sight, rear view, like a feather-bed."

The Mayas had mastered most of the eastern and southern parts of the cape, the frontier sections, but were not strong in the more populous northwest. Sierra's description of the situation to Buchanan earlier in the year had not been exaggerated: "The barbarians have destroyed by fire four towns and more than fifty hamlets; they have caused the destruction of as many as two hundred farms and as many other cotton and sugar plantations; they have laid waste immense tracts of land sown with seed; they have killed hundreds of white families. . . ." When the American volunteers arrived late in the year, however, the government was forcing back the Maya bands. Troops found it hard to defeat them, as Sierra wrote: "The numerous hordes of that race fall with surprising rapidity on the defenceless hamlets, leaving them reduced to ashes, and then, withdrawing to the woods and thickets, flee from our troops, tiring, discouraging and driving them to desperation. The fact that that race requires nothing, the facility with which they bear every condition of privation, the extraordinary rapidity of their movements, all this has already given them an almost irresistible superiority."[26] The Americans from the north were to find that their experiences in Mexico had not trained them for this kind of warfare.

The volunteer regiment remained only a short time in Mérida, starting out the second week of December on a 150-mile march eastward to the village of Tihosuco, where a government garrison was besieged by Mayas. The regiment arrived at Tihosuco on December 23, rested the next day, and on Christmas day went out in search of the enemy, and, Tobin said, "on my word they were not hard to find." It was at this time, apparently, that Tobin began to understand the nature of the conflict in Yucatán, called in Mexican histories a caste war. "I had thought, at first, this was a mere irruption of savage Indians," he wrote, "but I now discovered it is in reality a sort of servile war, and the Spartacus is a half-breed—a cross betweeen a British subject and a native of the soil; he is called Prince Pat, and is said to be a man of talent, education and wealth." Tobin's Prince Pat was Jacinto Pat, cacique of the tribe at Tihosuco whose ranch nearby had been a depot and assembly point at the start of the rebellion.

Tobin praised Pat's military ability on the first foray of the Americans against the enemy. "Our road has been cut through a dense chaparral, and was very tortuous," he related. "At almost every angle, Prince Pat displayed his talents in the construction of barricades (here called trancheros), and their sites were chosen with a skill that would not be discreditable to the most accomplished engineer from West Point." The Americans charged at the signal of a bugle and easily swept through the trancheros, but the Indians, slipping into the chaparral on either side of the trail, fired upon them from the flanks. When the bugle sounded retreat, the

Americans had suffered twenty-five casualties, five men killed on the spot and the others wounded, four of these, however, to die subsequently. "They are excellent soldiers—far superior to the Mexicans of the north," was Tobin's grudging praise of the enemy.

A Yucatecan historian, Serapio Baqueiro, wrote twenty years later that the Yankee volunteers knew nothing of guerrilla fighting. They advanced along the mule paths in a disorderly manner, talking loudly, joshing one another, and smoking pipes which signaled their advance to the lurking Mayas. When they went into battle, they emitted the loud yells that had disconcerted the Mexicans of the north and that here only aroused the wonderment of the Indians.

Another historian of the expedition, Edward H. Thompson, an archeologist who served as U.S. consul at Yucatán from 1885 to 1909, also reported that the Mexican War experience had not prepared the North Americans for jungle fighting. Thompson interviewed a survivor of the expedition who had remained in Yucatán who described a ruse that took them by surprise. In a skirmish near Culumpich the Mayas made concealed pitfalls in the path and placed sharp-pointed stakes at the bottom. When the white strangers approached, the Indians stood on the other side of the pits and shouted at them. The North Americans rushed to attack, the vanguard falling into the pits.[27]

After five days of skirmishing in the Tihosuco area, many of the North Americans felt they had seen enough of Indian fighting. "Here many of our officers tendered their resignations," Tobin related. "All were promptly accepted by Colonel White, and the result is that I have received the captaincy of a dashing company. . . ." About 200 of those who did not quit at Tihosuco took part in a foray led by White to Valladolid, about 40 miles away. This onslaught ended the participation of the Americans in the fight against the Mayas. They had experienced all they wanted of warring on an enemy who would not stand up and fight and who dug pits along the trails for them to fall into. Moreover, they had not received their monthly pay, and the promise of 320 acres of land—thin soiled, waterless, and barren—at the end of their service did not seem very attractive after they had seen it. They therefore decided to return to the United States.

Their arrival at New Orleans on March 13, 1849, was noticed by the *Delta*, which declared the "disbanding of this regiment, in the manner in which it was done, is disgraceful to the authorities of Yucatán." According to the paper's account, the regiment had done what it set out to do: defeated the Mayas. "The regiment was between three and four months in service," the paper said. "During that time they had several severe engagements with the Indians, and . . . drove the enemy before them until they now have possession of no position of importance. . . . The regiment was beseiged eight days in Tihosuco, and during that time was reduced to such an extremity that officers and privates had nothing to eat but cats and dogs. In several engagements, the loss in killed was from sixty to seventy, and from one hundred to one hundred and fifty were wounded." The article stated that, despite the hardships they had endured and the victories they had won, "the only requital offered the men is the paltry sum of ten dollars each." It ended: "Barbachano pleaded the poverty of the treasury, and Colonel White feeling there was no prospect of the stipulations entered into with the regiment being fulfilled, at once requested that it should be disbanded which was acceded to."

Later in the year, in September, the Yucatán government became worried over a report that White was assembling at New Orleans another armed force to descend upon the country to obtain the pay his regiment had not received and to exact other recompense to make up for the trouble of collecting it. So alarmed was the government that it dispatched 500 troops from Mérida to Sisal to oppose a landing. It was a report that also reached the ear of the Mexican vice-consul at New Orleans, who wrote Luis de la Rosa, minister to Washington, that an expedition gathering at Round Island a few miles off the coast of Mississippi was to be directed against Yucatán, Tampico, or some other point. Rosa reported this to Secretary of State John M. Clayton, who told him not to worry: whatever the destination of this expedition, the United States would frustrate it by invoking the neutrality laws.[28]

The report was true, in part. An expedition was being assembled at Round Island, but the Colonel White whose name figured in it was another man entirely, one Robert M. White, who had been a second lieutenant in the Independent Company of

Louisiana Volunteers, and the object was not Yucatán but Cuba. After months of negotiations and planning, the Cuban conspirators and their American supporters had raised the money, purchased arms, and enlisted men for an attempt to wrest the Pearl of the Antilles from Spain.

CHAPTER TWO

Plots That Failed to Hatch

The election of a Whig administration had not only emboldened the Spanish minister of foreign affairs to reject with scorn President Polk's offer to buy Cuba, but it had also threatened to upset the expansionist aim of bringing New Mexico, California, and Oregon into the Union. On receiving the news by telegraph on November 8, 1848, that General Zachary Taylor had won the presidency—it was the first national election held uniformly on the same day in all the states—Polk wrote disparagingly of the president-elect that having "no opinions or judgment of his own upon any one public subject" he would be compelled to depend "upon the designing men of the Federal party" and be made "to reverse, so far as the Executive can reverse, the whole policy of my administration."[1]

When, on March 5 (instead of March 4 as this was a Sunday), Polk rode in a carriage up Pennsylvania Avenue with Taylor for the inaugural ceremony on the steps of the Capitol, he was shocked at views expressed by his successor. "They were to the effect that California and Oregon were too distant to become members of the Union, and that it would be better for them to be an Independent Gov[ern]ment," Polk related. Polk recorded dryly that he made no response.[2]

An administration indifferent to incorporating contiguous territory into the Union could have little interest in taking up Polk's effort to purchase Cuba, especially after the sharp rebuff given Romulus Saunders. Taylor, though vague during the campaign and in his inaugural address about his foreign policy, was clearly not inclined to overseas adventures, citing the admonition "of our own beloved Washington to abstain from entangling alliances with foreign nations." His secretary of state, John M. Clayton, considered purchase of Cuba a dead issue and twitted his predecessor James Buchanan about his failure to buy the island in a letter early in April. "What will you give me to recall Romulus Saunders from Spain?" he asked. "Speak out—do not be bashful. Shall I try to buy Cuba after you have made such a botch of that business?" Buchanan refused to take the matter lightly, and replied: "We must have Cuba. We can't do without Cuba, and above all we must not suffer its transfer to Great Britain. We shall acquire it by a coup d'état at some propitious moment, which from the present state of Europe, may not be far distant."[3]

Clayton, in instructing the new minister to Spain, Daniel M. Barringer, wrote in August that "we do not desire to renew the proposition made by the late Administration," adding: "After all that has occurred, should Spain desire to part with the Island, the proposition, for its cession to us, should come from her;—and in case she should make any, you will content yourself with transmitting the same to your government for consideration." He reiterated the doctrine that the United States would be satisfied so long as the island continued to be a dominion of Spain, declaring: "The news of the cession of Cuba to any foreign power would, in the United States, be the instant signal for war."[4]

But the government's lack of interest in doing anything to acquire Cuba did not discourage such fervid Northern expansionists as John L. O'Sullivan and Moses Y. Beach, Mexican War veterans eager for more military action and acclaim, and Southern slaveowners. The latter, in particular, had what they thought compelling reasons to obtain the island. First, they feared that Spain, submitting to pressure from England, might abolish slavery in Cuba. This, one proponent of possession wrote John C. Calhoun, would constitute "a war on institutions of the South." If Cuban Negroes were given their freedom, sparks would shoot out that would "kindle a great conflagration throughout the South," and it would be impossible to prevent slave insurrections. Second, possession would increase the political power of the South, for the island could be divided into at least three states, which would give the slaveocracy control of Congress. Third, the island would provide rich land to be exploited by slave labor, as the one-crop plantation system of the South quickly depleted the soil and new territories had to be obtained to maintain it.[5]

This economic motive did not stop with possession of Cuba. More visionary Southerners saw their slave system extended throughout the Caribbean area—the other islands in the West Indies, Mexico, and Central America. The dream was described by the *New Orleans Delta*: "Wresting that whole region from the mongrelism which now blights and blackens it, and making it yield its riches up to the hands of organized and stable industry and intelligent enterprise, this idea is firmly fixed in the American mind, and, sooner or later, its development must become a great fact—a historical reality—manifest destiny accomplished."[6]

Nor did the refusal of the Taylor administration to renew efforts to buy Cuba dampen the ardor of the Creole planters for annexation. They continued their agitation to make this goal popular in the United States through their newspaper, *La Verdad*, published in New York, and collaborated with dissidents on the island attempting to start a revolt that they hoped the oppressed people would join.

To free the islanders from Spanish despotism and to introduce democratic self-government for which the United States was the world's model were high aims often proclaimed to justify the military expeditions that followed the failure to obtain Cuba by purchase. These motives were in part camouflage to divert attention from the slave-economy character of the annexation movement, but they were also powerful influences in attracting idealistic adherents, for the spirit of freedom was rampant at the time. Widespread sympathy was aroused in the United States for the efforts in Europe in 1848 and 1849 of the people to cast aside their kings and tyrants. When Louis Kossuth, leader of the aborted Hungarian revolution, came to the United States in December 1851 to enlist the support of freedom lovers in continuing his fight, cannons in New York's harbor were fired to salute his arrival, huge crowds gathered to cheer his speeches, and the entire nation was swept with enthusiasm for his cause.

The time was ripe for a leader to emerge to appeal to a broad range of people interested in Cuba's independence—American adventurers, enthusiasts of Manifest Destiny, partisans of the South and supporters of slavery, European revolutionary exiles, and Creole plantation owners and island patriots conspiring to start a revolution against Spain. He was Narciso López, who fled from the island to the United States in July 1848 after an attempt to touch off a rebellion was suppressed even before he could summon his followers to arms.

Then about fifty years old, López seemed to possess a personal magnetism and inner force that attracted people to him. A *Mobile Tribune* writer described him as having a "compact and well set" figure and one of his followers, the Hungarian exile Louis Schlesinger, reported him as being of "stout frame and very great muscular development and strength." "His face which is dark olive, and of a Spanish cast, is strikingly handsome, expressive of both intelligence and energy," the *Tribune* writer continued, "His full dark eyes, firm, well-formed mouth, and erect head, crowned with iron grey hair, fix the attention and convince you that he is no ordinary man." Mrs. Jefferson Davis, who met López when he offered the leadership of a filibuster expedition to her husband, described him similarly: a dark complexioned man remarkable for his glowing eyes and snowy hair. A cavalry leader in the Spanish army who had risen to the rank of field marshal, he exemplified the dash and daring associated with that branch of the army. In moments of peril, according to Schlesinger, his "behavior was admirably adapted to impart confidence and courage to the men," for it "was that of a man familiar of old with danger, and personally insensible to its extremest degrees."[7]

López had been born in Venezuela in 1798 or 1799, the son of a large land owner whose estates were destroyed in the rebellion of Simón Bolívar to free the country from Spain. As a boy López became an expert horseman on his father's ranches, a talent later to make him a peerless cavalryman, and at the age of about fifteen, after the defeat and scattering of Bolívar's forces at La Puerta in 1814, managed despite his youth to join the Spanish army. During his nine years' service, he rose to the rank of colonel and received the rare military honor of the Cross of San Fernando. In 1823, after a series of victories by Bolívar, the Spanish army evacuated Caracas and withdrew to Cuba. There López married into the noble and wealthy de Frías family and, though retaining his army rank, devoted his time to developing the properties brought to him by his wife.

On a trip to Spain in 1833 to sue for money seized by the government in Cuba, López joined the army group that supported the claims of María Cristina and her infant daughter Isabella to the throne upon the death of Ferdinand VII, the despotic ruler installed through the intervention of a French army, against those of the king's brother Don Carlos. Although López had no respect for the brilliant, bold, and avaricious queen, supporting her would mean restoration of the constitution of 1812, which she was forced to accept. López served during the Carlist war as aide-de-camp of the commander in chief, General Gerónimo Valdés, and the two men became friends.

After a decade of strife and turmoil in Spain, López wished to return to Cuba, and the opportunity came when Valdés was sent to the island as captain general. Under Valdés, López held such powerful positions as governor of Trinidad, commander in chief of the Central Department, and president of the Executive Military Commission charged with putting down dissidents to the rule of Spain. When Isabella, although only thirteen years old, was declared queen, Valdés was replaced as captain general in Cuba by the conservative General Leopoldo O'Donnell, who began at once a brutal campaign to suppress any movements for independence. Deprived of his lucrative government positions, López turned to promoting his business enterprises and iron and coal mines, properties called La Rosa Cubana. Under the financial bondage imposed by Spain, he failed to prosper and soon began to engage in intrigues to obtain independence.

Historians do not agree about the motivations that made López a persistent enemy of Spain: to foment an uprising on the island and after its suppression and his enforced flight to launch military expeditions from the United States, the last of which ended in his capture and execution by garotte. Was he an idealist devoted to abstract concepts of liberty, as maintained by some of his advocates in the United States? Was he merely embittered by the loss of his government emoluments and determined to regain his wealth by leading an insurrection that would place him in the seat of power? Did he favor separation from Spain to make Cuba an independent republic? Did he seek independence for annexation to the United States as a slave state? Since there is evidence for all these points of view, it is probable that, like Francisco Miranda and Aaron Burr before him, he was driven to use whatever means were at hand without much regard for ends.

While President Polk in the spring of 1848 was planning the strategy for the purchase of Cuba, Secretary of State Buchanan received from General Robert B. Campbell, consul at Havana, a letter dated May 18 saying that a revolution was impending on the island. Campbell added that he did not think it would succeed without help from the United States and that there was a widespread wish to delay the *grito* until such help was assured. But, he went on, "there is one general who is restrained with difficulty, he is brave, and of some experience and it is understood wishes to retire into the interior and make a pronunciamento immediately."[8] Although Campbell did not name the general, it was López, who since 1843 had been preparing the way for an uprising by establishing a personal following in the Cienfuegos area. He set himself up as a physician and dispensed medicine and mingled with the country folk at the popular cock fights, forbidden by the government to prevent public assemblies. The *Democratic Review*, an admirer of López, said of his efforts: "Aided by the respect due his rank, the brilliancy of his military reputation as the well-known bravest and boldest officer of Cuba, his generosity and character for humanity and good nature, he thus established an influence, such that he has always been confident that the whole region would rise at his voice, whenever he should summon the people to rally round the flag of liberty and independence."[9]

A constant meddler in Cuba's internal affairs, a confidant of both López and the Havana Club annexationists, and a tactless and belligerent defender of the rights of American citizens on the island, Campbell expressed his sympathy for the revolutionary cause and emphasized the friendliness of the people in the United States to it. As he had reported to Buchanan, López had so far advanced his plans that he had set a date for the *grito*: June 29, when the festival of Saints Peter and Paul would permit public gatherings. Afterward called the Conspiracy of the Cuban Rose Mines, the revolution would begin at Cienfuegos and spread to neighboring towns, so López hoped, until the whole island was in revolt.

As Campbell had written Buchanan, there were, however, objections to such an attempt at this time. They came from the Havana Club, which had already set afoot its scheme to obtain an American general to head an expedition of Mexican War veterans to the island.[10] There were several reasons why the planters looked with disfavor on López's project. For one, they feared that if the impetuous general started a revolt it might result in internal disorders in which the Negroes would rise up against their owners. For another, they were not sure that he could be relied on to seek annexation to the United States. Finally, they were not persuaded that the people would join a revolution, and in this they were more realistic than the visionary general. Campbell was not a perceptive person, but he was aware of the difficulties of rousing the people. He wrote that while the Cubans had a deep-rooted hatred of Spain and spoke freely of separation, there was nothing to prevent "an open outbreak but the listless, timid character of the population, a great distrust of each other, and fear of loss of property, and risque of life."[11] The Havana Club prevailed upon López to defer his uprising until the expedition from the United States could arrive. He assented reluctantly. He had attained the highest rank in the Spanish army, he had been decorated for valor, and he had filled important positions in the government. His pride was affronted by the plan that he be subordinated to an American general. He would, however, consent to defer the uprising for two weeks.

Since Polk had word of the López schemes through Campbell's letters and through reports from O'Sullivan, he had time enough to act to frustrate both the uprising on the island and an expeditionary force from Mexico to be led by Brevet Major General William Jenkins Worth, both necessary because either would interfere with his effort to obtain the island by legitimate purchase. Worth was the "distinguished general" whom O'Sullivan had told Polk would resign his commission to take part in the Cuban adventure. In June 1848 an agent of the Havana Club had approached Worth, marching his division from Mexico City to Vera Cruz to embark for the United States, with the offer to join in the annexation scheme of the Creoles by recruiting 5,000 soldiers to invade the island and defeat Spanish garrison troops. The sum held out to dazzle him was $3 million. The opportunity to win renown appealed to Worth as well as the rich reward in money. His taste for glory had been whetted earlier when editorials in the *New York Sun* and *New York Herald* touched off a minor boom for his nomination for the presidency. He was, moreover, a rabid advocate of Manifest Destiny and had written Secretary of War Marcy: "That our race is finally destined to overrun this whole continent is too obvious to need proof."[12]

It was a simple task for Polk to prevent an expedition from Mexico—only an order to General William O. Butler, who had replaced General Winfield Scott as commander of troops, that no ships with returning soldiers should touch Cuba and another recalling Worth. In any case, there is no indication the orders were needed, for Worth had not agreed to the proposition of the Havana Club. They were only a device to be used by the American minister to Madrid to show the Spanish government the friendly intentions of the United States. Instructions to Campbell to maintain strict neutrality and to warn Americans in Cuba not to take part in any insurrection were similar camouflage.

Polk succeeded in thwarting López by similar underhand machinations. Buchanan betrayed the plot to the Spanish minister in Washington, Angel Calderón de la Barca, and there are indications that Campbell revealed the plot to the captain general, the Count of Alcoy.* Alerted by the United States, the captain general on July 5 moved to suppress the intended revolt. López was summoned to appear before the governor at Cienfuegos on important business, but he evidently had been warned that the plot was known. He went instead by train to Cárdenas and thence by boat to Matanzas, where he took passage on a small sailing vessel for Providence, Rhode Island. Two of his fellow conspirators were arrested. The suppression of the revolt made it unlikely for the time being that there would be another attempt at insurrection. Campbell wrote Buchanan on July 17 that "universal panic" struck all agitators who were now "hushed as death" insofar as talk of revo-

*Buchanan's revelation to Calderón did not fully succeed. In November 1848 he received from the Spanish minister of foreign affairs, Pedro J. Pidal, a note expressing the pleasure of the queen over the information on the insurrection plans. Unfortunately for the gratification Buchanan might have derived from this, the letter also reiterated the determination of Spain to keep possession of Cuba. W. R. Manning, ed., *Diplomatic Correspondence of the United States, Inter-American Affairs, 1831–1860*, 11:452–53.

lution was concerned.[13] López, condemned to death *in absentia*, knew now that if he were ever to return to Cuba it would have to be as the head of an invading force.

Soon after reaching the United States, López went to New York, headquarters of the Cuban annexationists. He urged an immediate invasion of the island with himself as commander, but received only hesitant support because the Havana Club leaders considered him impetuous and unreliable. Their main objection, however, was that they thought the expedition should be headed by an American as insurance of annexation.

Though not repulsing López, the club sent an agent, Ambrósio José González, to renew the offer made to General Worth. A Cuban of good family, González had been a professor at the University of Havana when he became interested in the independence movement. Possessed of a gift of oratory, he was a persuasive advocate of annexation, and his pamphlet, *Manifesto on Cuban Affairs Addressed to the People of the United States*, issued in New Orleans in September 1852,[14] had a wide influence. Worth still expressed an interest in the scheme but was prevented from accepting the offer when he was suddenly ordered to assume command of the military departments of Texas and New Mexico, leaving Washington for his new assignment on December 5, 1848, to die of cholera a few months later.

Angry over the attitude of the Havana Club, López determined to act independently and founded his own junta in New York. The quarrel between the two factions, however, was not total. The club provided funds for López and he in turn sought an American military leader to command an invading force. He first turned to Jefferson Davis, then senator from Mississippi, who as a colonel had commanded the Mississippi Rifles in the Mexican War. Davis, wanting Cuba as a slave state, had already been in touch with island revolutionists. On June 23 he had called on President Polk with three members of the Cuban Council who had information that an insurrection would occur on the island the next day, the López revolt, which they did not know had been postponed. Davis asked the president to station troops at Key West and other points on the alert to protect American citizens on the island. He hinted that this would serve as an excuse for intervention if Americans were endangered in an insurrection, but Polk did not rise to the bait. Pursuing his scheme of purchasing the island, he merely replied that he would consider the proposal.[15]

The offer to Davis was a generous one, reflecting the heroic optimism of López, who had no resources except what the Havana Club gave him. The junta would deposit $100,000 before the departure to Cuba for the use of Mrs. Davis, and if the invasion succeeded Davis would receive an additional $100,000 or a large coffee plantation. Davis approved of López's plan but was unwilling himself to undertake command, suggesting instead his friend Robert E. Lee, a captain in the Engineer Corps in the Mexican War. Davis later recalled the proposal: "They were anxious to secure his services, and offered him every temptation that ambition could desire, and pecuniary emoluments far beyond any which he could hope otherwise to acquire." Lee went to Washington to consult with Davis about the offer but decided to refuse, because he felt it wrong to accept such a military post while he held a commission in the U.S. army.[16]

Failing to obtain a well-known person whose name would give éclat to the expedition (Lee hardly qualified in this respect), López decided to carry on with the project nevertheless, with González as his second in command. He pursuaded several young officers in the Mexican War to join him, including Robert M. White, a second lieutenant in the Regiment of Louisiana Volunteers, and Walter F. Bisco, a lieutenant in the Battalion of Louisiana Mounted Volunteers.

During the first months of 1849 López operated mostly in New York and Washington. On two occasions while López was in Washington, John C. Calhoun conferred with him and once arranged for him to meet with four other senators in a committee room of the Capitol to hear his plans. Calhoun was sympathetic to the cause but unwilling to become an active supporter, wishing to devote his fullest effort to solving the slave question dividing the nation.[17] Later in the year, on August 24, John L. O'Sullivan, a busy conniver in the scheme, serving as a liaison between the Havana Club and the junta and traveling about the country as López's business agent, wrote Calhoun asking his public support and quoting a remark by Calhoun presumably made at one of the Washington conferences: "The South ought (according to an expression which Gen. López has quoted to me from you) to flock down there in 'open boats,' the moment they hear the tocsin."[18]

The invasion plan was now well along. The Havana Club had advanced López $30,000 as the first installment of $60,000 promised him, and additional funds, about $70,000, came from sources in the United States. López acknowledged the Havana Club gift in a letter declaring that everything pointed to the "triumph of the common cause, *and the adding of the Star of Cuba to those which shine in the glorious flag of the American Union*." He had chartered three ships to sail from New York with arms and men recruited there and at Philadelphia and Baltimore and other vessels at New Orleans to transport Southern recruits to an embarkation point at Cat Island off the coast of Louisiana. Volunteers were offered the U.S. army pay and rations with a bonus of $1,000 and 5 acres of land when Cuba was free. One recruit in Philadelphia was quoted as saying he was persuaded to sign up by the offer of $1,000 and "plenty of plunder," and in New Orleans, where moneyless adventurers were eager to head for the goldfields of California, eligible men were regaled with the prospects of wealth to be found instead in Cuba. "The gold is already dug and coined for which you will fight," they were told.[19]

López was confident an expedition of 1,500 men was enough for a successful invasion, but his optimism was greater than that of some of his supporters. *The United States Magazine and Democratic Review* believed an invasion was feasible but set the required force of 3,000 to 4,000 Americans who would need sixty days to take over the island,[20] and the U.S. consul at Havana, Robert B. Campbell, said 3,000 men and ninety days would be required.[21] Even O'Sullivan, usually ebullient, was worried about prospects, and in his letter to Calhoun had urgently pleaded with him to rouse Southerners to Lopez's banner: "I write to you (being myself deeply interested in the movement and now on my way to N. Orleans on business connected with it) in the hope that you will appreciate at once the thousand and powerful reasons which seem to me to apply to your position, to cause you to strain every nerve at this moment for the promotion of the object. . . . Now, my dear sir, can not you write to fifty points and fifty proper persons to act and act with requisite energy, promptitude, head and heart in this matter?"

Both the Spanish minister, Angel Calderón de la Barca, and the Taylor administration maintained a close surveillance of the filibuster movement. On August 2 and again on August 13, Calderón wrote Secretary of State Clayton to protest the party "which plans and even openly seeks" to invade Cuba. Clayton replied on August 16 that Calderón could "rest assured that the strictest watch will be kept over the movements" to send forth an expedition. By August 8 Clayton had collected sufficient information to write Logan Hunton, U.S. attorney in New Orleans, to check on reports that a force of 800 men was to leave from Cat Island between August 20 and 25 for Cuba. He mentioned that "Colonel Biscoe" of New Orleans was concerned in the enterprise and that Whitney and Company of the city was reported to have on hand $250,000—a fantastic exaggeration—to aid in fitting out the expedition. If Huston could obtain evidence that would stand up in court, he was to arrest the leaders. Two days later the secretary of the navy ordered Commodore F. A. Parker, commander of the home squadron based at Pensacola, to patrol the coast of Mississippi and prevent the sailing of the expedition, reported now to be assembling at Round Island. To reinforce these orders, President Taylor on August 11 issued a proclamation setting forth the circumstantial reports of the expedition and warning citizens against taking part in an enterprise "grossly in violation of our laws and of our treaty obligations."[22]

The Southern volunteers recruited by Colonel White and Bisco had been taken to Round Island, off the coast of eastern Mississippi, rather than Cat Island, which was too close to New Orleans for comfort, and were awaiting the steamers from New York. By September 4 the island was blockaded by several naval vessels. They were not needed to stop the expedition, however, for the ships fitted out in New York were seized by orders of the U.S. attorney, J. Prescott Hall, on September 6. The small propeller ship *Sea Gull* had sailed but was delayed in quarantine; only the crew and a few other men were on board, but there was a cargo of 1,000 muskets "with powder and provisions in plenty," according to the *New York Tribune*'s report on September 8. The large steamer *New Orleans*, fitted out as a transport with accommodations for 900 passengers, and the smaller *Florida* were seized while at anchor in the harbor.

Naval officers in the blockade of the filibusters at Round Island reported that they were a wild lot. "It is my deliberate opinion," one wrote, "that if a *piratical* enterprise were, or could be, projected at this point to rob upon the high seas, that more than one-half of the 450 now assembled on Round Island would instantly volunteer to take part in it."[23]

President Taylor defended his order to halt the expedition in his message to Congress on December 4 and went on to express his concern about relations with Latin-American countries. "The United States stand as the great American power," he said, "to which, as their natural ally and friend, they will always be disposed first to look for mediation and assistance in the event of any collision between them and any nation." He touched upon several topics that in the next few years were to figure importantly in the dreams of expansionists and filibusters. One concerned the Isthmus of Panama. In 1844 the United States had entered into a postal convention with New Granada (Colombia) for transporting mail across the isthmus; complaints had been received of New Granada's failure to fulfill provisions of the agreement and the administration would look into this. He expressed his hope that a proposed railroad would be constructed across the isthmus under a treaty with New Granada ratified on June 10, 1848, by President Polk. Of a transit route across the Isthmus of Tehuantepec, which Polk had attempted to obtain in the peace treaty with Mexico, Taylor said that he would not renew any proposition to purchase, declaring that right of passage should be equally secured to all nations. Of a canal route across Nicaragua, the rights of which had been obtained by a company controlled by Americans, he said he was negotiating a treaty pledging both governments to protect those engaging in the work and inviting other nations to enter into the same treaty stipulations. Extending the sphere of American interest to the Sandwich Islands (Hawaii), he said his desire was that they should maintain their independence and hoped that other nations concurred. "We could in no event be indifferent to their passing under the dominion of any other power," he declared.

The two failures of López to spark a revolt in Cuba, one the Conspiracy of the Cuban Rose Mines and now the Round Island expedition, determined the cautious Havana Club to have nothing more to do with him and to pursue annexationist goals by peaceful means. The club dissolved the Cuban Council in New York and organized El Consejo del Organización y Gobierno Cubano, whose main activity was publication of *La Verdad*.[24] López thereupon announced in the newspapers the organization of the Junta Promovedor de los Interéses Politícos de Cuba with headquarters in Washington. The junta would act openly "without infringing on the laws of this country," and friends of Cuban liberty were invited to contribute any aid "honorably and legitimately in their power." The Spanish minister, Calderón, protested strongly to Clayton this "extravagant and improper" manifesto on January 19, 1850.[25]

Although López had some strong supporters in the North, he realized that his real strength lay in the South and while operating from Washington as a base decided to transfer his headquarters to New Orleans. A number of Southerners he met urged this step. One was John Henderson, a Mississippi cotton planter, lawyer, and former U.S. senator who favored annexation of Cuba as a move in developing a slave empire in the Caribbean and who promised to give financial support. Another was a Kentuckian, Theodore O'Hara, decorated for bravery in the Mexican War, who promised to return to his home state and raise a regiment for an expedition. A handsome, dark-haired Irishman with the charm and manner of a Southern gentleman, O'Hara also had the gift of eloquence of Southern orators. He is remembered as the author of a once-famous poem, "The Bivouac of the Dead," written on the reburial at Frankfort of Kentuckians slain in the battle of Buena Vista. Lines from it carved in marble or cast in bronze appear on soldiers' monuments or over the gates of military cemeteries around the country.

Traveling south in March by way of the Ohio and Mississippi Rivers, López and González stopped for conferences along the way with persons interested in the Cuban venture. They found recruitment centers in Ohio and Kentucky headed by friends of O'Hara. In Cincinnati, the leader was William Hardy, a veteran of the Mexican War, and a promoter of the movement was Richardson Hardy, publisher of the newspaper *Nonpareil*. Richardson Hardy was to become a historian of the enterprise, publishing late in the year *The History and Adventures of the Cuban Expedition*.[26]

A significant meeting for the Cuban annexation movement took place in mid-March at Jackson, Mississippi, when López and González called on the flamboyant John A. Quitman, who had been sworn in as governor on January 10. In his inaugural address Quitman had delivered a magniloquent defense of slavery as a good rather than evil institution which was "looked upon favorably by God." The governor received López and González cordially and expressed his enthusiasm for their plan. As a result, they submitted to him on March 17 a formal contract on their own account and in behalf of their "coadjutors in the United States, and of the people of Cuba." They offered him the position of general in chief of the army of a freed Cuba while López would head the civil administration. Liberal financial rewards were promised Quitman and all soldiers who took part. To carry out the scheme, López would go to Cuba "with all dispatch," raise the standard of Cuban independence, and "from the field of revolution" furnish Quitman with evidence that the people supported him and would welcome his presence.

Quitman's friend and biographer, John F. H. Claiborne, wrote that the governor was strongly tempted by the offer. "Quitman was ambitious, and these grand ideas of revolution and progress, of changes to be accomplished by liberal principles and energetic rule, were his own," Claiborne said. "To lead such a movement in aid of an oppressed people, and for the introduction of American civilization and Southern institutions, had been the dream of his life. The battle-field and its glory, the clangor and the charge rose up like a gorgeous pageant to dazzle his imagination." Nevertheless, on March 18, Quitman wrote López and González declining the offer. His "devotion to the cause of civil liberty" urged him to accept, but he was "bound by official engagements to the people of my own state," which he felt he could not abandon.

Quitman, however, did not reveal that he had another reason to refuse. This was that on December 13, 1849, and again February 23, 1850, he had received urgent requests from the Havana Club to join its movement. The first letter stated that club members had lost all confidence in López and declared that if Quitman could unite Southern advocates of annexation in "one great and bold blow" such an accomplishment "would be worthy of the gallant hand that unfurled the American flag" over Mexico City.

Quitman had apparently said, in earlier correspondence, that agitation over slavery was on the increase and that he felt this must be settled before Southerners could whole-heartedly get behind the Cuba movement, an opinion shared by Calhoun, but by February the Havana Club believed that the situation had changed with the introduction in the U.S. Senate in January by Henry Clay of his compromise resolutions to resolve differences between the North and South. Mentioning the prospect of speedy settlement of the slavery question and the danger of the "impetuous anxiety" of López to go to Cuba, the second letter pleaded again for him to head the movement that would "serve Southern conservative interest" while at the same time serving the planters' interest in Cuba. The wealth of the Havana Club leaders was mentioned, with the assurance that at least a million dollars could easily be raised if Quitman's name were used. "It would be almost unnecessary to say that Cuba would lavish on you her wealth, as well as the honor and gratitude due to the achievement," Quitman was assured. Thus, Quitman turned down López so as not to foreclose more promising arrangements with the Havana Club.[27]

Going on to New Orleans, López and González found enthusiasm for their project among young men eager to match the derring-do of romantic tradition in the exploits of the pirate Jean Lafitte and his men who had raided the shipping and the coastal towns of the Caribbean and such heroes of the Texas revolution as Davy Crockett, William B. Travis, and James Bowie. Moreover, all over the South there were "young bloods" that General William Tecumseh Sherman a few years later was to describe: "War suits them, and the rascals are brave, fine riders, bold to rashness, and dangerous subjects in every sense. They care not a sou for niggers, land or anything. . . . As long as they have good horses, plenty of forage, and an open country, they are happy. This is a larger class than most men suppose, and they are the most dangerous set of men that this war has turned loose upon the world. They are splendid riders, first-rate shots, and utterly reckless."[28]

Such a one was the struggling young lawyer Chatham Roberdeau Wheat, to win fame in the Civil War as leader of the Louisiana Tigers. He had been a member of the First Tennessee Mounted Regiment and had fought under General Quitman in the Mexican

War and afterward had studied law in New Orleans and been admitted to the bar in 1849. He had been imbued with the far-ranging ideals of Manifest Destiny in the columns of J. B. D. De Bow's *Review*, an influential spokesman for national expansion in the interest of extending slavery as a cure for the South's economic ills. Wheat presented himself to González, begging to be allowed to join the expedition. "I told him we had no transportation for him," González wrote later, "but he removed the objection by offering to procure it if I only gave him the authority to form also a skeleton regiment of Louisianians. This having been done, he obtained money from young gentlemen friends of his, to charter the brig *Susan Loud*, provisioned her, etc., all for the mere privilege of going."[29]

Another was J. C. Davis, who with Hardy was to be one of the annalists of the expedition, his *History of the Late Expedition to Cuba* appearing late in 1850.[30] He expressed the motives of young men of his class in taking part. The inhabitants of Cuba wished to be free, but if they revolted "the blacks would be armed and turned loose upon them." "No government," Davis declared, "capable of conceiving such an idea, or making such a threat, either deserves the respect or allegiance of its subjects." He believed "it to be right and proper to propagate republican principles . . . and multiply republican governments," because if it were praiseworthy for Lafayette to join the American Revolution, "how much more glory would there be in striking the first blow for an oppressed people." Moreover, "it was whispered about certain places that there was *gold* as well as *glory* in Cuba." And, finally, "it would be a very pretty little operation for the summer," though there might be "a right smart brush or so" because Spain had 25,000 troops on the island.

There were hundreds of young men like Wheat and Davis ready to join up in a spirit of adventure, although they did not disregard the "gold" as well as the "glory" they might win; but there were also hundreds of stranded war veterans, hangers-on in the saloons, and "riff raff," as even a leader of the expedition called them, attracted by the army pay of $7 a month and rations, not to mention a $4,000 bonus—inflation seemed to be operating—and a grant of land in Cuba. Such munificent promises cost nothing, but the cash had to be on hand to charter ships and to buy muskets, artillery pieces, and ammunition. There had to be men with money to put up for the expedition, and López found them in New Orleans also. Money was raised by issuing 6 percent bonds pledged on the "public lands and property of Cuba." Two million dollars worth of bonds were issued and they were purchased by speculators, but no grand sums were obtained since they sold at 10 cents on the dollar. Perhaps $40,000 or $50,000 was thus raised to fit out the expedition, about one-half actually contributed by one man, the planter and lawyer John Henderson. One of López's most important New Orleans supporters was Lawrence J. Sigur, owner of the *Delta*, who promoted bond sales and recruitment in his newspaper, made his home into the headquarters for the general, and in other ways involved himself deeply in the conspiracy.

Meanwhile, in Ohio and Kentucky Major Hardy and Colonel O'Hara had completed their recruitment drive and had chartered a steamer, the *Martha Washington*, to transport the men to New Orleans. The battalion under the command of Hardy—it was made up of 120 Ohioans and 130 Kentuckians—sailed from Cincinnati on April 4. O'Hara, with a small contingent from Frankfort, sailed on a separate vessel, the *Chancellor*, from Evansville.

On the trip down the river those on the *Martha Washington* passed the time engaging in such military exercises as could be carried on in the confines of the crowded boat. They had been instructed to reply to all questions about their destination that they were bound for the goldfields of California, but no one who saw them when they poured ashore at the stops along the way was fooled. At Vicksburg, Richardson Hardy reported, an onlooker improbably sang out as he saw the men walking up and down the levee: "Cuba, by G-d! No such men as these go to California to dig. Did you ever see such a body of men! D—d if they ain't all gentlemen! What fire, intelligence and energy glows in every countenance."

They reached Freeport, about 3 miles from New Orleans, early in the morning of April 11 and there encountered one of the typical instances of the slapdash management that characterized López's leadership. "Owing to some woeful misunderstanding," Hardy wrote, "we had arrived ten or fifteen days too soon." Lodgings at Freeport being inadequate for these harum-scarum adventurers, they moved next day to Lafayette, which was nearer the city of bright lights. Hardy reported that the officers had their hands full keeping them "within the bounds of prudence and propriety . . . in such close proximity to New Orleans." As for their pretensions of being bound for California, Hardy wrote: "Our object and destination was then as well known in New Orleans as it could be. We had been the subject of several newspaper notices, and the Cuban expedition was barroom conversation all over the city."

López had evolved an elaborate plot by which he hoped to mislead the Spanish, whose spies were everywhere and reported regularly to the consul, Juan Y. Laborde, and to circumvent the neutrality laws of the United States. The Kentucky battalion would sail on a ship cleared for Chagres, Panama, ostensibly bearing emigrants to California. In reality, it would stop at Mujeres, an island a few miles off the coast of Yucatán, where it would be joined later by the Louisiana battalion being organized by Wheat and the Mississippi battalion with which López would sail.

Arrangements for a vessel to transport the Kentucky battalion, the bark *Georgiana*, were finally completed, and on the afternoon of April 25 the men went aboard. A large crowd had assembled by nine o'clock to cheer the departure when a tug came alongside and towed the craft down the river. The next morning, at the mouth of the Mississippi, the *Georgiana* anchored and waited for a fishing smack that had left the day before in the charge of Sigur with arms for the battalion. Sailing south toward the arm of Yucatán extending into the Gulf of Mexico, the *Georgiana* had favorable winds, but when the coast was sighted after five days the unhappy discovery was made that the bark was 80 miles west of Mujeres. After four days of fighting the winds, the *Georgiana* reached the tiny uninhabited island of Contoy a few miles north of Mujeres. Conditions for sailing were so adverse and the men so rambunctious that the captain decided to put them ashore here for the time being. He anchored in "a pretty little bay" and the battalion disembarked the next morning, May 7. The men cheered the opportunity to leap into the surf to wash off the sweat and grime of the two weeks of confinement in the bark, but they soon learned why the island had no people: it was merely a sandy cay and the only water to be found was in a small salt lake in the center. Efforts in the next four days to sail on to Mujeres failed and the men settled down in a cantankerous mood to await the arrival of the other battalions, signaling their location by fires kept burning day and night.

Back in New Orleans, Colonel Wheat was completing his recruitment and planning for his departure on the bark *Susan Loud*. Richardson Hardy, who came to know the men of the Louisiana battalion later on, had a low opinion of them. They were "worthless characters and blackguard rowdies . . . of New Orleans, who had applied for and been refused admission into the Kentucky battalion." This was not the view of New Orleanians, who feted them as heroes and regarded their leader, the twenty-four-year-old Wheat, as even nobler. "He was a pet with the generals of the Mexican War," wrote one of his followers in a diary published in the *Delta*. "The ladies of the Crescent City frequently speak of his flashing, dark eyes, his frank ingenuous countenance, and his Herculean, but graceful, frame." On the night of May 2, about the time the *Georgiana* made a landfall at Yucatán, the *Susan Loud* cast off her moorings and under sealed orders sailed down the Mississippi and into the gulf with about 150 men making up the Louisiana battalion.

Unlike the voyage of the *Georgiana*, that of the *Susan Loud* began as a rough-and-tumble one of buffeting winds and frequent squalls of rain, according to J. C. Davis's history. But on May 6 the skies cleared and the wind abated, and, shortly after noon when the captain had taken the ship's position, the men were assembled aft. Wheat soon appeared waving a paper, which he told them he had been handed by one of General López's aides with instructions to break the seal at Latitude 26° N. Longitude 87° W. His orders, he said, were to remain at this spot until May 7, when he was to sail south. About May 9 they could expect to meet up with the steamer *Creole*, on which the general would sail May 7 from New Orleans with the Mississippi battalion. Then Wheat launched upon an oration, given *in extenso* by Davis, that sounded all the themes expressed in the propaganda for the liberation of Cuba.

"I have addressed you as Fellow Citizens, because it is perhaps the last time I shall ever address you as Citizens of the United States," Wheat said. "Long ere the sun has sunk beneath the world of waters which now surround us, we shall perhaps have consummated an act that will throw us beyond the protection of the Stars and Stripes under whose auspices we have sailed thus far. . . . The moment we organize, that moment we pass beyond the protection of our own government we have no longer any right to sail under her flag. . . . I shall therefore henceforth address you as Soldiers of the Liberating Army of Cuba." He continued in this vein for some minutes until, upon a prearranged signal, the lone star flag of the Republic of Cuba was raised at the masthead.* Dramatically pointing to it, Wheat exclaimed: "Liberators! Behold your flag! Three cheers for the Cuban flag!"

The Cuban banner was also hoisted in the United States on the day of the departure of the *Creole*—on the flagstaff of the *Delta* in New Orleans by Sigur and that of the *Sun* in New York by Moses Y. Beach. Both displays angered Calderón de la Barca and he complained petulantly on May 8 to Secretary of State Clayton of these manifestations of flagrant partisanship for the revolutionary conspirators and declared they were a scandal. Calderón wondered why, after he had kept Clayton informed of the expedition, which was publicized in the newspapers as well, the government had not prevented López's departure. A week later he warned Clayton that, if the American "pirates" were captured, no interposition would be made by him or the government of Spain to prevent their "deserved chastisement." Clayton replied on May 18, acknowledging that there was substance to Calderón's complaint but pointing out that the government could not stop individuals leaving the country ostensibly as citizens going to California.

Calderón had additional reason to feel unhappy when the New Orleans newspapers printed proclamations that López had left to be published after the sailing of the *Creole*. In one addressed to the filibuster force López exclaimed over the flag of the Cuban Republic under which the men would fight: "The Flag on which

*The flag, designed by a friend of López, consisted of a white star in a red triangle upon three broad blue stripes separated by white stripes. The lone star was apparently chosen as an inspirational reminder of Texas in winning her independence from Mexico.

you behold the Tricolor of Liberty, the Triangle of Strength and Order, the Star of the future State." In the other, to be issued to the people of the island, he again referred to the flag: "And the Star of Cuba, today dark and obscured by the fog of despotism, will emerge beautiful and shining, on being admitted with glory into the splendid North American constellation, where destiny leads it."

The *Susan Loud* and the *Creole* came to their rendezvous as scheduled on May 9, one of the few times that López's plans for this ill-fated venture worked out. The men in the Louisiana battalion had passed the time playing poker with large amounts of the bonds of the Cuban Republic as stakes—they might as well have been matchsticks insofar as their monetary value was concerned. A day was spent in transferring the adventurers to the *Creole*, whose course was then set for Mujeres. The Louisianans, according to Davis, were disappointed by the size of the Mississippi battalion, as it numbered only about 130 men when they had expected 500, "the very flower of the Mississippi Volunteers in Mexico."

After three days that passed almost without an incident worthy of being recorded by the historian Davis, those on the *Creole* sighted Yucatán on the afternoon of May 13 and early the next day, rounding a point on the cape, glimpsed the *Georgiana* anchored at Contoy. As the *Creole* sailed into the bay the men on board and those ashore commenced to cheer, "the Kentuckians giving some of those famous Old Kentuck' yells, which used to terrify the Mexicans." At a council of war attended by the battalion leaders and López, it was decided to land the men from the *Creole* to organize and drill on the beach while the steamer went on to Mujeres for water. On her return the next day all three battalions would be taken on board the *Creole*, which would sail at once for Cuba.

López, though he might be guilty of oversight in anticipating practical difficulties, had come prepared with a printed proclamation describing his vision of conquest. Distributed to the men upon the arrival of the *Creole* at Contoy, it "greatly elevated their previously high ideals of the glorious mission on which they had embarked," Richardson Hardy wrote. It addressed the filibusters as "soldiers of the Liberating Expedition of Cuba" and played up to their patriotism as Americans by referring to "the men of the field of Palo Alto and Churubusco." It urged them "to strike from the beautiful limbs of the Queen of the Antilles the chains which have too long degraded her, in subjection to a foreign tyranny . . . to do for your Cuban brethren what a Lafayette, a Steuben, a Kosciusko, and a Pulaski are deathless in history for having aided to do for you."

Ashore companies were organized and uniforms issued consisting of "a red flannel shirt, a black cloth cap, with a Lone Star cockade, and 'any sort' of pants." The red shirts had been chosen as the color worn by the European revolutionists of 1848. But the glorious prospects unrolled before them by López had not addled the senses of all the men, especially those of Wheat's Louisiana battalion. They observed that the liberating army would be made up of barely 600 troops and that the *Creole*, now seen to be old and unseaworthy, would be dangerously overcrowded when the Kentuckians were taken aboard.

Wheat rose to the crisis and assembled his men on the beach where he sought to reinspire them for the venture through his oratory, as he had probably concluded that the grumblers were more than half right in their apprehensions. He depicted the condition of the people of Cuba, "the theatre of brutal oppression, unprecedented in the most diresome periods of a Nero or a Caligula, and this too, within a short distance of a land that boasts of a Washington, an Adams, a Hancock and a Patrick Henry." The speaker went on to say that the "kindly interposition of a superintending Providence" was apparent in the steps they had already taken, and he assured them that their future safety was also thus secured. "And now, my brave boys," he concluded, "let us, under the command of our noble chieftain, rush to the field of glory."

Meanwhile at Mujeres, where the *Creole* had gone to obtain water, there was disaffection among the ranks of those in the work force. When it came time to leave, thirteen refused to board the ship, saying they would capture a smack of Yucatecans fishing off the island and sail it to the United States. López prevented this by taking the smack in tow and hauling it to Contoy, leaving the deserters without arms or food on the island. The next day, May 16, when all three battalions were loaded on the *Creole*, López decided to get rid of potential mutinous elements by announcing that all who wished to quit the venture could return to the United States on the *Georgiana*. Thirty-nine accepted the offer, some of them having sailed only because they thought they were going to Chagres where they could desert and go on to California. Their desertion and that of the men at Mujeres cut the original force of 570 men to about 520.

López briefed his battalion officers on the campaign on the first day at sea. The expedition would land at Cárdenas, a port of about 3,000 people on the north coast. Taken by surprise, the town would be easily captured, and the filibuster army, swelled by the Cubans who would flock to join it, would go by railroad to attack Matanzas, a city of 30,000 lying 25 miles from Cárdenas and 70 from Havana. López expected this phase of the campaign to be completed within twenty-four hours. At Matanzas he would send a picked body of 100 men eastward to blow up a bridge on the railroad to hinder the dispatch of Spanish troops from the capital. With Matanzas as his headquarters, he would send out recuiters and in a short time he expected to have an army of 30,000 men to lay siege to Havana.

At about ten o'clock on the night of May 18 the *Creole* passed the lighthouse at the tip of the peninsula on the west side of the bay at Cárdenas and made her way into the harbor toward the town 15 miles away. The moon was full and the ship went slowly to time her arrival after it had set. The men, armed with muskets or rifles and sixty rounds of cartridges—some also carried revolvers, sabers, or bowie knives—stood silently for hours on the deck as the ship crept along, passing the cays and anchored vessels, with the only sounds breaking the stillness the cry of the leadsman taking soundings or an occasional clank of a saber. When the *Creole* approached a dock at one o'clock in the darkness, the mate, Callender Fayssoux, jumped overboard with a line to tie up at the wharf. Fayssoux, a native of Missouri, had served as a midshipman in the navy of the Republic of Texas and he had been a crewmember of one of the ships chartered by López for his thwarted 1849 expedition. With only a single plank from ship to wharf to land the more than 500 men, the disembarkation went slowly, and it was five o'clock before all of them, beginning with the Kentucky battalion followed by the Mississippi and Louisiana battalions, were ashore.

General López's strategy was to send two companies to seize the railroad station within the town and the yards just outside while the main force attacked the garrison occupying barracks on the plaza. He expected the soldiers to surrender immediately upon his call and he then would embark his forces on the train and proceed to Matanzas. Only the first part of his battle plan succeeded. A company from the Mississippi battalion, commanded by Captain Achilles Kewen, quickly captured the railroad station and one from the Kentucky battalion, commanded by Lieutenant Colonel John T. Pickett, had no trouble in seizing the locomotive and rail cars in the yards. But he was unrealistic in his belief that the garrison would surrender without resistance.

At five o'clock in the morning the streets were deserted except for muleteers bringing in produce, and the three battalions quickly marched upon the plaza by three different routes. Taking the central street from the pier to the plaza, Colonel O'Hara led his column along until he reached the Spanish garrison; the Louisiana column, commanded by Colonel Wheat, took a street to the east, and the Mississippi column one to the west. At the barracks, O'Hara was challenged by sentries and replied in English "Friends and López!" Instead of emerging to welcome their savior at this cry, the troops answered with a burst of fire that wounded O'Hara. General López then came forward and demanded that the garrison surrender. Instead, the Spaniards fled by the doors facing the plaza and took refuge in the governor's palace on the opposite side. At this moment the column commanded by Wheat debouched from the road entering the plaza on the east. Wheat, thinking the firing was a salute to López, cried out, "López and liberty!" and rushed gallantly into the plaza at the head of his Louisianans. They were met by a volley from the Spaniards escaping into the palace. Wheat, struck in the shoulder, fell to the ground, crying: "Louisianans! Your colonel is killed! Go and avenge his death!" His wound, however, was not so fatal as he had thought, but it put him hors de combat. The Spaniards barricaded themselves in the palace, which was surrounded by the Americans, who, unable to break in, set it afire. At eight o'clock the besieged men displayed a white flag and surrendered.

The plan for the speedy attack on Matanzas had been frustrated by the unexpected resistance of the garrison, and before the day was well along the outlook for the raiders began to look ominous when rumors reached them that 3,000 men were on the road from Matanzas and would arrive before midnight. The reports seemed to be confirmed about three o'clock when López received a message that a company of lancers was galloping about the outskirts of the town reconnoitering the situation. Unable to advance toward Matanzas from which a large body of troops had been sent to stop him, as López believed, and fearful of barricading himself at Cárdenas because warships could blockade the harbor and cut off all retreat, he decided to reembark on the *Creole* and make another landing—at Mantua on the western point of the island.

With his facility for seeing silver linings, López persuaded himself that this plan was just as good as the one that had just failed. He was well known and had many friends in the west, so he believed, and word of the capture of Cárdenas would precede him so that he would be hailed as a leader with a splendid victory to his credit, the first landing being taken as a feint to set troops at Havana off on a fool's chase. He had, moreover, strengthened his forces by capture of the arms of the Cárdenas garrison. Finally, at Mantua he would be closer to New Orleans from which it would be easy to obtain supplies and reinforcements. He accordingly sent out word at four o'clock for the troops to assemble in the plaza and prepare to reembark.

The reembarkation, however, could not be done in a few moments, for supplies and arms taken to the railroad station had to be hauled back to the pier and put aboard. While this was being done, a part of the Kentucky battalion was stationed in the plaza to fight off the Spaniards in case they attacked. The situation was worse than López realized, for the lancers had been reinforced by an infantry company. The Spanish commander, in an effort to surround the filibusters in the plaza, sent his lancers down the east road bordering the plaza and the infantry down the west one. The tactic, however, did not succeed, for companies from the Kentucky battalion were sent to intercept them while the main body of troops retreated down the center road to the pier.

Reaching the pier, the Americans drew up behind hastily

erected barricades of sugar hogsheads to cover the loading of the *Creole*. The Spaniards did not attack in force and by nine o'clock the steamer had cast off and was heading down the bay. The day's activity had been a costly one for the American invaders. The Kentucky battalion had about forty casualties, including fifteen men killed, and the smaller Louisiana battalion about half as many. The Mississippi battalion, which had not been in much action, suffered the least, about half a dozen casualties.

Although the *Creole* was once more under weigh, the situation of the invaders was serious as their vessel would have to clear a tricky harbor in the darkness and enemy warships might arrive at any time. The scene on board was one of complete disarray, the decks blocked by boxes of provisions and arms and, Hardy wrote, littered "with loaded muskets, rifles, pistols, sabres, and bowie knives, thrown down by the exhausted men, who lay down to sleep in the very jaws of death." Worse was to come, for the *Creole* had not gone 5 miles when she went aground on a sand bar. In a desperate effort to free her before daybreak, provisions, arms, and ammunition were thrown overboard. Still she did not budge, and more than 100 men were landed on a nearby cay. Relieved of much of her load by these expedients, the *Creole* at last floated clear and, as the sun rose, left the harbor and stood out to sea.

Despite the night's difficulties López's spirits rose with the rising sun, and he was eager to set the course for Mantua. But the liberating army had other ideas. The officers, at a council of war, pointed out that most of their arms and provisions had been jettisoned and that the captain general of the island, surely by now informed of the expedition, would attempt to prevent another landing or if one was made would have troops on hand to do battle before Cuban patriots could rise to López's call, and their experience at Cárdenas had made them less than hopeful of this. Colonel O'Hara denounced López's new scheme as madness, and he was supported by other officers; Colonel Wheat and Adjutant General González, who had also been slightly wounded in the day's battle, were still willing to follow López. Unable to reach agreement among themselves, the officers decided to put the question to a vote of the troops. Their ardor for freeing Cuba had cooled and they voted almost to a man to return to the United States.

Heading toward Key West, the filibusters were lucky in missing Spanish warships patrolling the straits. At nightfall they came to anchor about 40 miles east of their destination. In the morning, the captain of a fishing boat was commandeered to pilot them to the port, but the *Creole* had sailed only 14 miles or so when the Spanish ship *Pizarro*, which the day before had visited Key West in search of the expedition, was sighted in the southwest. The *Pizarro* came up to fire upon the *Creole*, her sidewheels spinning in an attempt to stay out of range. Having a lighter draft than the *Pizarro*, the *Creole* was able to sail over reefs that the warship had to avoid and kept well ahead. She was not, however, in the clear, for the coal gave out and provisions and uniforms were shoved into the fireboxes to keep up steam. Panting like a spent horse, the *Creole* at last staggered into port and anchored near a navy surveying schooner, the *Petrel*, winner of the race by a few minutes. López, though defeated in his third attempt to seize Cuba, had escaped to try again to raise the lone star flag over the island.

CHAPTER THREE

Defeat and Death in Cuba

The arrival of the *Creole* at Key West with her several hundred armed passengers—a ruffianly looking lot after days spent aboard the crowded steamer and the brief but brisk fighting at Cárdenas—frightened U.S. officials there. Both Samuel J. Douglas, collector of customs, and W. C. Maloney, U.S. marshall, wrote President Taylor asking that army or naval forces be sent to protect the citizens. No arrests could be made, Douglas wrote, because the civil authority could not enforce any court orders against such a large group, which, Maloney wrote, exceeded "the number of effective male inhabitants." Their fears, however, were unwarranted.[1] The residents, according to the accounts of the expedition's historians, welcomed the filibusters as heroes and helped them to make a speedy getaway to avoid arrest. The *Creole*, hastily abandoned, was seized by a revenue officer accompanied by a body of sailors dispatched from the *Petrel*.

The expedition members who had deserted at Mujeres and Contoy fared worse than those who had stayed with López to attack Cárdenas. It was several weeks before the castaways at Mujeres could leave for Yucatán, where they were able to survive only by beggary and stealing before obtaining passage home. The *Georgiana*, left at Contoy to transport the deserters to the United States, was captured—as well as the *Susan Loud*, which had reached the island after the departure of the *Creole*—by two Spanish war vessels sent out to intercept the expedition. Taken to Havana, the thirty-nine filibusters and fifteen crew members were imprisoned on charges of piracy.

Secretary of State Clayton, chagrined at the failure to stop the expedition and worried about the fate of the Contoy prisoners, moved quickly to conciliate Spain by ordering U.S. district attorneys in the South to arrest López. The general, who had gone by ship to Savannah, was taken into custody on his arrival on May 25 but at a hearing that night was released as there were no witnesses available to testify against him. At Mobile, through which he passed on May 30, the district attorney in a letter to Clayton excused his failure to make an arrest on the same grounds.[2] In the history of filibusterism it seems that nothing succeeded like failure. López's trip from Key West was the triumphal passage of a conquering hero. Crowds greeted his appearance wherever he stopped. At Gainesville, Mississippi, for example, he was saluted by cannons and there was a parade in which appeared "a band of music, some one hundred ladies, the pupils of the academy, Gen. López and friends, the masonic brethren, and the Sons of Temperance."

In Congress, too, Southern advocates of annexation spoke out in his favor and protested the dispatch by President Taylor of naval vessels to prevent the expedition from landing. In both the House and Senate, resolutions were introduced condemning the president's action. David L. Yulee of Florida led the attack in the Senate. He declared that the expedition was not illegal under the Neutrality Act of 1818 and accused the president of usurping powers not given him by the Constitution. Daniel Webster, soon to become secretary of state after the death of Taylor on July 9, defended the president. He reviewed the nation's relations with Spain and treaty obligations that committed the government to protect that country's possession of the island and pointed out that the neutrality law made it mandatory for the chief executive to suppress military expeditions set afoot in the United States against any country with which the nation was at peace.[3] The Yulee and Webster speeches threatened to open a long debate, but Henry Clay, trying to force his omnibus bill to settle all issues arising over slavery through the Senate, succeeded in squelching this diversion.

Neither administration policy nor public opinion would permit the government to ignore the plight of the captured deserters at Contoy and the crews of the *Georgiana* and *Susan Loud*. Clayton, in letters to the U.S. consul, Robert B. Campbell, to the Spanish minister, Calderón de la Barca, and to the American minister to Spain, Daniel M. Barringer, took the stand that the men should not be tried in Spanish courts and that they should be returned to the United States to be prosecuted under the neutrality law. He wrote Campbell on June 1 to warn the captain general that "if he unjustly sheds one drop of American blood, at this exciting period, it may cost the two countries a sanguinary war." Two days later he wrote Calderón that the Spanish government, having captured these citizens on a Mexican island, had no right "to convey them to Havana and punish them capitally for crime."

Calderón in his first reply presented a view that was substantially to be maintained by his government and the captain general. Clayton must remember, Calderón wrote excitedly on June 7, "that these persons made part of an expedition fitted out in the U.S. with the intention of invading Cuba, burning and sacking her cities, plundering and murdering her inhabitants, and committing every act which could put them in the rank of buccaneers and pirates, and as such entitled to the protection of no government, but worthy only of the execration of mankind." Clayton replied on June 25 that the filibusters were not guilty of piracy, a crime that could be committed only on the high seas, and that they were guilty only of violating laws of the United States.[4]

In the meantime the government persisted in its efforts to bring López into court. When the general reached New Orleans on June 7 he was arrested, and two weeks later the district attorney obtained indictments against him, nine officers of the invading force, such abettors of the project as John Henderson, Lawrence J. Sigur, and John L. O'Sullivan, and several Mississippi officials— Governor John A. Quitman, Supreme Court Judge Cotesworth Pinckney Smith, and General Donahen Augusten of the state militia.[5]

These indictments may have persuaded the captain general, the Count of Alcoy, to modify his attitude toward the Contoy prisoners, for on July 8 he released the passengers on the *Georgiana* after investigation revealed that their intention had been to go to Chagres and they had declined to go on the expedition to Cárdenas. Proceedings against the officers and crews of the *Georgiana* and *Susan Loud*, however, would be continued, a matter that was to concern the U.S. minister to Madrid for months and to involve other European chancelleries when Spain issued a circular to her envoys to request other governments to make solemn protests to the United States for failing to fulfill international obligations by not stopping the military raid on Cuba.[6]

Governor Quitman protested the indictment against him in a letter of October 2 to H. J. Harris, U.S. district attorney in Mississippi. His personal inclination, he wrote, was "to meet the baseless charges," but his official position forced him to disregard his own feeling "when the consequences of my action might result in a suspension of the executive power of a sovereign state to which my primary allegiance is due." He promised to appear in court as soon as his term of office ended. This was unsatisfactory to federal officials, and Quitman, responding to them, reiterated his refusal to appear voluntarily in a second letter. Meanwhile, he discussed with associates the question of whether he should resign and, as his friend Claiborne put it, "thus precipitate a collision between the federal and state authorities, which would, in its sequel, involve the other Southern States." He did take this course when he was served on February 3, 1851, with an arrest warrant issued on January 13. At a hearing before the U.S. Circuit Court in New Orleans on February 7, Quitman was held for trial and released on his own recognizance in bail of $1,000.[7]

The trials of the others indicted had been delayed in the meantime because of legal technicalities except for that of John Henderson, who had chosen to test the case against the defendants in court at once. In three trials the juries could not agree on a verdict, and in March Logan Hunton, the district attorney, entered a nolle prosequi against all the defendants. He explained in a letter to Secretary of State Webster that he could adduce no stronger evidence against any of those indicted than he had used against Henderson and therefore could not hope to obtain convictions, especially in view of the difficulty of impaneling an impartial jury when he was restricted to residents of New Orleans—that hotbed of filibusterism—in the selection of members.

During the summer and fall of 1850 Calderón fired a series of missives to Clayton and his successor as secretary of state, Webster, alleging filibuster movements reported to him by Spanish consuls. Some of these reports, when checked by U.S. district attorneys, proved baseless, but some indicated that there was widespread activity, not only in the South but in such northeastern ports as New York, Philadelphia, and Baltimore. On June 3 Juan Y. Laborde, the Spanish consul in New Orleans, felt himself endangered by violence, writing Calderón that the consulate had been vandalized by men who shouted threats that "they would catch the Consul by the neck and throttle him." "The pirates and their abettors do not appear to have become discouraged in the prosecution of their ominous schemes," he said, "but are still making fresh enlistments, circulating false notices to give an air of plausibility to their intentions, and using every endeavor to make people believe that their nefarious projects will yet succeed."[8]

Persuading people that a new venture, even after two failures, would succeed was not difficult, but money was not easily come by. John Henderson wrote Quitman from New Orleans on November 6 that López's present plan was to embark for Cuba from the coast of Georgia where arms were to be stockpiled in advance. He mentioned that $25,000 was needed but only one-half this sum had been obtained in New Orleans. He alluded to his own contribution to the Cárdenas expedition, but now he was impoverished. "With my limited means, I am under the *extremest* burdens from my endeavors on the former occasion," he wrote. "Indeed, I find my cash advances for the first experiment was *over half* of all the cash advanced to the enterprise, and all my present means and energies are exhausted in bringing up arrearages."[9] Lawrence J. Sigur became the chief contributor when he sold his interest in the *Delta* to finance the charter of a ship. Smaller sums were obtained from other true believers and through the sale of Cuban bonds.

In New York the chief activist supporting López continued to be John L. O'Sullivan, busy seeking money and making arrangements to purchase arms, charter a ship, and recruit men. He was soon joined by Louis Schlesinger, one of the European exiles who had fought as an officer under Louis Kossuth, the Hungarian nationalist. Visiting New Orleans in January 1851, Schlesinger met López and at once became an admirer. "To sympathise warmly with the cause of liberty in Cuba was natural enough to any one," Schlesinger wrote later; "to offer it such services as my military education and experience might qualify me to render, was equally so to one thus circumstanced."[10]

A lack of coordination in the activities of the filibuster leaders and ineptitude as practical men are brought out in the report of a spy who infiltrated the organization and sold his information to Spanish officials. He was one Dr. D. Henry Burtnett, who in the fall of 1850 under the name of Duncan Smith joined a company in New Orleans engaged in drills in preparation for fighting in Cuba. He related that his intention was to "defeat the objects of these common disturbers of the peace of the world and pirates upon mankind." His motive, however, was not actually so altruistic. Records show that he put in a claim for $25,000 for his services but had been induced to accept $12,000; he seems actually to have been paid only $8,000. When Burtnett went to New York in April 1851 and met O'Sullivan, he had so well established himself with the conspirators that details of the operation were confided to him and he was asked to charter sloops or schooners to transport recruits from the port to the steamer *Cleopatra*, which had been obtained for the expedition and which would take on passengers at a rendezvous at sea off Sandy Hook.[11]

Under the arrangements Burtnett made with O'Sullivan, he was to be paid $750 for his services in obtaining sloops to transport 250 recruits from the New York vicinity and 150 from New Jersey and Philadelphia to the rendezvous with the *Cleopatra*. The *Cleopatra*, according to the plan, would sail to a point in Florida where she would join other vessels fitted out in the South. Several landings would be made simultaneously on the north coast of Cuba to "distract and divide" the forces of the captain general and permit the invaders to amalgamate with native insurrectionists, of whom it was believed 14,000 had been enrolled under island leaders. Burtnett revealed the scheme to the Spanish consul in New York and to the U.S. marshal and district attorney.

Unaware of Burtnett's betrayal, the filibusters went ahead with plans for embarking the troops on the night of April 23. According to the schedule, the *Cleopatra* was to leave her berth in New York at six o'clock for the rendezvous at sea. The *William Roe*, one of the sloops chartered by Burtnett, was to sail from South Amboy with the New Jersey and Philadelphia recruits, commanded by Armstrong Irvine Lewis, captain of the *Creole* in the Cárdenas expedition, at eight o'clock. Burtnett was to sail with the New York recruits on the *Nahantee* at nine o'clock. They were to recognize the *Cleopatra* by three lights suspended vertically from her stem pole. The counterplot of the government was for the U.S. marshal to patrol the area in a steamer and halt the *Cleopatra* after the filibusters were taken aboard.

The filibusters' scheme did not work out as planned. Burtnett had loaded his passengers on the *Nahantee*, moored at the end of Eighteenth Street, when O'Sullivan arrived in great excitement with the information that the *Cleopatra* had not sailed because the crew had become intoxicated and refused to go to sea without an advance of wages. Burtnett debarked his passengers and procured provisions for them while they waited for the sailing of the *Cleopatra*, it was hoped, next day. He then took a cutter to Sandy Hook to intercept the *William Roe* and spent a futile night looking for her—she had in fact not sailed, having been detained at South Amboy when government officers discovered a defect in her papers.

After this night of errors it would seem that nothing worse could happen, but it did. The next day O'Sullivan reported to Burtnett that a libel had been placed upon the *Cleopatra* by the man from whom she had been purchased because of $3,000 still owing him. O'Sullivan had only $1,400 in cash. While he attempted to raise the money to free the *Cleopatra*, the U.S. district attorney obtained an indictment against him as well as Schlesinger and Lewis and had them arrested on April 26.[12]

To forestall further filibuster expeditions, President Fillmore on April 25 issued a proclamation charging that the *Cleopatra* invasion was set on foot "chiefly by foreigners who dare to make our shores the scene of their guilty and hostile preparations against a friendly power, and seek, by falsehood and misrepresentation, to seduce our citizens, especially the young and inconsiderate, into their wicked schemes." With the Contoy prisoners in mind, he warned that participants in such ventures would "forfeit their claim to the protection of this government, or any interference on their behalf no matter to what extremities they may be reduced in consequence of their illegal conduct." Neither the arrest of the *Cleopatra* conspirators nor the president's proclamation acted as a deterrent to filibuster activity. Developments in Cuba led the leaders on to even more frenetic endeavor during the summer.

The Count of Alcoy had been replaced by a new captain general, José de la Concha, who, on reports of the new filibuster movement in the United States issued a proclamation warning that "a new incursion of pirates is preparing, similar to the one which took place at Cárdenas during the last year" and instructing officials to be vigilant to prevent any disturbances of the peace. Nevertheless, there were scattered attempts at revolt reports of which, reaching López in highly distorted and exaggerated accounts, led him to believe his arrival was all that was needed to coordinate them into a mass insurrection.

Discomfited but by no means disheartened by the failure of the *Cleopatra* expedition, López had set to work at once to obtain another ship. He was caught unprepared, however, on July 28 when newspapers told of uprisings that had begun on the island on July 4. The *New Orleans Delta* carried the exclamatory headlines:

> GLORIOUS NEWS FROM CUBA!
> THE REVOLUTION COMMENCED!
> FIRST BATTLES ON THE FOURTH OF JULY!
> THE PATRIOTS TRIUMPHANT!
> THE GOVERNMENT PANIC STRICKEN!

The revolution, so the reports said, had begun at Puerto Principe (Camagüey) in the central part of the island. The leader was Joaquín de Agüero. He had issued a Declaration of Independence on the day celebrated in the United States as the beginning of the revolt of the colonies against England. At the foot of the Cascorro Mountains insurrectionists numbering 200 men had engaged 300 government troops and routed them completely, a battle, one newspaper said, that "inspired very great confidence among the people" who rapidly joined the insurgent forces which, at the last accounts, "were known to number 1,000 men and more." Later reports said that three regiments of government troops had gone over to the insurgents and that rebels had taken over at Tunas, Nuevitas, and San Juan de los Remidios, the implication being that the whole central part of the island was in the hands of the insurgents.

The same newspapers that reported these insurgent victories also published a statement of Captain General Concha that government troops had encountered small rebel bands at Puerto Principe and Tunas and had dispersed them and that except at Nuevitas the whole island was tranquil. His statement was discredited by the American press, one paper declaring: "The Government has published that every symptom of insurrection has been quieted. The object of this is to intimidate the people and induce them to forgo any measures of resistance they may have contemplated. The representations of the Government are all false." The *New York Tribune*, strongly condemnatory of López, accepted this view and reported that exiled Cubans in the city were certain of success.

Louis Schlesinger, after being released on bail for his part in the *Cleopatra* affair, had decided to join López in New Orleans. He arrived the day reports of the insurrection first appeared in the newspapers. "New Orleans, the gay and spirited metropolis of the South-West, I found all in a blaze of sympathising excitement about Cuba and for Cuba," he related. "The mere traversing of the streets revealed in a few minutes to the stranger the public sentiment by which the community was strongly moved. The Cuban flag . . . was to be seen in almost every direction, displayed in ample folds from buildings, or in miniature form in windows. Placards on the walls invited to public meetings, and Cuba, Cuba, Cuba was the topic of the newspapers, the Exchange, the street corners, and the bar-rooms."[13]

Schlesinger found López, unable to get off at once to Cuba, "chafing at the delay like an imprisoned lion." He showed Schlesinger letters from Cuba expressing anxiety for his arrival and declaring that his presence, together with a supply of arms, was all that was needed to make the revolt island-wide. López himself feared that if he did not reach the island at once the revolt would be crushed without the inspiration of his presence and his organizing genius. But a ship recently purchased by Sigur for the expedition, the *Pampero*, a coasting packet, was on a voyage to Galveston, and had not returned. She at last arrived on Saturday, August 1, and López was disconcerted to learn she was having engine trouble that would require several days to repair. Worse, one of his chief aides, William L. Crittenden, employed at the custom house, reported that orders had been received to seize the ship on Monday. To prevent this, López announced that the embarkation would be on Sunday night in the hope repairs could be made while the ship was sailing down the river before putting out to sea. The *Pampero* was moored at Lafayette and López went on board at one o'clock in the morning, "greeted with wild hurrahs both from the officers and men already collected on board and from the thousands of citizens who were assembled to witness the departure," Schlesinger related. He estimated the crowd at 10,000 persons, most of whom remained on hand until coal and provisions were put on board and the ship was taken in tow at four o'clock for her trip down the river "in the midst of the most enthusiastic cheers of applause, good wishes, and farewell, from the crowded masses we left behind." When the *Pampero* reached the mouth of the river and anchored to complete repairs, she was crowded with about 500 men and the decks were piled high with barrels of provisions, boxes of arms, and the trunks, bags, and knapsacks of the volunteers.

On August 4 López reduced the number of volunteers by about 100 men. His force now included about fifty Cubans, twenty or so Hungarians and Germans, one infantry battalion of Americans of 232 men, and an artillery battalion of 122 to handle the guns to be loaded on board at St. Johns River in northern Florida. When the *Pampero* put out to sea next day, Schlesinger expressed his admiration for the Americans "whose impelling motive was simply a gallant enthusiasm to fight for liberty in aid of a tyrannized people" against 20,000 to 30,000 Spanish troops on the island.

Despite this good opinion of Schlesinger for the Americans, his history of the expedition contains frequent criticisms of them. In his opinion, they were "raw and undisciplined." He noted an instance of their lack of discipline involving the distribution of provisions shortly after the *Pampero* got under weigh. "Both men and some officers broke through all restraint, and would seize upon what they wanted, almost by force," he related. "Barrels and boxes were broken, and a great deal was extravagantly wasted."

But such difficulties as these were minor compared with the discovery on August 10 that the *Pampero* was running out of coal. In the haste of the departure the specified coaling for sixteen days of sailing had been incomplete and now, after only five days at sea, there was fuel left for only three days. Considered as being capable of doing 15 knots, the *Pampero* had been able to average only 8 or 9. On this date she should have been at the St. Johns River, but actually she had not reached Key West. By now the enthusiasm of the men when they left New Orleans had abated. "So much ill feeling had been generated, out of the discomfort of the crowded, hot and protracted voyage, together with some jealousies and dissatisfaction," Schlesinger wrote, "that there were some of the officers, who seriously contemplated, and even talked about abandoning the expedition." But when Key West was reached and residents swarmed around the *Pampero* in boats, greeting her with "hurrahs and waving of handkerchiefs," and the volunteers heard roseate accounts of the progress of the revolution, their enthusiasm was revived, and they "were now impatient to strike straight across for the nearest part of the Island." This was indeed López's new plan, suddenly evolved, when he realized that it would be impossible to sail up the coast of Florida to the St. Johns River to obtain the stockpiled guns and ammunition and thence to the northern coast of Cuba.

The expeditionists left Key West happily under the delusion they would arrive on an island where the people, raising the banner of revolt, had won victory after victory and had occupied town after town. In actuality, there had been only two small uprisings, quickly put down, and the official reports of the government at Havana carried in the American press that the situation was well in hand had been correct. The *grito* for revolution had been sounded prematurely by Joaquín de Agüero, who had formed the Sociedad Libertadora and issued proclamations clandestinely throughout the island calling for uprisings coordinated with López's expedition. The captain general, José de la Concha, aware of what was happening, had sent a ruthless commander, Marshal José Lemery, to Puerto Principe to "frustrate the realization of the criminal purposes of Her Majesty's enemies." Agüero, like López a reckless and impetuous man, inclined to act before considering the consequences, had decided, on learning of the seizure of the *Cleopatra* and the consequent postponement of the expedition, to issue his call for revolution to hasten the departure of a force from the United States.

The Cuban conspirators had used the *noms de guerre* of

Franklin, Washington, and other leaders in the American Revolution, and Agüero in tribute to them had issued his own Declaration of Independence on the Fourth of July. "The Island of Cuba is unanimously declared to be independent of the Government and Peninsula of Spain," his proclamation said, "in order that she may be recognized before the world as an independent nation, which has spontaneously placed itself under the protection and auspices of the Republic of the United States whose form of government we have adopted."[14]

The revolt had been revealed to Marshal Lemery when Agüero's wife and other women of the town ordered masses to be celebrated in the churches for its success. Sixteen of the ringleaders had been arrested, but Agüero had succeeded in escaping with about fifty followers to the mountains near the city. On July 7 he had decided to begin his war of liberation with an attack on the town of Tunas, but his small force had been quickly repulsed by government troops and he himself had been captured. The only other uprising occurred a few days later at Trinidad, where a friend of López, Isidoro Armenteros, had assembled a small force of about fifty horsemen. Government troops had been sent out against them and they had been surrounded and captured.

After leaving Key West about ten o'clock on the night of August 10, the *Pampero* made slow progress, having to stop for several hours for engine repairs. At ten o'clock in the morning, instead of approaching Bahía Honda, the ship was found to be sailing directly toward Havana harbor within view of sentinels at Morro Castle. She had been carried off her course by the current, and the compass, moreover, had been inaccurate, due, Captain Lewis said, to the iron in the musket barrels of the expeditionists. The *Pampero* fled to the west with López expecting Spanish warships to come out in pursuit, but none appeared and he directed the course to Bahía Honda. Later on he stopped a fishing schooner and took the captain aboard the *Pampero* to serve as a pilot.

In the afternoon López, with his ready ease in changing plans, put in at the Bay of Cabañas, a few miles from Mariel, in the belief this would be as good a landing place as any. It might have been except for the fact that anchored in the bay were two Spanish warships, a frigate and a sloop. Once more the *Pampero* was forced to flee, pursued this time by the frigate, which, being a sailing ship, could not keep up with the steamer. At nightfall the *Pampero* reached Bahía Honda, but entrance was delayed when the kidnaped pilot protested that he did not know the depth of the water. Callender Fayssoux, hero of the Cárdenas landing, took a small boat with several sailors to take soundings. Again danger was encountered when he was challenged by sentries at a small fort, but he quickly returned to the *Pampero*, which escaped in the darkness. Two hours later López decided again to land, this time at Morrillo, a coastal village of a half-dozen houses about 60 miles from Havana. Sailing into the bay, the *Pampero* was grounded about half a mile from shore, but the unloading of men, provisions, and arms was successfully completed by four or five o'clock. López had fulfilled his promise to return to Cuba.

Despite the narrow escapes during the day, the optimism of the filibusters was high. "Were these three warnings of Providence, against our landing on a coast destined to be so disastrous to so many of our gallant little band?" Schlesinger asked. "Three times within that day, in our crippled condition in regard to speed, had we thus stood in straight upon destruction, coming first within sight of the Morro itself, next almost under the guns of a Spanish frigate and sloop, and now again under the battery of a fort. If they were warnings, they were lost upon us in the enthusiasm which reigned among us." He interpreted these hairbreadth escapes as being a sign that luck was with the expedition. They were just the reverse. As word of the sightings of the *Pampero* filtered in at Havana, General Concha knew where to send his troops to surround the expedition, which like a fly in a spider's web, was ready to be pounced upon.

When López himself went ashore, resplendent in white jacket and pantaloons and a red sash tied around his waist, his first act was to kneel and kiss the soil of his "querida Cuba"; this was an impressive rite to his romantic followers, who did not stop to recollect that, born in Venezuela, he had fought against the liberator Bolívar and in Spain and Cuba had served as an officer in the army of a detestable monarchy.

Shortly after dawn the provisions and arms had been carried ashore, and the *Pampero*, free of her cargo, was once again afloat. López directed Captain Lewis and Fayssoux to return to Florida to get the artillery pieces at St. Johns River and to embark another expedition that would land east of Havana where the people were thought to be in revolt. He would himself establish a base in the mountains in the west and rally to his banner disaffected Cubans in this part of the island. To this end he hastened inland with the bulk of his force to the village of Las Pozas, leaving behind the artillery battalion to guard the supplies until carts and oxen could be obtained to transport them. The commander of this battalion was Colonel William L. Crittenden, a member of a well-known Southern family and nephew of the U.S. attorney general. A graduate of West Point, Crittenden had fought in the Mexican War. "It was not imagined that the separation would be for more than a few hours," Schlesinger related. "For most of those who then parted, it was for life."

The march to Las Pozas 10 miles inland was hardly a display of military smartness. It was hot and the mosquitoes attacked in force, drawing the first blood of the campaign, Schlesinger related; the men straggled along the road in disorder so that the advance guard had to stop on occasion to permit the rear to close up. At about two o'clock the marchers ascended a ridge and saw spread out below them a little village of fifty or so houses. Word of their approach had reached the people, and with the exception of the owners of the town's two stores and a few Negroes all had fled. Although there was hardly anyone left to see them, López posted copies of a proclamation assuring the populace that his troops had come only as friends and protectors against their Spanish oppressors. He requested provisions from the store owners, issuing receipts payable in the coin of the future republic, and commandeered two carts and two yokes of oxen which he sent to pick up the supplies and arms left behind with Colonel Crittenden.

Shortly after dispatching the carts, López received word from a native who had come from Bahía Honda that Spanish troops had been landed there from the warship *Pizarro*. General Concha, informed of the sightings of the *Pampero* the day before, had lost no time sending troops to the area. Alarmed by the prospect of being attacked with his force divided, López sent messengers to Crittenden directing him to leave the supplies and arms behind and to push forward to join the expedition at Las Pozas that night. He hoped to evacuate the town early in the morning, planning to fall back into the Cuzco Mountains to establish his base for operations.

According to an account of the expedition by Captain J. A. Kelly of the artillery battalion, Crittenden left Morrillo about eleven o'clock. The cumbersome carts made such slow progress that Crittenden was able to advance only 5 miles in about six hours. He stopped at a country store, or *tienda*, to prepare breakfast, and only then, Kelly said, did he get the message from López. Meanwhile, López, believing his order had been received the evening before, waited anxiously for him all night. "When day broke and still *no Crittenden*! the General was extremely disturbed," Schlesinger related. "To lose Crittenden and his force now, nearly a third of the Expedition, would be a dreadful blow, both from the weakening of our actual number, and still more from the bad moral influence such a calamity would have on the country!"

The men at Las Pozas were at breakfast—several cattle had been rounded up and killed—when they were surprised by a volley of musketry from Spaniards occupying a house at the crest of the ridge rising above the village. The pickets who should have alerted the general of the approach of the enemy had left their posts to have breakfast. Although taken by surprise, the companies were quickly organized and deployed to face the enemy, the main body of which formed a column along the road leading to the village. Under the accurate fire of the Americans, the Spaniards, in less than two hours of fighting, were forced to retreat.

Schlesinger estimated that the Spanish force numbered 800 men, but General Concha's reports said it was only 400. The figure may be supposed to be somewhere between, but, considering the lack of training and drill of the expeditionists, they acquitted themselves well in their first engagement. Their casualties were about twenty men killed and twenty-five wounded. Colonel Robert L. Downman, a Mexican War veteran who commanded the infantry battalion, and General Pragay, a Hungarian who was López's chief of staff, were among those seriously wounded.

About the time of the assault on Las Pozas, Crittenden's battalion at the *tienda* was attacked by the enemy, being fired upon by a body of troops that, according to Kelly's narrative, numbered about 350 men. The Spaniards, however, withdrew after one or two volleys fired by the defenders of the *tienda*. When after some time they did not reappear, Crittenden decided to take about eighty men and go after them, leaving Kelly with about forty men to guard the supplies until his return. Kelly waited three or four hours without receiving a report from Crittenden. Some of the men wanted to return to the coast in the hope of somehow getting off to the United States, but Kelly was able to persuade them that they should press on to join the main body of the expedition at Las Pozas. Knowing that the road would be dangerous because of the Spanish troops, they were compelled to make their way through the woods, their guide a Negro who had driven one of the oxcarts from Morrillo. Just before nightfall they came upon a farmhouse, where they learned that a battle had been fought at Las Pozas although whether the Spaniards or the Americans had won was not known. Toward ten o'clock they found themselves near the village, and the guide went ahead to discover if it was occupied by Spaniards or Americans. He returned with the information that the men wore blue shirts, the uniform of the Americans, and the thirty or so men remaining in Kelly's company then entered Las Pozas.

After the morning battle López had sent out patrols to learn what had happened to Crittenden's battalion, but these returned with the news that there were so many Spaniards in the area it was impossible to make contact with him. "We still indulged a hope," Schlesinger wrote, "that, since at the last news he had repulsed the enemy, and had even moved in pursuit of him, he had kept his corps together, and, in pursuance of his orders to join us at Las Pozas, might still come in under the cover of the darkness, as Captain Kelly had done."

Expecting another attack in the morning by a larger body of Spanish troops, López had already planned to evacuate Las Pozas during the night. At two o'clock his army, diminished by the eighty men with Crittenden, the forty-five casualties, including not only the dead but also the wounded because they could not be carried along, and about ten stragglers from Kelly's company who had not made it to the village, marched off in a southeasterly direction for the mountains. Of leaving the wounded behind, Schlesinger wrote: "We could only trust to the hope that the Spaniards might for once belie their character for bloody cruelty, and at least so far respect the decencies of common humanity as to spare the lives of the wounded, especially after the brotherly kindness which their own wounded had received at our hands, and which they remained there side by side with ours to attest." Afterward he learned that this hope was unfulfilled—when the Spaniards entered the village they slew all the wounded except General Pragay and a Cuban officer who, as a precaution against torture, had committed suicide.

Schlesinger said nothing of the spirits of the expeditionists when they left Las Pozas. They could not have been very high. In less than two days after landing, their number had been reduced by more than one-fourth, they were without provisions, and they had only the muskets and ammunition they carried with them. They were in a strange land occupied by hostile troops who far outnumbered them. As invaders of another country, they could expect little mercy from the enemy if they surrendered. About all that was left for them to do was to stay with López in the hope that somewhere before long the promised Cuban supporters would materialize.

Their departure from Las Pozas in the darkness of the early morning of August 14 was the beginning of ten days of wandering about the countryside during which they were to learn that López had no supporters and no plans except hastily improvised ones based on vague rumors picked up at isolated farms they happened upon. One of these was that the people of Pinar del Río had revolted and that those of San Cristóbal were on the verge of doing so. Schlesinger in his history repeatedly criticized the Americans for their loss of faith in López and repeatedly lauded him as a great leader who would have succeeded if only his followers had exhibited a more soldierly spirit. Yet at the same time he reported fully the disasters the expeditionists met almost daily and López's delusions that around the next turn of the trail or over the next hill rescue or relief was at hand.

After leaving Las Pozas at two o'clock in the morning, the expedition marched steadily until nine o'clock when they stopped for a scanty breakfast. Then they resumed their weary progress, which continued until the late afternoon when they stopped at a farm house and had a substantial meal of roast oxen that López paid for, as he was always punctilious in doing in commandeering provisions, with his worthless receipts in the name of the future republic. After camping for the night, they were off again before daybreak, August 15, and at ten o'clock stopped at a coffee plantation where cattle were purchased, killed, and roasted for another meal—one that they were not fated to enjoy. It was interrupted when a Cuban arrived with the information that they were only a few miles from Bahía Honda from which troops were being dispatched to attack them—their march, instead of being a forward one into the interior, had been in a circle.

At the muster before setting off, López attempted to reassure his men that all was well. "He told them that he looked to each of them to set an example to the men in the cheerful endurance of fatigue and hardship," Schlesinger related. "He believed it would not be long before they would unite with insurgent parties of the Cubans, and acquire such force as to be able to take up positions in which all their wants would be supplied." After abandoning their meal, the expeditionsts plodded steadily on until eleven o'clock that night, when they stopped to make camp on a mountainside. Early the next morning they were again on their way, "marching up and down steep ascents and descents, over ground extremely rough, tangled, and fatiguing." López's strategy now was this: "Constant motion . . . so as to baffle the efforts of the troops to attack us with their superior forces, until we should be strengthened." At the end of the day a farm was reached and for the first time in forty-eight hours cattle were available for a meal. From a peon who came along they heard again of the rumored insurrection at Pinar del Rio and the impending one at San Cristóbal. "The general," Schlesinger related, "determined to move in that direction, to ascertain the disposition of the people and the force of troops in that neighborhood, and to act according to circumstances." Another day of marching brought them, on August 17, to the Cafetal de Frías, a coffee plantation owned by the family of López's wife. Schlesinger in his account of the expedition regularly mentioned in horror the fact that some of the Americans had been so unsoldierly as to throw away their muskets. Now, four days after leaving Las Pozas, he reported that the force consisted of only 260 men, about thirty having dropped behind or deserted, and that only 200 still carried their muskets.

At Las Frías, the men, instead of entering the enclosed quadrangle formed by the house and outbuildings of the plantation, bivouacked in a grove of mango trees on a hill some distance away. This was a fortunate circumstance, for they had not been camped long when the plantation buildings were attacked by a company of about 150 Spanish cavalrymen supported by an infantry force of several hundred. Seizing their rifles, the Americans fired upon their foe and so accurate were their volleys the Spaniards retreated in a panic. It was a notable victory, for the expeditionists lost only three men and General Ena, the Spanish commander, was killed.[15]

Fearful of a return attack by a larger Spanish force, López could only resume his plan of rapid movements to avoid an encounter. Once more he took to the back country though still progressing toward San Cristóbal. The men were by now in a terrible condition. Their boots were worn out, their clothing was in tatters, and they were exhausted by the constant wandering and lack of food. Their misery was made greater because the rains had set in. At a muster on August 19 it was found that only ninety of the men still bore their muskets, some in poor condition from the rain and about fifteen useless because of lack of ammunition. In consequence, when they were discovered by a company of Spaniards at a cafetal called Candelaria all they could do was flee into the woods, where the enemy fortunately decided not to pursue them. On August 21, after four days of storm during which they had been without food, López sacrificed his horse to provide a meal for the 160 men remaining.

The next day the expeditionists formally protested to López that their hardships could not be endured any longer and that they had been deceived in the project for no bodies of Cuban patriots had been found to join them. They demanded that they return to the coast where they might perhaps obtain a vessel on which they could escape from the island. By this time they were almost completely incapable of defense should they be attacked. Only forty men had muskets, but probably only ten of these could be fired even if ammunition were available and it was not because their cartridges, soaked by the rain, were useless.

Schlesinger related that López blamed the men for the situation in which they now found themselves, asking: "Where were the hundred and twenty or thirty of our people who, for want of obedience and care, had strayed off, or been left or dropped behind, to fall certain victims to the ferocity of a foe, cruel in proportion to his cowardice before them in the field? Where were the arms and ammunition of the men now here, which had been recklessly thrown away to lighten fatigue, or in some cases for even worse reason, and the loss of which had so reduced our means of resistance to have forced us to fly into these inhospitable wilds, from before an enemy whom otherwise we could have defeated as easily as we had defeated the same troops, or their comrades, twice before?" But he still held out hope: "The time could not be far when reinforcements must arrive from the United States, and he still expected to unite with friendly bands of the people of the island in insurrection. . . . "

The end came the next day when the forlorn band descended from the mountains to the plains near San Cristóbal with apparently no plan except to find food, of which there had been little since the sacrifice of the general's horse four days before. They were straggling along a trail when the warning was given of an attack. Now with no arms for defense, without the spirit to use them if they had, they sought only to escape by turning into the bushes on either side of the road as they had at Candelaria a few days before. "This, our dispersion, took place at about six o'clock in the afternoon," Schlesinger related. "We had landed on the morning of the 12th. Las Pozas was fought on the 13th; Frías, on the 17th; and the affair of Candelaria was on the 18th; the hurricane in the mountain followed and now, on the 23rd, this was the end of the Expedition, which after this cannot be said to have had any military existence."

Utterly routed in this last attack, the expeditionists who were not captured hid in the woods in small groups to avoid seizure. About fifteen were killed in the attack and others were shot on the spot when captured. On August 26 orders from General Concha reached San Cristóbal that those who surrendered would be spared and sent to Havana. Separated from López, Schlesinger wandered about with a half-dozen members of the band until August 28 when he was finally captured. General López was taken the next day. He was led into San Cristóbal with his arms tied behind his back and a rope around his neck.

General Concha's *indulto* for the prisoners taken at San Cristóbal was in contrast to his treatment of the first ones taken two weeks before—the fifty men under Colonel Crittenden who had been unable to rejoin the main force at Las Pozas—on August 13. After leaving Captain Kelly with the supplies at the *tienda*, Crittenden had been repulsed when he encountered a force of Spaniards. Escaping into the woods, the men spent two nights and a day in hiding before they decided it would be impossible to push on to Las Pozas. Retreating to the coast, they took four small boats that they found at Morrillo and put out to sea in the hope of reaching Key West.

On the second day they were picked up by the frigate *Habanero* and taken to Havana, where General Concha, whose proclamation about the expedition had said that all invaders would be executed without trial if caught, ordered that they be shot by a firing squad at seven o'clock the next morning, August 16. Because the men had not been captured on the island but at sea, although within the territorial waters of Cuba, he permitted a four-hour delay while lawyers interviewed them to obtain confessions, hoping thus to avoid embarrassing questions of international law if summary executions were carried out.

They were permitted during this time to write letters, and Crittenden, having "not the heart to write any of my own family," wrote a friend in New Orleans. He related the details of his separation from López and the capture at sea and declared that he and his men had been "deceived grossly." "During my short sojourn on this island I have not met a single patriot," he wrote. "We landed some forty or fifty miles to the westward . . . and I am sure that in that part of the island López has no friends. When I was attacked López was only three miles off. If he had not been deceiving us as to the state of things, he would have fallen back with his force and made a fight, instead of which he marched on immediately to the interior."

Reports of the executions reaching newspapers in the United States described Havana as being in a holiday mood, with as many as 20,000 people on hand at eleven o'clock to cheer the shooting of the Americans led out two by two—some papers said in groups of ten—to suffer the doom pronounced by Concha. The papers gave gory details of the bodies being thrown to the crowd to be dragged by the heels and mutilated in "a manner our Indian savages would revolt at." But all, the papers reported, met their deaths bravely and stoically in the tradition of American heroism. The *New Orleans Crescent* related that Crittenden refused to kneel with his back to the firing squad. "An American kneels only to his God, and always faces his enemy," he is reported to have said.

On September 1, sixteen days after Crittenden met his death, López himself at seven o'clock in the morning mounted a platform on the point opposite the Morro to die by the garotte. The city had celebrated during the night, buildings being illuminated and torchlight parades of rejoicing crowds being held. At dawn 10,000 soldiers and as many citizens had gathered to view the execution. Newspaper reports said that López ascended the platform with a firm and steady step. Facing the huge conclave, he gave a short address, ending with the words: "I die for my beloved Cuba." He then took his seat in the death machine, the metal neckband was adjusted, and at the first twist of the screw his head dropped forward—and he was dead.

CHAPTER FOUR

Filibusters in the Campaign of 1852

Reports of the execution of Crittenden and his men reached New Orleans on the morning of August 21. Newspapers, calling it a "massacre," said that some of the prisoners were clubbed with rifle butts as they were dragged before the firing squads and their bodies were thrown to the spectators, who stripped them of their clothing, mutilated them, and cut off ears and fingers to be carried away as souvenirs. Enraged New Orleans crowds roamed the streets to destroy anything Spanish. One group attacked *La Unión*, a newspaper that had published an "extra" carrying praise for the captain general of Cuba, and other groups sacked tobacco shops and coffeehouses owned by Spaniards. Late in the afternoon a mob descended on the Spanish consulate, tore the flag to shreds, and defaced a portrait of the queen. Juan Y. Laborde, the consul, fled to the country to hide at the home of a friend.[1]

Indignation over the executions was also expressed in other cities north and south—Boston, New York, Philadelphia, Baltimore, Cincinnati, Louisville, Savannah, Nashville, Mobile, Key West. Speakers at mass meetings denounced the slaughter of the Americans and assailed the government in Washington. In Nashville, protesters adopted a resolution declaring that the president had no right to hinder persons leaving the country for Cuba and after the meeting formed a procession led by men carrying a banner with the motto, "God and Liberty—Cuba." In Boston, a speaker declared that "the blood of the slaughtered patriots of Cuba cried out for vengeance." In Philadelphia, a resolution demanded that the United States propose to Spain immediate autonomy for Cuba and if this was refused that the nation go to war to set the island free. Anger against the Spanish was so great at Mobile that a mob threatened to attack fifty hapless sailors brought there after the wreck of the brig *Fernando VII* off the coast. Violence was avoided when the vice-consul chartered a schooner to remove them to Havana.[2]

The Spanish minister, Angel Calderón de la Barca, protested the New Orleans outrages to President Fillmore and demanded indemnification for damages to Spanish property.[3] The president, vacationing at White Sulphur Springs, Virginia, was so upset by the national agitation that he hastily returned to Washington on August 30. Three days later, in a letter to Secretary of State Webster, he wrote that since his return he had devoted his efforts almost exclusively to Cuban matters. "In times like this," he said, "the telegraph in the hands of irresponsible and designing men, is a tremendous engine for mischief, aided as it is in many places by a mercenary and prostituted press. Agitation and excitement seem to pervade all the large cities, and this is greatly aggravated by unscrupulous partizans who desire to turn it to political account against the administration." His concern about the political implications was well founded because a presidential election year was in the offing. The Democratic press assailed him, and Charles Eames, assistant editor of the *Washington Union*, chortled in writing William L. Marcy on September 14: "You see the blows we are dealing him." Eames predicted: "It is general opinion here that Cuba has killed Fillmore."[4]

The excitement in New Orleans over the executions continued for days, with mass meetings held almost nightly to raise money to mount an expedition to avenge their deaths. The *New Orleans Courier* expressed the sentiment of many: "American blood has been shed! It cries aloud for vengeance—vengeance on the tyrant! Our brethren must be avenged! Cuba must be seized!" Among the most enthusiastically applauded orators was Chatham Roberdeau Wheat, who had not sailed on the *Pampero* but had remained behind to be one of the leaders of a second expedition, to include a Kentucky regiment and two regiments raised in New Orleans. Of his appearance at a rally on August 26, a newspaper said that he "made a truly brilliant and spirit-stirring address in which anecdote and argument were so happily mixed up, that the effect on the audience was indeed electrifying." So popular had he become that two days later at another rally "there was a stretching of necks, glistening of eyes and tremendous cheering" as he rose to speak.

There was no shortage of men eager to sail to Cuba. Adventurers poured into the city and encampments were set up to take care of them. The *Delta* said that 5,000 expeditionists could be transported in twenty-four hours if steamers were available. But they were not. The reason was that, though many were eager to give their lives for Cuba, few were willing to give their money. A committee of thirty-three appointed to manage the fund-raising campaign found businessmen reluctant to contribute, donations at the rallies produced only small sums, and benefit performances likewise were not very successful. Altogether, only about $8,000 was raised during a week of intensive effort.

During this time the fate of López and the other expeditionists was unknown, and anxiety increased as contradictory reports were received. At last, on September 4, a mail steamer brought the disastrous tidings that he had been captured with the remnants of his army. So overwhelming was the news that the entire city was cast into gloom, and the newspapers took up the cry for no more expeditions: they would only result in further reprisals against the captured men who had sailed on the *Pampero* and further loss of lives. Editorials appealed to the two or three thousand adventure-bound men who had descended on the city to break camp and leave for their homes. Violence was threatened when these men, received as heroes but now looked upon as potential trouble-makers, declared they had to have money if they were to leave the city. But their demands could not be met, as the Cuban committee had already spent what money it had collected in supporting them. Police were called to break up their camps and the men dispersed.[5]

In the heated atmosphere created by the executions and the attacks on Spaniards, President Fillmore continued the policy of conciliation that had marked most of his life. Never regarded as a strong leader in the Whig party, he had been nominated for the vice-presidency largely to placate the followers of Henry Clay. Upon his succession to the presidency after Zachary Taylor's death, the opinion of many was reflected in an aspersion cast by the New

York senator William H. Seward: "Providence has at last led the man of hesitations and double opinions where decision and singleness are indispensable." His policy in the Cuban affair supported this description: he sought to pacify Spain for the outrages committed by U.S. citizens against her and to persuade the annexationists he was doing everything he could for the American prisoners. Calderón was a thorn in the flesh. As soon as he had satisfied himself that there was no danger of an invasion of Cuba, the Spanish minister began registering complaints with the secretary of state against the treatment of Spanish nationals. He protested the "apathy, the disobedience, and, sometimes, the connivance" of officials who failed to stop filibuster ships and reported that he found it difficult to obtain consuls to serve in some cities because they feared for their lives. He climaxed these protests on October 14 with a demand for "full satisfaction" for the insults to the Spanish flag in New Orleans and for indemnification for the property losses sustained "at the hands of an infuriated and licentious mob."[6]

In the case of the prisoners taken at Contoy the year before, the United States had good grounds to protest punishment of them by Spain. This was not so of those who had survived the Bahía Honda expedition: they had invaded the island, seized the property of civilians, and attacked and killed members of the armed forces. Yet American sentiment in their behalf had to be satisfied. Robert B. Campbell, the consul in Havana for years almost persona non grata to successive captain generals, had been replaced by Allen F. Owen, whose reports provided little evidence the president could offer the people indicating that he had acted energetically to prevent the executions. When William S. Derrick, acting secretary of state during an illness of Daniel Webster, wrote Owen asking him what he had done, the reply was—nothing. For one thing, the executions were carried out so hastily that there had been no time for him to intervene; for another, he thought protest would be useless, because he had been told by Captain General Concha that "no quarter" would be shown the invaders, that if they were caught they would be shot. He had followed—too literally, Fillmore thought—the instructions given him when he was sent to Havana to replace the meddlesome Campbell not to involve himself in Cuban politics.[7]

The course adopted early in August by Fillmore to persuade officials to act leniently with the 162 prisoners taken to Spain was one of apology and appeal for clemency. In the way of apology, Webster wrote Calderón on November 13 effusively regretting the insult "to the flag of a nation so ancient, so respectable, so renowned as Spain." In the way of clemency, he told the minister in Madrid, Daniel M. Barringer, to admit that the prisoners had no legal claim for the protection of their government, but, he continued, "they are men" and as such "objects of compassion," which it was not unreasonable to look for "from the Sovereign of a great nation." Barringer's task to persuade Spain to forgive the invaders was not an easy one, for the Marqués de Miraflores, minister of foreign affairs, played with him as a cat with a mouse, insisting upon adequate demonstration by the United States of regret "for the insult to their flag & consular office in N. Orleans." At last, on December 11, Miraflores notified Barringer that "the Queen, my Lady, by a proper and spontaneous act of her magnanimous heart and yielding to the natural impulses of Her inexhaustible clemency," had pardoned all the prisoners.[8]

Both England and France had followed the López affair with great interest and some concern. Their attitude was expressed in part in an editorial in the London *Times* of September 9:

> In a naval point of view the possession of the port of Havana by the Americans would be an occurrence of first rate importance. . . . It would place under their guns the vast line of traffic which more and more connects the eastern and the western oceans; it would leave almost at their mercy the islands and colonies of European States, which would speedily become fresh objects of their ambition. . . . If the Southern States are allowed to incorporate Cuba, and to strengthen the slave-holding interest in the Union by that enormous acquisition, the North will turn in self defence upon the nearest territory of which it may seize to restore the balance of power, and that territory is our own. One act of rapine and violence will follow another, until the cry will be for the expulsion of European authority from the North American continent and the West India Islands.

Both nations instructed their naval commanders in the Caribbean to prevent, by force if necessary, the landing of adventurers with hostile intent, but they refused a proposal from Spain that they guarantee her possession of Cuba. They became interested instead in another project—a treaty in which Britain, France, and the United States should declare that none of them would seek to obtain possession. Fillmore in his message to Congress on December 2 served notice to France and England that the orders to their naval commanders would be resisted. "No American ship," he declared, "can be allowed to be visited or searched for the purpose of ascertaining the character of individuals on board, nor can there be allowed any watch by the vessels of any foreign nation over American vessels on the coast of the United States or the seas adjacent thereto."

This strong statement, however, provided no reassurance for the expansionists, for the president was equally firm in the expression of his intention to enforce the neutrality laws and his opposition to territorial aggrandizement. He deplored the fact that "thoughtless young men have been induced by false and fraudulent expectations of assisting to accomplish political revolutions in other states, and have lost their lives in the undertaking."

The president's warning went unheeded by the filibusters, who had formed in the fall a new organization, the Order of the Lone Star, to mount an expedition to Cuba in the summer of 1852. It was purported to be a secret society, organized along the lines of the Masonic order with a ritual of a religious character, but its activities were regularly reported in the newspapers. Its constitution, issued from the office of the *Delta* in New Orleans, stated in a preamble that its aim was "extending the area of liberty" to Cuba and annexing the island to the United States. Within a few weeks local chapters were formed in as many as fifty towns in eight states and a membership numbering in the thousands was claimed. By early spring, plans were well along. An expedition would get off in June to support an insurrection to be fomented on the island by Francisco de Frías, brother-in-law of López.[9]

Reports of this new expedition reached Calderón early in the year, and he wrote Webster on March 1 to protest. The *Pampero*, which had been seized on her return from Bahía Honda and later sold at auction, he said, was being fitted out at Savannah for the new foray. John L. O'Sullivan, still under indictment for his part in the *Cleopatra* affair, was alleged to have advanced money for the purchase. Calderón quoted a Charleston correspondent: "There is great talk in this city, of new preparations for an expedition against the Island of Cuba, and there is ground for apprehending a repetition of the events of last summer." Calderón wrote again on May 14 that the Order of the Lone Star, "organized as its name indicates, for the purpose of revolutionizing and invading" Cuba, was actively at work and that recruits in the New York area were being sent to Mobile, New Orleans, and other Southern cities. Among them—gluttons for punishment, apparently—were survivors of the Bahía Honda expedition who had been pardoned by the queen. But on July 1 Calderón reported to Webster—he did not reveal his sources—that the June invasion had been deferred though he cited newspapers as saying preparations for an expedition were still being made.[10]

One reason for the postponement was that this was a presidential election year—a Democratic year from all political weather signs—and the Whig administration, hostile to Cuban adventures, would probably be replaced by a friendly Democratic administration. The Democrats, meeting at Baltimore on June 1, had been able to patch up their quarrels over slavery and unite behind a dark-horse candidate for president, Franklin Pierce, but the Whigs, meeting on June 16, had still remained divided over this issue when on the fifty-third ballot they wearily nominated Winfield Scott. Both party platforms accepted the Compromise of 1850 and condemned further agitation over slavery. In the campaign the personalities of the candidates, rather than their programs—these were almost indistinguishable on the slavery issue—offered the principal choices to the electorate. But Pierce had the support of the most vocal Cuba annexationists and Manifest Destiny advocates calling themselves Young America.

The Young America movement did not take in all expansionists. Its members were chiefly those of the most radical sentiment fed up, so they proclaimed, with the "Old Fogies" who had been playing their political roles for years. Young America was a catchword rather than a party or faction; it had no organization, held no meetings, and elected no officers. The name may have derived in part from a lecture, "The Young American," which Ralph Waldo Emerson read before the Mercantile Library Association in Boston on February 7, 1844, in which he declared that America, a nation so young as not to have a past, would be the country of the future, its eminent citizens "willing to stand for the interests of general justice and humanity." The leadership of the world, Emerson implied, should be the Young American. But a more explicit and immediate call for leadership by the Young American was sounded in a commencement address to the South Carolina College the next year by Edwin de Leon, a lawyer and journalist. He pictured the United States as being in its youth, for "nations, like men, have their seasons of infancy, manly vigor, and decrepitude." European nations, old and tired, could not hope to stand against the young giant of the west in the full flush of "exulting manhood." De Leon subsequently became one of the prime movers of Young America, and was especially influential after 1850 when he was invited by Southern members of Congress to go to Washington and edit, with Elwood Fisher, *The Southern Press*.[11]

But the man who made the amorphous concept of Young America, which appealed to such diverse groups as rebellious literary coteries and social and economic reformers of various ideologies, a more particular one that became a political force in 1852 was an audacious Kentuckian, George N. Sanders, who had played a small part in Kentucky politics in supporting U.S. claims to Oregon and annexation of Texas. He went to New York in 1845 and soon became involved in the schemes of capitalists speculating in the public lands, in railroads and steamship lines, and in mail contracts, promoting their interests as a lobbyist and political wire-puller.

One of the financiers Sanders served was the burly and belligerent George Law, who beginning as a contractor in canal construction had gone on to invest in railroads and shipping lines, including the United States Mail Steamship Company, which had a lucrative contract to provide biweekly mail service between New York, Havana, New Orleans, and Chagres, Panama. In 1848 Sanders was Law's agent in the purchase from the Department of War of 144,000 muskets made obsolete by adoption of the new percussion lock. Sanders had seen an opportunity to sell the muskets at a profit to French revolutionists and hurried to Paris to make the sale. The revolt, however, was crushed before the sale could be completed, and Sanders returned to the United States, where he had muskets enough to equip an army but no soldiers to bear them. As the most likely purchasers were the European democrats, Sanders became an enthusiastic supporter of Louis

Kossuth, exiled leader of the Hungarian revolution who arrived in the United States in December 1851 to gain American support for the movement.[12]

Since 1852 promised to be a Democratic year, there was no lack of candidates for the party nomination for president. The best known was Senator Lewis Cass of Michigan, now sixty-nine years old, who had also been the nominee in 1848. He was noted for his ability to straddle an issue as long as possible, but he could be counted on to favor expansion. His running mate in 1848, William O. Butler of Kentucky, fifty-eight years old, was brought forth by such friends of Andrew Jackson as Francis Blair and Thomas Hart Benton, who thought they could manage this one-time protégé of "Old Hickory." James Buchanan, who had angered James K. Polk in finagling for the 1848 nomination while violating his oath not to seek office while serving in the cabinet, thought his time had come, and from his home, Wheatland, in Pennsylvania the sixty-year-old cautious but persistent politician was busy writing letters to his friends to further his candidacy. Finally, among the party elders was William L. Marcy, sixty-five, like Cass and Butler an old Jacksonian, who now seemed well along toward winning the support of both the Barnburners, the radical and reform wing of the party in New York, and the Hunkers, the conservative wing.

These veterans of many campaigns and legislative battles, adroit in the ways of politics, recipients of the offices and gifts of the nation, were not men who could arouse enthusiastic response in any large portion of the public. What enthusiasm there was in the early stages of the campaign came in the emergence of Stephen A. Douglas of Illinois as a front-runner. George N. Sanders saw incarnated in the Little Giant, thirty-eight years old in 1851, the bold and energetic spirit needed to revitalize the Democratic party. He believed that a crusade to aid the European republicans would divert attention from sectional controversies to the end of increasing the market for American goods as well as fulfilling the American mission to further the cause of freedom. By April 1851 Sanders had become one of Douglas's closest advisers. "I have great confidence in your judgment & discretion," Douglas wrote him early in the campaign, and to a supporter in New York he said: "Our friend George S will keep you advised of all movements here. Entire confidence can be placed in his discretion. He is invaluable to us & will remain here at the point where he can do most."[13] Douglas was to learn soon that his reliance on Sanders' discretion was one of the greatest political mistakes he ever made, but he was correct in his estimate of his value at the time because his friendship with Law and others among the "steamboat crowd" brought them into his campaign as his principal financial backers.

Young Americanism had a magnetic attraction for bold and unconventional men, and therefore it is not surprising that a rising Louisiana politician with a romantic background and grandiose visions of his own future enlisted under its banner. He was the exiled French revolutionist, Pierre Soulé, who had fled to the United States after his conviction in Paris for publishing an inflammatory attack on the government in 1825 and who had emerged as a leader of the Democratic party of Louisiana in 1849 through his defeat of John Slidell for the U.S. Senate. In the Senate he had championed the extreme Southern secessionist cause, advocated the extension of slavery, and opposed the admission of California as a free state.

Soulé, like John L. O'Sullivan, also allied to the movement, and Sanders seemed to see no contradiction in his defense of slavery and his advocacy of American aid for the European revolutionists of 1848. Voluble, impetuous, and a notable orator, he impressed friends and opponents alike as an attractive and winning person. Charles Sumner, a Whig and abolitionist, thought him "the most polished speaker and gentleman of the Senate," and Harriet Beecher Stowe saw in him "an impersonation of nobility and chivalry," although she wondered also how he could be at the same time "the tool of tyranny." Soulé became one of the most fervent supporters of Douglas. "In siding with Douglas," he wrote a friend, "I was prompted to give my help in a struggle whose object was the overthrow of the old party-dynasties that had assumed power, and lost all elasticity of mind, all energy of will, all courage in action, so necessary to those who wish to govern a great people."[14]

Late in 1851 Sanders obtained control of *The United States Magazine and Democratic Review*, which O'Sullivan, devoting most of his time to filibuster expeditions, had let slide downhill, and made it the chief organ of the Douglas campaign. In the

January 1852 number he sounded the call for a Young America program in an article, "Eighteen-Fifty-Two and the Presidency." The article attacked the Old Fogies of the Democratic party, paying particular attention to Butler and Cass. Butler, not noted for temperance, was "a judicious bottle holder" and Cass was a "beaten horse." "The statesmen of a previous generation, with their personal antipathies and their personal claims, with personal greatness or personal inefficiency, must get out of the way," the article declared. The man for whom they must make way must be a man with "world-wide ideas," a "State-rights man," "a man of large soul and open heart, who will maintain in the teeth of the despots of Europe the democratic doctrines upon which his popularity and success are based here; a bold man, who can stand the brunt of foreign war, and . . . crush the despots of the world in their very dens. . . . "

The article created a sensation, an adverse one for Douglas. His less hare-brained supporters wrote him that it went much too far in advocating support of European revolutionists and would create enemies in the Democratic party. Douglas was quick to see this and wrote Sanders urging him to avoid attacks on the other candidates. The appeal had no effect, Sanders promising that the February number would contain an attack on Butler "more terrific than was ever made against mortal man before." Two months later Douglas appealed again to Sanders to desist. "If you cease now," he wrote, "and make no more attacks upon anybody and especially none on Gen'l Cass, possibly I may yet regain my lost position. If those attacks are repeated my chances are utterly hopeless, and I may be compelled to retire from the field and throw my influence in favor of one of those whom the Review strives to crush."[15] Douglas did not retire from the field, but he was correct in his belief that the blows dealt by the *Democratic Review* had bruised him more than they had his enemies. The assessment of Andrew Johnson, two months before the convention, that Douglas was "a dead cock in the pit" was not far from wrong.[16] But though the Young Americans were not able to make Douglas the Democratic nominee, they were victorious in other ways, for the Old Fogies of the party also went down to defeat and the dark-horse victor, Franklin Pierce, was a man whom they could wholeheartedly support.

Sanders, O'Sullivan, and other Young America leaders appropriated Pierce and attributed to him the policies they wanted to pursue. In the *Democratic Review* Sanders demanded repeal of the neutrality laws to facilitate filibuster expeditions, upheld the right of exiled revolutionary groups to seek aid in the United States, and condemned President Fillmore's apology to Spain for the sacking of the consulate in New Orleans.

Douglas, eager to win friends in the party again, promised "to spend the whole vacation upon the stump" for Pierce. Some of his speeches sounded as if they had come out of the *Democratic Review*. Speaking in Richmond, he accused Spain of "butchery" in executing Crittenden and his men and declared that the president in his apology to Spain had trailed the Stars and Stripes in the dirt before the banner of Castile. He attacked British encroachments in the Caribbean, especially in Honduras and Nicaragua, and asserted that the United States should take possession of the transoceanic crossings at Panama, Nicaragua, and Tehuantepec.[17] Pierre Soulé, too, came to the support of Pierce and carried on a whirlwind speaking campaign that took him through the New England and Middle Atlantic States as well as the South.[18] Louis Schlesinger, believing that he could win the foreign vote for Pierce, campaigned vigorously in cities of the Northeast.

Sanders additionally sought to tie Pierce to the Young America program by promising him the financial support of George Law. The Democrats were having trouble raising funds, and Pierce's New York backers, in particular William L. Marcy, feared that if it became known the disreputable Law had contributed money the respectable element would not support the ticket. The needed money came instead from the German-born August Belmont, who had come to the United States in 1837 as an agent of the banking firm of the Rothschilds and who, establishing his own firm, had achieved great personal wealth. From 1844 to 1850, mostly for business reasons, he had served as Austria-Hungary's consul general in this country, resigning because he was sympathetic to the Kossuth revolution.* An admirer of Buchanan, Belmont had

*Belmont's support of the Democrats was scathingly attacked by the leading Whig newspapers in New York City, Henry J. Raymond's *Times* and Horace Greeley's *Tribune*. Editorials contained references to "Jew gold" from abroad being used to buy votes and, appealing to the native American sentiment to give

supported him for the presidential nomination, but like other Democrats now gave his support to Pierce.[19]

Even before the people went to the polls to turn the antiexpansionist Whigs out of office, the Cuba annexationists who had acted clandestinely as the Order of the Lone Star came out into the open. This was very likely done to create a last-minute issue in a dull election campaign. Calderón complained of the order's activities to the secretary of state on September 30. "Impiously availing themselves of a religious ceremony, as a pretext, some of the agitators have made public demonstrations, and delivered incendiary harangues . . . provoking a new invasion of Her Catholic Majesty's dominions," he wrote. Cuban refugees and American citizens, he continued, had formed military companies and were holding public drills and target practices, and newspaper articles urging revolution in Cuba had been sent to Havana with the intent to "foment agitation." Acting Secretary of State Charles M. Conrad—Daniel Webster was incapacitated by an illness that was to end in death on October 24—replied that the government had not been inattentive to these activities but added: "It does not, however, attach as much importance to them as Mr. Calderón seems to think they deserve, and believes that they are the work of a few obscure individuals, who have all along been known as actors or agitators in this business."[20]

A sizable Cuban group had sprung up that did not seek annexation to the United States. On October 19 a new junta formed in New York issued a long manifesto, published in the newspapers, that set forth, like the American Declaration of Independence, the crimes of the mother country against Cuba and that appealed to lovers of freedom to help in obtaining independence for the island. It said nothing, however, about becoming a part of the Union.[21] Annexation had also not been mentioned by Ambrósio J. González in *Manifesto on Cuban Affairs Addressed to the People of the United States* on September 1 in New Orleans. He appealed for support from the United States but declared that although López had received no help from Cubans on the island "the Cuban

rise to the Know Nothing party later, attacked him for maintaining his ties with foreign kings because of his service as the Austrian consul. Irving Katz, *August Belmont*, pp. 13–15.

revolution has been, by our efforts, replanted upon its native soil, where it now progresses."

The Cuba question was brought more prominently to the fore during the campaign, however, when the captain general, to prevent the importation of the incendiary publications of which Calderón had complained, refused to let one of George Law's steamers land passengers and mail on its regular trip from New York to New Orleans via Havana. The insult involving U.S. commercial rights was ready-made for the annexationists. It provided an opportunity to challenge the Whig administration that seemingly had sided with Spain against the filibuster movement, but even better it might lead to obtaining the island by fomenting a war against Spain. Law by intransigent actions in refusing to obey orders issued by officials of the port at Havana and arrogantly demanding redress by the U.S. government did everything he could to make the incident serve as a *casus belli*.[22]

The order against Law's ship, the *Crescent City*, was issued after the purser, William Smith, was quoted in New York newspapers on August 19 about conditions on the island. Harsh measures, he was quoted as saying in an article in the *Times*, were being taken to suppress the issuance of revolutionary publications, many Creoles being "thrown into prisons that have been untenanted for twenty years." The *Crescent City* was one of the steamers operated by Law under his mail contract. Although owned by him, the ship was given official status by being commanded by a U.S. naval officer, Lieutenant David D. Porter. On September 3, the captain general, Valentín Cañedo, issued an order barring American newspapers carrying articles critical of Spain from the island and after the publication of the interview with Smith another order saying no vessel on which he was a passenger could stop at Havana. On October 1, when the *Crescent City* reached the island on her regular trip from New York to New Orleans, Captain Porter was told he could not enter the harbor because Smith was aboard. Porter nevertheless sailed on into the harbor but was refused permission to land his sixty or so passengers and the mail, though he was able to send ashore a protest accusing authorities of violating treaty agreements between the United States and Spain and declaring that the steamship company could not be held responsible for newspaper articles.

When the *Crescent City* reached New Orleans on October 6, indignation meetings protesting the insult to a ship flying the American flag were held and there were demands for war against Spain. At one, the expansionist U.S. senator, Judah P. Benjamin, declared that if Spain refused to give full satisfaction, then Americans had "the right to appeal to the God of battle and annex Cuba." Other protest meetings were called by the Order of the Lone Star, and the annexationist press took up the cry. One newspaper declared that if the government did not support Law he "should convert his mail steamers into warships, put his muskets to use, and expel the Spaniards from Cuba." A Lone Star organizer, Francis V. R. Mace, wrote John A. Quitman, a member of the Supreme Council of the order, that Porter should return to Havana and should retaliate if the *Crescent City* were fired upon.[23]

The belligerence of the annexationists was matched by that of Law, whose agent, Marshall O. Roberts, wrote Acting Secretary of State Conrad on October 6 urging that the firm's ships be protected or that the company "be allowed to redress the grievance and repel the insult to our national flag, with such means in such manner as we can." On the *Crescent City's* return voyage, with the purser still on board, she stopped again at Havana and again was denied permission to land passengers or mail. On passing Morro Castle in departing from the island, Porter raised the American flag and fired a gun at the fort, an action that drew from Calderón in a letter to Conrad the comment that it was "a demonstration which although puerile and in bad taste, was considered significative and offensive."[24] On October 27 Law wrote Conrad stating that no reply had been received to Roberts' letter of October 6 and asking what course of action the steamship company should follow. He received the reply that the department had protested to the Spanish government against the treatment given the *Crescent City* as not being in accordance with standard practices in the commercial intercourse of nations and as amounting almost "to a declaration of hostility" to the United States.[25]

To ease the situation, the government directed the steamship company to transfer Porter and Smith from the *Crescent City* to another ship that did not go to Cuba, but Law refused. Hence Smith was still serving as purser when the *Crescent City* left New

York on November 1 for New Orleans. At Havana the steamer was allowed to unload her passengers and the mail, but Smith was refused permission to take care of his business ashore. The captain general announced firmly that in the future the vessel would not be permitted to enter the harbor if Smith were aboard. Law was determined to continue his game of stirring up trouble by keeping Smith as the purser on the *Crescent City* and divulged his intention to Hugh Maxwell, collector of the port at New York. In some excitement, Maxwell wrote President Fillmore of Law's plan, which was that the ship "will go to Cuba, and enter the port of Havana in defiance of the Spanish authority." He said Law had asked "whether he is right in persisting in the pursuit of his lawful business" and had promised that "if the Government shall tell him he must not go, he will not go." On the other hand, if the government said nothing against his going he would infer that he had a right to go.

This placed the president on the horns of a dilemma. He could hardly say Law had no right to sail his ship to Cuba, for that was the government's stand in the correspondence with Spain, nor could he say the government gave Law permission to go, for that was what the government was seeking from Spain. Fillmore resorted to a diversionary tactic, saying in a letter to Maxwell made available to the newspapers that he did "not admit the right of Mr. Law, or any other citizen, to threaten a war on his own account for the purpose of seeking redress for real or imaginary injuries and then to call upon the Government to say, whether it approves or disapproves of such conduct, and assume its approbation unless the act is forbidden." As president he was "resolved at every hazard to maintain our rights in this controversy as against Spain" and "equally resolved that no act of our own citizens shall be permitted to place this Government in the wrong." Law replied in a letter written to the *New York Times* saying he had sought only to find out what the consequences would be if the ship were fired upon. He added that he thought such an insult would constitute a matter over which the country would go to war or he was "mistaken in the character of the American people."

Law's effort to stir up a war against Spain might have gone further if Spain, as in the diplomatic exchanges over the Contoy and Bahía Honda prisoners, had not recognized the strategic moment for retreat. She was able to save face because of an affidavit signed by the purser Smith, transmitted to Calderón by Edward Everett, appointed secretary of state on November 6, denying that he had ever written or published anything critical of the government of Cuba or had ever carried messages from revolutionists on the island to their fellows in the United States. Captain General Cañedo effectively cooled the indignation in the United States by accepting the truth of Smith's declaration and lifting the ban on the purser.[26]

While the Cuban Guards of the Order of the Lone Star were marching in the streets, while island exiles were issuing new manifestoes, and while George Law was attempting to provoke a war, the election campaign ground drearily on. When the nation went to the polls in November, Winfield Scott carried only four of the thirty-one states and won only 42 electoral votes to Franklin Pierce's 254. The crushing defeat was generally considered the death blow of the Whig party. To the Young Americans it was their victory. They had helped elect Pierce and thought their goals would be his goals. Conspicuous at the bonfires and torchlight parades celebrating the Democratic victory were banners with such slogans as "The Fruits of the late Democratic Victory—Pierce and Cuba," "May the Queen of the Antilles Be Added to Our Glorious Confederacy under the Prosperous Administration of Pierce," and "The Lone Star—nightly it beams and beckons onward."[27]

The acquisition of Cuba was the leading concern of both the Senate and House during the short session of Congress that convened in December. Debates on the question were prompted in part by President Fillmore's annual message, in which he reported on the uneasy relations between the United States and Spain caused by the *Crescent City* affair. A "strong" remonstrance had been made to Spain, he said, and he had no doubt that "due respect" would be paid to it by the government at Madrid. He then went on to introduce a subject that had been kept secret: a proposal of France and England that the United States join them in a tripartite treaty disclaiming any intention on their part to obtain Cuba and guaranteeing possession by Spain. The proposal, he said, had been rejected for reasons that he did not feel it necessary to give in detail but that led him to conclude such a treaty would be "of doubtful constitutionality, impolitic, and unavailing."

Had Fillmore contented himself with this brief statement he might not have raised an issue, but he went on to state that he had directed the ministers to France and England to assure these nations the United States had no designs against Cuba but on the contrary regarded "its incorporation into the Union at the present time as fraught with serious peril," explaining: "It would bring into the Confederacy a population of a different national stock, speaking a different language, and not likely to harmonize with the other members. It would probably affect in a prejudicial manner the industrial interests of the South, and it might revive those conflicts of opinion over slavery between the different sections of the country which lately shook the Union to its center, and which have been so happily compromised."

The reading of the president's message produced an immediate reaction in Richard H. Weightman, delegate to the House from New Mexico, who declared he resented the slur against the Spanish-speaking people of Cuba and of his own constituency. Thereafter, the Cuban question was injected into debates in both chambers on almost any subject. It received a thorough airing in the Senate in the next two months, climaxed by a speech by Pierre Soulé, who was considered a spokesman for the views of the president-elect.

On December 21 James M. Mason of Virginia, chairman of the Committee on Foreign Relations, introduced a resolution asking for the correspondence on the rejection of the tripartite treaty. As soon as it was read, he took the floor and spoke at length on the topic. He wondered why France and England had made the proposal, as the United States policy toward Cuba was well known: that so long as the island belonged to Spain this country would not interfere with it but would resist the attempt of any "grasping potentate" of Europe to obtain it. He went on to express his view that acquisition by the United States, however, was inevitable, declaring: "We know that in the fullness of time the fruit will ripen, and fall from the parent stem." Mason's view was indorsed by Senator Cass, who said further that he would be willing to hasten obtaining the fruit by purchase "at a liberal, even an extravagant price."

The debate on Cuba was resumed on January 3 when Cass introduced two resolutions in which he sought to set forth a definite policy for the future. One was prompted by British activity relating to the Mosquito Coast in Nicaragua and the Bay Islands off Honduras and reported French projects in the Sonora department of Mexico. A restatement of the Monroe Doctrine, the resolution declared that the American continents "are henceforth not to be considered as subjects for future colonization by any European power." The other reiterated the disclaimer of any intention of the United States to annex Cuba in any way inconsistent with the laws of nations and warned that should any other nation seek to obtain possession this would be considered an unfriendly act "to be resisted by all the means in their power."[28]

After some discussions of the resolutions, it was moved that they be referred to the Committee on Foreign Relations; but Soulé, who had not spoken in earlier debates, moved a postponement until January 25, when he delivered a speech that was regarded as the expression of the expansionist wing of the Democratic party. His speech was a well-argued statement that won even from Cass, with whom Soulé took issue, the comment he had not heard one in the Senate that surpassed it "either in power or beauty."

Soulé began by stating his disagreement with Cass and Mason in their favorable opinion of the administration's course, which in his opinion was "peculiarly unwise and undignified." First, he condemned Fillmore's proclamation against filibuster expeditions branding participants as "outcasts" and dooming them "to indiscriminate slaughter." Instead of being "marauders," Soulé maintained, the 500 young men who had taken part in the last López expedition were heroes. Next, he wondered why senators should be so "supremely fastidious" about "marauding" when they themselves admitted that they only awaited "the ripening of the fruit." "Will the plucking of it when ripe be less 'marauding' than the plucking of it while still green?" he asked. He then went on to attack the administration's timidity in the *Crescent City* embroglio and praised George Law's patriotism in standing up against the captain general of Cuba.

Soulé denounced the hypocrisy of those who advocated purchase of Cuba in the face of their repeated asseverations that the only wish of the United States was that Spain should retain possession. He defended annexation by outlining present instances of "marauding"—England's conquests of India and France's in Africa—and past instances both of the United States and other countries—the Miranda expedition to Venezuela supported by Alexander Hamilton, the West Florida adventures after the purchase of Louisiana, the repeated "filibuster" support of Texas attempting to gain independence from Mexico. As for himself, Soulé said, he was against attempting to purchase Cuba, because of the Castilian pride that could not be dealt with "through mere dollars and cents." He advised Spain to accept the historical necessity of giving Cuba independence. "As long as the Powers of Europe shall not presume to interfere with the relations which its proximity to our shore, and the possibility of its being made an obstruction to one of our great commercial outlets create between her and us, she need apprehend no tampering on our part with any scheme that may be devised against remaining longer under her dominion," Soulé said.[29]

The debate continued for several days, but Soulé's address had the most far-reaching repercussions. France and England, attacked because of their tripartite proposal and their own colonizing methods, were made angry; the defense of López and the filibusters and the support of George Law's intransigence in the *Crescent City* affair were anathema to Spain; and the disdain for the idea of purchasing Cuba and the tacit approval of cooperation with the revolutionary movement on the island were exultantly received by the expansionists. With the inauguration of Franklin Pierce as president, they thought, the nation's Manifest Destiny would be fulfilled.

CHAPTER FIVE

Franklin Pierce: Expansionist President

Franklin Pierce in his inaugural address of March 4, 1853, announced a policy of territorial acquisition that would "not be controlled by any timid forebodings of evil from expansion." His country's position on the globe, he said in a statement of the geographical imperative, made "the acquisition of certain possessions not within our jurisdiction eminently important for our protection." He was the first president in history to proclaim territorial aggrandizement an aim of the incoming administration.

Pierce realized that the greatest danger to his ambition lay in the strife over the question of slavery. Both the Whig and Democratic campaign platforms had accepted the finality of the Compromise of 1850 and condemned further agitation over the institution, and in his inaugural address he expressed the wish that "no sectional or ambitious or fanatical excitement may again threaten the durability of our institutions or obscure the light of our prosperity." The way to prevent this, he thought, was to mollify all factions, even the most extremist, by careful distribution of the rewards within his power as chief patronage dispenser. Consequently, the suppression of internal strife rather than enlargement of the country's borders was the dominating influence in his selection of his cabinet. It was a ruse destined to fail. The slavery controversy would not lie down and die. Instead, it took on a new and more vigorous life in the issue of organizing the Kansas and Nebraska territories.

For secretary of state Pierce chose William L. Marcy, shrewd, experienced in the divisive ways of New York politics, and strongly opposed to the extension of slavery. To balance this appointment, he named Jefferson Davis, as willing to break up the Union over slavery as Marcy was to preserve it, as his secretary of war. Another man with Southern rights sentiments, James C. Dobbin, of North Carolina, whose announcement at the Democratic convention that his state was voting for Pierce had set off the stampede leading to his nomination, was chosen Davis's opposite number as secretary of the navy. Pierce's choice of his New England representative in the cabinet, Caleb Cushing, was also known for his pro-slavery beliefs, even his subservience to what Northern free-soil editors called the Southern slave oligarchs. Pierce felt that he owed something to James Buchanan and his following and considered naming him secretary of state though he did not want him in the cabinet. He compromised by appointing Buchanan minister to England and choosing one of his Pennsylvania adherents, James Campbell, known only in his own state, as postmaster general. The Northwest, whose spokesman in national affairs had long been James Cass, received its sop in the appointment of Robert McClelland, then serving his second term as governor of Michigan, as secretary of the interior. The other section that had to be reconciled, the border states, was represented in the sturdy and competent James Guthrie, a Kentucky businessman who had made a fortune but had little experience in politics outside serving in the state assembly.[1]

Thus Pierce's cabinet represented insofar as it was possible ingenious success in paying political debts and appealing to sectional interests. It represented, too, the friends of all the prominent Democratic contenders for the presidency except Stephen A. Douglas and his claque, the exponents of Young America. But if they missed out in the major appointments they were amply compensated in the foreign service appointments. From ministers plenipotentiary down to consuls and commercial agents, Pierce's choices were often spectacularly unsound. They included adventurers with questionable pasts, intriguers in all sorts of shady enterprises, and erratic characters intent upon carrying out their own fantastic schemes.

In naming Marcy secretary of state, Pierce made an appointment that was generally well received, although the Young Americans

—Pierre Soulé, George Sanders, and John L. O'Sullivan—were critical of giving this high office to an Old Fogy. Creator of the slogan, "To the victor belong the spoils," Marcy soon found that these went to Pierce and not himself, for the president had the prerogative of making the minor as well as the major diplomatic appointments as a part of the huge patronage he had to dispense—within a few weeks after his inauguration he had filled more than 700 positions. There was then no foreign career service and such posts as chargés d'affaires, consuls, and clerks were used to pay political debts without even the secretary necessarily being consulted. Marcy might dislike seeing the spread-eagle expansionists given sensitive posts abroad, which he did, but there was little he could do to prevent their being sent forth to all parts of the world.[2]

Before completing his cabinet, Pierce had written Buchanan seeking his advice on appointments. He had slyly excluded Buchanan from consideration in the sentence: "I think I am expected to call around me Gentlemen who have not hitherto occupied Cabinet positions." Almost a month after the inauguration he offered Buchanan the mission to England. It was not a gratifying offer to the Sage of Wheatland. His friends whom he had recommended for office had been rejected, and he could not accept with alacrity the idea of working under Marcy, whose appointment belied Pierce's own statement to him that he would have no members of Polk's cabinet in his.[3]

Another member of the Polk cabinet, the old-school Virginian, John Y. Mason, secretary of the navy, was appointed minister to France, largely to please the president's Southern supporters and to placate the Old Dominion, whose delegates at the Democratic convention had been among the first to swing to him. Although an Old Fogy, he was acceptable to Young America because of his approval of Polk's effort to purchase Cuba. An easy-going man interested in his own comfort—his chief preoccupation in Paris was to be that of making sure of an adequate supply of Virginia hams, Virginia tobacco, and good potables—he was not expected to get along well in the French court of Louis-Napoleon.[4]

During the period of Pierce's cabinet making, the name of Pierre Soulé was frequently brought forth in the public speculation, especially in the South, as an appointee. When the cabinet was announced and his name did not appear, the speculation turned to which diplomatic post he would receive. Since he was a leading exponent of Pierce's announced goal of expansion, it seemed only logical that he would get one. The arch-enemy of slavery, Charles Sumner, reflected a widespread belief when, predicting Soulé's appointment to Spain, he wrote John Bigelow, one of the editors of the *New York Evening Post*: "The tone of the Administration on Foreign Affairs will be indicated by Soulé's nomination. *This I know*." In view of the difficult relations with Spain because of the enthusiasm in the country for the acquisition of Cuba by any means, the mission was perhaps the most delicate in the diplomatic corps. The appointment of Soulé was one that flouted reason. His agitation for annexation, his praise of López, and his attacks upon the Spanish government for the execution of Crittenden made him repugnant to Madrid, a minister a less distracted government than Spain would reject. It was also one that the French and English would find antipathetic and it was one that would be received without enthusiasm in other European capitals because of Soulé's reputation for rabid republicanism.[5]

Shortly after the announcement of the cabinet, the *New York Times* had described the attitude of the new secretary of state: "Gov. Marcy is rigidly conservative. His influence will be exerted directly against any recognition by this Government of the existence of tumult in Europe, except so far as may be necessary to preserve our own immediate material interests." It was a shock to Marcy, therefore, when Pierce appointed, besides Soulé, another advocate of intervention in European affairs, George Sanders, as consul at London. Sanders had exerted all his considerable talent to prevent Marcy's appointment. Knowing that Marcy would object to his receiving any foreign assignment, Sanders insouciantly had a letter read at Tammany Hall in which he declared he would obtain an office in the face of the secretary's opposition. Marcy was so irked by the appointment he refused to sign the papers accrediting Sanders to London. In London Sanders was to make his home the headquarters for the revolutionary exiles—Louis Kossuth, Giuseppe Garibaldi, Giuseppe Mazzini, and others—and with them hatched plots for renewing the uprisings that had been put down in 1848 and 1849. His tenure as consul, however, was a short one. He left the country before his nomination was confirmed, and when news of his activities abroad reached the Senate in February of 1854 it was rejected.[6]

Another appointment that was to cause trouble in London was Buchanan's selection of a dynamic and unscrupulous New York Democrat, Daniel E. Sickles, as secretary of his legation. A member of an old Knickerbocker family, the Van Sicklens, Sickles had been a youthful rebel. Against the wishes of his father, he had withdrawn from school to learn the printing trade. Later he had obtained his father's reluctant permission to prepare for college in the home of Lorenzo Da Ponte, the Italian opera impresario and librettist to Mozart, where he learned to speak several languages and became acquainted with the culture of Europe. He went on to study law, became a member of the bar, took part in Tammany politics, and was elected to the state assembly, winning from Marcy the praise: "As a debater he excels any man of his years in political life." As a supporter of Pierce at the Democratic convention, Sickles felt he was entitled to a political plum and among the jobs available was that of first secretary of the London legation. After an interview with Buchanan at Wheatland, he was given the job. Sickles was to be of no help as secretary of the legation. He lived extravagantly, created a scandal by remaining seated during a toast to the queen at a public dinner, and further embarrassed Buchanan by his ostentatious support of the European radical exiles.[7]

August Belmont, who had helped finance Pierce's campaign, was another Young American who sought a foreign post. He had some difficulties to overcome. He had been an original supporter of Buchanan, but the main objection to him was that he was "foreign" and was opposed by nativist groups. The *New York Tribune* referred to him slightingly as "Mr. August Schoenberg, formerly of Hanau, Germany—better known in this country by his Frenchified alias of August Belmont." Belmont was the author of a plan to obtain Cuba which he had presented to Buchanan and Marcy, both of whom urged it upon Pierce. His idea was that the holders of Spanish bonds, now very much depreciated, might combine in an effort to force Spain to sell Cuba to pay her debts. If he were named chargé d'affaires at Naples, where he had served as agent of the Rothschilds, he would be in a position to use his influence and contacts with bankers in Paris, Brussels, Amsterdam, and London as well as with powerful friends of the Spanish royal family. Buchanan was enamored of the idea, which, he wrote Pierce, had the additional merit that "Queen Christina, who is avaricious and exercises great influence over her daughter, the Queen of Spain, and her court, has very large possessions in the island, the value of which would be greatly enhanced by its cession to the United States." Belmont was sent instead to The Hague, considered even a better place than Naples as his base of operations.[8]

Pierce evidently felt that in the Belmont appointment he had acted more judiciously than he had with some of his other ones. He is reported as having lectured Sickles before he left for London: "Mr. Sickles, our foreign appointments have been too carelessly made—men have been selected without reference to their fitness for diplomacy or the particular place to which they have been accredited. In this matter I mean to take great pains to secure the services of gentlemen, who like Mr. Belmont, possess the confidence of discerning men and who have the qualifications which he possesses to serve the country abroad."[9] He might very well have had some qualms at this moment, for among his other appointments had been the agitator and intriguer John L. O'Sullivan as minister to Portugal and Edwin de Leon, who had given Young America its name, as chargé in Egypt.

There were also important New World ministers to name, one of them to Mexico. Almost five years after the signing of the peace treaty and the acquisition of New Mexico and California, expansionists still had their eyes on Mexican territory, which, like Cuba, was attracting the attention of filibusters. The boundary between the two countries had not been established, and Mexico complained of encroachment by settlers from Texas in territory she claimed as her own. United States interests, moreover, were still seeking transit rights across the Isthmus of Tehuantepec, and new plans had been put forth to obtain a strip of northern Mexico felt to offer the best southern route for a transcontinental railroad to California. The man Pierce chose for this important post was a South Carolinian, James Gadsden, upon the recommendation of Jefferson Davis. Of late years chiefly interested in extending rail lines westward, Gadsden had been a friend and military associate of Andrew Jackson. A strong states' rights man, he had broken up their friendship by supporting the South Carolina nullification movement of the 1830s; and a defender of slavery, he had been one of a group of Southerners who memorialized the California assembly in 1851 for permission to form a colony to which cotton planters would transport their slaves.[10]

Central America, too, was important in the eyes of expansionists. Many who wanted to annex Cuba as a slave state hoped to extend U.S. control through the whole Caribbean and create a vast slave empire. Aside from its attractions to these visionaries, Central America was of interest because of the expectation of constructing a canal across Panama, Nicaragua, or Tehuantepec to link the Atlantic and Pacific oceans. Great Britain, ever on the alert for commercial advantage, had acted to extend her influence in the area by assuming a protectorate over the Mosquito Indians of Nicaragua and seizing the Bay Islands off the coast of Honduras.

Secretary of State John M. Clayton had sought to settle some of these difficulties when he negotiated a treaty with the British minister to the United States, Sir Henry Lytton Bulwer. The Clayton-Bulwer treaty of 1850 had placed any projected interoceanic canal under the joint control of the United States and Great Britain, guaranteed its neutrality, and provided that transit tolls should be equal for citizens or subjects of both countries. It also had pledged the signers not to colonize, occupy, or exercise dominion over any part of Central America. It had not been a popular treaty with expansionists, and its ambiguity in phraseology—whether the colonization clause was prospective or retrospective—had opened up a Pandora's box of troubles.

Heretofore, U.S. representatives in Central America had been only of the rank of special agents and consuls. Early in its session Congress had authorized a full mission to Central America—the states of Nicaragua, Costa Rica, Guatemala, Honduras, and El Salvador—and Pierce had the task of finding a minister to send there. He offered the post to John Slidell, Soulé's chief rival for dominance in Louisiana politics before the latter's appointment to Spain had been decided on, and this was taken to mean that Soulé would not receive a major foreign assignment as it could not be expected that the patronage system would allow Louisiana to have two full missions. Slidell, however, cleared the way for Soulé's appointment when he refused the post because he preferred entering the Senate. To accept it, he thought, would be to be sent into exile; moreover, his unhappy experience as Polk's emissary to Mexico had made him wary of engaging again in Latin-American diplomacy.[11] Pierce next offered the post to Solon Borland, then serving in the Senate from Arkansas. A veteran of the Mexican War, Borland was bellicose, hot-headed, and strongly anti-British, a man who would stand up for American rights in Central America.

Aside from the raffish character given U.S. diplomacy through some of Pierce's foreign office appointments, Marcy himself contributed his bit to upsetting effete embassies and chancelleries by a dress circular issued on June 1. In it he directed the nation's representatives to appear "at court in the simple dress of an American citizen." His circular said that the "simplicity of our usages and the tone of feeling among our people" were well reflected by the homespun garb in which Benjamin Franklin appeared in Paris. His order meant that American ministers were limited in their costume to the conventional silk hat and black coat and trousers customarily worn by men in the United States for public occasions. Some of the diplomatists were a little put out by the dress rule. For one thing, their failure to appear in all the glory of gold braid and embroidery might be considered an insult to the potentates and ministers on whom they had to call, and, for another, they found the prescribed black clothing indistinguishable from the similarly garbed servants at the royal palaces and embassies.[12]

Despite the interest shown by the president and his two most important foreign policy advisers, Marcy and Buchanan, in the Belmont plan, none of the three could have much confidence in it in the wake of what had happened after Polk's attempt to buy Cuba. Instead, the administration policy during its first year in office seems to have been to hope for annexation through the island's gaining independence by revolution aided by filibusters from the United States. This is indicated in the very guarded instructions Marcy gave Pierre Soulé on July 23 before he left for his mission to Spain. Marcy emphasized that "the President does not deem it proper to authorize you to make any proposition for the purchase of that island" and set forth the expectation that Cuba would obtain independence by other means. Spain, he said, "cannot but see that at no distant period Cuba will release itself or be released from its present Colonial subjection," and if this occurred the island would fall "necessarily into the American Continental system."

The instructions repeated the familiar doctrine that the United States would do nothing to "disturb" Cuba's present connection with Spain but added the proviso "unless the character of that connection should be so changed as to affect our present or prospective security." Marcy cited past instances of enforcement of neutrality laws but by implication expressed the administration's sympathy for filibuster movements:

> Our country is open to the reception of the citizens and subjects of all nations. . . . Those who are born here as well as those who have come from foreign lands are not, and cannot be placed, under obligations to remain among us. Our government can lay no restraints upon their emigration if they have respected our laws while under its jurisdiction. It cannot make inquisition into the motives which induce them to withdraw from our country, nor restrain them on the ground of suspicion that they may not, while out of our country, respect the rights of those nations which are at peace with the United States. Wherever oppression has provoked revolt, the sufferers are ever the objects of sympathy. Ardent enthusiastic spirits rally to their standard. Should the rule of Spain over Cuba be so severe as to excite revolutionary movements in that island, she will undoubtedly find volunteers in the ranks of the Cubans from various countries, and, owing to very obvious case, more from the United States probably than any other; but it would be unjust to impute to this and the other governments to which these volunteers formerly belonged, an unfriendly disposition towards her, or a desire to aid clandestinely in the attempt to wrest that island from her.[13]

Officially, then, the administration would not countenance "detaching" Cuba, as Marcy put it, from Spain by any improper methods, but unofficially the president and the administration were kept in touch with the resurgent filibuster movement of the previous year in the formation of the Order of the Lone Star and the new Cuban junta in New York City. Once before, while governor of Mississippi, John A. Quitman had refused an offer of the junta to command a filibuster expedition to Cuba. On April 29, 1853, he received an extraordinary proposal from the reconstituted junta that he become the "exclusive chief" of a new movement to make the island "a sovereign and independent nation." With his political career now in eclipse since an extreme Southern rights group in 1852 had nominated him for vice-president on a ticket headed by George M. Troup of Georgia that had received no support even in the slave states, his ambition was fired anew by this offer. The articles of agreement signed later in the year made him the civil and military chief of the revolution "with all the powers and attributes of dictatorship" to cease as soon as a free government was established on the island. At the end of his service, in addition to regular pay, he was to receive $1 million from the new government.[14]

To what extent members of the Pierce administration were involved in Quitman's expedition is not clear. Quitman's biographer and friend Claiborne said that on a trip to New York to consult with the junta he stopped at Washington and communicated his plans to "distinguished persons" who assured him "not only that he had their sympathies, but that there could be no pretext for the intervention of the federal authorities." Undoubtedly such support was expressed by his expansionist friends Jefferson Davis and Caleb Cushing, but whether or not he had the approval of the president, which he seemed to think he had, is not known. Pierce's biographer, Roy Franklin Nichols, said that he did but gave no documentation. "Pierce hoped that Cubans aided by Americans would revolt and, like Texas, seek admission to the Union as a state," Nichols wrote. "With the President's knowledge, a Cuban junto was negotiating with his Mexican War associate, General Quitman, to lead such an expedition, and Pierce appointed the latter's intimate, Alexander M. Clayton, Consul at Havana."[15] Clayton, a former judge of the Mississippi High Court of Errors and Appeals, was familiar with Quitman's plans, writing him before leaving for Havana that he thought an independent government "after the fashion of Texas" would be "at first advisable."

Further evidence of the administration's connection with the Quitman movement is seen in the career of Pierre Soulé after his appointment as minister to Spain. The appointment of a foreign minister is not ordinarily the occasion for public demonstrations of enthusiasm, but that of Soulé evoked a series of them. He left Washington on April 20 to go to New Orleans to wind up his personal affairs before departing for Madrid. His reception at stops along the way was like that of a returning Roman hero. He seemed in no hurry to go abroad and lingered in New Orleans for almost two months before sailing for New York, on June 26, aboard a ship that stopped at Havana. In New York, which he reached on July 4, he was serenaded at his hotel by members of the Order of the Lone Star and the Cuban community. A New Orleans newspaper correspondent noted that he "gave no sign of approval, wisely considering his new relations as envoy to Spain." When he left Washington July 26, after almost a month spent in conferences with the president and secretary of state, he was honored with a serenade given by Young America colleagues. His address in response was appropriately diplomatic: his was a mission, he said, of conciliation and justice.

So far he had acted very circumspectly, and, though Spain might have found the serenades offensive, they drew no comment from that quarter because Calderón de la Barca had been recalled to Madrid and was soon to be named minister of foreign affairs and his replacement had not reached the United States. But in New York at a demonstration sponsored by the Order of the Lone Star and the junta, the discretion that Soulé had so far shown was abandoned. It was so brazen a demonstration for a free Cuba and annexation it could hardly have been held unless the sponsors felt they had the approval of the Pierce administration. The affair began with a torchlight procession, led by the popular Dodsworth's Band, from Fulton Street up Broadway to the New York Hotel, where Soulé was stopping. Banners and transparencies bore such slogans as "Cuba Must and Shall Be Free," "Free Thought and Free Speech for the Cubans," and "Young America and Young Cuba." One, triangular in form, had on one leg the word "Cuba," on a second "Pierce," and on the third "Soulé." The message was also conveyed in bad poems, one of which said:

The Antilles Flower,
The true key of the Gulf,
Must be plucked from the Crown
Of the Old Spanish Wolf.

When Soulé appeared on the balcony of his hotel to receive the plaudits of the 5,000 cheering Cuba supporters, Miguel Teurbe

Tolón, speaking for the junta, addressed him with the hope "that on your returning home, a new star shining in the sky of Young America may shed its dawning rays upon your noble brow." Soulé's fervid expansionism was expressed in his reply: "I could not believe that we were eternally to be encircled within the narrow limits described as the space assigned to us at the dawn of the Republic." As to his role as minister to Spain, he said that his official position made him no less an American citizen who "has a right to carry wherever he goes the throbbings of that people that speak out such tremendous truths to the tyrants of the old continent."[16]

Quitman's decision to head an expedition to Cuba quickly became known to followers of López, who wrote offering their services even before he signed the final papers with the junta in August. Louis Schlesinger, who had unsuccessfully sought a foreign service appointment under the new administration, wrote on May 18 saying he had "a private account to settle with old Spain" and offered to raise a regiment in New York. Quitman could get in touch with him through John L. O'Sullivan. Preparing to leave for his mission in Portugal, O'Sullivan found time to busy himself with invasion plans. He promised in a letter of August 29 to work through his relatives in Cuba to encourage an uprising to coincide with Quitman's invasion, and later, on September 8, warned that some impatient young Cubans were planning to go to Trinidad de Cuba as advance couriers, a dangerous scheme, he said, because they might act prematurely to upset a better organized program for rebellion. Chatham Roberdeau Wheat wrote of his eagerness to fight in Cuba again "beside an Apostle of Liberty."[17] Quitman chose as his chief assistant a former American resident of Havana, John S. Thrasher, a member of the Havana Club and editor of *El Faro Industrial*, a trade journal. He had gone to New Orleans after his arrest and subsequent release for involvement in the Bahía Honda expedition of López and had been employed on the *Daily Picayune* there.

Well aware that the López expeditions had been too hastily fitted out, that money was needed to acquire adequate arms and steamers, and that a few hundred men, even with support in Cuba, could not fight successfully against Spanish troops, Quitman had no intention of invading the island unless he was well prepared.

He would not let himself be pressured into a premature invasion by either his American or Cuban supporters. One of his New Orleans associates, Samuel R. Walker, wrote him on February 7, 1854, that inactivity was causing a loss in enthusiasm. The same complaint was made a month later by Felix Huston, a former general in the army of the Texas Republic, who said he had arrived in New Orleans and found "nothing done or doing" there and at Baton Rouge things were "just at a dead halt."[18]

The junta was also impatient and wrote him about the same time. Quitman replied on April 16 explaining why he was not ready to sail. He declared that 3,000 men was the minimum number required for a successful enterprise and that his commitment to the invasion was based on the raising of at least $220,000, which had not been reached. His conditions were not excessively high—one moderately armed steamer, and sufficient transportation otherwise." "I have not expected that it would be in our power to procure transportation of the very first class," he said. "In this, economy as well as safety should be consulted. Of this, however, I must be the judge under professional advice." In respect to support of patriots on the island, he said that this was "dependent upon contingencies which no human foresight can anticipate."[19]

The urgency for invasion had been heightened in September 1853 when Spain sent a new captain general to the island, Juan de Pezuela, with orders, so annexationists and Creole slaveowners believed, to free the slaves. This was done, they thought, partly at the behest of Great Britain, which had threatened to withdraw support of Spanish ownership unless something was done to suppress the slave traffic and thus to make the island less attractive to U.S. annexationists. Pezuela's program was not so extreme as the annexationists and slaveholders feared, but it was bad enough. In a series of decrees issued in December, he announced heavy fines and banishment from the island of anyone caught importing Africans as slaves; gave citizenship rights to all *emancipados*, that is, Negroes illegally imported before 1835; and provided for the importation as "apprentices" of Indians, Chinese, and Africans to supply the labor shortage.

In reply to an inquiry from Marcy as to whether Spain, as rumored, intended to emancipate all Africans imported since 1820,

William H. Robertson, acting consul at Havana, said on April 21, 1854, he did not believe this had been commenced though he thought the December decrees were preliminaries to this action. "The natural consequence of this state of things," Robertson said, "would be that the Island would be entirely in the hands of the colored population, the whites would have to abandon it or be sacrificed." So frightened were island slaveholders that emancipation would come—the "Africanization" of Cuba was the term used—that through Robertson they sent appeals to President Pierce to send troops to prevent it. One appeal, decided upon at a meeting of several planters with Robertson in April, went so far as to include a draft of a proclamation to be addressed to the inhabitants of Cuba on the arrival of U.S. troops.[20] The administration was so concerned over the possibility that Marcy, in March, sent Charles W. Davis as a secret agent to Cuba to find out if Africanization was actually planned, how far it had progressed if so, and to what extent Great Britain was involved in the "conspiracy." If evidence of the truth of the program was obtained, the president would ask Congress for immediate action. "Our forbearance," Marcy said in his instructions, "is ceasing to be a virtue."[21]

The rumored program of Africanization created widespread hysteria in the South. Speakers at annexationist rallies and newspaper editorials warned that emancipation would kindle slave insurrections in the United States and that Cuba would become a haven for fugitive slaves. The junta capitalized on the agitation by issuing a manifesto warning that Cuba's Negroes would exact bloody vengeance on their owners, that the island would be completely desolated, and that only armed intervention could prevent these disasters.

Governor P. O. Herbert of Louisiana, early in March, sent a message to the legislature on the Africanization menace. On March 16 both houses adopted a memorial to Congress asking for action to prevent Spain and other European powers from establishing measures and institutions "prejudicial to our safety and welfare." The memorial declared that Africanization would have a pernicious effect on slavery in the United States, that it would destroy the social and political existence of Cuba, that it would "materially affect the natural law of American progress by precluding forever the admission of Cuba in this Union," that it would "create almost in sight of our shores a government administered by an inferior and barbarous race under the immediate influence of European interest and ideas," and that it would menace commerce carried on at ports on the Gulf of Mexico. Louisiana's senators, John Slidell and Judah P. Benjamin, presented the memorial to the Senate on May 1, when Slidell submitted a resolution asking the Foreign Relations Committee to look into the expediency of authorizing the president to suspend by proclamation the neutrality law so as not to hinder American efforts to aid Cuba.[22]

The Slidell resolution provoked no extended discussion and was routinely referred to the Foreign Relations Committee. It was addressed to a Senate wearied by a long and tumultuous controversy over the extension of slavery in the debate on the Kansas-Nebraska Act that Stephen A. Douglas had introduced on January 4 and that the Senate had finally passed on March 4. But while the Senate at this time could not be aroused to concern itself with the acquisition of Cuba, the situation was such that President Pierce decided the time had come to pursue the goals he had announced in his inaugural address.

CHAPTER SIX

Antic American Diplomacy

For almost a year during which Pierre Soulé's chief diplomatic concern had been protesting seizure at Havana of an American commercial vessel, the *Black Warrior*, he had been under instructions to make no offer for purchase of Cuba. This policy was suddenly reversed on April 3, 1854, when Secretary of State Marcy authorized him to begin negotiations to obtain the island. Marcy gave two reasons for thinking the situation had changed so that Spain might be amenable to an offer. One was the unsettled condition of political affairs in the country, and the other was the threat of uprisings in Cuba over the new policies of the captain general. Marcy referred to the Polk offer in 1848 to pay $100 million for Cuba and, although Pierce felt this was a liberal price, Soulé was told he could increase it by $20 million or $30 million. There were other reasons Marcy did not mention—Spain's troubled financial situation and the assurances of James Buchanan in London and John Y. Mason in Paris that neither England nor France, their attention turned to the Crimea, had any plan of joint action to protect Spain's ownership.

Marcy recognized the difficulties Soulé faced and the likelihood he might fail. In this eventuality, Soulé was to direct his efforts "to the next most desirable object, which is to detach that island from the Spanish dominion and from all dependence on any European power." Marcy gave no hint as to how Soulé might go about this. His use of the word "detach" has puzzled historians. This was not, however, the first time Marcy had used the word in connection with Cuban independence. In his July 23, 1853, instructions to Soulé he had written: "There is reason to believe that Spain herself, as well as other European governments, suspect[s] that the people of the United States are desirous of detaching Cuba from its present transatlantic dependence . . . with a view of annexing it to this Union; and that our government was disposed to connive at the participation of our citizens in the past disturbances in that island, and would again do so on the recurrence of similar events." He then had hastened to disavow such an "unfounded suspicion," but now he hinted that the United States might support a revolution.

Marcy pointed out that the Cubans had no political voice in how they were ruled and no local government agencies to deal with Spain about island affairs. "No body of men are permitted to associate for the purpose of accepting or offering terms," he wrote. "Should the despotic rule now established be so far relaxed as to allow of any association the United States would readily countenance and aid its efforts to release the Island from dependence on Spain." Marcy refrained from any statement that would lead Soulé to conclude that he could present this view to Spain as a threat; he left it instead to Soulé's discretion, saying: "This government would look with favor upon such an arrangement, and aid in any useful way to bring it about; but without knowing whether anything can be done to effect that object, or what part the United States could properly take in furtherance of it, it is not possible to give you any special instructions for your action in such a contingency."[1]

The favorable outlook for making an offer came at a time when the Manifest Destiny hopes of Pierce were at high tide. His minister to Mexico, James Gadsden, who had been charged with settling a boundary dispute with the neighbor to the south, had submitted a treaty now being discussed by the cabinet which added more than 45,000 square miles to the country by the purchase of a strip regarded as a desirable route for a railway to the Pacific, a territorial addition that by no means satisfied the president but that was the first fruit of his inaugural address promising expansion. With Great Britain and France allied to prevent Russia from taking the Crimea from Turkey, Pierce and his imperialistic supporters saw that the opportunity was at hand to push other schemes for aggrandizement. On the day after directing Soulé to make an offer to Spain, Marcy wrote his agent at Honolulu authorizing him to make a treaty with the Hawaiian king for annexation of the Sandwich Islands. In November 1853, Marcy had sent William Cazneau to Santo Domingo to investigate conditions in the Dominican Republic, from which France was seeking a cession of Samaná Bay in return for aid against a feared invasion from Haiti. Cazneau had returned to the United States with a glowing report of the island's rich natural resources awaiting American development. Informed by Mason in Paris that France, because of the Crimea situation, had given up her efforts in the Dominican Republic, Marcy sent Cazneau back to the island with instructions to lease Samaná Bay as a U.S. naval station. Cazneau, like Sanders, O'Sullivan, and others among Pierce's foreign agents, had a fine capacity for intrigue dating from his early efforts to help Texas gain independence from Mexico. He had married the journalist Cora Montgomery, Moses Y. Beach's associate in the efforts of the editor of the *New York Sun* to annex Cuba, and the couple were alike in their enthusiasm for expansion.* John Bigelow, writing in the *New York Evening Post* about their first trip to the island, had said: "She has not hesitated to assure the people of St. Domingo that the country could belong to the United States in six months."[2]

The traditional attitude of Spain for keeping the Pearl of the Antilles was not the only obstacle to the revived plan to purchase Cuba. Another was the popularity in the South of the Quitman filibuster expedition, which Senator Slidell had sought to give governmental sanction by a resolution calling for suspension of the neutrality laws for a year. The resolution had been referred to the Senate Foreign Relations Committee without much discussion, but

*Cora Montgomery was the pen name of Jane McManus, born in New York on April 6, 1807. Her filibuster activities may be said to have begun in 1833 when with her father and a brother she took part in an unsuccessful colonization scheme in Texas, where she met the man who was to be her second husband, William Cazneau. She related her experiences in a book, *Eagle Pass or Life on the Border*. She supported the annexation of Texas and other expansionist projects in newspaper articles over a period of years. John Bigelow, one of the editors of the *New York Evening Post*, described her as being "famous as a filibustera," and Henry Watterson, editor of the *Louisville Courier-Journal*, said she was "a born insurrecto and a terror with her pen." Walter Prescott Webb, ed., *The Handbook of Texas*, 1:122; Charles C. Tansill, *The United States and Santo Domingo, 1798–1873*, p. 179; Edward Wallace, *Destiny and Glory*, pp. 245 ff.

late in May James M. Mason, the chairman, informed Pierce that the committee had decided to report favorably on it. The news upset the president, for a real filibuster threat would interfere with his plan to purchase the island. He called the Democratic members of the committee and Thomas H. Bayly, chairman of the House Foreign Affairs Committee, to a conference with himself and Jefferson Davis—for some reason Marcy could not attend—for a conference at the White House on May 30. He took the firm stand that invasion plans must be halted. He explained that he had directed Soulé to open negotiations for purchase of the island and that with the concurrence of Congress he intended to send two special commissioners—"distinguished citizens," as Marcy later wrote Soulé—to be associated with him in obtaining the end in view. To emphasize his intention to prevent any rash acts by filibusters during the period of negotiations, he would issue a proclamation against the mounting of an expedition.

Slidell, who in introducing his resolution had said he was convinced Spain intended to Africanize Cuba and who had no confidence in the diplomatic abilities of his political foe Soulé, angrily objected to the proclamation. It would be a betrayal of the South and the ardent workers for Cuba's freedom. Unable to persuade Pierce to give up his plan, Slidell then sought a delay until the president transmitted a message to Congress requesting a commission. It should be worded, he said, in a way "to satisfy our people in New Orleans that he was prepared to pursue an energetic policy & thus induce them to abstain from any hostile expedition." Pierce, averse to assuming this responsibility, suggested instead that Slidell himself telegraph the district attorney at New Orleans that "immediate & decisive measures would be taken in relation to Cuba." Slidell protested on the ground that such a message must be an official statement of government policy. It was finally agreed that the secretary of state should send the message to New Orleans.[3]

Slidell was not happy about the outcome and did not really expect Pierce to send a forceful message to Congress, which he did not do. The reason was that the administration, in supporting the Kansas-Nebraska Act so unpopular in the North, had exhausted its strength. It could hardly expect to obtain a Democratic majority in the Congress to uphold another measure favorable to the slave interests. The situation was summed up by Marcy in a letter to John Y. Mason in Paris: the Nebraska question had "sadly shattered our party in all the free states and deprived it of that strength which was needed and would have been much more profitably used for the acquisition of Cuba."[4]

On the day after the conference, Pierce issued his proclamation warning against engaging in a military expedition being fitted out for the invasion of Cuba. It angered Quitman and his associates, whose plans, after early setbacks, had progressed to the extent that negotiations were under way to obtain ships to take an army to the island. Exaggerated accounts of the readiness and imminence of the invasion had excited the South. The *Memphis Whig*, for example, reported it had learned that nearly a million dollars was available, that between 80,000 and 90,000 stand of arms had been collected besides ninety field pieces, and that eight steamers and four sailing ships had been purchased or chartered to take 10,000 men to the island. The expedition, the paper said, would sail in mid-July.

An expedition on such a grand scale had not been conceived by Quitman, and even his more modest goals were not in reach at this time, but the South was all agog over prospects. Alexander Walker, a New Orleans leader in the Order of the Lone Star, in a letter to A. G. Haley, one of Quitman's agents in Washington, intended for Davis's eyes, complained on June 15 that the proclamation violated the understanding Quitman had with the administration. It would not go down well with the South. "First, you must understand that the cause of Cuba now overwhelms all others in this section," Walker said. "This whole corner of the Union has been filibusterized. Cuba must be taken, and that shortly. . . ." He went on: "At present, it is like holding in a mettled race horse after the drum is tapped, to prevent an open declaration of the great mass of the Southern Democracy against the Administration."[5]

Quitman himself drafted a letter to Pierce protesting the plan to purchase the island, notes for which are among his papers in the Mississippi Department of Archives and History. The letter contained several threats that if it was actually sent might have given the president pause. He was told first that a treaty to purchase would stand little chance of approval in the Senate. He then was warned that if he delayed in acquiring Cuba "until the abolition plans of Spain [Africanization] can be matured, a fearful responsibility will devolve upon you and your advisers" and he would be held "accountable to posterity for the ruin of Cuba and perhaps that of thirteen states of this Union." Cuba and annexation, Quitman continued, were only "mere questions of political considerations" to the president, but to Southern slaveholders they were questions of vital interests, affecting "our happiness, our fortunes and our lives."[6]

In the North the Kansas-Nebraska Act repealing the Missouri Compromise and providing for the question of slavery in the new states to be determined on the popular sovereignty principle had produced mass meetings in opposition, its supporters had been burned in effigy, and there were other manifestations of outrage. In the South, though generally approved, it was considered of no great import. Slaveholders thought annexation of Cuba more vital to their interests. Alexander H. Stephens of Georgia expressed a widespread view when he said: "We are on the eve of much *greater issues*. The Cuba question will soon be upon us."[7] It was a view also widely set forth in the newspapers, the *New Orleans Picayune*, for example, declaring on June 9: "The measure upon which the Nebraska principle will be tested is that of the acquisition of Cuba."

A more damaging blow to the expedition than the president's proclamation, however, was an order by John A. Campbell, associate justice of the U.S. Supreme Court sitting as a circuit judge in New Orleans, binding Quitman and his associates to observe for nine months the laws of the nation in general and especially the neutrality law of April 20, 1818. Campbell had determined to act against the filibusters when he went to New Orleans in April to open the spring term of the U.S. Circuit Court. His determination may have been strengthened by the president's proclamation of May 30, but he had apparently acted without consultation with the administration. Appointed to the court by Pierce upon the recommendation of the other justices, Campbell was a brilliant Alabama attorney who had been admitted to the bar at the age of eighteen and was only forty-one when named to the nation's highest tribunal. Before going to Washington he had freed his own slaves and, though sympathetic to Southern interests, he opposed the extreme states' rightists who talked of secession. In New Orleans he instructed the grand jury to look into violations of the neutrality laws. On June 19 it subpoenaed as witnesses Quitman and his associates, John Henderson, Samuel J. Peters, P. Suave, a rich sugar planter, A. L. Saunders, and J. S. Thrasher, and in July reported that Saunders, Thrasher, and Quitman had refused to testify. Its presentment said that filibuster meetings had been held, that the Cuban bonds had been sold, and that arrangements for an invasion were being made.

Campbell called the three recalcitrant witnesses before him and asked them to show cause why they should not be required to post bond of $3,000 as a guarantee they would observe the laws. When they refused, he ordered their arrest. Campbell's action was attacked by New Orleanians, and the three filibusters were hailed as heroes. The U.S. marshal, J. M. Kennedy, who took them into custody and accompanied them to a banquet in their honor, offered the rhymed toast:

Cuba:
We'll buy or fight, but to our shore we'll lash her;
If Spain won't sell, we'll then turn in and *thrash-her*.

Quitman was disposed to go to jail rather than post the bond but was persuaded by friends that he had, in the words of his biographer Claiborne, "higher duties" to fulfill. The three were released after they had posted the bond under protest, Quitman asserting that Campbell's order was "an unconstitutional, illegal, and arbitrary exercise of power." Campbell responded to the attacks upon him in an article in the *Delta* in which he declared that Northern communities were being required to enforce the Fugitive Slave Act but they could not be expected to do so if Southerners persisted in their piratical attempts to extend slave territory by an invasion of Cuba.

Quitman had no intention of abandoning his expedition, but Campbell's interference had made it impossible to mount one in 1854, unfortunate from his standpoint because the junta as well as his own followers was pressing him for immediate action. To reassure them, he issued a circular in July saying that preparations were continuing and that only a little more money was needed. Activities were stepped up late in the summer and early fall. Samuel R. Walker went to Cuba in September to consult with annexationists there and on his return prepared an article for *De Bow's Review*, published in the November issue, in which he warned of the need for intervention to prevent Africanization. He declared that a war with Spain to obtain the island would not do, because the property of the Creoles would be confiscated and the slaves would be freed, and that purchase, even if Spain would sell, offered similar difficulties. The only road open, he argued, was for the U.S. government to hold off while the Cubans, aided by soldiers for freedom from this country, won their own independence. Then the United States would acquire the island in the same way Texas had been acquired. Quitman's activities included the attempt to smuggle into Cuba 5,000 muskets obtained from George Law to aid a revolutionary group at Nuevitas, but this failed when the gun runners were captured. To acquaint islanders with their American leader, a book, *Apuntes Biográficos del Mayor General Juan Antonio Quitman*, was published. By the year's end expedition plans were sufficiently well along for an invasion to be launched in February of 1855.[9]

If President Pierce thought he would have better success than President Polk in an offer to Spain to buy Cuba, he was being unrealistic. His unfortunate choice of Pierre Soulé as minister precluded any favorable outcome. He had been almost a persona non grata since his arrival at the Spanish court, which expected almost anything from this notorious democrat and revolutionist.

Soulé's first offense was a duel fought with the French ambassador over an insult to his wife. Shortly after reaching Madrid, the minister, his wife, a beautiful Creole of New Orleans, and their son Nelvil were guests at a ball given by the French ambassador, the Marquis de Turgo. At this affair the Duke of Alba was overheard by Nelvil to remark on the appearance of Mrs. Soulé, wearing a very décolleté dress: "Here comes Marie de Bourgogne," a reference to the dissolute wife of Louis X. Angered by this slur upon his mother, Nelvil challenged the duke to a duel, which they fought with swords but which was ended by the seconds before injury to either. Three weeks later, Soulé, who had been ill while his son was defending the family honor, felt it incumbent upon himself to take action. Instead of challenging the Duke of Alba, however, he demanded an apology from Turgo as host at the occasion. Turgo haughtily refused, saying such a demand could be replied to only at the point of his pistol. In their confrontation on the field of honor Soulé emerged unscathed but Turgo suffered a crippling wound in the right leg.[10]

Soulé's second offense came in his arrogant handling of official protests against the seizure at Havana on February 28, 1854, of the merchant vessel *Black Warrior* for an alleged error in her manifest. To Americans this seizure seemed to be a deliberate insult, as if Spain, made bold, as Marcy wrote Soulé, by the recent support of France and England in affairs involving the island, wanted to demonstrate that she could retaliate for filibuster threats from the United States. The usually equable Marcy was so angry over the action that he told the Russian chargé that if he had had warships available he would have sent them to Havana, Congress called upon the president for information about the insult, and Pierce responded with a message declaring that if peaceful protests failed he would use any power the legislature would grant to "vindicate the honor of our flag." In instructing Soulé to demand redress for the "outrage" Marcy said the president wished to settle the affair peaceably but would not "brook any evasion or delay."[11]

Soulé took literally Marcy's instruction that Spain's usual dilatory routine in dealing with disputes with the United States would not do in this exigency. He presented a threatening demand for immediate redress to the foreign minister, Calderón de la Barca, on April 8 and after three days when no reply had been received submitted a new demand, the payment of an indemnity of $300,000, the value of the ship and cargo, and dismissal of all persons, whatever their rank, responsible for the seizure. Calderón merely trotted out the excuse made so often in the past in protests made regarding Cuban affairs—no decision could be reached until his government was in full possession of the facts, these to be obtained from the captain general. Incensed by being thus put off, Soulé continued to apply "the lash," as he put it to Marcy, on Calderón's shoulders until finally, on April 13, he was informed of the decision of the Spanish government: the *Black Warrior* was to be returned to her owners and the $6,000 fine imposed for violation of port rules was to be remitted.*[12]

Thus when Soulé received from Marcy instructions empowering him to attempt to purchase Cuba, he saw no prospects of immediate success because of his unpopularity with the Spanish government. Having angered officials by his peremptory demands for satisfaction in the *Black Warrior* affair, he wrote Marcy on May 3 that there was no one with whom he could bring up "so delicate a subject." He suggested that the only way Spain could be brought to the point of considering a sale would be for Cuba "to rise in arms & assert its independence." If this should happen, Spain might be willing to make an offer in order to save what she could if the colony "ceased to be of any possible value to herself."[13]

But within a few weeks the situation in Spain changed completely. Earlier in the year revolutions in Zaragoza and Barcelona had been suppressed, but the discontent of the people with their poverty and the oppressions of a sovereign they despised had grown. By the end of June the revolutionary movement had spread and insurgents were preparing to march on the capital. Soulé, who had earlier pinned such hopes as he had for obtaining Cuba on his friendship with the Queen Mother María Cristina, saw possibilities in the revolution.

"I am up on the watch," he wrote Marcy on June 28. "Who knows, but something may grow out of all this that may afford me some chance of advancing the great object?" But he did more than merely observe. He met almost daily with rebel leaders and promised them financial support. "I have drawn them to make a specific offer of relinquishment to us of the Island of Cuba," he

*The dispute with Spain over the *Black Warrior* affair continued for another year. On Feb. 21, 1855, Claudio Antón de Luzuriaga, Spanish minister of foreign affairs, admitted that Havana authorities had been wrong in their application of port regulations to the *Black Warrior* in not taking into account the precedents allowing the vessel to enter the harbor with her cargo listed as in ballast and said that damages would be paid as soon as the proper amount could be determined. Finally, on Aug. 4, 1855, these were set at $53,948.96. W. R. Manning, ed., *Diplomatic Correspondence of the United States, Inter-American Affairs, 1831–1860*, 11:841–43, 877.

informed Marcy on July 15, "on terms which would be deemed reasonable, and they now propound it for our acceptance provided we can help them to a succour of three hundred thousand dollars." His enthusiasm grew when the insurgents entered Madrid and Queen Isabella and María Cristina barricaded themselves in the royal palace. "Madrid is at last in full insurrection . . . ," Soulé enthusiastically wrote Marcy on July 18. "What a moment for taking in our hands that question of Cuba. . . ."[14]

Soulé was not alone in thinking the revolution provided the opportunity for seizing the island jewel. Mason in Paris wrote Marcy that it presented "a most favorable moment to press the settlement of the Cuban question," and Buchanan in London wrote that if the Cubans were wise they would "seize the present propitious moment" to declare their independence and suggested that the United States should decide what steps to take to assist an island revolution.[15]

The glowing hope that Cuba could be obtained through the revolution was extinguished when, so Soulé reported in a series of dispatches to Marcy, the insurgent leaders were hesitant to assume control of the government and there was growing dissension among them. Baldomero Espartero, who had been regent during the childhood of Queen Isabella, was recalled to head a new ministry and during August succeeded in establishing a fairly stable government. Writing Marcy on August 30, Soulé said that very little could be expected to be done until the Cortés met and that, as his health was bad, he would repair to a watering place, Aulus in the French Pyrenees on the border, to await fresh instructions.[16]

If Soulé's machinations had resulted in failure, so had those of Pierce in Washington.* In March, in connection with the seizure of the *Black Warrior*, the president had sent the House a message

*A pronouncement on the failure of Soulé's mission was given by the secretary of the legation for five years, Horatio J. Perry, in a long, self-exculpating letter to Marcy on Sept. 6. Perry did not like Soulé and resented that the minister had not properly appreciated his knowledge of Spanish affairs and had paid no attention to his suggestions, but his opinion of his superior may be considered a fair one: "Sir, the policy which Mr. Soulé has represented at this court and urged with all his talent and all his resources is a complete and utter failure. He has not an individual of any influence in any party who supports him at this moment, or would listen to any proposition from him. He has not a friend or a dependent even, who could serve him for anything in politics. He is isolated in Spain. . . . "

suggesting "the propriety of adopting such provisional measures as the exigency may seem to demand." One of the measures he sought was approval of his plan to send the special commission of distinguished citizens to Spain, and for this he needed an appropriation. It was not a request likely to be received favorably in view of the opposition of Northerners to annexation and the support of Southerners for a filibuster expedition, and it did not because the House took no action.

When the revolution broke out in Spain, Pierce had turned again to Congress to obtain resources—$10 million was suggested—to be placed at his disposal. As all administration measures were having trouble in Congress, he needed an opportunity by which he could diplomatically present his request. He thought this could be done if a resolution were introduced in the Senate asking if relations with Spain had changed in a way to make his request for "provisional measures" unnecessary. He asked Slidell to be his agent in this maneuver but received a chilly refusal. Next, James M. Mason of the Senate Committee on Foreign Relations was approached and, consenting, submitted the resolution on August 1. The president's response had been prepared in advance and reached the Senate in time to be read the same day. In it Pierce reported that the unsatisfactory relations in March still existed and the need for measures by Congress still remained. A canvass of senators revealed to Mason there was no support for doing anything, and he reported the resolution three days later with no recommendation, softening the blow to the president by saying the committee would have approved the provisional measures except for the fact that the present session was so near an end there was no time for "maturing them."[17]

This rebuff in the Senate meant that no money would be available to send the special commissioners to give weight to Soulé's efforts to obtain Cuba. Marcy announced the abandonment of the plan in a letter to Soulé on August 16, assuring him that it had not been intended to imply any lack of confidence in his work. Soulé had in fact resented the proposal. This inference had been drawn in Ma-

---

W. R. Manning, ed., *Diplomatic Correspondence of the United States, Inter-American Affairs, 1831–1860*, 11:802.

drid in press reports and he had written Marcy that it had made his position highly delicate and painful.

But in a second dispatch with the same date Marcy divulged a new plan of the president—a consultation of the ministers at London, Paris, and Madrid to discuss means of obtaining Cuba or "at least to clear away impediments to its successful consummation." Marcy was vague about what the three ministers could accomplish, though he seemed to think that Buchanan in London and Mason in Paris could remove the "impediments" of the opposition of both France and England to cession of Cuba to the United States. In any case, he wrote, it was desirable that the three ministers bring their "common wisdom and knowledge to bear simultaneously upon the negotiations at Madrid, London and Paris."[18]

Pierce's belief that somehow the three ministers in a meeting of minds could come up with a workable idea indicated that he was clutching at straws. Soulé's bluster over the *Black Warrior* affair had so irritated Spanish officials that even a man of his effrontery did not dare to bring up the matter of purchasing the island, and his efforts to put in a revolutionary government favorable to cession had failed when Espartero came to power. Clearly, achieving anything through Soulé was a lost hope. Nor could much reliance be placed on a revolt in Cuba. The president had effectually frustrated this by his efforts to prevent the Quitman filibuster expedition. The only project not tried was the one proposed by August Belmont in 1852 of bringing financial pressure to bear on Madrid through the holders of Spanish bonds. This indeed seemed to be the main impetus behind the decision for the extraordinary meeting of the ministers.

The idea may have had its inception in a letter of Buchanan to his friend and supporter for the presidential nomination in 1852, John Slidell. In the letter, dated May 23, Buchanan said he was "wholly ignorant" of what was being done to acquire Cuba. He then mentioned the plan which Belmont had proposed to him, saying that Belmont, appointed minister to the Netherlands, had sounded out influential persons and still believed it would work. Slidell had a personal interest in the scheme, because Belmont was married to a niece of his and he had been his nephew-in-law's political adviser, and replied on June 17 that he had urged Pierce to use the influence of Buchanan, Mason, and Belmont to settle the

Cuba question at Madrid. This would seem to be the first definite proposal of a conference of the European ministers. Buchanan followed up the idea in a letter to Marcy on July 11 directing his attention to the Belmont scheme he had urged on Pierce. "I shall by no means despair of success," he said, "should the plan . . . be steadily pursued in concert." Slidell was consulted by Pierce and his advisers on the Cuban problem and ten days before Marcy issued his instructions to the three European ministers informed Buchanan of the conference plan: "The idea now is to have you, Soulé & Mason to meet for the purpose of consultation. I have suggested that on account of the Rothschild influence at Madrid & Paris, it would be well that Belmont be brought either personally or by correspondence into your counsels."*

The lack of definite instructions in the diplomatic correspondence about what was expected of the three conferees was due to the fact that Marcy did not wish to set them forth in his notes to the ministers but left them to be given orally by the bearer of the dispatches—Daniel E. Sickles.[19] This decision, made by Pierce himself, contributed to making the meeting one of the most bizarre incidents in American diplomatic history.

In the selection of a secretary of the London legation, Pierce had suggested a young Ohioan, Don Piatt of Cincinnati, to Buchanan, who objected because he preferred Sickles, whose "manners, appearance, & intelligence are all that could be desired." The president concurred, as he had similarly been charmed by Sickles at a meeting in Washington.[20] Buchanan in his first months in London continued to express a liking for his chief aide, although later he was to say that he was a drag on the legation because his poor handwriting imposed the work of copying upon other members.

*This sequence of events is borne out in an explanation that Marcy gave to Peter D. Vroom, minister to Prussia, on Nov. 4: "Mr. Buchanan having suggested as I understand in a private letter to the president that it was probable that an influence might be brought to bear on Spain in regard to the sale of the Island of Cuba by the Spanish Creditors & bondholders in London & Paris the President was induced to believe that a conference of Mr. B. & Mr. Mason with Mr. Soulé might possibly result in some thing favorable to our negotiations with Spain. Mr. S. was therefore authorized to have a meeting with those two gentlemen at some convenient place to be designated by him. . . . " Quoted in Ivor D. Spencer, *The Victor and the Spoils*, p. 325.

Sickles himself disliked embassy routine and wrote a friend that he planned a trip to the United States—he was "tired of London and *of this mission*." He reached Washington on August 8 and called upon the president, smarting under his recent rebuff by Congress and studying his plan of a foreign minister's conference. The young and voluble visitor was like a fresh breeze in the summer heat of the capital. Pierce invited him to stay at the White House and heard from him the news of Europe and garrulously confided to him his plans for Cuba.

When the time came to send the instructions prepared by Marcy for the ministers' conference, Pierce selected Sickles to be his messenger, writing Buchanan on August 12: "Mr. Sickles' visit at this time is, on several grounds, very opportune, and if he has participated in the pleasure he has conferred, he will have no occasion to regret it. . . . Mr. Sickles will return with despatches for yourself, Mr. Mason, & Mr. Soulé, and he will have much to communicate verbally with regard to home and other affairs. . . ."[21]

Marcy, hesitating to commit the conference plans to paper, had been purposely indefinite in his instructions to the ministers. His discreetness was of no avail in the indiscreetness of the messenger. Flattered by the president's friendship as manifested in their convivial sessions at the White House, he conceived his role as being not just a messenger but the prime mover in affairs of vast importance. His visits to Buchanan in London, Mason in Paris, and Soulé in the Pyrenees, in which he interpreted after his own fashion the president's intentions, were so ostentatious that the European press was filled with speculation as to what he was about.

Neither Buchanan nor Mason could see any purpose in the grand conference of ministers. Buchanan wrote Pierce on September 1: "I can not for myself discover what benefit will result from a meeting between Mr. Soulé, Mr. Mason, and myself. I perceive that you expect from it 'useful information and suggestions,' but it is impossible for me to devise any other plan for the acquisition of Cuba in which I could be useful than what I have already fully presented to you. We are willing to purchase, and our object is to induce them to sell. One great means of accomplishing this object is to bring the creditors of Spain into our views by an appeal to their self-interest. The best agent for this purpose with whom I am acquainted would be Mr. Belmont. . . ." Mason conveyed his scruples in a letter to Buchanan, saying he was surprised at the plan and could "hardly see, in the results of his proceeding, any thing beneficial, either to the Country or to you or myself."

Buchanan had delayed in sending his protest to Pierce, apparently in some doubt as to its propriety; he added a strong postscript about two weeks later after hearing of Sickles' activities on the continent. He objected strongly to a meeting in Paris: "No more unsuitable place than Paris could be devised for such a meeting. The French espionage is perfect and all-pervading, and all its eyes would be upon us. Every object which you have in view can, in my opinion, be accomplished by correspondence." He also felt that the press reports of Sickles' activities had endangered the Belmont plan: "Capital and Capitalists . . . are proverbially timid, and nothing of this kind ought to be attempted until after the éclat by the public journals to Col. Sickles' journey to Paris and Madrid shall have passed away. Matters of this kind, in order to be successful in Europe, must be conducted with secrecy and caution."[22]

Before the end of the month the press of Europe was filled with speculation about what the United States was up to, for her foreign service officers seemed to be gathering by prearrangement in Paris. The chief of them was A. Dudley Mann, assistant secretary of state, known as a secret agent of Hungary during the revolt of 1849–50 against Austria and a notorious agitator for European republicanism. He had left August 6 for a short vacation in Europe and, though charged with no responsibilities by Marcy, had set about investigating conditions in Spain and had been under French surveillance when he had met with Soulé at Bayonne. John L. O'Sullivan, who could not resist the opportunity to involve himself in any intrigue concerned with the acquisition of Cuba, had arrived from Lisbon. August Belmont was there, summoned from The Hague by the officious Sickles. Also present although only incidentally were Lewis Cass, Jr., from Rome, who had gone to Paris on private business, and John M. Daniel, from Turin, who had gone there to escape the cholera in Italy. The press of Europe could be expected to wonder about what was in the air for, as the London *Globe* said, the "American diplomatic congress" was entirely without precedent.

Reluctant to attend the conference at all, Buchanan objected to suggestions by Soulé of proposed meetings at Spa, in Belgium, and at Basel, in Switzerland, Paris being out of the question because of the harassment by French spies. He preferred London, a large city where they would attract less attention than they would in a smaller place. Finally, the three ministers agreed on Ostend, in Belgium. Before leaving for the conference on October 7, Buchanan wrote a nephew prophetically that it would "probably make noise enough in the world."

By October 9 the ministers, traveling separately, reached Ostend to begin their discussions. As none of them kept notes of the meeting and they considered it undesirable to have a secretary present, their deliberations can only be surmised. After three days at Ostend they decided to transfer their conversations to Aix-la-Chapelle in Prussia, apparently because they may have thought they lacked the privacy they required, their arrival at Ostend having been made known throughout Europe by the newspapers. Soulé preceded Buchanan and Mason to the new meeting place, arriving on October 12, and immediately, so he later wrote Marcy, set down a draft for their joint statement. They resumed their talks on October 15 and on October 18 signed the document that has gone down in history as the Ostend Manifesto.[23]

The Aix-la-Chapelle report began innocuously enough with the proposal that the United States attempt to buy Cuba from Spain, certainly nothing earth-shaking because both Buchanan and Mason as members of Polk's cabinet had supported this move then and afterward and Soulé had been instructed by Marcy to make an offer. The authors stated that they could not anticipate a refusal by Spain except possibly "through the malign influence of foreign Powers who possess no right whatever to interfere in the matter." Their reasons for resuming an offer to buy, not given in detail, were the new government in Spain, the "wretched financial condition" of the country, the failure of Cuba to supply more than a million and a half dollars to the exchequer, and the threat of revolution on the island. To other nations, they held out the hope of profitable trade with Cuba if she became a possession of the United States. It was what the conferees proposed should Spain refuse to sell that made their report so infamous in American history, "The Manifesto of the Brigands," as Horace Greeley damned it in his influential *New York Tribune*.[24] Sanctimoniously saying that the United States had "never acquired a foot of territory except by fair purchase, or, as in the case of Texas, upon the free and voluntary application of the people of that independent State" and even territory obtained in the Mexican War had been paid for, they declared that the law of "self-preservation" would justify "wresting" Cuba from Spain if she refused to sell.

Almost four months were to pass before the world was to learn the results of the conferences at Ostend and Aix-la-Chapelle despite the public glare in which they had been conducted. American ministers reported that European officials had sought for hints of what was decided, Buchanan writing Marcy, for example, that Lord Clarendon in London had anxiously quizzed him on the subject.[25] Even the conspirators Daniel Sickles and John L. O'Sullivan had no inkling of what was decided. Newspaper correspondents in London and Paris, adept at ferreting out information, likewise could not obtain details and had to resort to speculation. It was not something the administration could emblazon to the world. Pierce's private secretary, Sidney Webster, wrote that "the whole document filled the president and all the members of his cabinet with amazement."[26] He might better have described it dismay.

One reason for this was not so much what the report itself said, though it seems bad enough, but in what Soulé said in his letter of transmittal to Marcy. Now was the time, Soulé said, to settle the question of Cuba; he hoped that it could be done peaceably. "But, if it were otherwise, if it is to bring upon us the calamity of war, let it be now," he declared, "while the great powers of this continent are engaged in that stupendous struggle [the Crimean War] which cannot but engage all their strength and tax all their energies, as long as it lasts, and may before it ends, convulse them all."[27] Another reason was that the report reached Washington when Congressional elections had revealed the country's repudiation of the Pierce administration. In the spring elections Democrats had lost in Connecticut, Rhode Island, Pennsylvania, Iowa, Maine, Ohio, and Indiana; this rout was completed in the fall elections when the anti-Nebraska men, Whigs, and Know-Nothings swept every Northern state but two, putting the Democrats in a minority in the House of Representatives.

To add to the discomfiture of Pierce and his advisers, the *New York Herald*, published by James Gordon Bennett, inimical to the administration because its editor, it has been related, had been denied the ambassadorship to France, was sniping at the president in editorials and printing reports that came so close to the truth about the decisions at Ostend that the president feared they were based on leaks, as indeed they may have been. On October 16 the paper had predicted that the Ostend conferees would declare to Spain: "What we must have is security for the future. This is to be found only in our possession of the island of Cuba. We tender to you twice the amount of its actual value. If you do not accept our proposal, we must take the island." The accuracy of this prediction was due to the fact that George N. Sanders, a friend of Soulé, was the *Herald's* London correspondent. Now the paper was reprinting this speculation and twitting the president for keeping the report a secret.

After nine days of discussions, Marcy drafted a letter to Soulé, copies of which were also prepared for Buchanan and Mason, designed to save the administration from embarrassment and to put a rein on Soulé's activities. As to renewing the offer to purchase Cuba, Soulé was to pursue the effort only if he found persons high in the government willing to listen and inclined to favor the proposal. As this was highly unlikely, Soulé was told in effect to drop this approach.* Marcy felt that the still unsettled *Black Warrior* claims provided a stronger basis for achieving a partial settlement of difficulties with Spain than the cession of Cuba and instructed Soulé to resume negotiations on this matter. His instructions here contained an implied rebuke of Soulé's previous high-handed demands: the president did not insist that the punishment of the offending Cuban officials required their removal and he wanted "all controversial points adjusted by negotiations and not coercion."[28]

This letter was a weasel-worded communication, studiedly evasive and vague, but it was not lost on Soulé. He replied in a curt letter on December 17 that the new instructions left him "no

*Horace Greeley's *Tribune* summarized Marcy's dispatch sarcastically: "Mr. Soulé, I have very little confidence in your discretion or wisdom, and I do beg of you to mind what you are about and not make a fool of yourself. Spain does not want to sell Cuba, as she has shown in a thousand ways, and don't you be running amuck in proposing to buy it." *New York Tribune*, Mar. 8, 1855.

alternative but that of continuing to linger here in languid impotence, or of surrendering a trust which, with the difficulties thrown in the way of its execution, I would strive in vain to discharge either to the satisfaction of the Government or to my own credit." He thereupon announced his resignation with the hope of being relieved from duty by the end of January.[29]

Before returning to Madrid from Ostend and Aix-la-Chapelle, Soulé had become involved in another embroglio that caused tongues to wag in the embassies of Europe and provided the press with new sensations. Instead of going directly to Madrid, which he had left almost two months before, he went to London to visit George N. Sanders, who had made his home the headquarters for the exiled revolutionists of Europe. Earlier in the year, on February 21, while still the American consul, Sanders had entertained some of them at a brilliant affair. Among those present were the Hungarian Louis Kossuth, the Italians Giuseppe Garibaldi and Giuseppe Mazzini, the Russian Alexander Herzen, the German Arnold Ruge, and the Frenchman Alexandre-August Ledru-Rollin. After the Senate turned down Sanders' appointment, he had remained in London engaging in plots to start revolutions in Europe, promising the republican exiles financial aid from the United States, and using diplomatic dispatch bags of the American legation to scatter his incendiary letters abroad. On October 4 he had issued a message to the French people urging them to revolt and advising the assassination of Louis Napoleon.

While a guest of Sanders, Soulé was feted by the exiles, including the French *proscrit* Ledru-Rollin. Departing after his long absence from Spain, Soulé was escorted to Dover by a bon voyage party of revolutionists headed by Ledru-Rollin. When Soulé reached Calais on October 24, he was informed that he would not be permitted to enter France. He protested strenuously to no avail and took the next boat back to Dover. During the following two weeks, while Soulé enjoyed the unexpected reunion with the exiles, his debarment from France was the occasion for a diplomatic flurry involving not only France and the United States but England as well. It was largely because of the insistence of the British foreign minister, Lord Clarendon, that France was led to withdraw the ban: with Sevastopol under siege in the Crimea, now was no time for the French to become embroiled in a dispute with the

United States. National honor was satisfied when it was agreed that Soulé could pass through France on his way to his post in Madrid but not stop along the way. He entered Calais on November 8 and reached Madrid on November 29.[30]

When Marcy's dispatch of November 13 reached Soulé, he sank into an apathy from which during his remaining time in Spain he was never able to rouse himself. A man of action, imperious and impetuous, he was not one capable of the quiet approach to diplomacy that was needed in Spain. He was a witness to the utter failure of his mission when, on December 18, the day after he had announced his resignation to Marcy, he sat in the diplomatic gallery of the Cortés and heard a pronouncement on the sale of Cuba as definite as that of 1848 when a predecessor was told that Spain, rather than see Cuba transferred to any other power, would prefer seeing the island sink into the ocean. Now Soulé, the center of attention, heard another minister of foreign affairs, Claudio Antón de Luzuriaga, declare that "to part with Cuba would be to part with the national honor." Soulé wrote Marcy that the statement was received with "frantic applause." "Thus was disposed of in a single session of that grave body, the Cortés," he wrote, "what of hope the United States might still retain of bringing their difficulties with this country to a peaceable & friendly adjustment through the cession to them of that Island."[31]

1. President James K. Polk, who wanted to buy Cuba from Spain, opposed the efforts of Cuban revolutionists and U.S. filibusters to send military expeditions to the island.

2. President Franklin Pierce entered office with ambitions of obtaining Cuba and huge areas of northern Mexico but found them impeded by the forays of filibusters.

3. Narciso López, exiled from Cuba after attempting a revolutionary coup, won a wide following in the United States in his efforts to win the island by filibuster expeditions.

4. *President James Buchanan suffered serious embarrassment in his isthmian and Mexican policies because of the actions of filibusters.*

5. *The shipping magnate George Law bought outmoded U.S. army muskets to sell to revolutionary armies in Europe in 1848. When he could not sell them there, he supplied them to filibuster expeditions to Cuba and Nicaragua.*

6. *Roberdeau Wheat, a New Orleans soldier-of-fortune, took part in the Narciso López expeditions to Cuba, fought in the army of a revolutionary general in Mexico, and joined William Walker's band in Nicaragua.*

7. *John L. O'Sullivan, a scholar and magazine editor, was one of the chief supporters of Narciso López in organizing his expeditions to Cuba.*

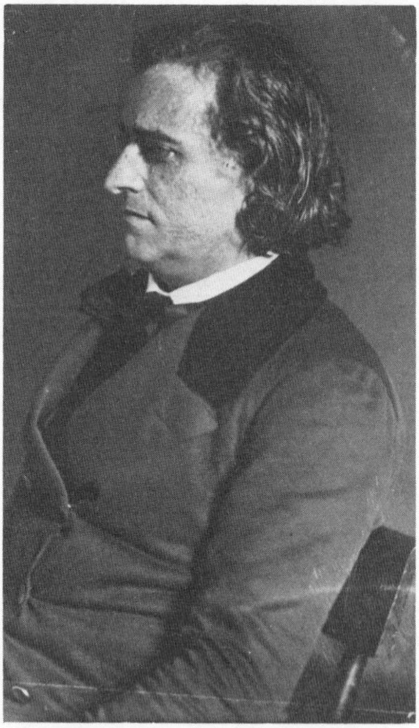

8. *Pierre Soulé, an expatriate from France who became a political leader in Louisiana, supported the filibuster expeditions to Cuba and was appointed minister to Spain by President Pierce to wheedle that country into selling the island.*

9. *The first attempted landing here by* Narciso López *in his expedition of 1851 at Bahía Honda on the coast of Cuba was prevented by shots fired by a garrison of Spanish soldiers.*

10. *The grounding in 1851 of* Narciso López*'s ship, the* Pampero, *a half-mile from shore, delayed the landing of his troops at this small bay a few miles from* Morrillo.

11. *The village of Las Pozas, where Narciso López in 1851 established a camp after landing in Cuba and where his troops successfully defended themselves from an attack by Spanish soldiers.*

12. General John A. Quitman, a hero of the Mexican War, struggled unsuccessfully for several years to mount an expedition to Cuba.

13. Count Gaston Raousset-Boulbon, failing to find a fortune in the California goldfilds, led expeditions of his French compatriots into Mexico.

14. Guaymas, a coastal town on the Gulf of California, was the departure point for expeditions from San Francisco lured to the Mexican state of Sonora by tales of gold to be found in abundance.

PART TWO

El Dorado in Mexico

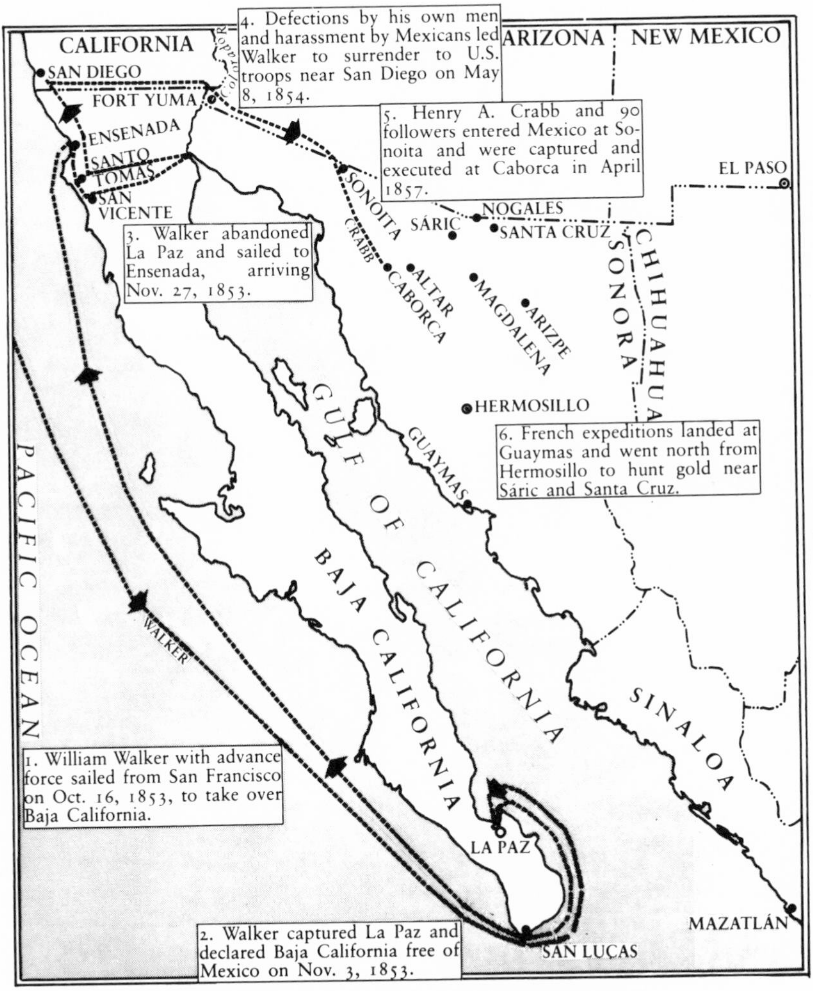
CALIFORNIA
SAN DIEGO
FORT YUMA
ENSENADA
SANTO TOMAS
SAN VICENTE
ARIZONA
NEW MEXICO
EL PASO
SONOITA
CRABB
NOGALES
SÁRIC
SANTA CRUZ
ALTAR
CABORCA
MAGDALENA
ARIZPE
SONORA
CHIHUAHUA
HERMOSILLO
GUAYMAS
GULF OF CALIFORNIA
BAJA CALIFORNIA
PACIFIC OCEAN
WALKER
SINALOA
LA PAZ
SAN LUCAS
MAZATLÁN
1. William Walker with advance force sailed from San Francisco on Oct. 16, 1853, to take over Baja California.
2. Walker captured La Paz and declared Baja California free of Mexico on Nov. 3, 1853.
3. Walker abandoned La Paz and sailed to Ensenada, arriving Nov. 27, 1853.
4. Defections by his own men and harassment by Mexicans led Walker to surrender to U.S. troops near San Diego on May 8, 1854.
5. Henry A. Crabb and 90 followers entered Mexico at Sonoita and were captured and executed at Caborca in April 1857.
6. French expeditions landed at Guaymas and went north from Hermosillo to hunt gold near Sáric and Santa Cruz.

The filibusters in Baja California and Sonora

CHAPTER SEVEN

Expeditions to Mexico

James K. Polk, cold and methodical in character, was seldom eloquent in utterance, and his statement in his last message to Congress of the chief accomplishment of his administration—almost doubling the area of the country mainly at the cost to Mexico of one-half of hers—was not a rousing one. "The acquisition of California and New Mexico, the settlement of the Oregon boundary, and the annexation of Texas, extending to the Rio Grande," he remarked colorlessly though not without a hint of boastfulness, "are results which, combined, are of greater consequence and will add more to the strength and wealth of the nation than any which have preceded them since the adoption of the Constitution." Many—the exponents of Manifest Destiny—wanted more, but Polk was satisfied with what he had gained. The problem now, he said, was to establish regularly organized governments in the new territories.

But there were large numbers of people not interested in settling down to the peaceful development of these regions. Lawless adventurers in Texas and disappointed gold-seekers in California during the next few years made repeated incursions into northern Mexico to implement Manifest Destiny by taking over more territory to bring into the Union. The southern part of Mexico, where the Isthmus of Tehuantepec offered a desirable transit route between the Atlantic and Pacific, also attracted the land-grabbers. During the decade after the signing of the Treaty of Guadalupe Hidalgo successive Mexican governments, all of them tottering affairs because the country was torn apart by repeated revolutions, feared that engulfment of the country by the predator to the north would continue. Mexico had never been able to maintain strong governments in her remote and immense territories of Alta California, New Mexico, and Texas, and after the war she did not do much better in the states immediately south of the Rio Grande. There, rebel leaders repeatedly arose to take control and declare themselves independent assisted by U.S. adventurers hoping to bring the regions into the Union. One of the most persistent, a scourge from 1851 to 1853, was José María Jesús Carvajal, who operated out of Brownsville, Texas.

Carvajal was born about 1810 in San Antonio and became a protégé of the Texas colonizer Stephen F. Austin, who aided him in 1823 to go to the United States to be trained as a surveyor. On Carvajal's return to Texas he worked as a surveyor and in 1835 was elected deputy from San Antonio to the legislature of Coahuila and Texas. Later that year he was ordered arrested for attempting to stir up a revolution to accomplish the sale of a large tract of land decreed by the legislature but opposed by the commandant. He fled to New Orleans, where with other revolutionists he chartered a vessel to carry supplies to Texas forces. The vessel was captured and Carvajal was imprisoned but succeeded in escaping and returning to Texas. In December at Goliad he was one of the signers of a declaration of independence issued by the troops and citizens of the town, and he was elected a delegate to but did not attend the convention at Washington-on-the-Brazos where on March 2, 1836, the Republic of Texas was declared.[1]

Carvajal was next heard of in 1839 as a member of the forces of General Antonio Canales, who for years had engaged in conspiracies to organize the northern Mexican states of Coahuila, Tamaulipas, and Nuevo León as an independent republic. Canales sought a coalition with Texas, and Carvajal was one of several hundred Texans who fought with the rebels against the central government. In one battle Carvajal, leading a company of Texas volunteers, was wounded and permanently lost the use of his left arm. Though nowhere victorious and compelled to retreat across the Rio Grande, Canales proclaimed the establishment of the Republic of the Rio Grande, in which Carvajal served as secretary of the governing council. This was a bit of bravura. Before long Canales's army became hardly more than a band of robbers and marauders, and he capitulated to federal troops the next year, dismissing his Texas auxiliaries and merging his Mexican soldiers with those of the government commander General Mariano Arista.[2]

Canales saw an opportunity to revive his plan for establishing a Republic of the Rio Grande in June 1845 when General Zachary Taylor was ordered to set up a base on the south bank of the Nueces River to protect Texas in case of an invasion from Mexico after the annexation of the republic by the United States. Though still a member of the Mexican military service, he sent an agent—Carvajal—to invite American help in a plot to destroy the army, "long the scourge of the nation," and to form a separate republic with "a constitution based upon the rights of man." Carvajal was authorized to seek arms for 3,000 men until the forces of Mariano Paredes y Arrillaga, who had assumed the presidency after overthrowing the government of José J. de Herrera, could be put down. In return, Canales would do all in his power to support American claims to Texas and would repay loans by customs arrangements or by adjustment of the boundary.[3] It was an offer that had attractions for the United States, for one of the plans of President Polk to prevent war with Mexico was by supporting secession of her northern states. Taylor submitted Carvajal's plan to Secretary of War Marcy, who replied on March 2, 1846, that in case of war "we should be ready to avail ourselves of all the advantages which could be fairly derived from Mexicans disaffected to their rulers." The United States, however, would not provide arms or money, Marcy said, for Mexicans wishing to resist Paredes.[4]

When war with the United States began, Canales was in command of 425 horse troops of the Mexican army but was so reluctant to take effective action against the enemy that General Francisco Mejía suspected him of being a traitor and only grudgingly supplied him with arms, horses, and men. A bandit at heart, Canales was gratified when Mejía after a series of defeats resorted to guerrilla warfare and he was given leave to harry the Americans in any way possible. He launched a campaign of brigandage under the color of the Mexican flag that won him the name of the Chaparral Fox. Canales continued to seek the support of the United States for his plot to detach the northern states from Mexico, but the administration in Washington was averse to guaranteeing them their independence after the war and moreover it had no confidence in the will of the Mexicans to strike for freedom and form a stable government and it distrusted the leaders, who were little better than bandits marked by unusual energy and cunning. Thus the Republic of the Rio Grande never came nearer to actuality than a scheme set down on paper in pronunciamentos of the ruffianly leader calling on the people to arise.[5]

After the war disorderly conditions prevailed along the border that contributed greatly to the creation of the filibuster spirit. Frontier regions are inclined to attract adventurous if not lawless types, and this was true of the regions north and south of the Rio Grande. The depredations of bandits and the popularity of smuggling operations as a convenient way of making money and Indian raids against settlers of both sides of the river made disorder the normal thing rather than the exceptional. Asked by the U.S. district attorney in Texas to investigate smuggling, Ovid F. Johnson, a Brownsville newspaper editor, reported that the end of the war had turned loose "a refuse population" that, stationing themselves on both sides of the border, were "ready for any enterprise, lawful or unlawful, that presents itself."[6] As for the Indian raids, the Treaty of Guadalupe Hidalgo required the United States to prevent incursions across the border from the territories obtained from Mexico, but it soon became clear that this was impossible. There were more than 160,000 Indians in these regions, and they were not peace-loving tribes. They made repeated raids into Mexico, which the United States with garrison troops held down to a string of forts along a 2,000-mile border, could not prevent. The countryside, Secretary of War Charles M. Conrad said, offered "wonderful facilities to escape and insurmountable barriers to pursuit."[7]

A leader soon emerged to gather around him the adventuresome and lawless spirits on the border by offering them, as did Narciso López in forming his filibuster expeditions to Cuba, the promise of land and loot. He won the support of traders by promising to reduce the tariff duties and the heavy fines for contraband. He was Carvajal, who with other former followers of Canales as early as 1848 had hatched a plan for a revolution in Tamaulipas and Nuevo León to set up a state to be called the Republic of the Sierra Madre.

As had the Cuba filibusters, these conspirators hoped to obtain recruits from ex-officers and ex-soldiers of the American army. One officer approached who expressed an interest in the scheme was General James Shields of the Illinois volunteers. Earlier, when Carvajal presented to General Taylor the Canales plan, he had also approached Shields. Shields had taken it up with zeal and had written letters to President Polk and members of his cabinet about it, although these seem not to have been dispatched.[8] The scheme never got very far along. Secretary of State James Buchanan wrote the American minister to Mexico on October 10, 1848, saying that circulars had been addressed to district attorneys at St. Louis, Little Rock, Natchez, Galveston, and Mobile instructing them to guard against a rumored attempt to mount an expedition to northern Mexico.[9]

Carvajal resumed his effort to capitalize on the unsettled border conditions to separate Tamaulipas from Mexico and set up the Republic of the Sierra Madre when, in September 1851, he assembled a number of insurgents at La Loba and promulgated what became known as El Plan de la Loba. His proclamation called for withdrawal of the centralist army from the northern frontier and promised a reduction in tariff duties and fines for contraband and the adoption of a rule to admit certain articles free of duty for a period of five years.[10] General Francisco Ávalos, commander of the Mexican frontier forces, sent troops to the border to arrest Carvajal, but he fled to Texas and began negotiations with merchants at Brownsville, the gateway town to Mexico, to support a revolution that he would lead. His proposals coincided with the disbandment of the Texas Rangers, many of them, Brevet Major General Persifer F. Smith, commander of the Eighth Military Department, reported to the adjutant general, "men of unsettled habits" who "were left without occupation or means of subsistence" and who "were ready for anything that offered to supply their necessities."[11]

One of these Texas Rangers "ready for anything" was Captain John Salmon Ford, who, serving in the Mexican War under Colonel John C. Hayes, was chiefly responsible for making the Colt revolver popular on the frontier. As adjutant of the regiment, he received the nickname "Rip" Ford, by which he was known later along the frontier, from his practice in issuing casualty lists of ending each with the words "Rest in peace," which, to save time, he reduced to "R.I.P." Ruthless, tough, profane, and unwilling to settle down to peaceful pursuits, he joined the Texas Rangers as a captain.[12] When his company of Rangers was disbanded, he and his men kept their arms and most of them enlisted in Carvajal's army, lured by promises of high pay and the prospects of plunder.

Reports of the Carvajal expedition were carried in newspapers of the United States, and in New Orleans adventurers attracted by the last López expedition and left purposeless and without prospects by its failure were excited by the promise of action across the Rio Grande. One of them, Chatham Roberdeau Wheat, was looking for a revolutionary hero to replace the lamented López, and, convinced that Carvajal was a patriot of like nobility, he in the spirit of a knight-errant hastened to Brownsville to offer his sword in defense of Mexican liberty.[13]

Carvajal started his revolution on September 19 when with a band of a hundred Mexicans and seventy Americans he assaulted and captured Camargo, a few miles south of the Rio Grande. This enterprise, though successful, was ill-timed, for Carvajal had not yet been joined by Ford's company of Rangers, who were not mustered out of service until September 23, and he was forced to remain in this unimportant village until October 9. In the meantime, the administration in Washington had learned of the invasion plans but not soon enough to take effective action. President Fillmore on September 24 dispatched orders to General D. E. Twiggs, commander of the western division of the U.S. army at New Orleans, and General Smith to stop the expedition. He did not issue a proclamation warning citizens against taking part in it, however, until October 22.

Carvajal marched his little army of about 400 men out of Camargo on October 9 and reached Matamoros on October 18. On this date from his headquarters of "Liberating Army of the Northern States," he notified foreign consuls in the town of his intention to attack and requested them to "take the necessary steps to place the persons and property of your countrymen in safety." General Ávalos, with a strong force, had prepared for the attack by evacuating women and children and erecting barricades. The attack began on October 30, and the insurgents won an initial victory by capturing an earthwork on the outskirts of the town.

Carvajal was so jubilant that he ordered the band to strike up some music in celebration, but afterward there were few occasions for victory airs. Carvajal, having only one piece of artillery, a six-pounder in the charge of Roberdeau Wheat, was not equipped to batter his way into town. This gun became almost useless when the ammunition ran out and Wheat was compelled to substitute bars of iron cut into short lengths for grape and canister. The only way the town could be taken, therefore, was by hand-to-hand fighting from building to building.

Four days after the siege began, Carvajal received word that a U.S. vessel was en route from the mouth of the Rio Grande with supplies for General Ávalos. He protested to J. S. Phelps, commander at Fort Brown, in a letter rhetorically defending his leadership of the revolution, possibly written by Wheat because it has all the bombast of his usual style. "When the people assembled to consider in what manner their rights and liberties could best be preserved, by common consent, without any agency of my own, I was chosen," Carvajal declared, "to lead this patriotic enterprise. . . . I have raised the standard of liberation, and hundreds of my aggrieved country men have rushed to its support. . . . The Americans who are acting with me will not shame either their country or their name—they are fighting in a cause as just and righteous as that which has inscribed on the same roll with Washington, those other names, noble as his allies, Lafayette, Kosciusko, and Pulaski. . . . " The *Texas State Gazette*, which published the effusion on November 5, said that it would "awaken an enthusiastic response in every American bosom not dead to every impulse of patriotism."

Carvajal sought on the same day to win the people of Matamoros to his support by an appeal to them to renounce the tyranny of Mexico and to fight under his banner. As his manifestoes demonstrated, Carvajal was thoroughly in command of the filibuster slogans of the time, but he could not turn them to account in winning battles. After ten days of fighting during which he had been unable to oust the defenders from the plaza, he suddenly, on October 30, ordered his men to withdraw. Harried by government troops, he retreated to Camargo, which he reached on November 16. Wheat reported on the situation in a letter to his mother: "The general is for the time being recruiting his forces. We may remain here two weeks; but shall then move towards the enemy who are very much afraid of us. . . . I am anxiously awaiting the arrival of some heavy pieces from the United States. . . ." Colonel Ford was sent on a recruiting expedition into Texas, but, without waiting for reinforcements, Carvajal led his men in an attack on Cerralvo, defended by 200 troops, about the same number remaining in the insurgent army. His hope was to capture the artillery pieces in the town. The defenders with their cannons advantageously placed held their attackers off for two days. Word reaching Carvajal that federal troops were approaching, he again retreated, his diminished forces scurrying to safety across the Rio Grande to Texas.[14]

Luis de la Rosa, Mexican minister to the United States, in a letter to Secretary of State Daniel Webster on November 13, sought to disabuse him of any idea that Carvajal was leader of a revolution of the Mexican people. His raid, Rosa said, was merely a scheme of smugglers. But, with the history of Texas in mind, he feared this trade might soon be given a political aspect. "Then," he continued, "the emigration of adventurers, from the United States, will become so numerous that the government of this republic will find it difficult to check it. . . ."[15] Even elements of the expansionist press in the United States did not regard Carvajal as a revolutionary patriot. The *New Orleans Picayune*, for example, reminded potential filibusters that this "guardian of the liberties of Northern Mexico" had emerged from the Mexican War with a reputation as the "most miserable freebooter and rapacious robber" in the Rio Grande Valley. Of the Americans who joined Carvajal—it perhaps had Wheat in mind—the paper said: "A love of adventure and a poetic temperament have disguised the real character of the expedition in which Carvajal has engaged their services. If the country was ripe for revolution, they would not have to explain the miscarriage of the late siege. The people would have risen en masse to welcome them as deliverers."[16]

While "Rip" Ford sought recruits for Carvajal, the general maintained headquarters at the small town of Rio Grande in Texas, where, according to General Persifer Smith's report, his men "resorted to plunder for subsistence" to "the great terror of our own people and of travellers." In January 1852 Ford in a special election won a seat in the Texas legislature, but even in this position he had little success in recruitment. Reporting to Carvajal, he said that "the class of men likely to engage in such service are seldom blessed with a superfluity of the good things of this world" and there were few who could arm themselves and obtain mounts.

Rumors were rife that a new expedition was being planned, the Mexican minister of foreign affairs, José F. Ramírez, informing the American minister Robert P. Letcher on January 22 that "articles of clothing, and other useful commodities are being prepared, at Brownsville, with the greatest speed." Almost a month later, on February 20, Carvajal assembled a small force, equipped with one piece of artillery under the command of Wheat, and began a march on Camargo. Attacked by Government troops under Canales, the filibusters were quickly routed and escaped again to Texas. On their way to Brownsville, however, a U.S. army squadron arrested Carvajal and eleven of his followers on March 8, 1852. Carvajal was released in bail of $5,000 and his men in bail of $3,000 for their appearance in the U.S. District Court in June. The case was postponed because of the absence of the judge and had not come to trial more than a year later when Manuel Larrainzar, minister to the United States, in a long bill of complaints to Secretary of State Marcy, said that Carvajal continued "to laugh at justice" and to treat with contempt the neutrality laws and the proclamation of President Fillmore.[17]

In May Carvajal was one of the main attractions at a fair at Corpus Christi promoted by the large-scale trader and rancher Henry L. Kinney, later to organize a filibuster expedition to establish a colony on the Mosquito Coast of Nicaragua. Kinney, born on June 3, 1814, in the Wyoming Valley of Pennsylvania, had gone to Brownsville in 1838 after a career as a farmer, merchant, and politician in Illinois and as a soldier in the wars against Black Hawk in Illinois and the Seminoles in Florida. Later he had moved north to Corpus Christi and begun buying up land from small ranchers, building a fort garrisoned by up to a hundred men at times to protect his property against Indian and Mexican marauders. He had served in the congress of the Texas Republic and in the Mexican War was a major in the quartermaster division of Texas volunteers. After the war, he amassed a huge property, said to total 500,000 acres, owned several ships that plied the Gulf of

Mexico ports, and operated a fleet of prairie schooners carrying freight from Corpus Christi to the interior of the state. His fair of 1852, on which he spent $40,000, was held to attact emigrants to Texas.[18]

Carvajal, introduced to a large crowd in the fair pavilion by Ashbel Smith, secretary of state for the Republic of Texas, orated at length on the "tyranny and oppression" of the Mexican government and appealed for funds and men to support his army of liberation. He was followed by General Hugh McLeod, leader of the Santa Fe Expedition of 1841, who castigated the administration in Washington for ordering Carvajal's arrest while at the same time it had taken into its arms and banqueted the European revolutionist Louis Kossuth.

Despite the rumors that Carvajal was planning another invasion, reported by Larrainzar to the American Department of State, the fact was that he was having little success in raising money and men. Roberdeau Wheat, disappointed in the prospects for action, prepared to return to New Orleans. He wrote his mother from Corpus Christi on May 25: "I saw Gen. Carvajal yesterday, he is downhearted. I shall not move again in the matter unless I am certain of success."

Not until March 26, 1853, was Carvajal able to send another force across the border. This, however, was not a full-scale invasion but a small raid of about eighty men who under the command of A. H. Norton, arrested with Carvajal in March of the previous year, sacked Reynosa. The raiders seized the alcalde and demanded a ransom of $30,000. The citizens, however, were able to raise only $2,000, which Norton accepted and then quickly retreated to the town of Rio Grande on the Texas side of the border. This last act of brigandage prompted Major Gabriel R. Paul, commander of an infantry company at nearby Ringgold Barracks, to arrest Carvajal in a surprise raid on his headquarters the night of March 31. Breaking down the door of Carvajal's house with axes, they seized him before he could dress, but Norton, perpetrator of the outrage at Reynosa, managed to escape. Three days later Carvajal and several of his followers who had also been arrested were arraigned before the U.S. commissioner at Brownsville, who set them free because no affidavits had been filed against them. The filibusters were elated, and "Norton now made his appearance," a newspaper reported, "and walked the streets with the air of one whose gallant conduct was the theme of universal approbation." Their jubilation was short-lived, however, for upon a complaint lodged by the Mexican consul they were rearrested and confined to jail until the latter part of May when they were able to furnish bail.[19]

Brought to trial the next year, Carvajal was acquitted. For the next two years, rumors that he was planning expeditions across the border continued to excite apprehension among Mexican officials, but though he made several attempts he never succeeded. He ceased to become a disturbing factor in the relations of the United States with Mexico when he changed his field of activity to join various rebel forces in the struggles for power in that country.

The filibuster spirit seemed to be as combustible as gunpowder in many parts of the United States—recruits came from the North, East, South, and West to join Narciso López and they were easily found for Mexican forays—but nowhere did it become so easily ignited as in California. There, no matter how dubious the auspices or how dangerous the project, adventurers enthusiastically joined invasion parties to the Mexican states of Sonora and Baja California, to the Sandwich Islands, to Ecuador, and finally, in one sailing after another, to Nicaragua.

In the first year after the discovery of gold more than 100,000 people poured into the territory by overcrowded ships from the United States, South America, the Pacific islands, and Australia and by wagon train across 2,000 miles of prairie, desert, and mountains from the settled regions of the nation. This influx was aptly described "the gold rush." The people had come, by the quickest means available, to obtain the precious metal whose discovery had excited the world and not to farm, engage in trade, or practice a profession. "Ho, for the diggings!" was one of the banners carried on covered wagons setting off from Missouri, and on reaching San Francisco the fortune hunters headed at once for the latest gold strike. Earlier westward migrations had been family affairs, for wives and children were needed to build homes in the wilderness; this one was chiefly of males—less than 8 percent of the California population in 1850 were women and in the mining regions less than 2 percent. Mostly young and unfettered, the arrivals were ready for anything that came along. "California or bust!" was another banner carried by caravans going west. It reflected the devil-take-the-hindmost attitude of the gold seekers. "Thrown upon his own resources midst strange surroundings, with quickened observation and thought, the enterprising newcomer cast aside traditional caution, and launched into the current speculation," the historian Hubert Howe Bancroft wrote; "for everything seemed to promise success whatever course might be pursued, so abnormal were the times and place. . . ." Bancroft compared gold-seeking to a lottery "wherein a vast number of blanks were overshadowed by the glitter of the few prizes."[20] Hence many who had spent all their money just to get to California soon became objects of charity. The *Alta California*, San Francisco's leading newspaper, in 1850 published stories of efforts to provide help for immigrants and in August reported that at the request of Mayor John W. Geary the San Francisco Immigrant Relief Committee had been set up to solicit aid for them.

It was from among this population, men for whom the wheel of fortune had not turned up a winning number, that the leaders of filibuster expeditions drew most of their recruits with the promise of wealth to be found in Mexico, Ecuador, or Nicaragua. Such a one was David Deaderick, who joined a Nicaragua expedition and told his story in a series of articles in *The Atlantic Monthly*, "The Experience of Samuel Absalom, Filibuster." One morning, after sleeping in the street at Oroville, he read in the local newspaper: "The heavy frost which fell last night brings with it at least one source of congratulation for our citizens. Soon the crowd of vagrant street-sleepers . . . will be forced to go forth and look for warmer quarters." Deaderick told himself: "I will shake California dust from my feet, and be gone!" The means to do so were found in San Francisco, where a filibuster expedition was forming, recruits being offered free passage to Nicaragua, $25 a month for service in the liberation army, and 250 acres of land when discharged.[21]

The first comers obtained the best mining claims and many later arrivals, without resources and reduced to working for others, were easily tempted by the stories of wealth in Mexico. Nuggets were scattered so profusely south of the Gila, according to the current mythology, that the Apaches molded them into bullets. Beginning with 1851, the northern state of Sonora became a promised land to those disillusioned by California. The central government of Mexico, with problems closer at home, was unable to send troops to protect the people from the Apaches, who raided settlements without hindrance, and the province was in a constant state of civil war between generals contending for power. Defenseless, sparsely populated and yet, according to legend, rich in minerals, Sonora was the object of a half-dozen gold-seeking and colonizing expeditions from California.[22]

The earliest, that of 1851, was mounted by the quartermaster general of California, Joseph C. Moorehead. He had been named to the post in December of 1849, when the first legislature established a state militia. In 1850 Moorehead, at the direction of the governor, headed an expedition to put down a threatened uprising of Yuma Indians in Colorado. The danger of a revolt disappeared before he reached the scene. "Still thirsting for blood and glory," the historian Bancroft wrote, "he received one of those invitations which rebel leaders in Mexico were not backward in extending, though slow to fulfill. The military promenade to Colorado, having served to point out to his followers an easier and more alluring method of earning money than by hard digging, an organization was quickly effected."

Only a few accounts of Moorehead's activities are to be found in government records and contemporary newspapers. The *Alta California* reported that in March a party of men armed with rifles and six-shooters had passed through Los Angeles. The newspaper said that they were a part of a band of 300 who were ostensibly on a prospecting tour to the Gila. The *Los Angeles Star* carried an article saying that during March and April several parties numbering from 25 to 100 had left the town with the avowed purpose of taking part in a revolution in Sonora.

Moorehead seems to have planned a two-pronged invasion, one by land via Los Angeles and one by sea from the bark *Josephine*, which he purchased from the proceeds of the illegal sale of militia arms and supplies. The *Alta California* related that the *Josephine* landed toward the end of April at San Diego, where most of the adventurers abandoned the expedition with the intention of returning to San Francisco because of rumors that Moorehead was to be arrested. The embarrassed governor on April 25 had indeed asked the legislature to make an appropriation for a reward for the capture of Moorehead or to dispatch agents to arrest him, but the request was denied. Moorehead, fearful of arrest at San Diego, seems to have sailed with a few followers to La Paz in Baja California, where it was reported that American adventurers supposed to be filibusters had landed in June with the intention of going from there to Sonora. The expedition, poorly planned from the start, ended like most filibuster forays. Bancroft related that "on reaching Mexico the broken bands found the aspect so changed or unpromising that they were glad to slink away under the guise of disappointed miners."[23]

While Moorehead was engaged in his fumbling expedition to Sonora, other pursuers of the will-o-the-wisp of fortune were turning their attention to the Sandwich Islands with the idea of bringing them into the American Union. Manifest Destiny, it seemed, was a doctrine capable of being stretched to take in any area the American eye might see and covet. "The inevitable destiny of the islands is to pass into the possession of another power," the *Alta California* declared. "That power is just as inevitably our own. . . . The pear is nearly ripe; we have scarcely to shake the tree in order to bring the luscious fruit readily into our lap." To the north, the *Oregon Statesman*, commenting on the growing trade with Hawaii and the number of Americans already settled there, predicted the quick absorption of the islands into the United States: "The fact is, where our countrymen migrate they sow seeds of self-government, which naturally find roots in the hearts of men and cause a longing for the free institutions of America; nor will they rest satisfied until they become incorporated into the glorious union. . . . It is the inevitable destiny of the Sandwich Islands."[24]

American influence in the islands had been felt since 1820, when the first missionaries from New England went there to convert the Polynesian population to Christianity. Although both Britain and France had on occasion attempted to claim the islands, diplomatic missions in 1842 and 1843 secured recognition of independence from these two nations as well as the United States. Then, in 1848, the arrival of a new French consul, Guillaume Patrice Dillon, created a threat to Hawaiian independence.

A native of Ireland, Dillon had been educated in Paris and afterward held several government posts. He was sent to Hawaii with instructions to obtain ratification of a new treaty. Going beyond his instructions, he made impossible demands on the government and, when these were refused, in collaboration with the rear admiral commanding two French warships in the harbor, occupied the fort and two public buildings at Honolulu. This show of force brought the king, Kamehameha III, to terms. Dillon's high-handed actions were disavowed by the French foreign office and he was recalled, sailing in September 1849 on one of the warships for San Francisco en route to France. Dillon, however, was irrepressible. Observing the large number of French immigrants in California, unrepresented by a consul, he proposed the establishment of a consulate there. He himself received the appointment as consul, one that he was to fill for several years displaying his innate ability to cause trouble by his overenthusiasm for the interests of his adopted country.

Dillon's successor at Honolulu, Louis Émile Perrin, also carrying on diplomacy under the guns of a warship in the harbor, renewed French demands in 1851. Fearful of a repetition of the 1849 attack, Kamehameha offered sovereignty of the islands to the United States in a document signed in March and given to the U.S. commissioner to the islands, Luther Severance. Severance, in his correspondence with Secretary of State Webster, favored annexing Hawaii. "We must not take the islands in virtue of the 'manifest destiny' principle," he wrote, "but can we not accept their voluntary offer?" Opposed to territorial extensions, Fillmore and Webster adopted a policy similar to that maintained in regard to Cuba: the United States had no desire to annex the islands but she could never consent to see them taken possession of by a European power.[25]

The administration's unwillingness to take a stronger attitude toward helping along the inevitability of Hawaii's destiny was not shared by the California delegation to Congress. The next year, in June, Senator John B. Weller secured passage of a resolution calling on the president to submit information about Kamehameha's offer. Fillmore refused on the ground of lack of American interest in the matter. Some months later the president was accused by Representative J. W. McCorkle of cowardice for his refusal of the annexation offer. "The possession of these Islands by the United States is not only of the highest importance to California and the

Pacific, as a matter of security in time of war . . . but their trade is of vast importance," McCorkle said, "and their possession almost necessary to the United States, in a successful prosecution of commercial enterprise with Asia and the Pacific Islands." Attacking Fillmore's diplomacy, McCorkle perorated: "Will he tell the American people that they shall not annex the Sandwich Islands from dread of offending France, England, or all of continental Europe? Let him tell them so; let Whig policy tell them so; but it will be found that the American heart will scorn such baseness, and assert our right and honor as a nation, if the shock of battle shake the world."[26]

The offer to cede the islands to the United States under the threat of seizure by France was a desperate remedy by Hawaii. There was, as a matter of fact, little interest in the islands for annexation, even in the foreign colony of about 1,500 persons, most of them Americans. One of the strongest opponents was the minister of foreign affairs, Robert C. Wyllie, a Scotsman who had stopped at Honolulu in 1843 while on his way to China. He had been persuaded to remain as acting consul and in 1845 accepted the appointment as head of the foreign office, a post he held until 1865. Though fearful of the French aggressions of 1849 and 1851, Wyllie was more fearful of filibusters from the United States. His paranoia was fed during the fall of 1851 by reports that an expedition to the islands was being mounted at San Francisco. The *Daily Evening Picayune* said on October 15: "A party of restless young bloods numbering about 160 are about sailing from this part for the Sandwich Islands for the purpose, it is said, of revolutionizing his Kanaka majesty." About two weeks later the *California Daily Courier* gave the information that the filibusters were "well armed and of that peculiar temperament that prefers a row of any kind." Wyllie issued a proclamation for every island to organize companies to meet the invaders, though, armed only with pikes and a few carbines, it was clear that they could not accomplish much.[27]

The reports of an expedition were true, but it was hardly of the magnitude that Wyllie was preparing for. It was led by one of the state's wealthiest men, whose improbable experiences could scarcely be matched in a land where the unusual was commonplace—Samuel Brannan. Brannan, a native of Maine, was publishing a Morman newspaper, the *Messenger*, in New York when he was chosen by the church in 1845 to lead an expedition of emigrants to establish a settlement in California, then a Mexican province. He chartered a ship, the *Brooklyn*, and sailed on February 4, 1846. The emigration party was made up of 70 men, 68 women, and about 100 children, and the ship carried a cargo of farm implements, machinery to construct flour mills, and a printing press and type. The party landed at Yerba Buena (later renamed San Francisco) on July 31, 1846. Brannan began immediately to establish a settlement on the sandhills of the beach but soon ran into trouble with his followers. Organized as an association for mutual support and protection, some of them became dissatisfied with Brannan's leadership and accused him of appropriating too much for himself. The issue was decided in Brannan's favor at a trial, and from this time on there was practically no check on his acquisitiveness. He constructed a sawmill, opened a store, erected buildings, and, on January 7, 1847, published the first newspaper in the territory, the *Star*.

Later in the year Brannan led a group of Mormons to meet Brigham Young's followers going westward to find a new home in the wilderness with the intention of directing them to California. He was angered when Young said that he had found the promised land in Utah. While on his way back to San Francisco, Brannan saw an opportunity to set up as a merchant on the south fork of the American River where John A. Sutter, a Swiss adventurer who had obtained title to huge tracts of land, was building his empire and employing scores of men to guard his herds and construct houses and mills. Brannan established a store to supply Sutter's workmen with provisions and equipment. On January 24, 1848, the superintendent of an undertaking by Sutter to construct a sawmill detected flakes of gold in the excavation for the building. Brannan may be credited with starting the gold rush when, excited by the discovery, he hurried to San Francisco and, holding up a bottle of dust in one hand and waving his hat in the other, he went through the streets shouting: "Gold! Gold! Gold from the American River!"[28]

Bold, unscrupulous, and domineering, Brannan late in 1851 decided to extend his business activities from San Francisco and Sacramento to the Sandwich Islands. Whether he had plans to take over the islands is not known, but the Hawaiian foreign minister, Wyllie, was convinced he did and organized his defense against an invasion. The reports that Wyllie received had been wildly exaggerated. Brannan sailed on the *Game Cock*, a ship bound for China, with about two dozen followers on November 1 and reached Honolulu two weeks later. It was by no means an armed expedition. William Cooper Parke, for thirty-four years marshal of the islands, thought Brannan's plan was to persuade Kamehameha, old, frightened that he might lose his kingdom to the French, and intoxicated most of the time, to yield his sovereignty if guaranteed a life annuity. Brannan would become the governor general, Parke thought, and he would appoint men to other offices. The foreign community did not look with favor on Brannan's little band of roisterers, fearing that they were the vanguard of a greater force to follow. If Brannan had plans to become governor of the islands, he soon saw that the scheme was not likely to succeed and returned to San Francisco. The *Alta California* noted his return on January 2, 1852, with the remark: "The *Golden Rule* brings back most of the persons who sailed from here some two months since with extravagant notions relative to a change in the Hawaiian government."

No other expeditions sailed to the islands, but officials were uneasy during the next several years that they might. The U.S. commissioner, Severance, wrote the Department of State on May 3, 1852, that the Hawaiians considered Americans their best friends but, "if harassed by marauding expeditions" from the mainland, they would seek allies in other governments. In later dispatches he reported attempts to remove the king under threats that if he did not abdicate filibusters would be invited from California. On November 12, 1854, the U.S. commissioner, David Gregg, wrote that "a group of filibusters from California, in concert with three hundred American residents, were ready to demand signatures of a treaty of annexation as the only alternative to the overthrow of the dynasty and the plundering of Honolulu." None of these projects, reported by worried officials and imaginative newspaper writers, materialized, perhaps because there were so many other expeditions competing for interest.[29]

One of these was organized by a persuasive exile from Ecuador, Juan José Flores, who since his removal as president in 1845 had roamed Europe, the United States, and Central and South America seeking support for an invasion to take over the country. He provided the funds for an expedition from San Francisco that sailed late in 1851 for Panama to join other forces being gathered there and at Callao, Peru, for a landing at Guayaquil to march on the capital.

Flores, born in Venezuela and of mixed Spanish and Indian blood, had as a youth joined the forces of Simón Bolívar fighting for independence from Spain. He had attained the rank of general when Bolívar sent an army to Ecuador in 1822 and defeated the royalists and was appointed intendant at Quito of the confederacy established under the name of the Republic of Colombia made up of Venezuela, Ecuador, and Peru. "But, he was of a restless, unquiet spirit, and soon began to betray uneasiness in this subordinate sphere," the U.S. chargé at Quito, John Trumbull Van Alen, wrote in 1850, "and, at length, he boldly aspired to independent authority, though at the risk of breaking up the Republic of Colombia." He soon declared the independence of Quito, a secession that succeeded because of the death of Bolívar, and was elected the first president of the republic in 1830. Years of turmoil and changes in the government followed, and Flores, on the losing side, was forced into exile in 1845.

He first went to Spain, where he persuaded Queen Cristina to abet his plans to seize power in Ecuador, her son by a second marriage, the young Don Juan, to be the sovereign and Flores to be regent. She was reported to have supplied two million pesos to carry out the scheme. Flores' plans to return to Ecuador were defeated in 1846 when British authorities forbade the sailing of ships that he had purchased and fitted out in London. Flores next went to the United States, where, late in 1847, he requested an audience with Secretary of State Buchanan, but received no support from the Polk administration for his scheme if that was his hope. Buchanan, in instructing the first diplomatic agent to Ecuador, Vanbrugh Livingston, informed him that the official policy, as set forth in a note to the Ecuadorian minister of foreign affairs, was that "intervention or dictation" of European governments in the affairs of the Western Hemisphere, which Flores' project was, would "never be viewed with indifference by the government of the United States."

Rebuffed in Washington, Flores went to Costa Rica to hatch his plots. In 1851 the U.S. chargé, Van Alen, described him as being "poor, pining and discontented in exile." Van Alen thought Flores, with his experiences abroad, his quick mind, and his persuasiveness, would make "the best Governor of a State, in South America." This was not the opinion of Van Alen's successor, Courtland Cushing. As president of Ecuador, Flores had done nothing to promote the public welfare, instead enriching himself by seizing gold mines and several estates as large as an American county and building a mansion in Quito at a cost of $80,000 for his family and another, at a lesser cost, for a strolling actress. Flores' current plans, in the winter of 1852, to mount an invasion from Panama and Peru would find no support in Ecuador. "This Government," Cushing wrote, "is at peace with all nations and there are no indications of a serious opposition at home."[30]

The leader of the expeditionary force financed by Flores at San Francisco was one Alexander Bell, who, according to the scant information about him, had fled from Mobile, Alabama, just before the Mexican War to escape prosecution for mistreatment of the crew of a steamboat that he operated on the Tombigbee River. The story goes that the crewmen, who had not been paid for some time, refused to load cotton at Montgomery for shipment to Mobile, but were finally persuaded to go to work with the promise that they would get their money at the end of the trip. When the last bales were being stowed, Bell battened down the hatches on the crew and dickered with the owner of the cotton for blacks to fire up the boiler and run the boat to Mobile. This was accomplished in the course of four or five days, and at Mobile the hungry and thirsty crew was dragged out. So horrified and indignant were the people at Mobile that Bell decided suddenly to emigrate to Texas. In the Mexican War Bell fought in the American army and after the war, when news of the gold strikes in California reached Texas, went overland to San Francisco in 1849.[31]

In 1851 Bell commanded an expedition of about forty Californians who sailed on the steamer *Lightfoot* to join the Spanish-American followers of Flores at Panama. By late March, Courtland Cushing reported to the Department of State, Flores had assembled a flotilla of one steamer, one brig, and two barks off Guayaquil with from 700 to 1,000 men ready to land and fight their way to

Quito to seize the government. No landing was made, however, because there was no support for the invasion among the Ecuadorians, and the little flotilla succeeded only in maintaining a blockade that interfered with shipping at the port. The San Francisco supporters did not arrive until early June. The Ecuadorian minister of foreign affairs, José Villamil, complained to Cushing on June 7 that the Americans, "brought here for the purpose of imparting greater activity to the work of destruction begun by the bandit Flores," had sailed under the U.S. flag on a steamer he called *Quickstep*, a close enough approximation to the actual name, *Lightfoot*. By this time Flores' forces had been weakened by the departure of about 250 Chileans. They had been enticed from their homes, Cushing related, in the belief that they would be taken to the mines in California.

After three months the Flores expedition still had made no progress, though raiding parties had landed about 40 miles from the city to loot farms and villages. More than 100 of them had been killed or captured. Cushing reported to the Department of State: "By desertion, death, and capture, the expedition has lost not less than 350 men, and although it has received some accessions from Peru and Panama, it is weaker than when it first arrived. . . ." Among those killed were fifteen or twenty U.S. citizens, who perished in an explosion that destroyed a vessel called *Providence*. By the end of the year the surviving Americans made their way back to the United States, "destitute, disgusted and utterly surfeited with military expeditions."[32]

When Guillaume Patrice Dillon after a trip to Paris returned to San Francisco to take up his consular duties on July 22, 1850, he encountered major problems because of the large number of his countrymen lured to the goldfields. During the first months of the gold rush, from November 1849 to June 1850, thirty-five vessels had brought more than 2,000 fortune hunters from France, and during the next year more than 4,000 arrived. These did not include the Frenchmen already abroad who, like adventurers of other nationalities, rushed from Central and South America, the Pacific islands, the United States, and other areas to the mines. Dillon, not one to understate his responsibilities, estimated in December 1851 that there were more than 28,000 Frenchmen in

California. This, however, was probably more than double the actual number, of whom perhaps as many as 5,000 had settled in San Francisco.

The attraction of California to so many Frenchmen was due not only to the hard times after the revolution of 1848 but also to the formation of stock companies bearing such enticing names as La Fortune, La Californie, and Toison d'Or to transport fortune hunters to what a poetic contributor to the *Alta California* called the Eureka State. The largest of these companies was the Société du Lingot d'Or, which attracted subscribers to a lottery with a grand prize of a golden ingot and 224 other prizes. The company promised to transport, free of charge, 5,000 emigrants to California and actually did defray the expenses of more than 3,000. On their arrival in San Francisco, however, the company failed to provide the clothing and equipment promised, and Dillon was burdened with the responsibility of obtaining food and shelter for them. Those who made it to the goldfields were derisively known as "lingots."[33]

In common with other foreigners, especially Latin Americans, early nicknamed "greasers," the French suffered from prejudice in the mine fields, and they were sometimes driven off their claims. This prejudice received official sanction in 1850 with the passage of a foreign miners' tax law, which provided that until federal regulations were adopted no foreigner could conduct mining operations without a license to be renewed monthly at a fee of $20. Foreigners were thus forced back into the towns, where they took up whatever work they could find to maintain their existence.[34]

The French were among the first to be attracted by the lure of the fabled gold of Sonora. Some, with the example of the United States before them, saw in this weak northern state of Mexico, thinly settled, ravaged by Apaches, and neglected by the central government, a huge territory, rich in minerals, which they could settle, perhaps make a part of the empire of France. Moreover, the idea of a French settlement was welcome to the Mexican government which, unable to garrison the frontier, feared that the hated Americans might find the region tempting and there would be a repetition of Texas. Thus when a French adventurer, Charles de Pindray, sometimes given the title of count and sometimes that of marquis, proposed to lead an expedition of Frenchmen to hunt gold in Sonora in 1851, he received offers of governmental assistance through the Mexican consul in San Francisco.

Pindray, described by the historian Bancroft as a "scion of decayed French nobility," had turned up in San Francisco in 1849, having gone there from Mexico. He was said to have left France hurriedly to escape arrest for counterfeiting, and his reputation was so unsavory that the French minister to Mexico refused to assume any responsibility for him. In San Francisco he made a living hunting game which he sold to the markets of the city. Early in 1851, while Moorehead was leading his followers into Sonora, Pindray projected, with the promised support of Mexican officials, a gold-hunting expedition. Other Frenchmen were eager to join him, even at a fee of $50 assessed for chartering a ship and equipping an expedition. He received the editorial best wishes of the *Alta California* when his first detachment of eighty-eight sailed on the *Cumberland* for Guaymas on November 21, 1851.

At Guaymas, Pindray was at first welcomed by officials eager to support an enterprise that promised to establish a buffer colony between the Mexican towns and the Apaches. With a force numbering about 150 men through a second contingent arriving from San Francisco, Pindray set out for the valley of Cocospera on the northern frontier early in 1852 and by March had established a settlement at an abandoned Spanish mission. The promised government help was not forthcoming, however, because Governor Miguel Blanco became fearful that letting foreigners settle in Sonora might threaten his power. Receiving no supplies from Guaymas, suffering attacks from Apaches, and quarreling with his followers, Pindray after several months saw his project ending in failure. One night some of the colonists heard a gunshot in Pindray's room; when they entered they found their leader dead of a bullet wound in his head. Whether he committed suicide in despair over the failure of his plans, was killed by disgruntled followers, or was assassinated by Mexicans to get rid of a man who threatened to cause trouble has never been determined. His death did not result in immediate abandonment of the settlement. Pindray's friend and lieutenant, Olivier de Lachapelle, was elected commander, and though many of the expeditionists left, a small group remained until the fall when they were able to join another French expedition that had gone to Sonora with the same hopes and with the same promises of Mexican help that had inspired Pindray.

The new French expedition was organized by Lépine de Sigondis, an agent of one of the Parisian emigration companies. His group sailed from San Francisco in two small steamers, the *Sonora* and *Hermosillo*, to work abandoned placer mines in the vicinity of Santa Cruz. The expedition of from sixty to eighty men was faced with more restrictions than had been imposed upon Pindray: Blanco on May 1 issued a decree requiring the colonists to become Mexican citizens, to be subject to military service, and to give one-tenth of what they produced to the state in return for grants of land. The expeditionists went on nevertheless to Santa Cruz, but they failed to find gold in the quantities expected, a day's work producing hardly a dollar's worth of gold. Finding life in this arid region unbearable, the expeditionists soon dispersed, some going to Guaymas to sail back to California and some returning overland.

Meanwhile, a third expedition was being organized in Mexico City and San Francisco by the most daring and ambitious of all the French adventurers in America, Count Gaston Raoux de Raousset-Boulbon. Of an ancient Provence family, Raousset-Boulbon as a boy was headstrong and proud, refusing to bow the knee to any authority. So untamable was he that he acquired the nickname *le petit loup*. As a young man he dissipated two fortunes, one inherited from his mother and a second from his father, and in the difficult times following the revolution of 1848 was caught up in the California gold excitement. He sailed in May 1850 third-class, a comedown for a cavalier of his expensive tastes, for America. Some three months later, after he reached San Francisco, where, like others of his countrymen, he soon discovered a fortune was not for the finding, he was forced to gain a precarious living as a laborer. He was to be seen, according to the *Alta California*, at six o'clock every morning at the foot of Long Wharf, clad in a red flannel shirt, britches, and a pair of top-boots and puffing away at his cigar or pipe while he hoisted boxes and bales of goods from his boat. At night, however, he exchanged this working-man's clothing for a black suit, white shirt, and white gloves to cover his calloused hands and fancied himself again the boulevardier he had been in Paris. He was subject to dreams of grandeur, of undertaking a bold adventure that, as he later wrote a friend, would lead either to success or death.

Inspired by Pindray's venture and jealous of his renown, it was said, Raousset-Boulbon planned an expedition of his own but on a grander scale. He consulted with the French consul, Dillon, who was eager to promote colonization in Sonora to ease his burden of looking after Frenchmen in California. Dillon wrote of the matter to André le Vasseur, French minister to Mexico, and receiving favorable reports from him urged Raousset-Boulbon to go to Mexico City to obtain permission for the project. With the support of Le Vasseur and a Franco-Mexican banking house, Raousset-Boulbon persuaded President Mariano Arista that his colonization scheme was the solution of the problem of northern Sonora. In April 1852 a mining company in which Arista and other officials were shareholders was organized to finance Raousset-Boulbon's expedition to work the mines and defend the frontier from the Indians. Returning to San Francisco, Raousset-Boulbon quickly recruited about 250 men and sailed for Guaymas on June 1, 1852.

At this coastal town Raousset-Boulbon soon ran into difficulties with General Blanco, who on one pretext and then another held up the departure of the expedition to the north. He finally permitted it to proceed but at Sáric, site of the mining operation, Raousset-Boulbon refused to obey an order to report to the general at his northern military headquarters at Arizpe. Angered by this disobedience of his summons, Blanco sent word to Raousset-Boulbon that he could choose one of three courses: his men might take the oath of allegiance to Mexico and place themselves at his orders, they might secure letters of safety permitting them to search for gold but could not take possession of land or mines, or they might reduce their party to fifty men and under Mexican leadership proceed with the plans of the mining company.

When the ultimatum was read to the expeditionists, they agreed with Raousset-Boulbon in rejecting the terms. This, in effect, meant war. Leaving Sáric, the band began a march to Hermosillo, the capital and chief city of Sonora. Raousset-Boulbon hoped to obtain recruits to join him and his 250 men in a rebellion from among the Mexican settlers, embittered by the failure of Blanco to protect them from the Indians, and he sent emissaries on ahead to go to San Francisco for reinforcements and stores. To give them time to complete their mission, he stopped at Magdalena, where he carried on a brief love affair with the blond daughter of an official, "the rose in a bouquet of black tulips," while his men enjoyed flirtations and danced the fandango with the village belles. But this dalliance could not continue for long and Raousset-Boulbon pressed on to Hermosillo, reaching the town on October 14. To prevent an attack, the prefect sent an emissary to treat with the expedition. Taking out his watch, Raousset-Boulbon noted that it was eight o'clock in the morning. "Tell the prefect," he said, "that within two hours I shall enter Hermosillo and by eleven I shall make myself master of it if opposition is shown." It was not mere rodomontade. Within an hour, at the loss of seventeen men killed and twenty-five wounded, Raousset-Boulbon fought his way into the town and took charge as the defenders fled.

It was an empty victory, however. Raousset-Boulbon's hopes that the Mexicans would join him were not fulfilled and, stricken by fever and so incapacitated that he had to be carried on a litter, he started with his followers for Guaymas, where he hoped he might have received reinforcements in response to the agents sent out from Sáric. Nearing Guaymas, he was met by the French consul, who urged him to make terms with Blanco. By now he was delirious and unable to exercise command, and his men reached an agreement with the general to disband when offered means to return to California.

When the count returned to San Francisco early in 1853, he found himself a hero, for the Californians admired men with his audacity. Instead of being dispirited over prospects in Mexico by this defeat, his ambitions only became the greater. In complaints to the United States about the attack on Hermosillo, Mexican officials said that Raousset-Boulbon had proclaimed annexation of Sonora to France. Edward Everett, then secretary of state, denounced the idea as preposterous.[35] But Everett underestimated the grandiose ambitions that a filibuster was able to nurse. "Je ne vivre sans La Sonore," Raousset-Boulbon said at the time, and he later wrote a friend: "Do not be surprised, my friend, to see me embrace all of Mexico; I dare not say that this is in my plans, but it is in the realm of possibility."

Sending an armed expedition to obtain possession of the riches of Sonora under the guise of protecting settlers from the Indians was not an idea that had escaped the attention of Americans with visions of glory. When Raousset-Boulbon reached San Francisco, he found that he had competition in a foray being planned by William Walker, who had gone to California in 1850 from New Orleans and had engaged in the law at Marysville and edited a newspaper in San Francisco. Walker's invasion of Sonora with the idea of revolutionizing the province and setting up an independent republic was the first step in a career that was to make him the most famous filibuster of the time.

CHAPTER EIGHT

William Walker: Special Agent of Destiny

Little in the appearance, personality, or experience of William Walker made it seem plausible that he could conduct an expedition of adventurers to Mexico, inspiring them to battle against government troops, fight off Apache marauders, and overcome a hostile environment in a campaign to establish his own rule. Filibuster leaders—López, Quitman, Flores, Raousset-Boulbon—were bold and flamboyant soldiers, commanding in physique, eloquent in speech, magnetic in their attraction for other people. Walker had few, if any, of these assets. Only five feet, five inches tall, weighing less than 120 pounds, soft-spoken, withdrawn in the company of others, he was an insignificant figure among the boisterous and rough-and-ready men of San Francisco.

Yet he possessed what was not outwardly evident, the conviction that he was destined to achieve greatness. Several years before, in a philosophical article in the *New Orleans Crescent*, of which he was one of the editors, he had written: "Unless a man believes that there is something great for him to do, he can do nothing great. Hence so many of the captains and reformers of the world have relied on fate and the stars. A great idea springs up in a man's soul; it agitates his whole being, transports him from the ignorant present and makes him feel the future in a moment. It is natural for a man so possessed to conceive that he is a special agent for working out into practice the thought that has been revealed to him."[1] In planning his foray into Mexico he was the instrument of destiny that, according to his belief, could lead to but one result.

His life heretofore had been one of sudden decisions and reversals. He had been born, twenty-nine years before, on May 8, 1824, in Nashville, Tennessee, the son of a Scotsman, James Walker, who had come to the city four years earlier to take over a store inherited from an uncle, and of Mary Norvell, a member of an old Kentucky family. His boyhood was not that of the stereotypical young bloods of the South in the cavalier tradition who early took to riding spirited horses, became expert rifle and pistol shots, learned to hold their liquor, and, outside their immediate circle of family and friends, tended to be roisterers and libertines. The Walker home was a Calvinistic household, the father a member of the Disciples of Christ, and the son was brought up under more Spartan and religious conditions than customary among people of his class in the South. Although the Norvells of Kentucky owned slaves, there were none in the Nashville household—James Walker employed free blacks as servants.

The boy William was closer to his mother than to his taciturn father. He was her first child—three others followed, two sons, Norvell and James, and a daughter, Alice. In William's early youth, his mother became an invalid, and he devoted his mornings reading to her, probably the romances of Sir Walter Scott, from whom many Southerners absorbed their ideas of chivalry. "He was very intelligent and as refined in his feelings as a girl," a friend of the family, Miss Jane H. Thomas, recalled. At the age of twelve, William entered the University of Nashville, a typical academy of the time. Strong emphasis was placed on religion, almost monastic in discipline and ritual. Meals began with a blessing and ended with the offering of thanks, chapel services were held twice daily, and there was an evening prayer session. Prescribed work included Greek and Latin literature, rhetoric, history, mental and moral philosophy, logic, political economy, and a miscellany of courses in mathematics, astronomy, chemistry, mineralogy, navigation, and other subjects. The instruction could not have been very thorough, for Walker completed the curriculum in two years, graduating summa cum laude at the age of fourteen, but nevertheless he must have been something of a prodigy.[2]

William's parents wanted him to study for the ministry, and he was sufficiently religious after his graduation to join the church, but he insisted upon preparing for medicine. He began his studies under the family physician and then entered the medical school of the University of Pennsylvania, receiving his degree in 1843. Biographers have seen significance in the fact that his graduating essay was on the iris, because his own eyes were his most striking feature. Journalists popularized the descriptive epithet, "the grey-eyed man of destiny," derived from a legend of Central American Indians that they would be delivered from Spanish oppression by a grey-eyed man. His eyes, according to one of his followers, were "keen in their scrutiny and almost hypnotic in their power," and a journalist described his visual organ: "It is large, blue, gray, or light hazel, as you may deem proper to decide; the mind that is behind it is not visible through its operation as in others, but seems to lie in wait behind the pupil, receiving the reflection of what is passing before it, and thus secretly forming judgment, without ever itself being betrayed."[3]

At the age of nineteen, Walker was too young to practice medicine, and his parents, wishing him to have the advantage of study in Europe, sent him abroad. He spent a year in Paris getting experience in the hospitals and attended medical lectures at Heidelberg; before returning to the United States, he passed some time in London and in Edinburgh, where he attended medical classes. When he reached Nashville in 1845, just turned twenty-one, he had received the best medical training available at the time and had been exposed to the culture of Europe. He should have been ready to begin his career but unaccountably decided to take up law, beginning his preparation in the office of a Nashville attorney and, after several months, moving to New Orleans.

After two years reading law, Walker was admitted to the bar. In a city with numerous attorneys, many of them histrionic characters who, in the Southern mode, relied on oratory as much as skill in legal argument, there was little place for Walker, undersized and boyish in appearance at twenty-five and unimpressive in speech. He developed one enduring friendship among the legal fraternity, Edmund Randolph, clerk of the U.S. Circuit Court. Randolph, of the Randolphs of Virginia, grandson of Edmund Randolph, attorney general in Washington's cabinet, was Walker's opposite, a handsome man with wavy hair rising above a broad forehead and brushed back over his ears and wearing a mustache and chin whiskers. He possessed a dominating personality and was a popular figure in the social life of New Orleans. Unlike Walker, he was impetuous in temper, full of poetry and enthusiasm, though in the courtroom he was adept at sarcasm and vituperation. "In arguing a case," a contemporary said, "if there was no cause for invective, he would find an occasion."[4]

Journalists and biographers have attributed Walker's indrawn spirit and his ambition to establish an empire to a disappointed love affair. The flamboyant California poet, Joaquin Miller, who among his false pretensions claimed to have been a filibuster with Walker in Nicaragua, described him:

A dash of sadness in his air
Born maybe, of his over-care,
And, maybe, born of a despair
  In early love.

The object of this early love has been found in the person of Ellen or Helen (the name varies) Galt Martin. The story as told by one journalist was that Walker met her while she was on a visit to Nashville and, smitten by her charms, followed her to New Orleans. "She was," according to this account, "a most attractive woman—the loveliness of face and form being enhanced by that endearing charm which helplessness to beauty lends. For nature, so lavish in her other endowments, deprived this beautiful creature of two most essential faculties—she was a mute. Strange as it may seem, these two young people, in appearance and character the apparent antithesis of each other, allowed friendship to ripen into an ardent and lasting affection. . . . Just before the date fixed for their marriage the breath of pestilence poisoned the Gulf breezes, and the dreaded yellow fever became epidemic in the coast cities. Among the first to fall victim to the scourge was Miss Helen Martin, and her death changed the entire life-current, if not the heart of William Walker. From the ashes of a buried love ambition rose supreme."[5]

A similarly sentimental version of this story is that Walker met Miss Martin after going to New Orleans, being introduced to her and her widowed mother by Randolph. The girl had lost her voice and hearing in an attack of scarlet fever at the age of five and had learned the sign language at a school for the handicapped near Philadelphia. She was well read and intellectual and despite her misfortune was popular at balls and parties, carrying a small pad and pencil which she used to engage in repartee with the beaux present. Walker, it was said, learned the sign language, and they carried on long conversations. "It was a courtship," one biographer has written with no evidence, "charged with tenderness, urgency, and intense concentration." A contemporary journalist wrote that Miss Martin's death "gave a tinge of melancholy" to Walker's thoughts and probably "produced the great change in his character which ensued—a change from the quiet, modest student to the bold, daring, dauntless revolutionist and warrior."[6]

Unsuccessful as a lawyer, Walker found in journalism an occupation in which he could wield influence and could earn the money to enable him to marry Miss Martin, if that was his intention.* He apparently joined the *New Orleans Crescent* in the summer of 1848. The paper was nominally independent politically, a salutatory editorial saying that it "would discuss the great questions of State and National policy with impartiality and freedom," but it was primarily known as a Whig organ. To what extent Walker influenced its policy cannot be determined, but he probably wrote many of its editorials from early 1849 on when the masthead carried his name and that of J. C. Larue, a former judge, as editors. Although his contributions cannot be identified, presumably he shared the paper's views. The *Crescent* editorialized frequently in favor of annexation of Cuba, a cause célèbre in the city, but was not willing to go to war with Spain to obtain the island, arguing that it should be obtained by purchase or by annexation after Cubans themselves had won independence. It did not support the López expeditions, declaring in a cliché of the time, "If we wait a little the ripened plum will fall into our laps." The paper did not condemn President Taylor's proclamation of August 1849, warning against participation in a López foray, berated generally in the Southern press, but it later attacked the naval blockade of

*The California historian Hubert Howe Bancroft wrote of Walker: "Slow of speech, swift in energy, with a sharp pen every ready for attack; brave and resolute to obstinacy; a slumbering volcano . . . and burning with ambition for a fame of wide range—herein lies an explanation why he abandoned the sedate medical path staked out for him, to enter the more seductive mazes of the law, and failing, to see as editor a vent for his pent-up aggressiveness." *History of California*, 6:593.

Round Island to prevent the departure of the expedition as an offense against the sovereign rights of Mississippi.

Late in 1849 J. E. McClure, the chief owner, sold his interest in the *Crescent* and the paper came under new management. Whatever Walker's hopes had been for his future, they did not now seem possible of fulfillment in New Orleans. His star of destiny pointed westward, and early in 1850 he sailed via Panama to California, where his one close friend, Edmund Randolph, had gone the year before.

Walker's decision to leave New Orleans very probably was due to an opportunity that Randolph created for him to go into journalism in San Francisco. A new state where politics not yet dominated by established party factions was a free-for-all open to any comers, Randolph's daring and flamboyance stood out, and he was elected, in November 1849, to the lower house of the first legislature. He needed a newspaper to promote his political ambitions and planned a new daily with John Nugent, a former member of the staff of New York City's popular and sensational *Herald*, published by James Gordon Bennett. This paper was their model when Randolph and Nugent established the *San Francisco Herald* on June 1, 1850, with their names appearing as editors. Walker joined the paper as one of its editors in July, Randolph leaving to devote his time to politics and the law.

In New Orleans Walker had written for a Whig newspaper, but in San Francisco the *Herald* expounded some of the sentiments of Southern Democratic extremists. Shortly after Walker joined the staff, it endorsed "dissolution" of the Union if the Fugitive Slave Act was ignored in the North, and recommended passage of a California law to prevent the migration to the state of Negroes, many of them no doubt fugitive slaves. The chief editorial topic of the *Herald*, however, was a series of attacks against corrupt public officials and the failure of police to enforce the law and the courts to convict. Officials were accused of being hand in glove with criminals, bold desperadoes who acted singly and in bands without danger of arrest and punishment.

On one occasion the campaign brought Walker into personal danger. He had written on January 10, 1851, that the public administrator and probate judge "had 'pickled' rather than 'preserved'" a certain estate. The judge, R. N. Morrison, accompanied by a friend, W. H. Graham, descended on the *Herald* office to give Walker a cowhiding but did not find him in. They left a note demanding an apology worded, it later was reported, in "the most abusive and insulting language, such language as one gentleman could not quietly receive from another." The result was that Walker challenged Graham to a duel, which was fought on January 12. Graham, who had appeared several times on the field of honor and was noted for his marksmanship, seriously wounded his adversary. Brought before a magistrate on a charge of assault with a deadly weapon, Graham was bound over to the grand jury, but his opponent, according to one witness who testified, could not be identified. The *Herald* printed an account of the hearing but did not name the second duelist; the name, William Walker, however, was given in the *Alta California*. Walker, in an editorial, "Snaffling Public Sentiment," declared that the *Herald* would continue its campaign though a half-dozen friends of the judge had threatened to prevent further criticism "*vit et armis*." The paper, he declared, would not submit to "pistol-and-bowie knife censorship."[7]

The next month Walker became embroiled in another controversy with a judge, Levi Parsons of the District Court. Because of the strictures of the newspapers against the failures of law enforcement, the district attorney had obtained indictments against several suspects. Parsons reproved the grand jury on the grounds that these were not based on evidence sufficient for conviction. Walker in a short editorial corrected Parsons as to the law—a grand jury acted on *ex parte* evidence and could indict if this was sufficient to show probable cause. "Whether his Honor, Judge Parsons, in this instance has laid down for the guidance of the Grand Jury, an incorrect rule of law, through haste, inadvertence or misapprehension it is immaterial to inquire," the editorial said. Incensed by this criticism, Parsons, calling the press "a nuisance," ordered the grand jury to issue a presentment charging the editors with contempt. This it refused to do. In one of his most scathing editorials, "The Press a Nuisance," Walker declared that the judge instructed the grand jury "to aid the escape of criminals" and that after laying down the law favorably to them it was no wonder he "should declare against the Press."

A few days later, on March 7, Parsons cited Walker and Nugent for contempt. It was an action that brought the other newspapers strongly behind the *Herald's* editors. The *Alta California* asked: "Has anything so monstrous, nay, half so monstrous ever before been attempted in this free nation? What becomes of our right of freedom of speech and freedom of press, if a judge have the right of deciding anything which he dislikes 'a contempt,' forcing the accused summarily to appear before him, and be punished by him, with no appeal from his decision?"

The hearing on March 8 was conducted arbitrarily by Judge Parsons from the opening moments when he overruled a motion of Walker's attorney, Edmund Randolph, that the charge be put in writing. Seldom diplomatic in utterance in arguing a case, Randolph described the judge's decision as "monstrous." This provoked a heated exchange in which both the judge and the attorney had to resort to shouting to be heard as the courtroom was packed with vociferous supporters of Walker. "Mr. Randolph," Parsons declared, "the Court cannot sit here to hear itself abused and its proceedings characterized as monstrous." After several additional exchanges, Randolph declared: "I regret that the circumstances of the case will not allow me to make an apology." The statement created a silence, for it immediately portended to those present resort to the code duello. Quickly replying, Parsons said, "We do not ask for an apology." The hearing then proceeded with Randolph expounding at length on the law of contempt. When Walker took the witness stand, he readily admitted authorship of the offending editorial. "I wrote and published that article," he said, "to promote—and not obstruct—public justice." Parsons found him guilty and imposed a fine of $500 and ordered him confined until the amount was paid. Walker announced his refusal to pay and was put in jail.

In response to handbills headed "Justice! Public Meeting!" calling upon citizens to protest Parsons' high-handed action, 4,000 people assembled on the plaza the next day. They were harangued by Randolph, who between shouts of "Let's bring the Judge out here!" and "Set Walker free!" secured resolutions condemning the jailing as an unwarrantable exercise of power and violation of law. It was announced that Walker's release would be sought on a writ of habeas corpus and that the district's senators and representatives would be asked to draft impeachment articles against the judge for presentation to the legislature. The Superior Court received the habeas corpus request on March 11 and on March 14 by a vote of two to one freed Walker. The effort in the legislature to remove Parsons, however, was not successful. Walker memorialized the state assembly, appearing himself before a committee to present his case. The committee, on March 26, recommended impeachment, but a later select committee named to investigate the charges reported that there were insufficient grounds for this action.[8]

The acclaim Walker had received in challenging the power of the courts seemed to mark out a career for him as a leading editor, but again, almost unaccountably, he switched occupations, resigning from the *Herald* to form a law partnership with Henry P. Watkins at Marysville. The reason may have been in part that the *Herald*, whose plant was destroyed by a fire that swept the city on the night of May 4, was publishing under difficulties and in part also that his appearance before the legislative committee to obtain Judge Parsons' impeachment had revived his interest in legal practice and perhaps politics, the law being the springboard to success in public affairs.

Marysville, at the junction of the Feather and Yuba Rivers, had sprung up almost overnight early in 1850 and offered opportunities to a beginning lawyer, and Watkins, who, as it turned out, shared Walker's addiction to dubious ventures promising glory and wealth, already had a foothold there. Stephen J. Field, brother of the New York attorney and free-soiler, David Dudley Field, who had located at Marysville before the town had a name and a government, paid ambiguous tribute to Walker as a lawyer in his reminiscences: "He was a brilliant speaker, and possessed a sharp but not a very profound intellect. He often perplexed both court and jury with his subtleties, but seldom convinced either." At Marysville, Walker refused to enter into the social and community life, another contemporary recalling that he "always maintained a stolid indifference for those around him, and confided in no man."[9]

The routine of law practice—drawing up deeds, representing clients in mine claims, probating wills—had little attraction for Walker, and he was interested when in early 1853 he was approached by one Frederic Emory with a plan to obtain a land grant near Arizpe in Sonora and establish a colony to operate the abandoned gold mines in return for protecting the Mexican inhabitants from the Apaches. The plan had been proposed the year before at Auburn by several men who contributed the money to send two agents, one of them Emory, to Guaymas to conduct the negotiations. Emory failed to obtain any support for the project because Count Raousset-Boulbon had preceded him, and when the Frenchman sailed for Sonora the Auburn group abandoned their scheme. The return of Raousset-Boulbon, his expedition a failure, prompted them to revive their plan, and to do so before the count could proceed with his object of making a second attempt. In mid-June Walker and Watkins sailed on the brig *Arrow* for Guaymas, arriving at the dusty little seaport on the last day of the month. Walker, in an account of the trip, wrote that before leaving San Francisco he and Watkins had obtained passports from the Mexican consul, but if so these were of no help because Guaymas authorities received orders from the governor, Manuel María Gándara, to detain them upon a report from the local commandant that their purpose was to invade Mexican territory.

A well-traveled adventurer in Guaymas was T. Robinson Warren, who met Walker and related that he was impressed by the filibuster's "astuteness and determined character." "Below the medium height, and very slim, I should hardly imagine him to weigh over a hundred pounds," Warren wrote. "His hair was light and towy, while his almost white eyebrows and lashes concealed a seemingly pupilless, grey, cold eye, and his face was a mass of yellow freckles. . . ." Altogether, he was "as unprepossessing-looking a person as one would meet in a day's walk." But, according to Warren's recollections, to judge Walker by his appearance was a mistake. "Extremely taciturn," Warren said, "he would sit for an hour in company without opening his lips; but once interested, he arrested your attention with the first word he uttered, and as he proceeded, you felt convinced that he was no ordinary person."

The U.S. consul at Guaymas heatedly supported Walker's request for permission to go to Hermosillo, but officials were too wary to risk admitting American citizens into the state and Walker prepared to depart. After his return to San Francisco, a newspaper report said that the Mexican government had offered a reward for his head and "he left the country to save the important member advertised." Though he had not got into the interior, Walker saw enough of the country to convince him "that a comparatively small body of Americans might gain a position on the Sonora frontier, and protect the families on the border from the Indians." He believed that this not only could be done but also that it should be done because the United States had not lived up to the Treaty of Guadalupe Hidalgo in preventing Indian raids into Mexico.

From this belief it was easy for him to progress to the conclusion that Americans should settle in the country, with or without the formal consent of Mexico, that "any social organization, no matter how secured, is preferable to that in which individuals and families are altogether at the mercy of savages." In this Warren, who had traveled throughout the countryside, might have agreed. "The Apaches, knowing the cowardice of the Mexicans, venture oftentimes within sight of the largest towns to commit their depredations," Warren wrote, "and on several occasions have been seen by the people of Hermosillo from the housetops, burning farm houses not a league distant. The central government every once in a while makes a great flourish of trumpets about sending troops to put them down; a commandant is appointed to lead them, and a regiment or two of soldiers are assembled at some agreeable town in the interior. Here the commandant establishes headquarters—and this is about all."[10]

While Walker and Watkins were in Guaymas, Raousset-Boulbon had found prospects propitious for a second French colonization scheme with the return to power in Mexico of Antonio López de Santa Anna. After two years as president, Mariano Arista, with three-fourths of the country in rebellion or threatening to rebel, had resigned on January 5, 1853. Two months of chaos followed until on March 17 the state governors and legislatures patched together an arrangement to elect a president with dictatorial power to act until a new national congress could be chosen and a new constitution adopted. They settled on Santa Anna as the man to bring about order. Santa Anna had served as president four times before, including the period of the war with the United States. After his defeat at arms, he had gone into exile in fear of his life. He now entered Mexico City hailed by the fickle people as the country's savior-to-be in a triumphal march with streaming banners, pealing bells, and floral wreaths.

With unhappy subjects ready to follow revolutionary leaders in most parts of the country, Santa Anna looked with favor upon a proposition of the French minister, Pierre Émile Levasseur, that the Raousset-Boulbon colonization scheme be revived to protect Sonora from the Indians. It was attractive in another way, since reports had reached the capital of an expedition being planned by Americans. Raousset-Boulbon arrived in Mexico City in May, but he found Santa Anna difficult to deal with. His Most Serene Highness, as the dictator had styled himself, was suspicious of the count's motives. Newspaper reports, if he had no other sources of information, would have led him to be so. The *San Francisco Evening Journal* of April 30, for example, had reported that Raousset-Boulbon was planning to invade Sonora with 2,000 men. This account had provoked a protest to Alfred Conkling, the American minister. Conkling replied in a note stating that the newspaper's story was false, being contradicted by other newspapers, and adding that the count would be lucky if he could get twenty men to join an expedition, a flagrant underestimation of the attraction of filibustering to Californians. After keeping Raousset-Boulbon dangling for several months with vague promises, Santa Anna finally offered him a colonelcy in the Mexican army. The count angrily rejected this and set out for California determined to enlist an army and seize Sonora by force.[11]

William Walker and Henry P. Watkins had returned to San Francisco to organize their expedition to Sonora and Raousset-Boulbon was still being subjected to the cat-and-mouse game played by Santa Anna when President Pierce made his first move to add more territory to the country as promised in his inaugural address. His objective was Mexico and his plans were tentatively set forth in instructions that Secretary of State Marcy issued on July 15 to the new minister to Mexico, James Gadsden. Marcy began his instructions with the understatement that "relations between the United States and Mexico are in an unsettled state." He then reviewed the major differences and suggested the policies Gadsden should follow in resolving them.

The most urgent matter, Marcy said, was determining the

exact border between the two countries. In the Treaty of Guadalupe Hidalgo provisions had been made for each nation to appoint survey commissions to fix the division line, but after four years no agreement had been reached. A major difficulty was that the map used by the treaty negotiators had been discovered to be inaccurate. The treaty declared that the southern boundary of New Mexico would begin just north of "the town called Paso" and extend west until it intersected the first branch of the Gila River, thence down the middle of this stream until it emptied into the Colorado River, and thence along the border of Upper and Lower California to the Pacific. Surveys showed that the map designated as official was in error: El Paso was not situated on the parallel 32°15' north latitude, as marked on the map, but on the parallel 31°45'.

The area in dispute was a fertile strip 32 miles wide, which had been settled by both Americans and Mexicans. In 1853 the population was estimated at 3,000 persons. Early in that year Governor Angel Trias of Chihuahua claimed possession and decreed that no one could own land there except Mexican citizens. American settlers appealed to the governor of New Mexico to protect them. Governor J. S. Calhoun, shortly to be replaced, declined, but his successor, William C. Lane, took it upon himself to claim the region for the United States and issued a proclamation to this effect. Governor Trias issued a counter-proclamation declaring that he would preserve the national honor of Mexico against this aggression. Secretary Marcy avoided a collision by instructing Conkling to inform Mexico that Lane's threat to hold the territory by force of arms was not the policy of the United States. Lane was correct in maintaining that by the Treaty of Guadalupe Hidalgo the territory belonged to the United States, Marcy told Gadsden, but this was a matter to be determined by negotiation.

Marcy then turned to the matter that had been a chief factor in the selection of Gadsden, one of the South's leading railroad promoters, as minister—the desire of Pierce to extend the border southward because the best southern rail route to the Pacific, according to the advice of surveyors, was "a marine league" below the Gila. Marcy did not know how much Mexican territory was needed, but he thought Mexico would be willing to give up a slice of territory for a "moderate sum" as she would derive as many advantages from a railroad as the United States.[12]

Of a famous South Carolina family, Gadsden's early years had been spent in military service, his advancement being aided by his friendship with Andrew Jackson formed during the War of 1812 and the war against the Seminole Indians of Florida. Making his home at Charleston in 1839, Gadsden became president of the Louisville, Cincinnati, and Charleston Railroad. He had hoped to extend the line to the Mississippi, and after the acquisition of New Mexico and California, to the Pacific. He had been removed from the presidency of the railroad in 1850, one of the stockholders declaring that while "the Grand and Western Extension" was a wonderful conception, it offered little consolation for those wanting returns on the capital they had invested.[13]

Gadsden's idea of carrying on a diplomatic negotiation was that of "striking boldly at the truth and leaving the rest to Providence." Soon after his arrival in Mexico City early in August he determined that following a strong line was the way to achieve his ends. He saw that Santa Anna desperately needed money and would be more concerned with how much he received than with how much he gave up in the way of territory. His control over the country was precarious. He was on a volcano, Gadsden wrote Marcy, which might explode in a month. Gadsden was so cheered by the prospects that, on September 5, he revealed to Marcy his belief he could obtain more territory than contemplated by Pierce, as much as "the Two or the Five States; bordering on the Rio Grande, the Gela & the Gulf of California."

Gadsden's dispatches were never very clear. Although a graduate of Yale, he apparently had not learned very much about English composition; his prose was so lacking in syntax as to be incomprehensible at times and he seldom completed a sentence, ending what started out as a statement or a question with a dash. He disliked the circumlocutions he found in the discourse of Manuel Diez de Bonilla, the Mexican minister of foreign affairs. Bonilla would never get down to the issue Gadsden considered foremost—cession of territory for the rail route. Instead, in note after note he stressed the failure of the United States to prevent Indian raids and to pay the claims for indemnity for them.[14]

Gadsden's early negotiations were hampered by the vague

instructions received from Marcy, and he repeatedly requested that these be clarified. His reports on Santa Anna's need for money and the danger his regime might be toppled led Pierce, on October 22, to send a special agent with instructions so secret they could not be committed to paper, the agent to memorize them and convey them to Gadsden orally. The agent chosen, Christopher L. Ward, was another instance of Pierce's proclivity for choosing emissaries who had private interests to promote rather than those of the president. A Pennsylvanian, Ward was a friend of James Buchanan and had taken a leading part in politics as a member of the Democratic national committee. More important from the standpoint of his mission to Mexico was that he was legal counsel for Americans seeking indemnity from Mexico for repudiation of a grant awarding them canal and transit rights across the Isthmus of Tehuantepec.

Pierce, believing Santa Anna to be in such a desperate situation he would be amenable to almost any proposition to obtain money, boldly instructed Gadsden to seek a border that would hand over to the United States large portions of Coahuila, Chihuahua, and Sonora and all of Baja California, altogether about 125,000 square miles. He was authorized to pay up to $50 million to obtain a desirable border. Pierce, however, was not confident enough to believe he could achieve the huge concession outlined and authorized Gadsden to fall back on four other border lines that progressively took in less of Mexican territory.[15]

Ward arrived in Mexico City on November 11 and immediately went beyond his instructions by telling Gadsden to include disposition of the Tehuantepec grant in the proposals for establishing a boundary. He was so insistent that Gadsden protested to Marcy on November 20 in his halting language: "Indeed to hear Mr. Ward talk; and seemingly under the confidential cloak of a private message. You might suppose that my mission was for the Tehuantepec grant if not at the sacrifice of higher claims; at least so to be connected as to render the recognition or adjustment of the latter indespensable with the former." He was outraged that Ward was seeking an indemnity of $5 million for the $600,000 spent on surveys before Mexico declared the grant null. Since "*money: & money alone*" would induce Santa Anna to "dismember" further the Mexican nation, Gadsden saw little prospect of obtaining a favorable treaty if Pierce insisted, as Ward asserted, that $5 million be deducted from whatever sum was offered to satisfy "the Cormorant appetite of Ward & Co."[16]

Marcy's reply explaining that Ward had been specifically told not to "embarrass" negotiations by taking up the Tehuantepec claims did not reach Gadsden until late in December after he had brought them into the treaty discussions. Santa Anna had appointed a commission on November 20 to treat with the American minister on the boundary question. To Gadsden's chagrin, the Mexicans would consider only a boundary that corresponded with the least favorable Pierce had suggested as a basis for negotiation. Gadsden, in a not very velvet-gloved threat, resorted to the Manifest Destiny doctrine in arguing for a larger territorial concession because its "mountain and desert outlines" would constitute a natural border. Despite the vigilance of the United States, he told Bonilla, the movement of the American people onto Mexican lands unimpeded by natural barriers was irresistible and "the spirit of the age" would ultimately cause the northern states to join the United States.

Later he complained to Marcy that the filibuster expeditions, about which he had received many complaints from Bonilla, were hindrances to reaching an agreement. In a series of six sessions from December 10 to 30 the negotiators, however, succeeded in drafting a treaty. From the view of the extravagant hopes Pierce had nurtured for territorial aggrandizement it was a disappointment, because it obtained an area close to the minimum he had sought. Gadsden accepted a line that, though it took in about 45,500 square miles, including the Mesilla Valley, was chiefly valuable only in providing for a rail route west of the Rio Grande. In return, he obtained abrogation of the Treaty of Guadalupe Hidalgo provisions dealing with Indian incursions. The United States would pay Mexico $15 million and assume American claims against Mexico, including those of the holders of the transit grant.[17]

Although Gadsden would seem to have been outmaneuvered by Santa Anna, he was proud of the treaty and indeed had a right to be, for if he had been compelled to lower his sights he had been faced with formidable obstacles—a hostile Mexico, outside interferences, and the machinations of Ward. When he arrived at New Orleans on January 12, 1854, he replied to customs officials: "Sir,

I am General Gadsden. There is nothing in my trunk but my treaty."

The pact was the subject of cabinet discussions for a month before the president submitted it to the Senate on February 10. Engaged in debate on the Kansas-Nebraska bill, the Senate delayed consideration for another month. Even if Gadsden had succeeded in obtaining the huge tract of 125,000 square miles Pierce had set his eyes on, it is doubtful if the Senate would have approved the treaty. Northern free-soilers urged rejection; some Southerners opposed it because they thought enough territory should have been obtained to create a new slave state to offset free California; expansionists thought the area purchased too small; some thought $15 million too much to pay for a rail route in a region of no value otherwise; and advocates of the Tehuantepec transit interests were vociferous in their advocacy of the rights of the grant holders. In short, so many contending views were set forth that the original treaty was only a shadow of itself when the Senate finally agreed, if its approval can be considered an agreement, on a document.[18] Few in the Senate liked the treaty, Pierce did not like it, and neither did Santa Anna, who would have preferred to reject it but was so in need of money that though the amount he expected had been cut from $15 million to $10 million he approved it at once. Pierce's effort to enlarge the dominion of the United States was a failure: he had seen a mountain and had to settle for a hillock.

The visit of Walker and Watkins to Guaymas in June had been correctly interpreted by Mexican leaders as the preliminary to an invasion of Sonora, and Bonilla on August 20 called upon Gadsden to urge the United States to prevent any expeditions being planned. Gadsden assured him of the firm policy of the Pierce administration to enforce the neutrality laws and informed him that he had written California authorities to frustrate the "movements of hostile character by lawless individuals from that state."[19] Embarking himself upon his negotiations to obtain as much of Mexican territory as he could by purchase, Gadsden did not want them endangered by wild-eyed filibusters from the United States.

Gadsden's own mission was considered in San Francisco to be only a beginning. "If the acquisitions that may now be looked upon as certain are commenced by negotiations," the *Alta Califor-*

nia said on September 8, "it will not stop until Young America has secured all her demands, which will prove to be nothing short of the entire scope of territory lying between the Sierra Madre and the Rio Grande, Chihuahua, Sonora, Sinaloa, and Lower California, and the reserved right to take more by purchase or force whenever it may be wanted."

Once back in San Francisco, Walker and Watkins went ahead with the project to obtain Sonora by force. In May they issued bonds in the name of the Independence Loan Fund for $500, signed by Walker, entitling the holder to one square league of land in the Republic of Sonora. With the money raised, they chartered the brig *Arrow*, which had accommodations for from 150 to 200 men, and began laying in a stock of arms and supplies. A recruitment office was opened, and the *Alta California* predicted on September 12 that "there will be a party—perhaps two or three parties—formed in California in a short time, destined for an excursion down the coast." On October 1 the newspaper took note of Gadsden's request to officials "to keep a sharp lookout for any expedition," but said that nevertheless the expedition was expected to sail in the next two or three weeks.

By calling his movement an effort to secure "independence" for Sonora, Walker justified an armed invasion by the moral argument that it was the duty of the American people to relieve "the frontier from the cruelties of savage war." "Northern Sonora," he said, "was in fact, more under the dominion of the Apaches than under the laws of Mexico; and the contributions of the Indians were collected with greater regularity and certainty than the dues to the tax-gatherer. The state of this region furnished the best defence for Americans aiming to settle there without the formal consent of Mexico. . . . "[20] But many who bought the "independence" bonds and enlisted in the expedition force had less altruistic aims. The belief persisted that Sonora was one of the richest mineral regions in the world, undeveloped because the Mexicans were unenterprising and because the government was inept. It was also considered to have fine agricultural possibilities and if slaves were introduced to offer a means of wealth by farming.

As important as mission and money in the appeal of filibustering was the spirit of the American people, and particularly those of California. "What, our people seem to think, is the worth of life, wanting emotion, wanting action?" the contemporary authors of *The Annals of San Francisco* asked. "At whatever hazard, most persons here must have occasional excitement—new speculations, leading to personal adventure, change of scene and variety of life. Danger to life and limb and property will not stand in the way. They will overlook the fairest prospect close at hand, with its dull routine of duty and labor, to seek for an inferior one at a distance. . . . Thus a new land, where hope and fancy see all things, is to them a charmed land."[21]

About the middle of September the activities of the filibusters finally penetrated the consciousness of General Ethan Allen Hitchcock, commander of the Pacific division of the U.S. army. This extraordinary soldier since graduating from West Point in 1817 had been one of the most efficient, and some thought overly conscientious, officers in the army, his services including the command of a regiment under General Taylor and the post of inspector general under General Scott in the Mexican War, but his overriding interest was philosophical speculation. During the summer of 1853 he wrote in his diary 224 pages of commentary on Hinduism and its conceptions of God, eternity, substance, and the absolute. He put an end to these arcane matters when he made this entry: "Much as usual, when I have action in my life my notes cease." They had been cut off because of his hearing that an expedition was being planned to invade Sonora. He requested the collector of the port, R. P. Hammond, on September 22 to keep a watch upon vessels in the harbor, and learning, on September 30, that arms were being loaded on the *Arrow* consulted with the U.S. district attorney, who advised seizure of the brig. Accordingly, at ten o'clock that night, he sent a party of soldiers to take the vessel and deliver her to the U.S. marshal.

On the next day Walker obtained a writ of replevin in the Superior Court ordering the marshal to deliver the brig to the county sheriff. The matter was referred to Hitchcock, who refused, citing the authority given him by President Fillmore in ordering him to California to use the armed forces to stop the sailing of any filibuster expeditions. Reports that Walker planned to lead a raiding party to seize the brig, tied up at the wharf, led Hitchcock to have her hauled out into the stream. Both the district attorney and collector urged Hitchcock, in case the vessel was attacked, to surrender her without opposition since public opinion opposed seizure by the army. "Damn public opinion," Hitchcock replied, adding that if any body of men tried to get possession it would be at their peril. Both California senators, William M. Gwin, whom Hitchcock had seen conferring with the port collector, and John B. Weller, who had condemned the seizure in a speech, as well as other leading politicians were thought by Hitchcock to be active behind the scenes in securing release of the brig.

On October 9 the Superior Court ordered Hitchcock to show cause why he should not be adjudged guilty of contempt, and Walker filed a complaint of trespass against him, seeking damages of $30,000. At a hearing the next day the U.S. district attorney submitted President Fillmore's instructions and the letter of Gadsden about stopping filibuster expeditions as authority for Hitchcock's actions, but the judge ruled that this correspondence did not constitute an answer to the charge against him and he was given seven days to reply. On the morning of October 17 Hitchcock noted in his diary: "I am likely to have a judgment against me in the State court for 'contempt' in not delivering the *Arrow* to the county sheriff! I hear that he says it will do no harm to fine me $5, and he will add that I followed my insructions. Monstrous! The judge is in the hands of the adventurers."[22]

But no hearing on the contempt case was held on this date.* Impatient over the law's delay, Walker had chartered a schooner, the *Caroline*, loaded her with arms, and sailed shortly after midnight on October 16 with forty-five men, all that could be taken aboard the small craft, as the advance guard of the army that was to conquer Sonora and proclaim the state an independent republic.

*On Nov. 8, the parties to the case filed a stipulation to dismiss it and the judge so ordered. *Alta California*, Nov. 9, 1853.

CHAPTER NINE

The Conquest of Lower California

Two weeks after the hurried departure from San Francisco, the *Caroline*, carrying the First Independent Battalion of the Sonoran invasion troops, reached Cape San Lucas at the tip of the long and narrow peninsula of Lower California. With only forty-five men in his command, Colonel Walker, as he had styled himself, did not have the forces for a landing in Sonora, and his plan was to establish headquarters at some place on the peninsula until he could be joined by three other battalions to sail as quickly as possible from San Francisco. He did not expect to encounter much opposition, for Lower California with an area of about 57,000 square miles had a scattered population of fewer than 15,000 people and no sizable Mexican military forces were garrisoned there.

Walker's first military communiqué, dated November 7, said that at San Lucas "some little information of importance" was obtained and that his force sailed a hundred miles up the coast of the Gulf of California to La Paz, the capital.* This information was probably that the little town was unprotected by troops. Anchoring at La Paz on November 3, Walker ordered a party led by the battalion captain, Charles H. Gilman, to go ashore. Within thirty minutes the unsuspecting governor, Rafael Espinosa, was a prisoner, the Mexican flag was hauled down from the staff in front of his house and replaced by a flag with red stripes at the top and

*Walker issued no communiqués under his own name, assigning the task of writing them to his adjutant, Second Lieutenant Samuel Ruland. The first reports issued to the newspapers were signed "Independence"; later ones were signed either by Ruland's full name or his initials.

bottom and a white stripe in the center emblazoned with two red stars representing Lower California and Sonora, and Walker issued a twenty-three word proclamation: "The Republic of Lower California is hereby declared free, sovereign, and independent, and all allegiance to the Republic of Mexico is forever renounced."

With the same sangfroid with which Walker announced the founding of a new nation, he issued four days later two decrees, which of course he could neither communicate to his subjects nor implement. The first established free trade with all the world by abolishing customs duties and the second proclaimed the legal code of Louisiana as the law of the land. The officers of the government were Walker, president; Frederic Emory, secretary of state; John M. Jarnigan, secretary of war; and Howard A. Snow, captain of the *Caroline*, secretary of the navy.

No place for the rendezvous of the first battalion with contingents to follow had been set, and Walker decided on November 6 to return to San Lucas—his communiqué termed it moving "the seat of government"—and embarked on the *Caroline*, taking with him his prisoner Espinosa and such state archives as there were at La Paz. Before he could leave the harbor, a Mexican ship, the *Neptune*, arrived bringing a new governor, Colonel Juan C. Rebolledo, who had been appointed by Santa Anna to replace Espinosa. Rebolledo was quickly captured and joined his predecessor as a prisoner.

The raid on La Paz, however, was not to end without some show of hostility by the inhabitants. When a party of six men went ashore to gather firewood, they were attacked by townspeople. Walker opened fire with his ordnance and under this cover led a detachment of thirty men ashore to rout the Mexicans. "From the time of landing until the close of the action . . . was about one hour and a half," the report on the combat said. "The enemy's loss was six or seven killed, and several wounded. Our men did not so much as receive a wound, except from *cacti*, while pursuing the enemy through the chaparral, in the rear of the town. Thus ended the battle of La Paz, crowning our efforts with victory, releasing Lower California from the tyrannous yoke of declining Mexico, and establishing a new Republic."

Two days later, on November 8, the expedition put in at Cape San Lucas, but a Mexican cutter seen hovering off the coast the next day aroused apprehension in Walker and determined him to seek a safer anchorage farther removed from the Mexican mainland while he awaited the arrival of reinforcements. Accordingly, he reembarked and sailed up the Pacific coast to Ensenada de Todos Santos, about 80 miles south of San Diego, where on November 29 he went ashore and declared the little port to be the new capital of the republic that as yet existed only in the minds of himself and his followers.

The first news of Walker's exploit reached the outside world on December 2 when Frederic Emory arrived in San Diego bearing a report of the victory at La Paz and an address by President Walker "To the People of the United States," dated November 30. The *San Diego Herald* said "the capture of La Paz and the establishment of a new order of things excited our American population to the wildest bounds of joy." Similar jubilation was expressed in San Francisco when the *Herald* reached the city on December 7 and its accounts were reprinted in the newspapers. The flag of the new republic was run up at the busy corner of Kearny and Sacramento Streets, a recruitment office was opened, and volunteers thronged before it to enlist in the liberation forces.

Walker's address was a defense of his establishing a new republic independent of Mexico. "Mexico," he declared, "has not performed any of the ordinary duties of a government towards the people of Lower California. . . . Thus abandoning the Peninsula, and leaving it, as it were, a waif on the waters, Mexico cannot complain if others take it and make it valuable."[1] Although Walker's declaration of the independence of Lower California was widely held to be a *fait accompli*, saner minds had their doubts. Critics generally agreed that the raid was only a prelude to an invasion of Sonora, which with a population of 70,000 could not easily be occupied and controlled by a small filibuster force. Among the doubters was the *Alta California*, which on two successive days carried editorials pointing out the difficulties in the way of detaching Lower California and Sonora from Mexico and extending to them the American institution of slavery, which Walker's adoption of the legal system of Louisiana was interpreted as being his intention. The newspaper granted that Lower California might be held but added that "the booty did not suit the restless and ambitious invaders," who wanted Sonora as well. It warned that persistence in the piratical project might lead to war with Mexico, as there were "a lot of idlers, discontented persons, loafers and ragamuffins not only in California but also on the Atlantic seaboard who would like every opportunity to get into a great row, fight the weak and pillage the rich."[2]

Later news from Ensenada might have given some of the fervid filibusters pause before going on to the support of Walker if it had reached them in time. On the morning of December 13, the *Alta California*, under the headline, "Defeat of the Filibusters," carried a report from San Diego that on December 3 a foraging party of twenty men had gone out from the new capital to attack a ranch, La Grulla, and drive off the owner's cattle and seize his grain stores. A report of the robbery reaching the town of Santo Tomás 20 miles away, the inhabitants turned out in force, pursued the marauders, killing two and capturing two, and chased the rest into Ensenada. As of the last report, dated December 6, the filibusters were under siege. "It is deemed impossible that the American party can escape," the article said, "if indeed any remain yet alive." This was not a very accurate account of what had happened—the situation of the filibusters was not quite so bad—but it indicated that the inhabitants of Lower California did not look upon them as liberators. A few hours before the paper appeared on the streets, the second party of filibusters of 150 men led by Walker's law partner, Henry P. Watkins, boarded the 235-ton bark *Anita* and sailed for Ensenada.

After General Ethan Allen Hitchcock's failure to prevent the sailing of the first battalion, he had taken no more interest in the filibuster movement, immersing himself again in his metaphysical speculations and setting them forth at length in his diary. As he was the only official, federal or local, who had opposed the expedition, there was no interference with the preparations Watkins had been making to enlist recruits. The new republic's scrip sold openly at 10 cents on the dollar, moneyed men bought the $500 bonds issued, also sold at a discount, and more adventurers flocked to the recruitment office than could be taken care of.

Although expedition plans were known to everyone, some pretense of secrecy was maintained about the departure to protect officials from being condemned for failing to enforce the neutrality laws. A friend of Walker and later an associate in his Nicaraguan adventure, William V. Wells, wrote that ammunition, guns, and provisions were quickly and quietly dragged out of a store on Front Street, loaded on drays, hauled to the wharf, and passed on board the *Anita*. A crowd of more than 100 gathered to view this operation, carried on, Wells related, in a hullabaloo as orders were issued, friends took leave of one another, and volunteers in their cups gave "vent to the exuberance of their spirits by songs and denunciations upon the 'Greasers' who had made the reported attack" upon the Ensenada battalion. When the *Anita* cleared the bay, she cast off from her tow, the steamer *Thomas Hunt*, and, raising sail, set out on her cruise to the south "with square yards, a strong northeast wind blowing and the foam flying from her bows."[3]

This spirited account of a vessel setting off on high adventure was not supported in the story of a young recruit, who related that in casting off from the *Thomas Hunt*, the *Anita* tore away a large part of the port bulwarks. "A breeze was blowing, and I beheld a scene the like of which I never before witnessed, and which, under the same circumstances, I would fain never be compelled to witness," he wrote. "Almost all on board were more or less drunk, and for the management of the craft there were but two available hands—at least belonging to her—the captain and the mate. In consequence of the loss of the bulwarks, the sea washed the deck fore and aft, and the greater part of the stores being on deck, and but poorly secured, with every roll casks, barrels, and boxes would slide about. . . . After a while the blow increased to a pretty good storm, tearing the foretopsail and jib into ribbons, as there were not sober hands enough to furl them. . . ." Later, two or three men were swept overboard, he related, but the ship's boats having also been washed away no rescue attempt could be made. Some of the men demanded that the *Anita* return to port, but before long the storm subsided, and the men, sinking into drunken sleep or overcome by seasickness, had no will to complain and the voyage continued.[4]

What had happened at Ensenada was that on December 1, on the day after Walker's landing, he had sent a force of fifteen men to a nearby ranch, Guadalupe, belonging to Juan Bandini of San

Diego, a large landowner in both Upper and Lower California. Commanded by Frederic Emory, they descended on the ranch at three o'clock in the morning and took fifteen horses together with saddles, ropes, and other gear, giving a receipt signed by Walker as president of the republic—a leaf borrowed from the book of Narciso López. Emory proceeded with several of the men to San Diego and the others returned to Ensenada.

The next foray on the following day was also a predawn raid, this time on the ranch La Grulla about 12 miles south. Walker himself led it, and as at La Paz demonstrated his ruthlessness as a military commander. He tied up the people on the ranch, seized about twenty horses, and on leaving took two men along as hostages. This raid was a major mistake, for it made Walker an enemy who was to harass him with repeated attacks throughout his invasion of Lower California. At the ranch visiting his father was Antonio María Melendrez, whose chief activity heretofore seems to have been banditry and horse thievery. After the filibusters left, he rode to the town of Santo Tomás, a few miles south, and reported the incident to the military commandant, Francisco del Castillo Negrete.

A posse of about sixty men was formed and went in pursuit of Walker's party, overtaking it before it reached Ensenada. In the skirmish that took place one of the filibusters was killed and two were captured. Walker collected his force in a thick-walled adobe house at Ensenada to withstand a siege that began on December 5. It was not conducted very aggressively. Negrete, who had no heart for battle, withdrew with about one-half the besiegers after a few days, leaving Melendrez to fight on alone with twenty-five or thirty men. On the night of December 14, Walker sent out a patrol of some twenty men under the command of Second Lieutenant Timothy Crocker to attack the enemy encamped in a willow grove. Taken by surprise, the Mexicans fled in the darkness, leaving behind their arms and one small field piece. The filibusters lost one man in the siege, First Lieutenant John McKibbin. Ensenada was named Fort McKibbin in his honor.

News of the victory at Ensenada reached San Diego by courier on December 21 and San Francisco by boat on December 26. The information was incomplete but thereafter communiqués from Walker, written by his adjutant, Second Lieutenant Samuel Ruland, arrived with some regularity through a weekly pony express established between Fort McKibbin and San Diego. Since Ruland's dispatches contained only news favorable to the filibusters, no mention was made that the *Caroline* had departed during the siege with the major portion of the expedition's supplies that had been left aboard. The captured Mexican officials had bribed the first mate during an absence ashore of Captain Snow to take them to Guaymas.[5] The arrival of the *Anita* on December 20 with the reinforcements under Watkins' command did nothing to improve the living conditions of the advance troops because she carried few supplies: most had been lost overboard during the first rough night at sea.

Undaunted by these misfortunes, Walker moved to enlarge his control by sending an occupation force of sixty-five men to La Grulla under the command of Captain George R. Davidson and on December 24 issued a notice to the people of Lower California calling upon them to support the new government. "In entering the territory of Lower California," Walker proclaimed, "the force under my command had for its object, the amelioration of your social and political condition, and the improvement of the country, by all the arts which conduce to the civilization of people." Ruland's dispatches said that the order was favorably received. "The inhabitants are free in their intercourse with the officers and soldiers of the command," he wrote, "and all express a willingness to unite with the liberators in sustaining the new government. Frequent conferences have taken place between the wealthy rancheros and President Walker, and they are all amply satisfied with the existing state of things." Walker promised to pay for all supplies received and decreed a sentence of death to any persons under his command found guilty of plundering.

Ruland reported that Juan Bandini, who had gone from San Diego to his Guadalupe ranch, was on friendly terms with Walker. "Supplies for the troops have been furnished to a considerable extent by Don Juan, upon the order of the president," a dispatch stated, "and it is said that some have been offered by him gratuitously." What were gifts to Ruland was robbery to Bandini. "Walker's men made several forays on La Grulla and Santo Tomás, taking what they required or wanted, and neither Walker's own promises, which were made in his proclamation, nor the papers of safe-conduct given to several persons, were sufficient to insure safety or prevent abuses of power," Bandini wrote of the invaders. "Houses were broken into, families were forced to do the bidding of the invaders, and horses and saddles were taken from passing civilians. . . . Heaven help anyone who resisted or in any way refused to do what they commanded, for then the fury of the entire company was vented on him. . . ."[6]

The rout of Melendrez in the siege of Ensenada, the arrival of the *Anita*, and the successful raids in the countryside so colored Walker's visions of empire that on January 18 he proclaimed the formation of the Republic of Sonora, made up of two states, Sonora and Lower California, and issued four decrees to implement it.[7] The decrees were tersely written in dry, legalistic language, but Walker in addressing his assembled troops demonstrated that he had some talent for inspirational oratory:

> Soldiers of Sonora: You are about to undertake a most glorious enterprise.—You start to cross the Colorado in order to defend a helpless people, from the attacks of merciless savages. For years the population of Sonora has been the prey of the Apache Indians. Their property has been taken from them—their wives and children have been massacred, or consigned to a captivity worse than death, by the torturing fire of a ruthless foe. The men of Sonora have been forced to see their wives and daughters ravished—and babes at the breast have been torn from their mothers, and murdered before the eyes of captive parents. . . .
>
> You, soldiers! are now called upon to wrest the country from the rule of the Apache, and make it the abode of order and civilization. It is possible that in your chivalrous efforts you may be opposed by the Mexican government. If you are, when you meet the enemy, let the holiness of your cause, move your arms and strengthen your souls. When you strike at a Mexican foe, remember that you strike at an auxiliary of the Apache—at an accessory to the murder of innocent children, and the rape of helpless women. Fill your minds with these ideas, and victory will follow you on the plains of Sonora. In such a cause, failure is impossible, and triumph certain. The God of battles is with you, and you will be strong, and prevail against a host of enemies.[8]

Outsiders could only be aghast by Walker's presumptiousness —or amused. When news of his *coup de plume* reached San Francisco, the *Alta California* described it as "the climax of the ridiculous." Of Walker's naming himself president, the paper wrote: "He is a veritable Napoleon, of whom it may be said, as of the mighty Corsican, 'he disposes of courts and crowns and camps as mere titulary dignitaries of the chess board.' Santa Anna must feel obliged to the new president that he has not annexed any more of his territory than Sonora. It would have been just as cheap and easy to have annexed the whole of Mexico at once, and would have saved the trouble of making future proclamations."[9]

Walker's establishment of the Republic of Sonora was no more believable to many of the expeditionists than it was to the editor of the *Alta California*. In the month since the arrival of the *Anita* they had awakened from their dream of easy conquest and quick riches to the realities facing them. Their only food was what could be foraged in the arid countryside, and they were surrounded by unfriendly people. Moreover, the discipline Walker imposed, with his insistence on the petty observance of military etiquette, was difficult to bear by men who had never been able to adapt themselves to hard work and steady jobs. Accustomed to the egalitarian life of the goldfields, they resented the privileges rank gave their officers. Discontent had mounted and a week after Walker's proclamation there was a revolt in which about fifty men quitted the expedition to return to California.

Two versions of the rebellion appeared in the San Diego and San Francisco newspapers. The official version in a dispatch by Ruland dated January 25 related that Walker had heard murmurings among the troops for several days and, satisfied that some would not be content to stand guard and perform other military tasks, assembled the battalions in formation. Declaring his determination to have "none but soldiers in his command," he ordered those who would not pledge fealty to the expedition to leave the lines. "The departing men took some of their arms, and a party of ten was sent after them," Ruland wrote, "and, after some insolence on their part, and one bloody head, we recovered the arms and let them go their way."

Other information obtained by the newspapers, however, said that the increasing discontent was brought to the point of mutiny by an order of Walker's depriving Captain Davidson's company of horses and mules it had commandeered. At a muster Walker spoke at length on the purpose of the expedition and administered an oath requiring the men to hold up their right hands and swear "before Almighty God to stand by him until his flag was planted in Sonora." Twenty-six men in Davidson's company and about twenty others refused to take the oath. They started out for San Diego with their rifles but had not gone far when Walker came after them with a squad of fifteen men and told them to leave their arms. A young private who interrupted him was silenced by one of Walker's officers who struck him on the head with the butt of his rifle. Several did surrender their guns, but others smashed theirs against stone outcroppings.[10]

Thus, within a month after the arrival of the *Anita*, Walker found himself in a serious predicament, although his hopes were buoyed up by the expectation of receiving additional men because both Emory and Watkins had returned to California on recruiting missions. He also heard reports that many adventurers for whom there had been no accommodations on the *Anita* were taking passage on ships to San Diego to go overland to Fort McKibbin. (The *Alta California* said that 125 had sailed on the *Goliath* on January 26.) Actually, only a few men drifted into the filibuster camp from the north. Besides trouble within his own force, Walker faced an uprising against him from among the Mexicans, Melendrez being reported to be organizing a march against him. On February 10 the U.S. naval vessel *Portsmouth* anchored in the bay at Ensenada. Walker, in the belief the government had sent out a force against him, abandoned Fort McKibbin two days later, spiking his field guns and leaving behind eight seriously injured men.

Officers on the *Portsmouth* estimated that Walker now had about 140 men in his army, which even he must have realized was too small and too poorly trained to be an effective fighting unit. He determined upon a blustering expedient—to compel the Mexicans to submit to his government. With this in view, he marched his men to San Vicente, about 30 miles inland to the southeast of Ensenada, and on February 21 ordered all "inhabitants of this frontier of Lower California" to congregate at San Vicente five days hence "with the understanding that, should any of you fail to do so, you shall be punished very severely." Walker's depredations on the march were such as to terrorize the people. Arriving at Santo Tomás on February 14, the marauders slaughtered forty hogs belonging to one farmer, forcing him to appear before President Walker to take an oath of allegiance to the republic, seized whatever provisions could be found belonging to other residents, and on departing the next day took the alcalde, Manuel Retes, and a former Los Angeles resident, Augustín Horn, along as prisoners.[11]

The assembly of the people, in response to Walker's circular, took place on March 1, sixty-two natives renouncing their Mexican citizenship in an impressive ceremony, or so Ruland reported in a dispatch on March 3 to California newspapers.* A table was installed on the parade ground at the filibuster camp and two flags of the republic were placed before it on crossed staffs. President Walker, flanked by his cabinet, administered the oath of allegiance as one by one the Mexicans passed beneath the flags and stood before the table. A declaration drawn up by the assembly and presented to Walker said: "Sir, we doubt not that the establishment of the government in the new Republic will redound to the honor and happiness not only of ourselves, but of the country at large, because we believe that your Excellency, by means of a wise constitution and protective laws, will guarantee our property and interests for all time to come." The *Alta California* in printing the document introduced it with the tart comment: "The subjoined is the bombast declaration, prepared by Walker himself, which the poor natives were compelled, at the point of the bayonet, to sign or acknowledge."

This elaborate charade did little to improve Walker's situation. Augustín Horn, the chief source of information about the filibuster activities at San Vicente, later told the San Diego correspondent of the *Alta California* it was only through force that Walker was able to round up forty-two terrified inhabitants to attend the assembly, and fifteen of these were Indians who, except for two white men, were the only persons to take the oath voluntarily. The other twenty-five were induced to take it only upon

*Juan N. Almonte, minister to the United States, wrote a strong protest to Secretary of State William L. Marcy against this "audacious, scandalous and criminal" action by Walker. His version was that thirty-six Mexicans were rounded up and herded into the square at San Vicente. Walker read a proclamation to them and they were invited to swear fidelity to his government. Only eight persons, five of them Indians "who through clownishness and natural simplicity did not know what they were about to do," took the oath. Almonte's report continued: "Walker, irritated by this refusal, set those who had taken the oath at liberty, and told the rest that they should continue to remain prisoners, that they would be treated as enemies of the new Republic; that they did not enjoy *any* the threat of being killed.* After guaranteeing the Mexicans the safety of their property, Walker resumed his raids upon the country side. "The provisions of the impoverished inhabitants are exhausted," Horn said, "and starvation seems inevitable to those who may be unable to leave the country and escape the rapacity of these pirates of the land."

But Horn also revealed that the situation was not much better for the filibusters. Melendrez was in the vicinity with a small band, and although he never engaged the sorties from the filibuster camp in battle he constituted a constant threat. There were also threats within Walker's army because of the harsh living conditions and the unlikelihood that, now reduced to about seventy privates and fifty officers, it would achieve security at San Vicente let alone go to Sonora and convert the vast territory into a democratic state of peace and wealth.

Walker acted to discourage a rebellion. Ruland in his report of the oath-taking ceremony wrote: "We had to shoot two men today, because they so far mistook the object of our coming down here as to attempt to make up an organization, the purpose of which was to desert and go on a stealing and robbing and murdering expedition. Their names were T. F. Nelson and Arthur Morrison, and they were both from Illinois. Two others of the party were convicted, and one of them, Theodore Ryan, received fifty lashes, and the other, Edward C. Barnes, received twenty-five lashes, after which they both were drummed out of camp." The *Alta California's* correspondent, reporting this incident, commented: "If this be the fit doom of those accused of suspicious intentions, in the name of the God of Equity, what refinement of

right whatever, and that all their goods were confiscated." W. R. Manning, ed., *Diplomatic Correspondence of the United States, Inter-American Affairs, 1831–1860*, 9:710–12.

*Both Augustín Horn and Manuel Retes, the prisoners seized at Santo Tomás, refused to take the oath. As the chief Mexican official in the area, Retes later issued a circular explaining that none of the persons at San Vicente had taken the oath freely. He declared "null and void the oath extracted by barbarous violence . . . of defenceless inhabitants, surrounded by bayonets in the filibusters' encampment." *Alta California*, Mar. 25, 1854.

torture is the appropriate reward of the rest of the robbers of the gang, and the chief of them, the great arch-thief himself?"*

Despite Walker's ruthless punishment of the suspected plotters and the presence of Melendrez hovering about to attack, some of the filibusters did escape. The correspondent reported that ten or twelve deserters had reached San Diego and that a ranch owner who had just come into the town brought the intelligence that nine deserters had stopped at his place. These men said that about fifty others were preparing to desert and that Walker planned to leave San Vicente for Sonora or Texas on March 17. "This account, if true, will give color to the opinion held by some," the correspondent wrote, "that the Mexicans are in force in their immediate vicinity, and the President of the Republic is endeavoring to save himself and his followers by a precipitate retreat out of his dominions." The report was true in part: with about 100 men Walker had indeed set out for the Colorado River on March 20 with the intention of crossing it to enter into Sonora.[12]

Why Walker decided to invade Sonora is difficult to explain. With so few troops under his command he could hardly expect to establish even a foothold there, and it was unlikely reinforcements could reach him from San Francisco. Moreover, he could have maintained himself at San Vicente, at least for a time, and as a

*Walker later defended the execution of the two men as an example of civilized justice in contrast to the savagery of the Apaches and the failure of the Mexican government to protect its citizens: "A military execution is a good test of military discipline; for no duty is so repulsive to the soldier as that of taking the life from the comrade who had shared the perils of his arduous service. . . . But painful as was the duty, the men charged with the execution did not shrink from the performance of it; and the very field where the unfortunate victims of the law expiated their offense with their lives, was suggestive of comparison between the manner in which the expeditionists and the Mexican Government severally performed the duties of protection to society. The expeditionary force, drawn up to vindicate the law, by the most serious punishment it metes out to the offender, stood almost in the shadow of the ruins of the church of the mission fathers. The roofless buildings of the old monastery, the crumbling arches of the spacious chapel, the waste fields which showed no signs of former culture, and the skulking form of the half-clothed Indian, relapsing into savagism from which the holy fathers had rescued him, all declared the sort of protection Mexico had given to the persons as well as the property of the Peninsula." William Walker, *The War in Nicaragua*, pp. 22–23.

matter of fact left behind a detachment of about twenty men to hold the town. Except for the small band Melendrez had gathered, there was little danger from other inhabitants, few in number, unarmed, and demoralized by the filibusters' raids on the ranches in the area. There was always the chance, also, of receiving additional men from California.

For him to reach Sonora meant marching more than 200 miles to the north over barren mountainous terrain to the Colorado River where it empties into the Gulf of California and crossing the stream to Sonora. Neither Walker nor members of his army ever told the story of the trek in detail, and it can only be pieced together from the inconsistent reports in the newspapers from a variety of sources, mostly deserters who escaped to San Diego or Fort Yuma, where there was a garrison of the U.S. army.

The first information of the march reached Los Angeles in mid-April from a Dr. Thomas Foster on his return from a trip to Fort Yuma. It came from about a dozen of Walker's men who arrived at the fort "nearly in a naked and starving condition" on April 7. Walker had left San Vicente driving about a hundred head of cattle to provide the army with food. Crossing the mountains, a few men deserted and about twenty of the cattle were lost. In the latter part of the trek they were followed by a band of Indians who, when Walker camped about 6 miles above the mouth of the river, stole about thirty cattle. Five Indians were seized as hostages for the return of the cattle, three of whom were shot later while attempting to escape. The Colorado, at this point about 400 yards wide, was crossed on rafts about April 4. Walker was unable, however, to get the cattle across since they drowned when driven into the stream. Foster's informants said that Walker's whole command was "in a most miserable and destitute condition, wearing the same clothing with which they went to the country, and this is in tatters and rags." Walker himself was no better clad and had "but one boot and a piece of a boot."

"On the second day after the crossing," Foster's report continued, "there was much disaffection in camp, and in a barren country which they had invaded with hostile intentions, with few means of repelling attacks, exhausted, naked, starvation staring them in the face, many men prepared to abandon the waning fortunes of the expedition, and return to the settlements for an honest livelihood." Walker, too, saw that the Sonoran invasion was hopeless, and with about thirty-five faithful followers recrossed the river to Lower California and set out to return to San Vicente.[13]

Five days after starting the retreat, Walker and his bedraggled troops encountered Melendrez at a ranch called La Calentura, where two of his men were taken prisoner in a brief skirmish. Thereafter, Melendrez gave the filibusters no rest. Always avoiding a pitched battle if possible, the Mexican leader with his band of eighty men trailed along after the liberation army until it reached San Vicente on April 17, where Walker found that the small force he had left behind had been annihilated. Melendrez made his appearance on a hill opposite the town and "trailed the filibusters' flag in the dust and otherwise 'insulted' the party." The Mexicans fled, however, when Walker sent out a force to attack their position. Melendrez soon received support from Juan Bandini, informed by the Mexican guerrilla that Walker planned to make the Guadalupe ranch his headquarters. Bandini was able to supply about thirty men—himself, his sons and employees, and volunteers—to support Melendrez.

Walker's only hope now for survival was to seek safety across the border of the United States at San Diego. He left San Vicente on April 19 and a few days later occupied the Guadalupe ranch, where he was able to hold out until April 26, when he resumed his march. Melendrez, with his enemy now in retreat, sent under a flag of truce an offer promising Walker a free pass out of the country if he would lay down his arms and surrender. "Walker read the message and threw it beneath his feet, then, by a series of well applied kicks, ejected the courier from his presence," the *Alta California* reported.

The Melendrez strategy, according to Bandini, was to remain always on the defensive, "depriving the invaders of all means of sustenance, maintaining a strict watch on their movements, leaving them always an unobstructed outlet to Alta California, and preventing them from taking any road that would lead them to an easily fortified position." As a result, Walker was able to lead his men to the border, which under view of his Mexican tormenters and curious spectators from San Diego, he crossed on May 8 and surrendered to a detachment of U.S. troops under the command of Major J. McKinstry and Captain H. S. Burton.

Of the 200 or so men who had formed Walker's expedition, only thirty-three—thirteen officers and twenty privates, corporals, and sergeants—remained in his force and signed a "parole of honor" to report themselves to San Francisco to Major General John E. Wool, newly appointed commander of the Pacific division of the army, to answer to charges of violation of the neutrality laws. The *Alta California* editorialized on their arrival on May 15: "After months of hardship, toil, privation and suffering, the remnant of the Republic's army has returned to the place of its enlistment, with its banners trailing in the dust, with no wreath of laurel twined around its brow, received with no welcoming songs, such as proclaim the return of the defenders of their country's rights or honor, but in the humiliating position of prisoners, held to answer the violated laws of their country."[14]

While San Franciscans avidly read of Walker's adventures, they were almost equally excited by dramatic events at home, most of them acted out in the courtroom: the trials of Walker's collaborators for getting off the *Anita* expedition, of the Mexican consul, Luis María del Valle, for sending a party of emigrants, most of them Frenchmen, to Sonora to protect the province from filibusters, and of the French consul, Guillaume Patrice Dillon, for abetting this project.

The crackdown was due to the arrival on February 14, 1854, of Major General John E. Wool to replace Ethan Allen Hitchcock as commander of the Pacific department of the army. A hero of the War of 1812 and the Mexican War, Wool was known as a harsh disciplinarian in enforcing regulations and as a martinet in upholding military etiquette. In attempting to stamp out filibusterism, he believed he was obeying orders of his commander in chief, President Pierce, and the secretary of war, Jefferson Davis. Fearful that Walker and French filibusters would prevent ratification of the Gadsden Treaty, Pierce had issued a proclamation on January 18 calling upon civil and military officers to arrest any violators of the neutrality laws, and Davis had instructed him "to the utmost of your ability" to detect and stop the fitting out of armed expeditions. Wool acted promptly, within two weeks obtaining enough information to take action against Count Raousset-Boulbon, Henry P. Watkins, and other Walker associates.

In Mexico City President Santa Anna had also acted, in an ingenious way, to thwart American filibusters. When news of the invasion of Lower California reached Colonel Manuel María Gándara, governor of Sonora, he issued a blood-thirsty proclamation calling upon the people to resist and describing the interlopers as "a contemptible band of plunderers" who "should be cut into a thousand pieces." Gándara's exclamatory call to arms did not instil confidence in Santa Anna that the people could put down an invasion. He was worried not only about the Walker expedition but also about the continued activity of Raousset-Boulbon, who, on returning to San Francisco after his frustrating visit to Mexico City, had set about enlisting his compatriots for another foray into Sonora. Documents discovered after his departure revealed that he had been in contact with rebel leaders in Sonora and Sinaloa to support them by bringing in French troops.

Santa Anna, through his foreign affairs minister, Manuel Diez de Bonilla, protested, on January 17, to the French chargé d'affaires, Alphonse Dano, about the count's criminal plans. But not expecting very much to come of this, Santa Anna hit upon a scheme to circumvent Raousset-Boulbon. It was to instruct Del Valle, on February 1, to sign individual contracts with foreigners of the Catholic faith to defray their expenses to Guaymas for settlement in Mexico. Frenchmen were to be particularly sought, to separate them from Raousset-Boulbon's schemes. As His Serene Highness conceived the project, it would solve all his problems. "By this measure, the Government proposed to defeat the notorious illegal plans of Raousset," Bonilla later explained, "and while it would thus avoid disagreeable discussions with the United States, it would encourage emigrants to settle in the country. . . . "

Del Valle acted immediately to recruit emigrants by inserting notices in the San Francisco newspapers. The *Alta California* praised the project: "We hope to see the Mexican consul succeed in his efforts to send the whole number of 1,000 men as advertised for. They will give life to business in Sonora, and in a market to be supplied from San Francisco. It is said that Americans are not specially invited, and it appears highly reasonable that it should be so. . . . Santa Anna would be more of a fool than he is generally reckoned to be, if he would at this moment send 1,000 armed Americans to Guaymas to be commanded by Mexican troops."

Del Valle was assisted in obtaining enlistments by Dillon despite instructions received by the consul on January 21 from the French chargé d'affaires in Mexico City to prevent his countrymen from taking part in the Raousset-Boulbon scheme because the government would consider every invader, whatever his nationality, as a pirate. The instructions, however, did not forbid Dillon from responding to Del Valle's requests for enlisting Frenchmen in Santa Anna's emigration scheme. He cooperated fully, to the extent that, as he wrote Del Valle on March 29, he had enrolled 450 Frenchmen, advancing them subsistence money on the promise of reimbursement from the Mexican government.[15]

Meanwhile, General Wool had maintained a close surveillance over the activities of Watkins and Raousset-Boulbon. He believed that the two were working together to send men to reinforce Walker at Ensenada. To stop them he obtained the arrest on March 1—the same day Walker was exacting his oath of fealty from the frightened Mexicans at San Vicente—of Watkins, Major John N. Baird, a state senator, Captain George R. Davidson, and a Dr. Hoge, Walker's physician. Raousset-Boulbon, however, avoided arrest, having left, Wool was informed, for Santa Barbara. The grand jury that heard evidence of the filibuster plans, however, issued indictments only against Watkins and Davidson. Two weeks later, Frederic Emory, as a result of the president's proclamation, was arrested by the naval commander at San Diego and sent to San Francisco for trial.

Wool quickly became suspicious of the Mexican emigration scheme being sponsored by Del Valle and called on him for details. When the consul explained that the intent was to detach as many Frenchmen as possible from Raousset-Boulbon and to swear them to allegiance to the Mexican government, Wool asked if they could be relied upon. The answer was "yes," as they would be recommended by passports issued by the French consul. "I informed him that he had been deceived," Wool related, "and that the party, instead of settling in the country and doing fealty to the government, would become a filibustering one, and I had no doubt would be commanded by Count Raousset de Boulbon, who intended to relieve Walker from his perilous position."[16] Wool was wrong in his belief that Raousset-Boulbon planned to unite with Walker in an attempt to take over Sonora, and possibly wrong in suspecting Dillon of conspiring with the count to send Frenchmen to Guaymas, "all red republicans and revolutionists," as he regarded them, to take possession of the country in the name of the French government. But whether the count and the consul were working together was immaterial. Assuming command of the Frenchmen when they reached Guaymas was Raousset-Boulbon's intention, and it is what he did when they went to Sonora later in the year. Santa Anna's cleverness in seeking to circumvent Raousset-Boulbon merely provided him the means, at no cost, to get his men into Mexico.

Henry P. Watkins' trial opened in the U.S. District Court on March 20, the same day that Walker set out from San Vicente for Sonora. The district attorney, S. W. Inge, introduced witnesses who testified that Watkins had taken the leading part in fitting out the *Anita* and enlisting recruits. Watkins' attorneys, Edmund Randolph and Henry S. Foote, a former governor of Mississippi, did not attempt to rebut the facts in the case but relied mainly on the argument that there had been no violation of the law. Randolph in his closing speech maintained that Watkins had committed no hostile act against Mexico until he had left the jurisdiction of the United States: his only hostility while in the country had consisted in *thinking*, and he could not be tried for what he *did* because his only actions took place in Mexico. Foote's argument was that the neutrality laws were unconstitutional.

The jury deliberated five hours before reaching a verdict of guilty with a recommendation for mercy. Judge Ogden Hoffman, an avid adherent of filibusterism himself, imposed a fine of $1,500, a light punishment, he explained, but he regarded the law vindicated by the conviction alone. A month later the district attorney entered a nolle prosequi in the case of Captain Davidson with the explanation that he had been unable to obtain enough evidence to satisfy a jury. The following week Emory pleaded guilty to the charge against him, receiving a $1,500 fine, as had Watkins. Both professed inability to pay. Instead of being jailed, however, they were released by Judge Hoffman, who said he would take the matter under advisement. "Thus are matters managed in California," the authors of *Annals of San Francisco* commented on the way in which filibusters were allowed to escape punishment.[17]

The Mexican and French consuls did not have such an easy time in the courts. They had enrolled 800 men and had chartered a ship, the *Challenge*, to transport them to Guaymas. The ship was ready to sail on March 23, but her departure, upon the insistence of General Wool, was held up on the technical ground that the number of passengers, 540, was greater than the number she was authorized to carry. He permitted her to sail on April 2, however, when the number of passengers was reduced and he was assured by both Del Valle and Dillon that they were merely colonists.

Del Valle, however, had been arrested two days before the sailing and his case came to trial on April 18. There was considerable public sentiment in his favor, the *Alta California* characterizing him as "a quiet old gentleman" whose only offense was trying to send a few Frenchmen to Guaymas. Prosecution witnesses testified that Del Valle conspired to transport 1,000 men to Sonora for one year's service in the Mexican army at a rate of pay of $30 a month upon the completion of which they would be entitled to a grant of land. The trial created no excitement until Dillon refused to appear as a witness for the defense on the ground that, according to a treaty between France and the United States, consuls would not be compelled to appear as witnesses before the courts. When Judge Hoffman decided, however, that he should be brought into court and ordered his arrest for contempt, from 1,000 to 2,000 animated and voluble Frenchmen gathered at the consulate bent on freeing him. The *Alta California* commented that "no event in the history of San Francisco has created more general and intense excitement." The excitement abated next day when Judge Hoffman dismissed the charge. Del Valle's trial ended on April 28 when a jury, after fifteen minutes' deliberation, returned a verdict of guilty.[18]

The filibuster situation in San Francisco held little interest until May 15, when the city was again aroused to excitement by the indictment of Dillon for violation of the neutrality laws and the arrival of Walker, with the remnant of his army, on the steamship *Southerner* from San Diego. Both Watkins and Walker were subpoenaed to tell what they knew of the relations between the two consuls at Dillon's trial, which opened on May 23, but they refused to testify on the ground of self-incrimination. After deliberating six hours, the jury was unable to agree on a verdict.

The prosecution of the two consuls ended on May 29, when the district attorney, who only reluctantly on pressure exerted by Wool had begun it, entered a nolle prosequi in the case of Dillon and moved to suspend further proceedings against Del Valle. The reason may have been that Wool had lost interest on the receipt, on May 18, of a reprimand from Jefferson Davis that it was not a part of his duties to "initiate arrests and prosecutions for civil misdemeanors." Wool in a tart reply defended his actions as coming well within the instructions contained in President Pierce's proclamation and Davis's own orders to him. "It is, however, too late to refer to my instructions," he wrote. "The work, whether for good or for evil, has been done." Alluding to the arrests and trials, he expressed the hope that an end had been put "at least for a time, to filibustering, and leave me more able to attend more strictly to my professional duties."[19]

General Wool was mistaken in his belief that he had stopped filibustering, for he had been unsuccessful in catching in his net Raousset-Boulbon, who, he had written Davis, was "cautious, and accomplishes his ends through the medium of others." He had put a crimp, however, in the count's plans. Alarmed by the arrests of Del Valle and Dillon, Raousset-Boulbon's financial backers hesitated to risk money on his venture, and he was able to obtain only a two-ton, unseaworthy pilot boat, the *Belle*, to take arms to the Frenchmen who had sailed on the *Challenge*. Loading on board only 180 carbines and ammunition—the schooner was too small to take a field gun he had bought—Raousset-Boulbon sailed on the night of May 23 with four companions. Battered by storms, the schooner several times came near to capsizing, once the rudder broke and she could not be steered, and once she ran aground, requiring two weeks' delay until repairs could be effected to continue the voyage. Finally, toward the end of June, Raousset-Boulbon was able to bring her into Punta Colorada, a few miles west of Guaymas.

In the meantime, the passengers on the *Challenge* had been received at Guaymas and permitted to organize themselves into military companies. Their arrival on April 19 had caused some consternation in General José María Yañez, recently named head of the military forces there. He had been instructed by Santa Anna to accept the emigrants into his own forces, but he was unprepared for such a large number coming all at once. His own troops numbered only about 200 men and he was faced with the problem of assimilating more than 400 foreign soldiers, about 300 of them Frenchmen and the others Germans and men of other nationalities. Captained by Leon Desmarais, an ex-sergeant of the French army designated by Raousset-Boulbon as his second in command, the Frenchmen were not amenable to any proposals of Yañez, as they were well paid and well fed, had no duties to perform, and saw that Yañez was too weak to compel them to do anything.

For two weeks after Raousset-Boulbon's arrival he and Yañez were two indecisive commanders. The count was irresolute because he was not sure of the support of all his compatriots and the Mexican because his troops were outnumbered and he did not dare to act until he received reinforcements from Hermosillo. A state of uneasy truce existed until the night of July 12, when several Frenchmen became involved in a fray with townspeople. The next morning Raousset-Boulbon sent a message to Yañez demanding that "in view of the hostile dispositions" taken against the Frenchmen he be given guaranties of their safety in the shape of hostages, munitions, and artillery. Yañez replied that though he had no intention of attacking he could not agree to these terms. Emboldened by this conciliatory attitude, Raousset-Boulbon addressed his followers, appealing to them to take up arms and earn "the glorious appellation of Frenchmen." Lacking Raousset-Boulbon's enthusiasm for glory, they only reluctantly agreed to assault the Mexican barracks, attacking in four companies of seventy-five men each. The better-trained and better-armed Mexicans repulsed them and they fled in disarray, many to the French consulate to put themselves under the protection of their government.

Subsequently, the Frenchmen were dispersed into the interior or sent out of the country by one route or another, although except for a few they were not permitted to return to San Francisco, where it was assumed they would be likely to join another filibuster attack on Sonora. Raousset-Boulbon, however, was court-martialed and sentenced to be shot. During his period of captivity, he showed great fortitude and calmly went about writing farewell letters to his family and friends. Just before sunrise on August 12 he was taken to a plaza where a huge crowd was assembled to view his execution. His death was as histrionic as had been his life. He is reported to have addressed the firing squad: "Allons, mes braves! Do your duty; aim well—at the heart!" The next moment came the volley and he fell to the ground.[20]

While Raousset-Boulbon was sailing the *Belle* down the coast of Lower California, Walker and two of his officials in the Republic of Sonora, John M. Jarnigan, secretary of war, and Howard A. Snow, captain of the *Caroline* and secretary of the navy, were brought into court on June 2 to face charges of violating the neutrality laws. They pleaded not guilty and asked for a postponement of the trial to obtain the testimony of the republic's secretary of state, Frederic Emory, who had left San Francisco after being discharged from his sentence. The postponement was granted and the three defendants were released on bail bond of $10,000 each.[21]

Walker returned to Marysville to resume his practice of law, very likely with the intention of seeking a career in politics as he was elected a delegate from Yuba County to the state Democratic convention, which opened at Sacramento on July 18. Walker went to the convention committed to a faction led by David C. Broderick, a former Tammany politician in New York who headed the Northern radical and antislavery wing of the Democratic party in California and was the political boss of San Francisco. Broderick's political enemy was California's first U.S. senator, William M. Gwin, who represented the Southern wing of the party, known as the Chivalry, which favored the extension of slavery into the territories seeking statehood.[22]

Because of Walker's work for Broderick at the convention, he was invited to join the staff of his organ, the *Democratic State Journal*, published at Sacramento. He worked on the paper only a few weeks, however, resigning to return to San Francisco as editor of the *Commercial-Advertiser*, which had recently been purchased by a young New Englander and former Boston editor, Byron Cole, who was involved in a number of get-rich-quick projects, including one scheme for developing the gold regions of

Honduras. Walker had been accused of wanting to introduce slavery into his Republic of Sonora, but in the *Demoratic State Journal* he supported the antislavery policies of Broderick and in the *Commercial-Advertiser* opposed the "hot-headed and narrow-minded" Southerners who had been willing to repeal the Missouri Compromise to support the Kansas-Nebraska Act of Stephen A. Douglas. He sided with the Southern moderates on the slavery question and condemned the "ultra-slavery men" who were "the most active and efficient agents abolitionists can have in the Southern States." "The true friends of the South," he said in one editorial, "are those who repudiate the ideas and acts of the South Carolina school and who believe the true policy of the slave States is conservative and not aggressive."[23]

Walker's trial for violation of the neutrality laws opened on October 13. His attorneys were his friend Edmund Randolph and Calhoun Benham, but he himself took part in the cross-examination of prosecution witnesses and acted as his own attorney in conducting his defense. In his opening statement, he said he would introduce evidence to show that at the time of leaving San Francisco his intention was to go to Guaymas and thence to the northern frontier and that only after he had got out to sea did he change his plan and land at La Paz. He called only two witnesses. James L. Springer, a resident of Marysville, testified that Frederic Emory, when he first broached the Mexico scheme to Walker, had outlined a plan to go to Sonora and develop the abandoned mines, the original intention being to go overland from the United States. The other witness was Howard A. Snow, captain of the *Caroline*, who testified that he had made a contract with Emory to carry the expeditionists to Guaymas at £20 a head. The decision to land at Cape San Lucas, he said, was made only two days before the arrival there, and no force was used at La Paz or San Vicente to get the residents to swear allegiance to the republic. In his argument to the jury, Walker said he had assumed his defense only to vindicate his honor and that of his followers who were "bound on an errand of humanity" in going to Mexico. When the case went to the jury, it was out only eight minutes and returned with a verdict of not guilty.[24]

Shortly before the trial, Byron Cole had sold the *Commercial-Advertiser*, which was losing money, to pursue his gold-mining scheme in Honduras, and Walker had returned to the staff of Broderick's *Democratic State Journal*. One of Cole's associates was William V. Wells, a fellow Bostonian who had been an agent and explorer for several mining and commercial enterprises. In August the two, with a third associate, James D. Whelpley, sailed for Central America to gather information about gold prospects. They landed at San Juan del Sur in Nicaragua to go overland to Honduras. At León, headquarters of a revolutionary junta attempting to seize the government, Cole's interest was diverted from the mining scheme to a colonization scheme in Nicaragua. Francisco Castellón, leader of the revolution, wishing to obtain American soldiers to strengthen his rabble of an army, proposed that "the renowned Walker" be invited to land a force that would help in the liberation of Nicaragua.

Cole agreed to a contract in which Walker would head an expedition of 300 Americans to join the Nicaraguan rebels and if victorious against the government would at the end of their service be allotted land from a grant of 21,000 acres to be given him. He hurried back to California to present the proposal to Walker. It was not entirely satisfactory. Walker thought the land grant offered too little inducement in view of the risks of the enterprise and the contract to send a military expedition would violate the neutrality laws. Cole returned to Nicaragua to obtain a contract arranging for sending colonists to Nicaragua and increasing the land grant to 52,000 acres. In this he was successful and dispatched the new contract to Walker on December 29. Thus was a new opportunity opened for Walker to fulfill his destiny.[25]

PART THREE

The Golden Transit of Nicaragua

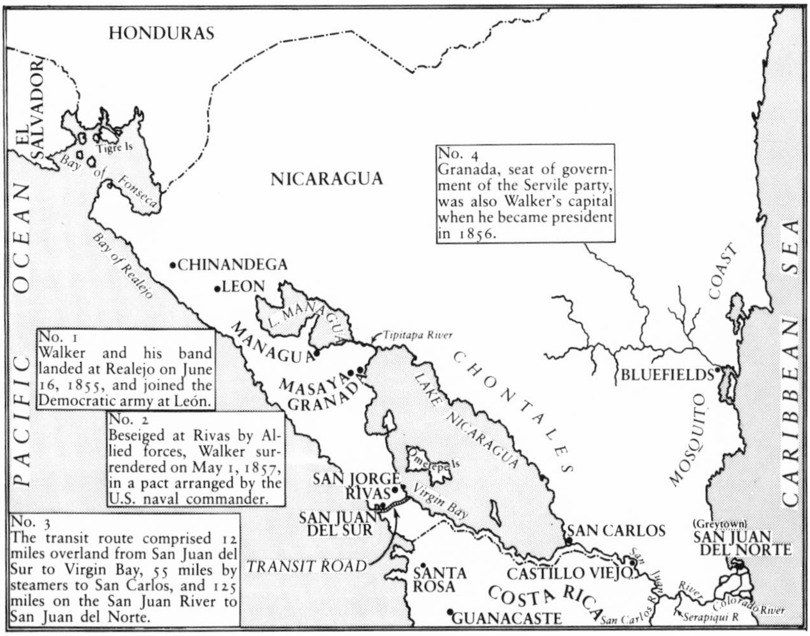
HONDURAS
EL SALVADOR
NICARAGUA
PACIFIC OCEAN
CARIBBEAN SEA
Tigre Is
Bay of Fonseca
Bay of Realejo
•CHINANDEGA
•LEON
L. MANAGUA
MANAGUA
Tipitapa River
MASAYA
GRANADA
CHONTALES
LAKE NICARAGUA
Ometepe Is
SAN JORGE
RIVAS
Virgin Bay
SAN JUAN DEL SUR
TRANSIT ROAD
SANTA ROSA
GUANACASTE
COSTA RICA
SAN CARLOS
CASTILLO VIEJO
San Juan River
San Carlos R
Serapiqui R
Colorado River
(Greytown)
SAN JUAN DEL NORTE
BLUEFIELDS
MOSQUITO COAST
No. 1
Walker and his band landed at Realejo on June 16, 1855, and joined the Democratic army at León.
No. 2
Beseiged at Rivas by Allied forces, Walker surrendered on May 1, 1857, in a pact arranged by the U.S. naval commander.
No. 3
The transit route comprised 12 miles overland from San Juan del Sur to Virgin Bay, 55 miles by steamers to San Carlos, and 125 miles on the San Juan River to San Juan del Norte.
No. 4
Granada, seat of government of the Servile party, was also Walker's capital when he became president in 1856.

William Walker's operations in Nicaragua

CHAPTER TEN

To Unite the Two Great Oceans

More or less ignored by the United States before President Polk through the acquisition of California and New Mexico had given continental dimensions to the country, Central America in recent years had assumed an importance to the nation of an artery in the human body. The rapid development of California after the discovery of gold had made it essential to maintain lines of communication between the east and west coasts, difficult because of the vast expanse of unoccupied land between the two sections. The Central American isthmus offered the readiest means of passage, and as a result the attention of Americans more and more turned to the five states in the region—Nicaragua, Costa Rica, Honduras, Guatemala, and El Salvador.

From the days of Spanish imperialism, a ship passage across the isthmus that would provide a shorter trade route with the Orient than sailing around Cape Horn had been sought. After it was found that a natural waterway did not exist, schemes were proposed to build canals, especially after the break-up of the Spanish empire and the establishment of independent republics in the 1820s when dozens of routes were considered. The chief projects were canals across Panama, Nicaragua, and Tehuantepec. But though a canal was to be only a dream for years to come, overland routes offered no insurmountable obstacles. The first developed was at Panama, where the isthmus is only about 50 miles wide, its neutrality being guaranteed by a treaty signed betweeen the United States and New Granada (Colombia) in 1848. The second was in Nicaragua, where American business enterprise, specifically that of the shipping buccaneer Cornelius Vanderbilt, made it a strong competitor for dominance of passenger and cargo traffic between the oceans.

The Vanderbilt enterprise in Nicaragua had been in operation four years before the little country, torn by civil strife, became the objective of filibusters, not only William Walker with his contract to send an expedition from California but also the land speculator and developer Colonel Henry L. Kinney, who in 1852 had attracted national attention when he held his fair at Corpus Christi to lure settlers. A year before Walker signed his contract with Francisco Castellón to supply soldiers for his rebel army, Kinney had formed the Nicaragua Land and Mining Company in New York and had advertised for colonists to go to Nicaragua. The struggle extending over several years for control of transit rights on the isthmus is an essential part of the expansionist history of the United States and of Manifest Destiny in which the filibusters figured so prominently in the 1850s.

An early official expression of U.S. interest in the construction of an isthmian canal came in 1835 when President Jackson appointed Colonel Charles Biddle of Philadelphia a special emissary to investigate "the present state of the projects for uniting the Atlantic and Pacific oceans." Biddle, relying on hearsay rather than on first-hand investigation, decided that the only feasible route was at Panama, and he joined a syndicate formed to build a combined steamboat and railroad passage from the mouth of the Chagres River on the Caribbean across the isthmus to Panama on the Pacific. He obtained a concession for the project from New Granada, but his death soon afterward caused his associates to drop the plan.

A little over a decade later the United States, more by chance than intention, secured the rights for the government or her citizens to a Panama transit and became the guarantor of the sovereignty of New Granada over the route. This came about when President Polk sent Benjamin A. Bidlack to New Granada as chargé d'affaires with instructions to arrange a commercial treaty. The New Granadan government, fearful that Great Britain or some European nation might seize the isthmus, insisted as a condition for the treaty upon a pledge by the United States to protect her

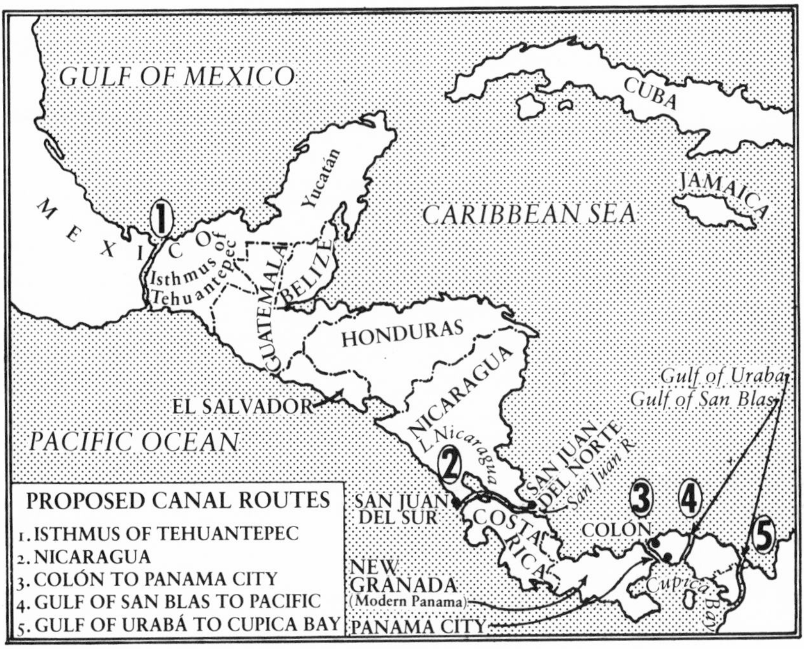

possession of it. Partly because of Polk's preoccupation with the Mexican War, Bidlack's repeated requests for instructions went unanswered; finally, he decided to act on his own responsibility and signed a treaty on December 12, 1846, that included the protection clause. Received with no great interest by Polk, the treaty was sent to the Senate on February 10, 1847, with a recommendation for approval. So slight was the interest in it that more than a year elapsed before the Senate finally got around to approving it on June 3, 1848.[1]

When gold was discovered in California and thousands of fortune-hunters set out for the west coast, their passage by way of Panama had been prepared for by the establishment of steamship service from New York and New Orleans to Chagres and after crossing the isthmus from Panama to California and Oregon. The government had been instrumental in financing the service through subsidies for carrying the mail. In March 1847 Congress had passed bills authorizing the postal department and the navy—the idea had been that merchant vessels could easily be converted to auxiliary warships—to contract with private firms for a service to Oregon.

The contract for the Atlantic route, offering an annual subsidy of $290,000, was let to Albert G. Sloo, who had established a steamship line on Lake Pontchartrain shortening the route between New Orleans and Mobile for which he had obtained a liberal mail contract he later had sold at a profit. Sloo sold the Atlantic concession to a group of New York capitalists headed by the rough-and-ready financier George Law. Although the Pacific route was not so attractive as the Atlantic route, the contract offering a subsidy of only $199,000, it was picked up by William Henry Aspinwall from Arnold Harris, a Tennessee politician and promoter, who like Sloo had obtained it as a speculation. After the California gold discovery, scores of ships at first and then hundreds sailed from eastern ports to Chagres, where the passengers disembarked and crossed over to the Pacific.

With their regular service and large ships, the United States Mail Steamship Company of George Law and the Pacific Mail Steamship Company of William H. Aspinwall soon dominated the transportation of passengers to and from California and the shipments of gold to the financial centers of the East. In 1848 only 355 passengers went to California via Panama; the number rose by leaps in the years that followed—4,624 in 1849; 11,299 in 1850; 15,464 in 1851; and 21,263 in 1852. After 1848 the backward trek began—of those who had made their fortune or those who had failed—in lesser but nevertheless large numbers: 1,629 in 1849; 7,770 in 1850; 14,189 in 1851; and 11,845 in 1852. Gold shipments were almost exclusively by way of Panama, rising from $4,140,200 in 1849 to $40,233,915 in 1852. The profits to the owners of the two lines and their stockholders were enormous despite the intense competition of other companies, and possessing ships was a surer way to wealth than searching for gold.[2]

The successes of Law and Aspinwall aroused the combative instinct as well as the cupidity of the multimillionaire Cornelius Vanderbilt, known as "Commodore" since being given this appellation by a newspaper because of his militant tactics in the shipping wars of the previous four decades fought around the harbor of New York. Vanderbilt had made his fortune by boldly entering into competition with established shipping lines, slashing fares and rates, and, when his opponents began losing money, selling out to them at a profit. In the winter of 1848–1849 he could be seen poring over Central American maps and nautical almanacs at his townhouse in New York City. His interest, however, was fixed not on Panama but on Nicaragua.

Born on Staten Island in 1794, the son of a farmer who occasionally operated a boat in the harbor, young Cornele, a big, robust youth who had quit school at the age of eleven and had done a man's work since, borrowed $100 in 1812 to buy his first vessel, a two-masted, flat-bottomed craft, and set up in business ferrying passengers and freight to New York City. During the war with England he obtained a government contract to carry supplies to forts in the vicinity and after the treaty of peace bought a schooner for $1,000 to enter the coastal trade. In 1818, at the age of twenty-four, he estimated his worth at $15,000 and seemed on the way to greater success as the owner of a prosperous line of sailing ships when he surprised his friends by selling out and going to work for Thomas Gibbons, who was bucking the steamboat monopoly granted Robert Fulton in the New York waters. The reason for this sudden decision was that he realized steamships would eventually clear the seas of sailing vessels and he would be paid to train himself in the new system of transportation. He remained with Gibbons' line for almost ten years, helping Gibbons smash the Fulton monopoly and learning every aspect of steamboating from designing vessels and handling them as pilot and captain to managing them as financial enterprises. When, in 1829 at the age of thirty-five, Vanderbilt decided to establish his own independent line, he was as well equipped as anyone to go into and survive in this ruthless business.

Competing first for the shipping on the Philadelphia route, Vanderbilt dismayed the opposition by bringing on such a cut-rate war that it decided if this new rival could not be crushed he could be bought. It was a tactic Vanderbilt was to employ in establishing other routes—a kind of blackmail that brought him increasing wealth. For example, when he established ships on the New York-Albany run on the Hudson River and destroyed the profits of competitors by his low rates, he agreed to abandon it for ten years in exchange for $100,000 in cash and an annual payment of $5,000. Afterward, he invested in real estate and railroads. Five years later, Moses Y. Beach of the *New York Sun*, in *Wealth and Biography of the Wealthy Citizens of New York City*, estimated Vanderbilt's fortune at $1.2 million and described him as having more "go-aheadativeness" in building and driving steamboats than any other Dutchman. By 1850 his fortune was estimated at $11 million. Though not above shady dealings, Vanderbilt had made his way by sheer competence and doggedness: he designed and built better ships than other men, he sailed them more efficiently, and he provided better facilities and service.

Possessing one of the great fortunes of America and able to live royally on the increment if he chose, Vanderbilt at fifty-five was not ready to settle down to a life of ease. He saw that the land transit at Panama was not the final answer to a trade route to the Pacific, that a waterway to avoid transshipment of goods and passengers was needed. His studies indicated that Nicaragua was probably the best location for a canal, but he needed to know more before he could act. He therefore sent an army engineer, Colonel David L. White, to Nicaragua to investigate the situation and to contract with the government for transit rights, preferably a canal, if the project seemed promising.[3]

A canal across Nicaragua was not a new idea. As early as February 1825 the Nicaraguan minister to Washington had proposed to Secretary of State John Quincy Adams that the two countries co-operate in construction of one. Upon becoming president, Adams instructed his secretary of state, Henry Clay, to have the American chargé d'affaires study the possibilities, but nothing came of this. The next year, however, the New York merchant Aaron Palmer obtained a concession for the Central American and United States Atlantic and Pacific Canal Company, one of the directors of which was the builder of the Erie Canal, former Governor De Witt Clinton. The company was never able to raise the capital to start the project.

American interest in a Nicaraguan canal was revived in 1838 when a group that included Aaron Clark, mayor of New York City, petitioned Congress to sponsor construction of an inter-oceanic waterway. President Van Buren appointed the traveler and adventurer John Lloyd Stephens, whose books on his trips through Egypt, Arabia, the Holy Land, Turkey, Greece, and Russia had enchanted readers by their graphic descriptions and their narrative drive, on a nebulous mission to Central America to find out if the political situation was of the sort to permit negotiations and treaties.

The Central American Federation of former Spanish colonies, Costa Rica, Nicaragua, El Salvador, Guatemala, and Honduras, had fallen apart, and Stephens "travelled over all Guatemala looking for the government to which he was accredited, and which he never could find." His survey of Nicaragua led him to conclude that a canal was a dubious proposition. Though he did not find much promise in the future of the country, he became interested in the past of the isthmus and out of his experiences wrote *Incidents of Travel in Central America, Chiapas, and Yucatán* and *Incidents of Travel in Yucatán*, widely read volumes that told of lost civilizations whose monuments and temples had long been covered by the jungle vegetation.

In the next several years French and Dutch promoters interested themselves in Nicaraguan canal projects, but it was not until the gold rush that American capitalists returned to the field. Cornelius Vanderbilt was not alone in noting the importance of Nicaraguan transit rights. In February 1849 William Wheelwright of the Pacific Steam Navigation Company sought this concession, and the next month Dr. David Tilden Brown sought it for the Compañía de Tránsito de Nicaragua and was successful to the extent that he obtained a contract that was ratified by the Nicaraguan congress and failed only through the disapproval of the president. But before then the matter had become immensely complicated by the machinations of Great Britain seeking strategic locations for dominating the trade of the region before it fell to the expanding commerce of the United States.[4]

Great Britain had maintained tenuous claims to certain Central American territory since the 1750s when the pirates, many of them Englishmen, who raided the gold-laden ships of Spain from the hidden bays along the coast began to find this industry no longer remunerative. In Southern Yucatán, where the Belize River empties into the Gulf of Mexico, the buccaneers were gradually replaced by loggers who cut logwood for its valuable dye ingredient and hardwood for shipment to Europe. To the south in the Bay of Honduras the Bay Islands, just north of Honduras and commanding the channels leading to Guatemala, the British had sought to establish settlements from time to time, but they were completely deserted for long periods and were acknowledged as belonging to Spain. Finally, there was the Mosquito Coast of Nicaragua, extending roughly from Cap Gracias a Dios at the north to Bluefields at the south, named after the Mosco or Mosquito Indians over whom Britain had assumed, through no appeal on their part, a protectorate. Unobtrusively but nevertheless surely, Great Britain in recent years had sought to expand and secure a firm grasp on these areas, unopposed by the Monroe Doctrine and President Polk's reaffirmation of it. This neglect, of course, changed after the acquisition of California and the discovery of gold brought forward the importance of a transoceanic crossing in Central America.

Of special importance in this respect was Great Britain's assumption of a protectorate over the Mosquito Indians. The history of this development contains so many absurdities that it is difficult to take the British claim seriously, but nevertheless it was of crucial importance in Central American affairs and the competition for an isthmian transit.

The Indians known as Mosquitos, a corruption of the name Miskitos, were according to reports of early explorers among the most backward of the tribes of the New World. The coastal area they occupied, a stretch of about 200 miles, had been bypassed by the Spaniards in their search for precious metals: if there was treasure in Mosquitia, it had not been discovered by the aborigines. The coast had provided, however, places for attack and retreat for the buccaneers raiding the Spanish Main. The Mosquitos became a racially mixed people, partly Caucasian with genes from the buccaneers and their descendants who remained on the coast after the age of piracy and from English planters who settled there, and partly Negro from blacks who escaped from a wrecked slave ship, fugitive slaves from adjoining Spanish settlements, and slaves brought in by the English. A mixed race and apparently not physically attractive, the Mosquitos were also called "Sambos," from the Spanish "zambo," a word for "knock-kneed."

Coming late to the Caribbean after it had been preempted

by the Spaniards, the English, who had seized Jamaica in 1655, sought to extend their control to Central America by crowning as a king one of the Mosquito chiefs and offering him their protection. The Indian chosen for this honor found the ceremony so little to his liking that "he pulled off the European clothes his friends had put on him, and climbed to the top of a tree." When England became engaged in a war with Spain in 1739, the government conceived the scheme of rousing the Mosquitos against the Spaniards with the goal of fomenting revolts in her other colonies. Captain Robert Hodgson, the agent sent to direct this semimilitary maneuver, held meetings with the Mosquitos, explained his plans to them and through liberal dispensation of rum obtained their agreement. The plot failed, but Hodgson remained as superintendent of the region. Thereafter, despite intermittent protests from Spain, the British maintained their assumption of sovereignty over Mosquitia until 1783 and 1786 when treaties were signed with Spain in which the British agreed to leave.

The independence movement of Spain's New World colonies provided the opportunity for England to resume her aggressions in Central America. Under the treaty of 1783 the English had been permitted to continue to cut logwood at Belize, but though forbidden to establish permanent settlements and restricted to limited areas they had nevertheless managed to occupy more and more territory. The weakness of the new independent states led to the effort to make Belize a crown colony, soon achieved under the name of British Honduras.

In respect to Mosquitia, England resorted to her former charade of selecting a likely Indian to crown as king and ruling the country through him as a puppet. The first given the crown and scepter in the restored dynasty turned out badly—"he combined the bad qualities of the European and Creole, with the vicious propensities of the Sambo, and the capriciousness of the Indian"—but fortunately he was killed in a drunken brawl. Another was equally unsatisfactory—too late it was learned that he favored the Spaniards—and he was forced to abdicate. The next in line was Robert Charles Frederick, who received the crown, dressed in a British major's uniform with resplendent gold buttons and epaulettes, in ceremonies at Belize in 1825. On Frederick's return to Mosquitia, he aroused consternation in the British by making grants of land to favorite traders who contributed to his well-being by furnishing him rum. He was taken back to Belize where he could be more easily kept under observation, and his grants were declared void. Before Frederick's death in 1842, he affixed his mark to a will designating Colonel Alexander Macdonald, the British superintendent at Belize, as regent during the minority of the heir, George William Clarence, who was placed under a guardian at Bluefields, where he grew up into a muscular and agile young man who was "seemingly satisfied with his title and total freedom from want—his requirements being attended to by the English government."[5]

Although Nicaragua is almost three times as wide as the Isthmus of Panama, it offers certain advantages for a canal route because it is almost completely traversable by natural waterways. From the Atlantic vessels can sail up the San Juan River from the port of San Juan del Norte about 125 miles along a winding course to Lake Nicaragua, about 100 miles in length and about 45 miles wide, in the southwestern part of the country. A canal only a dozen miles long would connect the lake with the Pacific. In the 1850s the river was the chief trade route to the interior, indigo, brazilwood, and hides being brought downstream to the little town of San Juan del Norte for shipment abroad. The volume of trade did not amount to much—between $400,000 and $500,000 annually. Both passengers and freight were carried by great canoes, called bungos,* some hollowed from a single tree and others made of cedar wood. Capable of carrying loads up to 10 tons, they were manned by from eight to twelve oarsmen using long sweeps. Sails bent on detachable masts, however, were used on the lake and in the harbor. The passage from the mouth of the river to the lake usually required from ten to fifteen days.[6]

As the eastern terminus for an interoceanic water route, San Juan del Norte became one of the chief objects of British encroachment in Central America, possession of it being the main reason for the protectorate over the Mosquitos. These Indians had never

*The craft is spelled "bongo" in Ephraim G. Squier's *Nicaragua, Its People, Scenery, Monuments, Resources, Conditions, and Proposed Canal*, but other contemporary writers usually spelled it "bungo."

lived this far south, but this was no deterrence to Alexander Macdonald. The boundaries were indeterminate and they could be extended at will in the absence of resistance by Nicaragua, which had a weak government because of dissensions—soon to reach the stage of civil war—between the two major Central American parties in all the Latin-American states, the Serviles (Conservatives) and Liberals. In August 1841 Macdonald sailed with Frederick to San Juan in a British ship, claimed the port in the name of the Mosquito king, and ordered the Nicaraguans to leave by March 1 of the next year.

The gradual enlargement of the spheres of British influence—extension of the boundaries of Mosquitia by edict, establishment of the independent colony of British Honduras in 1834, and seizure of Ruatán, one of the Bay Islands, in 1840—had received little attention in the United States, expansionists being more interested in absorbing the contiguous areas of Mexico. In these encroachments the British Foreign Office had acted circumspectly so as not to arouse the United States. Officials were led to adopt a less cautious policy when, foreseeing the outcome of the Mexican War, they realized that the acquisition of California would result in Central America's becoming more important to the United States. In consequence, the Foreign Office instructed its Central American consul general, Frederick Chatfield, to notify Honduras and Nicaragua that the British government would not view with indifference any attempt to encroach upon the rights or territory of the Mosquito king. This was followed in October 1847 with a note to Nicaragua saying that Nicaraguans would be given until January 1, 1848, to withdraw from San Juan del Norte. Once again a British ship was sent to the port, the Nicaraguan flag was hauled down, and that of the Mosquitos was raised. There were one or two skirmishes, but Nicaragua, too weak to defend her rights, was forced to accede to Mosquito, or British, control of the port. San Juan del Norte was named Greytown in honor of Sir Charles Edward Grey, governor of Jamaica, British warships were stationed in the harbor, and a British agent was appointed collector of customs. About a dozen miles inland the San Juan River divides into two channels, the San Juan proper and the Colorado, emptying into the Atlantic a few miles to the south of the port. The southern boundary of Mosquitia, which had been extended to the San Juan River, now was stretched southward to the Colorado branch to ensure control of both banks.[7]

Preoccupied with the Mexican War, President Polk had given little thought to the British encroachments, and the seizure of San Juan del Norte did not arouse in him any sense of urgency. He decided, however, to send a representative to Guatemala, capital of the former Central American Federation, to strengthen relations with the five states that had made up the union. The man named was Elijah Hise of Kentucky, designated chargé d'affaires. Secretary of State Buchanan, in his instructions to Hise on June 3, 1848, set forth the situation accurately: "I have no doubt that the dissolution of the confederacy of Central America has encouraged Great Britain in her encroachments . . . under the mask of protecting the so-called Kingdom of the Mosquitos. We learn that under this pretext, she has now obtained possession of the harbor of San Juan de Nicaragua. . . . Her purpose probably is to obtain the control of the route for a railroad and canal between the Atlantic and Pacific oceans through the lake Nicaragua. . . . Under the assumed title of protector of the Kingdom of Mosquito, a miserable, degraded and insignificant tribe of Indians, she doubtless intends to acquire an absolute dominion over the vast extent of sea coast. . . ."

Delayed by ill health, Hise did not reach Central America until late in October. Once on the scene, he quickly became suspicious of British intentions and attempted to rouse the administration to the need for frustrating them. Writing Buchanan from Honduras on October 26, he warned that the small isthmian states could do nothing to prevent the spread of British dominion over the whole area unless the United States "interferes firmly and shall carry out that celebrated declaration made by President Monroe." On December 20 he wrote that an American man-of-war occasionally making an appearance in Central American ports—an early instance of gunboat diplomacy—would give the states moral support and suggested that he be given authority to make treaties with all of them, especially with Nicaragua, "to secure the right of way over and through such communications by land or water between the oceans as now exist or may be hereafter made." Hise received no reply and he decided to act upon his own responsibility. On June 21, 1849, he signed a treaty with Nicaragua that granted to the American government, or its citizens, the right of way for transit purposes. In return, the United States pledged herself to protect Nicaragua in all her territory.[8] It was an otiose agreement. The Democratic administration of Polk had been voted out in the election of the fall of 1848 and replaced by the Whig administration of Zachary Taylor. The new secretary of state, John M. Clayton, had on April 2 sent Hise notice of his recall and on May 1 issued instructions to the new chargé at Guatemala, Ephraim George Squier.

The new chargé was a versatile and energetic man of twenty-eight who had started out to become a civil engineer but who later had turned to journalism. He had been born in Bethlehem, New York, and his first journalism was done for Albany newspapers. He was editor of a Whig paper in Hartford, Connecticut, a short while before going to Chillicothe, Ohio, where for some years he published the *Scioto Gazette*. He became acquainted with Dr. Edwin H. Davis, a physician and amateur archeologist, who interested him in the past of the plains Indians. Between 1845 and 1847 they opened about 100 Indian mounds and together they wrote *The Ancient Monuments of the Mississippi Valley*, the first publication of the new Smithsonian Institution in Washington. Squier, like his predecessor antiquarian in Guatemala, John L. Stephens, utilized the opportunities afforded by his diplomatic mission to study the archeology of Central America. In traveling from San Juan del Norte to the seat of government at León, the chief city of the western part of the country, he made side trips, accompanied by the artist J. W. Orr, to examine the antiquities half concealed by vines and creepers—monstrous idols in human and animal shapes, stones with grotesque paintings and designs, and the ruins of ancient temples.

Representing a Whig administration opposed to expansionism and not firmly dedicated to the Monroe Doctrine, Squier nevertheless was aroused to anger at the attempts of the British to acquire territory in Central America, and his aggressive efforts to combat them were to put him at odds with his superiors in Washington. His instructions from Secretary of State John M. Clayton were in some ways ambiguous. In an able exposition of the British protectorate over the Mosquitos, Clayton could find the claim to have no support in history or international law—the mere statement of "the pretension," he said, was enough "to startle an impartial inquirer"—but at the same time he emphasized that while Squier could express the "liveliest sympathy" to Nicaragua, he could promise only that the United States would "employ any moral means" in her power to thwart the designs of Great Britain. He instructed Squier to assist Cornelius Vanderbilt, who in a move to obtain canal rights had sought the support of the government, but also cautioned him "distinctly to understand how important it is deemed by the President so to conduct all our negotiations on the subject of the Nicaraguan passage as not to involve this country in any entangling alliance on the one hand or any unnecessary controversy on the other."

Squier arrived about June 10 at San Juan del Norte—he indicated his sympathy with the Nicaraguans by using this name rather than the British-imposed Greytown—from which he wrote Clayton that he thought it time to give up the "shallow disguise" of "Mosquito authority." The British commerical representative was a de facto dictator who signed his edicts "*not* as the *Agent of the Mosquito King*, but as 'H.B.M. Vice Consul.'" With stops and side trips to examine the archeological wonders of the country, Squier did not reach León until about August 1. He was enthusiastically welcomed, being escorted into the city by "the principal civil, military and ecclesiastical officers of the State" and "a large cavalcade of the leading citizens."

Vanderbilt's agent on the scene, David L. White, had made no headway in obtaining a canal contract, but Squier in less than a month secured one for Vanderbilt's American Atlantic and Pacific Ship Canal Company and concluded a treaty that granted the United States the exclusive right of way across the isthmus and the right to fortify the route in return for a guarantee of the neutrality of the transit route and the protection of Nicaraguan sovereignty so long as the canal remained under the control of U.S. citizens. The charter allowed twelve years for completion of the project and was to extend for eighty-five years. The company was to pay the state $10,000 upon ratification of the charter and $10,000 annually during the twelve years of construction. Nicaragua was to share in the profits from transit tolls, 20 percent during the first twenty years of operation and thereafter 25 percent. All nations were entitled to use of the canal subject to uniform tolls set by the company.

Squier was jubilant when on September 10 he submitted the charter and treaty to Clayton, saying: "I have the satisfaction of informing the Department that I have succeeded in accomplishing the objects of my mission to this Republic." His satisfaction was not entirely shared by the secretary, who in the meantime had undertaken negotiations with England which, he wrote Squier on November 20, he trusted would bring about an "amicable adjustment of all controversies" involving Central America and who found the Hise treaty more favorable on one or two points.[9]

Clayton's hope was to obtain by direct negotiation with Great Britain a canal treaty in which both countries would deny any territorial claims to an isthmian route that, as a great world highway, should never be the exclusive possession of any one nation. He instructed the American ministers, first George Bancroft, the Polk appointee whose replacement had not arrived in London, and then Abbott Lawrence, the Taylor appointee, to sound out the British foreign secretary Lord Palmerston on the question. From the start, the negotiations were carried on in an atmosphere of mutual distrust and not without some evasiveness and duplicity by the British Foreign Office. The American ministers were to express the view that the claims of the Mosquito Indians, as set forth by Britain, were invalid and that San Juan del Norte should be restored to Nicaragua.

Bancroft at an interview with Palmerston was assured that Britain had no interest in new colonies in Central America and that the occupation of San Juan was only temporary. The statement about San Juan was mendacious, of course, for then and later Palmerston maintained that the town and the lower part of the river belonged to the Mosquitos. When Lawrence reached London, he suggested, in conformance with his instructions, that the two nations sign a treaty guaranteeing the independence of Nicaragua, Honduras, and Costa Rica and disposing of the Mosquito claims by payments to the Indians by Nicaragua for the right of occupancy to any of their lands required for a canal. He suggested also that Britain sign with Nicaragua a treaty along the lines of the one Squier had just completed and sent to Washington. Palmerston replied equably that his government would take great pleasure in cooperating with the United States in securing and protecting an interoceanic transit, but he was adamant in upholding the Mosquito claim, indeed warning that any attempt of the United States to force the return of Greytown to Nicaragua would be an unprovoked aggression against Great Britain.

In the meantime, the agents of the two powers in Central America, Squier and Chatfield, were engaging in their own aggressions dangerous to the attainment of any accord. With the seizure of San Juan del Norte, Britain controlled the Atlantic outlet for a canal. What Britain now needed was control of a Pacific outlet. For some time Chatfield thought this design could be achieved by obtaining Tigre Island, which commands the Gulf of Fonseca in Honduras, to settle debts owed Great Britain. His suggestions to Lord Palmerston that this be done had been rejected, but Squier's success led him to act on his own and he issued a threat to Honduras in pressing for payment. Convinced that the proposed Nicaraguan canal must terminate on the Gulf of Fonseca, erroneously as it turned out, Squier acted to frustrate Chatfield's design by negotiating with Honduras, on October 10, 1849, a treaty along the lines of the one he had completed with Nicaragua but with a provision that portions of Tigre Island were ceded to the United States to be held in trust for the canal company. Chatfield acted promptly to forestall Squier, and at his order a British naval force seized the island.

This high-handed action, coming on top of the seizure of San Juan del Norte two years before, resulted in manifestations of outrage in the United States. The Democratic press accused the administration of supinely permitting Great Britain to extend her control over the isthmus in violation of the Monroe Doctrine, and resolutions appeared in both houses of Congress asking for the correspondence relating to Central American affairs.

Shortly afterward, the negotiations between Great Britain and the United States were shifted from London to Washington with the arrival of the new minister to America, Sir Henry Lytton Bulwer. Since both countries were agreed that the primary object should be an interoceanic canal, they were able to relegate to the background the question of the Mosquito claims. On April 19,

1850, a treaty was signed that reflected a compromise on the canal and left ambiguous some of the territorial issues. Both nations agreed that neither would "ever obtain or maintain for itself any exclusive control over the said ship-canal" and that neither would "occupy, or fortify, or colonize, or assume or exercise any dominion over Nicaragua, Costa Rica, the Mosquito Coast, or any part of Central America." This seems clear enough, but actually it was not. The British view was that the treaty pledged the government in the future not to occupy any areas or fortify any places not already under their control and that it did not affect their possession of Belize or the protectorate over the Mosquito Coast. The U.S. view was the opposite, that the treaty was retrospective rather than prospective and that the British had agreed to give up their claims to these territories.

Clayton was exultant over his statesmanship, writing Bulwer: "There is not a good man in the world who will not glory in what we have done." Clayton left office upon the death of President Taylor, being replaced by Daniel Webster. He therefore did not receive the letter from the Nicaraguan minister of foreign affairs, who wrote the Department of State on November 13, 1850, that the treaty had changed nothing insofar as his country was concerned: there still existed "the same Mosquito nation, the same savage King, and the same armed protection of Her Britannic Majesty."[10]

The treaty did not mention Cornelius Vanderbilt's American Atlantic and Pacific Ship Canal Company as the prospective builder of the canal, but both the principals in the negotiations approved of the contract given it. Clayton had consulted with Vanderbilt and his legal counsel, Joseph L. White, who had no objections to modifications proposed to conform to treaty provisions, and Bulwer wrote letters of introduction for Vanderbilt to use when the Commodore went to London in the fall of 1850 to obtain British financial backing. The powerful *Times* supported the American project, defending the company against critics favoring an all-British canal, and was so optimistic as to announce on October 15 that satisfactory financial arrangements had been completed. This was premature. London bankers, though interested, were unwilling to commit themselves until they received the reports of engineers sent by Vanderbilt to make surveys for the canal route and to arrive at estimates of the construction costs.

Besides rushing off to England to raise money, Vanderbilt had acted quickly to get construction started and to enter the competition for the isthmian passenger and freight shipping. He engaged as his surveyor the civil engineer in charge of enlarging the Erie Canal, Colonel Orville W. Childs, who was in Nicaragua with his crew by August. He also ordered construction of steamers to make the Atlantic and Pacific runs and smaller vessels to operate on the San Juan River and Lake Nicaragua. And, before he was ready to carry passengers or freight at all, he commenced his price-cutting tactic against competitors by memorializing Congress with an offer to carry the mails from New York to California in six steamships for $180,000 a year as compared with the combined totals of $389,000 paid George Law and William H. Aspinwall.

Since a canal would require years for construction, if one could be constructed at all, Vanderbilt had no intention of waiting for problematic profits in the future. His plan was to place shallow-draft ships immediately in operation on the San Juan River and Lake Nicaragua and to complete the transit by land to the Pacific coast. But he had run into an immediate snag when the wooden sidewheel steamer *Orus* of 210 tons, which he had purchased and directed David L. White to sail up the river to the lake, was wrecked in the Machuca rapids, one of the five in the upper part of the stream before it reaches the coastal plain. Despite White's reports that the only way to make the river navigable by boats larger than bungos was by construction of canals to bypass the rapids, Vanderbilt was not convinced and decided to go to Nicaragua to see for himself. In December he sailed from New York in the *Prometheus*, his new 1,200-ton steamer designed for the Atlantic run, towing a small steamer, the *Director*, that he planned to use on the river. His engineers warned him when he reached San Juan that it would be impossible to sail the *Director* up the stream, that she could not possibly traverse the rapids, but the Commodore, who had been sailing boats since boyhood, considered their objections to be namby-pamby. He would show them, and he did.

The first of the rapids, those known as Machuca, would have been sufficient to daunt most men, for there the *Orus* had come to grief and she could still be seen caught in the rocks. One of the engineers on this hazardous trip recalled that "the Commodore insisted upon 'jumping' all the obstacles, and tied down the safety valve, put on all steam, and compelled the little steamer to scrape and struggle over the obstructions into clear water again." Succeeding rapids proved not so difficult until those at Castillo Viejo were reached. The castle, built in the early days of the Spanish conquistadors, had been reconstructed in 1747 as a fort but now was largely in ruins. The rapids here really deserved the name of falls, pouring over a rocky ledge eight feet high. It took the bungos about three hours to cross this obstacle, since cargo and passengers had to be landed and the boats hauled over the impediment by ropes. Vanderbilt used the same technique. He directed the warping of the *Director* over the ledge by means of ropes bound to the ship's capstans and wrapped around trees on the shore. The rest of the trip from Castillo Viejo to Lake Nicaragua was comparatively easy. On New Year's Day of 1851 the *Director* sailed past Fort San Carlos at the head of the river and into the beautiful lake. Vanderbilt, by sheer will power, had sailed the first steamboat the entire length—more than 100 difficult miles—of the San Juan River.

Fort San Carlos, like Castillo Viejo, was in ruins. It occupied a promontory cleared of trees and was surrounded by about twenty thatched huts where customs officers, soldiers, and their families lived. A traveler across Nicaragua in 1850 described the scene as it was viewed by Vanderbilt: "At the foot of the hill a broad sheet of water is spread, studded, in the immediate neighbourhood, with some green islands of diminutive dimensions, and extending, in a northwesterly direction, as far as the eye can reach. To the left, a low wooded shore begins at the outlet of the lake, and continues in that direction till it is lost in the distance of the western horizon. A chain of high mountains, cast in a shroud of dark forests, rises in the rear, covering an unknown region of Costa Rica. It comprises several active volcanoes. . . . To the right, the view does not extend beyond the nearest hills. . . . On the distant horizon in the centre of the view the two cones of the island of Ometepec are seen, faintly traced, and as their forms are lifted up by refraction, they seem to swim over the water."

But Vanderbilt was not interested in scenery, the lives led by the natives, or the fauna and flora; he spent only a few days exploring the lake, his sole concern the discovery of the route by which he could most quickly and most easily transport passengers and freight to the Pacific. He decided that this route was to sail straight across the lake from San Carlos to a small indenture on the opposite shore known as Virgin Bay, at the time unsettled, and thence by land less than a dozen miles to the little coastal town of San Juan del Sur.[11]

When Vanderbilt returned to San Juan del Norte and departed for New York after less than a month spent in Nicaragua, he had his whole plan completely in mind. The *Prometheus*, a fast steamer that made a record run from San Juan to New York on his return voyage, would be used in the Atlantic, and a 1,000-ton steamer, the *Pacific*, would travel the route from San Juan del Sur to San Francisco. He would construct two stern-wheelers, protected by iron-plated hulls, for the sailings on the San Juan River, to be called the *John M. Clayton* and *Sir Henry Bulwer* in honor of the negotiators of the Anglo-American isthmian treaty. They could not navigate the falls at Castillo Viejo, but this was no matter: passengers and freight would be transferred at this point to the lake steamers, the *Director* and the *Central America*, to be added to his fleet later, which could sail the upper reach of the river.

One year after the ratification of the Clayton-Bulwer Treaty and six months after Vanderbilt's visit to Nicaragua, he inserted advertisements in New York and San Francisco newspapers announcing service between the two cities via Nicaragua. The *San Francisco Herald* in an article possibly written by William Walker praised the new service: "The presence of the enterprising and indefatigable Commodore Vanderbilt will insure the perfection of all arrangements to make the transit connection complete." The *New York Herald* had equal confidence in Vanderbilt but went further and predicted: "The rivalry which has now commenced between Commodore Vanderbilt and his associates on the Nicaragua route, and George Law and his associates on the Panama route, will hasten the state of things which is destined soon to occur, when the government and institutions of the United States will be extended over the whole of Mexico and Central America."

Vanderbilt's new service quickly became popular because the Nicaragua route was about 400 miles shorter than the Panama route and passengers could save four or five days in making the complete New York-to-San Francisco trip. It was also considered more healthful, because malaria and other tropical fevers were believed to be less prevalent in the more northerly climate. The chief reason for its popularity, however, was the low fares which Vanderbilt inaugurated to capture the business of the established lines of Law's United States Mail Steamship Company and Aspinwall's Pacific Mail Steamship Company.

Vanderbilt initially had set his first class through fare at $400, but within a year he cut it to $150. His line soon became the dominant single passenger carrier to and from the Pacific. Starting his service in July 1851, he transported during the second half of the year 5,102 passengers across Nicaragua. The number making the transit by Panama was 29,653 by several competing lines. The next year one-half the passenger traffic was carried by Vanderbilt, 16,484 going via Nicaragua and 33,108 via Panama. In 1853 Vanderbilt further reduced the edge held by the Panama route: 20,083 made the trip via Nicaragua and 27,277 via Panama.[12]

The operations of the Nicaragua transit very soon became highly complicated by a series of financial manipulations conducted by Vanderbilt. He had early seen that the charter given the American Atlantic and Pacific Ship Canal Company would cause problems in carrying passengers by land and inland waterways before completion of the ship canal within the twelve years agreed upon. He therefore, on August 14, 1851, completed an arrangement with the Nicaraguan government by which the privileges granted for construction of the canal and for passage by other means—the inland waterways and by railroad or carriage road—would be separated. He secured a charter for a new company, the Accessory Transit Company, by which the construction of a canal would be the sole function of the first company and transportation by river, lake, and road would be the function of the second company.

On the New York Stock Exchange the transit company shares rose in a few months from $20 to $50. With the report of Colonel Childs early in 1852 that a ship canal could be built in six years at a cost of $31,538,319, stock in the canal company, for which there had been slight demand at $800 a share, rose to $3,600. The *New York Times* warned the investing public against this rapid rise, reminding readers of the Mississippi Bubble. The canal company in the meantime had sent a delegation, which included Childs, to London to obtain financial backing. It was not forthcoming. The canal planned by Childs was considered too small for major ocean ships, the proposed toll of $3 a ton was too high, and the tonnage needed to yield a profit of 6 percent probably could not be reached for years. When this information reached the public, the stock plummeted and soon was dropped from the exchange. Vanderbilt was accused by the *New York Herald* of holding back the adverse report until he had unloaded his stock at the high price of $3,600 a share. The next year Vanderbilt made a further stupendous profit when he transferred the steamers built for the runs between New York and San Juan del Norte and between San Francisco and San Juan del Sur to the Accessory Transit Company for $1,200,000 in cash and $150,000 in the bonds of the company to be payable within twelve months.[13]

Early in 1853 Vanderbilt conceived of a project that afterward was to associate the family name with the ostentatious display of wealth—a voyage to Europe in a $500,000 steam yacht, the *North Star*, built after his own design, purely as a pleasure cruise. The newspapers devoted columns of flowery prose to descriptions of the luxury yacht. Before starting on his trip, Vanderbilt acted to relieve himself of some of the responsibilities of managing the Accessory Transit Company by bringing into the firm two other aggressive businessmen to manage the New York and San Francisco offices. Charles Morgan, a one-time grocery clerk who had entered the shipping business by provisioning vessels and who had by bold enterprise developed lines dominating the trade in the Gulf of Mexico and the West Indies, became the director of the Atlantic operations. The Pacific operations were turned over to Cornelius K. Garrison, who had started out as a cabin boy on a Hudson River sloop and who, when he was invited to join the Vanderbilt firm, had achieved wealth as head of a commercial and banking house he had established at Panama early in the gold rush. Resigning as president of the Accessory Transit Company, Vanderbilt entrusted the management to these two agents. It was the kind of mistake Vanderbilt seldom made. During his absence the two through stock manipulations and other maneuvers seized control of the company. Commenting on this financial coup, the *New York Herald* predicted that "trouble is anticipated upon the return of Commodore Vanderbilt." It was an understatement. Vanderbilt exploded and dictated a letter to the two men that was memorable for its succinct threat: "Gentlemen: You have undertaken to cheat me. I won't sue you, for the law is too slow. I'll ruin you. Yours truly, Cornelius Vanderbilt."[14] Vanderbilt was not able immediately to carry out this intention, and his war against the two traitors was to continue for several years and figure prominently in the affairs of Central America and the filibuster activities of William Walker.

CHAPTER ELEVEN

The Year of the Filibusters, 1855

It was a chastened Franklin Pierce who, halfway through his presidency, sat down in November 1854 to write his State of the Union Message. Winning office by an overwhelming electoral vote, he now found himself repudiated in the recent congressional elections, largely because of passage of the Kansas-Nebraska Act, an administration measure. The course of events that were to result in "bleeding Kansas" was well along following formation of the Massachusetts Emigrant Aid Society in April and an invasion of about 1,700 armed men from western Missouri of the territory to elect a delegate to Congress. Scarcely taking cognizance of the passions that the issue of extension of slavery was arousing at home, the president's message stressed foreign policy. It was not a subject to inspire enthusiasm, Alexander H. Stephens of Georgia commenting: "Everything is flat. Nobody cared a cent for the message or anything else."[1] Pierce himself could not have approached the topic with much interest. With the exception of the Gadsden purchase, his expansionist program had been a failure, and what he had obtained from Mexico was so much less than what he wanted that when the treaty was under attack in the Senate he had more than once felt like tearing it up. Pierre Soulé had failed in Spain to get even a polite hearing on his offers to buy Cuba, and the extraordinary foreign ministers' conference at Ostend had resulted in a report the president hoped he could keep secret.

His message was a somewhat petulant defense of his expansionist policies in a world given over to imperialism. His efforts had been "the legitimate exercise of sovereign rights belonging alike to all nations," he said, and he had done only what France and England had been doing. Pierce's strongest foreign policy statement was his defense of the razing of Greytown by bombardment and fire in July by a U.S. warship in retaliation for interference by some of its citizens in the operations of the Accessory Transit Company and an attack on the American minister to Nicaragua, Solon Borland.

Great Britain, in upholding her claim of a protectorate over the Mosquito Indians, had declared the little town of fewer than 500 persons a free city that had its own elected officials, collected customs duties, and imposed harbor fees. The destruction of the defenseless community had been condemned in the United States and abroad. It had so enraged the British foreign minister, Lord Clarendon, that he had sputtered to the American minister, James Buchanan, that it was an outrage "without a parallel in the annals of modern times."[2] It had been expected that the president would disavow the action as one taken by a naval officer who had exceeded his authority. Instead, Pierce, irked by the insistence of Clarendon that the Mosquito protectorate and the occupation of the Bay Islands did not violate the Clayton-Bulwer Treaty, chose instead to defend the bombing, in the process of which he gave a distorted history of what happened.

Cornelius Vanderbilt's Accessory Transit Company had several times encountered trouble with Greytown officials. The Commodore, visiting Nicaragua in 1851, had determined the imperious policy the company would follow when one of his ships, the *Prometheus*, was boarded by officials demanding payment of $123 in port dues. Since his contract with Nicaragua stated that the company would be subject to no imposts, Vanderbilt asked the captain of the port by what authority the fee had been assessed. The reply that it was by mandate of the King of Mosquito caused Vanderbilt to explode. "My government recognizes no Mosquito king or kingdom," he declared. Upon the request of the British consul, the captain of the British brig *Express* halted the *Prometheus* on her departure by firing two shots across the bow.

This firing on an American ship was not an incident to go unnoticed in the United States. Newspapers exploited it as an outrage, the *New York Herald*, for example, declaring that it demanded "the most ample apology and reparation," and speakers in Congress protested vociferously. The British Foreign Office was slow to respond to a complaint by Secretary of State Webster, but the tempest abated when the American minister in London was assured that orders had been sent to the naval squadron in the Caribbean to desist from enforcing payment of fees at Greytown and that the action of the commander of the *Express* was disavowed by the government.[3]

Next year British pretensions that Greytown was a free city became more of an actuality when the consul, who as agent of the Mosquito king served as chairman of the town council, announced his withdrawal from participation in civic affairs. Under a new constitution the residents, many of them North Americans, organized the government. The transit company operations in the following two years were shifted from the town to Punta Arenas, a narrow spit of land that forms the outer edge of the harbor. This deprived Greytown of the profits to be made from ship passengers, and the business people sought to return the operations to the town. Their efforts resulted in the next disruptive incident in February 1852.

Neither Greytown nor Punta Arenas had attractions that would cause travelers to stop there any longer than they had to. Elisha S. Capron, who made the journey to California in the spring of 1853 as an agent of a New York mercantile house, described the land as being so low that viewed from the *Prometheus* the few buildings on both sides of the bay appeared to rise out of the water. The vegetation—grass of broad, hard blades growing in tufts, trees from which hung tropical vines, and the forests made impenetrable by the underbrush—was unattractive. Nowhere did he see a cultivated field, a garden flower, or a fruit tree, nor was there a cow, sheep, or other farm animal. Greytown had only one main street and there were few modern houses, most of the buildings being low huts constructed of bamboo with thatched roofs of plantain or palm leaves.[4]

Early in 1853 the Greytown council directed the Accessory Transit Company to vacate Punta Arenas within thirty days. The company ignored the order and appealed to Washington for protection. Instructed by Secretary of the Navy James C. Dobbin to sail to Greytown to prevent any interference with the company,

Captain George N. Hollins arrived on the sloop-of-war *Cyane* on February 10 after the town had already dismantled some of the company's buildings. He notified the authorities that he would resist by force any further efforts to destroy the property and used marines to prevent this when the town marshal landed with an armed band under orders "to tear down the buildings." Clarendon protested the American show of force to Secretary of State Marcy but in so conciliatory a manner—his government was under attack in the U.S. Senate for the earlier firing on the *Prometheus*—that the incident was not allowed to develop into a major dispute.[5]

The bad feeling between Greytown authorities and transit company officials, however, grew progressively stronger over a series of other unpleasantnesses. When Solon Borland, the new U.S. minister to Nicaragua, arrived at Greytown in August 1853, he found little semblance of any sort of government. Thieves raided the company warehouses and officials refused to make any attempt to arrest them or recover the stolen property. For its part, the company made no effort to improve relations, continuing to refuse to pay port charges and delivering no mail or freight to the town.

Borland was to become one of the chief figures in the series of events that in July 1854 resulted in the naval bombardment of Greytown. An expansionist of the extreme Southern viewpoint, Borland had resigned as U.S. senator from Arkansas to take the post of minister to Nicaragua. Strongly anti-British, he wrote letters to Marcy that were diatribes against the Clayton-Bulwer Treaty—he had voted against it in the Senate—and that urged its abrogation on the grounds it excluded the United States from Central America. In a speech in Nicaragua he declared it his greatest desire to see the country become a bright star in the flag of the United States. On December 30, 1853, Marcy wrote Borland, then at Granada, reprimanding him for his attacks on the treaty. Denouncing the rebuke as "offensive" and "uncalled for," Borland wrote President Pierce on February 22, 1854, to announce his resignation—he felt that Marcy's letter had been such an indignity he could not bring himself to inform the secretary of state of his decision.[6]

Feeling injured and resentful, Borland sailed on one of the transit company boats, the *Routh*, on May 16 for Greytown. Near the end of the trip, the steamer struck a bungo. The master of the bungo, a Negro, angrily protested to the commander of the *Routh*, Captain T. T. Smith, who suddenly turned away and started for his cabin, saying, "I must shoot the fellow. He has used threatening language that shall cost him his life." When Smith returned to the deck with his rifle, he calmly shot the man dead. Borland might have acted to prevent this callous slaying but uttered no word of protest, saying later in a report to Marcy that he was "decidedly of the opinion" the captain was justified in all he did.

That evening while the *Routh* was transferring passengers to the ocean steamer *Northern Light*, a bungo with about twenty-five armed men, mostly Negroes, came alongside from Greytown. Several of them, led by a man who said he was the town marshal, climbed aboard and presented a warrant for Smith's arrest. Smith had armed himself and was holding the men at bay when Borland came aboard from the *Northern Light* and took command, telling the marshal the United States did not recognize the authority of Greytown to arrest an American citizen. When others on the bungo prepared to board the steamer, Borland took a rifle from a bystander and warned them to keep off. His resolute attitude was effective, and the men withdrew.

That night Borland went to Greytown to confer with the U.S. commercial agent, Joseph W. Fabens, for the past several years a consul at Latin-American ports. A schemer alert as much to his own commercial interests as those of his country, Fabens was negotiating for one of the land grants given away by the Mosquito king Robert Charles Frederick, and he had supported the transit company in all its complaints against Greytown residents. Shortly after Borland's arrival, a group of men armed with muskets knocked loudly at the door of Fabens' house and on being confronted by the consul announced their intention of arresting Borland. Again Borland's courage in facing down a rabble was evinced when he came to the door and warned the men of the serious consequences that would follow if they persisted and they withdrew to talk over the situation. While this colloquy was going on, someone in the crowd threw a broken bottle at Borland that lacerated his face. Next morning when Borland returned to the *Northern Light*, he decided that the persons and property of Americans were not safe at Greytown and prevailed upon fifty passengers to remain as an armed guard until he could obtain protection from the United States.

When Borland reached Washington with his story of the incident, recounted in indignant detail in the newspapers, Captain Hollins was ordered to proceed to Greytown in the *Cyane*. "It is very desirable that these people should be taught that the United States will not tolerate these outrages, and that they have the power and the determination to check them," Dobbin instructed Hollins on June 10.[7]

The administration heard about the situation from another source, Joseph L. White, attorney for the transit company, who complained that the firm had been plundered to the amount of thousands of dollars by "a camp of savages" pretending to exercise authority over Greytown and that the lives of citizens were imperiled. When the *Cyane* was dispatched to Nicaragua, White on June 16 jubilantly wrote Fabens: "Capt. Hollins leaves here next Monday. You will see from his instructions that much discretion is given to you, and it is to be hoped it will not be so exercised as to show any mercy to the town or people. If the scoundrels are soundly punished, we can take possession, and build it up as a business place, put in our own officers, transfer the jurisdiction, and you know the rest."[8] In short, the government had been inveigled into supporting a scheme of a private corporation to establish its own reign over the port and the transit.

Fabens, even before the arrival of the *Cyane*, had acted upon instructions from Washington to enforce claims of the transit company against Greytown by demanding reparations of $8,000 for the destruction of the buildings at Punta Arenas. On the arrival of Hollins on July 11, the two conferred and agreed to renew the demand for damages and added a claim of $16,000 for later losses. For the indignity offered the United States in the attack on Borland, Fabens wrote town officials, "nothing short of an apology, promptly made, and satisfactory assurances given to Commander Hollins of future good behavior on the part of said authorities and people . . . will save the place from the infliction which its late acts justly merit." Fabens' communication went unanswered, and on July 12 Hollins issued a proclamation warning that if the demands were not met he would at nine o'clock on the next day bombard the town "to the end that the rights of our country and citizens may be vindicated." Next day the *Cyane's* batteries were opened on the town, which was subjected to three separate bombardments.

The destruction of the town was execrated in the United States. "We cannot recall any public question with regard to which there has been such unity of opinion," the *New York Tribune* declared. "Journals habitually opposed on every other subject, representing every shade of party feeling, every divergence of interest, and every antagonism of nationality, concur to declare the destruction of San Juan a needless, unjustifiable, inhuman exercise of warlike force." Both Secretary Marcy and the president were taken aback by the totality of the destruction. Marcy wrote Buchanan in London: "The place merited chastisement, but the severity of the one inflicted exceeded all expectations."

Nevertheless, in view of the attitude taken by Great Britain toward the Clayton-Bulwer Treaty—Buchanan had been told bluntly in April that it was "entirely prospective in its operation" and did not cover "existing possessions in Central America"—Pierce decided to test the policy in respect to the Mosquito protectorate.[9] In his message he inveighed against those "adventurers" who had taken over San Juan del Norte, changed the name to Greytown, and acted "as the subjects of the fictitious sovereign of the Mosquito Indians" in setting up an independent government. Pierce's reply to his critics at home and abroad did not lead to a disruption of relations between the two countries, for British public opinion would scarcely support a war over the dubious protectorate and the world at large would condemn it.

If Pierce was disheartened at the close of 1854 about prospects for expansion, if destiny seemed not so manifest as it had before, the same could not be said of a great many other people. The disastrous outcomes of all private expeditions—those of López to Cuba, of Flores to Ecuador, of Carvajal to Tamaulipas, and of Raousset-Boulbon and Walker to Sonorà—might have been expected to deter men from engaging in such ventures but they did not. Instead, as 1855 opened, the spirit of filibusterism burned as ardently as ever. Cuba, Mexico, Ecuador, and a new region—Nicaragua—all were the objectives of expeditions projected for the year.

After many postponements, General John A. Quitman was ready early in 1855 to mount his expedition to Cuba. He had been given dictatorial powers by the Cuban independence leaders in the agreement signed in 1853 for "overthrowing the Spanish government in the island of Cuba," but he soon found himself at odds with the junta chiefs in New Orleans and the revolutionary plotters on the island because he refused to act until he had more resources than had López in his thwarted expeditions. His efforts had also been hampered after he and his lieutenants were put under bond to obey the neutrality laws in June 1854. Money had come in slowly, but now ships had been chartered and plans completed for an invasion timed for an uprising on the island set for February 12.[10]

Interest in an Ecuadorian expedition was revived in 1855 through the continued efforts of General Flores. Since the fiasco of his invasion in 1851, supported by a California force headed by Alexander Bell, Flores had hatched various plots for an invasion by troops enlisted in the United States. These plots, or rumors of them, worried the government in Quito; and the U.S. chargé d'affaires, first Courtland Cushing and later Philo White, Pierce's appointee, received frightened protests from the president and foreign affairs minister. In August 1853 Cushing had written Marcy that Flores's son was reported on his way to California to organize an expedition. He had been asked by President José María Urbina, Cushing said, to request President Pierce to issue a proclamation against an expedition. Cushing thought any attempt would fail, because Flores had "scarcely the shadow of a party in Ecuador." Marcy, after checking with officials in California, replied that a proclamation was unnecessary, as there was no evidence of any designs being plotted against Ecuador. White in 1854 received similar complaints from Ecuadorian officials of a California expedition, and he also was informed none was being planned.

Unsuccessful in California, Flores turned in 1855 to the eastern part of the United States. News of his efforts reached the press on March 9 when the Washington correspondent of the *New York Herald* reported that the leading spirit of the new filibuster was Senator Jeremiah Clemens of Alabama. The threat aroused alarm in Quito a little later, according to a report from Aaron H. Palmer, Ecuador's consul general at Washington. Clemens, trained for the law but avid for military glory, had fought in a volunteer company against the Cherokee Indians, in the Texan war for independence, and in the Mexican War. On his return to civilian life, he had entered politics and was elected to the Senate in 1849. With the Quitman Cuban expedition still in prospect, Southerners did not rally to the Flores banner, and nothing came of the Clemens project. White in Quito calmed the fears of officials by assuring them, so he wrote Marcy, that even if enough "lawless men" were recruited "capitalists of our country could not be seduced into risking their funds in such criminal and hazardous adventures."[11]

No new leaders had arisen to head expeditions into Mexico after the execution of Raousset-Boulbon and the return of William Walker and his half-starved band, but scores of Americans joined the army of General Juan Álvarez, who led a revolt in the southeastern state of Guerrero early in 1854 against Santa Anna that spread throughout the country and resulted in the flight of His Serene Highness to Cuba in the fall of 1855. Among these was Roberdeau Wheat, who had gone to Cuba with López and fought with Carvajal in Tamaulipas. Bored by his law practice in New Orleans, Wheat had been excited by the news of Walker's declaration of the independence of Lower California and Sonora, and in April 1854 set out for California to fight for the spread of liberty under the two-star flag of the new republic. Wheat had known Walker in Nashville, where the filibuster's younger brother, James, had been his college chum and classmate.

Arriving in San Francisco on March 23, too late to join the Sonora expedition, Wheat remained in the city about four months, however, keeping himself in military readiness for whatever might come by joining the California guard as an honorary lieutenant. During this time he became interested in the Álvarez revolution. When he left San Francisco early in August, the city's newspapers speculated that he was off to join the Quitman expedition or, as the *Chronicle* put it, he was one of those intending "to wed the 'Queen of the Antilles' to his Excellency, Uncle Sam." But Quitman's delay in getting his expedition off led Wheat to return to Texas, where there seemed to be more immediate prospects for action because he had heard that Carvajal was still attempting to lead a revolution in Tamaulipas. Nothing developed from this, however, and early in 1855 Wheat accepted an offer to join

Álvarez as a brigadier general. His daring and impetuous temperament appealed to Álvarez, and he soon became one of the general's favorites. "I . . . hope ere long to have plenty of money," Wheat wrote his mother. "If the revolution succeeds I shall have my pick and choice of lands." Later, as the revolution proceeded and victory over Santa Anna seemed near, Wheat wrote again: "General Álvarez has given me the command of the column which will march on the Capital. I shall have American Riflemen and Artillerists and 4,000 Indians. Should we succeed . . . I shall then be rich and powerful. . . . "[12]

The most powerful magnet for filibuster enterprise in 1855, however, was not Cuba or Ecuador or Mexico but Nicaragua. Interest in this isthmian country had largely been aroused by a project promoted by the Texas land developer Henry L. Kinney. He had obtained title to one of the land grants given away by the inebriate Mosquito king, Robert Charles Frederick, and had formed the Central American Land and Mining Company to colonize the coast. Newspapers had printed reports of the project since early in 1854, and now a year later Kinney was ready to sail with several hundred followers. But there were other Nicaragua schemes afoot not so well known. Visitors to Nicaragua such as Byron Cole, who late in 1854 had obtained a contract for William Walker to lead an expedition in support of the Liberals in the civil war being fought with the Serviles, saw opportunities in the disorganized state and roamed the countryside making deals to bring in Americans to support this or that faction.

The Cuban expedition of General Quitman planned for early 1855 was to be the most formidable ever launched against Spanish rule of the island. Three steamers were chartered to transport forces optimistically set at 4,000 men to the island to support an insurrection led by Ramón Pintó. The signal for the uprising was to be the assassination of the captain general, José G. de la Concha, while he and other government leaders were in attendance at the opera.[13] Unfortunately for this plan, General Concha was kept well informed of the Quitman arrangements by agents in the United States, and on January 28 summoned the acting American consul at Havana, William H. Robertson, to a conference to issue a warning against the invasion. He told Robertson that "he knew all the particulars," the consul reported to Secretary of State Marcy; the expedition had been delayed until the conspirators learned the outcome of Pierre Soulé's mission to Spain, Concha told Robertson, and he was prepared "to meet the invaders if the Government of the United States allowed them to escape."[14]

On February 9, three days before the assassination attempt was to be made, the correspondent of the *New York Tribune* at New Orleans reported that the city was in a state of "considerable excitement" as large numbers left for points in Florida to take part in an invasion. "The papers here are all silent on the subject," he wrote, "and it is evident do not wish to place any impediment to the departure of the expedition." Nevertheless, it was no secret for nothing was talked about but Cuba. The steamer *Massachusetts* and the veteran filibuster ship *Pampero* were to take the men gathered on the Florida coast, while the *United States* was to sail from New Orleans with the Mississippi contingent under Quitman's direct command.

But before the expedition could get off, bad news for the filibusters came from Cuba. General Concha on February 7 had acted to prevent the rebellion by arresting Pintó and about thirty-five other conspirators, adding to his bag forty more the next day. In a proclamation he announced the breaking up of "a vast plan by plotters putting themselves under the orders of foreign adventurers" and declared that troops and ships had been disposed to meet the invasion.

The *Tribune*, alluding to these developments, said of the projected expedition: "No doubt such an invasion—should it be attempted—would be most vigorously welcomed." It added sarcastically for the benefit of filibusters ready to sail "to the scene of glory": "However, we advise them all, from generals down to corporals, not to start till they hear of a more successful revolution in the island than that just nipped in the bud, and meanwhile we trust the authorities will keep an eye on their movements, and put the necessary embargo on the sailing fleet." The same unattractive prospects for the expedition were described by the Spanish minister in Washington, Leopoldo Augusto de Cueto, who wrote Marcy: "The elements of defence and prevention which are at the disposal of Her Majesty the Queen in Cuba, developed and invigorated in consequence of the conspiracy just now discovered, are more than sufficient to repel and punish the aggressions of adventurers."[15]

The discovery of the plot may have disheartened but did not demoralize the filibusters. The New Orleans correspondent of the *New York Times* reported on February 26 that he had just returned from "the grand encampment of filibusters" at a plantation below the city. "I found the men," he wrote disparagingly, "to be a rather hard set of cases, a large number having for a long time been 'members of the *bar*' and loafers about the grog-shops of St. Charles Street." He ridiculed a statement in the *Picayune* that no expedition was planned. "Why, every man, woman and child in this city is aware that there is an expedition afoot," he wrote. "Everybody talks about it, and the city is full of men who are going to Cuba."

The Quitman expedition was one to arouse apprehension in President Pierce over the effects of the Ostend Manifesto if its provisions became known. News reports had aroused widespread interest in this unusual meeting, and on December 4, after the reading of Pierce's State of the Union Message in which he omitted mention of it, Augustus R. Sollers of Maryland asked unanimous consent of the House to offer a resolution calling on the president for information about it. Administration supporters defeated the motion, but Sollers brought it up again next day in order, he said, "to satisfy the curiosity which is almost general, from one end of the country to the other" about this "most unprecedented" conference. Protesting secret diplomacy, Sollers wished to know if the meeting had "for its object some new aggression, some new filibuster movement calculated to bring about discord and war between foreign governments and our own." Although few congressmen knew enough about the matter to discuss it intelligently, they managed to do so at length, their remarks filling six closely printed pages of the *Congressional Globe*. After prolonged skirmishing, the resolution was adopted on February 23, 1855.[16]

Aware that publication would add to the critical attacks being directed at the administration, Pierce and his advisers debated whether to comply with the House resolution. To refuse, they concluded, would be worse than to spread the story before Congress and the public, and on March 5 the president submitted the documents though in much edited versions. Marcy's authorization to Soulé to "detach" Cuba from Spain, for example, was deleted. The correspondence would have been censored more extensively if Soulé, blaming the administration for his failure in Spain, had not objected to additional deletions. Publication on March 7 elicited the barrage Pierce had feared. Whig newspapers and antislavery newspapers of the North were especially virulent. Horace Greeley's *Tribune*, under the heading, "Manifesto of the Brigands," called it a "buccaneering document" in which was seen "the brutalizing march of slavery." William Cullen Bryant's *Evening Post*, describing the participating ministers as "The Three Wise Men of Ostend," declared the report was so "weak in its reasoning and so atrocious in its recommendations that some sensible persons have actually doubted its authenticity." The press of Europe, as could be expected, denounced the American notion of diplomacy exposed in the strange conference, and Marcy received letters from embassy staff members expressing fears that publication of the documents—coming, as it were, "like a criminal, dragged out with the stamp of cabinet condemnation on its front," as Don Piatt, secretary of the Paris legation, put it—would have dangerous effects on the country's foreign relations.[17]

The election reverses, the clamor in Congress over the Ostend conference, and the news of the suppression of the Pintó revolt made it clear to Pierce that if he permitted the Quitman expedition to sail to defeat, which was likely in view of the defensive measures invoked by General Concha, his administration was heading for disaster. Because what political support he had left was in the South and he did not want to lose this by arresting Quitman, he met with the filibuster leader in Washington late in February or early March to persuade him of the inexpediency of his enterprise.

Details of this meeting have never been divulged, but evidently threats of official action against Quitman and his lieutenants and evidence of the formidable defenses of the island led him to see there was little promise of success. Two months later, on April 30, Quitman submitted without explanation to the Cuban junta a briefly worded letter of resignation. His abandonment of the expedition was generally recognized as being due to pressure from Washington. The *New York Tribune* said: "The Adminstration . . . have thrown every obstacle in the way of the departure of Quitman; and but for the determined course pursued by the President and the Cabinet to defeat the enterprise, Gen. Quitman and an army of 4,000 men would now be on the Island of Cuba. . . . "[18]

Early in 1855 the Quitman expedition still had the ability to arouse the enthusiasm of Southerners for the cause of Cuba, but in the North it had been eclipsed in interest by Kinney's projected colony in Nicaragua. Kinney's land grant had originally been made by the Mosquito king Robert Charles Frederick to two brothers, Samuel and Peter Shepherd, natives of Georgia, who had operated trading vessels in the Caribbean and who had won the king's favor, so the story goes, through ample supplies of rum, his favorite beverage. Kinney had obtained title from the surviving brother, Captain Samuel Shepherd, now decrepit with age and half blind, who spent most of the time in a hammock at his house in San Juan del Norte. One of the town's notable citizens, he enjoyed the visits by travelers passing through and regaled them with his garrulous reminiscences.* In the 1840s the Shepherds had organized a company to sell stock in a settlement project, but it came to nothing. In 1853 a New York lawyer named Bryce, who had gone to San Juan in search of adventure, heard about the claim and returned to New York with plans for a colonization scheme. Among the speculators who took up his project was Kinney, and the Central American Land and Mining Company was organized to promote it.[19]

News reports of the enterprise came to the attention of the Nicaraguan minister to Washington, José de Marcoleta, who informed his government in Managua. President Mateo Mayorga instructed the minister, on February 19, 1854, to protest to Secretary of State Marcy. Mayorga, who considered the denomination of the "savage Indian" a king by the British "a ridiculous farce," said that if the Kinney company sent settlers to the territory they

*Ephraim G. Squier, when he went to Nicaragua in 1850 as the American minister, called on Shepherd on the second day after arriving at San Juan del Norte. No report on the town could be complete, Squier wrote, without a description of the venerable trader. From a locked seaman's chest, Shepherd would produce the parchment documents with "his X mark" of "Robert Charles Frederick" granting title to "all that tract of land lying between Blewfields River on the north and San Juan River on the south." *Nicaragua, Its People, Scenery, Monuments, Resources, Conditions, and Proposed Canal*, pp. 55–58.

would be repelled as invaders. Marcoleta's protests to Marcy went unanswered until November 24, when he obtained a disappointing response to his plea that the neutrality laws be invoked against the Kinney expedition. Despite the fact that the United States had never recognized the Mosquito king's sovereignty or the British protectorate, a fact to which Marcoleta had directed attention in his complaints, Marcy replied that his government could not intervene to stop an expedition. The Central American Land and Mining Company, he wrote, was merely an association for business purposes and was not engaged in fitting out an expedition that had any hostile intentions against another nation. The United States could not stop people from leaving the country in a peaceful pursuit, he explained, and could not seek to control their conduct after they had left its jurisdiction.[20]

Accustomed to large land promotions in Texas, Kinney had eagerly taken the lead in the grandiose project involving 22,500,000 acres of land in the Shepherd concession. Although the title must have seemed dubious to anyone who looked into it, he had no trouble in obtaining associates in the scheme in New York, Philadelphia, and Washington. The company offered 225,000 shares of stock at $25 a share to raise operating capital of $5,625,000, and bonds were issued in the sum of $30 million. The president of the board of directors was James Cooper, of Philadelphia and Washington, a former U.S. senator, and the members included Charles Morgan, who with Cornelius K. Garrison had wrested control of the Accessory Transit Company from Cornelius Vanderbilt, and the company's legal counsel, Joseph L. White. Financially interested in the project were three close associates of President Pierce —Sidney Webster, his secretary, and John W. Forney and A. O. P. Nicholson, editors of the *Washington Union*, the administration organ.[21] One of Kinney's most important recruits was the U.S. commercial agent at San Juan del Norte, Joseph W. Fabens, who himself had obtained one of the spurious Frederick land grants, 700,000 acres in the Chontales district, and the two dreamers of empire joined forces. Possession of the Chontales, a highland area between Lake Nicaragua and the Bluefields River, was more attractive than the low, swampy coastal area claimed by Kinney, for it was reputed to contain gold in abundance.[22]

In his promotional literature Kinney emphasized the peaceful intentions of his expedition. One pamphlet, titled *A Home in Nicaragua!*, described the lands to be occupied as a paradisical region for the farmer and gave an alluring account of the mineral wealth of the Chontales. The company formed to colonize the lands, the pamphlet said, offered to all persons taking passage within the next three months, "for the purpose of becoming actual settlers," from 160 to 640 acres. The steamship *United States* had been fitted out to convey the expedition to Central America at passage fares of $80 for after-saloons, $60 for forward saloons, and $40 for steerage. "Each person," the pamphlet advised, "should outfit himself for three months—clothing, tent, domestic agricultural and mining implements and weapons for sport and defense."[23]

The antiexpansionist press did not believe this propaganda. The *New York Tribune*, in an editorial, "The Plot of the Day," on January 5, 1855, attacked the scheme as just another military expedition got up to invade an unoffending foreign country. The paper charged that the leaders were so confident of success they had reached an agreement with the Accessory Transit Company to issue it a new contract once Kinney and "his condottieri" succeeded "in conquering the present State of Nicaragua and in getting possession of its territory in its sovereign powers." Exposures of the plot in such newspapers as the *New York Times*, the *Washington Union*, and the *Boston Post* were cited; and yet "in the face of this public notoriety" Secretary Marcy affected "a total ignorance of the design" and replied to Marcoleta that he had "no official information" concerning it. The paper believed Kinney's ultimate plan was to establish slavery in Nicaragua and to annex the country to the Union.*

In the meantime, Marcy had become troubled over the questions raised by the newspapers and summoned Kinney to a conference on January 28 to obtain answers. At the close of the

*Newspaper condemnation was so widespread that Kinney, on Jan. 8, 1855, replied in a letter to the Washington *National Intelligencer*. The letter did not halt the spate of criticism, and soon Washington correspondents were predicting that the government would hold the expedition in violation of the neutrality laws. The *New York Courier and Enquirer*, for example, said on Jan. 24 that there was little doubt the administration would "soon issue instructions to break up the Kinney expedition and prevent its departure."

interview, Marcy asked Kinney to put his statement in writing, and this was printed, together with Marcy's rejoinder, in the *Washington Union* on February 7. Kinney wrote that it was his "purpose to occupy some suitable place, and to establish municipal regulations for the immediate government of the colonists." Quoting this back to Kinney, Marcy in his reply declared it could not be assumed the expedition would take up land in a place where a government did not already exist. The significance of this was that any government set up by Kinney anywhere would violate the sovereignty of the state in which he intended to settle. Marcy pointed out that both Nicaragua and Costa Rica claimed ownership of parts of the Mosquito country and warned that the government held that the Mosquito Indians were a savage tribe, and though they had rights as occupants of the country they possessed no sovereign authority by which they could transfer to individuals title to the lands on which they lived. His letter was phrased in the guarded language he customarily employed but nevertheless made it clear the administration took a dim view of the expedition and would certainly intervene if it were proved to be a military one.

Newspaper accounts of the Kinney project had whetted public interest in Nicaragua, and editors met the demand for information by printing long reports on conditions there. The country was torn apart by one of the frequent civil wars—so frequent as to be almost continuous—between the two traditional party factions, the Liberals and the Serviles, that had marked her history. It was a situation creating opportunities for restless filibusters, as Byron Cole and William V. Wells had discovered in August 1854 on their way to explore mining opportunities in Honduras. The nation's organic law of 1838 provided for a legislative body of two chambers and a president, called the supreme director, elected biennially. A Servile, Fruto Chamorro, had won the election in 1853, taking office on April 1, but his victory had been challenged by the Liberals, who said it was obtained by fraud and violence. The losers, as was customary in such a situation, immediately began engaging in plots to overturn the government, but Chamorro, now in command of the army, forced them to flee the country under threat of arrest. They took refuge in Honduras, then controlled by the Liberal party led by Trinidad Cabañas. To secure himself in power, Chamorro had the legislature at Managua revise the constitution to give the supreme director greater powers and to extend the term of office to four years. He promulgated the new law on April 30, 1854.

Less than a week later, on May 5, a band of Liberal exiles in Honduras of about fifty men sailed from Tigre Island with arms supplied by President Cabañas for Realejo, a town of about 1,000 people on the coast, to lead an uprising against Chamorro. The Occidental District with its capital at León, the nation's most populous and thriving city, was the stronghold of the Liberal party, and the invaders expected the people to join the revolt. In a series of attacks they drove the Serviles from the towns, including León, and on June 11 proclaimed the establishment of a new government with Francisco Castellón as the provisional director. The Liberals, designating themselves Democrats, adopted a red ribbon as their color; the Serviles became known as Legitimists from the motto on their white colors, "Legitimidad o muerte." Chamorro withdrew to the traditional Servile stronghold, Granada, a town of 10,000 people at the northern end of Lake Nicaragua, which he proclaimed the seat of government. Máximó Jérez, commander of the Democratic army, attacked Granada in June, but his troops were repulsed in their first assault and he settled down to a somewhat desultory siege. Such was the state of affairs in August when Byron Cole, meeting Castellón at León, persuaded him that 300 well-armed soldiers under William Walker could turn the tide of war.[24]

The idea of enlisting Americans to fight under the red or white colors of the contending factions in Nicaragua was not new. John Bozman Kerr, who succeeded Ephraim George Squire as chargé d'affaires, protested in 1851 and 1852 against the practice to Nicaraguan officials and complained of it in letters to Secretary of State Webster. Kerr reached Nicaragua in July 1851, but the country was so disorganized that it was some time before he was able to find an authority to which he could present his credentials. His difficulties began shortly after his arrival at León on July 28, when the supreme director, José Laureano Pineda, and several of his ministers were seized in a revolt headed by General José Trinidad Muñoz and a new provisional government was established. It did not last long, for Muñoz was captured and exiled on November 10, but while temporarily in power he sought to strengthen his hand by recruiting Americans from among the travelers crossing the newly established transit from California. Kerr wrote Webster: "You may imagine my position here, when the success of the revolutionary movement is regarded by Muñoz and his junto as mainly dependent on the assistance thus to be secured." With 100 Americans, Kerr added, Muñoz would not hesitate to march upon Granada.[25]

The practice of recruiting Americans was still being followed three years later when Charles W. Doubleday, an English-born adventurer who had traveled over the American West, landed at San Juan del Sur on the Pacific in June 1854 from one of the mail steamers. He had recently been visiting the California mining camps and on reaching San Francisco thought it might be pleasant to "sail away and wander among the tropical forests." Arriving shortly after General Jérez had begun his siege of Granada, Doubleday decided to offer his soldierly skills to the Democratic army and began at once to recruit a company of like-minded adventurers whom he found mostly, he related, in the rum shops of the town. "Though their farewell potations doubtless gave an impetus to the forward movement," Doubleday wrote in his reminiscences in the jocular vein of other filibuster authors, "they caused a divergence from a straight line, which was not even partially corrected until we got beyond the last *pulpería* of the town." When Doubleday and his band reached General Jérez's headquarters at Jalteva, a village near Granada, they were accepted into the Democratic army and saw action in occasional skirmishes with troops sent out from the city.[26]

While Doubleday was taking part in the siege of Granada, several other Americans arrived in Nicaragua to make contacts with the Democrats to bring in filibusters to their aid. One of these was Henry A. Crabb, a boyhood friend of William Walker in Nashville. A lawyer who had his fingers in Tennessee politics, Crabb had joined the gold rush in 1849, partly because of the unpleasantness resulting from his killing a man in a duel fought over a dispute in the election of 1848. He had served in the first California legislature as a Whig. Passing through Nicaragua in 1854 to visit the Mississippi Valley, Crabb learned that revolutionists were seeking the aid of Americans, and in New Orleans persuaded two friends to join him in a project to obtain a contract to bring in an expedition from California. They were C. C. Hornsby, a native of North Carolina who had fought in the Mexican War as a captain of volunteers and who had become acquainted with Crabb while serving as sergeant at arms in the California legislature, and Thomas F. Fisher, a soldier of fortune then living in New Orleans.[27] Sailing to Greytown late in December 1854, they encountered another adventurer, Julius de Brissot, who was on his way to Ecuador as the agent of a company formed to obtain the guano from a rich deposit he reported he had discovered on the Galapagos Islands. De Brissot had learned at Greytown that the richness of the guano deposit had been greatly exaggerated, and he cast in his lot with Crabb.[28]

The arrival of this opportunity-seeking quartet in Greytown coincided with that of the new U.S. minister to Nicaragua, John H. Wheeler, and soon the newspapers were carrying reports that they were traveling about the country as members of his official party. Wheeler was a North Carolina lawyer whose political career had been only moderately successful. He had served in the state legislature but had been defeated in his races for higher offices. He had been named minister on the recommendation of his fellow North Carolinian, Secretary of the Navy James C. Dobbin. Wheeler's immediate object was to settle claims of persons, chiefly British subjects, whose property had been destroyed in the bombardment of Greytown. The town was "slowly rising from its ashes, but without any government, or law, or rules whatever," Wheeler wrote Secretary of State Marcy on December 22. Two weeks later he reported outrageous claims—evidence of the "swindling character" of the people—totaling $1,182,679 when "the whole town in its palmiest day was not worth more than $100,000."

Late in January Wheeler left Greytown for the interior with the filibuster quartet as part of his entourage to decide which of the two warring factions constituted a government to which he could present his credentials. According to Doubleday's reminiscences, at Granada he was able to arrange a truce between the Legitimists and the Democrats, the first during the war, to meet General Jérez at Jalteva. It created an opportunity for the filibusters, under the protection of the American flag, to present their California expedition plan to the general, who, after several months during which he had been unable to defeat the Legitimists, welcomed the offer. Crabb hastened on to San Francisco to begin the work of organizing an expedition while Hornsby, Fisher, and De Brissot remained behind to conclude arrangements with Jérez. The three then set out to follow Crabb to California, but Hornsby and De Brissot became sidetracked at Rivas, a town a few miles from the west coast of Lake Nicaragua, when they were persuaded by Máximó Espinosa, governor of the district, to lead a band of native troops in an effort to capture Castillo Viejo, the fort that commanded the San Juan River whose possession by the rebels would shut off the Legitimists on the east as they were now shut off on the west.

Meanwhile, Wheeler returned to Greytown to complete the taking of evidence in the bombardment damage claims and shortly afterward presented his credentials to the Legitimist government at Granada. He was glad to quit Greytown, writing Marcy: "Nothing but a sense of duty, and instructions from your Department, could compel me to remain two more such months here; for there has not been an hour that the safety of myself and family has not been jeopardized."[29]

The New Orleans correspondent of the *Alta California*, in an account of memorial services held in September 1854 on the anniversary of the death of Narciso López, was led to wonder about the popularity of filibuster expeditions in the face of their consistently unhappy outcomes. He had heard reports that San Francisco was "nursing formidable battalions for filibustering purposes" and asked: "Has not the wretched failure of the Sonora expedition damped the ardor of your chivalrous sons? . . . Has the fate of the López expedition or the Walker bubble produced no salutary effect upon their ideas of foreign conquest?"

These were questions bothering some of the country's leading editors. Horace Greeley, the oracle of the *New York Tribune*, considered filibusterism a "natural outgrowth of the peculiar character of our political and material development." Linking the projects of 1855 to the settlement of Texas in the days of Sam Houston, he wrote:

The reckless character of American enterprise delights in just such emigrating stampedes. Bands of men shoulder their muskets, put their personal traps into wagons or ships, and go forth to plant themselves upon unoccupied soil, wherever it is to be found. Obeying a natural impulse common to the emigrant everywhere, inflamed by the love of excitement and adventure, these crowds drift over the boundaries of our territory and alight upon whatever country is most enticing to their imaginations, or most promising to their cupidity. The mere matter of the existing government of such, they view with little regard, having been educated and always having lived, in the faith that every country should be governed by the people who inhabit or migrate to it. . . . Thus it is difficult to make them view as a crime, the peopling of uninhabited countries, or countries where there is plenty of room for more, with Anglo-Saxon stock and giving such all the improvements of American civilization, including the blessing of self-government as they understand it.

Henry J. Raymond of the *New York Times* noted that from Aaron Burr down to Colonel Kinney "disaster and defeat" had been "the portion of all filibusters," yet expeditions for conquest still attracted followers. He thought that they were probably prompted by "the same spirit of adventure which sent De Soto to Florida and enticed our ancestors across the Atlantic, to found the empire of which we now boast."

William Cullen Bryant of the *Evening Post* attributed filibusterism to the nature of the Anglo-Saxon people. "The piratical instinct of our Anglo-Saxon forefathers is active yet," he wrote. "We will say nothing of the British conquests in India, which are robberies on a large scale; we have examples in point nearer home. In our country the old instinct is continually breaking out, and keeping a part of the population in a restless state. At one time Canada was its object; at present the spirit of piratical adventure seeks a southern direction, wisely preferring to strike at a feebler prey. Repelled from Cuba it pounces upon Central America."

Rather than a racial or national trait, the *Alta California* found the impulse to filibusterism arising primarily in the misfits of society. The first step in forming an expedition, the paper said, was to find "some individual who has speculated through half a dozen different professions, and failed in them all . . . ; has become convinced of the injustice of the world towards him; is strongly impressed with the idea that the world owes him a fat living; and reasoning from the vanity of human affairs, is not disposed to scruple at the means by which he can attain that living." Such a person, the paper continued, will attract as followers similar spirits, equally "maltreated and unappreciated by the world." The next stage is to choose the promised land, to be found "in any territory not occupied by Europeans or North Americans." Then the expedition must be financed, and this can be done by striking off bonds secured by the public lands of the state to be taken over, which are sold at a huge discount with the implication "that the buyers can lose little and may make a princely fortune." With money thus obtained, captains and lieutenants can be recruited by hunting up "the disappointed office seekers, the bankrupt speculators, the briefless lawyers, the worn out politicians, and all others too good to work and too afraid to steal." The ranks are easily filled by the promise of "all kinds of honors in the case of success" and by assurances that "the fighting at worst with the Spaniards will be mere fun, to be followed by the partition of all kinds and any quantity of booty." Then the expedition is given an aura of sanctity by being proclaimed as "undertaken to overthrow some tyrant, to spread the blessings of civilization and true Christianity, and to establish a free government that will soon apply for admission to the American Union."[30]

Whatever their motives, the leaders and members of the two expeditions simultaneously sailing for Nicaragua in the summer of 1855 were possessed of a recklessness that was irrational. Walker, who was to set out with only fifty-eight followers, whom he later designated "The Immortals," and Kinney, who was to be able to depart with only eighteen followers, had few qualms, it seems, that with their small numbers they could possibly fail. Walker described his crew as being "tired of the humdrum of common life, and ready for a career which might bring them the sweets of adventure or the rewards of fame." Kinney's expeditionists seemed to have been a similar collection of devil-may-care adventurers. The historian of the voyage was William Sydney Thayer, a twenty-five-year-old New Englander who had gone to work on the *Evening Post* in 1853 and who had resigned to join the enterprise in which he owned several shares of stock. "Our companions on the voyage," he wrote the paper, "were mostly young, unmarried men, mechanics and merchants, with a sprinkling of western frontiersmen, who had been more inured than the rest to the hardships of out-of-door life."[31]

15. The filibuster William Walker became a popular hero in the United States when he succeeded in making himself dictator of Nicaragua.

17. Ephraim George Squier, sent to Central America as chargé d'affaires in 1849, opposed British enroachments in the region and signed an agreement with Nicaragua for American construction of an interoceanic canal.

16. The financier Cornelius Vanderbilt, angry when William Walker sold the Nicaraguan transit franchise to a business rival, relentlessly fought the filibuster and eventually contributed to his downfall.

18. Cornelius K. Garrison, west coast manager of operations of the shipping company given the Nicaraguan transit franchise, abetted William Walker in his depredations in Central America.

19. A straggle of thatched huts and small wooden buildings, San Juan del Norte on the Atlantic coast of Nicaragua had few attractions to delay travelers on their way to California.

20. San Carlos, on the eastern shore of Lake Nicaragua, where the San Juan River has its origin, was an important command post in the control of the transit route across Nicaragua.

21. *The volcano Ometepe at sunrise, with a bungo in the foreground, as seen from Virgin Bay on the west shore of Lake Nicaragua.*

22. *Travelers from California landed at San Juan del Sur to begin their trip across Nicaragua to sail to the eastern United States.*

23. Charles Frederick Henningsen, who had been a soldier in revolutionary armies in Spain, Russia, and Hungary, joined William Walker in Nicaragua and for a time was his second in commmand.

24. Henry L. Kinney, owner of a vast tract of land in Texas, sought to enlarge his empire by establishing a colony on the Mosquito Coast of Nicaragua.

25. The city of León, capital of the Democratic government in the 1850s, with the Cathedral of St. Peter, largest structure in Nicaragua, in the background.

26. A scenic view of the mountain at the confluence of the San Carlos and San Juan Rivers; the boat in the foreground is a bungo, the chief means of navigation on the rivers.

27. Callender I. Fayssoux took part in two expeditions of Narciso López to Cuba and was one of William Walker's chief aides in Nicaragua.

28. S. A. Lockridge, commander of William Walker's forces on the San Juan River, lost several battles to Costa Rican troops.

29. Lake Nicaragua steamers landed or picked up transit passengers and cargo at Virgin Bay on the west shore. The volcano Ometepe is in the background.

30. A Nicaraguan volunteer in William Walker's army.

31. Navy Commander Charles H. Davis saved William Walker's starving soldiers from annihilation early in 1857 at the town of Rivas by negotiating with the Central American command for surrender of the filibuster and his men to the United States.

32. Commodore Hiram Paulding broke up William Walker's second expedition to Nicaragua late in 1857 by arresting him in the harbor of San Juan del Norte and shipping his 150 followers back to the United States in a naval vessel.

CHAPTER TWELVE

Expeditions to Nicaragua

The new contract that Byron Cole arranged with Francisco Castellón, provisional director of the Liberal government at León, to give William Walker's planned expedition to Nicaragua the camouflage of a colonization project and to increase the amount of land to be won as booty reached him at Sacramento early in February 1855. He resigned his job with the *Democratic State Journal* and hurried to San Francisco to commence operations. Walker related in his own account of his experiences, *The War in Nicaragua*, which he published in 1860, that his friend Henry A. Crabb arrived shortly afterward with news of the contract he was negotiating with General Jérez. Walker's enthusiasm for the Nicaraguan adventure was heightened by Crabb's "glowing report of the natural wealth and advantages of the country." The arrival of Thomas F. Fisher, who had remained behind to complete arrangements with Jérez, with a report of the eagerness with which American military aid was sought also increased Walker's ardor for the expedition.

Crabb lost interest in the Nicaraguan scheme when he saw an opportunity to put himself at the head of the Know Nothing movement in California and offered the contract brought by Fisher to Walker. Walker refused to have anything to do with it, because it was a military scheme that would violate the neutrality laws, the flaw he had found in the first arrangement negotiated by Cole. Fisher was reconciled to giving up the Jérez contract when he was offered a commission in Walker's army, as were Hornsby and De Brissot when they reached San Francisco a little later after the failure of their attempt to seize Castillo Viejo.

Confident that the contract with Castellón, explicitly described as a colonization scheme, could not be objected to by federal officials, Walker cleared it with the U.S. district attorney, S. W. Inge, and General John E. Wool, commander of the Pacific division of the army. Inge found no legal bar to the expedition, and Wool, smarting under the reprimand of Secretary of War Jefferson Davis over his zealousness in trying to stop the Sonora expeditions, was not inclined to interfere.

There was a greater hindrance to the project, however, than obtaining official sanction—the lack of money. On February 22 the San Francisco banking house of Page, Bacon, and Company suspended payment, and the next day three more banks closed and there were runs on others. The best that Walker could do was to obtain $1,000 from Joseph Palmer, whose bank had managed to remain open.

At Palmer's home Walker met Colonel John C. Fremont, who had recently passed through Nicaragua on his return to California from serving in the U.S. Senate, and found him in favor of the project. Some historians have insisted that Walker in his forays in Sonora and Nicaragua had no intention of introducing slavery, but his own history indicates that this proposition is dubious. In relating the meeting with Palmer and Fremont, next year to be the antislavery candidate for president of the new Republican party, Walker wrote cryptically: "It is due probably, to both Colonel Fremont and Mr. Palmer, to state that they were not fully aware of all the views Walker held on the subject of slavery; nor, indeed, was it necessary at that time for those views to be expressed."

Walker's efforts to raise money were also hindered by what he ambiguously reported in his history as "an injury in the foot, which kept him in his chamber until the middle of April." What had happened was that on March 15 he had fought a duel with a former Sacramento man, W. H. Carter, a veteran of several duels in which he had wounded his adversary with his first shot; the same fate befell Walker when they faced each other at eight paces and the filibuster received a pistol bullet in the foot.[1]

Although Walker was able to raise only "a pitiful sum of money," he obtained enough so that by early April he was able to charter a leaky old sailing brig, the *Vesta*, and buy arms and supplies. All was set for the sailing to Realejo on April 20 when Walker became enmeshed in legal entanglements that were to hold up his departure for three weeks. The expeditionists had gone on board when the sheriff seized the vessel upon a writ of attachment obtained by a creditor of the owner, one Lamson, sending aboard a party of ten men armed with revolvers to prevent an escape. To make doubly sure the ship did not depart, the sheriff unbent the sails and took them ashore.

A few days later a second writ of attachment obtained by merchants who had furnished supplies and accepted stock in the enterprise in payment and who had on second thought decided they wanted cash was served by the U.S. marshal. He placed a deputy aboard and, to ensure that the vessel did not leave, stationed the revenue cutter *W. L. Marcy* astern. As Lamson was a friend of Crabb's, he was persuaded to grant easy terms for release of the vessel as well as to urge dismissal of the writ of attachment of the merchants who owed him money, Walker related, but his action was not entirely induced by goodwill toward the expedition: it was pointed out to him it might not be safe for him to keep the expeditionists in San Francisco.

Now cleared of legal entanglements, Walker was ready to sail except for one thing: the sheriff's fees for serving Lamson's writ and the cost of employing guards had risen to more than $300, and the filibuster, down nearly to his last cent, could not pay him to obtain release of the sails. Walker managed to get around this obstacle, however, by prevailing upon the sheriff to return the sails because, ignorant of the dismissal of the writs, he thought the *Marcy* would prevent the *Vesta* from sailing. In any case, the sheriff still had one of his deputies aboard, E. P. Purdy, a former state assemblyman.

On the evening of May 3 Walker notified the commander of the *Marcy* that the *Vesta* had been freed of the attachments against her and obtained his promise to send sailors from the cutter aboard the brig to bend on the sails. He prevented Purdy from interfering by asking him to look over some papers in the cabin below decks. Once in the cabin, Purdy was informed that the *Vesta* was getting ready to sail and that no harm would be done him if he remained quiet. Walker is reported to have addressed him: "There, sir, are segars and champagne; and there are handcuffs and irons. Pray take your choice." It was an easy one for the deputy. The sailors from the *Marcy* came aboard at ten o'clock and bent on the sails and shortly after midnight the steam tug *Resolute* came alongside and towed the *Vesta*, carrying fifty-eight expeditionists, to the harbor entrance where the now cheerfully disposed Purdy was taken aboard. The harbor cleared, the *Vesta* was cast off from the *Resolute* and, as the *Alta California* described the departure, was "away under a spread of sail to the southwestward, with a stiff northwest breeze after her."[2]

William Walker, in San Francisco where indulgent officials offered no opposition to his expedition, had only to solve his financial difficulties, which he did with the cunning of a confidence man. But Henry L. Kinney in New York faced not only financial problems but also an administration in Washington that had become alert to the political dangers of foreign adventures like the Quitman expedition and the projected one to Nicaragua and had decided to suppress them.

Secretary of State Marcy had warned Kinney that the government would invoke the neutrality laws if his expedition was found to be a military one. Such evidence was soon to be presented to him by an unexpected opponent of Kinney's—the Accessory Transit Company. Joseph L. White and Charles Morgan had become members of the board of directors of Kinney's company shortly after its incorporation. Their withdrawal was revealed January 8 by the *New York Tribune*, which printed a report that they had informed the minister from Nicaragua, José de Marcoleta, they would no longer support the expedition because its character had changed from a peaceable enterprise to a "warlike and even piratical" one.

This was hardly the full story. The company the year before, through the collaboration of the Pierce administration in bombarding Greytown, had destroyed the free city so that it could no longer interfere with its business operations. Now Kinney appeared on the scene with plans to take over the port, set up his own government of aggressive Americans, and place himself in a position to control the Atlantic end of the transit route. To prevent this, White became legal counsel to Marcoleta and supplied him with documentary evidence of the expedition's military character to submit to the secretary of state and federal district attorneys. The result was that legal action was taken to prevent the sailing of the expedition.

On April 21 New York papers carried the information that the long-planned expedition was almost ready to sail, that the steamship *United States*, which recently had set a record in a run from Havana, was moored in the East River at the foot of Eighth Street and would depart May 7 with several hundred passengers for San Juan del Norte. A week later there was news of a different nature. On April 29 the papers announced Kinney's arrest on charges of planning a military expedition against a friendly nation. Joseph W. Fabens, named in the same indictment, was arrested five days later in Washington and taken to New York. They were brought to trial on May 7, but when the case was called the U.S. district attorney, John McKeon, sought a postponement on the ground that two of his witnesses were absent. Because the trials of Cuba expedition leaders had indicated that New York juries would not convict accused filibusters, Kinney was confident he would be acquitted and therefore opposed the postponement. Delay would harm him more than the trial. The charter of the *United States* had cost him $21,000, and every day her sailing was held up he was out of pocket about $2,500 in harbor charges and the expense of feeding and housing the several hundred registered expeditionists. Nevertheless, the judge passed the case over to the next term of court, and the defendants were released on their own recognizance in $1,000 bail.

Since Kinney and Fabens were not compelled to post a high bond, the editor of the *New York Times*, Henry J. Raymond, took this as meaning that the *United States* could sail at any time. Marcoleta was of the same belief. On May 9 he wrote Marcy requesting that the government post guards on the ship to prevent her departure. He considered a "characteristic circumstance" of "the mad enthusiasm produced by the excitement of, and the thirst for, adventure" the distribution of a map of Nicaragua embellished with likenesses of Kinney and Fabens and with new towns marked out bearing the names Montezuma, Cortes, Fabensville, and Kinneyville. He complained that Fabens still held his post as commercial agent at San Juan del Norte. Marcy had anticipated Marcoleta in respect to Fabens' official status: on the same day that Marcoleta wrote, the secretary of state had notified Fabens of his dismissal.[3] He did nothing, however, to prevent the sailing of the *United States*.

Marcoleta and White redoubled their efforts to cause Kinney trouble, interviewing witnesses to obtain evidence of the military character of the expedition and presenting it to government officials. They scored a success in Philadelphia, where a grand jury indicted Kinney and he was arrested. The *New York Times* commented: "One court, in the district where Kinney's offence, if any, was committed, has released him; and yet a foreign adventurer, aided by the speculating attorney of a speculating company which fears the establishment of a rival to its monopoly, are permitted to go into another court, in another district, and obtain a new indictment upon the same charge. It looks very much as though the prosecuting parties are determined to *harass* the life out of the Kinney enterprise." The *Evening Post*, too, considered the government's position, if it could be said to have one, as being somewhat duplicitous, declaring editorially: "Meanwhile the administration . . . appears to look on the whole with a masterly inactivity and unconcern, prepared, if Kinney should find a happy issue out of all his inflictions, to rejoice in the extension of American enterprise and institutions over Central America; and, if his project should be suppressed, to announce it to the world as evidence of the Government's sensitive regard for the rights of a sister Republic, and its determination to crush even the semblance of filibusterism."[4]

Arraigned in the U.S. District Court in Philadelphia on May 21, Kinney was again unable to obtain the speedy trial he requested. Newspaper predictions that despite the charges pending against him the sailing of the expedition would not be delayed prompted President Pierce, after a cabinet discussion of the situation, to order the Department of the Navy to post ships in New York harbor to blockade the *United States*. Facing two trials and with his vessel under guard by warships, Kinney was finally forced to a desperate expedient to launch his expedition.

The night before Kinney and Fabens were to come to trial in New York, the wharf in the East River where the *United States* was moored was the setting for a rally of 3,000 persons called to protest the blockade, most of them seamen and shipyard workers. Next morning when the filibuster case was called in court, Kinney was absent. The case was put off until the next day and again the chief defendant did not appear. When, on the following day the case was again called, the district attorney was forced to inform the judge that the trial could not proceed: Kinney, he had been told, was on the high seas. As indeed he was. While the attention of officials was centered on the protest rally, Kinney had slipped aboard a schooner, the *Emma*, and sailed with eighteen expeditionists for San Juan del Norte, leaving public notice to be issued after his departure inviting others to follow on the next ship to Central America and attacking the "high-handed measures to oppress private citizens in the pursuit of lawful business" taken by "a most extraordinary coalition—that of the Government of the United States and the Accessory Transit Company of Nicaragua."[5]

During the voyage of the *Vesta* south, Walker's expeditionists must have worried at times if they would ever reach their destination. A twenty-nine-year-old brig whose timbers had sprung leaks during years of sailing the Pacific, she made slow progress, and in crossing the Gulf of Tehuantepec she encountered a gale that sent such huge waves over her decks she several times was in danger of foundering. After five weeks, she finally reached the Bay of Fonseca and anchored off Tigre Island. There Walker was met by an emissary from Francisco Castellón, Gilbert Morton, captain of the vessel that had taken the revolutionists from Honduras in 1854 to start their campaign against the Serviles, sent to conduct him to the Nicaraguan port of Realejo.

During the short cruise to Realejo, reached on June 16, Walker learned from Captain Morton of severe reverses suffered by the Democrats since the first of the year. In January, General Jérez, who had been severely wounded, was forced to abandon the siege of Granada. His forces retreated to León, covered by a small band of expert marksmen led by "el capitan California," Charles W. Doubleday, or so this adventurer related. The Serviles now occupied Rivas and Managua, and the Democrats were confined to the area around León. Jérez had been replaced as commander of the Democratic army by José Trinidad Muñoz, who was ranked as one of the ablest soldiers in all Central America and who since leading an aborted revolt against the government of José Laureano Pineda in 1851 had lived in Honduras. The Legitimist president, Fruto Chamorro, had died, to be replaced by José María Estrada. By following a moderate course, Estrada was gaining favor in the Democratic towns, and he could feel confident in the strength of his government to which two foreign ministers had been accredited, John H. Wheeler of the United States and Facundo Goñi of Spain. Muñoz, Walker learned, had followed a dilatory course, mainly of a defensive nature, and he was thought to have given up his fiery republicanism and to favor a compromise between the two contending parties.[6]

Instead of being discouraged by the poor prospects of the Democrats as reported by Captain Morton, Walker was cheered. "He felt that the more desperate the fortunes of the Castellón party were," Walker wrote in his history, in which he referred to himself in the third person as his model, Julius Caesar, had done in his account of the Gallic wars, "the more deeply would they be indebted to the men who might rescue them from their danger, and the more thoroughly would they be committed to any course or policy the Americans might propose."[7] It was with such supreme self-assurance that he left the *Vesta* when she came to anchor in the Bay of Realejo and made the trip with his small force by bungo 5 miles up the river to the town, established so far from the coast to escape raids by buccaneers in the seventeenth century. There were a few soldiers about wearing the red ribbon with the identification "Ejército Democrático," who guided them to their quarters. A few hours later a welcoming delegation from Castellón made up of Captain Doubleday and Colonel Félix Ramírez reached the village. Doubleday related that he found the streets seemingly crowded with Americans, "who, in true California style, were having things their own way," chiefly a merry and boisterous one through their taking over the *pulperías*.

The next morning Walker, accompanied by Timothy Crocker, who had been at his side in the Lower California invasion, and C. C. Hornsby, who had been one of the contractors with General Jérez for bringing in an American force, set out by horseback for León. Once en route, on the outskirts of the ancient town of Chinandega, Walker noticed a company of the native soldiery resting in the shade of a huge ceiba tree. He observed that they were carefully watched by their officers for fear some of them might take advantage of the halt to slip away and "so escape the hated service" into which they had been impressed.*

Walker, like other visitors to Nicaragua, was greatly taken by his first view of León. Emerging from the forest to the plain in which the city is set, the traveler saw the lofty line of volcanoes to the east extending from the Gulf of Fonseca to Lake Managua, with the towering spires of Momotombo to the south and Viejo to the north. The houses on the outskirts, typical of Nicaraguan towns, were of cane covered with thatch, though sometimes plastered with mud, but those within were solidly built of adobe. Ephraim George Squier thought the public buildings of León among the finest in all Central America. Its most notable structure was the Cathedral of St. Peter, built of stone and mortar and completed in 1743 after thirty-seven years of labor.[8]

Castellón, though disappointed to discover that Walker's force numbered only about one-fifth of the 300 men expected, received the filibuster cordially. Walker, quickly sizing up the Nicaraguan, came to an adverse opinion of him. "There was a certain indecision, not merely in his words and features, but even in his walk and the general motions of his body," Walker recalled; "and this trait of character seemed to be aggravated by the circumstances about him." The chief circumstance was that he appeared to be nervous about General Muñoz's reactions to the arrival of the Americans. Earlier Muñoz had recommended that Castellón send a commission to discuss peace terms with General Ponciano Corral, commander of the Legitimist army, who was at odds with his government since he had expected to be named supreme director upon the death of Fruto Chamorro and was disappointed when the office went instead to José María Estrada. Nothing had come of the peace overtures, however, because of the recent series of victories of the Legitimists. At this first interview, Castellón told

*Neither the Legitimist nor the Democratic generals could rely on their native troops. A former U.S. consul in Nicaragua just before Walker's arrival, Peter F. Stout, reported that the method of recruitment was to round up farmers and laborers and force them into military service. Barefoot and dressed in loose cotton shirts and pantaloons reaching the calf, they were harshly treated, for minor offenses being tied to a post and whipped with leather thongs or gun ramrods. *Nicaragua: Past, Present and Future*, pp. 53–54.

Walker that he would like to have the filibusters enter the service as a separate corps, *la Falange Americana*.

That evening Muñoz called at the house of the provisional director to meet Walker. The two accounts of the meeting—those of Walker and Doubleday—indicate that the American and the Nicaraguan took an immediate dislike to each other. "Between the two," Doubleday recalled, "as marked an antipathy was observable as that exhibited in the sudden encounter between a dog and a cat." Walker's laconic and abrupt speech and plain appearance were in contrast to the Latin grace of Muñoz and his handsome uniform of a major general. Walker was put off by what he considered Muñoz's pretensions of military knowledge, "exposing his ignorance in every sentence." The general intimated that he opposed bringing the American volunteers into the army, and Walker for his part informed Castellón later that if he enlisted it would be with the distinct understanding he would not serve under Muñoz. It was a view Castellón could accept, because, as Doubleday related, he "felt himself about equally exposed to destruction from the hostile acts of the enemy in arms against his government and the machinations of General Muñoz, commanding his own army."

Walker was eager for action, understanding, as Doubleday said, that "by success as a soldier only could he claim consideration in the country." He proposed to Castellón that he lead the falange, supported by native troops, in an attack on Rivas, a town a few miles west of Lake Nicaragua whose occupation by the Democrats would give them control of the transit road to San Juan del Sur. It was a plan that solved Castellón's dilemma. It would give Walker a command independent of that of Muñoz, and if he obtained a footing on the transit road he could more easily obtain recruits for his force and supplies from California. Thus Walker during his first days in Nicaragua established the military goal he was to pursue in all his operations thereafter: control of the transit route, which would give him control of the country.

Rejoining his troops next day at Chinandega where the falange was now quartered, Walker immediately set about organizing a corps that would be supported by native soldiers recruited by Colonel Ramírez. He appointed Achilles Kewen, a veteran of the López expeditions, his second in command with the rank of lieutenant colonel.* Walker's young follower in the Lower California foray, Timothy Crocker, was commissioned a major and made third in command. Walker held him in great affection, writing of him after he fell in action in the first engagement at Rivas: "A boy in appearance, with a slight figure, and a face almost feminine in its delicacy and beauty, he had the heart of a lion. . . . To Walker he was invaluable; for they had been together in many a trying hour, and the fellowship of difficulty and danger had established a sort of free-masonry between them."[9]

Walker wasted no time in preparing for his first battle. Within two days he had moved his men to Realejo and on June 23 set sail in the *Vesta* for a landing at the south, Brito, a few miles north of San Juan del Sur, to start the march on Rivas. His native support was to have been made up of 200 men, but when they were mustered on deck he was disappointed to find there was only half this number. The failure of Ramírez to recruit the promised number of men was no surprise to Doubleday, who had decided to join the falange, reluctantly because in the past he had been given considerable freedom as "el capitan California." Doubleday had warned Walker that Ramírez was unreliable, a "morose and inconspicuous officer" who, he had been told, was a tool of Muñoz. "Walker, to whom I imparted this information, seemed to care but little about it," Doubleday related. "The reason for his indifference was his inordinate confidence in the ability of his handful of Americans to conquer, unassisted, any number of the enemy." This overconfidence was the fatal flaw Doubleday saw in Walker. Like Napoleon, who was his great exemplar, Walker "conceived himself to be an instrument of destiny before whom all lesser influences must give way" and "this confidence in his destiny led him to disregard obstacles which might have deterred other men."[10]

After four days "tossed hither and thither by contrary winds," according to Doubleday's account, the overloaded brig reached Brito at nightfall. The debarkation was made in bright moonlight,

*Kewen was a brother of a San Francisco friend and later one of Walker's most active supporters, Edward J. C. Kewen, a lawyer who had practiced in Columbus, Ohio, and St. Louis, Missouri, before going to California in the gold rush.

but by midnight, when the march inland began with two local Democrats serving as guides, a heavy rain had set in. The falange, the members carrying nothing but their arms and blankets and two days' provisions in their haversacks, was at the head of the column, and Ramírez and his command formed the rear. They advanced slowly through a heavily forested area, slogging with difficulty over the muddy ground and wet to the skin from the torrential rain. Walker pressed on, not stopping until about nine o'clock in the morning, when an abandoned adobe house was reached that provided a place for the men to have breakfast and rest.

Walker wrote with the pen of a poet when he described the resumption of the march under clear skies, and the men breathed in the unfamiliar and balmy air of the tropics. "You felt," he said, "as if a thin, and vapory exhalation of opium, soothing and exhilarating by turns, was being mixed at intervals with the common elements of the atmosphere." But the second night was a repetition of the first, a night of heavy rain, so retarding the march that Walker saw he could not reach Rivas, as he hoped, before morning. There was an additional delay when the force reached a village, Tola, about 8 miles from their objective, where they surprised a small detachment of Legitimists, who fled, after a brief skirmish, to carry the news of the attacking force to their commander.

Despite the difficulties of the two nights of marching and the knowledge that the enemy had received warning of an assault, it was a cheerful band that set out from Tola about eight o'clock in the sunshine of the new day, July 29. The North Americans used the few Spanish expressions at their command in chaffing the market women returning from the town with fruit baskets on their heads and were struck with wonderment when, reaching a turn in the road, they saw spread before them the lake and the slender cone of Ometepe rising from it, the classical student Walker was reminded, like Venus from the sea.

Halting less than a half mile from Rivas, Walker outlined to his officers his attack plans, details of which differ in the Walker and Doubleday accounts. Walker's version was that the falange, led by Kewen and Crocker, would advance toward the plaza, driving the enemy from the streets if possible, and that the native command under Ramírez would follow close after, protecting their flanks and rear. But according to Doubleday, Ramírez was instructed to divide his force, two groups to guard the outlet roads to San Juan del Sur and Granada to prevent the escape of the enemy if they attempted to do so and a third to cover the rear of the Americans advancing into the town. Doubleday related that he remonstrated with Walker over this strategy. He believed that Walker, whose battle experience had been confined "to the sage-brush nurtured inhabitants" of Lower California who "were ready to fly at the sound of their own guns," undervalued the fighting qualities of the strongly barricaded forces in Rivas; moreover, he thought it inadvisable to send the Ramírez troops out of reach to guard the roads until it was determined whether they were needed for the attack on the plaza.

The falange intrepidly entered the town, driving the defenders from their street barricades but suffering from the deadly rifle fire from the houses. They discovered they were in a precarious situation when, at the top of a hill near a large adobe house, they observed that Ramírez and his men had still not entered the town. Doubleday related that it was at his suggestion that Walker ordered the falange into the adobe house to gather strength for renewing the offensive if possible, retreat seeming suicidal at this point. Charged by the enemy, the Americans kept up such a fire from the house that the bodies of their attackers soon littered the streets. The enemy lost men by the scores, but the falange also suffered woefully, fifteen being put out of action through wounding and death. Among those killed were Colonel Kewen and Major Crocker. To remain in the building would mean death for the whole falange, and Walker determined upon a sally out. He described the escape from the besieged structure: "At the moment of leaving the house, a shout was raised by the sallying party; the nearest of the enemy turned and fled in confusion; and the main body of the Legitimists, paralyzed, as it were, by the offensive appearance of the American movement, waited, expecting everywhere an attack. Thus the Falange escaped from its difficult position with the loss of only one man killed."

If the Legitimists had pursued the Americans fleeing from the town, they could have put an end to the Walker expedition then and there, but they did not. Leaving in the town six men killed and five so seriously wounded they could not be moved—Walker's "one man killed" revealed his tendency to refuse to admit his losses—the reduced force took the road to San Juan del Sur, halting just before nightfall near the village of San Jorge to form their plans and redistribute the ammunition. Walker learned only at this time of what had happened to the native troops when two or three stragglers emerged from a thicket and told him Colonel Ramírez had set out on the road to Costa Rica.

When the bedraggled Americans resumed their march for the transit road a few miles to the south, the pace was not as fast as Walker would have liked, for the ground was muddy, his men were tired, and some of them were badly wounded, two of them officers with leg injuries, Captain Julius de Brissot and Lieutenant Francis P. Anderson, a member of a New York regiment in the Mexican War. Captain Doubleday was also in poor shape. He had been hit on the head by a glancing rifle ball and though it had not put him out of action he was weak from loss of blood and dizzy with pain. Finally, at midnight, Walker called a halt at a small cattle ranch with the transit road still some distance away.

In the morning the troops feasted on roast ox supplied by the frightened ranchero and his wife, who had been held under guard to prevent their informing the Legitimists of the location of the falange. Shortly after the filibusters emerged from the thorny thickets through which they had been forcing their way onto the graveled transit road near Virgin Bay on Lake Nicaragua, they were met by a horseman, one Dewey, a desperado and gambler who had found California inhospitable, with the news that there were no Legitimists in San Juan del Sur, the garrison there having been withdrawn for the defense of Rivas. Cheered by this information, the soldiers pressed on for the port, arriving just before sunset, their clothing torn to rags by the underbrush through which they had fought their way and some of them without shoes, which they had lost in the mud of the backcountry trails. They presented an appearance not unlike that of the remnants of Walker's band who a little more than a year before had crossed the Mexican border south of San Diego and surrendered to the U.S. army after the failure of the Lower California expedition.

San Juan del Sur offered only a temporary refuge, however, for it was beyond all reason to believe that Legitimist forces had not been sent out, or soon would be, to resume battle. Walker had lost none of his confidence in his destiny. "The appearance of the Falange at that moment was not imposing," he wrote; "but he who knew how to read men might see from the looks of these, that they bore with firmness the blows of adverse fate." He himself acted with decision after occupying the vacant barracks near the beach. He took possession of the small boats in the harbor and sent a detail under Captain Hornsby to seize a schooner flying the Costa Rican flag, the *San José*, whose captain was preparing to weigh anchor and leave. Walker's hope had been that the *Vesta*, which had been instructed to cruise off San Juan del Sur, would appear to remove the falange. As there was no news of the brig, he put his men aboard the *San José* to sail in search of her.

Waiting for the tide to change so that the schooner could leave the harbor, those on board saw a fire blazing ashore. It was found upon investigation to be the barracks, which Dewey and a beachcomber named Sam had set afire in retaliation for mistreatment they fancied they had suffered at the hands of the townspeople. What followed was another instance of Walker's peculiar ideas of justice and his delusion that all his actions were motivated by the desire to bring law and order to an abandoned people, just as at San Vicente he had executed two men he thought intended to pillage the countryside. The firing of the barracks, he feared, would be blamed on the Americans who out of revenge for their defeat at Rivas had attempted, "like savages," to burn up an inoffensive town. For the good of his enterprise, no such vandalism could go unrebuked. He thereupon took the two miscreants in custody and hastily summoned a court martial, which found them guilty and sentenced them to be shot.

Walker justified this high-handed execution of men not even members of his force: "I have minutely narrated the circumstances attending Dewey's death, because they made a deep impression on the native mind, and gave a certain and decided character to the Americans in the democratic service. The Nicaraguans conceived from these events a respectful idea of American justice. They saw that the men they had been taught to call 'filibusters,' intended to maintain law and secure order wherever they went; that they had the will to administer justice, and would, when they had the power, protect the weak and the innocent from the crimes of the lawless and abandoned." There is no evidence that the Nicaraguans interpreted the incident according to Walker's warped thinking, if indeed they ever heard of it at all.

Late in the day the *San José* came upon the *Vesta* sailing northward and the falange went aboard the familiar vessel to complete the voyage to Realejo. The next morning, July 1, the volcano Viejo was sighted due north and in a short time the *Vesta* was again at anchor, neither Walker nor his expeditionists, now numbering forty-five men, knowing where their chief's star of destiny would lead them next.[11]

The news of Walker's defeat first reached the United States in the issue of the *New York Herald* of July 9 from the paper's correspondent at Virgin Bay, the embarkation point on Lake Nicaragua of transit passengers after their passage over the road that had been constructed from San Juan del Sur. Dated June 30, the dispatch contained no details, however, the meager information given having been obtained from Colonel Ramírez's troops heading for Costa Rica. It had been brought by the steamer *Northern Light*, which had sailed from San Juan del Norte, or Greytown, on July 1 and had reached New York seven days later.

San Francisco, where the filibuster had originated, did not get the news until July 16. The papers there had fuller information obtained from passengers on the *Sierra Nevada*, which had left San Juan del Sur twelve days before. Because transit steamers made the trip to and from Nicaragua only on a twice-a-month schedule, it was not until late in July that American readers received the full story. The general opinion was that the debacle at Rivas signaled the end of Walker's expedition. Writing from Rivas on July 13, the *Herald*'s correspondent said: "It was, indeed, a great foolishness—more craziness than anything else—to believe that a force of fifty-six men could take a country, as weak as it might be, and is, and keep it."

The correspondent learned that in fleeing the town Walker had lost his coat containing all his papers—the original contract between Byron Cole and Castellón, letters between Cole and Walker, and Castellón's recent correspondence with Walker. Documents were found also that revealed Walker's difficulties in raising money—receipts for loans of as little as $10 obtained from well-wishers and information that the expeditionists paid $40 for their passage from San Francisco. There were also share certificates in the Nicaragua Colonization Company formed by Cole and signed March 1 by Walker as his agent. The capital stock of the company was $100,000 and each share was valued at $1,000. "I send you one signed in blank, in case you should like to have an interest in the concern," the correspondent wrote. "There are plenty more here, and to be bought very cheap."[12]

While news of Walker's misadventures was slowly reaching the American public, it was learning also that the parallel expedition of Colonel Kinney was having difficulties. Kinney had last been heard of when he sailed from New York harbor on June 6; seven weeks later, on July 18, the *Evening Post* printed the first dispatch from William Sydney Thayer, dated June 27 at Turks Island in the southeastern Bahamas.[13] The *Emma*, despite some rough weather after leaving New York, had made a good voyage until June 19, when she entered Turks Island Passage and the captain, having lost his bearings, had difficulty in navigating. About eleven o'clock that night the passengers were jarred out of their berths when the schooner crunched upon a coral reef south of the Caicos Islands. She continued "jumping and thumping" over the reef before her progress was stopped by hauling down the sails.

At daybreak it became clear that the schooner, now lying on her side and grinding against the coral 3 feet below the surface of the water, could not be got off the reef. But land was close at hand, Blue Caicos Island, 3 miles off, and Kinney determined to save as much of his cargo as he could by the lifeboat and a raft that he had constructed. Helped by some of the fifty or sixty inhabitants of the island, the task was completed by nightfall. Working in water up to his chest all day, lifting heavy loads, and fighting against the sea when his followers would have given up, Kinney might have been in despair when he finally left the reef, the wrecked schooner apparently writing finis to his project, but he was not. "He has never quailed before any obstacles heretofore," Thayer wrote, "and even now, while so sick that he can with difficulty move about, he works with the despatch and energy of ten ordinary men in full health, to forward his great design."

After two days on Blue Caicos Island, the expedition sailed in two small sloops to Grand Turk Island 90 miles away, which they reached on June 25. Here they were received by the U.S. consul, a former congressman from Maryland, John L. Nelson, who decided to join Kinney when he sailed in the sloops for Kingston, Jamaica, on July 8. The expedition remained at Kingston only long enough for Kinney to charter a schooner, the *Huntress*, to continue his trip to San Juan del Norte, reached on July 16.

Before the *Huntress* dropped anchor, news was received from ashore that about fifty men had arrived the night before, fully armed, from the transit company's ship, *Star of the West*, to prevent a landing by Kinney. The colonel was told that they had been employed by the Nicaraguan government but assumed that in actuality they were hirelings of the company. They were posted at Punta Arenas to prevent the debarkation of the expedition from the *Emma*, now of course broken to pieces on the reef of the Caicos Banks. The wreck had at least this fortunate outcome: the transit company's force did not know that the expedition was aboard the *Huntress*. The report of the hostile welcoming force was true. The Nicaraguan minister, José de Marcoleta, and Joseph L. White, consul for the Accessory Transit Company, had employed about fifty immigrants from Europe and enlisted them for four months' service. They had sailed from New York on July 5.[14]

Colonel Kinney took the precaution of slipping ashore from the *Huntress*, leaving Nelson to explain to the harbor master the intentions of the passengers seeking to land. According to Thayer's report, the local citizens were enthusaistic when Kinney's arrival was made known. "They had long been waiting for him," Thayer wrote, "and now on the third day after the first anniversary of the town's bombardment by Captain Hollins, they turned out to welcome the man whom they expected to rebuild and make it prosperous."

Such was Kinney's persuasiveness that he was able to put to rest doubts the commander of a British warship in the harbor, Captain W. H. Dobbie of the *Buzzard*, and the British consul, James Green, might have about his intentions. Kinney explained to them that his was a peaceful colonization project on lands to which he believed he had a valid title, but if this was disproved he would abandon it. The British officials very likely saw no danger from a band so small and made no objection when the expeditionists took up quarters ashore, and there was likewise no opposition from the band dispatched by the transit company to prevent their landing. Before long it was dispersed, John H. Wheeler said in a report to Secretary of State Marcy, some returning to New York, some taking jobs with the transit company as laborers, and some joining Kinney's group.

Reports from Marcoleta to the Legitimist government at Granada had aroused such fears of the expedition that on June 2 a proclamation had been issued calling on citizens to defend their country "now menaced by a party of adventurers" attempting to make themselves masters and ordering Kinney's arrest and that of Joseph W. Fabens if they set foot on national territory.[15] With his few followers, Kinney realized he would be confined to San Juan del Norte unless he could obtain permission from the government to found his own settlement, and he decided to send an emissary to Granada to explain his position. John L. Nelson, who as U.S. consul at Turks Island had at least a shadow of American authority behind him, undertook the mission and left for Granada on August 8. Despite twice being arrested and released en route, he was received in a friendly fashion by President Estrada and General Corral, and he returned to San Juan del Norte with a letter to Kinney offering to cooperate with him in any arrangements that might be helpful to both parties.[16]

Kinney had hoped that when news of his arrival in Nicaragua reached the United States his supporters in the hundreds would sail to join him, but only a small group departed on August 5 in the brig *Ocean Bird*. Among the supplies shipped were a printing press, type, and paper for a newspaper to be established and edited by Colonel William H. Young, identified in the *Evening Post*'s notice of the sailing as being from Corpus Christi, Texas.[17]

With the capacity of all filibusters to be blind to current unpleasant realities in their visions of a roseate future, Kinney on August 15 issued an address to the American people setting forth his prospects: "I have now reached, under most favorable auspices," he proclaimed, "the shores of a country whose capabilities and natural riches have long been proverbial, and which, on personal exploration in the interior, thus far have exceeded my most sanguine anticipations. I have, moreover, the fullest confidence in the opinion that not many months will elapse before Central America will throng with industrious Anglo-American farmers and artizans, who need only the enterprise and business habits of their native land to insure an ample reward for their labors in developing its resources."

Blaming the Accessory Transit Company for preventing the sailing of his expedition from New York and angry that it had employed foreign mercenaries to attack him on his arrival, Kinney devoted most of his address, however, to a tirade against Marcoleta and White even if it meant exposing the collaboration of his associate Joseph W. Fabens in the destruction of Greytown. The company, Kinney charged, realized that a free Greytown stood as a barrier against its aggressive schemes and White went to Washington and represented that it was being made the victim of marauding residents. "At his suggestion," Kinney declared, "a ship-of-war is sent out, and the town is bombarded and destroyed." He quoted a letter of White's to Fabens of June 16, 1854, directing him to cooperate with Captain Hollins in destroying the town as evidence supporting his accusations.[18]

The next month, on September 6, Kinney summoned residents of the town to a meeting to establish a government. They showed so little interest in the project that those at the meeting were confined chiefly to the members of his own party, and it is no surprise that most of the offices went to the North Americans. So few were they that almost all had either a title or was a member of the town council. Kinney was "elected" civil and military governor; Thayer, secretary of the government; and Young, who had only just arrived on the *Ocean Bird*, government attorney.[19]

Kinney wasted no time in attempting to obtain recognition of his regime, informing the U.S. vice commercial agent, E. F. Mason, and the British vice consul, James Geddes, of the actions of the "mass meeting," as he called the farcical gathering over which he had presided. As the representative of the United States, Mason, in a fulsome letter, recognized the government at once. "For my own individual part," he closed his letter to Kinney, "I have seen this movement in favor of a government and the establishment of law with great satisfaction, and am confident that it will be productive of great good to this place; and I cannot refrain from congratulating you, and the citizens through you, that this has been brought about with so much harmony and unanimity."

The British reaction was strongly adverse. Geddes conferred with I. W. Tarleton, commander of H.M.S. *Eurydice*, then in the harbor, who set forth his objections in a letter on September 13 to be made known to Kinney. Tarleton pointed out that Greytown already had a government established under the constitution of 1852 and said that he had received from the majority of the inhabitants a protest against the usurpation of control by Kinney. "From this protest," Tarleton said, "I learn that only a small minority of holders of property in Greytown took part in that election, and that it was mainly effected by the presence of some twenty persons, lately arrived and having no legitimate qualifications to vote."[20]

News of Kinney's spurious coup reached the United States from the columns of his biweekly newspaper, *Central American*, the first number of which appeared on September 15. The paper, extensively quoted in the American press, was designed to advertise the resources of Nicaragua and attract immigrants. One historian has commented that there was "a kind of melancholy humour in the extensive advertisements of Greytown lawyers, merchants, schools, traders, physicians, hotels, and places of amusement, all of which owed their existence to paper, printer's ink, and a vivid imagination."[21] Hotel advertising, for example, described the Central American Hotel, "elegant, spacious, and well ventilated"; the San Juan House, where "delicacies of the tropical clime" were served; and a third that offered French cuisine.

Thayer, who had publicized the expedition in his articles for the *Evening Post*, was sent by Kinney to Washington late in the month to see the British minister, Sir John Crampton, to seek his support of the dubious government. Thayer was instructed to have Sidney Webster, Pierce's secretary, and John W. Forney, co-editor of the administration organ, the *Washington Union*, accompany him on this mission, further evidence of the collusion of the president's aides in the filibuster project. It was, of course, a futile mission.[22]

Meanwhile Walker, who returned to Realejo on July 1, endured a period of delays and frustrations—almost two months—that had he been less self-confident would have led him to give up his endeavor. Although defeated at Rivas, his little band was considered a formidable force that Castellón wished to retain. The heavy losses of the Legitimists, though outnumbering the Americans eight to one, William V. Wells wrote in his history of the expedition, inspired the Nicaraguans "with a dread and respect of General Walker's prowess, and a proper idea of the indomitable bravery of our riflemen."[23] Wells's language was high flown and chauvinistic, but the fact was that Castellón believed retention of the falange, with the probability of obtaining additional Americans for his army, was essential to the Democratic cause.

Walker, in his report to Castellón on the battle, charged that the desertion of Colonel Ramírez had been at the instigation of General Muñoz and demanded an inquiry. If it were not made, he threatened in behalf of his men to "seek elsewhere than in Nicaragua a field for their faculties and enterprise." The ultimatum upset Castellón. He momentarily expected an attack on León, especially since the arrival a few weeks before of the feared General Santos Guardiola from Guatemala, who in earlier wars had won the name of the Tiger of Central America, to command a Legitimist force, and he could not offend Muñoz, who had amibitions of his own. Walker recognized Castellón's painful dilemma and made the most of it. Castellón urged him repeatedly to take the falange to León, but Walker delayed doing so for weeks. The city was thrown into almost daily panics by rumors that General Corral was attacking from Managua, rumors that Walker discounted, because cholera was sweeping the countryside and in his estimate the Legitimist general was not sufficiently venturesome to engage the enemy and would instead retire to Granada.

Regarding the transit road as the key to control of Nicaragua, Walker proposed to Castellón that he be given command of a force of 200 men to assault Rivas again, but the provisional director was markedly ill at ease at the idea. He suggested a meeting with Muñoz and General Jérez to plan a broad scale campaign against the Legitimists. Muñoz proposed that the falange be broken up into groups of ten to be attached to several bodies of native troops for an attack from several directions against Granada, but Walker interpreted this as a ruse to weaken his position and refused, returning to Chinandega with his men.

Earlier, Byron Cole, who after turning over his contract with Castellón to Walker had gone to Honduras, had turned up at Chinandega. He was accompanied by a Prussian, Bruno von Natzmer, who several years before had come to Central America in a German colonization project that had failed and who now was interested in joining Walker. Cole was Walker's agent in working out a new arrangement with Castellón. In this contract, the pretension of a colonization project was dropped, and Walker was authorized to enlist 300 men in California for military service at a pay of $100 a month and the award of 500 acres of land at the end of the campaign. Walker was also authorized to represent the government in settling differences and outstanding accounts with the Accessory Transit Company.

When Walker returned to Chinandega, it had been with the intention to seize the transit road with or without the aid of the provisional government, establishing himself at the head of a third movement for control of the country. It was egomania at its most egregious. In the first place, the Americans were few in number —only forty-five men—and there was disaffection among them, brought about, Walker believed, by idleness. He sought to keep up their spirits, he related, by speeches and talks with individual men in which he attempted to "fill them with the idea that small as was their number they were the precursors of a movement destined to affect materially the civilization of the whole continent."

There was also the problem of transport. The *Vesta* had sailed under charter from San Francisco, and the captain, M. D. Eyre, wished to return but had no crew, the ship having been manned on the voyage by members of the expedition, and no sailors were available for hire at Realejo. Walker, always seeking a legal justification for doing what he wanted to do, found an excuse to obtain possession of the brig by having the men who had sailed her sue for their wages and pressing the harbor master to collect port fees. He thus pronounced judgment against Eyre, who had no money to pay these claims, and the vessel was sold on credit to two of the expeditionists for less than $600.

Then, there was the problem of obtaining powder, caps, and lead for bullets for the falange rifles. This was a task entrusted to Doubleday as commissary and quartermaster, and he went about the countryside confiscating what materials could be located.

Finally, there was the problem of obtaining a native officer willing to join the expedition with or without the consent of Castellón. Walker found his man in Colonel José María Valle, sub-prefect at Chinandega, who had been injured in the siege of Granada and was not now on active service in the Democratic army. Valle, an Indian, could neither read nor write, but "with a certain rude eloquence he was accustomed to stir the hearts of the people with a recitation of the wrongs they had suffered from the Legitimist Government." He succeeded in recruiting 175 men for the falange to go to the transit road and demonstrate the warrior qualities of the Nicaraguans.

About the middle of August Walker marched the falange to Realejo, where he was joined by the troops under Valle's command. The force was ready to board the *Vesta* when a courier arrived from Castellón with a message that Muñoz had been killed in a battle with Guardiola at Sauce, a village northeast of Chinandega. Muñoz's death removed the chief obstacle standing in the way of Walker's influencing Castellón, but he refused the provisional director's urgent request that the falange return to León. On the morning of August 23 the *Vesta* weighed anchor and cleared the port to sail to San Juan del Sur.[24]

CHAPTER THIRTEEN

Walker Victorious: Forming a Government

Manned by inexperienced sailors and blown about by unfavorable winds, the *Vesta* was six days in reaching San Juan del Sur. She dropped anchor shortly after dark, and news was received from ashore that the small garrison of Legitimist troops had left when the brig was sighted. Next morning the Accessory Transit Company ship *Uncle Sam* arrived from San Francisco. "It was a glad sight for the Falange, inasmuch as it suggested the fact that they were now in communication with the friends of youth and manhood," Walker wrote, "and there would now be an opportunity to swell their numbers from the passengers crossing the Isthmus."

In actuality, the travelers were not friendly toward the filibusters, who were delaying their trip. Walker, to prevent information about his force reaching the Legitimists, opposed letting them continue, and the muleteers who provided transportation to Virgin Bay would not come into town for fear that their animals would be seized for use by the Democratic army. "Two of our passengers who were acquainted with Walker, volunteered their services in procuring mules," one of the travelers told the *Herald* on finally reaching New York. "They called on Walker, and the one by threats of the company's vengeance, the other by personally guaranteeing that no communication should reach the enemy, succeeded, though with great difficulty, in their object."[1]

Already at San Juan del Sur was a Californian with a reputation as a rogue, who sent Walker word that he had just returned from Granada and would like to see him. He was Parker H. French, whom Walker had encountered in San Francisco early in the year. French then had promised to obtain the support of Cornelius K. Garrison, the transit company's western agent, but no help came from this source. Garrison was in trouble at the time: he was mayor of the city and under indictment for embezzlement of $75,000 in municipal property. Aside from French's ill repute, Walker was wary of him because of a report that he had gone to the Legitimist headquarters to join the army as an artillerist. French nevertheless obtained his interview and told Walker his purpose in going to Granada was to observe the defenses of the city. Walker was not convinced but loath to refuse any offers of help authorized him on his return to San Francisco on the *Uncle Sam* to enlist men to serve in the Democratic army.

It was a commission that enabled French to associate himself with Walker and follow a brief career as a filibuster. His history up to this time had been marked by a superior talent for chicanery. He had set out for California from Illinois in 1850 and turned up in San Antonio bearing letters of credit from the firm of Howland and Aspinwall to outfit an emigration train that he would lead to the goldfields. He obtained the wagons, stores, and ordnance for the trek, but when the train reached El Paso it was overtaken by a cavalry unit from San Antonio under orders to seize the property and arrest him. The letters of credit had been discovered to be forgeries. French escaped with a few desperadoes into Mexico and made his way to Mazatlán, where he was arrested and thrown into prison. He was able to escape, losing one of his arms when the elbow was shattered by a musket ball, and reached Los Angeles in 1853. Clever and persuasive, he was elected to the state senate, became editor of the *State Tribune* at Sacramento, and engaged in a variety of financial deals, including, it was revealed later, selling and mortgaging ranches of constituents from whom he had obtained powers of attorney.[2]

Although Walker had under his command only the forty-five men forming the falange and about 125 Nicaraguans commanded by Valle, he determined to take the initiative in the war against the Legitimists by a show of strength. His intelligence was that General Guardiola, after a defeat at Sauce a few weeks before, had returned to Granada and, eager to restore his fame as a commander, had marched with 200 troops to Rivas, vowing to sweep the filibusters into the sea. His total force was believed to number about 500 men.

On the afternoon of September 2 Walker began loading his supplies on packmules and in carts and shortly after midnight left San Juan del Sur for Virgin Bay. His intention was not to occupy the village but to show that he did not plan to remain on the defensive by keeping his troops confined to San Juan del Sur. "The night was fine and pleasant," he related, "the road good, and the spirits of the command high." They stopped once to rest at an inn called the Halfway House and reached the bay at about nine o'clock in the morning. A guard of about a dozen of Valle's troops were posted on the transit road and the remainder of the force were at breakfast when musketry fire was heard. Soon the pickets were seen retiring slowly along the road, shooting at intervals at a body of troops flaunting the white ribbons of the Legitimists. The slow retreat of the pickets gave the falange and Valle's command time to take defensive positions. Nearing the bay, the Legitimists fanned out left and right to surround the village. Walker sent one-half of his falange to a height at the north to fight off a flanking movement and the other half to the low ground at the south while Valle and the natives were assigned to meet the onslaught from the transit road at the center. "Thus the democratic force stood with its back to the lake . . . , its front and flanks simultaneously threatened by the enemy," Walker wrote. "It thus became necessary to fight well or be cut to pieces. . . ." The battle did not last long. Before ninety minutes passed, the Legitimists had fled in disarray. It was learned later that General Guardiola had left Rivas the day before to attack San Juan del Sur but on reaching Halfway House had been told the Democratic forces had gone to Virgin Bay.

Walker reported that Guardiola lost about sixty men killed and an undetermined number wounded. There were no fatalities among the Americans and only two or three among the native allies. There were several narrow escapes, however. A package of letters Walker carried in his coat pocket was cut to pieces by a musket ball, and he was knocked down by a spent ball striking him in the throat. Captain Doubleday suffered a wound in the side, and two other filibusters were injured. After the battle, squads sent out by Walker picked up about 150 muskets thrown away by the panicky Legitimists.[3]

Next day Walker marched his victorious troops back to San Juan del Sur and sent a message to Castellón at León to report the defeat of the Legitimists and to request additional arms and men.

The news reached the city as Castellón was on the point of dying of the cholera, and the reply congratulating Walker came from the new provisional director, Nasario Escoto, who promised all help possible, though little was forthcoming because of the cholera epidemic.

At San Juan del Sur, however, Walker received additions to his force from native volunteers. He would not permit his Nicaraguan officers to draft men into the army, and in this way won the goodwill of the people. "It was difficult at first to check this inveterate habit of catching a man and tying him up with a musket in his hand to make a soldier of him," Walker wrote, "but seeing the good effects of the policy the officers afterward desisted from a practice which seemed to have become almost second nature to them." He also added a few Californians to the falange when the steamer *Sierra Nevada* arrived from San Francisco on September 20, and at the end of the month his army included sixty Americans and about 200 Nicaraguans.

To raise money, Walker levied contributions on the town's few traders and innkeepers. In his history Walker complained of the difficulty of collecting taxes. He related one incident—the subject of a letter written to Secretary of State Marcy—concerning the U.S. consul, John Priest, who kept an inn. Priest refused to pay the tax, and Walker brought him to terms by placing a guard at the door under orders to prevent customers from entering. In his letter to Marcy, Walker defended the tax on Priest and his taking up arms for the Democrats: the war was more than just a Nicaraguan war but one being fought throughout Central America between the Liberal and the Servile parties; his hope was to place the Democrats in power in Nicaragua. Reports of the tax collections reached San Juan del Norte from transit passengers, and William Sydney Thayer, in one of his articles, said that a levy of $6,000 was imposed on the transit company. Walker considered this legal because of the authority given him by Castellón to deal with the firm.[4]

While Walker was gathering strength at San Juan del Sur, Doubleday was the confidant of his dreams and expectations during walks they took together on the beach, "the rhythmic wavebeats seeming to emphasize the gigantic plans of empire he unfolded." "In his plan," Doubleday said, "the present popular movement was to obtain a temporary success in order to demonstrate to the hierarchical oligarchy their necessity for his aid, by which he would in the end wield the temporal power over Central America and Mexico in union with the policy and influence of the mother Church." With himself as the central figure, Walker would rule from Mexico to Panama.

Doubleday, put off by this program for empire because it envisioned the reestablishment of slavery in Central America, made the mistake of remonstrating with Walker. It was a mistake that later associates of Walker were also to learn was fatal. He would bear no criticism. As a result of Walker's anger over his speaking his mind, Doubleday decided to leave the army and continue the journey to New York that he had interrupted the year before when he assembled a company to fight with the Democrats under General Jérez. Walker wrote of his departure: "He left at this time because having, without invitation, stated to Walker his opinion about certain movements being made, the commander remarked, that 'when his commissary's opinion was required it would be asked for.'"[5]

Shortly after General Guardiola's defeat at Virgin Bay, Walker heard from Legitimist deserters that General Corral had left Granada to go to Rivas to reorganize his forces for operations against the Democrats. Late in September came a report that Corral had left Rivas to advance against the Democrats, the artillery to be taken by boat to Virgin Bay and the infantry to go by land. Thinking to surprise the enemy, Walker left San Juan del Sur on the night of September 25 and established an ambuscade on a hill about 5 miles distant overlooking the transit road. The Legitimists did not appear, and in the morning Walker went on to Virgin Bay. Here he learned that Corral had started out from Rivas to attack San Juan del Sur, but on receiving reports the Democratic army had left he had returned to his headquarters. Walker himself returned to San Juan del Sur. He concluded from this experience that he "had only to leave San Juan del Sur, apparently for Rivas, in order to paralyze any advance movement his opponent might make." More important, however, dispatches to Corral from Granada seized when a courier was captured at Virgin Bay revealed the dire situation at the capital and the inability of the government to raise more troops to send to his support.

On October 3 the falange was augmented by thirty-five recruits who had sailed on the *Cortes* from San Francisco on September 20. They were commanded by Charles Gilman, who had lost a leg in Walker's Lower California expedition but who was still loyal to the leader of this ill-conceived venture. With the falange now numbering almost 100 men, Walker organized it into three companies forming a single battalion. Commanders were C. C. Hornsby, promoted to colonel, and Gilman, given the rank of lieutenant colonel. "By the arrival of the force on the *Cortes*," Walker wrote a San Francisco friend on October 4, "I am placed in a position for offensive operations. I am constantly receiving recruits from the natives, and my force is now about 400 effective men—100 Americans and 300 natives. The native force is well officered—has confidence in the skill and courage of the Americans—and will therefore fight well."

Knowing from the captured dispatches at Virgin Bay that most of the Legitimist army had been sent from Granada to reinforce Corral at Rivas, Walker determined upon a surprise attack on the capital. If successful, the loss of their capital would demoralize the Legitimists and demonstrate the invincibility of the Democrats. His plan was to march quietly to Virgin Bay, seize the transit company's lake steamer, *La Virgén*, put his troops on board, and land them during the night near Granada preparatory to assaulting the city.

Accordingly, on the morning of October 11, the battalion left for Virgin Bay. A San Francisco correspondent considered the American soldiers to be "truly striking" in appearance. "Their dress," he wrote, "consists of heavy felt hats, with red ribbons, blue woolen shirts, coarse pants, and heavy boots; a strap around their waist contains revolver and knife, and rifle in hand finds them fully equipped." On reaching Virgin Bay, the men were assigned quarters about the town to await the scheduled arrival of *La Virgén* at dusk. When she had anchored, Colonel Hornsby with a detail of fifteen men came out in a schooner and went aboard against the protests of her commander, Captain Joseph N. Scott. Next day both Scott and the transit company agent at Virgin Bay, Courtland Cushing, protested against the seizure of the ship, maintaining that she sailed under the American flag. Walker had a legalistic answer to this: the company was chartered by Nicaragua and therefore any of its ships were committed to sailing under Nicaraguan colors.

About four o'clock in the afternoon Walker embarked his whole command on the steamer and sailed for Granada, anchoring at about ten o'clock 3 miles north of the city. Disembarkation in the darkness was a slow process, and it was not until three o'clock that all the men were ashore and the march on the city began. The troops entered the town when "the first rays of the rising sun had begun to warm the eastern heavens," Walker wrote, and he gathered from the startled looks of the people that they were completely surprised by the sudden appearance of the Americans. Led by the American troops, the battalion charged into the plaza, with only a few shots being fired at them from the Government House. "In fact, the Legitimist force in the town had been trifling, and the encounter between it and the Democrats could scarcely be dignified with the name of an action," Walker wrote.

Ordinarily in Nicaraguan warfare the seizure of a town would have meant a spree of looting, but Walker acted at once to prevent this. Seeing some of his native soldiers heavily laden with spoils, he ordered them to halt and, drawing out his sword, commanded them to restore the stolen articles to their owners. He then charged the falange with the responsibility of preventing any pillaging and of protecting the lives of Legitimist soldiers.[6]

One of Walker's first actions was to issue a proclamation to assure the people they need not fear any persecution by the Democrats. In this he had the assistance of a merchant, Carlos Thomas, who because of his knowledge of Nicaragua and facility with the pen became his chief proclamation writer. The "swell of his sentences was perfectly Ciceronian," Walker wrote, and, direct in speech himself, he was somewhat annoyed at seeing his signature "appended in print to an address teeming with the rhetoric which characterizes Spanish-American productions." Walker's first proclamation on the morning of October 13 declared:

> At six o'clock this morning I took possession of the plaza of this city, after slight resistance on the part of the troops belonging to the supposed Legitimate government. In the skirmish three or four of the enemy soldiers were unfortunately killed, but since the triumph which I of course gained, no one has received a personal injury. . . .
>
> My duty as chief of the expeditionary force of a government free in

its principles and which looks to the vital interests of the state, protection to the laboring man, security to the citizen, progress to the arts, sciences, agriculture, etc., was to preserve order and cause it to be preserved. And therefore, although I have imprisoned Dionicio Chamorro, Toribio Jérez, and other persons of high consideration, the principal agents of the government of legitimacy, I have done nothing with them but give them into the custody of responsible persons.

I shall take possession of the remaining towns of the state, and he shall perish who opposes the commanding march of my forces, who admit to their ranks, without distinction of color, all who wish it. . . . Behold it—a democratic government in its true signification, guaranteeing progress and liberty.[7]

Next morning Walker attended the eight o'clock mass in the cathedral conducted by Padre Augustín Vijil. This was a part of his plan to win over the church to his program, and in Father Vijil he found a sympathetic supporter. A German traveler, Julius Froebel, who had visited Nicaragua in 1850 and 1851, wrote of the priest: "The Padre Vijil is a man of enlightened views in religious matters, who has always belonged to the liberal party of the country, and has ever been favourable to foreigners. Religious toleration and hospitality towards them were the constant theme of his sermons delivered in the cathedral of Granada during the time of my residence." His sermon on this Sunday morning called for suspension of the civil strife that racked the country and the quenching of political passions that had brought misery to the people. More important than his sermon, however, was his offer to put himself at the service of Walker in restoring peace.[8]

Later in the day at a meeting of citizens, a resolution was adopted offering Walker the provisional presidency of the country. Wishing to secure an end of hostility between the Legitimists and Democrats and believing this could be accomplished by bringing the two parties together in the government, Walker declined. He proposed instead that General Corral be selected to head the state if peace could be negotiated and that he himself become commander in chief of the army.

This proposal was accepted and two commissions were appointed to carry it to Corral at Rivas. The U.S. minister, John H. Wheeler, offered to be one of the bearers, to sail on *La Virgén* to San Jorge, the port of Rivas, and then proceed to the town to meet with the general. The other commission, consisting of two Granada citizens, would go by land. When Wheeler, accompanied by John Ruiz, the Legitimist minister of War, reached Rivas next day, he found that Corral had left with a body of troops on an expedition toward León. Before Wheeler could depart for Granada he was arrested despite his protestation that he was a representative of the United States. Two days later, when nothing had been heard from him, it was learned he was being held a prisoner, and Walker sent a message that unless he was freed Rivas would be attacked, a warning that was effective in securing his release. A letter from Corral to Wheeler, dated October 17, indicated that the Legitimist general was not very favorable to Walker's peace feeler. Corral wrote that he would not be responsible for Wheeler's safety after "having interfered in our domestic dissensions."[9]

During the year and a half of civil war, transit passengers had crossed the country in perfect safety. Now, with Walker intent upon taking control of the transit route, they became victims of the crossfire of the opposing factions as the result of an attempted military coup by Parker H. French. On reaching San Francisco, French had spread the word that he was to head an expedition to come to Walker's aid and soon won the cooperation of Cornelius K. Garrison. Recruits were accepted at the office of the transit company for departure on the steamer *Uncle Sam* on October 5. Officials received word that arms belonging to the San Francisco Blues, a militia company, had been stolen and put aboard the steamer. While a warrant was being obtained to search the ship, she left the wharf and anchored in the stream, soon being boarded by a party of filibusters from a schooner. Upon the personal order of Garrison, the *Uncle Sam* sailed before the search for the stolen property could be conducted.

French brought only sixty men to Nicaragua, but they were well armed, a respectable addition to Walker's forces. According to a passenger on the *Uncle Sam* whose story was reported in the *New York Tribune*, French was disappointed on arriving at San Juan del Sur on October 15 that Walker had seized Granada—"it was judged that all the battles were fought, all the victories won, and all the glory carried off." But French had the ability to rise above circumstance, and when the passengers reached Virgin Bay to board *La Virgén* to cross the lake to San Carlos he decided upon a bold coup—to capture the fort in the name of the Democrats and present it to Walker as a gift.

His armed band going aboard the steamer with the transit passengers, French took command when she sailed for San Carlos. The port on the opposite side of the lake was reached at eleven o'clock on the morning of October 19. "Here a bombastic proclamation was prepared," the *Tribune* reported, "to the effect that the *Virgin* had 210 armed men on board, and that their humane commander, wishing to avoid bloodshed, demanded an unconditional surrender of the fort." The steamer's captain was sent ashore with the ultimatum, but he and his two oarsmen were seized and the fort commander replied with shots from a 6-pound cannon that fortunately fell short of the vessel. After a council of war with his company officers, French decided to send a force of twenty-five men ashore for reconnoitering purposes. They returned with the information that 200 soldiers were garrisoned at the fort and an assault would fail. Thereupon French ordered the steamer to return to Virgin Bay, where at midnight the passengers were unceremoniously landed. Next morning, with only the filibusters aboard, she sailed to Granada.

Meanwhile, the San Juan River steamer *San Carlos* reached the fort bearing passengers bound for California who had sailed from New York on the steamer *Star of the West*. While the *San Carlos* was passing the fort to enter the lake, the garrison commander fired a cannon ball into the ship, killing a woman and her child. Though badly damaged, the vessel proceeded on to Virgin Bay with the passengers, to find that the Americans put ashore there by French had been attacked by 200 Legitimist troops sent out from Rivas. Unarmed and unable to protect themselves, they had fled into the jungle. Six had been killed and about a dozen wounded before the attack was halted when it was discovered that there were no filibusters among them. Next day, after the abandonment of Virgin Bay by the Legitimist force, *La Virgén* arrived from Granada and the passengers were taken aboard to go to the Legitimist capital to remain until some way could be found for them to continue on to San Juan del Norte.

Walker was irate over French's presumptousness in deciding on his own to attack San Carlos. His later opinion was that French had engaged in "a most foolish if not criminal act" but that "existing circumstances made it necessary to overlook" it, presumably his securing the collaboration of Garrison in shipping recruits from San Francisco. Walker's wrath at the result—the shooting of the passengers—was turned instead against the Legitimists. "Such conduct," he wrote, "on the part of officers, acting under color of the Legitimist government, called for retaliation and punishment in order to prevent its recurrence." If such were the case, it could be supposed that his course would be to attack those who were guilty—the commander and the troops at Rivas. Instead, he determined upon the execution of one of the Legitimists imprisoned at Granada—the young secretary of foreign affairs, Mateo Mayorga; he was a member of the Legitimist cabinet and therefore "morally responsible for the outrages and barbarities practised by those holding a military commission." The execution was carried out in the main plaza on October 22.[10]

In capturing Granada it had not been Walker's intention to maintain permanent occupation, because the city was 50 miles from the transit route, control of which he considered essential for obtaining sway over the country and introducing American settlers. But now he changed his plans, for possession of the city and the Legitimist army supply depots placed him in a position to impose peace terms on General Corral. His first proposal had been rejected, but the attack on the transit passengers at Virgin Bay, for which he had held Mayorga accountable, suggested a new weapon for coercion. On the morning of October 22 he sent a courier to Corral, who had barricaded his forces at Masaya, about 12 miles distant from Granada, to inform him of Mayorga's execution and to threaten that unless he agreed to sign a peace pact other government officials would meet the same fate. Although Corral was given until eight o'clock the next day to respond, he decided to submit immediately and the courier returned to Granada at ten o'clock that night with his reply: he would go to Granada to discuss terms with Walker.

Early next morning Colonel Fry was sent with a mounted escort to meet Corral, and shortly after nine o'clock they were reported on the outskirts. Walker went out to greet the Legitimist general, and the two, side by side on horseback, rode down the main street to the plaza. There the entire falange was on parade as well as the transit passengers, many of whom had been given arms "to impress Corral," Walker wrote, "with an idea of the American strength of the Democratic army." The two commanders then retired to the Government House to enter into negotiations.

Under terms of a treaty, which Walker said were mainly proposed by Corral—a doubtful assertion as they stripped the Nicaraguan of power—hostilities were declared ended and a new government was to be formed under a provisional president to serve a term of fourteen months or until an election was called. Chosen provisional president was Patricio Rivas, an elderly and well-esteemed man, then at San Juan del Norte, who in earlier Legitimist governments had held minor offices. A council of ministers, to be appointed by the president, was to consist of ministers of war, foreign and internal affairs, the treasury, and public credit. It was specified that Walker, designated commander in chief of the army, would issue orders to Democratic forces attacking Managua to withdraw to León, reducing their number to 150 men, and that Corral would reduce the Legitimist forces to 100 men at Managua and to fifty men at Masaya. Corral was to deliver the Legitimist arms and munitions to Walker. The colors of the army of the new republic were to be blue ribbons bearing the inscription "Nicaragua Independiente."

In signing this treaty on October 23, neither Walker nor Corral had been given authority by the governments they ostensibly served. In effect, what they did was to act as field generals in negotiating out of existence two contending governments and establishing a third. When the treaty was presented to the Legitimist president, José María Estrada, at Masaya, he agreed to it under protest because he was powerless to do otherwise. On October 28 he declared his government dissolved and left the country to take refuge in Honduras, where the liberal government of Trinidad Cabañas, supporter of the Democrats in Nicaragua, had recently fallen. The Democratic government at León approved the treaty, and its leaders set out for Granada to take part in forming the new republic.

On the afternoon of October 23 a transit company steamer, the *Central America*, arrived from San Carlos with the news that Legitimist garrisons at the fort there and at Castillo Viejo had disappeared. The San Juan River from Lake Nicaragua to San Juan del Norte was now again open for the safe passage of travelers crossing the isthmus, and the California passengers staying at Granada embarked on the *Central America* to continue their journey.

The seizure of the city and the peace treaty indicated to a recently arrived agent of the Accessory Transit Company that Walker was now the most powerful man in Nicaraguan affairs. The agent was Charles J. Macdonald, who had been a passenger on the *Cortes*, which brought the first recruits from San Francisco on October 3. He had just reached Granada and was introduced to Walker by Gilman as the representative of Cornelius K. Garrison. To assure acceptance of the transit company's rights by the new government, Macdonald proposed to advance $20,000 to be taken from bullion in transit from California to New York. The loan would be secured by the annual payments the company made to the state for its franchise.

The delivery of General Corral's troops to General Walker took place on October 29. Walker, to be prepared for any last-minute treachery, stationed the falange and native troops in line of battle on the west side of the plaza opposite the cathedral. At noon the Legitimist troops entered the city. It was a time of high tension. "The accidental discharge of a single musket or rifle," Walker wrote, "would have led to serious consequences, for each party was suspicious of the good faith of the other." Both generals, mounted on elaborately caparisoned horses, met in the center of the plaza, embraced, dismounted, and walked arm in arm to the cathedral, where they were met by Padre Vijil. The *Te Deum*, a prayer of thanksgiving, was chanted, and the priest preached a short sermon calling upon all to support the new government "to bring peace, prosperity, and happiness to this blood-stained, unhappy country."

Patricio Rivas arrived from San Juan del Norte the next day. The inauguration ceremony took place in the Government House, where a crucifix and an open copy of the Gospels were placed on a table before which the provisional president knelt and took the oath of office. To Walker's surprise, Corral indicated that they also were to take an oath on this occasion. Without hesitating, he did so. Later in the day, Rivas issued his first decrees, naming Corral minister of war and Walker commander in chief of the army. At their installation next day, Corral again insisted upon the administration of an oath, and again Walker acquiesced. At the inauguration, Walker had seen nothing sinister in Corral's wishing him to go through this ceremony, but now he suspected that it was intended to embarrass him. "Although Walker had been educated a Protestant, he had no objection," Walker wrote, "to kneeling before the crucifix—the symbol of salvation to all Christians—and if the legitimist expected to gain a point by the refusal of the American to take the oath, he was, as in the case the day before, disappointed."[11]

In the first days of the new government, Walker observed that Corral's bearing seemed to intimate that he had Rivas "in his keeping," and an incident he related gave evidence of this. Walker had established his headquarters at the home of a popular woman of the city, Niña Yrena, whose family name, Ohoran, indicated she was probably a descendant of an Irish officer in the Spanish service before independence. She was a friend of Legitimist officials and had been useful in acquainting Walker with the people and practices of the city. He overheard Corral, passing her house one afternoon, reply to a question about what he thought of the coalition with the Democrats. Walker related that Corral replied in the language of the cockpit: "We have beaten them with their own cock."

Corral's confidence came from the circumstance that he had been appointed minister of war, Rivas had named, at his request, Norberto Ramírez, a former president, minister of foreign relations, and the provisional president seemed inclined to appoint other Legitimists to council positions. In the struggle for power, Walker, however, had friends among the Granadinos, who made it clear to Rivas the coalition government could not succeed unless Democrats were also named to office. Walker came into a better position to play his hand when General Máximó Jérez and other leading Democrats arrived from León on October 31. He proposed that Jérez rather than Ramírez be named minister of foreign relations. Corral objected that he did not think it possible for him and Jérez to serve in the same cabinet, and he disliked even more the suggestion that Buenaventura Selva, the Democratic government's war minister, receive the post. Walker prevailed, however, and the office went to Jérez. There were fewer difficulties with the other appointments. Both generals were agreed that Fermin Ferrer, a highly respected attorney and judge in Granada, was qualified for the post of minister of credit, and, as it was now assumed that the cabinet must be a balanced one, Walker's nomination of Parker French for minister of hacienda was accepted.

Victorious over Corral in obtaining the appointment of Jérez, Walker succeeded in another coup when, as he termed it, the army under his command was placed on a peace footing. All soldiers wishing to return to their homes were offered discharges, and since most of the Legitimist troops had been impressed into service, more than 1,500 of them left the ranks. Walker's falange and the troops under Valle remained as the only military force in the country.

General Corral had apparently underestimated Walker from the first. He no doubt thought that Walker, as leader of a swashbuckling band of soldiers, fearless in battle, bold in enterprise, and unerring in marksmanship, was himself a military man not up to the niceties of diplomacy. Instead, when they met for the first time to draft the peace treaty, he encountered a mild-mannered, soft-spoken, and undersized man who seemed to be willing to let him dictate the terms. A skilled intrigueant in Nicaraguan politics, Corral believed that Rivas, who had never risen to a high position in the government, would be easily controlled, and the appointment of Ramírez to the important post of minister of foreign affairs gave him confidence. This confidence, revealed in his remark to Niña Yrena, evaporated when he discovered that Walker, rather than being an easily led subject, had a will of iron. Walker, it developed, had the winning fowl in the cockpit.

In great perturbation about the way things were going, Corral on November 1 wrote messages to General Guardiola, who had returned to Guatemala after his defeat at Virgin Bay, and to Pedro Xatruch, who had been left in command of the force at Rivas when Corral went north to attack León and who had fled to Honduras, begging them to obtain help at once lest the Legitimist cause be entirely lost. His hurriedly written notes dispatched by courier were intercepted by General Valle, who delivered them to Walker on November 5. Walker called a meeting of officers of the new government and produced the letters revealing the effort to invite Serviles in other states to invade Nicaragua. Corral was court-martialed the next day on charges of high treason and conspiracy to overthrow the government. The court was made up entirely of Americans: there were few army officers in the city other than Democrats since Walker had disbanded the Legitimist forces and in any case Corral preferred to put his fate in the hands of foreigners rather than in those of his own countrymen against whom he had fought. The court-martial found him guilty and condemned him to death, but unanimously recommended mercy in forwarding the verdict to Walker.

Walker pondered long over whether to affirm the sentence of death. It was an instance of indecisiveness he had not shown before. After his defeat at Rivas, he had suffered no moral qualms about the death sentence meted out in a hasty court-martial of the two renegades who had set fire to the barracks at San Juan del Sur; later one of his Nicaraguan officers had been sentenced to death and shot, on October 6, for having terrified the owner and customers of a tavern while drunk and violent; a week later, while Walker was at Virgin Bay preparing to attack Granada, a Legitimist "spy" had been captured, condemned to death by a court-martial, and shot on the spot; on October 22, without a court-martial, he had himself ordered the death of Mateo Mayorga; and as late as November 3 he had approved the death sentence in the case of one of the new recruits from San Francisco who while drunk had exhibited his skill as a marksman by drawing a bead on a native boy and shooting him.

But in the case of Corral there were political considerations to be taken into account, for he had been a popular leader and Granadinos expressed their sympathy for him, Padre Vijil as well as other influential persons interceding in his behalf. On the other hand, Corral's death would demonstrate to the people that "there was a power in the State capable and resolved to punish any offences against their interests" and mercy to him would be an "invitation to all the Legitimists to engage in like conspiracies." Then there was Walker's own sense of right and justice to be taken into account. "Walker had solemnly sworn, with bended knee on the Holy Evangelists," he wrote, "to observe . . . the treaty of the twenty-third of October; and he was responsible before the world, and especially to the Americans in Nicaragua—as well as before the throne of Heaven—for the faithful observance of his oath." Such lofty considerations as well as practical exigency could lead to only one conclusion: Corral must die. Walker did not mention one of his considerations: that Corral's death would get rid of the one man who had shown himself capable of interfering with his plans for Nicaragua. Corral's execution brought into the cabinet a willing disciple of Walker, Buenaventura Selva, minister of war in the Leónese government.[12] Walker now controlled the cabinet and apparently President Rivas as well.

From the day of the Democrats' seizure of the undefended capital, the American minister, John H. Wheeler, had supported Walker and his band of filibusters. Writing Secretary of State Marcy hastily on the day after the coup, he said: "I hope that this may settle this distracted, yet beautiful country." A week later he reported his unhappy experience as bearer of peace messages to Corral and complained of the insult to the United States, ignoring the fact that this trip was, as Corral wrote him, a gross interference in the internal affairs of the country. When the provisional government was organized under President Rivas, Wheeler informed Marcy he intended to recognize the regime under the historic principle "that every Nation possesses the right to govern itself according to its own will." Accordingly, on November 10, he presented his credentials—those he had some months before presented to the Legitimist government—to President Rivas, declaring: "I request that you will regard the letter of the President of the United States, as addressed to you, as President of the Republic of Nicaragua, and that you rely with confidence on his sincerity in the expression of friendship entertained by him and the people of the United States for this republic. . . ." He went on to set forth, in lofty language, his hopes for the new republic, "the 'golden gate' between the Atlantic and Pacific oceans, which opens the commerce of the world."[13]

News of Walker's success reached both San Francisco and New York papers on November 4 from transit company ships, the *Uncle Sam* sailing from San Juan del Sur and the *Star of the West* sailing from San Juan del Norte. Ordinarily, accounts of happenings in Central America were sketchy, information being supplied by ships' captains and pursers, passengers, and correspondents' letters that were irregularly dispatched; but full details of what had occurred were now available in reprints of articles published in an organ, *El Nicaragüense*, which Walker had established a week after seizing Granada. In publishing his own newspaper, a leaf borrowed from the book of Colonel Kinney at San Juan del Norte with his *Central American*, Walker had an effective instrument for propaganda in the United States, for its articles were widely reprinted so great was the interest in Nicaragua.[14]

Walker has been given the historical epithet "the gray-eyed man of destiny" as the fulfillment of a tradition of the Indians that they would be delivered from Spanish oppression by "the Gray-eyed Man." This fiction, similar to the legend of the Aztecs awaiting the Fair God, Hernando Cortés, the conqueror of Mexico, was a creation of *El Nicaragüense*. It cited as authority for the legend a Baptist missionary, Frederick Crowe, who in a work published at London in 1850 said that if the Gray-eyed Man arrived he would be of the Anglo-Saxon race, and most likely an American as Americans were taking "a lively interest" in Central America at the time. The editor of *El Nicaragüense* did not need much evidence, if any, to confirm the prophecy. "The Gray-eyed Man has come," he wrote. "He has come not as Attila, or a Guardiola, but as a friend to the oppressed, and a protector of the helpless and unoffending."[15]

After Walker's rout at Rivas in July in his first battle, he had become an object of ridicule in much of the U.S. press. Recalling the fiasco of his Lower California expedition, the *New York Herald* had sarcastically written of his failure in Nicaragua: "This is the end of the great annexation project of Col. Walker, ex-President of Sonora." The *New York Tribune* had been even more adverse, as well as inaccurate, in saying: "Fourteen of his cut-throat followers were killed in the mad attack which they made on the town of Rivas, and he himself barely escaped with his life, leaving behind him guns, swords, ammunition and the like, even to his pantaloons and shirt."

But success, as the *Alta California* pointed out, changes "rebels and traitors into patriots and heroes." The paper, heretofore opposed to him, was now willing to admit that in his Nicaraguan campaign he had "exhibited a good degree of skill." "Now that the country is in the hands of Walker, as it really is," the paper continued, "strong efforts will doubtless be made to induce immigration, and thousands will without doubt, flock to Nicaragua, tempted by the novelty and apparent openings for enterprise, capital and labor." Even the antiexpansionist *New York Evening Post* was willing to concede that his usurpation of power might prove beneficial and justified this belief on the principle of Manifest Destiny. "He may fail," the paper said, "but there is reason to believe that in Nicaragua at least the sceptre has departed from the degenerate descendants of the Spanish conquerors, and that the destiny of Central America is now more manifestly than ever placed in Anglo-American hands. An efficient republican system may yet be adopted there under Yankee auspices, and the perplexed 'Central American question' . . . may be settled by the irresistible law of modern colonization."[16]

Walker was unwilling to wait for this irresistible law to become operative. The loan of $20,000 from the shipment of gold bullion made by Charles J. Macdonald suggested that further cooperation with the transit company might be possible, and he wrote his San Francisco friend, Alexander P. Crittenden, saying any arrangements he might make with Cornelius K. Garrison to transport 500 men into the country would be "fully approved."[17] The falange now numbered about 150 men, with the additions of thirty men brought by Charles Gilman and the sixty brought by Parker French.

In the first week of November Walker received another sizable contingent, seventy-eight men brought by Edward J. C. Kewen, brother of Achilles Kewen, killed in the attack on Rivas. The *Alta California*, reporting the departure of the band on October 20, said that Kewen, one of the city's leading men, had sailed "to avenge the slaughter of his brother." On November 17 Kewen, appointed financial agent by Walker, returned to San Francisco to sell bonds of the new republic and to recruit additional men. With these new enlistments, Walker had doubled the size of his American force. According to a roster published in *El Nicaragüense* on November 17, it consisted of 213 men organized under a general staff headed by Walker as commander in chief.[18]

Attached to the general staff as a first lieutenant was one of Walker's younger brothers, Norvell, who had been a passenger aboard the steamer that in July carried the band of foreigners the Legitimist minister in Washington, José de Marcoleta, and the transit company's attorney, Joseph L. White, had sent to break up the Kinney expedition. Informed of this by his brother, Walker decided that the transit company in dealing with the contending parties in Nicaragua had only one guiding principle—to be left free to make money transporting travelers and freight.[19] This decision was to have an influence on his relations later on with the company.

Walker's exploit had created so much enthusiasm in California that Kewen on his return to San Francisco quickly recruited a band of 150 men, the largest to enlist under the banner of the new republic, who sailed on the *Sierra Nevada* on December 6. Among them was a young ex-Missourian, James Carson Jamison, who recalled his experiences in a book, *With Walker in Nicaragua, or Reminiscences of an Officer of the American Phalanx*. He was at Georgetown in Eldorado County when he heard that recruits for Walker were being sought. "My blood grew hot at the thought of the stirring adventures that awaited me if I could attach myself to Walker's army," he recalled. He was successful in joining the band recruited by Kewen, and in the election of officers for one of the companies was chosen a first lieutenant. When Jamison received his commission from Walker at Granada, he found that the leader lacked the commanding presence he had expected. "A woman's voice was scarcely softer than Walker's," Jamison wrote, "and so imperturbable was he that his praise of a valorous deed or his announcement of a death penalty were equally calm in tone and deliberate in enunciation. Though affable in intercourse, he suppressed his emotions, whether of joy of sadness, and did not permit himself to be startled by surprise." Like many of Walker's followers, Jamison respected his leader though he always found him an enigma.[20]

In contrast to Walker's success, Kinney was experiencing failure. The fear of José de Marcoleta and Joseph L. White that he would be able to control the port of San Juan del Norte and interfere with operations of the transit company turned out to be unjustified. His early euphoria in electing himself governor had dissipated when the British refused to recognize him and the townspeople were indifferent to his decrees. Accordingly, he issued a notice on September 23 announcing his resignation.[21]

Nevertheless, Kinney endeavored to keep his scheme alive by

publishing in the *Central American*, widely quoted by American newspapers, articles glowingly describing the opportunities in the Mosquito territory. News letters from San Juan del Norte refuted these. A *New York Herald* correspondent, for example, wrote: "Kinney is here without money, credit, supplies or men. . . . The stories circulated by Kinney and his friends about farms, coffee, sugar, corn, are all humbug. Not an acre has been cleared, nor will be, and not a coffee tree nor stalk of cane will ever be planted by Kinney or his followers. . . . Lying around bar-rooms, drinking liquor, and running in debt for board, lodging, rum and segars . . . is all they have done. . . ."[22] Joseph Fabens had brought in a few men when he sailed to San Juan del Norte in September, but otherwise there had been no additions to Kinney's colony.

Walker's victory at Granada made Kinney realize that he must come to terms with his California rival, and in the first week of November he sent Fabens to the capital with a proposal of accommodation. Fabens was accompanied by a Captain Swift and about twenty of Kinney's followers, apparently sent to persuade Walker that the Americans were in a strong position at San Juan del Norte. If so, it was a futile stratagem, for Walker had no illusions about the colony; only a week before, on October 27, *El Nicaragüense* had carried an article, "Colonel Kinney's Progress and Pretensions Reviewed," exposing the hollowness of his claims of progress.

According to a correspondent of the *San Francisco Herald*, Walker courteously received the two "ambassadors" from Kinney on November 7. Kinney's proposal was that if Walker would recognize the rights Kinney had acquired in the Mosquito kingdom he in turn would recognize the new government at Granada. Although Walker received the message with a countenance "as placid as ever," the correspondent wrote, he nevertheless told the messenger "that if Kinney was taken within the limits of Nicaragua or the Mosquito kingdom . . . he would within a very limited period of time terminate his dreams of Central American ambition by facilitating his involuntary exit from earth through the instrumentality of a hempen auxiliary." This journalistic elevation of language was not reached in another version of the interview, that of William V. Wells. He quoted Walker: "Tell Mr. Kinney, or Col. Kinney, or Gov. Kinney, or by whatever name he styles himself, that if he interferes with the territory of Nicaragua, and I can lay my hands on him, I will most assuredly hang him."[23]

Fabens and Captain Swift knew when a ship was sinking and decided to desert Kinney and join Walker. Fabens, in particular, would be useful to Walker because of his relations with members of President Pierce's cabinet, and received a high government position, that of director of colonization. He entered into his duties enthusiastically, placing advertisements in American newspapers within the month offering under a decree issued on November 23 land grants of 250 acres to single settlers and 350 acres to families that would emigrate to Nicaragua.

During the busy first weeks of the Rivas government in which Walker had placed his own men in office, had reorganized and strengthened his army, had entered into negotiations with the transit company to obtain its assistance, and had made arrangements for bringing in American settlers, one of his most enthusiastic supporters had been John H. Wheeler. On October 30 and again on November 12 the American minister had written Secretary of State Marcy that Walker would succeed in restoring the Central American confederation.[24] Marcy, however, was provoked by the Walker filibuster, which intensified the bad relations existing with Great Britain over the Central American question and the interpretation of the Clayton-Bulwer Treaty. Four days after newspapers carried the reports of Walker's success, he wrote Wheeler: "It appears that a band of foreign adventurers have invaded that unhappy country, which, after gaining recruits from among the residents, has by violence overturned the previously existing government, and now pretends to be in possession of sovereign authority. The knowledge we have of their proceedings does not authorize the President to recognize it as the *de facto* government of Nicaragua, and he cannot hold, or permit you to hold in your official character, any political intercourse with the persons now claiming to exercise the sovereign authority of that state." A month later, after he had been informed of Wheeler's unauthorized recognition of the government, Marcy wrote a letter of reprimand, emphasizing earlier instructions that he "at once cease to have any communication with the present assumed rulers of that country."[25]

Walker may have been misled about the Washington view

by Wheeler's expressions of goodwill when he made a disastrous choice in appointing a minister to the United States—Parker H. French. Walker later confessed that the appointment was made "with a view of getting him out of the Hacienda Department and out of the country," explaining: "He was utterly unfitted for the administration of the hacienda, having little knowledge of either the principles or details of public business, and not having either the modesty to be sensible of his defects or the patience to overcome them. Moreover his rapacity made him dreaded by the people of the country, and, as a measure of policy, it was necessary for the Americans to get rid of him."[26]

When French appeared in Washington in mid-December, it was generally agreed in the press that Marcy would not receive him, especially as the story of his forgeries at San Antonio in equipping his California wagon train was revived. The *New York Times*'s Washington correspondent wrote that should French call on Marcy he would meet with a cold reception, for "I know of no man who possesses greater facility than the Secretary of State of turning an unwelcome visitor into an icicle." French wrote Marcy on December 19 requesting an interview to present his credentials. The rejection was as frigid as the *Times* had predicted. The president, Marcy replied, "has not yet seen reasons for establishing diplomatic intercourse with the persons who now claim to exercise the political power in the State of Nicaragua." The refusal was a blow to Walker. The administration would act to frustrate the emigration schemes he had set in motion and its failure to recognize the government would provide neighboring states with an excuse for withholding diplomatic recognition and encourage the conservative parties in them, as Walker foresaw, "to take active and decided measures against the Rivas government."[27]

CHAPTER FOURTEEN

The Costa Rican War against Walker

When Parker H. French left San Juan del Norte on December 3, 1855, bearing his credentials as minister plenipotentiary to the United States, the *New York Herald*'s correspondent wrote that his "amiable character and polished manners" would win him hosts of friends. The correspondent's impression of French was typical—he did possess charm for those who did not know him well or had not been victims of his chicanery. It had not taken Walker long to see through him, but he had been helpful in persuading Cornelius K. Garrison to support the filibusters. Perhaps he would be as successful in obtaining the help of Charles Morgan, the New York agent of the transit company, for in addition to serving as envoy at Washington, French was instructed to arrange with Morgan to send recruits from the east coast as Garrison was already doing from the west coast.

El Nicaragüense published articles boasting of the popularity of the new regime with the Nicaraguans, but even if this were true, which it was not, Walker realized that he could keep control only by bringing in more Americans. Without money to finance colonists, he could obtain them in large numbers only if they could be transported free of charge. Offers of 250 or 350 acres of land were an inducement, but not much for those lacking the wherewithal to pay their passage. This transportation, however, was not wholly a bribe of the transit company to keep its rights of passage. The costs were to be charged against money that both the Legitimists and Democrats claimed was owed the government under the charters granted the American Atlantic and Pacific Ship Canal Company and the Accessory Transit Company.

Under these arrangements, Nicaragua was to receive $10,000 annually until the completion of a ship canal or, if construction of a waterway was not feasible, a railway or other road across the isthmus, and 10 percent of the net profits. The transit company had made the annual $10,000 payments but not those based on profits, maintaining that there were none because of money spent on improving the route, salaries, and equipment. This was not very believable in view of the thousands of passengers who made the transit annually and the millions of dollars in bullion and the thousands of tons of freight transported. In June 1855 the Legitimist government had sent two commissioners to New York to come to an accounting with the company, and they offered to settle for $40,000. The company refused in August, and the matter was submitted to arbitration.

President Castellón had given Walker authority in July to deal with the company and notified it that any settlement made by the Legitimist agents would not be recognized. On September 3, after the victory over General Guardiola at Virgin Bay, Walker had taken up the matter with the company's agent there, Courtland Cushing, but nothing had come of this. Walker pursued the matter after the Rivas government was established, requesting on November 12 that the company appoint commissioners to meet with new Nicaraguan commissioners to arrange a settlement. Thomas Lord, the company's president, upon the advice of its attorney, Joseph L. White, refused. The question, White said, was now under arbitration by commissioners appointed by both parties—and the power to negotiate had passed into their hands under the legal doctrine that a change of administration in a country did not invalidate earlier acts of its government. Walker was angered by White's instructing him on the law and declared it was a "mere evasion." Lord had suggested that if both parties agreed they could appoint new commissioners, but Walker, ignoring this solution, planned a bombshell for the company after his friends Edmund Randolph and Alexander P. Crittenden arrived at Granada on December 18.[1]

It was a devious plot that the three worked out, one designed to mislead President Rivas as well as the San Francisco and New York agents of the company. Walker's friends were accompanied to Nicaragua by W. R. Garrison, son of Cornelius K. Garrison, and they brought more than 100 recruits for the army. The plan was for Rivas to issue a decree declaring the charters null and void because the provisions they contained had not been met and to draft a new charter offering better terms to the company. Copies of the new grant were to be taken to New York for Morgan's approval by W. R. Garrison and to San Francisco for the elder Garrison's approval by Charles J. Macdonald. The plan, however, did not envision awarding the charter to either but to Randolph and Crittenden. Walker's duplicity did not end there, for he also considered it necessary to keep knowledge of the plan from President Rivas.[2]

While this plot was being hatched, French had proceeded to Washington, where Secretary of State Marcy refused to receive him on the ground that his government did not have the support of the Nicaraguan people.[3] Neither this rejection nor the newspaper articles recalling French's past sins—the public had been regaled by them before in a pamphlet, *The Sufferings and Hardships of Parker H. French's Overland Expedition*, published in 1851—could deflate French. He went on to New York, took a suite at the St. Nicholas Hotel, and, lavishing champagne and cigars on newspaper reporters, provided the city with dramatic stories of his own part in the Nicaraguan civil war and began negotiations with the transit company to send emigrants to Nicaragua. Given authority by Walker to settle the claims against the company, he airily dismissed them: inasmuch as the company had advanced the new government $20,000 from the bullion shipment, they could not amount to much. Instead, he arranged for the company to transport emigrants at $20 each chargeable to the government, the question of the claims to be settled later.[4]

The shipment of emigrants from New York, however, was not to be so easy as it was from San Francisco, where permissive officials did not interfere with the departure of transit company ships carrying men as passengers that everyone in the city knew were sailing to join Walker. After news of Walker's accomplishment reached the United States, newspapers published stories that hundreds of persons were eager to join expeditions to Nicaragua. President Pierce issued a proclamation on December 8 warning against such ventures and through Attorney General Caleb Cushing instructed district attorneys in port cities to prevent the sailing of ships bearing men planning to enlist in the Nicaraguan army.[5]

One reason for the proclamation was that Pierce was preparing his annual message to Congress, in which he wished to place himself in an advantageous position in reporting on negotiations with Great Britain over the Central American questions raised by the Clayton-Bulwer Treaty. In the fall he had instructed the American minister, James Buchanan, to obtain a definite and final answer on Great Britain's continued claims to the Bay Islands and the protectorate over the Mosquito Coast. The reply was the same as before: the treaty was prospective in intention and did not require Great Britain to relinquish holdings acquired before 1850. Another reason was that during the summer the administration had protested against British officials enlisting recruits in this country to fight in the Crimean War. It was Pierce's intention in acting against the filibusters to show that his administration was impartial in enforcing the neutrality laws. He could not wink at the violations, or suspected violations by Americans, while he was prosecuting British agents and planning to demand the recall of the minister to the United States, John F. T. Crampton, for his part, a leading one, in obtaining the enlistments.[6]

French in New York held a series of secret meetings with several men who had been prominent in the López expeditions as a result of which about 300 recruits were enlisted to sail for Nicaragua on the *Northern Light* the day before Christmas. Anonymous tipsters, however, informed the U.S. attorney, John McKeon, of the plan, and he warned French that he would be arrested if the men sailed and Joseph L. White that the vessel would be seized. McKeon called on French at the St. Nicholas Hotel to issue his warning, and the unaccredited ambassador blandly denied knowledge of any wrong-doing. "My country invites immigration," he told McKeon, "but I am too well aware of the duties of my position, and of the Argus eyes with which I am watched by all the world, to do aught that would embarrass me or entangle the negotiations now pending in Washington." He admitted, however, that the transit company, to build up trade with Nicaragua, had agreed to transport emigrants at a rate of $20 each.

On the morning of December 24 the *Herald* revealed the secret details of the filibuster recruitment effort and the detective work of the district attorney's office in collecting evidence. Because of the paper's revelations, several thousand persons gathered at the No. 3 pier on the North River to see the excitement when the *Northern Light* cast off. Just as the gangplank was about to be raised, McKeon, leading five U.S. marshals, went aboard. He attempted several times to read a message from President Pierce authorizing him to hold the vessel, each time being shouted down by the passengers.

"Gentlemen," McKeon addressed the men on deck, "I have here a despatch from the President, which I wish to——"

"Well why don't you read it at once, old Puddenhead?" shouted a passenger.

"Down with him!" was the cry from another.

"Let's duck him in the river!" yelled a third.

Unable to make himself heard, McKeon withdrew to the wharf, leaving two of the marshals aboard. In a few minutes the *Northern Light* cast off and was on her way down the river, with the encouraging cries of "Go it!" from those on the pier. The ship did not go far, however; as she was passing Governor's Island, she was brought to by a blank shot fired by a revenue cutter, and later a naval vessel was sent to blockade her.

McKeon's prevention of the sailing of the *Northern Light* was the most serious effort made by any of the district attorneys directed to "detect and defeat" all filibuster enterprises, but as it turned out he was scarcely more effectual than those in other ports, New Orleans and San Francisco in particular, where officials were less energetic in enforcing the law. A difficulty lay in the fact that filibusters were no longer recruited to sail in chartered ships to the country to be invaded but sailed as passengers on the transit company ships. Attorney General Cushing in a letter to S. W. Inge in San Francisco acknowledged "the difficulty of detecting criminal intent by persons when they embark in passenger ships."

When McKeon sent marshals aboard the *Northern Light* to take off those intending to join Walker, he found only forty suspects among the 500 passengers, and these were suspects only because they had no tickets. About the only result of McKeon's activities, headlined "The Nicaragua Excitement" on successive days in the *Herald* and reported in voluminous detail, was to hold up the sailing for two and a half days. There were several arrests, however, Scott himself, Joseph R. Malé, editor of *El Nicaragüense*, who had gone to New York to purchase printing supplies, and three men identified as officers in a regiment formed to join Walker. One famous filibuster who escaped McKeon's net was Louis Schlesinger, the European revolutionist who had fought with Kossuth and who had joined López on his last expedition to Cuba. Schlesinger escaped detection by shaving off his moustache and donning the monkey jacket and tar-spattered pantaloons worn by crewmen. He boasted of his exploit in a letter to the *Herald* written in the belief, he said, that it might find a place because of the paper's desire "to publish facts which may have a tendency to enlighten or amuse" its readers.[7]

The jeering and hooting by the crowds on the wharf as marshals went aboard the steamers to arrest filibusters on subsequent sailings of transit company ships were echoed in much of the press comment on the futile searches.[8] The *Northern Light* affair had provoked a bit of doggerel which began:

> The officer a warrant had to search the vessel through;
> From deck to keel, from stem to stern, he must his duty do.
> Beneath her coal, within her berths, were articles of war;
> Between her sheets were rogues and thieves, and lawless men a score.
> Her traffic was against the State, her boilers full of treason.
> In fact, for her detention he gave most urgent reason.

The *New York Atlas* demanded: "When will this child's play cease? Like India rubber, North American filibusters jump higher every time they are stricken down; and all such opposition recently made to their movements, by the instructions of the President and his cabinet, only increases their numbers and emboldens them to cling more tenaciously to their enterprise."[9]

While Walker was plotting with Randolph and Crittenden to seize the property of the transit company, at the same time using it to bring immigrants to the country, Cornelius Vanderbilt was nearing the end of his campaign to "ruin" Garrison and Morgan. He had declared in his famous letter announcing his intention that he would not sue them because the law was too slow, but he did resort to the courts in actions against the company to settle disputed accounts. The legal situation was a complex one as the transit company was a Nicaragua corporation, and the *Herald*, which reported the litigation in detail, commented on the difficulty of getting "at the bottom of this mysterious, mixed-up matter."

Vanderbilt, with the capital at his command, could have regained control of the transit company by buying up the stock, but the effect of this would be not to ruin his enemies but to enrich them by raising the value of the shares. Instead, he depressed the market by unloading his stock in such large blocs that he became known as the "Great Bear" on Wall Street. Then, in January 1854, he entered the isthmian competition against the Accessory Transit Company, the United States Mail Steamship Company, and the Pacific Mail Steamship Company by forming the Independent Line with Edward Mills, a California shipping magnate. The Independent Line offered such low rates for the Panama passage that its competition was ruinous to the other lines. Before the end of the year they were glad to buy him out by paying $800,000 for his ships and a secret bonus of $40,000 a month so long as he stayed out of the competition. The *Alta California*, which did not know about the bonus, predicted: "Vanderbilt is slippery, very much like an Irishman's flea, and we should not be surprised if a line of opposition steamers were puffing away in the course of six months, established, at least indirectly, through his means."

Although Vanderbilt made a huge profit in this deal, he derived little satisfaction from it because Garrison and Morgan remained at the head of the transit company. Their financial position, however, was shaky since the civil war in Nicaragua had lowered the value of company shares. Vanderbilt contributed to a further drop, in addition to unloading his personal stock, by instigating a suit early in 1855 accusing Morgan and Garrison of mismanagement and misuse of funds. The stock was further depressed in November when the company sought to borrow money at 7 percent interest to meet current indebtedness. During this time Vanderbilt and his friends obtained a majority of the stock at the depressed value. In December he was elected a director of the company and on February 1, 1856, he had himself appointed the president.

Vanderbilt had ruthlessly and persistently carried out his threat against Morgan and Garrison, but it was a triumph he was not to enjoy for long, for Walker had easily persuaded President Rivas to assent to revocation of the transit company charter. In the meantime, Vanderbilt was continuing to carry out the policy established by Morgan and Garrison of cooperation with Walker in transporting immigrants to Nicaragua, although he attempted to clear himself with the government and to stop the searches of his vessels for filibusters by writing McKeon on February 6 he would "most cheerfully" join in any "mode you may point out to save trouble that may arise."[10]

Walker's proposed decree of revocation citing the failure of the transit company to meet its charter obligations was signed on February 18 by President Rivas "not only without hesitation but with undisguised pleasure," since Nicaraguans, including Rivas, who had been a collector of customs at San Carlos, disliked its high-handed operations over the years. But Rivas balked when, after indorsing the document, Walker submitted a new contract giving the franchise to Randolph and Crittenden. In talks with Fermin Ferrer, then acting as "minister general," the president described it as "a sale of the country." Walker was forced to make modifications in the contract and to exert pressure on Rivas to obtain his signature to a decree implementing it on February 19.

Walker did not publish the revocation decree at once, however, to prevent news of it reaching New York by passengers from San Francisco making the transit crossing. The delay would give the new holders of the contract two weeks to put ships into operation before the company halted its sailings. Walker related with some glee an unexpected dividend from this delay. A company vessel leaving New Orleans on February 27 carried more than 250 passengers for service in Nicaragua paid with drafts by Domingo de Goicouria, for years a leader in the Cuba filibuster movement and the associate of López in his ill-fated ventures, on Cornelius Vanderbilt.[11]

Walker's eventual downfall was in part the outcome of the decrees of October 18 and 19. They resulted in the alienation of Rivas and others in the government, who soon joined his enemies in other Central American states planning a war against him, and they created a powerful opponent in Vanderbilt, who could not endure being bested by anyone in a financial deal.

One of the first acts of the Rivas government had been to send circulars to the other Central American states giving the terms of the treaty of October 23 and declaring the desire of Nicaragua for harmony and fraternity with her neighbors. The only reply came from El Salvador, whose Liberal government congratulated Nicaragua on the restoration of peace. Guatemala and Costa Rica, controlled by Serviles, opposed the Nicaragua regime, as did Honduras, also in the hands of conservatives since July when José Trinidad Cabañas, who had helped the exiled Democrats return to lead the revolution against the Legitimists, was driven from office and fled to El Salvador.

Walker attributed the hostility of these three states to the bringing of Americans into the government.[12] There was a stronger reason, however, and this was the belief, not unfounded, that Walker's success was only a prelude to attacks on the other states. Antonio José de Irisarri, the minister of both Guatemala and El Salvador in Washington, expressed this fear in a letter on November 30 to Secretary of State Marcy. Irisarri complained that Walker planned to lead expeditions to overthrow the governments of the other states and said that these republics could not lay down their arms until they had driven from Nicaragua "the intrusive rulers of the country." Similar fears were expressed by Luis Molina, Costa Rican chargé d'affaires at Washington, who wrote Marcy on December 6 that his government could not remain passive before the threat of the American invaders. These protests might have won more sympathy from Marcy if they had not accused the United States of bad faith in failing to prevent the departure of filibusters on ships of the transit company. He replied somewhat stiffly that the envoys were mistaken in ascribing the revolution in Nicaragua solely to the intervention of Americans, pointing out that they had been invited to Nicaragua by her own citizens.[13]

Walker's grand design was to reunite the five Central American states into a confederacy, but this was a project that would have to wait for the future. In the fall and winter of 1855 his chief concern was to bring in recruits to consolidate his power in Nicaragua. This was indicated when Cabañas went to Granada in November to plead for help in his effort to regain the presidency of Honduras. His reception on December 3 was a state affair, but his request for military support was denied. Cabañas confided to Wheeler, in an interview on December 15, that he was unhappy about conditions in Nicaragua. "The belief was current," he said, "that all the offices and emoluments of office would be absorbed by North Americans." It was a danger others in the Granada government had begun to perceive, and the refusal of aid to Cabañas provoked the defection of two Democrats in the cabinet. General Jérez resigned as minister of foreign affairs on January 8, saying that it compromised "the honor and true interest of Nicaragua," and Buenaventure Selva resigned a short time later as minister of war. Their resignations left only one person in the cabinet, Fermin Ferrer, who received the title of minister general.[14]

Walker in his objection to interference in Honduran affairs had sought to demonstrate the lack of aggressiveness of the Americans toward the neighboring states. To demonstrate further his peaceful intentions he had Rivas issue, on January 12, a circular to the other states asking them to receive a commissioner for discussion of restoring the union of Central American States. It was a proposal not likely to be well received. In Guatemala the president was Rafael Carrera, violently opposed to confederation. He was, in the words of the historian Hubert Howe Bancroft, "of a violent, irascible, and uncommunicative disposition" and through brigandage and warfare had made himself dictator. He had a counterpart in General Guardiola, who achieved the presidency of Honduras in January 1855, a man Bancroft described as possessing "all the vices" as he was guilty of "all the crimes known to man." The president of Costa Rica since 1850, Juan Rafael Mora, was a man of a different stripe. A wealthy merchant, he had traveled abroad and, according to Bancroft, possessed "rare intellectual powers." He was, however, as opposed to the Americans as the other heads of state. In fact, he was the first to condemn the new Nicaragua regime, describing Walker and the falange in a proclamation of November 20 as "a band of adventurers, the scum of all the earth," who "are planning to invade Costa Rica and seek in our wives and daughters, our houses and lands, satisfaction for their fierce passions, food for their unbridled appetites."[15]

Mora's animosity, however, was based on more than his fear of the Americans pursuing the career of rapine and looting he emotionally described. Their domination of Nicaragua would put an end to his hope of obtaining control of the lucrative transit route he had for years asserted was owned by Costa Rica. When the United States and England in the Clayton-Bulwer Treaty agreed on guaranteeing a free transit of the isthmus, Costa Rica had protested, claiming joint sovereignty with Nicaragua over San Juan del Norte and the San Juan River and navigation rights on Lake Nicaragua. Under ancient grants from Spain, Mora maintained, Costa Rica held title to the southern portion of the harbor and the southern banks of the river and the lake besides a district extending from the lake to the Pacific coast known as Guanacaste. Secretary of State Daniel Webster in negotiations with John F. T. Crampton, the British minister to the United States, in 1851 and 1852 had worked out an agreement for resolving the disputes in a quadruple treaty with Nicaragua and Costa Rica. Costa Rica assented to the plan, but it was rejected by Nicaragua.[16]

Thus the Rivas appeal to the neighboring states to receive commissioners to discuss restoration of the confederation went unanswered. Even El Salvador, where Democrats were in power, ignored it because, *El Nicaragüense* in its issue of February 9 charged, Cabañas, irked by the refusal of aid in his own behalf, had returned to the country and was inciting the people against the Americans.

Walker might have found support in Colonel Kinney at San Juan del Norte—a weak reed, to be sure—but he guaranteed that this would not be forthcoming by a decree, signed on February 8 by Rivas, asserting Nicaragua's title to all of Mosquitia.Two days later Granadinos were astonished when Kinney himself disembarked from one of the lake steamers and announced that he was on a diplomatic mission. He called first on Walker, whose reception of him, according to *El Nicaragüense*, was cold but polite. Kinney proposed, the paper said, that Nicaragua be divided into two states, one to be known as Mosquitia, which he would govern. Walker ended the interview by rising and declaring: "Your antecedents preclude the possibility of the state's placing you in any official position." Kinney was then arrested but was permitted to return, under guard, to San Juan del Norte. A slightly different version of the meeting was given by E. A. Pollard, a San Francisco editor on his way to New York. He related that Kinney had merely proposed a mutual assistance pact in "the great enterprise of Americanizing" Nicaragua, he to direct civil affairs in Mosquitia and Walker to direct military affairs.[17]

Despite the failure to receive responses to the invitation for discussions on restoring the Central American confederacy, Walker on February 4 dispatched a commission to Costa Rica for the purpose of improving relations headed by Louis Schlesinger, whom Walker, impressed by his military background as an officer in Kossuth's army and as a leader in López's last expedition to Cuba, had made adjutant general. The other commissioners were W. A. Sutter, son of the discoverer of gold in California, who had brought in a company of recruits from San Francisco in January, and Manuel Argüello, a former Legitimist serving in the government.

Egotistical, arrogant, and overly sensitive of his honor as an officer, Schlesinger was not a man to do well on a goodwill mission. When the commissioners reached the town of Guanacaste, they were delayed by the governor until he heard from the capital, San José, whether they would be received by President Mora. Insulted as he fancied by a Costa Rican soldier, Schlesinger "promptly punished the offender on the spot," the *New York Tribune*'s correspondent at Virgin Bay reported, "and told the governor if any such conduct was tolerated by the authorities ample satisfaction would not only be demanded by his government but enforced." After eight days, word arrived from San José that the commissioners would not be received. Ordered from the country, they were subjected to other insults as they proceeded to Punta Arenas on the Pacific coast to embark on a schooner to San Juan del Sur, Schlesinger threatening war and the wrath of Walker for the indignities he had suffered.[18]

Mora's summary dismissal of Schlesinger was inspired in part by support Costa Rica was receiving from Great Britain, secret negotiations having been conducted since January to obtain guns and ammunition. On February 27 he obtained from the congress authority to take up arms, either alone or with other states, against the Americans "to drive them utterly from Central America." On March 1 he addressed the people in a grandiloquent proclamation calling them to arms to free Nicaragua and declaring that "we war only on filibusters." "To the conflict then, Costa Ricans!" he exclaimed.

Mora set out with 3,000 troops on March 4 for Punta Arenas in the Gulf of Nicoya preparatory to an invasion of Nicaragua from Guanacaste and dispatched a detachment to dislodge a garrison of Americans at Hipps' Point on the Serapiqui River at its confluence with the San Juan River. Mora's strategy, as was Walker's, was to obtain control of the transit route. If he could defeat Walker in the west and dominate the river by seizing Hipps' Point, he would effectually shut off American recruits arriving on every ship from San Francisco and New York.[19]

While Mora was rattling his sword in San José, Schlesinger returned to Granada with the report of the rejection of his mission. Walker was irate. Four months after the establishment of the coalition government in Nicaragua, it was now clear that there was no hope of winning the friendship of the other Central American states. On March 10 Walker, in ignorance of the martial preparations in San José, declared war against the Serviles. Invited to Nicaragua by the Democrats, the Americans, he said, had struggled to carry on the principles of the party and had sought to end civil strife by amalgamating the warring parties in the provisional government. Their effort had been of no avail. The Legitimist party, Walker declared, had repulsed all efforts of conciliation and had maintained communication with Serviles in other states. These in turn, Walker said, had "treated with scorn and disdain" the government's overtures to peace on the sole ground of the presence of the American forces. Therefore, he continued, the only course open to the Americans was "to declare eternal enmity" to the Serviles in all the states. The declaration ended: "The troops of the army of the republic will assume and wear the red ribbon."

In issuing his proclamation Walker hoped, he explained later, to secure the zealous cooperation of the Nicaraguan Democrats as well as that of the Liberals in the other states "in the war immediately impending." Actually, it was an assertion of the independence of the Americans from both parties. The reason he could do this was that in the past several months about 2,000 Americans had come to Nicaragua on the transit company ships, and prospects, in his belief, were bright for the stream of immigration to continue.

He took as the occasion for his attack on the Serviles the induction into the army 250 men brought to Granada by Domingo de Goicouria. The son of a Havana merchant, Goicouria had been deported to Spain for revolutionary activities on the island; he later came to the United States and was associated as a member of the Cuban junta with López and Quitman in their expeditions. Since Quitman's abandonment of his project, Goicouria had lived in New York, where he had grown a long, flowing beard, which he vowed to wear until the island won her independence. He had followed with interest Walker's exploits, and in December had sent an agent, Francisco Alejandro Lainé, to Granada with a proposition that the two work together. They signed a written contract on January 11, 1856, in which Goicouria promised to provide soldiers for Walker's service in return for which Walker would assist him in mounting an expedition to Cuba.

President Mora's declaration of war did not reach Granada until March 11, the day after Walker proclaimed the Serviles in all the states as his enemies. President Rivas issued a proclamation of war against Costa Rica, and Walker issued a general order for the army to hold itself in readiness to commence operations.[20]

Walker wrote that the American forces in Nicaragua before the arrival of Goicouria's recruits, about one-half of them German and French immigrants, consisted of about 600 men organized into two battalions, the rifles and the light infantry. In addition, there were more than 500 Americans capable of bearing arms engaged in business and labor either at Granada or along the transit route. Contemporary newspaper reports indicate that Walker understated, as he usually did, the forces at his command. The *New York Herald*'s correspondent wrote on March 9, 1856, that there were about 1,200 Americans in the army and about 500 others in the country "ready to shoulder muskets." The *New York Tribune*'s correspondent, reporting on the disposition of the troops on March 12, estimated that there were 1,975 men, including those brought in by Goicouria. A muster of the army for 1855–56 preserved by Callender I. Fayssoux, a hero in the López expedition to Cárdenas in 1850 who became Walker's aide de camp in April, lists more than 900 officers and men exclusive of the Goicouria contingent.

Walker himself confessed that his troops at the time lacked the spirit and discipline needed by an efficient army. Fever and other illnesses had carried off several of his most competent officers, and he regretted the need for maintaining the bulk of his men in Granada as protection against the Legitimists there instead of stationing strong garrisons in other places. "The quantity of liquor there," he wrote, "and the fondness of many officers for drink, not only injured the health of the troops, but tended materially to prevent growth in military virtue."[21]

Facing Costa Rican attacks from the south and fearing an invasion by Hondurans and Guatemalans from the north, Walker adopted as his chief strategy guarding the transit route "with more tenacity than any other part of the state." Garrisons already posted on the San Juan River at Castillo Viejo and Hipps' Point could give warning if the Costa Ricans attacked on the east, and he saw the need for an observation post on the west below the road between Virgin Bay and San Juan del Sur. He accordingly determined to send a force into Guanacaste with the aim of striking "the first blow of the war on territory held by the enemy" and of guarding "against any surprise on the line of American travel across the isthmus."

The force chosen for this mission was the latest addition to the army, the Goicouria battalion that had been organized into four companies, one of Germans and one of Frenchmen and two of Americans. Schlesinger had been appointed battalion commander because he spoke the three languages used by this polyglot group. Without any training and quickly supplied with muskets and ammunition, they were shipped from Granada to Virgin Bay on March 12. On the next day they marched along the transit route to San Juan del Sur and three days later set out for Guanacaste, a sparsely populated district of hilly country in which there were few farms and roads. The nearly 300 troops penetrated this wilderness along rough footpaths that kept them to single file.

Proceeding in the full heat of the day from ten to four o'clock, they were an exhausted band when they reached a hacienda, Santa Rosa, about 12 miles north of the town of Guanacaste on March 20, where a camp was set up for them to rest and recuperate. Next day the force was lounging about the camp when a picket rode up shouting, "The greasers are coming!" Schlesinger could not be located to give orders, and the men milled about in confusion. The captains of the two American companies, however, were able to position their men to meet the attack, the French company, too, was hastily assembled, but the German company did not form at all. Early in the attack Schlesinger, followed by the Germans, fled into the thickets behind the hacienda, and the American companies, receiving no support from the foreign companies, were forced to retreat. Walker reported the debacle: "In five minutes, the whole command, led by its colonel, was in full and most disorderly retreat."

All accounts of Santa Rosa blamed Schlesinger for the rout, and most of them accused him of cowardice. The *New Orleans Picayune*'s correspondent wrote: "His march was marked by a want of military knowledge at every step, and at the time he was surprised, although he knew that he was within a few miles of the town which it was publicly announced he intended to attack, yet he took no precautions. . . ." The history of the Walker expedition by William V. Wells, however, indicated that the battalion was not equipped to do battle. Many of the weapons, Wells said, were of "a very inferior character," and those of the Germans "hardly worth bringing along." "Many were without so much as a screw to draw the charge," he continued, "and some of the foreigners were so ignorant of the use of arms, that they did not know which end of the cartridge to bite off in order to load." It was a criticism that might have been better directed against Walker, because he was the person who issued the marching orders to this untrained and poorly armed force.

After the flight from Santa Rosa, Schlesinger made no effort to reassemble his troops, who found their way back to Virgin Bay as best they could singly or in small squads. The *New York Herald*'s correspondent wrote on March 26 of Schlesinger's return: "He presented a different figure to my view from that which came on board the *Virgin* about three weeks before, bombastically announcing that he had just declared war against Costa Rica." Schlesinger did not delay at Virgin Bay but continued on to Rivas to report to Walker, who had removed his headquarters there from Granada to be nearer the transit road. Reports of Schlesinger's incapacity and cowardice had preceded him, and Walker convened a court of inquiry which recommended that he be court-martialed.*

*The court martial on May 5, 1856, found Schlesinger guilty. He was sentenced to be shot, but before the execution could be carried out he escaped and joined the Legitimists.

The attacking force of Costa Ricans at Santa Rosa consisted of 500 men, the vanguard of 3,000 soldiers President Mora had led to Punta Arenas. It was commanded by the president's brother, José Joaquín Mora, who exuberantly reported on the night of the victory: "Our army fought with so much valor and determination that the attack did not last over fourteen minutes." A later communiqué said that ninety of the enemy were killed and that nineteen prisoners taken were tried immediately and executed. He set the Costa Rican casualties at about fifteen men killed. The number of Schlesinger's troops who lost their lives was not reported officially by Walker or *El Nicaragüense*. Captain D. W. Thorpe, a New Orleanian who commanded one of the companies, told reporters on his return to the United States that between fifty and sixty Americans fell in the defense of Santa Rosa, and other news reports said that about seventy men were killed or missing in action.[22]

While Schlesinger was leading his troops into Guanacaste, Walker was concentrating his other forces at Granada, ordering garrisons at various points to the capital, as he expected the three other Central American states to join Costa Rica in the war against him. He learned almost immediately that he would receive no reinforcements from the United States because of his coup in seizing the Accessory Transit Company property. Vanderbilt, on hearing of this, had published an announcement that his ships would lie at their wharves until the U.S. government had sufficient time "to examine and look into the outrage" committed by the Nicaraguan government. The new transit franchise had been assigned to Edmund Randolph and Alexander P. Crittenden, but they had reassigned it immediately to Morgan and Garrison, who had hastily arranged to put two ships into operation, the *Sierra Nevada* on the Pacific run and the *Orizaba* on the Atlantic run, too late, as it turned out, to help Walker in the crisis created by the war with Costa Rica.

During this period Walker was officially placed in supreme command of the Meridional and Oriental Departments when President Rivas removed the seat of government, for reasons that are not clear, from Granada to León. He may have done so because Walker's labeling of the Serviles as the enemy of the American contingent made it advisable to return the capital to the Democratic stronghold in the Occidental Department. The president also, perhaps with the aim of freeing himself from the chief office of a government supported by neither the Legitimists nor the Democrats, issued a proclamation calling for elections to be held in April of deputies and senators to the legislature to convene at Managua in May and of a permanent president as provided for in the constitution of 1838.

Walker in his history of the war described the rout at Santa Rosa as a "disaster." He believed it would shake the confidence of the people in the ability of his forces to protect the state from its enemies, neglecting to mention that the Costa Ricans had declared war not on the Nicaraguans but the American interlopers; but worse than this he noted that it had shaken the confidence of his army, mentioning that "a general depression seemed to pervade officers as well as men."

This lowered morale was noted by correspondents of the *New York Herald* and the *New York Tribune*. The *Herald*'s correspondent, friendly to Walker, wrote that the troops disliked the move to Rivas and "sighed for Granada," where there was more entertainment available. He reported that a group of officers, among them Walker's brother Norvell, a captain, engaged in a prolonged carouse and that Walker angrily reduced him to the ranks as an example to the others. The *Tribune*'s correspondent, who had only recently arrived in Nicaragua, wrote unflattering descriptions of Walker and Norvell. Walker was reputed to be a man of varied talent—a doctor, a lawyer, a journalist—but the correspondent doubted that he was very good in any of these professions. "He, however, possesses common sense enough to say very little, and that little with caution," his article said. "His brother Norvell is the very opposite in the latter respect. When he is not drinking he is talking, and when not talking he is drinking."

The Santa Rosa debacle was a blow to Walker's expectations, but a little more than a week after receiving the report of it he received additional disconcerting information—that a large force expected from San Francisco on the *Cortes* reaching San Juan del Sur on April 1 had not been permitted to land but had been carried on to Panama. Details were brought to him by W. R. Garrison, who had sailed as a passenger to complete arrangements for the new transit. Commodore Vanderbilt had sent out via the Panama route an agent to stop the sailing of his ships from San Francisco, as he had already done those at New York. The agent was aboard a Pacific Mail Steamship Company vessel that encountered the *Cortes* before she entered the port and conveyed the order that she was not to put in at San Juan del Sur. Garrison told Walker that the new transit company could not send a ship out from California in less than five or six weeks.

After only a week at Rivas, Walker ordered the entire army to march to Virgin Bay to embark on the lake steamer *San Carlos*. This movement and subsequent ones mystified his officers and the correspondents, and Walker's own explanation of them in his history is more confusing than enlightening. Domingo de Goicouria, who had been appointed quartermaster general with the rank of brigadier general, could not understand the reason for abandonment of the Meridional Department and asked that he be placed in command of a company of American troops supported by native troops to resist enemy attacks on the district. Goicouria was not well acquainted with Walker, and he received the same response as others who questioned his leadership—a sharp rebuke. Walker wrote in his history: "The conceit of Goicouria, excited by his new rank and title, had turned his head; and although he had scarcely been a month in the country, he foolishly presumed to thrust his opinion unasked on his general-in-chief."

The 800 troops fit for duty embarked on the lake steamer on the night of April 5 and arrived next morning at San Carlos, whose garrison was taken on board. She continued down the river to Castillo Viejo, where a fresh company was sent ashore to relieve the garrison there. Then, to the mystification of everybody, the ship returned up river to San Carlos and then sailed on to Granada, where, on April 8, the troops were landed. The *Herald*'s correspondent on board the steamer believed at the start of the movement that Walker's intention was to invade Costa Rica, writing that the general kept his plans secret, even his "most confidential officers" not being informed of them until the last minute, but the return to Granada was so unexpected that he could not even guess what Walker had in mind.

Walker's own explanation was that this apparently aimless

movement had been made to deceive the enemy. When he learned from Garrison there would be no more recruits from the United States for more than a month, he had decided there was no need to hold the transit route and he could take the army north to León, where President Rivas was fearful of an invasion from El Salvador and Guatemala. Walker was ignorant of the fact that President Mora was marching at the head of 3,000 troops through Guanacaste to attack his lifeline and thought that if word reached Costa Rica of his trip to the San Juan River the enemy would be misled into believing he intended to attack the capital, San José, or to leave Nicaragua.

Walker considered the ruse a success, writing: "Thus the movement northward was, for a time, concealed from the people of the Meridional Department, among whom the enemy had numerous spies, and the impression was temporarily created, that the Americans intended to move either out of the country or toward San José." The stratagem was too successful; Walker had outsmarted himself. Mora, who had reached the frontier, was informed of the departure from Rivas and the embarkation of the army on the steamer and had permitted it to leave without attacking. On the day after Walker sailed, Mora took possession of San Juan del Sur and Virgin Bay and shortly afterward occupied Rivas.[23]

At Virgin Bay the Costa Ricans vented their hatred of Americans in an attack on transit company employes in what newspapers in the United States called a "massacre." The American minister, John H. Wheeler, a week later obtained affidavits from survivors that indicated the epithet was not undeserved. "The conduct of the Costa Rican troops," one of them said, "was barbarous and savage, for after the unarmed persons were shot and lay gasping for life on the ground, they brutally stabbed the wounded—through and through—many times with bayonets and swords."[24]

Walker's realization that his stratagem to mislead his foes had served only to give them the opportunity to enter the Meridional Department unopposed came to him within an hour after the disembarkation at Granada. Walker, however, was at his best in an emergency. He could not endure inactivity for long—hence perhaps his decision to abandon Rivas a week after moving his headquarters there. In moments of crisis he could act promptly and decisively. He at once issued orders for his force to be ready to take the field next morning, April 9.

Walker set out from Granada at the head of about 550 troops, leaving two companies to garrison the city, on a march of 55 miles to Rivas with the hope that he could occupy the town before it could be taken over by the Costa Ricans. He received the bad news early in the afternoon that the Costa Ricans had preceded him from a band of native troops who had fled Rivas. That night refugees from the town brought the word that the enemy force was a large one—2,000 or 3,000 men, a number Walker could hardly believe was true. After another day of marching in the torrid heat, his troops camped for the night some miles from Rivas. They were roused at two o'clock on the morning of June 11 to complete their march to the town. They proceeded slowly because of the darkness and the roughness of the trail, reaching the outskirts shortly after eight o'clock. Market women returning to their farms brought the information that the Costa Ricans were not aware of the approach of the army. Attacking by surprise, the Americans quickly gained the plaza before the defenders were able to commence firing. Once over the first shock, the Costa Ricans, however, subjected the attackers to heavy fire from buildings around the square before retreating to houses in the northwest section in which they barricaded themselves.

Without any artillery, the only way of dislodging the enemy was by direct assault, but, as Walker related with the unusual objectivity with which he frequently was able to view events involving himself, it was impossible to rouse his troops to storm the houses. "Many of the men, exhausted by the first charge, actually set their muskets against the walls, and throwing themselves on the ground, could scarcely be driven to any active exertion," he wrote. Seeing the attackers thus halted, Costa Rican forces sought to get into houses on the plaza but were successfully driven off. They were, however, able to set fire to some of the buildings, and one company occupying a church tower harried the Americans with occasional potshots.

Walker's previous battle experience had been against unenthusiastic foes who fled after a vigorous first attack. He now faced a numerous one that seemed capable of holding their positions surrounding his own force that without food and water could not hold out very long. Seeing the inevitability of annihilation if he remained, he decided to withdraw from the town under cover of darkness. When night fell, he moved the most seriously wounded of his men into the church, placing them around the altar in the hope, apparently, that found in this holy area they would not be killed, and shortly after midnight slowly and silently left the town.

Seventy-two hours after leaving Rivas, Walker and his weary troops reached Granada. His assault on Rivas had not been a victory, but it had not been a defeat either although his losses, considering the small number of men under his command, were large: fifty-eight killed, sixty-two wounded, and thirteen missing. Walker estimated that the Costa Rican casualties numbered about 600, of whom 200 were killed. In a boastful report sent to San José, Mora minimized his casualties; including those killed, they would not exceed 110 men. But, as Walker wrote in his history, although he had not succeeded in driving the Costa Ricans from Rivas, he had struck a blow that paralyzed the enemy. More heroic in speech than in action, Mora did not send out troops to pursue the retreating foe but remained at Rivas, explaining in his bombastic report of victory that his men were exhausted and it was necessary to give his attention to his wounded, although if his report of casualties was anywhere near correct this could not have been much of a task.[25]

While the second battle of Rivas was indecisive in a military sense, it was the final hostile encounter between the invading Costa Ricans and the Americans. As Walker put it, "an enemy fiercer and more malignant" than soldiers entered the fray, attacking the camps. At Granada before the war began a tropical fever had carried off many of Walker's men; after his return from Rivas it struck in an aggravated form and more men died. The disease was more virulent in Rivas, where Mora, instead of burning or burying his dead, had thrown them into the wells or left them in the streets.

Receiving reports of a political movement against him at San José, Mora toward the end of the month departed for Costa Rica, leaving his brother-in-law, José María Cañas, in command with orders to abandon the stricken town and to get the men out of the country. It was a most horrifying retreat, the correspondent of the *New York Herald* wrote, in which dead and dying were left by the roadside from Rivas to Virgin Bay and from Virgin Bay to San Juan del Sur. After the departure of the remnant of the army by boats for Punta Arenas, dead bodies for days floated ashore at San Juan del Sur.

Walker, getting reports of the situation at Rivas, had made no move against the town, but when he heard that the Costa Ricans were departing he loaded rifle and light infantry battalions on the lake steamer and sailed to Virgin Bay. There was no occasion for further fighting. Shortly after he disembarked, a messenger arrived bearing a note from Cañas, dated April 26, saying that he had been forced to abandon Rivas because of the cholera and that he was leaving behind "a certain number of sick" who could not be carried away without danger to their lives. He invoked "the laws of humanity in favor of these unfortunate victims of an awful calamity." So ended the war of extermination that the Costa Ricans had begun against the Americans less than two months before with Walker still in control in Nicaragua.[26]

CHAPTER FIFTEEN

The Dictator of Nicaragua

On May 3, a few days after the departure of the Costa Ricans, the first anniversary of the sailing of the *Vesta* from San Francisco was observed at General Walker's headquarters by the Immortals still at Granada. Only seventeen were present to celebrate the beginning of their historic adventure. Among these comrades-at-arms the reserved and abstemious Walker, called "Uncle Billy" by the "*Vesta* boys," unbent and joined in the toasts, songs, and cheers that marked the occasion.[1]

But in the situation facing Walker there was little to celebrate. The cholera and fever that had killed the Costa Ricans by the hundreds also ravaged Granada. In addition to providing food and medicine for the army, Walker faced the problem of caring for 450 California passengers who had landed at San Juan del Norte on April 16 from the *Orizaba*, the first ship to be placed in operation by Garrison and Morgan under their new franchise. It had taken them two weeks to ascend the San Juan River, and they had been disembarked at Granada because of the occupation of the transit route to San Juan del Sur by the Costa Ricans.

To protect the health of the army, Walker moved the main body of his troops from the pestilential city to Virgin Bay and sent out detachments to various points with the view, he related, of restoring the confidence of the people in the strength of the Rivas administration. This involved putting down Legitimist guerrillas who had been emboldened to activity by the Costa Rican invasion. General Goicouria was sent to the Chontales district, where he ferreted out persons believed to be opposed to the provisional government, summarily executed some, and levied "contributions" upon the residents. In the Segovia region Walker's old Indian ally, General Valle, stamped out any opposition that existed there. The fate of "disloyal" Legitimists was dramatically impressed upon the populace by Walker in the execution by hanging of a wealthy Granadino, Francisco Ugarte, who had joined the Costa Ricans and been taken prisoner. "This mode of punishment for such offenders being unusual in the country—shooting being resorted to rather than hanging—the execution of Ugarte," Walker related, "made a strong impression on the people, and infused a salutary dread of American justice among the plotting Legitimists."[2]

Walker's prospects were improved early in May by the arrival of about 200 men brought from New Orleans by C. C. Hornsby, now a brigadier general, who had gone to the United States to enlist recruits. Among the newcomers was Walker's youngest brother, James, given the rank of captain in the second light infantry battalion. James's army career was a short one. Commanding a company sent to Masaya, he became ill with fever and died on May 14.[3]

The Legitimists thrown into disarray, Walker turned his attention to improving his relations with the United States, proposing to President Rivas that Father Vijil be appointed minister to Washington. It was an appointment that the *New York Herald* correspondent thought would benefit Nicaragua. "The worthy Padre," he wrote, "will lay before the people of the United States, on the authority of the church, of which he is the leader here, a statement of the affairs of Nicaragua, its past history and prospects, that will be of infinite advantage."[4] Walker in his history mentioned without explanation that Father Vijil was accompanied by an old acquaintance from Nashville days, John P. Heiss. It was a circumstance that boded well for the success of Vijil's mission, for Heiss had long been an influence in the Democratic party. As publisher of the *Nashville Banner*, Heiss had supported James K. Polk for the presidency and during his administration was business manager of his organ, the *Washington Union*. Since 1851 he had been one of the owners of the *New Orleans Delta*. Interested in mining possibilities in the Chontales region, he had gone to Nicaragua in February 1856, his trip being facilitated by Secretary of State Marcy, who had given him credentials as a messenger bearing dispatches to the legation at Granada. The *Herald*'s correspondent wrote that Heiss had "the most favorable reports" of the resources of the Chontales and that he completed at Granada arrangements for working the mines, arrangements embracing an immigration project to populate the district with settlers from the United States.[5]

When Father Vijil and Heiss reached Washington in mid-May, they found the administration leaning toward recognition of the Rivas government. An important reason for the change in attitude was British interference in Central American affairs. Relations between the two countries had so worsened over their contrary interpretations of the Clayton-Bulwer Treaty that there was now talk of war in both capitals. President Pierce had brought the dispute to the attention of Congress in his annual message of December 31, declaring that while the treaty "holds us to all our obligations, it in a great measure releases Great Britain from those which constituted the consideration of this government for entering into the convention."[6]

In Senate debate the president's stand was upheld, and there were no divisions, as in earlier discussions of the matter, according to party lines. Several senators set forth their belief that Walker's activities in Nicaragua stood in the way of reaching an amicable settlement of the dispute, including the treaty's negotiator, John M. Clayton. He commented March 17 on the unanimity in the debate but went on to attack Walker's "seizing the territories of Nicaragua with a band of adventurers." The debate ended on March 24 with the adoption of a resolution submitted by William Seward requesting the president to provide information on the seizure of the property of the Accessory Transit Company as well as other Nicaraguan matters.[7]

Newspaper reports of the denunciation of him in the Senate reached Walker at Granada after the battle of Rivas when his prospects for winning the war against the Costa Ricans were at their most discouraging. They prompted him to write his friend, Senator John B. Weller of California, complaining of the odds against him in his efforts to create a republican government in Nicaragua. He charged that the neighboring states were being stirred to opposition by Great Britain, citing the interception of letters of the Costa Rican consul general in London showing that the British government was willing to provide arms to his enemies.

This correspondence had been obtained shortly after the beginning of hostilities with Costa Rica when Walker seized the English mail for San José at Hipps' Point. One of the letters, dated February 4, 1856, was from Edward Wallerstein, the Costa Rican consul general, to the Earl of Clarendon, the British foreign minister, thanking him for promising to send a warship to Costa Rica "for the protection of British interests." Another letter, dated February 9, was from the British Foreign Office to Wallerstein promising to furnish 2,000 smooth-bore muskets for the Costa Rican army. Walker turned the correspondence over to John H. Wheeler, who sent it on to Marcy on March 31; and the *New York Herald*'s correspondent obtained copies of the letters, which were published in the newspaper on April 30.[8]

Describing his difficulties in the war with Costa Rica, Walker wrote Weller: "I may not live to see the end, but I feel that my countrymen will not permit the result to be doubtful. I know that the honor and the interests of the great country which, despite the foreign service I am engaged in, I still love to call my own, are involved in the present struggle."[9] Walker's letter furnished Weller with the occasion to defend his course in Nicaragua and to offer a resolution calling for the correspondence between the government and the American minister at Granada.

Mentioning the importance of the isthmus in communicating with California and the need for establishing a stable government in Nicaragua, Weller declared that the true policy of the administration should have been to encourage rather than discourage emigration. "You will have no stability in any of the Central American States," he said, "until you have infused a large amount of North American blood into their veins." In reply to this Seward expressed his fear that a government established in Central America by Americans, or under the influence of Americans, would lead immediately to a demand for annexation, a step "so momentous" he was not prepared to address himself to the subject now. Stephen A. Douglas, who heretofore had not taken part in the debate, now rose to express his view that the present government of Nicaragua should be recognized. "I hold that the government is as legitimate as any which ever existed in Central America," Douglas declared. He saw no objection to recognition because an American was in command of the Nicaraguan army or indeed if all the offices of the country were filled by Americans.[10]

Public anger was stirred against Great Britain by the Senate debate, an anger that was heightened by the action of a British naval commander in interfering with the landing of 480 passengers, all but about sixty bound for California, from the steamer *Orizaba* on its arrival at San Juan del Norte on April 16. Cornelius Vanderbilt, attempting to prevent his business enemies from profiting from the cancellation of his charter and seeking to punish Walker, was the evil genius behind the troubles that the *Orizaba* encountered, both at her departure from New York and her arrival in Nicaragua.

When the steamer was casting off from the wharf at the foot of Beach Street on April 8, she was boarded by U.S. marshals with orders to arrest members of a military expedition to join Walker believed to be aboard. The *Herald* reported that the information about the expeditionists was supplied by Vanderbilt agents to the district attorney's office. Only three men who could be identified as filibusters were found.

At the end of the voyage while passengers were disembarking, the *Oriziba's* captain, E. L. Tinkelpaugh, a veteran on the Nicaraguan run as commander of Vanderbilt's *Northern Light*, was notified by Captain I. W. Tarleton of the British sloop-of-war *Eurydice* that they would not be permitted to land. Tinkelpaugh called on Tarleton to protest and was told that the reason for the stoppage was that he had been informed the *Orizaba* had 500 men aboard intending to join Walker. Tinkelpaugh replied that this information was incorrect—he had more than 400 passengers bound for California and the others had tickets only to San Juan del Norte. The passengers were permitted to land after Tarleton boarded the *Orizaba*, looked over her waybill, questioned a number of the travelers, and found no evidence that any of them were filibusters. When Tinkelpaugh returned to New York, he signed an affidavit before a U.S. commissioner protesting the "assumption of the right of search" by the British naval officers.

Hearing at Granada of the affront to the American flag, John H. Wheeler went to San Juan del Norte to investigate. He received the bland explanation from Tarleton that the objection to letting the passengers land was that provisions were scarce in the town and no accommodations for so large a number of persons were available. Reporting to Marcy, Wheeler hinted darkly that Tarleton doubtlessly had acted under orders of his government, "whose reasons lie deeper than those expressed by him to me."

Vanderbilt's role in the incident was revealed in the publication of a letter to one Hosea Birdsall, who had been dispatched on a mission to regain possession of the transit company's river boats. In case filibusters on the *Orizaba* attempted to seize the boats to ascend the San Juan River, Birdsall was to ask the assistance of the commander of the British sloop-of-war to prevent their doing so. Vanderbilt's letters to Marcy asking for intervention by the government to recover his property had been unavailing; by his latest plot he demonstrated his willingness to create an international incident that could lead to war in attempting to rouse feeling against Great Britain for interfering with a ship flying the American flag.[11]

That the time for recognition of Nicaragua had come was also indicated by the popular support for filibusters not only in the South but the North as well. An impressive rally for Walker was held at National Hall on Canal Street in New York on April 8. Organized by men who for years had taken part in filibuster movements, it billed as speakers such figures as Lewis Cass, John A. Quitman, Robert Toombs, John B. Weller, Stephen A. Douglas, George N. Sanders, and Daniel F. Sickles. Not all of them appeared, but telegrams declaring their support were read to the cheering crowd. The meeting was strongly anti-British. A huge transparency hung outside the hall proclaimed: "No British Interference on the Continent of America," and a resolution adopted declared: "That it is time the aggressive and interfering spirit of the British government in the affairs of the southern portion of this continent should receive a check; and that the savage warfare waged by Costa Rica against the republic of Nicaragua, aided and encouraged by that government, demands the rebuke of this nation and calls loudly for the practical enforcement of the Monroe doctrine."[12] In New Orleans, Pierre Soulé opened a drive to collect money to send to Walker at a rally held on April 28, setting a goal of $200,000 to be sent him as a loan. Soulé predicted that, as soon as Walker's present difficulties were surmounted, the five states of

Central America would form a confederation that would in time through American energy and industry become "the seat of empire of the commerce of the world."[13]

For various reasons, then, Father Vijil received a favorable welcome when he presented his credentials to the secretary of state on May 14. His appointment had been an exemplary one, for there could be no objection to him as a person, as had been the case with Parker H. French. He was a native Nicaraguan, well respected in his own country, and his assurances of the stability of the Rivas government and its adherence to democratic principles, though not unchallengeable, could be accepted. The president's decision to receive Father Vijil, however, had been opposed by Marcy, who regarded Walker as "a pirate and an assassin." Pierce used as the occasion for the announcement of the acceptance of Vijil a message to Congress in response to the March 24 request for information on Central American affairs.[14]

Since the invasion by the Costa Ricans and the removal of the seat of government to León, Walker had not been able to keep in close touch with President Rivas. A suspicion that Rivas was plotting against him was aroused when Edmund Randolph, who had been at the new capital since April, returned to Virgin Bay about May 20 and communicated his fears that "there was something wrong at León." Accordingly, Walker decided to go to León to find out what was going on, leaving on May 31 with a command of 200 men.[15] This visit led to developments of such a nature that when John H. Wheeler received instructions from Marcy to resume diplomatic relations with Nicaragua—Marcy had delayed until June 3 in sending them—the U.S. minister had a new president to deal with: Walker, who had rid himself of his native opponents and had set himself up as the head of the state.

There were two main matters for discussion at León between the general in chief and the civil government represented by Rivas as provisional president and Máximó Jérez, who had rejoined the government as minister of war. These were protecting the northern border against attack from El Salvador and Guatemala and replacement of the provisional government established by the pact of October 25. Rivas told Walker of an offer from El Salvador to recognize his government if the American forces were reduced to

200 men. Rivas wished to accept the offer, because it would ensure the friendship of El Salvador, but Walker angrily rejected it, interpreting it as a move to get the Americans out of the country. Until the state was ready to pay his men for their services, he declared, Rivas need not expect his cooperation in such a scheme. The question involving the establishment of a permanent government following the election held in April was whether officials chosen at this time represented the will of the people. Voting had been conducted during the Costa Rican invasion in districts not disturbed by the fighting, that is, chiefly in the Occidental Department, and the votes for president had been distributed among Rivas, Jérez, and General Mariano Salazar, commander of native troops in the area. So irregular and incomplete had been the balloting that Walker insisted upon calling a new election.

Thus far Walker had been content to rule through Rivas as his puppet, but he now realized that the provisional president wanted to get the Americans who had put him in power out of the country. If a new election was held, Walker believed he would receive the popular vote for president, especially in the Meridional Department where the Granadinos feared that if the April votes were allowed to stand the capital might be permanently fixed at León. His belief that this was the time to strike for the presidency was reinforced when General Goicouria reached León with the news of Father Vijil's recognition in Washington and the arrival of nearly 200 recruits from New Orleans under the command of John A. Jacquess. The reception of Vijil, Walker wrote, "strengthened the American influence in Nicaragua, and while it tended to make the prospect of hostilities from San Salvador more remote, it gave an additional reason for fixing the government on a firm basis by an appeal to the popular will."

What was needed to persuade Rivas was a show of force, and Walker hit upon a pretext for this by arresting General Salazar, who had sold some brazilwood to the government, a deal that violated army regulations. The arrest so frightened Rivas that on June 10 he issued a decree calling for an election, and next day when Walker departed for Granada with two of the companies he had brought to León, leaving one behind under command of Colonel Bruno von Natzmer, the provisional president accompanied him for several miles, assuring him of his support and goodwill.[16]

Walker's visit to León made it clear to Rivas that the filibuster intended to dominate the government, that Nicaraguans would have no vote in the affairs of their own country, and the troops left behind under the command of Natzmer added to his fears. Trouble broke out the day following Walker's departure when Natzmer replaced the native troops serving as guards around a building housing the military stores with Americans. Rumors spread that he intended to kill Rivas and his ministers, and hundreds of people ran into the streets, crying "Death to the Americans!" Natzmer, fearing an attack, assembled his troops in the plaza and occupied the cathedral. General Jérez sent orders for Natzmer to evacuate his troops, to be replaced by natives who would maintain order in the city, but he refused, dispatching a courier to Walker to receive instructions. Before a reply could come, both Rivas and Jérez as well as Salazar departed for Chinandega.

Walker was at Masaya, where the troops under the command of Colonel Jacquess had just arrived, when he received Natzmer's message. He sent orders for him to obey the command of the minister of war to withdraw his troops from León. He himself began a countermarch to León and had reached Nagarote, a village a few miles to the south, when information came that Rivas and Jérez were at Chinandega, erecting barricades and pressing natives into military service. Walker's explanation of his evacuation order was that Jérez had wanted Natzmer to refuse to recognize his authority to create an excuse for retaliation against the Americans and he himself was not disposed to have the coming struggle for power based on such an issue. When Natzmer joined him at Nagarote, Walker set out again for Granada with the entire command, seeing the need to concentrate his forces in one place because he did not know to what extent the defection of Rivas and Jérez would spread and because Guatemalan troops were reported at the northern border ready to invade the country.[17]

As almost always in moments of crisis, Walker now acted with boldness and decision. As soon as he reached Granada on June 20 he issued a decree declaring Rivas and Jérez traitors and appointing Fermin Ferrer provisional president until an election could be held according to the proclamation issued June 10. In an address to the people, Walker gave an emotional explanation for his edicts. He and his soldiers had come to the country to secure peace and prosperity; they had endured the pestilence at Granada and had shed their blood at Rivas; and yet the government had refused to provide them with the bare necessaries of life. "It is thus manifest that the late Provisional Government has not only failed to fulfill its promises to the Americans and its duties to the people," Walker declared, "but is guilty of the enormous crime of instigating its citizens to civil war. And to aid in these objects it has coalesced with the armed and declared enemies of the Republic . . . to pour over the plains of Nicaragua."[18]

In the meantime, Rivas had negotiated a treaty of amity and alliance with El Salvador in which Nicaragua was pledged to reduce the foreign forces to 200 men and El Salvador to interpose her friendship and good offices with the other Central American states. With the assurance of outside support, Rivas returned to León and on June 26 issued a proclamation declaring Walker "an enemy of Nicaragua" and divesting him "of the authority with which he had been honored by the Republic." The American soldiers were ordered to forsake their commander, but those who chose could become Nicaraguan citizens and be accepted into the military forces of the republic. Those who remained with Walker, whether foreign or native, were to be dealt with as traitors.[19]

In accordance with the election proclamation of June 10, Walker had tables set up in the towns of the Meridional and Oriental Departments where the people could have their choices for president tallied by recorders; there was no voting in the Occidental Department as the country around León was in the hands of men he considered traitors. The results announced by town criers at Granada on July 10 and subsequently published in *El Nicaragüense* were predictable: Walker was the overwhelming choice, receiving 15,935 votes to the 4,447 cast for Ferrer, 2,087 for Salazar, and 867 for Rivas.

The inauguration took place at noon on July 12 in the plaza at Granada. Walker, dressed in his military uniform and escorted by Ferrer and the bishop of Granada, ascended a platform and, kneeling on a cushion before the Bible and crucifix, took the oath of office. He then delivered his address in English, after which it was read in Spanish by Lieutenant Colonel Francisco A. Lainé, the Cuban associate of Goicouria whom Walker had appointed his aide-de-camp. It was an address in which Walker expressed his supreme confidence that he was destined to bring peace and prosperity to Nicaragua. "The Republic has reached an era in its history not second in importance to the day of her independence from the Spanish monarchy," he declared. He asked the people for their support in ending the internal disputes that had involved the country for so many years in civil strife. Then he assailed other Central American governments massing troops at the borders to attack. "Conscious of their own weakness, and fearful lest the prosperity of Nicaragua should detract from their wealth, these neighboring states are enviously endeavoring to interrupt our progress by force of arms," he fulminated.[20]

Although Walker realized that his enemies in the neighboring states were organizing against him and indeed that a contingent of Guatemalans had reached León under the command of General Mariano Paredes, he gave his first attention as president to civil rather than military matters. He felt secure from immediate attack because a company of about 100 Rangers had just returned from a reconnoitering trip in which they had ventured into the suburbs of León without opposition. The allied forces behind their barricades in the plaza were intent on defense rather than offense, he decided, and would not move against him until they had increased their numbers. In any case, his own army had been substantially strengthened since the exodus of the Costa Ricans by about 400 fresh troops. The 200 brought by Colonel Jacquess early in June were followed by about 100 on June 29 brought by Colonel John Allen of Kentucky and by about 100 others who had come in small groups early in July from New York, New Orleans, and San Francisco.

Late in June he was able to add a "navy" to his military might with the seizure at San Juan del Sur of the schooner *San José*, owned by Mariano Salazar. Salazar had made over half-ownership to Gilbert Morton, the skipper who had met Walker and conducted him to Realejo after the *Vesta* reached Tigre Island, and the vessel flew the American flag, a circumstance that did not deter Walker, who considered the transfer a ruse by which Salazar could profit from the war. The *San José*, converted into a war vessel by the installation of two 6-pound guns, was rechristened the *Granada*. Julius de Brissot was given the highest rank in the new navy, that of commodore, and Callender Irvine Fayssoux, hero of the López Cuban expeditions, was placed in command of the ship with the rank of lieutenant. Fayssoux had arrived in Nicaragua early in April and had served in the army first as an aide to Walker and then as a paymaster. As an officer in the navy of the Republic of Texas and on the López filibuster ships, he possessed the seamanship to command a ship, and his exploit in swimming ashore with a rope between his teeth to tie up the *Creole* at the wharf at Cárdenas marked him as a bold and enterprising sailor.[21]

John H. Wheeler had been notified by Secretary of State Marcy on June 3 that President Pierce had received Father Vijil as minister from Nicaragua and instructed to establish diplomatic relations with "the existing government of the State of Nicaragua." But the government that Pierce had decided to recognize in May no longer existed. In view of the changed circumstances, it might have been expected that Wheeler would delay recognizing the new government until he heard from Washington. Instead, on July 17 he called on Walker and informed him of his instructions to establish diplomatic relations. Walker, though realizing that it was impolitic for Wheeler to present himself at this time, was happy to receive him. It would vex Pierce, whose message to Congress on the reception of Father Vijil he considered "marked with the weakness and hesitation of American diplomacy," and Marcy, who had been "always averse to any action which might favor the Americans in Nicaragua." The formal reception two days later was a ceremonial affair. Wheeler, in an oration which appalled Marcy when he heard of it, declared that "the government of the United States hopes to unite cordially with you in the fixed purpose of preventing any foreign power that may attempt to impede Nicaragua's progress."[22]

President Rivas had welcomed the immigration of North Americans because they supplied the soldiers that maintained him in office, but he had not comprehended Walker's purpose, which was to make the Americans dominant in the country. According to estimates of Ephraim George Squier, there were only 30,000 whites in a population that included 18,000 Negroes, 96,000 Indians, and 156,000 persons of mixed blood. The language of the country was Spanish, but, to facilitate the takeover by the northern whites, Walker decreed on July 14 that all laws should be published in English as well as in Spanish and that all documents, whether worded in English or Spanish, should be of equal value. In legal matters, therefore, those who spoke both Spanish and English were given the advantage over those who knew only Spanish, and the tendency, Walker explained in his history, would be "to make the ownership of the lands of the State fall into the hands of those speaking English."

The language device to give the edge to North Americans in taking title to land was followed on July 16 by two more decrees that served this end more directly. One declared the property of all enemies of the state forfeited and named a board of commissioners to take possession, publish the lists of seized property, and sell it to the highest bidder. The confiscation decree—property listed to be sold was valued at $753,000—was designed to attract speculators from the United States. The other decree required all titles to property to be recorded within six months. As there had been no state registry law heretofore, the decree would benefit settlers from the United States familiar with the system of their own country and injure Nicaraguans to whom the practice was a mystery.[23]

Walker's assumption of the presidency of Nicaragua and Pierce's message in May recognizing Father Vijil as the minister in Washington had given a new direction to the thinking of expansionists in the United States. Where Cuba once was their chief interest, they now thought of Nicaragua; and, a contributor to *Putnam's Monthly* wrote, "theories of the indomitable Saxon race, the march of empire, the republicanization of the continent, superior and inferior people, all the sentimental variations of manifest destiny. . . become very conspicuous in newspapers and conversation."[24] Adventurers in a number of earlier expansionist schemes now sponsored rallies to go to the aid of Walker, and a number soon turned up in Granada to offer their help in person.

One of these was Appleton Oaksmith, who had been a leader in organizing the rallies for Walker in New York. A native of Portland, Maine, he had traveled in Africa and the Orient as well as in Central and South America and had recently been associated with Domingo de Goicouria in fund-raising activities for the liberation of Cuba. Reputed to be wealthy as a shipowner and promoter, he was welcomed by Walker. The subject of a toast by John Tabor, editor of *El Nicaragüense*, at the inaugural banquet, Oaksmith responded with a long speech in which, among dozens of flowery tributes, he predicted that the Twelfth of July, the date of Walker's inauguration, would be celebrated as the day of independence for Nicaragua as the Fourth of July was in the United States.

Although Oaksmith had only just arrived in Nicaragua, Walker appointed him the new minister to the United States to succeed Father Vijil. The priest's venture in diplomacy had been disillusioning, and he had been unhappy in Washington. Representatives of other Central American states wrote Marcy protesting his reception and were cool to him, and Catholic priests convinced of Walker's anticatholicism wondered how he, in the words of the archbishop of Baltimore, could come to the United States "to labour against his church and his native land." On June 23, less than six weeks after his arrival in Washington, he designated John P. Heiss chargé d'affaires and sailed for Nicaragua.

In submitting Oaksmith's name to Pierce in a letter of July 16, Walker wrote that he was "a Nicaraguan citizen of acknowledged integrity." A citizen of the country less than two weeks, the new minister plenipotentiary wrote Marcy on August 15, immediately on reaching Washington, asking to be received, and met with the secretary of state on the nineteenth. Almost a month passed during which Oaksmith wrote Marcy a half-dozen letters urging a quick decision on his acceptance before Marcy finally informed him, on September 13, in a curt letter that because of the present condition of political affairs in Nicaragua President Pierce had come to the conclusion not to receive him as minister. Oaksmith's letters had mentioned that John H. Wheeler had resumed diplomatic relations upon instructions from Pierce and complained that he could not understand the delay in accepting him as minister. The reason was that both the President and Marcy were furious that Wheeler had presumptuously recognized the Walker government without consultation with them. To prevent further embarrassment from Wheeler, Marcy on September 18 directed him to leave Granada and go to San Juan del Norte to await additional instructions, which came in a letter of September 27 recalling him to the United States.[25]

Two other adventurers attracted by the prospects in Nicaragua were Cora Montgomery and her husband, General William

L. Cazneau. Cora Montgomery, after her efforts to annex Cuba through her association with Moses Y. Beach of the *New York Sun* and her editorship of the junta paper, *La Verdad*, had married Cazneau, a soldier in the Texas war for independence. They had located in Eagle Pass, Texas, where they had supported Mexican revolutionary movements and urged the annexation of the northern states to the United States. Marcy had appointed Cazneau in 1853 a special commissioner to Santo Domingo to negotiate a commercial treaty and to obtain Samaná Bay as a coaling station for U.S. ships. Neither Cazneau nor his wife had been very discreet, the *New York Evening Post* reporting that shortly after their arrival on the island she had "not hesitated to assure the people of St. Domingo, that the country would belong to the United States in six months." Cazneau's mission had come to nothing, and the couple had returned to the United States in 1855. During their stay in Granada, celebrated by a laudatory article in *El Nicaragüense*, they arranged a contract to bring in 1,000 colonists within a year to be established in settlements of not fewer than fifty families, each settler to be given title to 80 acres of land.[26]

The most prominent of the visitors was Pierre Soulé, who arrived on August 20 to complete arrangements for Nicaraguan bonds to be offered for sale in the United States secured by 1 million acres of public lands. They were to be sold for $500,000 through the firm of S. F. Slatter and Mason Pilcher of New Orleans. Walker had reason to welcome Soulé other than as a financial agent. In April Soulé had addressed a New Orleans rally to raise funds for his support and at the national Democratic convention in June at Cincinnati, when James Buchanan was nominated for the presidency, had secured passage of a platform plank expressing the deep sympathy of the American people "with the efforts which are being made by the people of Central America to regenerate that portion of the continent which covers the passage across the interoceanic Isthmus." *El Nicaragüense* extolled Soulé's visit in an editorial, declaring it was a sign that "before long rich capitalists will come with wealthy merchants and energetic entrepreneurs who with their knowledge, capital, industry, and art will bring to the country a true element of public wealth"; John H. Wheeler held a reception for him at the American legation; and Walker noted that he "made a deep impression on the people of the country, peculiarly sensitive as they are to the charms of feature and manner."[27]

Walker's proclamation decreeing use of both the Spanish and English languages in all legal matters, confiscating the property of opponents of his regime, and ordering registration of land titles had been designed to facilitate the domination of the country by the Anglo-Saxon race. To make immigration more attractive, especially to Americans with capital, he saw the need, as he put it, for "the reorganization of labor" for development of the country's resources. The evidence was before him that the Nicraguans themselves would not do this. The acreage under cultivation had declined during the civil wars and the towns, Granada, for example, were crowded with vagrants once employed on the land. Walker's plan in part was to establish a system of peonage. On September 25 he decreed that persons without visible means of support would be adjudged guilty of vagrancy and sentenced to forced labor on public works. He followed this next day by a decree declaring that a person who contracted to work for another and failed to fulfill the contract would similarly be condemned to forced labor.

His most important labor reorganization decree, however, was one issued on September 22, "the act," as he described it, "around which the whole policy of the administration revolved." It was a decree restoring African slavery in Nicaragua. Walker went about this in a curiously circuitous way. The constitution of the Central American Federation adopted in 1824 had abolished slavery. When the union was dissolved in 1838, Nicaragua had continued in force all the acts and decrees of the federation that were not contrary to her own constitution. Walker's proclamation merely declared null and void these acts and decrees of the federation without mentioning the provision forbidding slavery.

That the decree restored slavery was the immediate interpretation, however, by newspaper correspondents in Granada and by his closest supporters. The *New York Herald* correspondent wrote: "The institution of slavery is, therefore, in effect, now recognized and authorized in Nicaragua. . . . Thus it will be perceived that the late decree of President Walker is highly important to planters and others in the southern portion of the United States, who desire to emigrate with their property to this 'garden of the world.' And it is presumed, that in the recent purchase of Mr. Soulé, for $40,000, of one of the most valuable cacao ranches in Nicaragua, that distinguished American statesman anticipated the issuance of this important decree."

Soulé seems to have carried the word to New Orleans in advance of the decree. The *Delta*, in an editorial reminding readers that it had always insisted Walker must introduce slavery into Nicaragua if he wished to maintain his government, declared: "We also alluded to significant assurances we had received from authorized sources that Walker designed, as soon as he could prudently do so, to publicly legalize slavery within his dominions, and invite slave-holders to immigrate thither with their slaves. We knew, some weeks since, that a decree to this effect had been drawn up, and we now learn that it has been promulgated. . . . Numbers of slave-holders have already written to us to know if they could safely take their slaves into Nicaragua. . . . We have always assured our correspondents that, though slaves were not recognized by law in Nicaragua, we had no doubt they would be secured to their owners during Walker's administration, and that, ultimately slavery would have an existence there of law as well as fact."

Walker's subsecretary of state, John L. Richmond, cited the decree in a letter of October 30 to Charles S. Morehead, of Kentucky, extolling the opportunities to be found in Nicaragua and sending a list of confiscated property to be sold that would enable Americans who wished to do so to "procure estates intrinsically more valuable than the best of the southern portion of the United States." He added: "I must also mention, that gentlemen from southern states, wishing to emigrate to this country with their slaves, are invited to come; and a decree has been issued by this government giving to all persons the privilege to do so, the object being to invite slave labor, without which the resources of the country can never be fully and profitably developed; upon this subject you need not entertain a doubt."[28]

Walker's decree, he explained later, was based on the belief, apparently arrived at in the year he had been in Nicaragua, that on the restoration of slavery "depended the permanent presence of the white race in that region." "The introduction of negro-slavery into Nicaragua," he wrote, "would furnish a supply of constant and reliable labor requisite for the cultivation of tropical products. With the negro-slave as his companion, the white man would become fixed to the soil; and they together would destroy the power of the mixed race which is the bane of the country. The pure Indian would readily fall into the new social organization; for he does not aim at political power, and asks only to be protected in the fruits of his industry."

It was also, he said, a "positive act" designed "to bind to the cause for which the naturalized Nicaraguans [i.e., Americans] were contending some strong and powerful interest in the United States" at a time when his forces were threatened by those of the four allied Central American states. "The policy of the act," he continued, "consisted in pointing out to the Southern States the only means, short of revolution, whereby they can preserve their present social organization."

Heretofore, Walker's actions and writings had not indicated that he held strong views in favor of slavery. He did not come of a slave-holding family; the newspaper for which he wrote in New Orleans, the *Crescent*, was conservative on the question; in California he had supported the antislavery candidate for the U.S. Senate, David C. Broderick, rather than the proslavery William M. Gwin; and some of his closest associates and trusted officers were northeasterners unsympathetic to slavery.

But his defense of his decree revealed that he had arrived at extreme views as to the inferiority of Africans and other colored people. "If we look at Africa in the light of universal history," he wrote, "we see her for more than five thousand years a mere waif on the waters of the world, fulfilling no part in its destinies, and aiding in no manner the progress of general civilization. . . . But America was discovered, and the European found the African a useful auxiliary in subduing the new continent to the uses and purposes of civilization. . . . Then only do the wisdom and excellence of the divine economy in the creation of the black race begin to appear with their full lustre. Africa is permitted to lie idle until America is discovered, in order that she may conduce to the formation of a new society in the New World. . . . Is it not for this that the African was reserved? And is it not this that one race secures for itself liberty with order, while it bestows on the other comfort and Christianity?"[29]

Much of the enthusiasm in the South for filibusterism in Cuba and Nicaragua had its basis in the hope of annexation—the bringing of new slave states into the Union to maintain control of Congress. The strength of the free-soil movement made it clear that extension of slavery into the new states to be formed of the territories, dramatized in the war going on in Kansas, was a losing proposition. Yet Walker, though in issuing his decree with the aim of binding "the Southern States to Nicaragua as if she were one of themselves," considered it at the same time a disavowal of the desire for annexation. Southerners should support him not to bring new states into the Union but to establish a strong Latin-American nation as an ally in the irrepressible conflict to come. It was becoming apparent in 1856, he argued, that all territory acquired by the federal government would "enure to the use and benefit of free labor." The people of the free states moved easily and readily into new territories, and the surplus of population was greater in the North than in the South so that the majority in any new territory would be from the antislavery regions. The South, moreover, had no surplus of labor to send either westward or southward, and indeed the Gulf states were "crying out" for more Negroes.

Holding these views, Walker was not alarmed when Domingo de Goicouria in November released to the New York press correspondence revealing that the plans for reconstruction of Nicaraguan society did not include annexation. The publication was the result of a final and irreparable rupture between the two filibuster leaders. Both egotists, they had clashed several times before, and this may have been the reason Walker had urged President Rivas to appoint Goicouria minister to England. It would get a troublemaker out of the country.

Goicouria left Granada on June 21 with instructions while in the United States to do what he could to obtain loans for Nicaragua. He stopped first in New Orleans, where he found the prospect dim for investments in Nicaraguan securities, and proceeded to New York, where capitalists advised him that loans could not be negotiated so long as Walker had to reckon with Vanderbilt as an enemy. In the meantime, Walker had succeeded in driving Rivas from the presidency and usurping the office himself. He wrote Goicouria on July 25 to delay his departure for London until he received a letter of instructions.

Goicouria's canvassing of the possibilities for financial aid revealed that American capital was interested only in the transit right, and he soon decided it had been a mistake for Walker to turn the charter over to Edmund Randolph, who had gone to New York in July, apparently to sell it to the highest bidder. Goicouria wrote protesting the grant on August 1, telling Walker he had not thought "such a vital and most important business would be made a subject of individual gain." Randolph, he said, had gone to Vanderbilt with an offer to sell the transit privileges for $300,000. "This large demand of compensation," Goicouria said, "caused that no arrangement could be made in the undertaking in question with the only party who could, at the moment, give you transportation and supplies immediately to carry out your plan of regeneration." Going to Randolph, he related, he discovered that the charter had been sold to Garrison and Morgan. Goicouria did not think they would provide adequate services because, though wealthy, they would not be able to raise the capital they needed in the face of Vanderbilt's enmity.

Believing that Randolph had ruined Nicaragua's chances to raise money, Goicouria himself approached Vanderbilt and obtained an offer that he reported to Walker on August 21. Vanderbilt would pay $100,000 in cash on the day his first steamer sailed to the isthmus on the basis of the new contract and $160,000 more during the next year, payable every four months, on the condition that all the confiscated transit company property was returned to him. Goicouria's August 1 letter complaining of Randolph had in the meantime reached Walker, who on August 20 wrote him a curt letter declaring: "You will please not trouble yourself further about the Transit Company. The matter is definitely settled. As to anything about Mr. Randolph, it is entirely thrown away on me. . . . As the government has given you no power, you cannot, of course, promise anything in its behalf."

Other recriminatory letters followed. When Appleton Oaksmith was refused recognition as the minister from Nicaragua, Goicouria wrote Walker that he thought it useless to expect himself to be received in London and that he was delaying his departure. Walker replied on September 27 that this decision disposed him to place more confidence than he had had before in reports "concerning your conduct in the United States" and that if he would not go on the mission someone else would be sent in his place. This provoked an angry reply from Goicouria in which he announced to Walker the severance of their relations.

Angry that Walker had rejected his efforts in behalf of Nicaragua, since his aim had been to raise "abundant pecuniary supplies, so as to enable you to meet your immediate necessities and sustain an American immigration" and also "to put a stop to a powerful opposition" in the person of Vanderbilt, Goicouria released their correspondence to the *New York Herald* on November 21. The publication provoked replies from John P. Heiss, chargé d'affaires for Nicaragua since the departure of Vijil, and Edmund Randolph. Heiss in a long letter defended Walker's conduct of affairs and berated Goicouria as a traitor. Randolph did not bother to answer at length. He wrote a note to correct a statement in a *Herald* editorial that Walker's decree confiscating the transit company's property assigned the charter to Morgan in February 1856, whereas Morgan had not become a party to it until July. As to Goicouria, he said: "I have only to remark further, that in this Transit business Don Domingo Goicouria is an intruder, with a dishonest and treacherous intent, and that knowing the import of the language I use, I shall remain at the Washington Hotel, No. 1 Broadway, until one o'clock to-morrow, and longer if it is the pleasure of Don Domingo Goicouria."

Goicouria did not take up this challenge to a duel but instead wrote the *Herald* a long communication accompanied by additional correspondence with Walker containing even more sensational revelations than any brought out in the publication three days before. Saying that his own aim first and last was to obtain the independence of Cuba, Goicouria related that he had joined Walker only because he thought Nicaragua was "a mere stepping stone to Cuba." He had not realized, he said, what sort of man Walker was until he received his instructions as minister to London in a letter dated August 12. In this Walker had told him his main objective was to get Great Britain to agree to the transfer of the sovereignty of the port of San Juan del Norte to Nicaragua.

"With your versatility, and if I may use the term, adaptability,

I expect much to be done in England," Walker had written. "You can do more than any American could possibly accomplish because you can make the British cabinet see that we are not engaged in any scheme for annexation. You can make them see that the only way to cut the expanding and expansive democracy of the North, is by a powerful and compact Southern federation, based on military principles." Walker's letter ended with a slap at annexationists in the United States in the statement that "Cuba must and shall be free, but not for the Yankees." "Oh, no! that fine country," he added, "is not fit for those barbarous Yankees. What would such a psalm-singing set do in the island?"

This letter, Goicouria said, determined him to delay his trip to England. "It revealed to me for the first time Walker's hostility to the Democratic principles of America," Goicouria continued, "and his design to establish a southern despotism as a counterbalance to the United States." He was further dismayed when he heard that Walker intended to restore slavery in Nicaragua, an act that coming at this time he held to be "preposterously stupid." Feeling completely betrayed by Walker, Goicouria declared: "I therefore denounce Mr. Walker as a man wanting in the first element of every kind of ability, viz., good faith; I denounce him as wanting in ordinary sagacity and discretion; I denounce him as false to the interests as well of Cuba as of the United States."[30]

While Walker was busy putting his administration in order, Nicaragua's neighbors to the north—El Salvador, Honduras, and Guatemala—were in spite of mutual jealousies slowly combining in an alliance against him. On July 18 they completed a treaty engaging to unite their naval and military forces to overthrow "the adventurers who have presumed to usurp public power in Nicaragua, and who, while they oppress the republic, threaten to destroy the independence of the other states of Central America." Costa Rica, unable to send a delegate to the conference, was invited to join the alliance. On September 18, under the overall command of General Ramón Belloso, a Salvadorian, about 1,800 troops moved out of León toward Managua to begin the war against the North American claimants to the control of Nicaragua.

CHAPTER SIXTEEN

The Allied War against the Filibusters

When the allied forces of the Central American states began their invasion, neither side was in a strong position to wage war. But two victories by Legitimist guerrillas over American forces in skirmishes in the Chontales region emboldened General Belloso to open hostilities. Walker now had little native support anywhere in the country, but the Chontales was, in the words of one newspaper correspondent, the "most disaffected" region. It was, however, of great value to Walker as the chief source of food. Unscathed by the civil war and by the invasion of the Costa Ricans, the Chontales was the only area where cattle and grain could be commandeered in large quantities to provision the army at Granada.

The skirmishes took place at a cattle ranch, San Jacinto, a few miles northeast of the town of Tipitapa on the Tipitapa River, which connects Lake Managua and Lake Nicaragua. Late in August a foraging party was attacked by guerrillas while driving cattle toward Tipitapa, where there was a bridge that could be crossed to reach the road leading to Granada. The commander of the garrison at Tipitapa, Lieutenant Colonel E. H. McDonald, was ordered by Walker to cross the river into the Chontales to put down the guerrillas. He found their base to be San Jacinto. With about forty men, McDonald attacked but he was met with such resistance that he withdrew. Two of his men were killed and four wounded.

To drive the guerrillas from San Jacinto, a force of about forty-five volunteers left Granada on September 12 and an additional fifteen or twenty were added at Masaya. At Tipitapa Lieutenant Colonel Byron Cole, assistant quartermaster general, who used the river town as a base for procuring cattle, took command and led the band to San Jacinto, reached about five o'clock on the morning of the 14th. Situated on an elevation with open approaches on all sides, the ranch was a formidable objective for men armed only with revolvers and rifles. Nevertheless, the Americans, organized in three companies, charged up the height under the heavy gunfire of the defenders. About one-third of the attackers fell, either killed or wounded, and in a few minutes the others withdrew and retreated to Tipitapa. Among those killed was Cole, who, though the prime mover in the start of the expedition to Nicaragua, had been content to serve Walker in relatively minor capacities. Walker wrote of his death: "For months preceding the arrival of the Americans at Realejo, he had traveled and toiled in their behalf; and the only reward of all his labor and anxiety was death on the first field where he met the foe of the principles he had aided to advance."[1]

Since going to Nicaragua Walker had received about 1,200 recruits, but when hostilities began he could count only 800 effective troops. He had permitted the Allies to assemble at León without interference in order to complete arrangements with Cornelius K. Garrison and Charles Morgan over the transit route to ensure bringing in more men. "It would have been folly to advance against León without having the Transit secure and communication with the United States certain," he wrote in his history. "León was well barricaded, and the Americans had not the numbers to spare for an assault; neither had they artillery to aid their attack, even if the roads had admitted of its easy transportation." Despite the addition of several units to the army in the past several months, it had not grown in number because of deaths and desertions.

As a commander, Walker was wasteful of manpower in sending small bands to attack much larger forces in fortified positions —his two assaults on Rivas, first against the Legitimists with his few Immortals and unreliable native support and then against the Costa Ricans were instances of this. The cholera that had defeated the invading Costa Ricans had also taken its toll at Granada. And, as Walker admitted in his history, a new and more dangerous disease began to make its appearance in August—desertions. "Walker's own men were deserting upon every occasion," a *New*

York Tribune correspondent wrote on August 17. "Whole companies are ready to leave him on the first favorable moment." Even *El Nicaragüense*, devoted to glorifying Walker, did not conceal the situation. To discourage defections, the paper on August 3 published an account of the execution of four men in the Masaya garrison who had tried to escape from the army. It carried names and descriptions of other deserters and announced rewards of $30 to be paid for their apprehension.

Among the hundreds attracted to Nicaragua, relatively few shared Walker's ambitions for reconstructing the society. Many were loafers, ruffians, and criminals lured by the offer of regular soldier's pay and keep, the land bonus upon completion of their enlistment, and the opportunity for pillage. They included also many recently arrived immigrants to the United States such as those General Goicouria had brought from New Orleans or the 200 who reached Granada from New York on September 15. Of this latest contingent, Walker wrote: "A very large proportion of them were Europeans of the poorest class, mostly Germans who cared more for the contents of their haversacks than of their cartridge-boxes. . . . The promise of free quarters and rations seemed to have carried the most of them to Nicaragua. . . ."

Few people in the United States knew of the difficult life of the Americans in Nicaragua, a life that many sought to escape by heavy drinking. Most of what was known about the country was found in the glowing accounts of opportunities reprinted from *El Nicaragüense* or almost equally favorable reports sent by newspaper correspondents. A *New York Tribune* correspondent wrote after returning to the United States in June that reporters did not dare anger Walker by telling the truth about conditions, and later in the year the *New York Herald* said that correspondents had no choice but "to eulogize Walker and magnify his successes."[2]

The life of the recruit was described by a young adventurer who went to Nicaragua in June, managed to desert, and returned to his home in San Francisco in December. Interviewed by the *Bulletin*, he related that he debarked at San Juan del Sur with a band of about thirty-five men. At Granada their billet was a church, a damp, filthy place "not fit for hogs," and since they were issued no blankets they had to sleep on the ground in the dirt and litter. Rather than being assigned to military duty, he was set to burning charcoal. He had been told he would receive $25 a month in pay, but all he ever collected was $6. In a few weeks he became ill with fever and spent three months in the hospital, somehow surviving despite the filth, lack of food, and neglect by the drunken doctors. "Soon after my arrival, as soon, in fact, as I saw Granada," the youth related, "I commenced devising means of escaping. This, however, is a difficult matter, after one is once there. No person is allowed to go from place to place without a passport. No person, either citizen or soldier, is allowed to leave Granada without one; and if a soldier is caught endeavoring to do so, he is taken as a deserter and shot." He himself managed to get out of the country after he obtained a furlough to go to Virgin Bay to recover his health. Instead of stopping there, he went on to San Juan del Sur, where he obtained passage—he had $25 himself and luckily was able to borrow another $25 to pay his fare—on the *Sierra Nevada*.[3]

The low morale and lack of purpose among the Americans were offset, however, by dissensions among the Allied forces. President Rivas had designated the Salvadorian Ramón Belloso commander in chief, but this did not suit the Guatemalans, who, coming from a larger state, thought the position should go to their own General Mariano Paredes. Neither Paredes nor his subordinate, General Víctor Zavala, was inclined to take orders from a man they thought their inferior. The dissension at the top of the command extended down through the ranks to the common soldiers. The army was made up of men who had fought under the banners of the Servile and Liberal parties, and old animosities were not easily forgotten. So powerful were these differences that troubles between the adherents of the two factions became common, and, Walker wrote, their leaders hardly dared to place them in the same camp.[4]

When the Allies determined to open hostilities, Walker was in nominal control of all the country except the region around León. The bulk of his army was at Granada, but there were garrisons at Managua, Masaya, and Rivas. A ranger company of about eighty men occupied Managua under the command of Major John P. Waters, who had fought in the Mexican War, being severely wounded in the battle of Monterrey, and who had joined one of the first wagon trains to go to California after the discovery of gold. He had gone to Nicaragua in October 1855 at the head of a party of twenty-five men he had recruited in San Francisco. At Masaya there were about 250 men commanded by Lieutenant Colonel I. McIntosh, in whom Walker had little confidence, considering him "sadly deficient both in knowledge and force of character." General C. C. Hornsby was in command of several infantry companies and the artillery company in the Meridional Department, maintaining his headquarters at Rivas.

Walker made no attempt to hold either Managua or Masaya. He sent Waters orders to withdraw from Managua to Masaya on the approach of the enemy, which he did on September 18. Though with the addition of the Rangers and a small force from Tipitapa there were 400 Americans well positioned behind barricades at Masaya, Walker, in a blunder that was to cost him dearly, withdrew the entire garrison to reinforce those at Granada. Thus, as he had during the Costa Rican invasion when the enemy forces had been allowed to barricade themselves at Rivas, he now permitted the Allies to establish themselves at Masaya in a fortified town that could be taken only by assault.

In the meantime, Walker's forces at Granada had been strengthened by the arrival on October 4 of about seventy recruits from California and on October 7 by about 100 brought from New York by Colonel John Allen. His arms at the same time were increased by the arrival of two howitzers, though the carriages by some blunder had not been sent and substitutes had to be improvised, and by 400 Minié rifles and ammunition. The new recruits brought his numerical strength to more than 1,200 men.[5]

Believing the time had come to strike a blow at the Allies, "if for no other purpose than to show them that the Americans were not thrown entirely on the defensive," Walker determined to attack Masaya. Accordingly, to the sound of martial music a force of 800 troops on the morning of October 11 was assembled and set out on the road to the town about 15 miles distant from Granada. Reaching their destination at nine o'clock that night, they camped on an elevation overlooking the road. The *New York Herald*'s correspondent, who accompanied the force and wrote a long and laudatory account of the battle, wondered why the enemy had not posted pickets to warn of an attack, but during the night a cavalry patrol discovered the camp and roused the sleepers by shooting into their midst. The shooting lasted only a few minutes and there were no further disturbances during the night, but the opportunity for a surprise attack was lost.*

Walker began the assault at daybreak with a rush down the road to the town, putting to flight the enemy soldiers who took refuge in the main plaza, difficult to attack because of street barricades and the solid rows of buildings that enclosed it. The two howitzers proved largely ineffective, the fuses being too short and the shells bursting in the air before reaching the target, and sappers and miners were set to work to cut through the walls of the buildings on both sides of the main street leading to the plaza. Sporadic fighting during the day drove all the defending soldiers from the houses into the plaza, and when night came and the fighting ceased only the buildings directly fronting it stood between the foes.

The Americans grounded their arms and lay down to sleep confident that in the morning they could drive the enemy from the plaza, but they were surprised not long after midnight when they were aroused and ordered to evacuate the town and march back to Granada. The reason for this was that early in the night Walker had dispatched a party to Granada to bring back more ammunition. Reaching the city, they discovered that it had been attacked at noon and occupied by Allied troops. A messenger brought the news to Walker at midnight, and he decided to return to the aid of the 200 Americans left there, most of them civilians and sick or disabled soldiers.

What had happened was that the entire Allied force was not gathered at Masaya, as Walker had thought when he marched out of Granada, but a few days before had been split into two groups, about one-half—700 men—moving to the village of Diriomo a few miles to the south. Those at Diriomo were Guatemalans under the command of General Zavala. When Masaya was attacked General Belloso sent orders to Zavala to strike at the rear of the

*The correspondent related that Walker, who did not bother with a tent while in the field and had reclined on a rubber blanket and covered himself with a woolen one, was unperturbed. Awakened by the shooting, Walker did not leap to his feet but, lifting himself up on one elbow, ordered an officer to find out what the trouble was. He maintained "the coolness of an icicle while all around was tumult and anxiety." *New York Herald*, Nov. 17, 1856.

Americans, but the Guatemalan, having received word that Granada had been left defenseless, decided instead to move against the capital. It was a lucky decision for Walker, for his troops, caught between two fires, might have been utterly destroyed.

The Americans at Granada had spent a quiet Sunday morning and were taken by surprise when the enemy entered the city shortly after one o'clock. They took refuge in the cathedral while the soldiers left in the command of Brigadier General Birkett D. Fry mounted cannons at the streets entering the plaza and discouraged the attackers from making an assault. Instead, they ranged through the city looting houses and shops and killing foreigners unfortunate enough to fall into their hands.

After leaving Masaya at three o'clock in the morning, Walker's troops made a quick countermarch to Granada, reaching the outskirts about nine o'clock. At a height on the road going into the city, the Guatemalans had erected a barricade and mounted a cannon, but they fled when the American troops rushed up the hill. Nor did they attempt resistance within the city, vacating it within an hour after Walker's arrival and retreating toward Masaya.

In the onslaught on Masaya, the Americans lost five men killed and fifteen wounded, and in the battle of Granada twenty killed and eighty-five wounded. The casualties of the Allies were much greater, more than 100 dead being found at Granada. One of Walker's favorites, his aide-de-camp, the Cuban Francisco Lainé, was taken prisoner and shot by the Guatemalans. In retaliation, Walker executed two Gautemalan officers captured at Granada.[6]

A few days after the Guatemalans were driven from Granada, a soldier of fortune arrived from the United States who was to play an important role in the subsequent career of Walker. He was Charles Frederick Henningsen, who had fought with revolutionists in Spain, the Caucasus, and Hungary and who had been sent to Nicaragua as the agent of the steamship and railroad magnate George Law, one of the chief supporters of the Cuban expeditions of Narciso López.

During the summer and fall Charles Morgan and Cornelius K. Garrison had made their transit company competitive with the Panama route by putting into operation three steamships on the Atlantic run and two on the Pacific run. Lowering fares to $150 for first-class passengers, $120 for second-class, and $50 for steerage, they had recaptured a large part of the travel trade at the expense of the United States Mail Steamship Company and the Pacific Mail Steamship Company. Law had been a close observer of the war between Morgan and Garrison and Cornelius Vanderbilt and apparently had seen an opportunity for himself in the unsettled state of affairs in Nicaragua. He had come to the aid of Walker by sending him in the charge of Henningsen some of the U.S. army muskets that he had bought in 1848 at a bargain thinking he could sell them to republican revolutionists in Europe but that, with the exception of some given to López, had since been in storage. The *New York Herald* speculated that Law's interest in Nicaraguan affairs was to supersede Walker with Henningsen and get the transit charter for himself.

Within two days after Henningsen reached Granada, he was appointed a brigadier general in command of the artillery and chief of ordnance, the rank and offices formerly held by General Goicouria. *El Nicaragüense* reported, without explanation, the removal of Goicouria's name from the army rolls and the appointment of Henningsen on the same day. Walker related that there was dissatisfaction among his officers over the rank given the newcomer, excited by prejudices aroused against him because he was not an American. Then forty-one years old, Henningsen, according to the recollections of James Carson Jamison, was a commanding figure of a man, 6 feet tall, spare in build, and of fair complexion with blue eyes and brown hair; like Walker, he was quiet in manner and a man of few words.

The son of a Scandinavian officer in the British service and of an Irish woman, Henningsen had been born in Belgium, but he claimed to be a Briton by birth. His boyhood had been spent in England, and at the age of nineteen he had joined the Carlist forces in Spain and won the rank of colonel. When Schamyl the Prophet led a revolution against the Russian tsar in the Caucasus, Henningsen had hurried to join his cause and fought valiantly in the snows of the mountains. His knight-errantry next had led him to join Louis Kossuth in his revolt in Hungary. When Kossuth came to the United States to obtain aid for the revolutionary cause in Europe, Henningsen had followed as his confidential secretary. He had subsequently married a wealthy widow, Williamina Connelley, niece of Senator John McPherson Berrian of Georgia, and the couple had established their residence in New York, where they were leaders in the international set. A prolific writer, he had produced long narrative poems lauding martial valor, histories of the wars in which he had fought, a biography of Kossuth, and learned and forceful discussions of political, social, and military conditions in several European countries.

Walker's hasty appointment of him as a brigadier general, however, was not in recognition of his fame but as a reward for his bringing arms, ammunition, and stores said to be worth $30,000. The arms included several thousand of the old muskets in Law's possession, which had been converted under Henningsen's supervision into weapons capable of firing the new Minié ball, a conical bullet that had a hollow base and expanded to fit the rifling when fired. The same rank had been given Goicouria when he brought 300 recruits from New Orleans, but Walker was better pleased with Henningsen, who set to work at once to instruct the troops in the use of the Minié muskets and to organize and drill two artillery companies and a company of sappers and miners. Walker said later that he "never had reason to regret the confidence he early placed in the capacity of Henningsen."[7]

During the next three weeks Walker remained inactive except for the work of drilling his troops. Meanwhile, the Allied army was steadily being increased in the north, and Costa Rica had entered the war by sending 600 troops under General José María Cañas to Guanacaste to attack from the south. Walker withdrew General Hornsby and his infantry battalion of 175 men from Rivas, quickly occupied by enemy troops sent out from Masaya, to Virgin Bay with the purpose of holding the wharf so that a force from Granada could be landed at any time. San Juan del Sur was protected only by the schooner *Granada* under the command of Lieutenant Callender Irvine Fayssoux. On August 4 Walker had, in a bombastic decree, directed "the naval forces of the republic of Nicaragua" to blockade all the Pacific and Atlantic ports of Central America, and Fayssoux did his best with the one warship available by cruising along the coast from the Gulf of Fonseca in the north to the

Gulf of Nicoya in the south but staying most of the time at San Juan del Sur to prevent the enemy, if he could, from occupying the town.

About three o'clock on the afternoon of November 7 Cañas reached the outskirts of San Juan del Sur and without resistance occupied the town. He sent G. H. Rozet, the U.S. consul, to the *Granada* with a message stating that if the schooner were not surrendered the lives of Americans in the town would be in danger. Fayssoux wrote in his log: "I replied I would not surrender, but not having the power to drive them from the town I thought it would be prudent to run out of the harbor." He remained in the vicinity, however, observing the events on shore.

The Costa Ricans soon were strengthened by about 300 Allied troops sent out from Rivas, and Cañas prepared against an attack from the Americans by occupying a ridge overlooking the transit road about 4 miles from the town. It was a strategic location, one used for an ambush by Walker earlier in the year when he had expected an attack from the Costa Ricans at Rivas in their first invasion.

On the morning of November 10, Hornsby, whose command had been strengthened by the arrival of 100 riflemen from Granada, marched from Virgin Bay against the forces at San Juan del Sur. When he reached the fortification on the transit road, there was a brief skirmish at the first barricade; but, observing the extent of the Costa Rican defenses, he deemed it imprudent to pursue the attack and withdrew to Virgin Bay. He went to Granada that night to report in person to Walker on the strength and placement of the invading army.

"It was all-important to keep the Transit clear of any formidable force of the Allies," Walker wrote in his history. "The enemy were well aware of its importance to the Americans when they styled the Transit the 'highway of filibusterism.'" Accordingly, he decided to launch an offensive to defeat the Costa Ricans, sailing from Granada on November 11 to Virgin Bay with 200 men. Immediately after landing in the afternoon, he marched his entire force of the new arrivals and Henningsen's troops along the route to the Halfway House, which was reached just before dawn. After a short rest, he resumed his advance and at daybreak his troops came under the fire of the enemy from their position on the heights overlooking the road. After about two and one-half hours of brisk fighting, the invasion forces retreated to San Juan del Sur. They were so demoralized that they did not stop there, the Costa Ricans taking the road to Guanacaste and the northern Allies the one to Rivas.[8]

Walker was satisifed that the day's fighting had made the transit road safe—that the Costa Ricans could not be rallied to action and that the forces at Rivas would not venture outside their barricades. Eager to return to Granada and renew the war against the greater threat of General Belloso's army, Walker marched his troops out of San Juan del Sur on the morning of November 13 to Virgin Bay and embarked them on the lake steamer for Granada. On the morning of the 15th he again took the road to Masaya with a force of 625 men, fewer in number than had left the capital one month before but stronger in artillery, including a 12-pound howitzer, two small brass cannons, and two mortars.

In contrast with the earlier march against Masaya, the men went at a slow pace. Although cheered by the victory on the transit road, they were not, as *El Nicaragüense* boasted, "enthusiastic in their desire to be led against the enemy." Most of them had been on the move for several days, without having been given time to rest, and now they were on their way to attack a fortified town that once before they had been unable to take. Their spirit was further lowered when, about halfway to Masaya, Walker detached 300 infantrymen under the command of Colonel John A. Jacquess to return to Granada and take the steamer to Virgin Bay to reinforce Hornsby's troops. Walker had received a report that General Jérez had gone out from Masaya to Rivas, and intent at all cost on protecting the transit road, he had decided to divide his forces.

In the earlier assault Walker's force on reaching Masaya had been able to establish a camp and rest during the night, but now, when they approached the town late in the afternoon, the enemy attacked in strength. Walker brought his artillery into play, General Henningsen pouring a heavy fire of grape and canister into the ranks of the Allied soldiers, who after a few minutes withdrew into the town, leaving the outskirts and the plazuela around the church of San Sebastian, from which the Americans in their earlier siege had attacked the main plaza, in the hands of the invaders.

During the brisk fighting the Americans suffered more than fifty casualties, including at least six men killed. When the troops camped for the night, Walker found them in a state of demoralization. "As the general-in-chief passed from one point to another, in order to see his commands executed, he found so many of the officers in such a state of languor and exhaustion, they were incapable of controlling their men," he related. "Some of them during the long march had taken a great deal of liquor, and this, as well as the excitement of the conflict dying out, left them utterly deprived of moral strength." It was only with great difficulty that he was able to get the wounded taken care of and pickets posted to ensure security during the night.

Next morning he resumed the attack, but during this day and the next his troops were unable to break into the plaza. Seeing no prospect of driving the enemy from the town and anxious about the safety of the transit road, Walker decided to give up the assault and return to Granada. "Accordingly, near midnight of the 17th, after a few hours' rest in the early part of the evening, the Americans silently abandoned the houses they held and took up the line of march for Granada," Walker wrote. His casualties during the three days of battle were more than 100 men, a third of his attacking force. Shortly after reaching Granada on the 18th, Walker announced to Henningsen his determination to abandon the city and make Virgin Bay his headquarters.[9]

Not only did Walker decide to abandon Granada, but he also decided to destroy the city, the symbol of Legitimist power; and, as "this duty required skill and firmness," he placed Henningsen in charge of the operation. Preparations for the evacuation began on November 19 when the two lake steamers, the *San Carlos* and *La Virgén*, were brought in to remove the troops, military stores, the sick and the wounded, and the civilians and their personal property. Next day Walker sailed on one of the steamers to Virgin Bay to get the troops there ready for a march on San Jorge or Rivas after the destruction of Granada.

Walker believed that Henningsen would be able to accomplish his task in two days, but an orderly evacuation soon became impossible. Soldiers and civilians wanted to take away as much of their property as they could, and they brought more of it to the pier than could be loaded on the steamer. As soon as word spread that the city was to be destroyed, looters began breaking into houses and shops to seize whatever valuables they could find, including spirits and wine which, to prevent their being wasted, they drank on the spot so that, as Walker related, nearly every man able to do duty was more or less intoxicated.

By the 22nd the sick and the wounded and most of the women and children—about 200 persons in all—had been removed to the volcanic island Ometepe in Lake Nicaragua with a guard of sixty men commanded by General Fry, and Henningsen had begun his work of demolition. It was not an easy task. Most of the buildings were of adobe erected on cut stone foundations and roofed with tiles, and the major ones—public edifices, churches, and convents—were so solidly constructed that they could, as they had in the past, withstand mortar shells. Word reached Henningsen that Allied troops would attack the next day, and he had barricades put up around the main plaza while buildings in the surrounding blocks were set afire, spreading an eerie pall of smoke over the city.

Next day, the 23rd, Henningsen ordered a company of sappers to fortify the church of Guadalupe, toward the edge of the city on the road leading to the pier from which he expected to sail when the steamer returned from Ometepe. When he went to inspect the church later in the day, he found that the men, drunk and carousing, had done nothing to fortify it. Next morning he again inspected the church and still nothing had been done. He removed the captain of the company and his lieutenant and sent additional men to do the job. When he visited the church again at noon, he found the barricades poorly erected and the men still intoxicated.

In the past three days enemy cavalrymen had been observed reconnoitering on the outskirts of the city, and Henningsen expected an attack at any time. It came from three directions at about 2:30 p.m. on the 24th. Henningsen had gathered the bulk of his force in the main plaza, closed off to the enemy by the barricaded streets and the burning buildings on all sides. The Americans were able to repulse two of the attacks, but the Allies captured the church of Guadalupe, cutting off a small party of twenty-seven men engaged in putting freight aboard the steamers at the wharf. The heaviest loss during the assault was twenty men in Guadalupe who, unable to escape, were massacred when the enemy broke in. Counting his troops the next morning, Henningsen found that he had 227 capable of bearing arms, but he was encumbered by seventy-three wounded men and seventy women, children, and sick persons. He had seven small cannons and four mortars in his artillery, but he was short of ammunition.

The only escape exit from the smoldering city was the road leading to the pier 1½ miles away, and Henningsen began erecting barricades along it with the hope of fighting his way to safety. There were two points on this route that would offer protection if he could possess them, the churches of Esquipulas and Guadalupe. Consequently, during the next three days he unsuccessfully sought to drive the enemy out of them. On the second day of the siege, Henningsen wrote later in his report to Walker, "we were slightly annoyed by some house fighting, which I suppose the enemy considered as attack." His foe was unable to do much more harm on the two days following. On the third day, the Americans were able to occupy the church of Esquipulas, with a loss of five or six men, and on the fourth they attacked Guadalupe with artillery but were compelled to fall back with a loss of sixteen killed and wounded.

On the 28th Henningsen removed the sick and wounded from the cathedral to a solid adobe building on the lake road and abandoned the main plaza. Not forgetting that his orders had been to destroy Granada, he set fire to all the buildings around the plaza that had not been demolished, placed 200 pounds of damaged powder in the cathedral tower, and set it off. Constructed more than 300 years before, the ancient church was shattered by the blast and debris rose high in the air just as enemy soldiers came running into the plaza.

After leaving the ruined plaza, Henningsen launched an attack against Guadalupe, first pounding it with artillery and then rushing it, and drove out the 200 or so defenders. In the church, he found about twenty unburied bodies of Americans, about a dozen unburied bodies of enemy soldiers, and about thirty graves covered with a few inches of soil. It was an unwholesome place, but it offered the only protection against the enemy, and the sick and wounded were moved into it that afternoon. There, for the next ten days, the beleaguered Americans withstood almost daily attacks while they set up breastworks on the road to protect their retreat to the lake shore. Food and ammunition were scarce. There was a little flour, carefully rationed out, and horses and mules were killed to obtain meat, as were cats and dogs that were occasionally caught. Round shot for the guns was obtained by cutting up a chain, inserting the links in clay moulds, and pouring into them the lead from cartridges that were unusuable because there were no caps.

Henningsen scornfully rejected two appeals from the Allied generals that he surrender. On November 28 a messenger carrying a flag of truce delivered an appeal from the four Allied generals inviting him "for humanity's sake" to give up "before we order our respective troops to fall upon you." He was told he could expect no help from Walker, who had been completely routed at Rivas and Virgin Bay. Henningsen replied that he would "have no parley to hold with men whom I know lie," and followed this statement with the impudent offer that if they laid down their arms in two hours their lives would be spared. If not, within six months he would in the name of the government of Nicaragua hang them "all as high as Haman."

Ten days later, when Henningsen had advanced his barricades and breastworks along the road to within 300 yards of the pier, he received a message from Zavala, as "one officer and gentleman to another," proposing that they hold a conversation to end the bloodshed. Zavala said that Walker could expect no reinforcements from either San Juan del Norte or San Juan del Sur, the implication being that the outlook for Henningsen was so hopeless he had no recourse but surrender. Again Henningsen's reply was scornful. He was much obliged for Zavala's good opinion, but he saw no need for any conference—he was strong enough to repel all attacks and break through the enemy lines when he thought fit. He would, he said, hold no parley except at the cannon's mouth.

In the meantime, Walker's infantry divisions at Virgin Bay were "in a very disorganized condition." Contemporary writers generally described Granada as being unhealthful, but bad as the hospitals were in the capital the fever-stricken and the wounded received better care there than in the village to the south. A member of Walker's army who had spent eight months in his service described the situation in both places in a series of articles, "A Ranger's Life in Nicaragua," for *Harper's Weekly*. In Granada before Henningsen began his work of demolition, two large buildings were used as hospitals. "In these might be found, at various times, from one-quarter to one-third of the military force," the Ranger wrote. "They lie along on each side of the vast rooms on cots, or on mattresses placed upon the floor. An oppressive odor of rank wounds, or of bodies decaying with malignant fever, floats in the hot air." Food shortages and lack of shelter from the rains, he wrote, made the situation worse at Virgin Bay, and each morning produced numbers of putrefying corpses. Walker himself wrote of the situation at Virgin Bay: "It being the close of the rainy season there was much fever in the camp; and the contrast between the quarters at Granada and at Virgin Bay, as well as the scarcity of vegetables in the rations at the latter point, depressed the spirits of the officers no less than the soldiers."

Walker's gloom, if not that of his men, over the situation at Virgin Bay was lightened on the 24th when the news reached him that the schooner *Granada* had engaged a Costa Rican brig, the *Onze de Abril*, so named to celebrate the repulse of the Americans in their attack against Rivas on that date, and in two hours of battle had sent her to the bottom. Lieutenant Fayssoux had sailed out from San Juan del Sur late in the afternoon of November 23 when the enemy vessel was seen, and, though the brig was twice the size of the schooner, had engaged her in battle. A lucky cannonball that struck the brig's magazine caused an explosion that blew her apart.

But this victory at sea did nothing to improve the situation on the lake. The Allies regularly received fresh reinforcements for the siege of Granada and the Americans at Virgin Bay were not prepared to go to Henningsen's relief. Walker had no means of finding out what was going on in the city. On the first day of the attack, the force of twenty-seven men loading the steamers at the wharf had set up barricades against the attackers. Walker, assuming that Henningsen was in no trouble, had withdrawn the steamers after supplying the loading party with ammunition and provisions. It was able to hold out two days before being overwhelmed. His communication with Granada cut off by the capture of the wharf, Walker daily sailed back and forth before Granada seeking in vain to discover the state of affairs in the city. When on occasion he returned to Virgin Bay, he found the troops, apprehensive of an attack from Rivas and worn out by sickness and heavy guard duty, in no condition to engage in any offensive action.

A volunteer surgeon in Walker's army, a Dr. Derickson, who sailed with the commander in front of Granada seeking to find out how the beleaguered Americans were faring, thought their situation was probably hopeless. "The exact condition of the Americans cannot be told," he wrote; "they must be suffering to some extent from cholera. The atmosphere is fearfully contaminated—the dead bodies can be smelled on board of Walker's steamboat." Derickson had, however, confidence in Henningsen, whom he considered "far superior to General Walker" as a military commander. Despite the suspense under which Walker labored, he seemed to Derickson to be in good spirits, or, rather, he wrote, "you cannot tell anything about him, for he is always as cold as ice, not feeling the loss of his dearest friends."

Besides Walker's concern over the weakness of his force of about 250 men at Virgin Bay, one-half of them ill and unfit for duty, and those fighting to the death in Granada, he was worried about the 200 sick and wounded men and the women and children landed at night on Ometepe. They had been left there in the belief that they would be safe from attack by the Allies, and during the two weeks of the siege of Granada Walker had ignored them. The island, about 10 miles off the western coast of Lake Nicaragua opposite Rivas, was inhabited chiefly by Indians. They had abandoned to the whites their huts built of mud and reeds, but without food, except for beef and plantains, and without medicine the death rate among the Americans in the days that followed had been appalling. The Ranger who related his experiences for *Harper's Weekly* wrote that a native oxcart called each morning at the huts to convey bodies of those who died during the night to a burial pit. He estimated that almost 100 of those who had gone to Ometepe died of fever and starvation.

About three o'clock on the morning of December 2 the pitiable refugees were aroused by "the *huppa* or war cry" of the natives attacking the village. They fled to the shore and into the forest but were not pursued and massacred, as they feared, because their attackers were interested chiefly in plunder. Three men who had been the first to reach the shore found a canoe without a paddle, climbed into it, and rowed out into the lake using the butts of their guns as oars. They were picked up by Walker, who had just left Virgin Bay on one of his regular trips to Granada. Walker set his course for Ometepe and approaching the island came upon a drifting barge crowded with men, women, and children desperately bailing out the water, the men with their hats and the women with their shoes. They were taken aboard the steamer and Walker proceeded to Ometepe. Deciding that the Indians would not attack again immediately, Walker left the Americans on the island with the promise that he would return within two days to remove all to the mainland. He then sailed on to Granada, where he discovered that Henningsen had established himself in some huts halfway between Guadalupe and the lake.

When Walker returned to Virgin Bay, he found that eighty recruits had arrived from San Juan del Sur, having sailed from San Francisco on the *Orizaba*. This infusion of new strength led him on the next day, December 3, to transfer his headquarters from Virgin Bay to the coastal village of San Jorge, 9 miles north and within striking distance of Rivas, situated directly west and 2½ miles inland. The unhappy immigrants and the sick and wounded at Ometepe were then removed to Virgin Bay. Walker's army was further bolstered on December 7 with the arrival of about 250 men brought from New Orleans by Colonel S. A. Lockridge, who had gone to the United States in the summer to obtain recruits. A native of Kentucky, Lockridge was an old Central American hand, having spent six years in Costa Rica before joining Walker.

At last Walker was able to come to the aid of the beleaguered Henningsen, and on December 11 several companies totaling 170 men under the command of Colonel John P. Waters were embarked on *La Virgén* for a landing near Granada. The steamer on the next day was anchored about 3 miles offshore, and within the city Henningsen observed that there were troops aboard. By now he had erected barricades almost to the shore and felt confident of being able to break through to the pier if Walker was able to effect a landing. He could not hold out much longer under siege. On that day he butchered his own horse for meat, and "the last dog but one was killed by the epicures in camp for dog mutton."

The rescue force aboard *La Virgén* sailed to a point 3 or 4 miles north of the city and began to disembark about nine o'clock that night. The landing was made without interference except for a few shots fired by advance pickets. At about eleven o'clock the men began their march toward Granada along a narrow strip of land bounded on one side by the lake and on the other by a lagoon. Three times during their advance they fought their way through barricades established on the road and about five o'clock reached the suburbs, where they were challenged by a formidable force that Waters estimated was made up of 500 men, who fired upon them from houses along the street and from behind their barricades. Waters directed flanking attacks against the enemy, and before long they retreated into the city.

During the night Henningsen was aware of the battle being fought along the beach to the north, but considered it imprudent to venture out from behind his barricades in the darkness to take part in the fighting. At dawn one of Waters' officers with a patrol sent forward to reconnoiter the situation entered Henningsen's camp with information on the night's fighting. Within thirty minutes, the two forces were united, and their commanders considered tactics to be used in extricating themselves.

Waters thought their best plan was to withdraw along the route he had followed in entering the city, but while they were debating this plan they perceived that the sheds and barricades at the pier were burning, set afire by the Allied force that had abandoned this position, leaving the way open for the Americans to go to the shore and embark on *La Virgén*. During the day and on into the night the work of carrying the sick and wounded aboard went on. Of the 419 persons under Henningsen when the siege began, 125 had died of fever or cholera, 110 were killed or wounded, about 40 deserted, and two were taken prisoner. Of Waters' force, 14 were killed and 30 were wounded. The last to leave the pier, Henningsen, a man addicted to flamboyant gestures, drove a lance into the ground bearing a strip of rawhide declaring: "Aquí fué Granada."

The complete destruction of this ancient city so that Henningsen could write its epitaph, "Here was Granada," was of no military importance to Walker, but the vandalism satisfied his vindictive desire to pay off his enemies. "As to the justice of the act, few can question it," he wrote; "for its inhabitants owed life and property to the Americans in the service of Nicaragua, and yet they joined the enemies who strove to drive their protectors from Central America. . . . By the laws of war, the town had forfeited its existence. . . ."[10]

However satisfied Walker was over the razing of the former stronghold of the Legitimists, his decision to destroy Granada had almost cost him a defeat from which it was unlikely he could recover. Instead, he came out of it very well. He had saved the artillery so necessary for his campaign, and, though the losses in men were severe, the new recruits had made up for these. Moreover, when he landed the next day at San Jorge he discovered that the Allies, panic stricken over their losses at Granada, had withdrawn from Rivas to Masaya. On the morning of December 16 he marched his troops into the town which three times before he had assaulted and from which he had been repulsed.

Walker now believed that he was again in control of the situation and sent his subsecretary of hacienda, William K. Rogers, on a trip down the river to San Juan del Norte to purchase the printing equipment of Colonel Kinney for reestablishing *El Nicaragüense*, whose machinery and type had been destroyed at Granada. On the boat also were Colonel Lockridge, returning to the United States to obtain more enlistments, and several officers and men given leaves of absence. They discovered a disaster, one of which Walker was to remain in ignorance for more than a month: the Costa Ricans had seized the river steamers of the transit company and had captured the forts along the San Juan garrisoned by Americans. Confident of being able to hold the transit route over the 12 miles from Virgin Bay to San Juan del Sur, Walker did not know that he could expect no more help from the United States. He was threatened with slow debilitation through disease and starvation and the ultimate collapse of his dictatorial regime even if the Allies continued to prove inept and reluctant in warfare.[11]

The man behind the Costa Rican successes on the San Juan River was Cornelius Vanderbilt, relentlessly pursuing his goal of revenge against Charles Morgan and Cornelius K. Garrison and seeking to punish Walker for the revocation of the transit company charter. In the summer of 1856 he had encountered an English adventurer,

William Robert Clifford Webster, who outlined to him a plan for defeating Walker's forces and repossessing the seized transit company property. Accordingly, on October 5, 1856, Webster sailed for Costa Rica as Vanderbilt's agent with the authority to approach President Mora with the offer of financial help and a military plan to capture the river steamers to prevent men and supplies from reaching the filibusters. Webster's checkered career, if newspaper reports can be believed, had included a term in jail in Baton Rouge for fraud and various other bits of chicanery that had brought him into the toils of the law. But he was of impressive appearance and had a persuasive tongue and assumed a grand manner that seemed to mark him as a man of imperturbable confidence and great ability.

Sailing with Webster were a former lieutenant in the U.S. army, George W. May, and a sailor who had knocked about the world as a mate, most recently on Accessory Transit Company boats in Nicaragua, Sylvanus M. Spencer. According to a letter written by May for the *New York Times*, he had been approached by Webster in August for "some military design he contemplated in Central America." Later Spencer was invited to join the venture. When they reached Panama, Webster chartered a schooner for $600 to take them to San José. On this trip, May and Spencer repeatedly asked Webster what his plans were, receiving only the mysterious answer: "Gentlemen, you will receive your orders on arrival at San José." May became ill with fever and was unable to take part in Webster's scheme, and thus lost his place in history. Spencer went through with it to the end, and his name became known to hundreds of thousands in the United States as the leader of the Costa Rican forces who captured the transit company's steamers and the forts on the San Juan River.

When reports of his coup reached the United States, people all over the country began asking, "Who is Sylvanus M. Spencer?" Nothing was known of him; he seemed to be a man without a history. It was not so, the *New York Times* reported; he did have a history that had occupied columns in the press. The *Times* was unable to discover where he had been born, but he had many acquaintances in the Thirteenth Ward, where he had been brought up by a family named Jenkins. Small in size but mean and quarrelsome, he was known as "Banty" Jenkins, and, the *Times* said, was like the author of *Leaves of Grass*, though in a different sense, "one of the roughs."

"The public school system had him in hand for a long time," the paper related, "but was not able to make much impression upon him. To the great gratification of the old ladies of his vicinity, and quiet people generally, he utterly vanished from public gaze for the space of ten years, when he suddenly turned up at Rio de Janeiro, on the charge of murdering Captain Frazier, of the clipper *Sea Witch*, of which vessel he had been the mate." Brought to the United States, Spencer was tried for murder in December 1855. During the voyage, the captain and the mate had frequently quarreled, it was brought out at the trial, and on the twelve-to-four watch one morning, Spencer found the captain in his berth, unconscious from wounds about the head and face. He died shortly afterward. Spencer took command of the ship, giving out that the death was due to hemorrhage. The trial ended in the acquittal of Spencer, and in 1856 he worked a few months as a mate on transit company steamers on the San Juan River, before quitting and returning to New York, where he fell in with Webster and was persuaded to join the Costa Rican venture.

Arriving in San José, Webster set himself up in style and spread the word that he was an agent of Commodore Vanderbilt, evidence of which he displayed in letters of credit drawn on the shipping magnate for $100,000, and of the banking firm of Glenn and Company of London. Before long he had the ear of President Mora and outlined a plan by which the American filibusters in Nicaragua could be defeated and Costa Rica enriched by obtaining possession of the transit route under earlier claims of sovereignty over the southern part of the harbor of San Juan del Norte and joint sovereignty with Nicaragua over navigation of the San Juan River and Lake Nicaragua.

On December 4 Webster received a grant signed by Mora and Secretary of State Lorenzo Montúfar giving him exclusive transit rights. The charter began with the declaration that should Costa Rican troops under the command of Captain Spencer take possession of the river and boats and other property of "the pretended transit company," the government agreed to pay Webster £25,000. Costa Rica would hold the seized property until the war against the filibusters was "happily concluded," when the boats would be delivered to Webster. Webster and his associates were then bound to lend the government £200,000, one-half to be paid six months after the successful seizure of the river and property. The grant gave Webster exclusive rights to the transit from San Juan del Norte on the Atlantic to Salinas Bay, about 25 miles south of San Juan del Sur, on the Pacific.[12]

While Webster remained behind in San José to devote his time to entertaining high officials, including President Mora as guest of honor at a banquet, Spencer, with about 300 troops—other commanders were a Costa Rican, a Frenchman, and an Englishman—began a march, so it was announced, to the Serapiqui River, one of the main tributaries of the San Juan River. At Hipps' Point, where the Serapiqui joins the San Juan, Walker had a garrison of forty men commanded by Colonel P. R. Thompson. The announcement that the Serapiqui was the goal of the force, however, was a stratagem to mislead the Americans. Shortly after the departure from San José, sealed orders were opened, and the force was directed to go instead to the San Carlos River, which enters the San Juan about 25 miles above the Serapiqui. When the San Carlos was reached, rafts were constructed on which the troops floated downstream to the San Juan on their way to Hipps' Point. The steamer bearing Rogers, Lockridge, and others to San Juan del Norte reached the mouth of the San Carlos at the time the rafts were entering the San Juan, but, though those aboard observed them and wondered what they were up to, they did not think them worth investigation.

The Costa Ricans landed about 3 miles upriver from Hipps' Point late in the day of December 21 and camped for the night. Next day they cut a path through the forest to the rear of the garrison, and as Thompson had posted no pickets, took it by surprise, the Americans being at dinner when the attack began. Most of the Americans sought to escape by leaping into the river, where about thirty of them were either shot or drowned. Thompson, who was "half-seas over," one newspaper reported, and one private were taken prisoner; eight men who fled into the woods turned up about a week later at San Juan del Norte after floating down the river on a raft.

Leaving forty men at Hipps' Point, the Costa Ricans descended the river in bungos and on rafts to Punta Arenas, opposite San Juan del Norte, which they reached about two o'clock on the morning of the 23rd. It was an easy task to capture the four small steamers in the harbor—the *Wheeler*, *Morgan*, *Bulwer*, and *Machuca*—because the crews had no loyalty to the transport company and for the most part were willing to man the vessels for the new owners when assured they would be paid regularly.

Spencer so far had carried out his project with sensational dispatch, but his mission was only half completed. To receive his share of the $100,000 that Mora had promised Webster, he must obtain control of the San Juan above Hipps' Point to Lake Nicaragua. Accordingly, without delay he embarked men on the seized steamers on Christmas day and sailed up the San Juan to the mouth of the San Carlos, where he expected that the Costa Rican army under the command of General José Joaquín Mora, the president's brother, would have arrived. General Mora had indeed reached the river with 800 troops, a remarkable performance in this sparsely settled region. Most of the supplies were borne on the backs of men, 600 being employed in this work, over trails that could not be traversed by carts and were difficult even for mules.

With General Mora now in command, troops were loaded aboard the boats and transported up the river to Castillo Viejo, where just below the rapids two other light-draft river steamers, the *Routh* and *Ogden*, were captured. Because the ancient fortress had not been garrisoned by Walker, it was quickly occupied. Nine miles above Castillo Viejo, the lake steamer *La Virgén* was anchored awaiting the arrival of Rogers from San Juan del Norte. Concealing men aboard the *Ogden*, Spencer then sailed up river to *La Virgén* and came alongside without arousing any suspicion of danger among her crew. The Costa Rican soldiers came out of hiding, boarded the larger vessel, and in a few minutes she was in their hands. *La Virgén*, of course, was the prize capture of Spencer's great exploits of one week, for she had quantities of ammunition and arms aboard and with the exception of the *San Carlos* was the largest of the ships available to Walker.

Embarking about 200 Costa Ricans on *La Virgén*, Spencer sailed upstream to San Carlos, where a garrison of Americans occupied a fort on a rocky hill overlooking the river, which has its source there as an outlet of Lake Nicaragua. Arriving about two o'clock on the morning of December 30, Spencer gave the prescribed signal for boats reaching the fort and Captain Charles W. Kruger, of New York, commander of the twenty-five-man garrison, was rowed in a bungo to the vessel. When he climbed aboard, according to Kruger's account given in an interview with the *New York Tribune*, Spencer demanded surrender of the fort, declaring that he had seized all the transit company steamers and was in control of the river. He displayed papers from Vanderbilt, Kruger said, authorizing him to seize the property in the commodore's name. Under threat of death, Kruger sent word ashore to the sergeant left in charge to surrender the fort.

Continuing his strategy of surprise, Spencer four days later was able to seize the *San Carlos* without resistance when she sailed into the San Juan River with about 175 transit passengers who had reached San Juan del Sur on the *Sierra Nevada* from San Francisco on January 2. The passengers had been told the transit was entirely in the possession of Walker, but they learned otherwise when the vessel sailed past Fort San Carlos and entered the river. A few miles below the fort, early in the afternoon of January 3, the lake vessel was halted and Spencer came aboard from the *Ogden* and informed the captain that as the agent of Vanderbilt he had taken possession of the route and there was no possibility of the passengers going through unless they submitted to his authority. There was some talk of resistance, but J. C. Harris, Morgan's son-in-law and a partner in the firm, was unwilling to risk the lives of the passengers and ordered the captain to surrender the steamer. Spencer posted a proclamation of President Mora, signed December 10, promising free and safe passage to San Juan del Norte and thence to New York to all Walker's officers and men who would abandon his army.

According to passengers who finally reached New York late in January, Spencer was talkative during the trip down the river after the transfer to one of the small boats and boasted of his feats of seizing the transit vessels and capturing Walker's garrisons, achieved without "the shedding of any American blood." "Spencer is a very loquacious man, talks like a mechanic, has a Yankee twang, is fond of telling that he was a common workman but a little while ago, and very much elated at what he has accomplished," one passenger told the *New York Tribune*.* Walker himself, though embittered that Spencer, an American, had opposed him, was forced to reluctant admiration in reporting his feats. His success, Walker wrote, "was the reward of rashness which, in war, sometimes supplies the place of prudent design and wise combinations" and "the fortune which proverbially favors the brave certainly aided Spencer much in his operations."[13]

*The *New York Herald*, of Jan. 29, 1857, described Spencer as being 5 feet 10 inches in height with hazel eyes, long fair hair, slightly freckled face, and "large coarse fair whiskers." He was about forty years old. He used "very emphatic language, well spiced with good strong adjectives."

CHAPTER SEVENTEEN

Walker in Defeat: Surrender at Rivas

Even before the occupation of the San Juan River by the Costa Ricans, Walker's precarious situation had aroused apprehension in his supporters in the United States. In Kentucky, always a ready source of recruits for filibuster expeditions, the *Louisville Courier*, for example, said that what forces he possessed were concentrated at Granada—the paper had not learned then of the abandonment of the city—and doubted if his 1,200 men could fight off the 8,000 reputed to be in the Allied army. "Even now it is admitted that his army is ill fed, while his foraging and scouting parties are in constant danger," the paper continued. "He may, perhaps, manage to keep open his communications with the lake, but if supplies are intercepted from that quarter it would be scarcely possible for him to maintain his position."

In New York, Appleton Oaksmith, General Duff Green, Joseph W. Fabens, John P. Heiss, Charles Morgan, and William L. Cazneau issued a call for a rally of Walker supporters on December 20. They adopted a slogan, "Americans to the rescue," and Oaksmith declared: "Walker is badly off, and needs money and men to hold his own." Roberdeau Wheat, who had not achieved the wealth he had sought in joining the revolution of General Juan Álvarez in Mexico and who had returned to the United States in July 1856, was one of the main speakers at the rally. He had fought with López, Carvajal, and Álvarez, and now he was eager to extend, as he put it, the boundaries of freedom at Walker's side. He described his friendship at college with James Walker, now dead in Nicaragua, and his admiration for William Walker. "I know his spirit—know that he will never give up," Wheat said. "Never will his foot be lifted from that sod unless it be victorious. He will establish a noble republic there; he will enfranchise and civilize a people before enslaved, or nobly fall a sacrifice to a glorious cause."[1]

Following rallies in the South, Walker's allies arranged for a ship to sail from New Orleans on December 28 with, it was announced, about 250 emigrants. Recruiting had been conducted openly, with advertisements being carried in the newspapers. At Nashville, where Norvell Walker had gone to enlist men, the newspapers printed a notice similar to ones appearing elsewhere: "Nicaragua—All persons desirous of emigrating to Nicaragua on the steamship *Texas*, which sails from New Orleans on the 28th inst., will address L. Norvell Walker, agent, Nashville, Tenn. Terms—Each emigrant pays his own expenses to New Orleans; passage from New Orleans to Nicaragua free. Two hundred and fifty acres of land, $30 per month paid to each emigrant. Each emigrant is required to remain in the country twelve months, unless sooner discharged from his obligations." Horace Greeley, in his *New York Tribune*, testily commented on these appeals: "To myriads of young men, it seems a slow business to delve ten or fifteen years for a scanty farm, when a 'rancho' and a 'hacienda' may be speedily had in Mexico or Central America by simply knocking over the owner."

The *Texas* arrived at San Juan del Norte on January 4, not long after the transit passengers on the *San Carlos* with Sylvanus Spencer in charge had arrived and gone ashore. The *Texas* recruits debarked at Punta Arenas, where they subsisted for two weeks, one of them related later, on a dry biscuit and a small bit of meat issued daily. Although not a military man, S. A. Lockridge took command of these recruits and began fitting out an abandoned transit company boat, the *Bulwer*, which Spencer had not bothered with because her boiler and engine had been removed, to ascend the river to attempt to recapture the forts and steamers. He called the boat *Rescue* as a description of her mission.

Meanwhile, the transit passengers were promised by the company agents transportation on the *Texas* on her return voyage to New Orleans and the *James Adger*, which arrived January 9 from New York with about forty recruits. One passenger on reaching

New York told newspaper reporters that while at Greytown he visited Colonel Kinney, still lingering there with the hope somehow of revivifying his own enterprise. Others related that a number of Walker's men at the port deserted upon the offer by President Mora of a free passage to Greytown and thence to New York, made in a proclamation issued on December 10.

The recruits brought by the *James Adger* were the remnants of an expedition of 300 men who had sailed from New York on the *Tennessee* on December 24. Shortly after leaving the harbor, the *Tennessee* ran into a severe storm and, on the third day, put in at Norfolk with a broken shaft. Most of the emigrants dispersed before the *James Adger*, sent by Charles Morgan, arrived to pick up the passengers and cargo and take them to Nicaragua. On board were Roberdeau Wheat, Colonel Frank Anderson, who had been in the United States recuperating from a wound, and Charles W. Doubleday, who had decided to rejoin his old comrades. Doubleday related that he had been unable to read of the Americans' early successes in Nicaragua without regretting he was not with them and that when the story of their reverses came out he could only feel his place was at their side.

The morale of the men at San Juan del Norte was low, and the reason was given by a young man, George W. Sites, one of the *James Adger* recruits. "We landed at Punta Arenas on the 9th of January," he told the *Tribune* when he returned to New York on April 16, "and proceeded up the San Juan River a distance of half a mile, to a point which was subsequently given the suggestive name of Point Misery. It was a swampy, miry piece of ground, and if a soldier got a place sufficiently large enough to lie upon without having some part of his body in the water, he considered himself fortunate." Sickness and the poor food, he related, soon led the men to seek every opportunity to desert by crossing over to Greytown.[2]

Before the end of January, two other expeditions sailed from the United States for Nicaragua. One group of 180 men was recruited by a hard-drinking belligerent man styling himself "Colonel" H. T. Titus from among the Border Ruffians who had warred against free-soil settlers in Kansas. His progress from Kansas and Missouri to New Orleans was publicized in the newspapers, and he was notorious when he departed with his force on the *Texas* on

January 28. When he arrived at Punta Arenas, loud-mouthed and boastful, he caused trouble by his overbearing attitude toward other officers. The other expedition sailed January 29 from New York on the *Tennessee* carrying 250 emigrants for Nicaragua, so the newspapers reported. When the ship was preparing to cast off from the pier, U.S. marshals came aboard with warrants for the arrest of Joseph W. Fabens and his associates for violating the neutrality laws, and they were taken ashore. The *Tennessee* reached San Juan del Norte on the evening of February 8, but according to the *Herald*'s correspondent the actual number of recruits turned out to be only sixty.[3]

Both the Americans and Costa Ricans recognized Greytown as a neutral area under British protection, but both also resented policies carried out by Captain John Erskine, senior officer present of the British fleet. With the Americans, resentment began when the river steamer *Joseph N. Scott* arrived with the passengers from California on January 3 after the capture of the *San Carlos* by Sylvanus Spencer. Lockridge was prepared to attempt to seize the vessel but was warned by Erskine against engaging in any hostile action. The recruits arriving on the *Texas* on January 4 probably could have seized the vessel, but they too were warned off by Erskine. The Americans became more incensed on January 16, when Erskine sent marines ashore at Punta Arenas and Lockridge was ordered to put his men on parade so that if there were any British subjects among them or any who claimed to be, they could leave. A number of Americans were among those who sought British protection as the only means of escaping from the filibuster forces. This incident was reported in U.S. newspapers as "interference" of the British in Central American affairs.[4]

The Cost Ricans were resentful that Erskine permitted the filibusters to make military preparations at Punta Arenas for ascending the San Juan River. Lockridge sailed upstream in the *Rescue* on February 6, attacking a small garrison of Costa Ricans at Serapiqui, and General Mora made a strong protest to Erskine on February 8. It was contained in a letter that never reached him, however, being part of correspondence Lockridge had been able to intercept. Mora expressed his surprise that "a band of pirates could have fitted out and organized, under the very eyes of her British Majesty's squadron" an expedition with hostile intent after he had received assurances the naval force would intercede to avoid conflict on the river.

Mora's letter noted that it was the desire of Costa Rica, as it was of Great Britain, to settle the territorial dispute over Greytown in a diplomatic way and then went on to threaten that he would be under the necessity of carrying the war to the port if in the future his country's enemies were permitted to use the neutral territory for hostile purposes. This threat, however, was rodomontade. Mora's letters to the Costa Rican minister of war, also seized by Lockridge, revealed that he had resisted Spencer's proposal that he take a force to attack the Americans at Punta Arenas, indeed that he was somewhat frightened of Vanderbilt's agent. He would not consent to the attack on Punta Arenas in the belief that sending a force downriver would deprive him of the men needed to maintain his position. Spencer, angry at the refusal, had left for San José to appeal to President Mora, and General Mora wrote his brother: "Don't think of sending Spencer on any war commissions, as he has not too much knowledge of military tactics, nor does he know how to manage our soldiers. Occupy him in urging on the house of Vanderbilt to help us with their influence and the materials of war."[5]

Unaware of the course of events on the San Juan River after the departure of the *San Carlos* from Virgin Bay with the transit passengers from California, Walker was still confident that he could once more gain the upper hand in Nicaragua. The rescue of Henningsen and the artillery pieces from beleaguered Granada merited in a way the headlines over accounts in San Francisco newspapers, "Walker Still Triumphant" and "Brilliant Victory at Granada," for the apparent irrepressibility of the filibusters had disconcerted the Allied commanders. General in Chief Belloso had withdrawn his Salvadorian force to Masaya, leaving the conduct of the siege to the Guatemalans under General Zavala. When Walker reorganized his combat forces at San Jorge, Belloso ordered General Jérez to withdraw the troops at Rivas to Masaya and General Cañas to return with his Costa Ricans to Liberia in Guanacaste. Cañas, not considering himself under the command of Belloso, refused to obey and accompanied Jérez to Masaya.

Shortly afterward, Belloso returned to León and the Allied

leaders held a council of war to elect a new general in chief. The post was conferred upon José Joaquín Mora, with Cañas the second in command at Masaya. The officers of the Allied contingents from the other states remained stationed at various points in the Meridional Department. The *Boletín Oficial* at San José had complained of dissensions in the Allied command before this arrangement was reached, declaring on January 3: "In consequence of these divisions, a band of filibusters have resisted, driven back, and finally laughed at the disorderly attacks of 2,500 men." According to the *Boletín*, there were about 2,000 Allied troops quartered in the Meridional Department under their own officers, while the remainder of the invading troops, the number not given, was at León under the command of Belloso.[6]

Belloso's evacuation of Rivas gave Walker the opportunity to occupy the city without firing a shot. Only 2 or 3 miles from the coastal village of San Jorge, which gave him access to Lake Nicaragua, and about a dozen miles north of the well-built transit road from San Juan del Sur to Virgin Bay, Rivas was a strategic place for Walker's headquarters while he awaited the arrival of recruits and supplies. He immediately set about preparing the city for defense by burning the huts and clearing away the tropical undergrowth on the outskirts and barricading the streets within.

Once a thriving city of 8,000, Rivas in the past two years had been the scene of battle so often that it had become largely a ruin. David Deaderick III, a twenty-one-year-old Tennessean who had been unsuccessful in digging for gold in California and who had joined a band of recruits that reached Nicaragua on January 2, 1857, was shocked by the city's appearance when he entered it, footsore and weary, after a march from Virgin Bay through a countryside that he had found very beautiful with its "broad-leaved plantains, bending oranges, tufted palms, and tropical fruit-trees." He wrote of his experiences in a two-part article, signed by the pen-name "Samuel Absalom, Filibuster," published in the *Atlantic Monthly*. The main plaza, he said, was about 100 yards wide and overgrown with grass. On one side was an ancient stone church or convent fallen to rubble out of which grew trees and vines, and the adobe structures on the other sides were largely "naked piles of dust and rubbish." Deaderick found Walker's men "melancholy" and "forlorn" and lacking animation in movement and conversation.

As on earlier occasions, Walker took harsh measures against deserters, sending out patrols to capture men who left the army and dealing out summary punishment—death before a firing squad. A deserter captured at San Juan del Sur in the morning was court martialed at noon and shot at sunset. Nevertheless, many succeeded in reaching Panama. The *New York Herald*'s correspondent there wrote: "I have spoken with many of the poor fellows who have escaped from Walker's clutches and found their way down here. They tell the most pitious tales of their treatment. . . . All hands agree in stating that nine-tenths of the soldiers would willingly leave if they had the means. . . ." Walker had little sympathy for men who reported in as sick. He stated that on January 3, when Deaderick reached Rivas, his forces numbered 919 men of whom 197 were sick, but many of these "had only chigoes [chiggers] in their feet, and were fully able to aid in the defence of the town."[7]

A few days after the *San Carlos* failed to return on schedule to Virgin Bay with California passengers for the *Sierra Nevada* awaiting them at San Juan del Sur Walker became uneasy, and as day after day passed and she still did not arrive his anxiety mounted. He could hit upon no explanation for the delay. Finally, on the morning of January 18, the steamer was observed lying at anchor before Ometepe island. When she got under weigh about ten o'clock, the transit company agent at Virgin Bay prepared to receive the passengers, but the ship instead steamed to the north and was met by *La Virgén*. Both vessels changed direction and disappeared behind the island.

The next morning they were again seen lying off Ometepe. At Rivas, Walker, informed of the mysterious movements, disbelieved the report, declaring that observers had mistaken bungos for the steamers. When he was notified the next morning that the ships had again been sighted, he hurried to San Jorge to see for himself. On this occasion he decided that the image seen through his glass was not two ships at anchor but a church on the island. Later in the day, *La Virgén* sailed toward Virgin Bay and, raising the Costa Rican flag, fired a few rounds at the port. Afterward both vessels sailed toward Granada, but the next morning, the 23rd, were again at their accustomed anchorage off Ometepe. Walker had refused to believe his own eyes or those of his informants, but now he had to accept the fact that the Costa Ricans, how he could not imagine, had obtained possession of the lake steamers. He did not learn the extent of the calamity he had suffered until the *Sierra Nevada*, which had left San Juan del Sur for Panama, returned on the 25th with an account of Spencer's exploits at Greytown and on the San Juan River.

Forced to admit that he had lost the lake steamers, Walker conceived of a daring, and as it turned out, infeasible plan to recover them. The story is told by Deaderick, who shortly after his arrival at Rivas had been assigned to the Rangers—provided that he could commandeer a steed at one of the haciendas in the countryside, which he did. He was one of a horse company posted on the transit road to escort the passengers from the Atlantic—the passengers who never arrived—to San Juan del Sur. At the pier at Virgin Bay was a recently acquired schooner being repaired for service. She had no engine and the wind blew too strongly from the northeast to sail her to attack the steamers that lay insultingly at anchor before Ometepe, but Walker thought she could be loaded with soldiers and towed across to the island for a surprise night attack by rowboats that had been brought from San Juan del Sur. It was a harebrained scheme and Walker gave it up when his naval expert, Callender Fayssoux, told him he did not think the feat was possible.[8]

In the meantime, Walker received word that the enemy with a force of 900 men had occupied the village of Obraje about 9 miles northwest of Rivas. He sent out a band of about 150 riflemen and a company of Rangers to reconnoiter and if possible dislodge the Allies from the hamlet. They camped about a mile away for the night, and a scouting party was sent out to probe the enemy defense. It encountered a picket of about 100 men, and three or four of the Americans were killed in the skirmish that took place. The next morning the filibusters made several futile attacks against the enemy outposts. When General Henningsen arrived in the afternoon with reinforcements, an attack was launched against the town, but the men were driven back by heavy gunfire. Henningsen received orders on the next morning to withdraw the entire force to Rivas.

The battle of Obraje was a turning point in Walker's war against the Allies. It was a defeat in his first battle with the foe since Granada, and it had "a most depressing effect upon the men," Deaderick wrote, "whilst it elated the enemy correspondingly." The worst result of the withdrawal, however, was that on January 28, the day after the Americans returned to Rivas, the Obraje troops marched to San Jorge and occupied the coastal village where they could be reinforced and supplied from the lake. Unless they could be dislodged, they posed a constant threat to Walker at Rivas. The occupation of San Jorge also made untenable the garrisoning of Virgin Bay and the troops there were also withdrawn to Rivas. San Jorge was to be the object of repeated attacks by Walker, but he was never able to drive out the enemy.

Walker's failure to order a large-scale assault against Obraje was a major mistake, and he later belittled the accomplishment in occupying San Jorge, saying that the Allies were afraid to meet the Americans in the open field. Nevertheless, he took the offensive the next day by sending a force of 400 riflemen and infantry under the command of Henningsen to take the town. The battle raged all day, but at nightfall the Allies still stood at their barricades and Henningsen withdrew with the intention of renewing the attack the next morning. Orders, however, came from Walker to return to Rivas. The American losses were heavy, about 100 men killed and wounded, one-fourth of those who had taken part.

That afternoon, Walker at the head of 250 men began a march to San Juan del Sur, "with the double view," he wrote, "of inspiring the troops with confidence by showing them that the Allies feared to meet them in the open field and of communicating with the steamer *Orizaba* expected in port about the first of February." The first objective was not achieved by this absurd gesture according to Deaderick, who wrote that from the day of the initial failure to capture San Jorge "General Walker's prospects clouded rapidly." About this time, he related, President Mora's proclamation of December 10 promising fugitive filibusters free passage to the United States found its way into Rivas. "The men had no sooner seen it than they began to leave as fast as they found opportunities to escape," he wrote.

After returning from San Juan del Sur with forty or fifty recruits who had arrived on the *Orizaba*, Walker decided to lead an onslaught against San Jorge himself. He formed a force of 300 men in the plaza at twelve o'clock on the night of February 3 and 4 for an attack, hoping to take the Allies by surprise. A detachment was able to penetrate the village, but under the fire of the defenders took refuge in the church. Deaderick, a member of the attacking party, related that Walker, sword in hand, came running up and in a frenzy threw himself first on one man and then on another to thrust them out of the building and into the fight. The men refused to do battle, and as the dawn broke Walker withdrew.

"This was now the third repulse we had sustained within a few days, with an aggregate loss, perhaps, counting wounded . . . not very far under two hundred men, and it became apparent that the filibuster day was over, unless General Walker could find some stratagem in his head, or some better mode of fighting than this confident rushing upon an overwhelming enemy, under strong cover, and grown bold with success," Deaderick wrote of this latest defeat. The infection of desertion spread, Deaderick said, and Walker wrote of this in his history. He said that a number of Rangers with a commissioned officer left with their horses and arms shortly after the assault on San Jorge—Deaderick's story indicates that he was a member of this group—and the morning report of February 6 showed twenty desertions.

Deaderick related that he was a reluctant member of the Rangers who took the trail to Costa Rica. They had been sent out on a foraging raid and were some distance from Rivas when he learned that they intended to desert. The few who objected were forced to accompany the others until the transit road was crossed, and Deaderick concluded that he might as well continue on as attempt to return to Rivas through a countryside infested with enemies. He believed that if Henningsen had replaced Walker as commander in chief the filibusters might have stood a chance of success. Walker was unfit, Deaderick wrote, because he scorned the Central Americans—"greasers" to the filibusters. But Walker was equally unsolicitous of the goodwill of his own men and was thoroughly hated by them. "Instead of treating us like fellow-soldiers and adventurers in danger, upon whom he was wholly dependent, until his power was established," Deaderick wrote, "he bore himself like an Eastern tyrant—reserved and haughty—scarcely saluting when he met us—mixing not at all, but keeping himself close in his quarters. . . ."

Four days after Walker's own failure to dislodge the enemy from San Jorge by his night attack, he made another attempt—

this time a cannonade directed by Henningsen. Henningsen fired about 100 rounds into the village plaza from his two 6-pounders, but the defenders were not routed. Describing the attacks on San Jorge as a series of "offensively defensive operations," Henningsen wrote a friend in New York that they had paralyzed the enemy forces. Walker considered the attacks important, while waiting the result of Lockridge's efforts on the San Juan River, "to let his troops see that they were not thrown entirely on the defensive."[9]

By tacit agreement both the filibusters and the Allies looked upon San Juan del Sur as a neutral port and neither attempted to garrison it though by proclamation Walker and President Mora had declared it blockaded. There was more substance to the filibuster declaration than the Costa Rican one, for Walker did have the little schooner *Granada* stationed there, whereas Mora had no naval vessel at all. Both the United States and Great Britain had sent ships there to protect their nationals—the sloop-of-war *U.S.S. St. Mary's*, commanded by Captain Charles Henry Davis, which arrived on February 6, and *H.M.S. Esk*, commanded by Sir Robert McClure, which arrived on the 10th.

Sir Robert, noted as an explorer of the Arctic, in an act of officiousness sent a lieutenant to the *Granada* on the morning of February 11 to demand by what authority she flew a flag unknown to other nations—a banner of blue, white, and blue horizontal stripes with a five-pointed red star in the central stripe. It was the new ensign adopted by Walker for his republic. Fayssoux replied that it was by authority of his government, Nicaragua. The British commander requested Fayssoux to come aboard the *Esk* to show his papers and on the filibuster's refusal threatened to haul the *Granada* alongside to obtain them. After Fayssoux boldly replied that he would resist a hostile boarding of his vessel, McClure gave up in his effort to intimidate the cocky commander of the little schooner.

Several days later Sir Robert went to Rivas to pay a visit to Walker and found him equally sensitive to his honor. Walker received him in his room but did not rise to greet him when he approached and said: "Being so near you, General, I thought I would come up and see you." Walker frigidly replied: "Yes, I hope you have come to apologize for that affair of the schooner." Taken aback, McClure said nothing for a moment, and Walker continued: "Your conduct, sir, to Captain Fayssoux was unbecoming an Englishman and British officer. I shall make such a representation of it to your government as will cause an investigation and insure an explanation." Sir Robert denied that any insult had been intended, and the two reached an agreement on the right of British subjects to leave Nicaragua without hindrance, the object of McClure's visit. The *New York Herald* in its account of the interview referred to Sir Robert's polar explorations and in a headline said: "Walker Receives Sir Robert in True Arctic Manner."

McClure's visit to Rivas was followed a few days later by one from the American naval commander, Captain Davis. Since becoming a midshipman in 1824, Davis had traveled to all parts of the world, but, Boston born and Harvard educated with a degree in mathematics, he had chiefly been distinguished for his scientific work for the navy. Before taking command of the *St. Mary's* in 1855, he had for several years been engaged in supervising publication of *The American Ephemeris and Nautical Almanac*.

Walker related that Davis treated him respectfully, studiously addressing him as "President," but did nothing to indicate that he was neutral in the filibuster cause. Davis requested that the small boats of a coal-ship, the *Narragansett*, which Walker had confiscated to use on the lake in his aborted plan to seize the *San Carlos* and *La Virgén*, be returned as the captain wished to leave San Juan del Sur. Walker agreed to return the boats—they were now of no use to him—but pointed out that the Costa Rican seizure of the lake steamers was analogous to his seizure of the *Narragansett*'s boats. If Walker could be asked to return property he had taken, then by the same token the Costa Ricans should be asked to return property they had taken.

Shortly after returning to his ship, Davis received a letter from General Florencio Xatruch of the Allies requesting that he prevent the landing of recruits for Walker from ships stopping at San Juan del Sur. Xatruch cited the neutrality proclamations of the United States and the efforts made to stop the sailing of filibuster expeditions and the blockade of San Juan del Sur declared by President Mora. Davis, in a letter of March 4, declined to interfere. President Pierce, in his last annual message to Congress, had declared that a state of civil war existed in Nicaragua and Davis's position therefore must be one of strict neutrality. He expressed surprise, however, at Xatruch's statement about the blockade. "You must know," he wrote, "that such a notification, without being accompanied by the principal thing which is essentially necessary to render it effective—that is, the presence of a competent naval force at or near the port—does not constitute of itself a legal blockade. In the present instance it is the more strange as the waters of this port are not only not in the possession of your force, but are actually held by a ship belonging to the opposite party—the schooner *Granada*."[10]

Except for two or three skirmishes between the Americans and the Allies on the transit road, in which Walker lost thirty or forty men killed and wounded, military operations had been quiet since the bombardment of San Jorge on February 7 while Walker dealt with the visiting naval commanders. He was able to take the offensive again with the arrival at San Juan del Sur on March 5 of a company of about eighty Californians recruited by William Frank Stewart who were incorporated into his army as the Red Star Guard.

Like many of Walker's cohorts, Stewart, a Mexican War veteran who had fought at Buena Vista, had been attracted by the promise of adventure and renown to be won in Nicaragua. He found San Juan del Sur to be a "deserted, dilapidated town," and on the quick march to Rivas was appalled to see the bodies of "unburied Americans blackening and festering in the sun," victims of a skirmish that had taken place the day before. Put off by Walker's "cold, passionless" manner at their first interview, Stewart soon learned that it was unsafe to question or criticize his generalship. Stewart was the author of the second book to be written about Walker, *Last of the Fillibusters*, printed at Sacramento in 1857 and written, he said in the preface, to "lift a veil from the eyes of the unwary youth of the land, and be instrumental in rescuing many a good fellow from the insidious snares which are now being laid to drag fresh victims into the hungry jaws of insatiable ambition." Walker paid his own respects to Stewart in his *The War in Nicaragua*: Stewart was "a noisy, talkative man, whose ideas about public affairs had been derived principally from grogshop assemblies in the mining villages of California."

The swearing in of the Red Star Guard was the occasion

for Walker to parade his army and make a speech with the object of improving morale after the recent losses on the transit road. "The address was brief," Walker wrote, "but it had an effect on those who heard it, and for several days the spirit of the garrison was better than it had been." Stewart, noting the starved look of the ragged and often shoeless soldiers, thought the parade a "ludicrous mockery of military pomp."

A week later, Colonel Titus arrived at Rivas from Panama and reported to Walker on the adverse situation on the San Juan River. Titus had quarreled with S. A. Lockridge after an unsuccessful attack on Castillo Viejo and had decided to join Walker on the west coast. Walker related that from the first he placed no confidence in Titus's report; he had, Walker said, "too much the air of the bully, to gain credit for either honesty or firmness of purpose." Nevertheless, he concluded that he could expect no immediate support from Lockridge and that his strategy of "offensively defensive" operations to gain time must give way to an all-out onslaught against the enemy.

The operation began at two o'clock on the morning of March 16 when Walker moved on San Jorge with about 400 troops, two iron 6-pounders, one 12-pound howitzer, and four small mortars to attack a force he estimated had grown to 2,000 men. The assault at dawn was a furious one and during the day the Americans entered the village and drove the enemy from the plaza. But the Allied army, instead of being routed, had merely withdrawn to occupy the road between San Jorge and Rivas to cut Walker off from Rivas and to attack the town. The Americans, suffering from the fire from the enemy positions along the road, succeeded, however, in withdrawing behind their barricades at Rivas. Walker's most strenuous effort had ended in defeat. A week later, on March 25, the Allies attacked Rivas with 500 troops, and though they did little damage they also suffered little. In the days that followed, with little resistance from the Americans, they succeeded in investing the town and had the Americans hemmed in so that only at great risk could they emerge to forage for food. The siege of Rivas had begun.[11]

The bad news that Titus had brought from the San Juan River was all too true. Early in January, Lockridge had completed repairs on the *Rescue*, and on several trips up the river had found the stream clear of the enemy as far as the mouth of the Serapiqui, where about 200 Costa Ricans had established themselves. On January 28 Lockridge opened fire on their fort, which they had named Trinidad, but inflicted no serious damage. With the arrival of Colonel Titus and his Border Ruffians, Lockridge felt that the time had come when he could commence in earnest his campaign to regain the river. Titus was an unknown quantity as a commander, but there were several officers whose valor and experience had been demonstrated: Colonel Frank Anderson, a Mexican War veteran and one of Walker's Immortals; Lieutenant Colonel Charles W. Doubleday; General Roberdeau Wheat, who had arrived on the *James Adger*; Major John M. Baldwin, who had been with Walker, serving as an aide-de-camp, since October 1855; and presumably Captain Norvell Walker, who had arrived with the New Orleans contingent in January.

Lockridge's troops were untried men, most of them young, a *New York Herald* correspondent saying that nearly one-half were under twenty-one years of age. Their personal stories, related after their experience in Nicaragua, revealed that many of them had quickly fallen ill shortly after arriving at Punta Arenas. Exposed to the rain, which was almost incessant, sleeping on the ground without blankets, and eking out existence on a diet of dry biscuits or crackers and salt pork, they were susceptible to tropical fevers and many suffered from the measles, which swept their camp.

In preparation for the campaign, Lockridge had established a camp about 25 miles up the river on the northern shore to which he moved the bulk of his troops, about 375 men, early in February. His first goal was two Costa Rican positions at the mouth of the Serapiqui, which empties into the San Juan from the south. Their stronger position was on the San Juan's south bank, where about 200 men were barricaded in the village of Serapiqui, or Trinidad; they had a smaller garrison across the river at a place known as Cody's Point.

On February 6 Lockridge embarked about 200 troops and sailed upstream with the intention of routing the garrison at Cody's Point before assaulting Serapiqui. The troops landed about 1 mile below the point under the command of Titus and Anderson, their intention to cut their way through the jungle to attack the breastworks on the point. Meanwhile, Lockridge would sail the *Rescue* past Serapiqui to draw the fire of the Costa Ricans there. The shore troops were given one hour and a half to reach Cody's Point, but the terrain was so difficult to traverse that they were four hours in reaching their objective. In this advance a reconnaissance party was ambushed with the loss of two or three men, but when the Americans charged the barricades they discovered that the enemy had deserted the position.

The Americans spent a week fortifying themselves at Cody's Point and mounting their artillery of three brass 6-pounders on a hill overlooking Serapiqui across the river. The artillery attack directed by Wheat began at six o'clock on the morning of February 15 to coincide with an assault by riflemen commanded by Anderson, Titus, and Doubleday who had landed with troops on the south shore of the San Juan during the night. Fighting continued all day, but the next morning the Americans discovered that the entire Costa Rican garrison had fled the fort. They left behind about forty wounded men, three 6-pound cannons, and 250 Minié rifles. The filibuster losses were slight, only three men killed and two wounded.[12]

Successful in his first operation, Lockridge decided to waste no time in moving up the river to attack the Costa Rican garrison at the ancient fort of Castillo, and, leaving Anderson in command at Serapiqui, he embarked about 150 men on the *Rescue* in the afternoon. Castillo Viejo had been constructed by the Spaniards on a craggy hill about 120 feet high on the south bank of the San Juan River, a hill that over the ages had become so eroded its scarped sides had almost the steepness and regularity of a pyramid. It had been taken by the English in 1780 in an attempt to seize the isthmus and divide the northern and southern possessions of Spain in an expedition of which Horatio Nelson was the naval commander. A nearby hill overlooking Castillo Viejo bore the name Nelson's Hill. Between the castle and the river was a flat expanse of land, almost at water level, called La Plataforma. The rapids, or rather falls, at Castillo Viejo were impassable by steamers, and passengers and freight had to be transferred by land to vessels above this obstacle. Facilities had been constructed on La Plataforma to take care of passengers detained here for several hours.[13]

Arriving in the *Rescue* below Castillo on February 16, Lockridge put Titus and his force ashore about 1 mile below to attack the fort from the land side while the steamer bombarded it from the river. On the approach of the *Rescue*, the Costa Ricans set fire to the buildings on La Plataforma and the two river steamers lying at anchor, the *Scott* and the *Machuca*, and retreated to the old castle on its pyramidal hill. Volunteer swimmers from Lockridge's force cut the *Scott* adrift, and she floated down the stream where she was boarded and the fire extinguished, but the flames had made such headway on the *Machuca* that she could not be saved.

Meanwhile, Colonel Titus under a flag of truce sent a message to the Costa Ricans to surrender and benevolently, on learning that the defenders numbered only twenty-five to fifty men, acceded to their request that they be given twenty-four hours in which to consider. They made good use of the period of grace, sending a messenger to General Mora at Fort San Carlos for reinforcements. Shortly before the truce period ended at seven o'clock the next morning, the besiegers were attacked from the rear. So disconcerted was Titus that he ordered a retreat and, according to all reports, was foremost of all the men who fled down the river.

After such a debacle, the only recourse left for Lockridge was to embark the demoralized soldiers on the *Rescue* and the *Scott*, which he took in tow, and descend the river to set up a camp until he could reorganize his forces. His staging area for the new assault, if it materialized, was on an island where the San Carlos River empties into the San Juan River from the south. Lockridge's interview with Titus has not been recorded, but he accepted his resignation with alacrity, according to newspaper reports, and speeded his departure from the army by taking him down the river to San Juan del Norte.

On March 3 aboard the *Rescue*, with the *Scott* in tow to undergo repairs at Punta Arenas, Lockridge sailed again to San Juan del Norte. There, as always on his arrival from up the river, he was met by a British naval force making the usual offer to receive nationals wishing to leave the filibuster army. This was not, however, to be a routine occasion. Titus, smarting under his ostracism by the Americans and made belligerent by drink, began abusing the lieutenant in charge of the boarding party for interfering with the Americans and proceeded from this to vituperation of the queen. Titus was arrested by the British but later was released and went into Greytown, with the proclaimed intention of going to Rivas by way of Panama to join Walker. No one regretted his departure, for all the Americans were disgusted by his "abusive language and violence," which were "none the less" when he was under the influence of liquor, a frequent condition.[14]

Despite the fiasco at Castillo Viejo, Lockridge issued a proclamation declaring that he had succeeded in opening the San Juan River as far north as the fort and that he offered the fullest guarantee that those using the river would be protected in their persons and property. He continued on at Punta Arenas, putting the *Scott* in condition for use on the river while he awaited the arrival of new recruits. He was ready to resume his campaign on March 18 with the arrival of a group of Texans calling themselves the Alamo Rangers under the command of Marcellus French and other Southerners who had been obtained by General C. C. Hornsby, altogether about 140 men.

In two and one-half months Lockridge had received about 700 men from the United States, but when he sailed from Punta Arenas in the *Scott* and *Rescue* on March 25 his command, reduced by sickness and desertion, comprised only 400. Two or three days were spent in landing supplies at the advance post on the island at the mouth of the San Carlos, and on March 29 Lockridge sailed with his force aboard the two steamers to Castillo Viejo. Scouts reported the next morning that the Costa Ricans were in an impregnable position with a large number of troops. In addition to fortifying the castle, they had occupied Nelson's Hill at its rear and mounted several cannons that would spread havoc among any attacking force. If Walker had been in command, he probably would have ordered the men to charge the fortifications, but Lockridge was a more cautious man and after a council with his officers decided not to make the attempt.

The next day after the troops had returned to the island outpost, Lockridge mustered them and announced that he had decided no help could reach Walker by way of the San Juan River. He invited volunteers to step forward who would return with him to San Juan del Norte and go to join Walker by way of the Panama transit. A recent recruit, Milton Shauman, related that about 100 did step forward, giving three cheers for Lockridge; the others thereupon gave three groans to indicate their desire of quitting filibusterism and returning to their homes. "Col. Lockridge," Shauman continued, "told them he would send them down to Greytown, and then they might either go home or to h—ll, just which they pleased, for all he cared—he didn't give a d—n where they went to."

The return trip began early in the morning of April 2 when the men, provisions, and arms were loaded aboard the two steamers. Approaching Serapiqui, the *Scott* ran aground on a sandbar. When steam was got up to back off, the vessel's boiler exploded, destroying the bow and setting fire to the deck. About twenty men were killed and forty wounded and twelve were reported missing. Two or three days were required before all the force could reach Punta Arenas.

The situation of the filibusters was abject—many were sick or wounded, their clothing was reduced to shreds, and they were without money. Lockridge looked upon the 300 who had refused to remain in the army as deserters and would do nothing to help them return to the United States. He had never been popular with them. "He was kind to the men when they were able-bodied," one recruit, Martin Schroeder, related, "but as soon as they became unfit for duty his treatment was very harsh." Another, George W. Sites, related that Lockridge would brook no insubordination or complaints. "Much dissatisfaction was caused by his knocking men down with the butt of his revolver and cursing them," Sites told the *New York Herald*. "If a man was sick or wounded, he might go to the d—l for all he cared."

When the *Tennessee* arrived from Aspinwall on her return run to New York, the captain would take on board only about fifty of the filibusters. The passage of the others was secured by an arrangement they entered into with the British commander, Captain Erskine, and Joseph N. Scott, the transit company's agent. They would be taken to Aspinwall on two warships if they surrendered their arms to the British, who would hold these for the company as security for the passage home on company ships. Charles W. Doubleday, who had been seriously burned in the explosion of the *Scott*, was among those thus returned to New York. "The failure of Colonel Lockridge to force a passage by the river San Juan, and thereby open a way to reinforce Walker, beleaguered in Rivas by an overwhelming body of the united troops of the Central

American states," Doubleday concluded, "was the virtual cause of Walker's ultimate defeat in Nicaragua."[15]

While Lockridge was failing in his attempts to regain the San Juan River, his arrival was the chief sustaining hope of the filibusters at Rivas. "'Lockridge is coming!' was the constant theme of the men," William Frank Stewart related. "Lockridge was our hope, solace and comfort—the promised military Messiah who was to bring us joyful deliverance." Before long they began to doubt that he existed, but Walker continued to count upon his coming to the rescue. In the latter part of February he had sent Major John M. Baldwin to San Juan del Norte via Panama with instructions that Lockridge, if he could not take Castillo and Fort San Carlos without too much sacrifice, was to cut a road through the jungle and march by land to Rivas. So that Lockridge would not be placed in "a false position," he would hold Rivas as long as provisions lasted.

The position at Rivas, however, became daily more precarious after the repulse of the major onslaught against San Jorge on March 16. Walker received an addition of about twenty recruits from California who reached San Juan del Sur on March 19, but with the strengthening by the Allies of their ring around Rivas his communication with the port after that date was limited to native couriers who could slip through the enemy lines. On March 23 the Allies made a dawn attack with 400 or 500 men but were repulsed with a loss to the filibusters of three men killed and six wounded. Thereafter, General Mora adopted a policy of starving out the Americans, keeping them on the defensive by randomly lobbing cannon balls into the town and sending platoons to fire upon it with their muskets. His strategy was successful. On March 27, the filibusters were forced to start killing their mules and horses for food. "We had neither bread, nor coffee, nor in fact, anything else to mix with our mule meat, except a very little sugar and sometimes a little cacao—or native chocolate," Stewart related. "Occasionally parties of foragers would bring in a few green plantains, but the work of getting them was always hazardous. . . . This state of things was hourly growing worse: even the mule-meat, poor food as it was, had to be sparingly dealt out . . . and it was not long ere the dogs and cats were dished up to eke out the scanty fare."[16]

At San Juan del Sur, Captain Davis of the *St. Mary's* received regular reports of the ordeal being endured by those at Rivas. When he heard that Walker planned to march out with his able men and leave the women and children together with the sick and wounded to the mercy of the enemy—there is no evidence that Walker contemplated this—Davis decided upon a humanitarian move: to remove the women and children from the town.* Accordingly, he sent one of his lieutenants and a sergeant of marines to the Allied headquarters on April 23 with a request that this be permitted. Two days of negotiation followed, and on the 25th between forty and fifty women and children, under protection of the American flag, left Rivas for San Juan del Sur.

Walker related that he was asked if he wished to send a message to C. J. Macdonald, the transit company agent at San Juan del Sur, but he replied that he had nothing to communicate. The lieutenant could tell Captain Davis that he considered his position safe so long as provisions lasted; when there was no more food, he would abandon the town and join Lockridge's forces on the San Juan River.[17] Almost exactly one month earlier, Lockridge had announced to his troops that he was giving up the attempt to capture Castillo Viejo and asked for volunteers to go with him via Panama to join Walker at Rivas.

Although Davis had no respect for Walker and condemned his object in going to Nicaragua, he was not satisfied that he had done all he could for the Americans at Rivas by bringing out the women and children. He wrote later that he felt a "horror of witnessing the slaughter of my countrymen . . . without the ability to succor them," for he feared that if they were not extricated from Rivas they faced wholesale execution by a vengeful enemy when they became so weak they could no longer resist. On April 30 he visited General Mora in the role of mediator between

*A *New York Herald* correspondent at Panama on May 19, 1857, attributed to Colonel Titus the concern of Captain Davis about the situation of the Americans at Rivas. At odds with Walker, Titus had gone to San Juan del Sur and told Davis of the disaster facing the besieged Americans. *New York Herald*, May 29, 1857.

the enemy forces. He found the Costa Rican eager to end the war and agreeable to a proposition that the Americans be guaranteed safe removal from Nicaragua if Walker would capitulate.

A letter to Walker was sent that night conveying the offer. He of course found it offensive, but, according to his history, in the belief Davis might have information he did not possess—apparently about Lockridge—made a conciliatory reply, inviting him to visit him at Rivas to discuss the matter. Davis, in his letter of refusal, wrote that Walker could not expect help from Lockridge and urged him to abandon his filibuster enterprise and leave the country. Not willing to end the negotiations, Walker proposed that he send two spokesmen, General Henningsen and Colonel John P. Waters, to confer with Davis.

In the conference, details of which were given in a long report written by Henningsen on May 2 and later published in full in U.S. newspapers, the two commissioners were told by Davis that Walker's position was untenable. The reasons were that Lockridge had retired from the San Juan River, leaving the enemy in possession; that the transit company intended to send no more steamers to San Juan del Sur; and that the force at Rivas was reduced to a few days' provisions and desertions had so thinned the ranks that even with food the men could not hold out for long. Walker's situation was so desperate, in short, that his only option was surrender under the guarantee of safe removal from the country.

Henningsen replied that there were other choices: the filibusters could break through the enemy's lines and march in any direction and if further weakened could always cut their way to the Pacific and embark on the schooner *Granada*. As to the last, Davis replied that he would not permit the *Granada* to leave port. The surrender conditions relayed to Walker were that he, under the guarantee of the U.S. flag, should with sixteen officers of his choice go to San Juan del Sur to be carried on the *St. Mary's* to Panama and that the troops left behind would surrender their arms and, accompanied by a U.S. officer, be transported by another route to Panama.

The terms were in effect an ultimatum, for, if Walker could not obtain possession of the *Granada* to leave the country, he and his entire band must perish. He reluctantly sent Henningsen back with the word that he agreed to the terms. The agreement contained the signatures of only Walker and Davis, Walker making the point that his capitulation was not to the enemy but to the United States. Although by provisions of the surrender the Americans, with the exception of officers permitted to keep their sidearms, were required to give up their guns and ammunition, Henningsen immediately set to work to destroy the arsenal at Rivas and the artillery pieces so that the enemy could not profit from them. It was an action that endangered those left after Walker's departure, for it enraged the Allies who considered it a violation of the treaty. Stewart, among those left behind, was outraged by this destruction by men of "overreaching, selfish ambition" willing to "jeopardise the safety and lives of that devoted band who stood firmly by them through so many sanguinary struggles."

Walker's unfeeling attitude toward his men was reflected again when they were assembled on the afternoon of May 1 in the plaza to receive official notice of the surrender. He did not appear before them to deliver a farewell address, but instead had departed earlier with his chosen favorites for San Juan del Sur. His general order commending them to the hands of Captain Davis was read by the acting adjutant general, Captain Philip R. Thompson. Walker's only personal words to his men delivered by proxy were: "In parting for the present with the brave comrades who have adhered to our cause, through evil as well as good report, the Commander in Chief desires to return his deep and heartfelt thanks to the officers and soldiers under his command." That was all. His next words put the blame for the defeat upon others: "Reduced to our present position by the cowardice of some, the incapacity of others, and the treachery of many, the army has yet written a page of American history which it is impossible to forget or erase. From the future, if not from the present, we may expect just judgment." This assurance of acclaim to come was poor solace for the 407 Americans Walker left behind at Rivas: 173 wounded and sick persons, 148 officers and enlisted men considered fit for duty, and 86 employees and armed citizens.[18]

Kept under close surveillance, Walker and his officers were taken to Panama and thence across the isthmus to Aspinwall, where they boarded a ship for New Orleans, arriving on May 27. His reception was like that of conquering Caesar returning to Rome. As Walker stepped from the gangplank, he was lifted to the shoulders of several men and borne through a cheering crowd to his carriage, and for the next several days he was the guest of honor at gala affairs in the city. A New Orleans lady composed a fifteen-stanza poetic tribute which ended:

> All hail to thee, Chief! Heaven's blessings may rest
> On the battle-scarred brow of our national guest,
> And soon may our Eagle fly over the sea,
> And plant there a branch of our national tree.[19]

Meanwhile in Nicaragua there remained several hundreds of his followers—the women and children taken from Rivas to San Juan del Sur and existing on charity, the sick and wounded abandoned at Rivas, the able-bodied who had survived the siege marching through the jungle of Guanacaste for the Pacific coast, and penniless deserters at a dozen ports hoping somehow to get transportation to their homeland—who would not return to the United States for weeks and months. There were more hundreds—those who had been killed in battle or had died of their wounds and those who had succumbed to cholera and tropical fevers—who would never return.

CHAPTER EIGHTEEN

The Years of Frustration

The report of the failure of Walker's plans in Nicaragua caused the *New York Herald*, whose stories of his adventures had made a superman of him, to pronounce his defeat as signaling the end of expeditions such as his. "We have had successive forays into Cuba and into Mexico,* and with the same termination to this last and most desperate, complicated and expensive Nicaragua experiment," the paper said, "and conclude that filibustering in behalf of 'manifest destiny' is used up."[1] The pronouncement was premature. The editorial writer had not taken into consideration Walker's faith in his own star of destiny and the enthusiasm with which his countrymen received him in New Orleans and during his progress northward to call upon President Buchanan in Washington.

The trip was made to obtain the promise of the president that the neutrality laws would not be invoked against his organizing a second expedition to Nicaragua. Walker's friends had told him that Buchanan, for years friendly to the South and elected largely by the votes of this region, would reverse the stand of the previous administration toward filibusters. He had been elected, in fact, upon a platform that contained one plank indorsing Walker and

*While Walker was basking in the sunshine of adulation for his exploits in Nicaragua, news reached the United States of a disastrous filibuster foray into Sonora led by his friend Henry A. Crabb. Crabb had entered Sonora with a band of about ninety armed colonists in January 1857 at the invitation of Ignacio Pesqueira, leader of a revolt against Governor Manuel M. Gándara. Succeeding in his revolution, Pesqueira treacherously denounced Crabb and his colonists as enemy invaders, defeated them in a battle at the village of Caborca on Apr. 6, and executed all of them except for a sixteen-year-old boy. Crabb's head was preserved in alcohol and placed on display as a symbol of victory.

another expounding claims of the United States to "ascendancy in the Gulf of Mexico." Walker's hope was additionally buoyed up by the fact that the man he considered a personal enemy, William L. Marcy, had been replaced as secretary of state by an expansionist who was one of the prominent persons frequently asked to speak at Walker rallies, Lewis Cass.

The president, adroit in politics and diplomacy, did not wish to do anything to alienate the South, where filibusterism was a popular cause, and granted Walker an interview on the evening of June 12. The press carried no details of the meeting and Buchanan's own papers and correspondence are also unrevealing, but Walker maintained later that the president approved his plans for a new expedition. Evidence that he was favorably received is indicated in a letter that Walker wrote the president three days later and gave to the newspapers with the explanation Buchanan had approved its publication.

Walker's letter was a vituperative condemnation of the role played by Captain Davis in effecting the surrender at Rivas. Asserting his claim as "the rightful and lawful" chief executive of Nicaragua, Walker began with a history of his career in that country. Then he entered into his tirade against Captain Davis. Instead of being motivated by a desire to rescue the remnants of the filibuster force at Rivas, the *St. Mary's* commander, Walker charged, had acted in behalf of the Central American Allies. He, Walker, had been betrayed all along in the surrender negotiations and had given up under threat that the schooner *Granada* would be seized. His force at Rivas was not so hard pressed that it could not have extricated itself, and, if it had been weakened by death and desertions, so had the enemy. The "dignity and honor" of Nicaragua, he wrote, were degraded when Fayssoux was forced to haul down the republic's colors at San Juan del Sur and to turn the schooner over to the enemy. His own honor as the head of an independent state was impugned when he was treated virtually as a prisoner aboard the *St. Mary's*.[2]

After giving his letter to the press, Walker set out for New York, where a huge crowd was gathered at Battery Park to greet him when he arrived on the evening of June 16 in a barouche drawn by "two splendid span of horses." The crowd had waited impatiently in a downpour of rain for their hero, and the crush was so great that only with difficulty was he lifted to the speaker's platform. A reporter for the *Herald* wrote, however, that many were disappointed by Walker's unimpressive appearance. "General Walker does not look like the terrible man he seems to be," the reporter said. "He speaks rather sharp and clear, and prompt, though when his features are in repose does not look like a man of much energy."

Walker remained two weeks in New York, occupying a suite at the Lafarge House with Colonel Lockridge, Colonel Waters, and Captain Fayssoux. Wherever he went he drew crowds, and at the theater his appearance in a box was the occasion for an ovation and demands for a speech, and Matthew Brady, "the well-known photographist of Broadway," invited him to his studio to sit for a portrait. He was in constant conference with his supporters, among them George Law, General Henningsen, General Wheat, and General Cazneau. "In conversation, General Walker exhibits a sort of diplomatic quietness, preferring, like a good general, to listen and talk as little as possible," the *Herald* said. "He is, however, by no means backward about expressing his determination to return to Nicaragua with sufficient force to make his return an event of interest."

The adulation of Walker was not unalloyed with criticism. On his arrival in New Orleans, Horace Greeley's *Tribune* commented about his admirers: "That crowds should flock to see Walker, just as every great criminal always draws a crowd in his train, we can well understand; but that anybody should have for him any admiration or respect, or should view him in any other light than that of a poor creature as destitute of ability as he is of honesty or humanity, we cannot very well understand." His aspersions against Captain Davis provoked adverse comment in other newspapers as showing ingratitude to a respected naval officer who had saved his skin at Rivas. Nor were all of the former associates who came to see him at the Lafarge House admirers. The *Herald*'s reporter wrote of seeing fifteen or twenty of Walker's soldiers gathered at the entrance of the hotel. "From the tenor of their remarks," he said, "they appeared to have got sufficient of the 'glories of war,' and to be anything but anxious to fight the battle of Nicaraguan freedom over again."

Walker's image as a hero was further tarnished on June 29

when the U.S.S. *Wabash* reached New York with about 150 of his followers. Commodore Hiram Paulding, sent to observe the situation in Central America, had received an order from the secretary of the navy to visit San Juan del Norte in his flagship the *Cyane* and if there were any Americans there who had engaged in the Walker expedition to take them to Aspinwall. The transit company had refused to accept any of the sick and wounded aboard its ships and would transport those in good health only as far as New Orleans at a charge of $40 for adults and $20 for children. Paulding decided that the only thing to do was to send these refugees in the *Wabash* to New York. The ship's arrival was the occasion for the newspapers to print long accounts of the miseries suffered by those who had believed in Walker's promises.[3]

Refusing to visit those who had made so many sacrifices in his behalf and doing nothing to help raise money to relieve their distress, Walker hastily left the city on July 1 on a vessel sailing to Charleston. He then traveled by easy stages to Nashville, where the city celebrated the return of its most famous native son. The Southern press continued its outpourings of praise, but the *New York Tribune* was indignant that this "notorious offender against the laws of the United States" was permitted "unmolested to perambulate the country" with the object of provoking "renewed crimes" and leading "the credulous in fresh misfortunes."

New Yorkers were to be regaled with more tales of distress of Americans arriving from Nicaragua in August. The frigate *Roanoke* arrived on the fourth with more than 200 refugees. The *Herald* quoted as a representative sentiment toward Walker the words of a wounded sergeant who accused him of deserting his followers without taking a single step to help them in their distress or alleviate their sufferings. The last group, 275 men, mostly deserters to the Costa Ricans at Rivas, arrived on the *Tennessee* on the 18th. The *Tribune* said of these disillusioned soldiers: "There is no power in pen to correctly describe their personal appearance; the artist's camera, only, is capable of doing justice to the sickly, sallow, ragged and threadbare picture of despair."[4]

By July Walker was well along with plans for the new expedition. Two organizations were formed to give legal color to the enterprise. One was the Mobile and Nicaragua Steamship Company, announced July 13 at Mobile by a leading businessman, Julius Hesse. The line would put two ships in operation for regular service between Mobile and San Juan del Norte, so it was advertised. The other was the Central American League, announcements of which were also carried in the newspapers, formed to send emigrants to Nicaragua.[5]

Early in September the Guatemalan and El Salvadorian minister to the United States, Antonio José de Irisarri, and the Costa Rican chargé d'affaires, Luis Molina, became so disturbed by Walker's activities that they protested to Secretary of State Cass of an expedition "so publicly and shamelessly proclaimed," and asked that warships be used to prevent the sailing of any expeditionary ship. Cass responded on September 18 with a circular directing officials in port cities to prevent the sailing of any military expeditions.

Walker on September 29 wrote Cass complaining of the presumption of the three countries "presenting themselves to the United States" as the protectors and guardians of Nicaragua: as the "rightful and lawful chief executive" of Nicaragua, he was the only person with authority to address the U.S. government in behalf of the country.[6] In writing this arrogant letter, Walker had a good point—the question of whether Nicaragua's neighbors could be her spokesmen in international affairs. The three countries had allied themselves to expel the Americans, but Nicaragua was not a conquered territory and now in fact had a government, though it was not Walker's. It was an unusual one, a *gobierno binario*, one with two presidents. With the departure of Walker and the Allied forces, the old dissensions between the Legitimists and Democrats had again threatened civil war. To avoid bloodshed, leaders of the two factions had agreed upon a provisional government with a dual presidency filled by General Tomás Martínez, representing the Legitimists, and General Máximó Jérez, representing the Democrats. They would hold office until a constitutional government could be established. They had designated Irisarri, the U.S. minister of Guatemala and El Salvador to the United States since 1855, to act also as the Nicaraguan minister.[7]

Walker, in his letter to Cass, rejected "with scorn and indignation" the charge that he intended to violate the laws of the United States, maintaining that he was merely enrolling emigrants to Nicaragua. The administration, however, looked upon the current activities as unlawful. During October and the early part of November Cass received reports from U.S. attorneys in Southern cities of the enlistment although, so they reported, there was insufficient evidence to obtain indictments. Finally, however, on November 10, U.S. District Judge Theodore McCaleb at New Orleans issued an arrest warrant against Walker upon an affidavit of three custom house employees declaring they had information Walker was preparing to embark upon a military expedition. Brought before the judge, Walker was released on $2,000 bail. The Mobile and Nicaragua Steamship Company's ship, the *Fashion*, was also seized but released when an inspection turned up nothing suspicious. Late that night a large party of filibusters boarded the vessel, and she slipped her mooring and set sail for Mobile. In the morning Walker appeared in court and his bail was continued pending an examination on the 19th. That afternoon Walker with his staff and about a score of other followers sailed as passengers aboard a mail steamer for Mobile.

The U.S. attorney at Mobile had received a warning from New Orleans to keep a watch on the *Fashion*, and when the vessel was reported at anchor a few miles below the city sent a customs inspector to determine if she were engaged in any illegal activity. The inspector found her clearance papers in order and about 270 passengers on board, apparently lawful emigrants. He left the ship to report to the district attorney as she was getting up steam to sail. Thus, with only token interference of the government, Walker sailed on the morning of November 14 on his second expedition to Nicaragua.[8]

As soon as the *Fashion* cleared the territorial waters, the pretense that she carried a body of peaceful emigrants was given up when they were organized into a battalion of four companies. John Tabor, editor of *El Nicaragüense*, was aboard and in an account of the expedition, published in the *New York Herald*, wrote that 200 troops, the actual number sailing, might be considered small to make a hostile landing on a foreign shore but they were "good and determined men" and included six of Walker's Immortals and about thirty others who had seen service in Nicaragua. Among them were such stalwarts as Brigadier General C. C. Hornsby, Colonel Frank Anderson, Colonel Bruno von Natzmer, and Colonel Thomas Henry. The *Fashion* would be followed, moreover, by additional expeditions being recruited by General Charles F. Henningsen, Colonel S. A. Lockridge, and Colonel John P. Waters.

Overloaded with men, provisions, and arms and encountering heavy seas, the *Fashion* was ten days in reaching Punta Arenas opposite San Juan del Norte. She did not put in at the harbor, however, but sailed 20 miles south to the outlet of the Colorado River, where fifty men under the command of Colonel Anderson were embarked in three small boats with orders to ascend the stream to the San Juan River to shut off communication from the points above with the port of San Juan del Norte. Then the *Fashion* returned to San Juan del Norte, lay offshore during the night, and at seven o'clock in the morning entered the harbor and tied up alongside one of the transit company steamer hulks abandoned at Punta Arenas. Within a few minutes the 150 troops aboard were on the beach.

The debarkation was made so quickly that Commander Frederick Chatard of the U.S. sloop-of-war *Saratoga*, under orders to prevent the landing of any filibuster expedition, was taken by surprise. In addition to ordering officials to prevent the departure of Walker's expedition, the president had directed Secretary of the Navy Isaac Toucey to send three ships to Central America to stop filibusters if they escaped from the United States. Commodore Hiram Paulding, commander of the home squadron, had been dispatched in his flagship the *Wabash* to Aspinwall, Commander Chatard to San Juan del Norte, and Lieutenant John J. Almy in the *Fulton* to Boca del Toro, Costa Rica. Their orders, however, did not very clearly set forth their authority. It was evident to them that a naval vessel could be used to prevent the sailing of a ship from a port in the United States, but there was no precedent for vessels stationed in foreign ports to be asked to enforce U.S. laws. Replies of Toucey to requests for clarification were vague. Commanders were not to act arbitrarily or on mere suspicion and should do nothing to interfere with lawful commerce, but, if a vessel was "manifestly engaged in filibustering," force could be used to prevent men and arms from being landed.

When the *Fashion* sailed into the harbor showing only about fifteen men on deck, Chatard assumed that she brought a party to reopen the transit route, and the landing of the troops was made so quickly that he could not interfere. "Somehow or other I was spellbound," he said in a letter to Paulding, "and so my officers seemed to be. . . . I beg you, sir, in the most earnest manner, to come here and advise me. I am in a very cruel state of mind and look gloomily to the future."

It was a week before Chatard could send Paulding by the British mail boat a report of his difficulties. It arrived on the same day, December 2, that a letter from Walker protesting harassment by Chatard was received. Chatard wrote that he had decided he could do nothing to interfere with Walker's activities ashore; but when Joseph N. Scott, the transit company's agent, requested protection of property left in his charge, the commander had sent a message to the filibuster that he would regard his force as hostile and prevent it, by shot and shell, from taking over the property or leaving Punta Arenas. A few days later Chatard sent another message stating that he had been informed Walker intended to seize the British mail from Costa Rica. "Now I warn you not to touch it, and allow it to come safely at hand here," Chatard wrote. Walker refused to reply, but he carefully avoided any collision with the naval force, protesting in his letter to Paulding the "unjust and illegal conduct" of Chatard.

A week after his first protest to Paulding of Chatard's harassment, Walker wrote again of continued indignities to which he was subjected. Several officers from the *Saratoga* had come ashore and ignored the challenge of a sentry at the filibuster camp. They were warned that if they did so again they would be fired on. Chatard dispatched a note saying that if one of his officers were touched, he would "feel justified to retaliate in the extreme." Another incident involved a naval party that landed at the outer end of Punta Arenas and engaged in gunnery practice over the heads of filibusters camped there. A note from Chatard to Walker warned him against letting any of his men get in the way of any shot the navy might have to fire in practice. "But it is useless to call your attention to the childish follies of these notes, as they are apparent to the most casual observer," Walker told Paulding. "Were they not signed by an United States officer they would not be dignified by notice on my part."[9]

Chatard's fumbling bellicosity would not have stopped Walker from proceeding with his invasion plans; instead, he was kept immobilized at Punta Arenas by the lack of boats to ascend the river to attack the Costa Ricans presumably still occupying the forts at Castillo Viejo and San Carlos. He anxiously awaited word from the expedition under Colonel Anderson that had been sent upstream by way of the Colorado River outlet. It finally came on December 6 when a bungo reached Punta Arenas with news of the capture by Anderson of Castillo Viejo, three river steamers, and the lake steamer *La Virgén* without the loss of a single man.

It seemed incredible, but it was true. After leaving the *Fashion*, Anderson and his men had rowed all night in a downpour of rain against a strong current upstream to Leaf's Island in the San Juan River, camping there until November 29, when they resumed their ascent of the stream, going ashore on the night of December 3 about 1 mile below the castle. For the attack on the fort, Anderson split his command into two groups. One occupied Nelson's Hill overlooking the fort while the other, led by Anderson, went along the shore to the castle. Tied up at the wharf was the steamer *Bulwer*, which was boarded without opposition and cut adrift to float downstream with a crew of five men. Two steamers upstream, the *Ogden* and *Morgan*, with only a few Costa Ricans aboard, were as easily and quickly captured. The *Morgan* was left to drift downstream while Anderson embarked the remainder of his company on the *Ogden* and got up steam for an attack on the fort. Subjected to fire from cannons, Anderson sailed up the river out of range. Later in the day, he moved the bulk of his force to Nelson's Hill, and sent a messenger carrying a flag of truce to the fort demanding the surrender of the Costa Ricans. There was no one there for him to parley with, however, for the small band of defenders had deserted it during the day. Two days later, on December 5, Anderson embarked a force on the *Ogden* to attack *La Virgén*, which he had learned was anchored up the river. There was again no resistance and he now was in possession of four vessels used in the transit operations.[10]

But Walker was to be unable to move his troops up the river, for on the same day that he received Anderson's report Commodore Paulding arrived at San Juan del Norte from Aspinwall. The next day Paulding received aboard the *Wabash* General Hornsby and Captain Fayssoux, bearing Walker's second letter protesting

Chatard's interference with the filibuster activity and requesting his intentions. Paulding wrote in his diary that he considered the letter objectionable in tone and that in his view the Americans were at Punta Arenas "irregularly" and had none of his sympathy. He did not reveal to Walker's two agents that he had determined to remove the "piratical assemblage" from Punta Arenas.

The naval operation to accomplish this was carried out the next day. In the morning Paulding directed Chatard to anchor the *Saratoga* off Punta Arenas opposite Walker's camp and to be ready for any contingency. Paulding transferred his flag to the *Fulton*, which had arrived from Boca del Toro in the afternoon of the previous day, and went aboard with 300 armed marines and sailors from the *Wabash*. The marines were deployed ashore to surround the filibuster camp, upon which the guns of the ships were brought to bear. He then sent Walker a letter that opened with a statement of his surprise at the "tone of audacity and falsification of facts" contained in the filibuster's two complaints to him and declared that Chatard's only mistake had been in not driving him from Punta Arenas when he went ashore from the *Fashion*. He ended by ordering Walker and his command to surrender their arms and embark on naval vessels that would take them to the United States.

Surrounded by an overwhelming force, there was nothing for Walker to do but capitulate. Observers reported that on this occasion Walker betrayed his emotion, that he was so shattered by the collapse of his enterprise he broke into tears when he boarded the *Fulton* to surrender. John Tabor of *El Nicaragüense* described the meeting: "The two took chairs to converse, when the General was so overcome by the great injustice of this sudden and appalling reverse . . . that his eyes were red with tears." And Paulding in a letter to his wife wrote that "this lion-hearted devil, who had so often destroyed the lives of other men, came to me, humbled himself, and wept like a child." Instead of sending Walker back to the United States with his followers on the *Saratoga*, Paulding gave him the option of sailing as a passenger on a commercial vessel upon his pledge that he would surrender to the U.S. marshal in New York. Walker reached the city on the *Northern Light* on the evening of December 27, forty-four days after he had sailed from Mobile on the *Fashion*.

In using force to break up the filibuster expedition, Paulding had not been sure in his own mind that he had acted properly. He wrote his wife on December 10 that his expelling Walker from a neutral territory might make him president or cost him his commission, and he felt called upon five days later, in a letter to Navy Secretary Toucey, to justify his action: "I could not regard Walker and his followers in any other light than as outlaws who had escaped from the vigilance of the officers of the government, and left our shores for the purpose of rapine and murder, and I saw no other way to vindicate the law and redeem the honor of our country than by disarming and sending them home."[11]

Paulding's self-doubts seemed to have been justified by events that followed Walker's arrival in New York. Newspapers carried reports that President Buchanan was of the opinion Paulding had exceeded his authority, and he was assailed by expansionist politicians and editors. Walker was confident the president would order no prosecution and took a bold stand. Paulding had violated neutral territory in arresting him, he told reporters, and the U.S. government owed him an apology. He would return to Nicaragua as that republic's legitimate president. If he had wept when confronted by Paulding aboard the *Fulton*, he impressed reporters now as being calm and assured. "He is not in the least depressed by this turn in his fortune," a *Herald* interviewer said, "but is on the contrary as hopeful and as sanguine as ever."[12] But Walker's unsuccessful effort to reassert his power in Nicaragua had consequences that, if he had been less blinded by his fanatical purpose, might have led him to worry about his future prospects.

For one thing, the expedition had won him the enmity of the president, whose Central American diplomacy was directed toward reopening the transit route. On November 16 Secretary Cass and Antonio José de Irisarri had signed the draft of a treaty by which the two nations jointly guaranteed its security, and Buchanan had spoken out against filibustering in his first annual message in December. "Such enterprises," he said regarding Walker's latest expedition, "can do no possible good to the country, but have already inflicted much injury both on its interests and its character." He asked Congress for legislation "as will be effectual in restraining our citizens from committing such outrages."

For another, the expedition succeeded in bringing about a

truce between the Legitimists and Democrats in Nicaragua and a settlement between Nicaragua and Costa Rica of their territorial claims to the transit route. The warring political factions in Nicaragua had been brought to a degree of cooperation in the duumvirate of Generals Jérez and Martínez, but this unstable arrangement was abandoned by the action of the constitutional convention, which appointed a single provisional president, Martínez, to assume command of the army and expel the filibusters. Since Walker's surrender at Rivas, President Mora of Costa Rica had pressed his country's claims for control of the transit and was prepared to wage war against Nicaragua to obtain it. Holding the river and lake steamers and occupying San Carlos and Castillo Viejo, he had been in a position to enforce his claims to the south bank of the San Juan River from Punta Arenas to Lake Nicaragua and to the Guanacaste region. On December 8, the day Walker surrendered to Commodore Paulding, the two countries signed a treaty of peace to end the dissensions between them while "their common independence is threatened by a new invasion of filibusters."[13]

Since the recall of John H. Wheeler as minister to Nicaragua in November 1856, the United States had been without a diplomatic representative in the country. In May of the next year President Buchanan appointed a special agent, William Carey Jones, to go to Central America to report on conditions. His efforts were to be directed toward reopening the transit route. He was told to prevent, if possible, the annexation of parts of Nicaragua by the adjoining countries and particularly to oppose the claims of Costa Rica to the transit route, which should remain solely under control of Nicaragua. U.S. citizens had been granted certain rights by Nicaragua, and whatever happened in Central America he must impress upon officials that these rights must be respected in the future.

A blundering, bibulous character, Jones went first to Costa Rica and then to Nicaragua, his travels being reported by correspondents who so delighted in tales of his befuddlement that when he prepared to leave one wrote that it was doubtful "whether he would be able to find his way out of the territory and thence home." On arriving in Costa Rica, without having seen any other parts of Central America, Jones wrote Cass that the Costa Ricans were a much superior people to the Nicaraguans and he saw no reason to object to their dominance of the transit. His next reports were so favorable to Costa Rica that, because they ran contrary to the president's policy, Cass ignored them and carried on negotiations with Irisarri, still awaiting recognition of Nicaragua by the United States. Cass wrote the Costa Rican chargé in Washington, Luis Molina, as well as Irisarri, on September 18, that the United States held to the view that the transit rights belonged to Nicaragua and that the government would see with reluctance the occupation of the route by Costa Rica.

While Jones wandered about Central America, losing his baggage, complaining to officials that his mail was intercepted, attempting to understand local politics, and sampling the native *aguardiente*, agents of American capitalists also gathered there to obtain the transit rights. Jones had difficulty in expressing himself, but he chose an apt quotation when he wrote Cass about the activities of these agents: "Where the carcass is, the vultures gather."

As Charles Morgan and Cornelius K. Garrison had supported Walker by bringing in filibusters, they were soon out of the running for the rights. The two leading contenders, only slightly less disliked, were Vanderbilt, claiming the rights granted to the Accessory Transit Company, and H. G. Stebbins, president of the Atlantic and Pacific Canal Company, aided by the schemer Joseph L. White, claiming them for this firm. Stebbins and White seemed to have won the game, because they had persuaded the minister-designate to the United States, Irisarri, to support them, and he had in turn, in June, received the approval of the duumvirate for a contract. A drawback to this was that Costa Rica possessed the river and lake steamers, and this was the hole card of Vanderbilt, who through his agent, W. R. C. Webster, the strategist in their seizure by Costa Ricans, had arranged to purchase them.

During the summer and fall Webster and Daniel B. Allen, Vanderbilt's son-in-law, were at Managua attempting to get the government to cancel the Stebbins-White contract and, according to newspaper reports, making progress. Vanderbilt, not inclined to overlook any means to obtain an end, still continued to promote his plot of Costa Rica's taking control of the transit. He wrote General Cañas, brother-in-law of President Mora, on August 5 urging him to open the route and assuring him the U.S. government would protect any regime that succeeded in doing so. He suggested that Cañas get himself appointed minister of both Nicaragua and Costa Rica to the United States. Irisarri, "thoroughly under the influence of Martínez and Jérez," would oppose granting the rights to Costa Rica, Vanderbilt said. "He will not be received," Vanderbilt assured Cañas. "I have hitherto prevented it, and shall continue to do so until I hear from your Excellency." Cass was provoked when informed of the letter by Irisarri, who had somehow obtained a copy. This may have speeded the official recognition of Irisarri as the minister of the provisional government of Martínez. On November 16, Cass and Irisarri signed a treaty of amity, commerce, and navigation in which their respective countries jointly guaranteed the security of the transit route.[14]

Walker, in accordance with his pledge to Commodore Paulding, presented himself to the U.S. marshal in New York City on the morning after his arrival from Nicaragua, December 28. The marshal, who had received no instructions from Washington, suggested that he turn himself in to officials at the capital, and in consequence he presented himself to Secretary of State Cass the next day. Walker was a hot potato the administration did not want to handle, and Cass told him the executive department did not recognize him as a prisoner and it was only through action of the judiciary that he could be lawfully held in custody to answer any charges brought against him.

Walker perceived the dilemma that faced the vacillating president: the administration would not countenance his filibuster activities but at the same time it would be on the defensive because of his arrest outside the country by Paulding. He took the offensive, publishing in the newspapers on January 4 an arrogant letter addressed to the president protesting "the illegality and injustice" of Paulding's actions at Punta Arenas. Declaring his determination to return to Nicaragua, he challenged Buchanan: "Permit your officers, if you can, to trample underfoot the constitution and the laws; pass unnoticed, if you will, the most violent invasions of individual rights and public duties; treat with scorn and contempt, if you choose, the demands for justice which we humbly and deferentially place at your feet—we will not be cast down or damaged."

The next day he wrote Henningsen: "The administration is bound to yield to the voice of the country in regard to our affairs. They will have no support in Congress unless they vary their Nicaraguan policy."

On the day Walker's letter to Buchanan appeared in the newspapers, both the Senate and House adopted resolutions asking for correspondence dealing with the arrest. Buchanan complied, sending a message with accompanying documents on January 7. It was a message that contained a sop for all points of view. The president admitted that Paulding had "committed a grave error" in arresting Walker; nevertheless, he continued, any filibuster expedition was a crime that could not be tolerated. "Disguise it as we may," he said, "such a military expedition is an invitation to reckless and lawless men to enlist under the banner of any adventurer to rob, plunder, and murder the unoffending citizens of neighboring States who have never done them harm." And yet he supported the Manifest Destiny aims of the filibusters: "It is beyond question the destiny of our race to spread themselves over this continent of North America . . . should events be permitted to take their natural course. The tide of emigrants will flow to the South, and nothing can eventually arrest its progress."

The president's message came up for discussion in the Senate on the day it was received, led by opponents who condemned Buchanan and Commodore Paulding. Jefferson Davis declared that the president had no authority to use the army or navy "as a constabulary force to stand at foreign ports and arrest persons suspected of a misdemeanor." Stephen A. Douglas, though opposing filibustering as retarding America's natural expansion, declared nevertheless that the president had acted unlawfully. "I am not willing to send out naval officers with vague instructions," he said, "and set them to filibustering all over the high seas and in the ports of foreign countries under the pretext of putting down filibustering." Similar views were expressed by John J. Crittenden of Kentucky, Albert C. Brown of Mississippi, George E. Pugh of Ohio, Robert Toombs of Georgia, and Stephen R. Mallory of Florida. Only James A. Pearce of Maryland expressed the belief that the president had the authority to send the navy beyond the territorial limits to arrest Walker's expedition. William Seward of New York was inclined to drop the whole matter, saying that the president had "balanced this case with exact justice." On the one hand, Walker and his expeditionists—"this band of lawless men who had escaped from the vigilance of the police, and had gone abroad to levy war against a State with which we were in amity"—had been allowed to go free. On the other, the president admitted that the officer who arrested them had violated the laws and had pronounced his censure. "What more can Senators ask than this in relation to either side?" Seward asked. But emotions had been too strongly aroused to let the matter rest. Next week, on January 13, James R. Doolittle of Wisconsin introduced a joint resolution requesting the president to have a medal struck off honoring Paulding for "his gallant and judicious conduct." The controversy continued for the next five months until on May 19 John P. Hale of New Hampshire asked if something could not be done to prevent this issue coming up every day and the Senate passed a motion that the resolution be postponed indefinitely.

The House debate followed a similar line, with Southerners generally condemning the president and Northerners defending him. There was discussion of but no action on opposing resolutions. The Committee on Naval Affairs on February 3 introduced a majority resolution declaring that Paulding had exceeded his authority and should be reprimanded. John Sherman of Ohio countered with a minority substitute resolution declaring that Paulding had "acted within the spirit of his orders" and deserved "the approbation of his country."[15]

Meanwhile, Walker, after issuing his blast against President Buchanan, began a tour of the South to raise money for a new expedition. At Mobile, on January 25, he replied to the president's message to Congress. Heretofore, he himself had not brought out all the facts but now, he said, he must disclose them. Walker said that he had satisfied himself of the administration's early goodwill toward him when, making no secret of his intentions to return to Nicaragua, he went to Washington. If he were engaged in a lawless undertaking, he would not have been received by the president but he was; and his letter recounting his experiences in Nicaragua had been published with the consent of the president. Moreover, before he left Washington, a cabinet member had assured him that he could sail in an American vessel under the American flag and that when he left the territorial waters no one could touch him. With such assurances, Walker asked, was he not right in assuming that the administration approved the enterprise?

Later in the year, however, this attitude had changed, Walker charged, and Secretary Cass had issued his circular warning against the expedition. Walker explained that the reason for the change was that the president was supporting American interests attempting to establish a railroad transit across the Isthmus of Tehuantepec. In October, Walker's tirade continued, one of his associates passed through Washington and was told by a cabinet member that the president now opposed the Nicaragua enterprise. It was suggested that Walker should direct his efforts elsewhere—ally himself with Mexico to bring about a war with Spain by which Cuba would be seized and he would be supported in this effort because of the desire of Buchanan, one of the authors of the Ostend Manifesto, to obtain the island.[16]

This last was such a harebrained proposal that even Walker, no stranger to giddy projects, expressed himself as being startled by it. There are several indications, however, that Walker's allegations might not have been imaginary. First, there was Buchanan's avidity for territorial aggrandizement. Early in his administration, he had instructed the minister to Mexico, John Forsyth, to make offers up to $12 million for purchase of Lower California, nearly all of Sonora, and part of Chihuahua. Forsyth, a holdover appointment from the Pierce administration, had been in Mexico long enough to know such a proposal would be rebuffed and so wrote Secretary Cass. Nevertheless, he presented the proposal, as "delicately" as he could, to the then president, Ignacio Comonfort, who replied that sooner than give up any territory he would throw himself from the palace windows.[17] Defeated in his effort to buy the territory, Buchanan in his second annual message to Congress recommended that he be granted the power to take military possession of the northern provinces because Mexico, in the constant throes of revolution, would never be able to maintain law and order there or to pay American claims amounting to more than $10 million. But the president had more than Mexico in view. In the same message, he reiterated the Ostend Manifesto doctrine that, if Cuba could not be obtained by purchase, circumstances might justify seizing the island "under the imperative and overruling law of self-preservation."

Second, though Walker had no interest in annexing Cuba, the idea of joining Mexico in creating a war against Spain to obtain Cuba had its appeal to two of his associates, Lockridge and Henningsen. Lockridge, resenting criticism of his failure to seize control of the San Juan River, had split with Walker, and in March 1858 wrote Governor Santiago Vidaurri of Nuevo León offering to bring in from the United States men and arms to support that province and the provinces of Coahuila and Tamaulipas, then in revolt against the government of the conservative Félix Zuloaga, who had turned out Comonfort in a coup d'état in January. Lockridge's only request was that if the liberal party was successful he be permitted to embark an expedition to Cuba from one of the Gulf ports. Vidaurri wrote Lockridge thanking him for his offer but saying that he could accept help only if hostilities between Mexico and Spain should break out and it became absolutely necessary to be supported by foreign troops.

Lockridge was at Brownsville, Texas, when Henningsen turned up in the region early in April. Lockridge wrote Vidaurri, on April 7, to warn him against Henningsen, declaring that he was an agent of Walker and was in Mexico for filibustering purposes. "You too well know what was the conduct of Walker in Sonora and Nicaragua," Lockridge said, "for it to be necessary for me to make known their intentions." In the meantime, a letter of Lockridge's published in American newspapers had come to Vidaurri's attention indicating that the offer of help had been in the interest of reviving the old Sierra Madre scheme of setting up an independent republic made up of the states of Nuevo León, Tamaulipas, and Coahuila for eventual annexation to the United States. Vidaurri replied on April 15 with the purpose, he said, of dispelling certain errors of Americans regarding the Sierra Madre scheme. The project, he declared, was that of "a traitorous party" and true Mexican patriots would never "suffer that foreigners, without any footing or station in our country, should interfere in our domestic affairs."

Henningsen, reading the correspondence in the official bulletin, wrote Vidaurri to protest, not very convincingly, Lockridge's charges. "I am no agent but a personal friend of Gen. Walker," Henningsen said, "and it is no violation of confidence to say that he, considering himself a Nicaraguan, neither mixes in nor could be induced, under any circumstances, to mix in the affairs of Mexico." This was true enough insofar as Walker's intentions were concerned, but the letter did not reveal that Henningsen himself was interested in the Mexican scheme. Walker, writing to Callender Fayssoux on August 5, expressed his belief that Henningsen was "lost to our cause." "My impression is that the General has had the Mexican notion in his head since last September —if not earlier," Walker wrote.[18]

Finally, Walker, in a letter to the *Mobile Register* on July 19, repeated his allegations against the administration and named Secretary of War John B. Floyd as the source of the suggestion regarding the alliance with Mexico. In several conversations with Henningsen, the letter said, Floyd proposed that "we turn our attention to Mexico" and that "while in the Mexican service we might by some act—such as tearing down the flag of Spain—bring about war between Mexico and Spain, and Cuba might then be seized by the former power." Henningsen was assured, Walker said, that "means would not be lacking for such an enterprise." Walker's allegations had not been of a kind that the administration could take cognizance of by issuing a reply, but they had been exasperating enough for orders to be issued to naval officers and port officials to maintain a close surveillance of the filibusters.[19]

Secretary Cass had told Walker that any prosecution for violation of the neutrality laws was being left to the judiciary. Three such prosecutions failed. When Walker reached Mobile late in January, he was arrested at the request of officials in New Orleans but was released upon a writ of habeas corpus. An effort about the same time to bring to trial Colonel Frank Anderson, five of his officers, and thirty-nine members of the expedition that had captured the transit company steamers and Castillo Viejo also failed. After Walker and his men were removed from Punta Arenas, Anderson had evacuated Castillo Viejo and sailed down the San Juan River in the *Ogden*. They had been arrested and taken to Key West, where, upon an affidavit signed by Paulding, charges were filed against them but a judge refused to hold them for trial. After Walker returned to New Orleans, he was indicted, but at his trial in May a jury could not agree on a verdict, voting ten to two for acquittal, and the U.S. attorney dropped the case.[20]

The defense of Walker in both houses of Congress, his enthusiastic receptions wherever he went in the South, and his victories in the courts had made him so confident that he went about planning his new foray without concealment. New Orleans papers carried frequent reports that he was planning some sort of joint operation with the exiled former president of Mexico, Ignacio Comonfort, who had taken up residence in the city, and they made much of the visits of Lockridge and Henningsen to Nuevo León. But Walker's sole interest was returning to Nicaragua.

Walker's main problem was raising money, and he traveled widely seeking funds, reporting his difficulties in frequent letters to Callender Fayssoux in New Orleans. His principal reliance was on selling the transit rights, but capitalists were unwilling to risk money on the improbable chance that he could again come into power in Nicaragua. He also offered bonds, signed by himself as president of Nicaragua, for land that could be taken up in the country, but there were few takers. He was not discouraged, however, and wrote Fayssoux September 9: "Tell all the Nicaraguans to be of good cheer; the day of our triumph begins to dawn."[21]

His activities worried port officials at Mobile, where he hoped to organize his new expedition. When the owners of the Mobile and Nicaragua Steamship Company obtained passage in the Alabama legislature of a bill incorporating the firm, Thaddeus Sanford, the port collector, wrote Secretary of the Navy Howell Cobb for advice on whether he should give clearance to the firm's steamship *Fashion* for coastal trade. Cobb replied that only upon very well-grounded suspicion of intent to violate the law could clearance be denied. Early in October Walker issued circulars announcing that a vessel would leave on November 10 for San Juan del Norte and inviting persons desiring to emigrate to gather at Mobile several days before the sailing. The nervous Sanford wrote Cobb that he had been notified of the intended sailing of the ship, a 700-ton bark, the *Alice Tainter*, by Walker and again asked for instructions. Walker had assured him, Sanford said, that about 300 emigrants would embark who would take with them only household goods and mechanical and agricultural implements. As before, Cobb replied that he could not give explicit instructions but there must be no repetition of the sailing of the *Fashion*, which had carried weapons, the year before.

So well publicized was the colonization scheme that Irisarri on October 27 issued an announcement warning that no travelers from the United States would be permitted to land at any port in Nicaragua unless they carried passports signed by himself. And, four days later, Buchanan issued a proclamation against the expedition. The enterprise, the proclamation said, was a hostile military expedition got up in violation of the neutrality laws; its leaders had sold bonds pledging the public land of Nicaragua and the transit route as security for their redemption, and the only way this could be achieved was by overthrowing the present government.

On November 9 Sanford notified Cobb that the firm of J. Hesse and Company, agent for the Mobile and Nicaragua Steamship Company, had requested clearance of the *Alice Tainter* and that between 300 and 400 "emigrants" were in Mobile ready to embark. He also reported that the passengers were said to have passports signed by Irisarri. Cobb replied that Sanford should withhold clearance. If the emigrants had passports, they were undoubtedly forgeries, because Irisarri had issued only seventeen for passengers sailing on a vessel from New York. A week later Hesse again applied for clearance, and again his request was denied. He then announced in advertisements that emigrants who had paid their passage to Nicaragua could obtain refunds. In the meantime, a grand jury had been assembled to investigate charges that Walker, in getting up the expedition, had violated the neutrality laws, but after several days of hearing witnesses failed to return a true bill. The emigrants, Sanford reported to Cobb, had left Mobile, the Hesse company had given up its charter of the *Alice Tainter*, and the vessel was now loading cotton for shipment to Hamburg. Walker's latest scheme, it appeared, had been frustrated.

But Sanford's difficulties with the filibusters were not over. On December 4 he telegraphed Cobb that Captain Harry Maury of the sailing schooner *Susan*, a 146-ton vessel, had asked for coasting clearance for Key West. As the owner, H. G. Humphries, was a friend of Walker's, Sanford feared this was a new maneuver of the filibusters to trick him. "What shall I do?" he asked. In a second letter he said that Humphries had called on him and threatened to keep him busy for a month to come as he intended to demand clearances daily and bring suit for each refusal. Humphries' threat of legal action, however, was a mere diversion to lead Sanford into thinking the *Susan* would not attempt to leave port without papers. Instead, on the night of December 5 and 6 about 120 passengers were embarked and the vessel was hauled into the bay by a steam tug. She could not sail out to sea, however, because the water tanks had to be filled at the fleet station about 30 miles below the city. Unable to make much headway during the next day and a half because of heavy fog and lack of wind, the *Susan* was overtaken by the revenue cutter *McClelland*. A lieutenant sent aboard was told by Captain Maury that the schooner had not yet received her clearance and that he was only preparing her for sea by obtaining water at the fleet station.

The lieutenant returned to the *McClelland* to report to Captain J. J. Morrison and after a short time reboarded the *Susan* and directed Maury to sail back to Mobile. A hot-blooded Southerner, noted for wounding a French count in a duel over a Mobile belle, Maury refused. Morrison himself then came alongside in a boat with an armed crew and, boarding the *Susan*, warned that he would fire on the vessel if his demand for surrender was not met. He then returned to the *McClelland*, leaving one of his officers aboard the *Susan*, Lieutenant George F. White. As Maury had a hostage aboard in the person of the lieutenant, he challenged Morrison by immediately raising sail to go down the bay in the belief that the cutter's commander would not endanger the life of one of his men by firing on the schooner. In this, Maury seemed to have been correct, for Morrison contented himself with following in the *Susan*'s wake. When Maury reached the entrance to the bay and prepared to stand out to sea, however, Morrison had the decks of the cutter cleared for action, and Maury turned back. The ridiculous chase continued during the rest of the day, and when night came the *Susan* dropped anchor and the *McClelland* followed suit. During the night Maury had the anchor quietly hauled in, hoisted sail, and with the binnacle lights shrouded in a blanket sailed down the bay and before dawn entered the Gulf of Mexico.

Walker himself, however, was not aboard. When the *Alice Tainter* was refused clearance and he was unable to mount a large and well-equipped expedition, he had changed his plan of operation. To avoid interference from U.S. or British naval vessels in Nicaragua, an advance expedition commanded by Colonel Anderson would land at Omoa in the Bay of Honduras, where it would await Walker's arrival with additional men. From Omoa the filibusters would march across Honduras to León to surprise the Nicaraguans by starting an offensive from the west coast rather than the east at San Juan del Norte.[22]

During the first two days after leaving the Bay of Mobile, the *Susan* encountered heavy seas, and, according to a log kept by Captain Maury, most of the men aboard were sick. Charles W. Doubleday, who had recovered from the injuries he received when the river steamer *Scott* blew up, was again with the filibusters. He did not have a high opinion of the *Susan*'s passengers. "They were mostly of the class found about the wharves of southern cities, with here and there a northern bank cashier who had suddenly changed his vocation," he wrote. On December 9 the *Susan* hailed a passing ship bound for New Orleans, and Lieutenant White, the hostage from the revenue cutter, was placed aboard, receiving "three cheers for a jolly good fellow" from the filibusters. During the game of tag played in the bay, White had caused no trouble, Maury related, taking things easy "as any sensible man would under the circumstances," that is, enjoying the liquid hospitality offered.

For the next several days the *Susan* sailed under sunny skies, but on December 15, cruising about 50 miles off the coast of the British colony of Belize, she encountered heavy weather and, not a very seaworthy vessel, became hard to handle. She continued without mishap during the night until about three o'clock of the 16th she struck a sunken coral reef. In a few minutes, with water rushing in from holes in the bottom, the schooner lay on one side. The masts and spars, swept by the waves rolling over the reef, threatened to beat the vessel to pieces until Maury cut them loose with an axe. The ship was partly righted, and as she still remained intact the hope arose that with daylight rafts could be constructed to take off all hands. Most of them were terror-stricken, and some broached casks of whisky which, Doubleday related, they drank in tin cups "as if it were water." At pistol point, they were forced to empty the casks in the bilge water "though fierce threats were indulged in, the men claiming the right to drink themselves insensible in view of impending destruction."

At daylight Maury was able to discover the position of the wrecked schooner—the reef surrounding Glover's Cays east of Guatemala. He dispatched the ship's one boat with the mate and four men aboard to discover if help were available at a cay sighted some 15 miles away and put the men to work constructing a raft. Shortly after noon on the next day, when the raft had been completed, a small craft was seen approaching the reef. She was the schooner *Wasp*, belonging to a family of fishers occupying one of the cays. During the next four days the men and cargo were transferred to the cay, and on December 22 Maury and Anderson set out in the *Susan*'s boat for Belize 50 miles distant to charter a vessel to convey the filibusters to their original destination. Two days later when they reached the port they found no ship commanders willing to charter their vessel for the trip to Omoa. New Orleans papers carrying accounts of the expedition had reached Belize, and it was feared that the lawless filibusters might seize any ship whose captain was foolish enough to give them passage.

Finally, Frederick Seymour, the British governor of the Bay Islands, requested Maury and Anderson to call on him. Receiving them courteously, he offered to transport the filibusters in the naval vessel *Basilisk* to Mobile. The stranded men at Glover's Cays were able to celebrate Christmas with joy when the *Basilisk* arrived and the next day they were taken aboard to sail to Mobile. They reached the city on New Year's Day.[23]

In the meantime, Walker had remained quietly in Mobile keeping in touch with his agents to organize an expedition to join the advance guard sent on the *Susan*. President Buchanan's proclamation in October and the measures to prevent the sailing of the *Susan* had made it clear that the administration would do anything to prevent his departure for Nicaragua, but he persisted in his plans. When he returned—it was *when* and not *if*—he would be bound to the inhabitants by a religious tie, for on December 31 in the cathedral at Mobile he knelt before the altar and took the vows of Roman Catholicism. Perhaps this conversion from Presbyterianism, if it were sincere, helped him the next day when the *Susan* expeditionists returned unexpectedly and he learned that his ambitions had again been frustrated. Charles W. Doubleday, bidding Walker good-by, told him that further expeditions would not be likely to prevail against the declared hostility of the world, but Walker replied sharply: "I am not contending for the world's approval but for the empire of Central America."[24]

CHAPTER NINETEEN

The Last Expedition: Death in Honduras

If the *Susan* expedition had attempted to land at San Juan del Norte, the result would probably have been equivalent to the shipwreck that did halt it, for both U.S. and British naval vessels were stationed at the port under orders to stop any filibusters who showed up. Secretary of the Navy Toucey had sent orders to Commodore James M. McIntosh, who had succeeded Commodore Paulding as commanding officer of the home squadron, to use "all lawful means" to prevent a landing of filibusters, and British naval officers had the same instructions from their government.

Toucey's first order of May 5, 1858, stressed that McIntosh should not act on "mere suspicion" and must be careful not to interfere with legitimate shipping. This was so vague that McIntosh, setting forth hypothetical situations, asked for clarification, because he had before him the example of Paulding, who had been publicly censured by the president for arresting Walker and removed from his command. Successive dispatches from Toucey did little to make things clearer, and the last sent in November directing him to station vessels at San Juan del Norte and Aspinwall to prevent a landing told him that he could only "intercept at *sea*" and could not act on land or within any harbor. McIntosh could not understand how if he encountered a vessel at sea he could know she carried filibusters or how if anchored in port he could detect that an arriving vessel had sailed in violation of the neutrality laws.[1]

But if the American commander was expected to operate

under incomprehensible orders, the British commander suffered under no such handicap. He had been instructed to prevent the landing of filibusters in Nicaragua and Costa Rica if requested to do so and further, without the need for a request from local authorities, to prevent any landing on the Mosquito Coast or at Greytown. Captain W. Cornwallis Aldham, the British commander, had no qualms about how he would act. On November 18 he sent officers aboard a U.S. vessel, the *Washington*, which had sailed from New York, and prevented the landing of 350 passengers bound for California. She had been sent by H. G. Stebbins and Joseph L. White of the Atlantic and Pacific Canal Company under the supposed grant of transit rights obtained from the ruling duumvirate of Generals Tomás Martínez and Máximó Jérez in June of 1857.

Earlier, on November 9, Secretary of State Cass had protested the orders given to the British naval force in Central America. For the British to use armed forces in Central America, Cass told Lord Napier, minister to the United States, would be clearly in violation of the Clayton-Bulwer Treaty. He warned that such action would excite strong feeling in the United States and "might be attended with the most serious circumstances." Napier agreed about the injurious consequences but nevertheless declared that his government would be inflexible in its policy. Cass was further provoked when informed that the British had requested France to send armed vessels to San Juan del Norte under orders to land forces to defeat the filibusters if asked by the government of Nicaragua.[2]

This collaboration of Britain and France was the result of U.S. diplomatic failures in Central America, where the successive Walker projects had created fear of invasion and suspicion of the administration's motives. In January 1858 Cass had recalled the bumbling William Carey Jones and appointed Mirabeau Buonaparte Lamar, a military hero of the Texas revolution and the republic's second president, minister to Nicaragua and Costa Rica. His instructions to Lamar were to restore relations between the two countries to what they had been before the war against Walker and to obtain approval of the treaty he and Antonio José de Irisarri, minister to Washington, had drafted in November 1857. When Lamar reached San Juan del Norte on January 18, his first impression was that "respect and confidence" prevailed toward the United States because of Paulding's capture of Walker, but he was soon disillusioned. A month later at Managua he decided that securing ratification of the treaty would be no easy task, writing Cass: "There is in all this country a deep-seated terror, that, when the Americans are admitted into it, the natives will be thrust aside —their nationality lost—their religion destroyed—and the common classes converted into hewers of wood and drawers of water." His efforts were to be further complicated by the machinations of W. R. C. Webster, Commodore Vanderbilt's agent, against the treaty, which presumably secured the transit rights for the Stebbins-White interests.

Lamar, however, made better progress than he had expected, for on April 28 he was able to announce to Cass that the treaty had passed the assembly by one vote the night before. But a month later he learned that, instead of being forwarded to Washington, the treaty had secretly been held back by President Martínez. It was an elaborate imposture. The treaty had been delivered in a sealed package to Louis Schlesinger, commander of the Walker force defeated at Santa Rosa in the first skirmish of the Costa Rican war, with the announcement that he would take it to Washington. Schlesinger had escaped from Walker and had joined the Legitimists. For some months he had been in Managua working in the Stebbins-White interests, and his designation as an official government messenger provoked scornful comment from newspaper correspondents. Lamar believed he himself had been the victim of Martínez's duplicity because he would have objected to certain amendments the president had directed Irisarri to propose to Washington.[3]

Newspaper correspondents, however, believed that Martínez had withheld his signature while awaiting a conference with a French promoter, Félix Belly, who had arrived in Costa Rica early in April and announced he was backed by huge amounts of European capital for construction of a canal across Nicaragua. This was the opinion also of Cass, who had received information about Belly's activities from the U.S. consul at Panama. The "strange proceedings" in regard to the treaty, Cass wrote Lamar, seemed to have been occasioned in part at least by the intervention of Belly in the competition for the transit route.

With no more tangible assets than a charming manner and

a persuasive tongue, Belly, known in Paris as a *littérateur* and *savant*, by sheer effrontery succeded in two months in bringing Presidents Mora and Martínez together to bury their differences and grant him the exclusive transit right. He had first appeared in the news when he arrived at San Juan del Norte on March 14 and it was reported he was on a mission to complete a historical study of Central America. Next he appeared at San José, Costa Rica, with a letter of introduction to Mora from the Costa Rican minister to France. Belly let it be known he had the financial facilities of the Crédit Mobilier behind him. Mora welcomed him effusively, as he had welcomed W. R. C. Webster when he showed up with the assertion that he had the backing of the Vanderbilt millions.

Belly's proposal that French capital be employed in reopening the transit appealed to both Mora and Martínez. Mora's desire for his country and Nicaragua to control the route jointly was opposed by the United States, and Martínez was reluctant to complete any compact with the United States by which Americans again would be allowed to come into the country. Thus Belly was able to persuade the two heads of state to meet at Rivas in April to consider a project that would settle the differences that had brought their countries to the verge of war, bring wealth to both, and keep out the hated Americans. Belly's was a remarkable diplomatic coup, or rather that of a confidence man. When the two presidents met at Rivas on April 22, carrying on their conversations in a bullet-riddled house in the town still in ruins after the siege ended by Walker's capitulation the year before, he succeeded in negotiating a contract by which he was given the exclusive canal concession for ninety-nine years. The presidents affixed their signature to the treaty and the contract on May 1, the anniversary of Walker's surrender at Rivas.[4]

Lamar was officially informed on May 14 of the treaty, but he was not told of the contract with Belly. On the basis of scant information given him, he interpreted the treaty as being designed merely to induce Costa Rica to aid Nicaragua in case of invasion by American filibusters. Disgusted with Central American politics, he wrote Cass on June 26 urging that the United States take measures of its own to reopen the transit by sending military forces to Nicaragua. It would come to this in the end, he said, for he did not believe that Nicaragua desired to reopen the transit and rather than do so under the auspices of the United States would place it under those of Great Britain and France.

Only later did he learn—it was from the columns of the *New York Herald*—of the intrigue played out by Belly, Mora, and Martínez. Mora and Martínez on May 1 had signed an amazing document placing their countries under the protection of "the three powers which have caused to be respected the independence and the nationality of the Ottoman Empire—France, England, and Sardinia." The statement opened with a preamble declaring that a new invasion of American filibusters threatened, that it was secretly approved by the U.S. government for the purpose of taking over all of Central America, and that all U.S. agents in Central America had been accomplices of the filibusters, the present minister boasting publicly of either taking possession of Nicaragua through the Cass-Irisarri Treaty or through the invasion being planned at Mobile.

In Washington, President Buchanan and Secretary Cass were outraged when, from European sources, they learned of the contract awarded Belly and the Mora-Martínez secret manifesto at Rivas. The president's first reaction, Cass wrote Lamar, was to recall him from Nicaragua and dismiss the Nicaraguan and Costa Rican ministers. If the offense had been given by "France or England, or by any other nation," this would have been the course followed, but because of the conditions prevailing in Central America the president had decided to delay acting until he learned if the manifesto was authentic. Lamar, therefore, was instructed to obtain a "yes" or "no" answer to the question of its genuineness.

Lamar wrote a note to Rosalio Cortez, the Nicaraguan minister of foreign affairs, on August 24 requesting a categorical answer to his question as to the authenticity of the document. Next morning, not having heard from Cortez, he dispatched a second note. An answer was in his hands that afternoon. In the euphoria of their Rivas meeting, Martínez and Mora had taken delight, if secretly, in plotting against the United States. Brought out into the open, their action did not now seem to be so fine a gesture. The Cortez answer to Lamar was an ingenuous example of evasiveness. In leaving Managua to meet Mora at Rivas, Martínez had for the time being relinquished his executive authority and his signing of the manifesto was the act only of a private citizen; it was not the act of the government nor was the manifesto a public or official document. Mora hastened to repudiate the manifesto, writing Lamar on September 16 that it had been an error. It had been based on suspicions that he now recognized as mistaken, and he apologized for having held them. After an exchange of letters with Mora, Martínez himself wrote Lamar on September 24 disavowing the document in almost the same words.[5]

Belly had been successful in arousing the enthusiasm of Martínez and Mora for his canal project, but when he left Nicaragua to obtain financial backing in the United States and England as well as in France he encountered the skepticism of hard-headed capitalists. His mission had been publicly repudiated by France, it had alarmed American expansionists and champions of the Monroe Doctrine, and his supporters in his own country had been denounced as a bad lot. President Buchanan, in a private letter to Lord Clarendon, the British minister of foreign affairs, summed up Belly's career the next year: "The little Frenchman, although repudiated by his Government, has made these silly people [the Central Americans] believe that he is going to dig a Ship Canal for them between ocean & ocean, a work which all the money in Paris would not accomplish. His plan is a subject of ridicule among capitalists both in England & this country; but the Nicaraguans venerate him as a perfect prodigy."[6] Belly's accomplishment, if it can be termed such, was the blocking of efforts in the United States to reopen the transit.

While Belly was promoting his canal scheme, Colonel Kinney, repining at Aspinwall after the collapse of his colonization project on the Mosquito Coast, determined upon a bold stroke to realize his own dreams of empire. On April 19 he turned up in Greytown with a half-dozen followers. A week later, on the 26th, they assembled in the plaza, hauled down the Mosquito flag, and hoisted the Nicaraguan flag. By this symbolic action, Greytown, a free city under the protection of the British, was restored to its proper government. Kinney, establishing himself at the Government House, then arrested the mayor and gave out that his actions had the support of Captain C. H. Kennedy of the U.S.S. *Jamestown*, at anchor in the harbor. For a few hours the town was pervaded by excitement, until Kennedy assured the residents and the British and American consuls that the flag-raising had been an independent action by Kinney. Kennedy saved Kinney and his followers from the vengeful townspeople by giving them asylum on the *Jamestown* and mediating an agreement by which they would leave the place and not return. Kinney left the ship with the intention of ascending the river to visit the capital at Managua.

Reporting the *opéra bouffe* performance to Cass, Lamar said that Kinney was induced to his "silly adventure" with the hope of rendering such an important service to Nicaragua that his colonial pretensions would be recognized; in this he failed, for his trip into the interior was halted and he was forced to return to Aspinwall. There, in debt and reduced to only a handful of followers, he decided that his colonization scheme was hopeless and on May 21 he sailed to New Orleans to return to Corpus Christi, scene of his earlier triumphs.*[7]

Hope sprang eternal in the filibuster breast, and Walker on January 13, 1859, wrote Fayssoux in New Orleans that his Nicaraguan invasion plans had been "somewhat deranged" by the failure of the *Susan* expedition a month earlier but they were again beginning "to resume form and substance." Two days later, however, he wrote that the outlook was "not as glowing as most imagine," but with a "little luck" he hoped to be in Nicaragua by April 11. A few days later he wrote that he was postponing the prospective return to July.

Unable to do much in Mobile, Walker spent the month of February in New Orleans, but found prospects for financial support so discouraging and heard such pessimistic talk among his confreres about the infeasibility of mounting another expedition from the Atlantic states that he determined to shift his operations to California. In his latest expeditions Walker had proclaimed his intentions publicly; now, because of a hostile administration in Washington, he saw the need for secrecy and in his letters to

*After his return to Texas, Kinney was elected to the state legislature but resigned in March 1861 because he was not sympathetic to the secession movement. He was lost sight of during the Civil War. One source says that he went to Matamoros, where he became involved in a dispute between warring Mexican parties and was killed in July 1861; other sources give the date as 1865. Walter Prescott Webb, ed., *The Handbook of Texas*, 1:962.

Fayssoux, his closest confidant, impressed upon him the need for circumspection. He committed few details of his plans to paper even in these communications. As far as can be determined from these guarded letters, the plan that ultimately emerged was to have his followers in the Atlantic states gather at Minatitlín on the Isthmus of Tehuantepec while he was in San Francisco recruiting additional men to dispatch to this assembly point. Evidently, then, the expedition was to depart from the eastern coast of Mexico. This, however, is not sure. Some of his advisers urged that the expedition sail from San Francisco for Realejo as the *Vesta* had done four years before, and Walker also seemed to have this in mind.

On March 4 Walker appointed Fayssoux his agent to act for him in all matters pertaining to Nicaragua and two days later sailed with Frank Anderson, C. J. Macdonald, and Bruno von Natzmer for San Francisco. There Walker found about the same situation as in New Orleans: men were to be had but money, "means" as he called it, was not available. After two weeks Walker was writing Fayssoux of his imminent departure overland for New York. "Since leaving New Orleans events have occurred to change very materially the aspect of affairs in Nicaragua," he wrote on April 19. "The development of M. Belly's plans gives a new phase to the politics of Central America. With the French in Nic.—and the schemes of Belly are admittedly backed by the French and English governments—I will not go thither with a limited force or limited means." He revealed that von Natzmer had been sent to Tehuantepec on a "delicate" mission which if successful would ensure the return to Central America "in the face of all opposition." "Do not fail to encourage good men to go to Tehuantepec," Walker exhorted Fayssoux. "Keep a list of all who go down."

Walker was playing his cards so closely to his chest that rumors abounded he was interested in an invasion of Mexico, and a false report reached newspapers in May that he had landed at Acapulco with a force of 300 men. Commenting on these rumors, Walker wrote Fayssoux: "People here think I have the idea of going to Sonora. Little do they know of me or the other Nicaraguans [his American followers]. Time will, I think, do us justice. In spite of France, England and the United States we will, I am persuaded, yet get back to our country—ours by every right legal and moral."

Walker left San Francisco on May 5—he took the overland route to avoid attracting attention—and reached New York almost exactly one month later, writing Fayssoux on his arrival that he found the "present moment propitious" and assuring him: "Our day of triumph approaches." On July 13 he was able to write that he had at last made arrangements for the return to Nicaragua and that Fayssoux should have passengers ready to leave New Orleans by August 20. Resorting to indirection to catch U.S. officials in New Orleans napping, Fayssoux confidentially revealed to newspaper reporters that Walker's New York trip was made to raise money for an expedition that would leave for Realejo from San Francisco in a ship provided by Cornelius K. Garrison.[8]

Walker indeed was making progress, as he wrote Fayssoux, but there were delays that kept him in New York longer than he expected. His sources of financial aid are not known. The *New York Times* hinted that one of them was Cornelius Vanderbilt. The steamer *Philadelphia*, which left New York in August for New Orleans with guns and ammunition for the expedition, the paper said, was one of the vessels that Vanderbilt planned to use to carry mail between New Orleans and Aspinwall under a contract with the government, and William W. Scott, the brother of the Accessory Transit Company's agent in Nicaragua, Joseph N. Scott, was the engineering officer.[9]

Walker preceded the *Philadelphia* to New Orleans to direct the embarkation of his expeditionists when the vessel reached the city. Despite the secrecy he had sought to impose, officials were on the qui vive, made suspicious by several circumstances, including the appearance in the city of well-known filibusters and an ill-disguised advertisement published by Captain Maury calling for men to go to the gold diggings at Chiriqui in Panama with a departure date set for October 5. A watch was set over the 200 or so recruits camped 10 miles below the city, and loose talk directed attention to the *Philadelphia*, whose commander's request for clearance to Aspinwall was denied. There then followed one of the comic chases that so often marked Walker's efforts to escape from officials bent on stopping him. On the night of October 4 the men camped below the city boarded a tugboat and sailed down the river with the intention of transferring to the *Philadelphia* when they reached the open sea. The *Philadelphia*, however, had not been permitted to sail, and the men returned to the camp next day. When army troops brought from Baton Rouge to arrest them arrived, the men jokingly told them they were only going on a fishing trip down the river. Only the leaders of the band were taken into custody—Maury, Fayssoux, and Scott—to be released later when a grand jury refused to indict them.[10]

In less than a month Walker was propounding new schemes for returning to Nicaragua, writing to Fayssoux of plans he had in mind and referring to the activities of Anderson, von Natzmer, and Macdonald by code names from the Greek alphabet—Sigma, Delta, and Gamma. But he was also involved in completing a project that had engaged his time "during a leisure thrust on me against my will," as he phrased it—the writing of a history of the Americans in Nicaragua. He confided to Fayssoux on February 17, 1860, from Mobile that he had seen a bookseller about publication. The bookseller, S. H. Goetzel, was enthusiastic, Walker wrote, and believed that he could dispose of 20,000 copies in Alabama. By the end of the month both Walker and Goetzel were in New York, Walker seeking support for a new filibuster attempt and Goetzel seeing the book through the press. At the end of March copies of the volume, *The War in Nicaragua*, were on their way to the South.[11]

The War in Nicaragua has been a chief source of historians, both those of the United States and Latin-American countries, for the battles fought by the American filibusters in their takeover of the country and those of the Allies in attempting to drive them out. In part this can be attributed to the sparseness of archival records maintained by the countries involved: subject to frequent revolutions, none of them had stable governments that preserved documents; and in part to the untrustworthiness of the communiqués of their commanders, who inclined more to rodomontade than to factual reporting of what happened.

Walker, choosing as his model Caesar's *Commentaries* and writing in the third person, was able to maintain remarkable objectivity. Quantities of information are available about the war in newspaper reports of correspondents and travelers arriving in the United States from Nicaragua; the official *boletínes* of the Central American governments, reprinted in newspapers at Aspinwall and Panama as well as in New York, New Orleans, and San Francisco; the collection of letters and military records preserved by Fayssoux, now in the Latin-American Division of the Tulane University Library; and the personal experience accounts of Walker's followers. A weighing of this confusing evidence leads to an acceptance more often than not of Walker's account insofar as dates and number of troops engaged are considered, losses in the American forces—the casualties of his enemies are generally exaggerated—and the way each skirmish and battle was fought.*

Walker, however, is untrustworthy in his presentation of Latin-American politics and society. He held the belief that it was the mission of Anglo-Saxon people—"the pure white American race," as he expressed it—to dominate the inferior "mixed Hispano-Indian race" that existed in Mexico and Central America. He defended his invasions in these words: "Whenever barbarism and civilization, or two distinct forms of civilization, meet face to face, the result must be war."[12] Holding these views, Walker could not be expected to give a fair and true account of the people on whom he chose to war.

These large, abstract views, however, occupy only a small portion of the book. They appear chiefly in a chapter devoted to his administration as president of Nicaragua, in which he defended his land decrees and restoration of slavery and in a short postscript of a propagandistic nature in which he sought support for the new invasion he was projecting. On the whole, the volume is a straightforward narrative of events that stoically records defeats without the expression of regret and victories without ebullition. His prose is singularly free from the influences that might be assumed to

*The historian William O. Scroggs wrote of Walker's book: "The facts are recorded with scrupulous accuracy, and the greatest compliment that could be paid him on this score has come from hostile Central American historians, who while impugning his motives and condemning his acts accept his version of the events without question." Scroggs cited the two-volume history by Lorenzo Montúfar, *Walker en Centro-America* (Guatemala, 1887), saying that the author "usually accepts Walker's version in preference to that of his own countrymen." *Filibusters and Financiers*, p. 380.

have shaped it—the florid rhetoric of his native South and the prolixity of the two professions that he practiced—the law and journalism. On occasion it was marked by a dry wit that in a phrase characterized a person or a policy. Henry L. Kinney "had acquired that sort of knowledge and experience of human nature to be derived from the exercise of the mule trade"; the ineptness of the native armies was due to "an inveterate habit of catching a man and tying him up with a musket in his hand, to make a soldier of him"; England was wise in appointing merchants as consuls because "the sting of self-interest keeps the sentry from sleeping on his post." There was occasionally a gleam of humor, as in his comment on an enemy general who had tried to increase the ardor of his men by plying them with *aguardiente* before a skirmish in which they were routed: "The empty demijohns which were picked up on the road after the action looked like huge cannon-balls that had missed their mark." His reading was sometimes reflected in a classical, historical, or literary allusion. Juan Rafael Mora, banished from Costa Rica by a political rival, drew from him the Dantesque reference: "Let us pass Mora in exile, as Ugolino in hell, afar off and with silence"; and the failure of the South, as he saw it, to awaken to the danger of the antislavery movement drew a comparison to the Earl of Strafford, who "sleeps though the axe of the headsman is whetted for his execution."[13]

Walker's annual expeditions, which in each case had ended in failure, made the prospects gloomy for raising money to mount a fourth in 1860. While planning the expedition to sail on the *Philadelphia*, he had written Fayssoux that he did not intend to attempt an invasion with "a limited force or limited means." He now seemed to have lowered his sights. He reported to Fayssoux from Mobile on February 17 that he had met a Dr. William H. Rivers, a wealthy Montgomery resident who had asked how much he required to return to Nicaragua. "I told him $5,000 would put me there with as many men as I wished for my purposes," Walker wrote. When Walker reached New York to complete arrangements for publishing his book and to obtain support for his expedition, he informed Fayssoux that he had obtained the aid of Francis Morris, a wealthy merchant who had an interest in one of the steamship lines carrying mail between New York and San Francisco via Panama. Morris was unwilling to contribute money but promised to provide transportation for Walker's followers. "There will be no difficulty he thinks in sending men by tens or twenties to Aspinwall," Walker wrote Fayssoux, "and I count on being able to devise means for getting them from A. to San Juan del Norte." The uncertain payment Walker held out for this assistance was that if he were once again in power in Nicaragua he would have at his disposal the lucrative transit rights across the isthmus. By March 12 Walker had completed arrangements for sending small groups to Aspinwall, to sail as prospective farmers and laborers intending to settle in the region. "If matters prosper we may get more hereafter," he wrote Fayssoux. "As for myself I do not disdain small beginnings."[14]

From Walker's letters to Fayssoux it is clear that he met with little enthusiasm for his Nicaraguan project. Aside from his own repeated failures, one reason was that the eyes of adventurers throughout the country were again on Mexico. Since 1858 civil war had raged there between the conservatives, led by Miguel Miramón, and the liberals, led by Benito Juárez. President Buchanan, in his message to Congress in 1859, had supported the Juárez party and asked for authority to send troops into the country to redress wrongs done American nationals, to obtain "indemnity for the past and security for the future." Congress had refused to act on the recommendation and so, the *New York Herald* said regarding the chaotic conditions across the border, the people were preparing to act. "In the West," the editorial continued, "in Cincinnati and St. Louis and Memphis, in the East, in Boston and Providence and New York, Philadelphia, Baltimore and Washington, and in the South, in New Orleans and Texas, preparations for migration are going on." There were "men of money and men of muscle" in the movement, and the only barrier between "these hardy pursuers of fame and fortune, and the rich placers and genial plains of Sonora and Chihuahua" was a boundary line "drawn with red ink on a map stowed away in some dusty pigeonhole of the State Department."[15]

Two of Walker's chief lieutenants, S. A. Lockridge and Charles F. Henningsen, had deserted his Nicaraguan cause in 1859 to involve themselves in intrigues to enter Mexico. Lockridge's defection had caused Walker no pain, but he had alluded bitterly to

Henningsen's in letters to Fayssoux. Henningsen never set himself up as a leader of a military force to enter Mexico, but Lockridge was one of the prime movers in the establishment of the Arizona Pioneer Emigrant Association which, according to newspaper reports, had recruited 600 men to establish themselves as miners and farmers in northern Mexico.

The most widespread campaign against the lands of Mexico, however, was being carried on by a secret organization, the Knights of the Golden Circle, established in 1854 with the grandiose aim of setting up a slave empire encompassing a great circle with Havana as a center and with a radius of 1,200 miles. It would take in the southern regions of the United States, all of Mexico and Central America, the northern portions of South America, and the islands of the West Indies. The promulgator of this fantastic scheme was George W. L. Bickley, a versatile man who was a novelist, historian, and doctor of eclectic medicine. Fluent in an inflated prose style suitable for the grandeur of his conception, he had over the years issued pamphlets and proclamations but had been unable to attract many followers until the fall of 1859 when he traveled over the South appealing for recruits to join him in going to Mexico to extend the area of slavery. "The Knights of the Golden Circle opens for you new fields of industry and enterprise," he declared in a proclamation calling for men to form local chapters, "castles" as he called them, of his organization for the invasion of Mexico. "It gives you the quarry from which to hew out the statue of your fortunes. . . . It tells you that your flag is glorious, and that you can and should keep it so; that the land is inviting and pleasant to look at; that there is fortune, fame, wealth, and glory for you."

Bickley's gospel was welcome to the ears of Southerners, and newspapers everywhere in the first months of 1860 enthusiastically supported the movement. Appealing for funds in a proclamation, Bickley listed agents and banks in more than a dozen cities that would accept donations, and by March hundreds of men on horseback and in wagons were entering Texas, where Governor Sam Houston was known to be eager to invade Mexico and where local "castles" had been formed in many towns. So numerous were they that Major General D. E. Twiggs, commander of the U.S. Army Department of Texas, issued a general order directing post commanders to scrutinize armed parties passing through the state professedly as emigrants and to arrest those discovered to be organized for any unlawful projects.[16]

Bickley's apocalyptic vision of the Golden Circle was similar to that of Walker in his appeals to Southerners for support of his movement for the "regeneration" of Central America. "The true field for the extension of slavery is in tropical America," he had written; "there it finds the natural seat of its empire and thither it can spread if it will but make the effort. . . ."[17] It might be assumed, then, that Walker would have expressed an interest in the new expansionist enthusiasm coursing through the country, at least to the extent of seeing if he could make use of it, but he did not. His single-minded objective was Nicaragua, and in none of his plans unfolded to Fayssoux did he mention the movement to invade Mexico.

While Walker was here and there obtaining dribbling support for his expedition, developments in Central America offered a new approach for an invasion with considerable promise of success. The possibilities were opened to him when he returned to the South the second week in April from New York* and Fayssoux revealed that he had talked with a resident of Ruatán who had come to the United States seeking "emigrants" to help the English settlers resist the cession of the Bay Islands to Honduras. What had happened was that President Buchanan's diplomacy had settled the long dispute with England over the interpretation of the Clayton-Bulwer Treaty. The hostility of the United States to

*Shortly after reaching the city, Walker found that his book had offended S. A. Lockridge. Lockridge met Walker on the street and denounced it as being "false in almost every particular" insofar as it related to him and declared he would formally demand an apology at an early date. Through a second he sent a note to Walker asking if in his book he intended to charge him "with acting as other than a gentleman of honor and courage." Walker rejected the challenge to a duel. He dispatched a reply that though curt was nevertheless considered by Lockridge's second as adequate apology. "For your satisfaction," Walker wrote, "I freely say that in the work alluded to I did not intend to impugn the honor or courage of S. A. Lockridge. When I aim to make charges against the character of any man let me assure you it shall be in words not easily misunderstood." Correspondence in Callender I. Fayssoux Collection of William Walker Papers, Tulane University; *New Orleans True Delta*, Apr. 14, 1860.

England's claims to authority over Ruatán and the neighboring islands in the Bay of Honduras and to the Mosquito Coast had resulted in a change of British policy: to develop the commercial resources of Central America rather than to hold territory that in the view of the United States violated the treaty. This new policy was implemented in separate treaties England negotiated with Honduras and Nicaragua. The treaty with Honduras, signed on November 28, 1859, surrendered sovereignty of the Bay Islands to Honduras, the English inhabitants to be guaranteed freedom of religion and the rights to property they held. The treaty with Nicaragua, signed on January 28, 1860, gave sovereignty over the Mosquito Coast to Nicaragua, the Indians to be confined to a reservation and Greytown, or San Juan del Norte, to be declared a free port. Writing Fayssoux from New York on February 29, Walker had said he thought the settlement of the Mosquito question would assist his plans, but it was the treaty with Honduras that opened the way for his return to Nicaragua.

English inhabitants of Ruatán had petitioned Queen Victoria to disavow the treaty with Honduras, and some of them had laid plans to declare their independence if it were ratified. It was to obtain Walker's aid in this independence movement that the Ruatán agent had interviewed Fayssoux in March. The plan was for Americans to go in small parties to the island by fruit ships sailing from New Orleans and assemble there by May 28, the day set for the transfer to Honduras. Walker dispatched a small party under the command of one of his Nicaraguan army officers, Captain J. S. West, to the island on April 29. West carried a letter to the leaders of the independence movement from Walker advising them on how they should proceed. More filibusters followed on two schooners that Walker chartered and as regular passengers on fruit vessels. West reported to Walker he found affairs at Ruatán in a mixed state. Negro inhabitants feared that the Americans intended to take possession of the islands and make slaves of them, public officials regarded them as filibusters and therefore dangerous characters, and there was no consensus on a course to follow among those favoring independence. What was needed, West wrote Walker, was a leader who would be supplied only if he were on the scene.[18]

Designating Fayssoux his agent with instructions to continue to recruit men and to obtain additional supplies, Walker sailed with a small band on the schooner *John A. Taylor* for Ruatán. He landed June 16 at Port McDonald, where his first contingents of liberators had gathered, and found, he wrote Fayssoux, matters in a "critical condition." One of his chartered vessels, the *Clifton*, had sailed for New Orleans to pick up men and cargo to be sent out by Fayssoux, but another, the *Toucey*, which had left the United States earlier, had not arrived. He was disturbed because the English at Belize had become suspicious over the number of men arriving there from New Orleans and proceeding immediately to Ruatán and because Governor Price had gone to the island with a body of troops two days before. Walker feared that his connection with the independence movement had been betrayed to authorities. The governor had returned to Belize, but the people of the island were "paralyzed" by the presence of the soldiers and the spirit of revolt had evaporated.

The *Toucey* fortunately arrived on the 17th, but Walker, considering it imprudent to remain at Ruatán in view of the watchfulness of the British, put all his men on board the *Taylor* and sailed for the island of Cozumel off the coast of Yucatán. He landed there on June 23 and sent the *Taylor* back to New Orleans for more men and supplies. By this time he had decided to abandon the effort of cooperating with the Ruatán rebels and using the island as a base for further operations. Instead, he would sail on the *Taylor* direct to Nicaragua to invade the interior, as Colonel Anderson had done in 1857, by going up the Colorado River in small boats. Captain Leonard S. Lombard, commander of the *Taylor*, had agreed to transport the expedition to Nicaragua, Walker wrote Fayssoux.

Because of the difficulty of keeping in communication with his agents and the need for secrecy in his movements, Walker was unable for more than a month to gather his forces in one place. The camp at Cozumel was no place to stay longer than necessary while awaiting Captain Lombard's arrival with recruits from New Orleans. The point at which the party landed was isolated enough for Walker's purposes, but only rough huts could be constructed to shelter the men and no provisions were to be had. Accordingly, when his chartered schooner, the *Dew Drop*, arrived with a squad of men on June 26, Walker embarked all his force on the vessel and cruised about the Bay of Honduras, putting in occasionally at island ports to obtain water and supplies. He returned to Cozumel on July 8 and waited there a week until the *Taylor* arrived from New Orleans. Walker dispatched Captain Lombard to Ruatán to load on board men and supplies that had been sent out on the *Clifton* from New Orleans ahead of the *Taylor* and set a rendezvous with him for July 20 off Guanaja, one of the Bay Islands. Walker wrote Fayssoux on July 14 from the *Dew Drop* outlining his plans: with the two schooners he would be able to sail to Nicaragua and land at or near the mouth of the Colorado and ascend the stream to the San Juan River in five whaleboats he had bought. "With the men on the *Clifton* I shall have the requisite number for all purposes," he said. "The resources now at my command make me confident of success."

On the day that Walker wrote Fayssoux so confidently of his expectations the *Clifton* arrived at Belize with reinforcements, twenty-four men under the command of Colonel A. F. Rudler and Captain William B. Newby. Cargo directed to Belize was unloaded, but the ship was not permitted to continue on to Ruatán when customs inspectors discovered that boxes manifested for the island as merchandise contained guns and ammunition. The men, however, were not arrested and on the 19th sailed on a chartered schooner to Port McDonald. When the *Taylor* failed to make the rendezvous at Guanaja on the 20th, Walker on board the *Dew Drop* became worried but remained at the appointed place until the 24th, when he stood in at Ruatán to obtain news. It was bad: Captain Lombard was still at Port McDonald awaiting the arrival of the *Clifton*, and an English warship, the *Icarus*, was reported searching the seas for the American expedition. Walker sent a message to Lombard to meet him off the northwest point of Ruatán as soon as possible, but it was not until the 27th that the forces were at last united.

The transfer of Ruatán and the other Bay Islands had been scheduled for May 28, but it had been postponed by President Santos Guardiola, whom the American falange had defeated at Virgin Bay in 1855, in his fright over the expected invasion by the filibusters. Now notices were posted on the island that the transfer would take place on July 30, but the day passed without this being done. Walker expressed the fear in a letter to Fayssoux that when

Guardiola accepted the islands the revolutionary plotters would be killed and said that he remained in the vicinity several days more to come to their aid when the Honduran flag was finally raised. But four more days passed and the transfer did not take place. Walker's voyage to Nicaragua had now been so long delayed that he had almost exhausted his provisions, and he decided he would have to alter his plans. "Always I have striven to take the course which would leave me as little as possible at the caprice of fortune," he wrote Fayssoux; "but 'man proposes, God disposes,' and I must certainly admit that in some respects we seem to have been forced by events entirely beyond our own control."[19]

His next move was inexplicable except from this view, for it was a diversion from his immediate goal of reaching Nicaragua. Acting with the unexpectedness that had often marked his movements in the past, he embarked all his force—about 110 men—aboard the *Taylor* on August 4 and set his course southeast to attack the town of Trujillo on the mainland. The harbor was reached in the late afternoon and about two o'clock the next morning the disembarkation began and all were ashore before daylight. One party attacked the fort and a second marched against the town. It was an easy victory. The fort was garrisoned by only seventy-five men and the citizens of the town, armed only with machetes and ancient muskets, could offer little resistance.

In establishing himself at Trujillo, Walker expected to be supported by the English at Ruatán resisting the return of the Bay Islands to Honduras and the Liberals of the country whom he hoped to rally under the banner of the former president, Trinidad Cabañas, in exile in El Salvador. He also expected aid from the United States, sending the *Dew Drop* and the *Taylor* to New Orleans with messages to Fayssoux to send additional men and supplies. "You know pretty well what our wants are, and I know you will do all you can to supply them," he wrote, ending on this note of confidence: "We have got a position from which all the forces of Honduras cannot drive us. If we get more men and the supplies they require we will guide the destiny of Central America."[20]

Two weeks after Walker had fortified himself at Trujillo and declared the town a free port, the British warship *Icarus* arrived and her captain, Commander Norvell Salmon, demanded that Walker lay down his arms and embark on ships to leave the area, the arms to be forfeited to Honduras as security against any further descents on the coast and the safety of the Americans and their private property to be guaranteed by the British flag until their departure. Walker's reply was conciliatory. He defended briefly his waging war against Honduras. It was due entirely, he said, "to the engagements which I consider I had in honor contracted with people desirous of living in Central America under the ancient laws and customs of the realm, claiming with them common interests under the institutions derived from the code of Alfred." He did not think it wrong to assist these Englishmen. He ended by saying that he deemed it no dishonor to lay down his arms to an officer of the British crown but asked for particulars about how the surrender would be carried out.

Salmon sent an officer with a note at five o'clock saying pacifically he was aware that in asking Walker to surrender he opened himself to rebuke from his government, but nevertheless to prevent the effusion of more blood he had assumed the responsibility of doing so. He replied dryly to Walker's explanation of the war against Honduras: "The supreme government of Honduras in a proclamation received by me this morning does not appear to wish the code of Alfred introduced in the manner that you propose, and the local government and inhabitants of Trujillo appear to be of the same opinion, judging from the numerous applications made to me for protection and assistance. . . ." As to Walker's request for details of embarkation, he must take care of the costs himself and there were two schooners in the harbor whose captains were willing to treat with him. Walker requested the officer from the *Icarus* to return at ten o'clock in the morning for an answer. It was one that Salmon was not to receive, for secretly in the night Walker evacuated the fort, destroying the guns and ammunition his men could not carry and leaving behind the wounded and the ill.

Walker's decision to escape from the fort was an indication that though Salmon offered him safety his own destiny required him to pursue his own goal in the face of whatever adversity befell him. He had written in *The War in Nicaragua*: "He is but a blind reader of the past who has not learned that Providence fits its agents for great designs by trials, and sufferings, and persecutions." He would not give up now although he had only eighty or so men with him when he struck out eastward along the coast, leaving behind him a hostile British warship and native troops sent to Trujillo by President Guardiola.

Two of those who accompanied him in this flight—Major Thomas Dolan, a veteran of the Nicaraguan campaigns, and Captain J. S. West, his advance agent sent to Ruatán early in May—said that his intention was to proceed to the mouth of the Roman River and somehow sail from there to Swan Island, where he could open communications with his friends at Ruatán and where supporters from the United States could be directed. Another survivor, Walter Stanley, recalled that Walker expected to form a union with forces assembled by the exiled Cabañas in El Salvador. Whatever Walker's hopes for gaining the initiative in the future, he was now concerned only with evading the enemy at his back. When he and his force reached the Roman River a few miles east of Trujillo late in the night, they had no way of crossing and began a march upstream to a place where they might find it fordable. Two days later, while camped at a place called Cotton Tree 30 miles inland, they were surprised by a company of about 100 Honduran soldiers. They grabbed up their Minié rifles and under their accurate counterfire the attackers fled. His only casualties were one man killed and five slightly injured, including Walker himself, who was hit in the face by a bullet that caused only a flesh wound.

Crossing the Roman River after this skirmish, the fleeing filibusters reached an abandoned camp once used by mahogany cutters. Here they were received in a friendly fashion by Carib Indians, but they remained only one day before pressing on to a small stream east of the Roman River called the Black River in newspaper reports. They had been camped there six days near a trading post operated by an Englishman about 3 miles from the coast when, on the morning of September 3, two boats from the *Icarus* loaded with about forty men arrived and Salmon and General Mariano Álvarez, commander of the Honduran force, stepped ashore.[21]

Salmon, "a burly, bluff young British officer of a very pompous, authoritative manner," according to a newspaper report, informed Walker that the *Icarus* and another vessel with 250 Honduran soldiers aboard were anchored at the mouth of the river and demanded that he surrender. "General Walker, with characteristic coolness and dignity, contrasting strongly with the pompous assurance of the British officer," the report continued, "asked whether this demand was made by Captain Salmon as a British officer, and whether if he surrendered it would be to the British authorities." Assured that this was the case, Walker agreed to lay down his arms.

Walker and his second in command, Colonel A. F. Rudler, were sent aboard the *Icarus* that night in manacles to be joined next morning by the remainder of his band. The *Icarus* reached Trujillo on the evening of the fourth, but the Americans and their leaders were not landed until the next day. Walker's followers under protection of the British flag were marched before the excited townspeople to prison, but Walker and Rudler were turned over to Honduran authorities, who incarcerated them in the fort they had seized a few weeks before.

A correspondent for the *New York Herald* was permitted to interview Walker before his removal from the *Icarus*. He found the Americans "all in bad health and as filthy as possible" and Walker angry at the betrayal by Salmon. Walker turned over to the reporter his correspondence on August 21 with Salmon and dictated a protest against Salmon's surrendering him and Rudler to Honduras. Dated September 5, it said: "I hereby protest, before the civilized world, that when I surrendered to the captain of Her Majesty's steamer *Icarus*, that officer expressly received my sword and pistol, as well as the arms of Colonel Rudler, and the surrender was expressly and in so many words to him, as the representative of Her Britannic Majesty." The correspondent detected that Governor Price of Belize was not happy about the situation. He was told, he wrote, that the British occupation of Ruatán would be prolonged six months, when the Hondurans must "skin their own varmints," that is, take care of themselves.

Shortly after his confinement in heavy irons at the fort, Walker sent for a priest, his only visitor during the six days that followed before he was tried, on September 11, by a court martial. He was informed of the verdict that night, that he would be shot by a firing squad the next morning. Rudler was sentenced, at the intervention of Salmon it was said, to only four years' imprisonment. At eight o'clock next day, guarded by a detachment of soldiers, Walker was marched out of the prison between two priests to the place of execution, followed by an excited crowd of Hondurans eager to see the end of the ogre from the north. A man who in his lifetime had seldom displayed emotion in victory or defeat, Walker, it was reported, walked erect and composed with uplifted crucifix to meet the death that with his rigorous sense of justice he had not quailed at in pronouncing for others. He received the last rites of the church from the priests and then waited motionless while a file of soldiers lined up before him, raised their rifles, and fired a single volley. A second squad fired another volley at the body, and then a soldier gave him the *coup de grâce* with a musket shot in the head that destroyed his features. The Catholic priests and some Americans at Trujillo obtained the body, which was buried with Christian rites in the Campo Santo.[22]

The news of Walker's death was received in the United States not with the outrage it would have provoked two or three years before but with sober and generally adverse appraisals of his career and a feeling of relief that it was ended. Popular support of his latest expeditions had steadily dwindled as they became recognized more and more to be the impossible projects of a fanatic that ended always in disaster for his followers. The attention of the people, moreover, was occupied with the coming election, which most felt would determine if the nation would remain one and indivisible.

Even in the South, where Walker had almost always been looked upon as a hero, there were few cries for revenge against Honduras or for war against England, whose representative had given him over to his enemies. A home-town paper, the *Republican Banner*, said of him: "There are thousands in this country who will hear of his death with regret,—as that of a man who had qualities and capacities entitling him to a better fate. Throughout his career he has shown a degree of steady courage, of unflinching tenacity of purpose under the most disheartening reverses, which would have earned for him a high position if they had been used in subordination to law and in harmony with the public good." The *New Orleans Commercial Bulletin*, in the past sympathetic to his cause, wrote while his followers were still prisoners at Trujillo:

"The mad and unwarrantable enterprise of the great filibuster has ended in disaster and defeat. Another band of brave, but recklessly impulsive, young Americans have, it is most probable, by this time met with the fate of their predecessors in Central America."[23]

In New York, where Walker was best known in the North and drew much of his support, the verdict was more adverse, although there was a grudging respect for the man in the condemnation of him. The *Times* editorial writer said of him when the report of his capture reached the city: "The most persistent enemy of Walker has found no trace of cowardice in his perverted character. He is merely a restless, reckless, ambitious man, devoid of all skill or judgment in the profession of arms, which he embraced without any preparation, and prosecuted with a most inhuman disregard of life and social order and happiness. . . . There is no reason . . . to believe that he will make any appeal to the sympathies of his countrymen; and there is every reason to believe that were any such appeal made, it would meet with no response save from that mad and wayward mob from which he has been accustomed to recruit his bands. The judgment of the country cannot be otherwise than that he has earned the penalty he is to suffer." *Harper's Weekly* summed up his career: "Walker was undoubtedly a mischievous man, better out of the world than in it. He never displayed any constructive ability; his energies were wholly destructive. He was brave, persevering, and energetic; but he had little or no foresight, no compunctions of honor or conscience, and not a spark of human pity in his breast. His works, from first to last, have been injurious rather than beneficial to the world."[24]

Many in the fall of 1860 felt that the issue of filibusterism agitating the country for more than a decade had been "laid in the grave of William Walker." There were few, like the *New York Herald*, that saw any future in it. In this paper's view, filibusterism at midcentury had appeared in two phases—the movement to liberate Cuba and annex the island and the movement of Walker in Central America. An editorial said that the first phase opened when Narciso López fled from the island in 1848 and mounted his two unsuccessful expeditions in 1850 and 1851 and ended when the more formidable expedition of General John A. Quitman was given up in 1854.

"The disbanding of the Quitman organization left the active

elements of filibusterism without a field," the newspaper said, "and prepared the way for Walker, who came forward in 1855 as a leader." But Walker, the paper continued, had neither the genius nor the wisdom to make the most of his opportunities. "The strong native party in the country that had at first accepted him fell away from him," the article said. "The monied interests here that had supported him tired of his mistakes and left him. The popular element that followed him felt the effects of the errors, and rapidly dwindled down to a small band of adventurous and brave spirits, with nothing to lose and everything to gain and the government found him, thus abandoned, an easy object to deal with." The paper saw a third phase of filibusterism in the making, one that with the emergence of a new leader of a more statesmanlike character than Walker would take advantage of the increasing weakness of the strife-torn nations to the south—Mexico, Central America, South America.[25]

There was to be no revival of filibusterism. When the antislavery party of the North elected Abraham Lincoln president, the secession movement in the South was translated from talk into action. Within a few months the energy of the nation that for more than a decade had populated the West, built railroads, developed manufacturing, and found an outlet in adventures abroad was concentrated in the struggle between union and disunion.

EPILOGUE

The Later History of Filibusterism

The filibusters of the 1850s were fallible agents of the force that since the founding of the nation had caused it to take a course of ever-expanding its borders. The impulse was manifested when leaders in the Revolution envisioned more than the independence of the thirteen colonies, John Adams declaring that Canada too "must be ours"; when settlers surged westward up the streams and through the mountain gaps beyond the Alleghenies; when Thomas Jefferson, doubting his constitutional authority, nevertheless bought Louisiana; when in the War of 1812 wresting Canada from England and Florida from Spain, her ally, stirred the war hawks as much as the freedom of the seas cited by President Madison in his war message; when first West Florida and then East Florida and Texas, as nature intended they should be, were annexed; when President Polk asserted American claims to the Northwest Territory and obtained New Mexico and California as the spoils of an aggressive war against Mexico, thus fulfilling the Divine Plan that the nation should reach from ocean to ocean. Now in the 1850s, as Senator Stephen A. Douglas declared, "the laws of progress which have raised us from a mere handful to a mighty nation" should continue to govern America's actions and compel the country to follow the course of its destiny southward.[1]

The rationale of expansionism underwent several permutations over the years. It encompassed belief in the American mission to extend the practice of government by free men to other places; in the geographical imperative that insisted on establishing natural boundaries of mountains or rivers though which when reached were not considered final but instead looked to an ever-widening perimeter; in the justice of acquiring land and resources by the people best qualified to utilize and develop them; in the right of security in attaching adjoining regions that might be used as bases for attack by other countries; and in the doctrine of natural development that a nation, like an organism, must either grow or die.[2]

But though these abstract forces can be cited to elucidate national expansionism, they are of little help in understanding the filibusters, whose motivations were personal. The leaders might profess goals of freeing the people of neighboring lands from tyrannical or inept rulers and of introducing the American way of government, but one and all they sought glory for themselves. Their followers might include idealists, but mostly they were young men out for adventure or down-and-outers attracted by promises of regular army pay and free land to be theirs after a brief period of fighting. Their financial backers were businessmen willing to wager a few dollars for big stakes when they bought at a discount the bonds of the proposed new republic or supplied funds for fitting out expeditions in exchange for securing commercial monopolies. Their political support came largely from Southern politicians seeking to enlarge the area of slavery. Filibusterism, then, was often not motivated by high idealism and was not necessarily the product of historical forces.

The daring of the filibusters provokes a certain admiration, as the struggle of men against great odds always does. It requires a valor not common for a handful of men to embark on the seas in leaky sailing vessels with the intention of conquering a country. The enterprises, however, were not so mad as they appear, for the governments attacked were weak, their people poor and oppressed and ready to accept a leader who could offer them security. In Cuba the misrule of Spain had caused widespread discontent, so that there were many eager to join any movement to cast off their fetters, and in Mexico and Central America there were seldom central authorities to maintain order, one regime after another being toppled after brief spells of control, often over only a small part of a country, by rebel leaders who could gather together an army of several hundred or a thousand men. Walker's falange in Nicaragua, never as cohesive and disciplined as he would have liked but reckless and aggressive in battle against reluctant native troops, was a force greater than its small numbers would indicate.

All the filibuster expeditions must be marked down as failures, but this is not to say they were not influential. They did have effects, and important ones. During the three presidential administrations following Polk's they were the principal concern of the nation's foreign policy makers. The diplomatic correspondence with Mexico, the Central American states, and Spain is filled with protests against filibuster enterprises and official disavowals of them by the government. They figure to a great extent also in the correspondence with England and France, because both countries hoped to obtain or hold territory to promote their commercial interests in Latin America and were fearful that the United States would seize and extend its authority over the region.

In this connection the filibuster movement has an important bearing on the development of the Monroe Doctrine. The doctrine declaring that the American continents would no longer be considered as subjects for future colonization by European powers had been seldom cited since its promulgation, but the surge of interest of the United States in Central America, due mainly to bringing California into the Union and the need for convenient communication with the west coast but also due in part to the efforts of the filibusters to extend American sway over the isthmus, made it assume a new significance in national policy. Appeals to the doctrine were not persuasive, however, to the objects of American aggression in view of the repeated military expeditions mounted against them. Mexico and the Central American states, frightened by the filibuster forays, appealed for aid from European powers, and Spain similarly sought to bind them in a treaty to protect her possession of Cuba.

The filibuster expeditions may have weakened the doctrine by arousing Latin-American animosities against it, but they may have strengthened it also. When Secretary of State John Middleton Clayton negotiated the treaty with Sir Henry Lytton Bulwer for joint protection of a transit across Central America, he was not dogmatically attached to the doctrine, but the popular excitement created by Walker resulted in its being cited more and more frequently in congressional debates on abrogation of this pact. Walker and his filibusters and the financiers who wanted the transit monopoly may not exactly be said to have forced Presidents Pierce and Buchanan to take firm stands against British encroachments in Central America, but they did; nor may the expeditions be said to have forced England to be conciliatory over the Central American question, but nevertheless she was. Maybe all that the filibusters accomplished was to exacerbate relations between the two countries, but England did give up her claims to the Mosquito Coast and did restore the Bay Islands to Honduras.

The influence of the filibusters was generally against the welfare of the states invaded even when collaborating with natives. By joining dissident rebel leaders, especially in Mexico and Nicaragua, they contributed to the misgovernment and division of countries already badly governed and divided, and their expeditions delayed Spanish reforms in the administration of Cuban affairs that kept the island in turmoil for years. Instead of bringing prosperity to Nicaragua, Walker destroyed what little existed by closing the transit route and preventing its reopening, which was one of the chief goals of the Buchanan administration. "Americanization," while it might have some attractions, quite clearly had drawbacks to Latin-American states. Filibusterism, which they thought was abetted by the U.S. government because it failed to stop expeditions, contributed to the fear of all Latin America of the growing nation to the north. The future expansion of the United States, the filibuster activities seemed to imply, contemplated hegemony over Latin America. And although the filibusters did not create the attitude that Latins and mestizos were inferior to the Anglo-Saxon Norte Americanos, they reinforced it. The "greaser" and the "gringo" have been words of disparagement ever since, standing in the way of mutual respect between the United States and her neighbors to the south.

Another effect of filibusterism was its influence on the widening division between the South and the North and the final decision of the South to secede. Territorial expansion to annex Cuba, the northern states of Mexico, the Caribbean islands, and ultimately Central America was supported by both Northerners and Southerners. It was, however, more widely and passionately taken up in the South, at first as a means of bringing new slave states into the Union to maintain control by the slavocracy over the national government and, should secession come about, to strengthen the confederacy by having a slave nation as an ally or even united with it. Abolitionists, opposed to slavery anywhere, and free soilers, willing to permit slavery to continue in the states where it existed but objecting to its extension into new states, were in consequence antiexpansionist. Thus in the North there were many who believed that expansion was merely a device to spread slavery, and many in the South who believed that it was essential to safeguard their interests. Filibusterism was one of the erosive elements in widening the chasm between the two sections.

Filibusterism was mainly a phenomenon of the 1850s when conditions were propitious for military expeditions against neighboring states. After the Civil War these conditions were lacking. The war, which ended slavery in the United States, destroyed the powerful forces in the South for extending the institution to adjoining countries. The Homestead Act, passed in 1862, opened up free lands to those who earlier would have been attracted by grants to be obtained in Cuba, Mexico, or Central America. The Pacific Railroad Act, passed the same year, authorized the Union Pacific and the Central Pacific to extend their lines east and west to be joined together in a transcontinental railway that reduced the importance of the isthmian transits at Panama, Nicaragua, and Tehuantepec. Capitalists who followed Cornelius Vanderbilt, George Law, Cornelius K. Garrison, and Charles Morgan had an outlet for their piratical ambitions in the railroad-building boom that followed the war—the huge land grants and millions of dollars in low-interest government bonds given the builders overshadowed anything that had ever been offered by Latin-American nations—and in the industrialization of the country that led to the era of great trusts and monopolies.

Moreover, the spirit of Manifest Destiny lost its popular appeal. Secretary of State William Seward, after the abolition of slavery, was eager to carry on the expansionist movement, predicting in 1868 that "in thirty years the city of Mexico will be the capital of the United States," but his projects found scant favor among the people. He grasped the opportunity of purchasing Alaska, but there was strong opposition to "Seward's Folly." When a reciprocity treaty with Hawaii was being considered in 1867, Seward would have preferred annexation, but did not press the matter because he saw that doing so would be useless. Two years later during a civil war in Santo Domingo, President Buenaventura Baez asked to be taken under the protection of the United States to save his government, but a resolution providing for annexation that Seward sought from Congress did not pass. Subsequently, to obtain a naval station in the West Indies, he completed a treaty with Denmark for transfer of the Danish West Indies to the United States, but the Senate was reluctant even to consider it and the Committee on Foreign Relations unanimously turned in an unfavorable report. Other regions also attracted his acquisitive attention and led him to explore the possibility of purchasing them—Cuba, Puerto Rico, Greenland, and Iceland—but to no avail.[3]

Nor did filibusterism and Manifest Destiny make much headway during the administrations of Ulysses S. Grant although, as one historian has written, expansion projects "with opportunities for action, glory, profit, escape from humdrum problems of peace, found plenty of advocates in Congress and in the Cabinet." The chief check on this ebullition was the secretary of state, Hamilton Fish. Cautious and conservative, Fish opposed any adventurism and reined in Grant when he tended to get out of hand after listening to advisers urging this or that expansionist project.

Throughout the Grant administrations Cuba was a continuing problem because of a revolution that broke out in 1868 and that was carried on for ten years by insurgents on the island aided by exiles in the United States. In the 1850s hundreds, perhaps thousands, of Americans would have embarked on ships to help secure the island's independence, but in the 1870s, though there was widespread support for the insurgents, the few expeditions planned in this country were confined mainly to small bands of Cubans organized by juntas in New York, Philadelphia, and other cities. Fish had expressed his concern over prospective expeditions in his instructions to the American minister to Spain, Daniel Sickles, in June 1869. It was no easy task, he wrote, "to restrain our citizens . . . and to repress the spirit of adventure and enterprise" when "the cry was in favor of liberty, emancipation, and self-government." His fears were groundless, for the times were different from those of the 1850s. The expeditions never materialized, and the chief aid sought for the Cubans in Congress and throughout the country was for recognition of the insurgents as belligerents, which would help them obtain arms. Fish had denounced the Ostend Manifesto as a policy "of the pirate and the bandit," and he doubted the ability of the Cubans, a conglomerate of Indian, Negro, and Spanish blood, to govern themselves. His belief that recognition of belligerency could be justified only when the insurgents demonstrated that they had a de facto government prevailed with the President.[4]

Not until 1895 when Cubans seeking independence once more revolted against Spain did popular enthusiasm for Manifest Destiny again arise. It might have been a source of wry satisfaction to John L. O'Sullivan, who died in New York on March 24, a month after the *grito* of revolution had been issued on the island. Then eighty-one years old, he was almost forgotten, receiving only brief obituaries in the *Times* and *Tribune*, which did not mention his advocacy of Manifest Destiny in the mid-1840s or his efforts in the Polk and Pierce administrations to annex Cuba in the 1850s. He was identified only as an intimate and friend of Nathaniel Hawthorne and as a widely known scholar, and his role in the movement that he had helped to inspire by his pen and promote as an activist was ignored. Appointed minister to Portugal by Pierce, he had been retained in that post by Buchanan but because of his pro-Southern sentiments lost it under Lincoln. After his removal in 1863, he lived in Europe and did not return to the United States until 1881. But the slogan to which he had devoted much of his life, Manifest Destiny, was ironically being repeated in the same newspapers that reported his death and the news of the new revolution in Cuba.

As if in anticipation of the revolution that was to revive American concern about the status of the island, a long-time expansionist, Senator Henry Cabot Lodge of Massachusetts, had written for the March number of *Forum* magazine an article, "Our Blundering Foreign Policy." He pointed out that for "more than thirty years we have been so much absorbed with grave domestic questions that we have lost sight of those vast interests which lie just outside our borders." Lodge had in mind President Cleveland's opposition to upholding American interests in the Pacific by abandoning Samoa, where the United States had obtained a naval base in 1878, to the British and Germans, and withdrawing a treaty to annex Hawaii, which had been negotiated after an uprising, inspired by sugar planters, chiefly Americans, overthrew the autocratic Queen Liliuokalani.

"In the interests of our commerce and of our fullest development," Lodge wrote, "we should build the Nicaragua canal, and for the protection of that canal and for the sake of our commercial supremacy in the Pacific we should control the Hawaiian Islands and maintain our influence in Samoa. England has studded the West Indies with strong places which are a standing menace to our Atlantic seaboard. We should have among those islands at least one strong naval station, and when the Nicaragua canal is built, the island of Cuba . . . will become to us a necessity."

This was a declaration that might have come from almost any expansionist of the 1850s, but Lodge went beyond the Western Hemisphere to take in the earth. "Commerce follows the flag," he continued, "and we should build up a navy strong enough to give protection to Americans in every quarter of the globe." This statement was an indication that the concept of Manifest Destiny was undergoing a transformation. It was a change that had been commented upon almost two years before by Carl Schurz, journalist, Republican party leader, minister to Spain, and a leader in civil service reform, in an article in the October 1893 number of *Harper's New Monthly Magazine*. "The new 'manifest-destiny' precept means, in point of principle, not merely the incorporation in the United States of territory contiguous to our borders," Schurz wrote in connection with Samoa and the Hawaiian Islands, "but rather the acquisition of such territory, far and near, as may be useful in enlarging our commercial advantages, and in securing to our navy facilities desirable for the operations of a great naval power." He recognized the appeal of farspread territorial aggrandizement to those wishing to see their "country powerful and respected among the nations of the earth," but warned of the difficulties of bringing peoples of different race and language into the Union and the doubtful prospects of tropical people conducting public affairs according to American principles of self-government.

The doubts expressed by Schurz about the inability of some of the peoples of the earth to govern themselves reflected another shift in the philosophy justifying annexation of distant lands arising out of the evolutionary theories of Charles Darwin. This was a belief in the superiority of the Anglo-Saxon people, a popular expounder of which was the historian and lecturer John Fiske. As early as 1885 in an essay, "Manifest Destiny," appearing in *Harper's Magazine*, he described the superior character of Anglo-Saxon institutions and the growth of Anglo-Saxon influence in the world through the imperialists par excellence, the English people. He considered their rise an example of the Darwinian concept of the survival of the fittest. Fiske wrote of Americans and Englishmen that "the two great branches of the English race have the common mission of establishing throughout the larger part of the earth a higher civilization and more permanent political order than any that has gone before." In a few years this mission was to be popularized in the slogan "the white man's burden," cited to justify seizure by the United States of the Philippine Islands after the Spanish-American War and projects to establish other outposts in the Pacific.[5]

The 1895 Cuban insurrection, treated skeptically at first by the American press, before long came to dominate the newspapers as Spain, with increasing ruthlessness, sought to defeat the insurgent forces and punish their sympathizers among the island populace. The atrocities committed aroused a wave of sympathy in the United States for the cause of *Cuba libre*. Americans attended mass meetings urging aid for the insurrection, and the two chambers of Congress echoed with calls for intervention. As in the 1850s, there were thousands of men ready to take up arms, or so they avowed, to help the Cubans win their freedom, and by the spring of 1897 the American Volunteer Legion, organized a few months before, reported that it had companies drilling in more than twenty states of men pledged to start toward Cuba on twenty-four hours' notice.[6]

This popular enthusiasm was exaggerated by the Yellow Press, which was exploiting the horrors inflicted upon the Cuban people by Spain, the offenses against U.S. nationals on the island, and the arrests of their daring correspondents for violating the censorship in sending out their stories from the island, but nevertheless it was strong and widespread. No major filibuster expeditions of Americans comparable to those to Cuba or Walker to Nicaragua, however, were mounted. Filibusterism was actively carried on in the three years of the insurrection before the United States entered into a war against Spain, but it hardly deserved the name of the heroic endeavors of the 1850s. The Cuban junta, which had been carefully planning the insurrection for years, was concerned chiefly with getting guns, ammunition, and supplies to the guerrillas, who sought to bring Spain to terms not only by winning battles but by destroying the economy through burning sugar cane and refineries and blowing up railroads. The need in this war was not so much of bodies of men to be shipped out from U.S. ports, which in any case would have been difficult because of strict enforcement of the neutrality laws by President Cleveland, but for matériel to keep the guerrillas in action. The junta maintained a fleet of what were called filibuster boats, small sea-going tugs well known in the newspaper headlines—the *Three Friends*, the *Commodore*, the *Dauntless*, the *Competitor*—that left from the coasts of Florida and South Carolina with munitions to be unloaded at night on the island by small working parties of Cubans. Filibusterism, in the 1890s, was chiefly gun-running by American captains and crews hired by the junta, a trade in contraband. No leader emerged with a dream of glory of establishing a tropical empire at the head of a conquering force of Americans come to free a down-trodden people. Filibusterism so-called continued even after the Spanish-American War in the illegal commercial pursuit of gun-running to supply arms for the Latin-American revolutions that were endemic, but it was a shady enterprise no longer associated with the grandiose projects of the private enterprise of American imperialists of the 1850s.

Source Notes

PROLOGUE

The Prototypal Filibusters

1. Information about Miranda is drawn largely from William S. Robertson, *The Life of Miranda*, and Joseph F. Thorning, *Miranda*.

2. Charles R. King, ed., *The Life and Correspondence of Rufus King*, 2:650 ff.

3. Edwin Erle Sparks, "Diary and Letters of Henry Ingersoll, Prisoner at Carthegena, 1806–1809"; "General Miranda's Expedition."

4. *Annals of Congress*, 10th Cong., 2nd sess., pp. 488–91, 511, 896–98; *American State Papers, Foreign Relations*, 3:256–59. *Abridgment of the Debates of Congress*, 1798 to 1856, 4:95–96, 142–47.

5. Burr's life is treated in Matthew L. Davis, *Memoirs of Aaron Burr*; Nathan Schachner, *Aaron Burr*; and Samuel H. Wandell and Meade Minnigerode, *Aaron Burr*. The conspiracy is considered at length in Thomas P. Abernethy, *The Burr Conspiracy*, and Walter F. McCaleb, *The Aaron Burr Conspiracy and a New Light on Aaron Burr*. See also James R. Jacobs, *Tarnished Warrior*, and Dumas Malone, *Jefferson and His Time*, vol. 6.

6. Isaac J. Cox, *The West Florida Controversy, 1798–1813*; Julius W. Pratt, *Expansionists of 1812*.

7. Richard B. Morris, ed., *Encyclopedia of American History*, pp. 157–58.

8. See T. R. Fehrenbach, *Lone Star*; Mattie Austin Hatcher, *The Opening of Texas to Foreign Settlement, 1801–1821*; Pratt, *Expansionists of 1812*; Harris G. Warren, *The Sword Was Their Passport*.

9. Cited in Albert K. Weinberg, *Manifest Destiny*: John Adams, p. 17; Samuel Adams, p. 22; Horatio Gates, p. 23; John Quincy Adams, p. 40; James Madison, p. 48; *Nashville Clarion*, p. 62; John L. O'Sullivan, p. 107.

10. Julius W. Pratt, "The Origin of 'Manifest Destiny'" and "John L. O'Sullivan and Manifest Destiny."

11. Sir William Cragie, ed., *A Dictionary of American English on Historical Principles*, pp. 970–71; Milford J. Mathews, ed., *A Dictionary of Americanisms on Historical Principles*, pp. 604–5.

12. William Walker, *The War in Nicaragua*, p. 429; Charles W. Doubleday, *Reminiscences of the "Filibuster" War in Nicaragua*, pp. 62–63.

13. *New York Herald*, Feb. 10, 1852.

CHAPTER 1
The Whetted Appetite for Territory

1. James K. Polk, *The Diary of James K. Polk During His Presidency, 1845 to 1849*, 3:446.
2. Ibid., p. 469.
3. Quoted in Robert G. Caldwell, *The Lopéz Expeditions to Cuba, 1848–1851*, pp. 29–30.
4. Polk, *Diary*, 3:476–77; 480–81.
5. Ibid., pp. 485–89.
6. Julius W. Pratt, "John L. O'Sullivan and Manifest Destiny"; *New York Times*, Mar. 27, 1895; *New York Tribune*, Mar. 26, 1895.
7. Julian Hawthorne, *Hawthorne and His Wife*, 1:160.
8. James Buchanan Papers.
9. Sources for Beach's mission are W. R. Manning, ed., *Diplomatic Correspondence of the United States, Inter-American Affairs, 1831–1860* (hereafter cited as *Dipl. Corr.*), 8:906–7; Frederick Merk, *Manifest Destiny and Mission in American History*, pp. 132–37; Justin H. Smith, *The War with Mexico*, 2:11–14, 65, 331–32.
10. Polk, *Diary*, 2:341–42, 476–77; 3:22.
11. *Dipl. Corr.*, 7:195–96.
12. Polk, *Diary*, 2:477.
13. Quoted in Basil Rauch, *American Interest in Cuba, 1848–1855*, p. 60. See also Frederick Merk, *The Monroe Doctrine and American Expansionism, 1843–1849*, pp. 248–49.
14. Sierra's correspondence is given in *Dipl. Corr.*, 7:974–80, 1021, 1027–28, 1061–73, 1075–78, 1080–82.
15. Polk, *Diary*, 3:78–79.
16. For the message and the debate that followed, see *Congressional Globe*, 30th Cong., 1st sess., 1847–48, pp. 709–13.
17. Polk, *Diary*, 2:444–45.
18. *Dipl. Corr.*, 11:54–64.
19. John Quincy Adams, *Memoirs of John Quincy Adams*, 11:197.
20. Quoted in Philip S. Klein, *President James Buchanan*, p. 192.
21. *Dipl. Corr.*, 11:456–59.
22. Ibid., 8:1085.
23. Louis de Armond, "Justo Sierra O'Reilly and Yucatán-United States Relations, 1847–1848."
24. Ibid.; *Niles' Weekly Register*, Mar. 28, 1849, p. 205; Nov. 15, 1849, p. 19.
25. See also Nelson Reed, *The Caste War of Yucatán*, pp. 110–14; Edward S. Wallace, *Destiny and Glory*, pp. 31–32.
26. *Dipl. Corr.*, 8:1076.
27. Edward H. Thompson, "A Page of American History."
28. *Dipl. Corr.*, 9:42, 345.

CHAPTER 2
Plots That Failed to Hatch

1. James K. Polk, *The Diary of James K. Polk During His Presidency, 1845 to 1849*, 4:184.
2. Ibid., pp. 375–76.

3. Quoted in Robert G. Caldwell, *The López Expeditions to Cuba, 1848–1851*, pp. 37–38.

4. W. R. Manning, ed., *Diplomatic Correspondence of the United States, Inter-American Affairs, 1831–1860* (hereafter cited as *Dipl. Corr.*), 11:69–71.

5. Summarized in Philip S. Foner, *A History of Cuba and Its Relations with the United States*, 2:31–35.

6. May 31, 1856.

7. Mrs. Jefferson Davis, *Jefferson Davis, A Memoir by His Wife*, 1:412; Louis Schlesinger, "Personal Narrative of Louis Schlesinger, of Adventures in Cuba and Cueta."

8. *Dipl. Corr.*, 11:439–40.

9. "General López, the Cuban Patriot," *United States Magazine and Democratic Review*, Feb. 1850.

10. Details are from Caldwell, *López Expeditions*, pp. 46–48; Foner, *History of Cuba*, 2:24–26; Basil Rauch, *American Interest in Cuba, 1848–1855*, pp. 75–76.

11. Campbell to Buchanan, May 18, 1848, *Dipl. Corr.*, 11:439–40.

12. Foner, *History of Cuba*, 2:24; Rauch, *American Interest in Cuba*, pp. 75–76; Edward S. Wallace, *General William Jenkins Worth, Monterrey's Forgotten Hero*, p. 185.

13. *Dipl. Corr.*, 11:441–43.

14. The González manifesto was printed in 1853 in the plant of the *New Orleans Daily Delta*, published by Lawrence J. Sigur, a supporter of López.

15. Polk, *Diary*, 3:499–500.

16. Caldwell, *López Expeditions*, p. 49.

17. John F. H. Claiborne, *Life and Correspondence of John A. Quitman*, 2:53–55.

18. John C. Calhoun, "Correspondence of John C. Calhoun," pp. 1202–3.

19. Caldwell, *López Expeditions*, pp. 48–50; Foner, *History of Cuba*, 2:43–44; González, *Manifesto*, p. 7; Rauch, *American Interest in Cuba*, pp. 113–14.

20. "Cuba."

21. Campbell to Clayton, Aug. 28, 1849, *Dipl. Corr.*, 11:471–72.

22. Ibid., 71–72, 470.

23. *Sen. Exec. Docs.*, 31st Cong., 1st sess., No. 57.

24. Foner, *History of Cuba*, 2:47; Rauch, *American Interest in Cuba*, pp. 121–22.

25. *Dipl. Corr.*, 11:473; González, *Manifesto*, p. 9.

26. Caldwell, *López Expeditions*, p. 58; González, *Manifesto*, pp. 9–10.

27. Claiborne, *Quitman*, 2:56–58, 379 ff.

28. Quoted in Edmund Wilson, *Patriotic Gore*, p. 195.

29. Biographical details from Charles L. Dufour, *Gentle Tiger*.

30. The narrative of the Cárdenas expedition is based largely on Richardson Hardy, *The History and Adventures of the Cuban Expedition*, and J. C. Davis, *History of the Late Expedition to Cuba*.

CHAPTER 3
Defeat and Death in Cuba

1. *Sen. Exec. Docs.*, 31st Cong., 1st sess., No. 57.

2. W. R. Manning, ed., *Diplomatic Correspondence of the United States, Inter-American Affairs, 1831–1860* (hereafter cited as *Dipl. Corr.*), 11:79–80.

3. *Congressional Globe*, 31st Cong., 1st sess., 1849–50, pp. 1030–35, 1055.
4. *Dipl. Corr.*, 11:77 ff., 523 ff.
5. Robert G. Caldwell, *The López Expeditions to Cuba, 1848–1851*, pp. 78–79; John F. H. Claiborne, *Life and Correspondence of John A. Quitman*, 2:68; "The Late Cuba State Trials."
6. *Dipl. Corr.*, 11:523.
7. Claiborne, *Quitman*, 2:63–76.
8. *Dipl. Corr.*, 11:496.
9. Claiborne, *Quitman*, 2:69–71.
10. Louis Schlesinger, "Personal Narrative of Louis Schlesinger, of Adventures in Cuba and Cueta."
11. His report was published in *Boletín del Archivo Nacional*, Havana, vol. 5, Jan. and Apr. 1906. A translation by L. M. Perez was published in *Publications of the Southern History Association*, Nov. 1906.
12. *New York Tribune*, Apr. 28, 1851.
13. The account of the Bahía Honda expedition is based largely on Schlesinger, "Personal Narrative." Though strongly biased in favor of López, Schlesinger seems to be reliable in his day-by-day account of events. Newspaper reports are so conflicting that it is difficult to obtain a clear account from them. The stories told to newspapers by survivors who returned to the United States in Sept. 1851 are useful records, as is Caldwell's *López Expeditions*.
14. The *New York Tribune* published the declaration in full on July 28, 1851.
15. Abstract of dispatches from General Concha to the Spanish minister of war, *Dipl. Corr.*, 11:606–8.

CHAPTER 4
Filibusters in the Campaign of 1852

1. *Sen. Exec. Docs.*, 32nd Cong., 1st sess., No. 1.
2. Robert G. Caldwell, *The López Expeditions to Cuba, 1848–1851*, pp. 114–16; Philip S. Foner, *A History of Cuba and Its Relations with the United States*, 2:61–62; Basil Rauch, *American Interest in Cuba, 1848–1855*, p. 161; Chester S. Urban, "New Orleans and the Cuban Question During the López Expeditions of 1849–1851"; *New York Tribune*, Aug. 26, Sept. 3, 8, 1851.
3. W. R. Manning, ed., *Diplomatic Correspondence of the United States, Inter-American Affairs, 1831–1860* (hereafter cited as *Dipl. Corr.*), 11:108–9, 602–4.
4. Both quoted in Rauch, *American Interest in Cuba*, pp. 162–63.
5. Urban, "New Orleans and the Cuban Question."
6. *Dipl. Corr.*, 11:609–10, 611, 620–22, 622–23, 623–25.
7. Ibid., 11:110, 611–12.
8. Ibid., 11:118–22, 124–28, 649–50.
9. Foner, *History of Cuba*, 2:66–67; Rauch, *American Interest in Cuba*, pp. 228–30.
10. *Dipl. Corr.*, 11:654–55, 661–62, 662–64.
11. Merle E. Curti, "Young America"; Rauch, *American Interest in Cuba*, pp. 218–21.
12. Curti, "Young America"; also his "George N. Saunders—American Patriot of the Fifties."
13. Stephen A. Douglas, *The Letters of Stephen A. Douglas*, pp. 215–16, 218–19.
14. Amos A. Ettinger, *The Mission to Spain of Pierre Soulé, 1853–1855*, pp. 101 ff.

15. Douglas, *Letters*, pp. 239–40, 246–47.
16. Quoted in Roy F. Nichols, *The Democratic Machine, 1850–1854*, p. 117.
17. John B. McMaster, *A History of the People of the United States from the Revolution to the Civil War*, 8:177; George Fort Milton, *The Eve of Conflict*, p. 92.
18. Ettinger, *Mission to Spain*, pp. 131–33.
19. Irving Katz, *August Belmont*, pp. 7–9, 18–19; Nichols, *Democratic Machine*, p. 162.
20. *Dipl. Corr.*, 11:135–37, 664–65.
21. *New York Times*, Oct. 20, 1852.
22. The complete history of the affair with official and private correspondence is given in the *New York Times* of Nov. 29, 1852. All citations except those otherwise indicated are from this account.
23. Foner, *History of Cuba*, 2:68–70; Rauch, *American Interest in Cuba*, p. 232.
24. *Dipl. Corr.*, 11:666–69.
25. Ibid., 11:137–41.
26. Ibid., 11:141, 670–71.
27. McMaster, *History of the People of the United States*, 8:181.
28. *Congressional Globe*, 32nd Cong., 2nd sess., 1852–53, pp. 12, 19, 139–40, 140–46, 199.
29. *Congressional Globe, Appendix*, 32nd Cong., 2nd sess., 1852–53, pp. 118–23.

CHAPTER 5
Franklin Pierce: Expansionist President

1. Roy F. Nichols, *Franklin Pierce*, pp. 227–30, 247–51; Allan Nevins, *Ordeal of the Union*, 2:45–51.
2. Ivor D. Spencer, *The Victor and the Spoils*, pp. 221–32.
3. Philip S. Klein, *President James Buchanan*, pp. 221–27.
4. Nevins, *Ordeal of the Union*, 2:59.
5. Amos A. Ettinger, *The Mission to Spain of Pierre Soulé, 1853–1855*, pp. 141–46.
6. Merle E. Curti, "George N. Sanders, American Patriot of the Fifties" and "Young America."
7. Buchanan to Pierce, July 29, 1853, and Buchanan to Harriet Lane, Aug. 4, 1853, *The Works of James Buchanan*, 9:31–33; Klein, *President James Buchanan*, p. 226; Edgcumb Pinchon, *Dan Sickles*, passim.
8. Irving Katz, *August Belmont*, p. 26.
9. *The Works of James Buchanan*, 7:493–99; Nichols, *Franklin Pierce*, pp. 357–58; Spencer, *The Victor and the Spoils*, p. 325.
10. Paul N. Garber, *The Gadsden Treaty*, pp. 74–82.
11. Ettinger, *Mission to Spain*, pp. 146–47; Nichols, *Franklin Pierce*, pp. 256, 262; Louis M. Sears, *John Slidell*, pp. 101–2.
12. Nevins, *Ordeal of the Union*, 2:59–61; Spencer, *The Victor and the Spoils*, pp. 233–39.
13. W. R. Manning, ed., *Diplomatic Correspondence of the United States, Inter-American Affairs, 1831–1860* (hereafter cited as *Dipl. Corr.*), 11:160–66.
14. John F. H. Claiborne, *Life and Correspondence of John A. Quitman*, 2:386–90.

15. Ibid., p. 195; Nichols, *Franklin Pierce*, p. 267; Basil Rauch, *American Interest in Cuba, 1848–1855*, pp. 262 ff.

16. Ettinger, *Mission to Spain*, pp. 167–77; Rauch, *American Interest in Cuba*, pp. 269–70; *New York Times*, Aug. 6, 1853.

17. Rauch, *American Interest in Cuba*, pp. 266, 273.

18. Ibid., p. 274.

19. Claiborne, *John A. Quitman*, 2:391–92.

20. Robertson to Marcy, Mar. 20, 1854, and Apr. 21, 1854, *Dipl. Corr.*, 11:748–49, 764–66.

21. Marcy to Davis, Mar. 15, 1854, *Dipl. Corr.*, 11:170–73.

22. *Congressional Globe*, 33rd Cong., 1st sess., 1853–54, pp. 1021–24, 1194, 1195 ff.

CHAPTER 6
Antic American Diplomacy

1. W. R. Manning, ed., *Diplomatic Correspondence of the United States, Inter-American Affairs, 1831–1860* (hereafter cited as *Dipl. Corr.*), 11:175–78.

2. Charles C. Tansill, *The United States and Santo Domingo, 1798–1873*, pp. 176–79; *New York Evening Post*, May 25, 1854.

3. Roy F. Nichols, *Franklin Pierce*, pp. 342–43.

4. Ibid., p. 343.

5. Quoted in Philip S. Foner, *A History of Cuba and Its Relations with the United States*, 2:86; Basil Rauch, *American Interest in Cuba, 1848–1855*, p. 286.

6. Foner, *History of Cuba*, 2:87.

7. Stephens to W. W. Burwell, May 7, 1854, Ulrich B. Phillips, "The Correspondence of Robert Toombs, Alexander H. Stephens, and Howell Cobb," 2:344.

8. John F. H. Claiborne, *Life and Correspondence of John A. Quitman*, 2: 196–200.

9. Foner, *History of Cuba*, 2:90; Rauch, *American Interest in Cuba*, p. 289.

10. *Congressional Globe*, 33rd Cong., 1st sess., 1853–54, p. 735; Amos A. Ettinger, *The Mission to Spain of Pierre Soulé, 1853–1855*, pp. 141–46.

11. *Congressional Globe*, 33rd Cong., 1st sess., 1853–54, p. 601; *Dipl. Corr.*, 11:168–70, 173–74.

12. *Dipl. Corr.*, 11:715 ff.

13. Ibid., 11:769–72.

14. Ibid., 11:798–99.

15. Buchanan to Marcy, July 21, 1854, *The Works of James Buchanan*, 9: 214–15.

16. *Dipl. Corr.*, 11:802–18.

17. Nichols, *Franklin Pierce*, pp. 353–54; *Congressional Globe*, 33rd Cong., 1st sess., 1853–54, pp. 2040, 2178.

18. *Dipl. Corr.*, 11:190–93, 193–94.

19. Louis M. Sears, *John Slidell*, pp. 11–12.

20. Pierce to Buchanan, July 27, 1853, and Buchanan to Pierce, July 29, 1853, *The Works of James Buchanan*, 9:30–31.

21. Nichols, *Franklin Pierce*, pp. 358–59; Pierce to Buchanan, Aug. 12, 1854, *The Works of James Buchanan*, 9:243.

22. Buchanan to Pierce, Sept. 1, 1854, *The Works of James Buchanan*, 9:251–53.

23. Ettinger, *Mission to Spain*, pp. 339–412; Philip S. Klein, *President James Buchanan*, pp. 239–41; Nichols, *Franklin Pierce*, pp. 366–71; *Dipl. Corr.*, 11: 824–26.
24. Mar. 7, 1855.
25. Oct. 31, 1854, *The Works of James Buchanan*, 9:267–68.
26. Quoted in Ettinger, *Mission to Spain*, p. 379.
27. *Dipl. Corr.*, 11:825–26.
28. Ibid., 11:196–201.
29. Ibid., 11:831.
30. Ettinger, *Mission to Spain*, pp. 412–48; H. Barrett Learned, "William Marcy," in Samuel F. Bemis, ed., *The American Secretaries of State and Their Diplomacy*, 6:205–8.
31. *Dipl. Corr.*, 11:832.

CHAPTER 7
Expeditions to Mexico

1. Ernest C. Shearer, "The Carvajal Disturbances"; Walter Prescott Webb, ed., *The Handbook of Texas*, 1:294.
2. Webb, *Handbook of Texas*, 1:288; *Diccionario Porrúa de Histórica, Biografía y Geográfica de México*, p. 297.
3. Justin H. Smith, "La República de Río Grande"; Webb, *Handbook of Texas*, 2:460.
4. Quoted in Smith, "La República."
5. Hubert Howe Bancroft, *History of Mexico*, 5:209, 214–15, 247, and *History of the North Mexican States and Texas*, 2:217–29; Justin H. Smith, *The War with Mexico*, 1:158, 165–66, 171, 174; 2:169–70, and "La República."
6. W. R. Manning, ed., *Diplomatic Correspondence of the United States, Inter-American Affairs, 1831–1860* (hereafter cited as *Dipl. Corr.*), 9:45–47.
7. *Sen. Exec. Docs.*, 32nd Cong., 1st sess., No. 1.
8. Smith, "La República."
9. *Dipl. Corr.*, 9:5; James Buchanan, *The Works of James Buchanan*, 8:192–95.
10. Shearer, "Carvajal Disturbances."
11. July 18, 1852, *Sen. Exec. Docs.*, 32nd Cong., 2nd sess., No. 1.
12. T. R. Fehrenbach, *Lone Star, a History of Texas and the Texans*, pp. 374–75, 500–2, 490–92; Webb, *Handbook of Texas*, 2:617–18.
13. Charles L. Dufour, *Gentle Tiger*, p. 64.
14. Shearer, "Carvajal Disturbances"; J. Fred Rippy, *The United States and Mexico*, pp. 89–91; *Dipl. Corr.*, 9:96, 414n; Dufour, *Gentle Tiger*, pp. 64–67; Bancroft, *History of Mexico*, 5:603–4, 612.
15. *Dipl. Corr.*, 9:426–32.
16. Quoted in Dufour, *Gentle Tiger*, pp. 66–67.
17. *Dipl. Corr.*, 9:555–62.
18. Biographical details about Kinney from Webb, *Handbook of Texas*, 1:962, and letters and reports in the William S. Thayer Papers, Library of Congress. An account of the fair appears in Shearer, "Carvajal Disturbances."
19. Shearer, "Carvajal Disturbances"; *Dipl. Corr.*, 9:557, 570–71.
20. Hubert Howe Bancroft, *History of California*, 6:225, 422–25.
21. *Atlantic Monthly*, Dec. 1859.
22. Bancroft, *History of California*, 6:582–84 and *History of the North Mexican States and Texas*, 2:673.

23. Bancroft, *History of California*, 6:584, and *History of the North Mexican States and Texas*, 2:672; Rufus K. Wyllys, *The French in Sonora, 1850–1854*, pp. 52–55; *Alta California*, Apr. 5, May 17, 1851; *Los Angeles Star*, May 26, 1851; J. Fred Rippy, *The United States and Mexico*, pp. 87, 100, 103, and "Anglo-American Filibusters and the Gadsden Treaty."

24. *Alta California*, Apr. 22, 1851; *Oregon Statesman*, Nov. 18, 1851.

25. Sylvester K. Stevens, *American Expansion in Hawaii, 1842–1898*, pp. 8–10, 50–53; Ralph S. Kuykendall, *The Hawaiian Kingdom, 1778–1854*, pp. 388–407; A. P. Nasatir, "Guillaume Patrice Dillon."

26. *Congressional Globe Appendix*, 32nd Cong., 1st sess., 1851–52, pp. 1083–84.

27. Andrew F. Rolle, "California Filibustering and the Hawaiian Kingdom"; Stevens, *American Expansion in Hawaii*, pp. 42–44; Kuykendall, *The Hawaiian Kingdom*, p. 408.

28. Frank Soulé, John H. Gihon, and James Nisbet, *The Annals of San Francisco*, pp. 174, 186, 748–53; James A. B. Scherer, *The First Forty-Niner*, passim; William Heath Davis, *Seventy-Five Years in California*, pp. 165–67, 233, 238.

29. Stevens, *American Expansion in Hawaii*, pp. 42–44; Rolle, "California Filibustering."

30. *Dipl. Corr.*, 6:264–68, 224–25, 272–74.

31. Horace Bell, *Reminiscences of a Ranger*, pp. 203–7.

32. *Dipl. Corr.*, 6:284–85, 274–75, 279–80, 821–22, 283–84, 286–87, 287–91; Bell, *Reminiscences*, p. 207.

33. The story of the French filibusters is told in Bancroft, *History of California*, 6:582–604, and *History of the North Mexican States and Texas*, 2:673–93; Helen B. Metcalf, "The California French Filibusters in Sonora"; and Wyllys, *The French in Sonora* and "The French of California and Sonora."

34. Soulé et al., *Annals*, p. 462.

35. *Dipl. Corr.*, 9:127.

CHAPTER 8
William Walker: Special Agent of Destiny

1. Quoted in Albert Z. Carr, *The World and William Walker*, p. 37.

2. Ibid., passim; William O. Scroggs, *Filibusters and Financiers*, pp. 9–17.

3. James Carson Jamison, *With Walker in Nicaragua*, p. 11; *El Nicaragüense*, Dec. 8, 1856; *Leslie's Weekly*, 4:27, June 1857.

4. Oscar T. Shuck, *Bench and Bar in California*, pp. 268–69.

5. James J. Roche, *By-Ways of War*, pp. 60–61.

6. Carr, *World and William Walker*, pp. 6–7; *New York Herald*, Jan. 30, 1856.

7. Hubert Howe Bancroft, *California Inter Pocula*, pp. 749–50; Carr, *World and William Walker*, pp. 57–59; Frank Soulé, John H. Gihon, and James Nisbet, *The Annals of San Francisco*, pp. 315–16; *Alta California*, Jan. 14, 1851; *San Francisco Herald*, July 2, Dec. 20, 1850, Jan. 14, 16, 1851.

8. Carr, *World and William Walker*, pp. 59–62; Scroggs, *Filibusters and Financiers*, pp. 15–16; Soulé et al. *Annals*, pp. 322–24; *Alta California*, Mar., 8, 9, 10, 12, 15, 1851; *San Francisco Herald*, Feb. 24, 27, Mar. 4, 5, 6, 7, 8, 10, 11, 13, 15, 28, Apr. 3, 10, 15, 1851.

9. Stephen J. Field, *Personal Reminiscences of Early Days in California with Other Sketches*, p. 70; Steve Addington, "Early Reminiscences of the Marysville

Bar," in H. S. Hoblitzell, *Early Historical Sketch of the City of Marysville and Yuba County*, p. 9.

10. William Walker, *The War in Nicaragua*, pp. 19–22; T. Robinson Warren, *Dust and Foam*, pp. 184, 211–14.

11. W. R. Manning, ed., *Diplomatic Correspondence of the United States, Inter-American Affairs, 1831–1860* (hereafter cited as *Dipl. Corr.*), 9:576–79; Hubert Howe Bancroft, *History of the North Mexican States and Texas*, 2:683, and *History of California*, 6:588–89; Helen B. Metcalf, "The California French Filibusters in Sonora"; Rufus K. Wyllys, *The French in Sonora, 1850–1854*, pp. 136–59, and "The French of California and Sonora."

12. *Dipl. Corr.*, 9:134–44.

13. Paul N. Garber, *The Gadsden Treaty*, pp. 74–82; Roy F. Nichols, *Franklin Pierce*, p. 266.

14. *Dipl. Corr.*, 9:607–9, 625–40, 649–50.

15. Ibid., 9:145–48 in memorandum dated Oct. 22, 1853.

16. Ibid., 9:667–69.

17. Ibid., 9:669–76.

18. Garber, *Gadsden Treaty*, pp. 109–45; James M. Callahan, *American Foreign Policy in Mexican Relations*, pp. 228–29; J. Fred Rippy, *The United States and Mexico*, pp. 148–67.

19. *Dipl. Corr.*, 9:601–3.

20. Walker, *War in Nicaragua*, p. 21.

21. Soulé et al., *Annals*, pp. 475–76.

22. Ethan Allen Hitchcock, *Fifty Years in Camp and Field*, pp. 399–403; *Alta California*, Oct. 1, 2, 3, 4, 10, 11, 18, 1853.

CHAPTER 9
The Conquest of Lower California

1. Hubert Howe Bancroft, *History of the North Mexican States and Texas*, 2:722–23; Frank Soulé, John H. Gihon, and James Nisbet, *The Annals of San Francisco*, pp. 478–79; William Walker, *The War in Nicaragua*, pp. 19–22; William V. Wells, *Walker's Expedition to Nicaragua*, pp. 24–28; *Alta California*, Dec. 8, 1853; *San Diego Herald*, Dec. 3, 1853.

2. *Alta California*, Dec. 12, 13, 1853.

3. Soulé et al., *Annals*, p. 472, 474; Wells, *Walker's Expedition*, pp. 30–32.

4. J. M. Reid, "The Ensenada," *National Magazine* 4 (June 3, 1854):502–5; reprinted by Arthur Woodward, ed., in *The Republic of Lower California, 1653–1854*, pp. 29, 37–43, 47–48.

5. Robert G. Cleland, "Bandini's Account of William Walker's Invasion of Lower California"; *Alta California*, Dec. 13, 27, 1853; Bancroft, *North Mexican States* 2:723; James M. Clarke, "Antonio Melendrez, Nemesis of William Walker in Baja California."

6. *Alta California*, Jan. 10, 24, 1854; Cleland, "Bandini's Account."

7. *Alta California*, Jan. 30, 1854; Wells, *Walker's Expedition*, pp. 28–30.

8. *San Diego Herald*, Jan. 28, 1854.

9. *Alta California*, Jan. 31, 1854.

10. *Alta California*, Feb. 4, 6, 1854.

11. *Alta California*, Feb. 22, Mar. 25, 1854.

12. *Alta California*, Mar. 15, 25, 1854; Cleland, "Bandini's Account"; Wells, *Walker's Expedition*, pp. 32–33; *San Diego Herald*, Mar. 11, 1854.

13. *Alta California*, Apr. 26, 1854, in a letter from the paper's correspondent in San Diego and in reprinted articles from the *Los Angeles Star*.

14. *Alta California*, May 16, 1854; Cleland, "Bandini's Account."
15. W. R. Manning, ed., *Diplomatic Correspondence of the United States, Inter-American Affairs, 1831–1860* (hereafter cited as *Dipl. Corr.*) 9:703–4, 708–710; *Alta California*, Mar. 15, Apr. 20, 1854.
16. Wool's correspondence with the French and Mexican consuls and with U.S. officials in San Francisco and his reports to the U.S. adjutant general and to the Department of War are given in *Sen. Exec. Docs.*, 33rd Cong., 2nd sess., Nos. 16 and 25. They were also published in the *New York Times*, Jan. 8, 1855.
17. Wool correspondence; *Alta California*, Mar. 22, 23, 24, 26, Apr. 4, 11, 1854; Soulé et al., *Annals*, pp. 524–25.
18. Wool correspondence; *Alta California*, Apr. 1, 2, 3, 11, 13, 14, 19, 25, 26, 27, 28, May 1, 1854; Soulé et al., *Annals*, pp. 531–35.
19. Wool correspondence; *Alta California*, May 16, 24, 26, 27, 28, 1854; Soulé et al., *Annals*, pp. 531–35; William O. Scroggs, *Filibusters and Financiers*, pp. 58–59.
20. Rufus K. Wyllys, *The French in Sonora, 1850–1854*, pp. 184–204; Bancroft, *North Mexican States*, 2:684–92; Helen B. Metcalf, "The California French Filibusters in Sonora."
21. *Alta California*, June 3, 1854.
22. David A. Williams, *David C. Broderick*, passim; Lately Thomas, *Between Two Empires*, pp. 56–61, 86–96, 104–7.
23. Scroggs, *Filibusters and Financiers*, pp. 68–70.
24. *Weekly Alta California*, Oct. 7, 21, 1854.
25. Walker, *War in Nicaragua*, pp. 24–25; Wells, *Walker's Expedition*, pp. 41–43.

CHAPTER 10
To Unite the Two Great Oceans

1. W. R. Manning, ed., *Diplomatic Correspondence of the United States, Inter-American Affairs, 1831–1860* (hereafter cited as *Dipl. Corr.*), 4:385–86; Gerstle Mack, *The Land Divided*, pp. 125–35; Mary W. Williams, *Anglo-American Isthmian Diplomacy, 1815–1915*, pp. 52–54.
2. Mack, *Land Divided*, pp. 137–42; John H. Kemble, *The Panama Route: 1848–1869*, pp. 7–25, 254.
3. Wheaton J. Lane, *Commodore Vanderbilt*, passim.
4. Mack, *Land Divided*, pp. 176–79; Ephraim G. Squier, *Nicaragua*, pp. 672–78.
5. Williams, *Anglo-American Isthmian Diplomacy*, pp. 14–18; Squier, *Wakina*, pp. 335–53; Peter F. Stout, *Nicaragua*, pp. 174–75; Dexter Perkins, *The Monroe Doctrine, 1826–1867*, pp. 18–20.
6. Squier, *Nicaragua*, p. 47.
7. Williams, *Anglo-American Isthmian Diplomacy*, pp. 46–51; Perkins, *Monroe Doctrine*, pp. 162–71.
8. *Dipl. Corr.*, 4:30–35, 289–90, 294–95, 375–86; Perkins, *Monroe Doctrine*, pp. 162–71, 212.
9. *Dipl. Corr.*, 4:36–51, 331–32, 346–47; Squier, *Nicaragua*, passim.
10. Williams, *Anglo-American Isthmian Diplomacy*, pp. 67–109, and "John Middleton Clayton," in Samuel Flagg Bemis, ed., *The American Secretaries of State and Their Diplomacy*, 6:44–70; Perkins, *Monroe Doctrine*, pp. 196–200, 201–15.

11. Lane, *Commodore Vanderbilt*, pp. 92–93; Squier, *Nicaragua*, pp. 645–46; Julius Froebel, *Seven Years' Travel in Central America, Northern Mexico, and the Far West of the United States*, pp. 20–24.

12. Lane, *Commodore Vanderbilt*, pp. 93–96; Kemble, *Panama Route*, pp. 60–61, 254.

13. Lane, *Commodore Vanderbilt*, pp. 98–100; Squier, *Nicaragua*, pp. 657–59, 689–90; *Sen. Exec. Docs.*, 34th Cong., 1st sess., No. 68.

14. Lane, *Commodore Vanderbilt*, pp. 104–10; J. O. Choules, *The Cruise of the Yacht North Star*, passim.

CHAPTER 11
The Year of the Filibusters: 1855

1. Quoted in Roy F. Nichols, *Franklin Pierce*, p. 374.

2. James Buchanan, *The Works of James Buchanan*, 9:248.

3. Wheaton J. Lane, *Commodore Vanderbilt*, pp. 100–101; Mary W. Williams, *Anglo-American Isthmian Diplomacy, 1815–1915*, pp. 120–21.

4. Elisha S. Capron, *History of California*, pp. 271–73.

5. Williams, *Anglo-American Isthmian Diplomacy*, pp. 171–73; Louis N. Feipel, "The Navy and Filibustering in the Fifties"; *House Exec. Docs.*, 33rd Cong., 1st sess., No. 126.

6. W. R. Manning, ed., *Diplomatic Correspondence of the United States, Inter-American Affairs, 1831–1860* (hereafter cited as *Dipl. Corr.*), 4:342, 348, 349, 358, 51–54.

7. Feipel, "The Navy and Filibustering"; *Sen. Exec. Docs.*, 33rd Cong., 1st sess., No. 8; *House Exec. Docs.*, 33rd Cong., 1st sess., No. 86; Williams, *Anglo-American Isthmian Diplomacy*, pp. 168–70, 174–75; Dexter Perkins, *The Monroe Doctrine, 1826–1867*, p. 229.

8. *New York Weekly Post*, Sept. 6, 1855.

9. *New York Tribune*, July 29, 1854; *The Works of James Buchanan*, 9:180–189.

10. Basil Rauch, *American Interest in Cuba, 1848–1855*, pp. 298–99; Philip S. Foner, *A History of Cuba and Its Relations with the United States*, 2:11, 93.

11. *New York Herald*, Mar. 9, 1855; *Dipl. Corr.*, 6:307, 308, 316–17, 322–23, 329, 356.

12. Charles L. Dufour, *Gentle Tiger*, pp. 77–87.

13. *New York Tribune*, Feb. 15, 17, 21, 1855.

14. *Dipl. Corr.*, 9:834–35.

15. *New York Tribune*, Feb. 15, 1855; *New York Times*, Feb. 17, 19, 1855; *Dipl. Corr.*, 9:852.

16. *Congressional Globe*, 33rd Cong., 1st sess., 1853–54, pp. 3, 9–15, 17, 83–84, 650, 692, 905, 1158; *Sen. Exec. Docs.*, 33rd Cong., 2nd sess., No. 93.

17. *New York Tribune*, Mar. 7, 1855; *New York Evening Post*, Mar. 7, 1855. Piatt's comment quoted in Amos A. Ettinger, *The Mission to Spain of Pierre Soulé, 1853–1855*, p. 394.

18. John F. H. Claiborne, *Life and Correspondence of John A. Quitman*, 2: 391–92; Foner, *History of Cuba*, 2:93; Nichols, *Franklin Pierce*, p. 394; Rauch, *American Interest in Cuba*, p. 300; *New York Tribune*, May 9, 1855.

19. Squier, *Nicaragua*, pp. 55–58; Capron, *History of California*, pp. 273–74; *Dipl. Corr.*, 4:404–9, 425–27.

20. *Dipl. Corr.*, 4:389–92, 404–9, 65.

21. W. S. Thayer Papers; *New York Tribune*, Jan. 5, 1855; *New York Times*, Jan. 30, 1855; Nichols, *Franklin Pierce*, p. 398.
22. *Dipl. Corr.*, 4:457–58; Squier, *Nicaragua*, pp. 654–55.
23. W. S. Thayer Papers.
24. Hubert Howe Bancroft, *History of Central America*, 3:238–44, 256–61; Comisión de Investigación Histórica de la Campaña de 1856–1857, *Crónicas y Comentarios*, pp. 38–43; William Walker, *The War in Nicaragua*, pp. 13–17.
25. *Dipl. Corr.*, 4:241, 245.
26. Charles W. Doubleday, *Reminiscences of the "Filibuster" War in Nicaragua*, passim.
27. Walker, *War in Nicaragua*, pp. 25–27; Rufus K. Wyllys, "Henry Crabb—a Tragedy of the Sonora Frontier"; *New York Herald*, Jan. 31, 1855.
28. *Dipl. Corr.*, 6:335, 336–39, 339–48, 349–50.
29. *New York Tribune*, Feb. 15, May 3, 1855; *New York Times*, Mar. 5, 1855; *New York Herald*, Jan. 3, 1855; Doubleday, *Reminiscences*, pp. 61–62; Walker, *War in Nicaragua*, p. 26; *Dipl. Corr.*, 4:432–33, 434–35, 445.
30. *Alta California*, Mar. 3, Oct. 7, 1854; *New York Tribune*, May 1, 1855; *New York Times*, June 6, 1855; *New York Evening Post*, July 9, 1855.
31. Walker, *War in Nicaragua*, p. 32; *New York Evening Post*, July 18, 1855.

CHAPTER 12
Expeditions to Nicaragua

1. William Walker, *The War in Nicaragua*, pp. 27–29, Frank Soulé, John H. Gihon, and James Nisbett, *The Annals of San Francisco, Continuation, Part 1*, pp. 36–37; William O. Scroggs, *Filibusters and Financiers*, p. 92.
2. Walker, *War in Nicaragua*, pp. 29–32; *Harper's Weekly*, vol. 1, May 16, 1857; *Alta California*, May 5, 1855; *San Francisco Herald*, May 6, 1855; William V. Wells, *Walker's Expedition to Nicaragua*, pp. 44–45.
3. W. R. Manning, ed., *Diplomatic Correspondence of the United States, Inter-American Affairs, 1831–1860* (hereafter cited as *Dipl. Corr.*), 4:458–59.
4. *New York Times*, May 16, 1855; *New York Evening Post*, May 15, 1855.
5. *New York Times*, May 16, 22, 31, June 7, 8, 9, 1855; *New York Herald*, May 18, 29, June 6, 7, 8, 17, 1855; *New York Tribune*, June 19, 1855.
6. Walker, *War in Nicaragua*, pp. 34–35; Charles W. Doubleday, *Reminiscences of the "Filibuster" War in Nicaragua*, pp. 76–77; Hubert Howe Bancroft, *History of Central America*, 3:261; Wells, *Walker's Expedition*, pp. 48–49.
7. Walker, *War in Nicaragua*, pp. 35–36.
8. Walker, *War in Nicaragua*, pp. 37–39; Ephraim G. Squier, *Nicaragua*, pp. 240–45.
9. Walker, *War in Nicaragua*, pp. 39–41; Doubleday, *Reminiscences*, pp. 109–10.
10. Walker, *War in Nicaragua*, pp. 41–44; Doubleday, *Reminiscences*, pp. 112–13; *New York Herald*, Aug. 7, 1855.
11. Walker, *War in Nicaragua*, pp. 42–64; Doubleday, *Reminiscences*, pp. 117–51.
12. *Alta California*, July 16, 17, 1855; *New York Herald*, July 9, 26, 28, Aug. 7, 1855.
13. Thayer's dispatches appeared in the *New York Evening Post* on July 18, 20, 28, Aug. 6, 7, 28, 29, Sept. 8, and Oct. 1, 1855.

14. *Dipl. Corr.*, 4:478–79; *New York Herald*, Aug. 8, 1855; *New York Evening Post*, Sept. 8, 1855.
15. *Dipl. Corr.*, 4:471–72.
16. *New York Herald*, Sept. 9, 1855; *New York Evening Post*, Sept. 8, 1855.
17. *New York Evening Post*, Aug. 6, 1855.
18. *New York Weekly Post*, Sept. 6, 1855.
19. *New York Herald*, Oct. 1, 1855; *New York Tribune*, Oct. 1, 1855; *New York Evening Post*, Oct. 1, 1855.
20. The correspondence is in the W. S. Thayer Papers and was published in the *New York Evening Post*, Oct. 15, 1855.
21. Scroggs, *Filibusters and Financiers*, p. 107.
22. Kinney to Thayer, Sept. 28, 1855, Thayer Papers.
23. Wells, *Walker's Expedition*, p. 53.
24. Walker, *War in Nicaragua*, pp. 64–85; Doubleday, *Reminiscences*, pp. 151–54.

CHAPTER 13
Walker Victorious: Forming a Government

1. William Walker, *The War in Nicaragua*, pp. 85–86; Charles W. Doubleday, *Reminiscences of the "Filibuster" War in Nicaragua*, pp. 155–56; *New York Herald*, Sept. 9, 1855.
2. Walker, *War in Nicaragua*, pp. 86–89; Horace Bell, *Reminiscences of a Ranger*, pp. 262–64; *New York Express*, Jan. 21, 1856, in Wheeler Scrapbook, 5:40.
3. Walker, *War in Nicaragua*, pp. 89–97; Doubleday, *Reminiscences*, pp. 157–64; William V. Wells, *Walker's Expedition to Nicaragua*, pp. 55–58; *El Nicaragüense* (as quoted in U.S. newspapers) Oct. 20, 1855.
4. Walker, *War in Nicaragua*, pp. 98, 101; Wells, *Walker's Expedition*, pp. 59–61; *Alta California*, Oct. 11, 22, 1855; *New York Herald*, Oct. 1, 1855; *New York Evening Post*, Oct. 1, 1855.
5. Doubleday, *Reminiscences*, pp. 165–79.
6. Walker, *War in Nicaragua*, pp. 101–15; Wells, *Walker's Expedition*, pp. 61–65; *Alta California*, Nov. 4, 17, 1855; *New York Herald*, Nov. 4, 5, 1855; *New York Tribune*, Nov. 5, 1855; *El Nicaragüense*, Oct. 20, 1855.
7. Walker, *War in Nicaragua*, p. 116; *New York Tribune*, Nov. 5, 1855; W. R. Manning, ed., *Diplomatic Correspondence of the United States, Inter-American Affairs, 1831–1860* (hereafter cited as *Dipl. Corr.*), 4:482.
8. Walker, *War in Nicaragua*, pp. 117–18; Julius Froebel, *Seven Years' Travel in Central America, Northern Mexico, and the Far West of the United States*, p. 45; Francisco Vijil, *El Padre Vijil*, pp. 140–44.
9. Walker, *War in Nicaragua*, pp. 118–20; Wells, *Walker's Expedition*, pp. 67–70; *Alta California*, Nov. 4, 1855; *New York Herald*, Nov. 4, 1855; *New York Tribune*, Nov. 12, 1855; *Dipl. Corr.*, 4:438.
10. Walker, *War in Nicaragua*, pp. 120–23; Wells, *Walker's Expedition*, pp. 70–76, 83–88; *Alta California*, Nov. 4, 1855; *New York Herald*, Nov. 4, 5, 1855; *New York Tribune*, Nov. 5, 1855.
11. Walker, *War in Nicaragua*, pp. 123–32; Wells, *Walker's Expedition*, pp. 76–81; *Alta California*, Nov. 17, 1855; *New York Herald*, Nov. 12, 1855; *New York Tribune*, Nov. 12, 1855; *El Nicaragüense*, Oct. 27, 1855.

12. Walker, *War in Nicaragua*, pp. 117, 130–39; Wells, *Walker's Expedition*, pp. 90–94; *Alta California*, Dec. 5, 1855; *New York Herald*, Nov. 29, 30, 1855; *New York Tribune*, Nov. 29, 1855; *El Nicaragüense*, Nov. 10, 1855.

13. Walker, *War in Nicaragua*, p. 141; Wells, *Walker's Expedition*, p. 95; *New York Herald*, Nov. 29, 1855; *New York Tribune*, Nov. 30, 1855; *El Nicaragüense*, Nov. 12, 1855; *Dipl. Corr.*, 4:481–82, 482–83, 484, 485–87, 487–88.

14. Walker, *War in Nicaragua*, p. 145; *Alta California*, Nov. 17, 1855; *New York Herald*, Nov. 30, 1855.

15. *El Nicaragüense*, Dec. 8, 1856.

16. *Alta California*, Nov. 17, 1855; *New York Herald*, July 26, 1855; *New York Tribune*, Aug. 7, 1855; *New York Evening Post*, as quoted in *National Intelligencer*, Dec. 1, 1855.

17. Walker, *War in Nicaragua*, p. 149.

18. *Alta California*, Oct. 21, 1855; Wells, *Walker's Expedition*, pp. 95–96.

19. Walker, *War in Nicaragua*, pp. 146–47.

20. James Carson Jamison, *With Walker in Nicaragua*, pp. 15, 58–64.

21. *New York Herald*, Nov. 5, 1855; Wells, *Walker's Expedition*, p. 142.

22. *New York Herald*, Oct. 13, 1855.

23. Walker, *War in Nicaragua*, p. 147; Wells, *Walker's Expedition*, p. 95; *Dipl. Corr.*, 4:487–88; *San Francisco Herald*, Jan. 12, 1856.

24. *Dipl. Corr.*, 4:484, 487–88.

25. Ibid., 4:74, 77–78.

26. Walker, *War in Nicaragua*, p. 166.

27. *New York Times*, Dec. 18, 1855; *Dipl. Corr.*, 4:496–97, 80; Walker, *War in Nicaragua*, p. 167.

CHAPTER 14
The Costa Rican War against Walker

1. William Walker, *The War in Nicaragua*, pp. 148–49; William V. Wells, *Walker's Expedition to Nicaragua*, pp. 208–10; W. R. Manning, ed., *Diplomatic Correspondence of the United States, Inter-American Affairs, 1831–1860* (hereafter cited as *Dipl. Corr.*), 4:545–49, 551–59; *New York Herald*, May 1, July 19, Aug. 31, 1856; *New York Tribune*, Sept. 1, 1856.

2. Walker, *War in Nicaragua*, pp. 150–53.

3. *Dipl. Corr.*, 4:80, 496–97, 503–4.

4. Vanderbilt to Marcy, Mar. 17, 1856, *Congressional Globe Appendix*, 34th Cong., 1st sess., 1855–56, p. 440; Vanderbilt to Marcy, Mar. 26, 1856, *Sen. Exec. Docs.*, 34th Cong., 1st sess., No. 68; Wells, *Walker's Expedition*, pp. 211–15.

5. *New York Herald*, Dec. 24, 1855; *Sen. Exec. Docs.*, 34th Cong., 1st sess., No. 68.

6. Mary W. Williams, *Anglo-American Isthmian Diplomacy, 1815–1915*, pp. 196–200; H. Barrett Learned, "William Learned Marcy" in Samuel Flagg Bemis, ed., *American Secretaries of State and Their Diplomacy*, 6:239–59; Ivor D. Spencer, *The Victor and the Spoils*, pp. 344–52; Roy F. Nichols, *Franklin Pierce*, pp. 429–31.

7. *New York Herald*, Dec. 24, 25, 26, 1855, Jan. 14, 1856; *New York Tribune*, Dec. 25, 26, 1855.

8. *New York Herald*, Jan. 10, 25, 30, 1856; *New York Tribune*, Jan. 30, 1856.

9. Quoted in William O. Scroggs, *Filibusters and Financiers*, pp. 147–48.

10. Wheaton J. Lane, *Commodore Vanderbilt*, pp. 111–17; John H. Kemble, *The Panama Route, 1848–1869*, pp. 69–74; Vanderbilt to Marcy, Mar. 26, 1856, *Sen. Exec. Docs.*, 34th Cong., 1st sess., No. 68.

11. Walker, *War in Nicaragua*, pp. 152–56; Wells, *Walker's Expedition*, 203–16; *Dipl. Corr.*, 4:506–8.

12. Walker, *War in Nicaragua*, pp. 159–60.

13. *Dipl. Corr.*, 4:488–89, 491–92, 78–80.

14. Walker, *War in Nicaragua*, pp. 160–62; *Dipl. Corr.*, 4:500–2; *New York Herald*, Jan. 30, 1856.

15. Walker, *War in Nicaragua*, pp. 163–65; Hubert Howe Bancroft, *History of Central America*, 3:125, 323, 336; *New York Herald*, Dec. 13, 1855, quoted from Boletín Oficial of Nov. 21, 1855.

16. *Dipl. Corr.*, 4:18–23, 313–19; Williams, *Anglo-American Isthmian Diplomacy*, pp. 110 ff.; Wells, *Walker's Expedition*, pp. 142–43.

17. *New York Tribune*, Feb. 29, 1856; *New York Herald*, Feb. 29, 1856; *New York Evening Post*, Feb. 28, 1856.

18. Walker, *War in Nicaragua*, pp. 163–65; Wells, *Walker's Expedition*, pp. 147–48; *New York Tribune*, Apr. 3, 1856; *New York Herald*, Apr. 3, 1856.

19. Walker, *War in Nicaragua*, pp. 175–76; Wells, *Walker's Expedition*, pp. 152–53; *New York Herald*, Apr. 3, 18, 1856; *New York Tribune*, Apr. 3, 1856; *Dipl. Corr.*, 4:515–17.

20. Walker, *War in Nicaragua*, pp. 179–81; *New York Herald*, Apr. 3, 1856; *New York Tribune*, Apr. 3, 1856; William O. Scroggs, "William Walker's Designs on Cuba."

21. Walker, *War in Nicaragua*, pp. 177–78.

22. Walker, *War in Nicaragua*, pp. 181–85; Wells, *Walker's Expedition*, pp. 153–68; *New York Herald*, Apr. 3, 17, 30, May 3, 1856; *New York Tribune*, Apr. 3, 17, 1856; *Alta California*, Apr. 11, 12, May 1, 2, 1856.

23. Walker, *War in Nicaragua*, pp. 186–94; *New York Herald*, Apr. 30, May 1, 2, 1856; *New York Tribune*, Apr. 17, May 1, 1856.

24. Walker, *War in Nicaragua*, pp. 193–94; Wells, *Walker's Expedition*, pp. 169–75; *New York Herald*, Apr. 30, 1856; *New York Tribune*, May 1, June 2, 1856; *Dipl. Corr.*, 4:514–15, 515–17.

25. Walker, *War in Nicaragua*, pp. 194–204; Wells, *Walker's Expedition*, pp. 175–88; *New York Herald*, Apr. 30, May 3, 1856; *New York Tribune*, Apr. 30, May 1, 1856; James Carson Jamison, *With Walker in Nicaragua*, pp. 72–78.

26. Walker, *War in Nicaragua*, pp. 206–11; *New York Herald*, June 2, 1856; *New York Tribune*, June 2, 1856.

CHAPTER 15
The Dictator of Nicaragua

1. William V. Wells, *Walker's Expedition to Nicaragua*, pp. 250–54.

2. William Walker, *The War in Nicaragua*, pp. 211–13; Wells, *Walker's Expedition*, pp. 258–60; *New York Tribune*, June 2, 1856.

3. Walker, *War in Nicaragua*, p. 205; *New York Tribune*, May 1, 1856.

4. Walker, *War in Nicaragua*, p. 205; Wells, *Walker's Expedition*, pp. 191–92; Francis Vijil, *El Padre Vijil*, pp. 201–3; *New York Herald*, May 2, 1856.

5. William O. Scroggs, ed., "Walker-Heiss Papers"; *New York Herald*, May 2, 1856; Roy F. Nichols, *Franklin Pierce*, p. 460.

6. *Sen. Exec. Docs.*, 34th Cong., 1st sess., No. 1.

7. *Congressional Globe Appendix*, 34th Cong., 1st sess., 1855–56, pp. 67–72, 75–79, 439–42.

8. Walker, *War in Nicaragua*, pp. 173–75; Wells, *Walker's Expedition*, pp. 149–53; W. R. Manning, ed., *Diplomatic Correspondence of the United States, Inter-American Affairs, 1831–1860* (hereafter cited as *Dipl. Corr.*), 4:509–11; *New York Herald*, Apr. 30, May 3, 1856.

9. Wells, *Walker's Expedition*, pp. 245–47; *Congressional Globe*, 34th Cong., 1st sess., 1855–56, p. 1070; *New York Herald*, May 3, 1856.

10. *Congressional Globe*, 34th Cong., 1st sess., 1855–56, pp. 1070–72.

11. Wells, *Walker's Expedition*, pp. 220–23; *New York Herald*, Apr. 9, May 2, July 19, 1856; *New York Tribune*, Apr. 30, May 1, June 2, 1856; *Dipl. Corr.*, 4:528–29, 556–57.

12. *New York Herald*, May 7, 10, 1856.

13. *New York Herald*, May 2, 1856; reprints of articles in *New Orleans Delta* of Apr. 26, 29, 1856, and *New Orleans Picayune*, Apr. 29, 1856.

14. *Congressional Globe*, 34th Cong., 1st sess., 1856–57, pp. 1238–39; Nichols, *Franklin Pierce*, pp. 460–62; Ivor D. Spencer, *The Victor and the Spoils*, pp. 371–72.

15. Walker, *War in Nicaragua*, pp. 214–15.

16. Walker, *War in Nicaragua*, pp. 216–23; *New York Tribune*, July 15, 1856.

17. Walker, *War in Nicaragua*, pp. 223–27; Hubert Howe Bancroft, *History of Central America*, 3:348–49; *New York Herald*, July 15, 16, 1856; *New York Tribune*, July 15, 1856.

18. Walker, *War in Nicaragua*, pp. 227–28; *New York Herald*, July 15, 16, 1856; *New York Tribune*, July 15, 1856; *Dipl. Corr.*, 4:538–43.

19. Bancroft, *Central America*, 3:349; *Dipl. Corr.*, 4:541–42.

20. *New York Herald*, Aug. 2, 10, 1856; *New York Tribune*, Aug. 6, 1856; *Dipl. Corr.*, 4:543–45.

21. Walker, *War in Nicaragua*, pp. 228–31; *Harper's Weekly* 1 (Mar. 28, 1857), p. 199; *Leslie's Weekly* 4 (June 27, 1857), p. 56; *New York Herald*, Mar. 21, 23, 27, 1857; William Frank Stewart, *Last of the Fillibusters*, pp. 11–12.

22. Walker, *War in Nicaragua*, pp. 231–33; *Dipl. Corr.*, 4:543–44.

23. Ephraim G. Squier, *Nicaragua*, p. 648; Walker, *War in Nicaragua*, pp. 251–54; *New York Tribune*, Dec. 17, 1856.

24. "Fillibustering."

25. *Dipl. Corr.*, 4:566–67, 568, 570–73, 86–87.

26. *New York Herald*, Sept. 1, Dec. 1, 1856.

27. Walker, *War in Nicaragua*, pp. 238–39; *New York Herald*, Oct. 19, 1856; *New York Tribune*, Sept. 2, 1856.

28. Walker, *War in Nicaragua*, pp. 254–56; *New York Herald*, Sept. 1, Oct. 19, 1856; *New York Tribune*, Oct. 20, 1856; "Fillibustering."

29. Walker, *War in Nicaragua*, pp. 256 ff.

30. Walker, *War in Nicaragua*, pp. 268–69; *New York Herald*, Nov. 21, 22, 23, 24, 1856.

CHAPTER 16
The Allied War against the Filibusters

1. William Walker, *The War in Nicaragua*, pp. 282–86; *New York Tribune*, Oct. 20, 22, 1856; *New York Herald*, Oct. 19, 1856; "A Ranger's Life in Nicaragua."

2. Walker, *War in Nicaragua*, pp. 239–40, 248–49; *New York Tribune*, Aug. 17, Sept. 2, 1856; *New York Herald*, Sept. 1, 1856.

3. *New York Tribune*, Dec. 29, 1856; item reprinted from *San Francisco Bulletin*.

4. Walker, *War in Nicaragua*, pp. 241–47; Hubert Howe Bancroft, *History of Central America*, 3:352–53.

5. Walker, *War in Nicaragua*, pp. 281–82, 290–91; *New York Tribune*, Oct. 22, 1856; *New York Herald*, Oct. 19, 1856.

6. Walker, *War in Nicaragua*, pp. 291–300; Bancroft, *History of Central America*, 3:353–54; *New York Tribune*, Oct. 31, 1856; *New York Herald*, Nov. 17, 1856.

7. Walker, *War in Nicaragua*, pp. 300–302; James Carson Jamison, *With Walker in Nicaragua*, p. 134; John H. Kemble, *The Panama Route, 1848–1869*, pp. 75–76; *New York Herald*, Nov. 17, 22, 1856.

8. Walker, *War in Nicaragua*, pp. 301–7; *New York Herald*, Dec. 16, 1856; *New York Tribune*, Dec. 17, 1856.

9. Walker, *War in Nicaragua*, pp. 307–12; *New York Herald*, Dec. 16, 1856.

10. Walker, *War in Nicaragua*, pp. 312–14; *New York Tribune*, Dec. 17, 1856, Jan. 26, 1857; *New York Herald*, Dec. 16, 18, 1856, Jan. 20, 25, 1857; "A Ranger's Life in Nicaragua"; Elleanore Ratterman, "With Walker in Nicaragua."

11. Walker, *War in Nicaragua*, pp. 342–43; *New York Herald*, Jan. 25, 1857; *New York Tribune*, Jan. 26, 29, 1857.

12. *New York Times*, Jan. 28, June 11, July 4, 27, Aug. 15, 22, Sept. 4, 1857.

13. Walker, *War in Nicaragua*, pp. 343–47; *New York Herald*, Jan. 25, 1857; *New York Tribune*, Jan. 26, 1857.

CHAPTER 17
Walker in Defeat: Surrender at Rivas

1. *New York Herald*, Dec. 18, 21, 1856.

2. *New York Herald*, Jan. 31, Feb. 23, 1857; *New York Tribune*, Dec. 22, 1856, Jan. 26, Mar. 21, Apr. 3, 17, 1857; Charles W. Doubleday, *Reminiscences of the "Filibuster" War in Nicaragua*, p. 176.

3. William Walker, *The War in Nicaragua*, pp. 357–58; *New York Herald*, Jan. 29, 30, 31, 1857; *New York Tribune*, Jan. 26, 29, 1857.

4. Walker, *War in Nicaragua*, pp. 355–57; *New York Herald*, Jan. 25, 26, Feb. 8, 23, 1857; *New York Tribune*, Jan. 29, 1857; Doubleday, *Reminiscences*, pp. 179–81.

5. *New York Herald*, Mar. 21, 1857.

6. *New York Herald*, Mar. 30, 1857; *Alta California*, Jan. 31, 1857; Hubert Howe Bancroft, *History of Central America*, 3:359; *New York Tribune*, Jan. 29, 1857.

7. Walker, *War in Nicaragua*, pp. 367–78, 370; David Deaderick III, "The Experience of Samuel Absalom, Filibuster"; *New York Herald*, Jan. 25, Feb. 14, 1857.

8. Walker, *War in Nicaragua*, 371–73; Deaderick, "The Experience of Samuel Absalom"; *Alta California*, Feb. 10, 1857; *New York Herald*, Feb. 23, 1857.

9. Walker, *War in Nicaragua*, pp. 374–84; Deaderick, "The Experience of Samuel Absalom"; *New York Herald*, Feb. 23, Mar. 21, 1857.

10. Walker, *War in Nicaragua*, pp. 385–88; *New York Herald*, Mar. 21, 23, 26, Apr. 30, 1857; *Alta California*, Mar. 29, 1857.

11. Walker, *War in Nicaragua*, pp. 388–99; William Frank Stewart, *Last of the Fillibusters*, passim; James Carson Jamison, *With Walker in Nicaragua*, pp. 154 ff.; *New York Herald*, Mar. 21, 27, Apr. 17, 30, 1857.

12. *New York Tribune*, Apr. 3, 17, 1857; *New York Herald*, Feb. 8, 23, Mar. 14, 21, Apr. 4, 1857; Doubleday, *Reminiscences*, pp. 179–85.

13. Ephraim G. Squier, *Nicaragua*, pp. 79–83.

14. *New York Tribune*, Apr. 17, 1857; *New York Herald*, Mar. 14, 21, Apr. 4, 1857; Doubleday, *Reminiscences*, pp. 185–87.

15. *Alta California*, May 16, 1857; *New York Tribune*. Apr. 17, 30, 1857; *New York Herald*, Apr. 17, 30, 1857; Doubleday, *Reminiscences*, pp. 187–91.

16. Walker, *War in Nicaragua*, pp. 403–8; Stewart, *Last of the Fillibusters*, pp. 30–35; Jamison, *With Walker in Nicaragua*, pp. 15 ff.; Louis N. Feipel, "The Navy and Filibustering in the Fifties."

17. Walker, *War in Nicaragua*, pp. 409–11; Stewart, *Last of the Fillibusters*, pp. 36–37; Elleanore Ratterman, "With Walker in Nicaragua"; Feipel, "The Navy and Filibustering in the Fifties."

18. Walker, *War in Nicaragua*, pp. 419–29; Stewart, *Last of the Fillibusters*, pp. 39–43; *New York Herald*, May 29, 1857; *New York Tribune*, May 29, 1857; *Alta California*, June 18, 1857; Feipel, "The Navy and Filibustering in the Fifties"; Charles H. Davis, *Life of Charles Henry Davis, Rear Admiral, 1807–1877*, pp. 102–4.

19. Quoted in William O. Scroggs, *Filibusters and Financiers*, p. 316.

CHAPTER 18
The Years of Frustration

1. *New York Herald*, May 29, 1857.

2. *New York Tribune*, June 18, 1857.

3. *New York Tribune*, May 29, 1857; *New York Herald*, June 17, 18, 19, 1857.

4. *New York Herald*, Aug. 5, 1857; *New York Tribune*, Aug. 19, 1857.

5. *New York Herald*, Dec. 14, 1857.

6. W. R. Manning, ed., *Diplomatic Correspondence of the United States, Inter-American Affairs, 1831–1870* (hereafter cited as *Dipl. Corr.*), 4:601; *House Exec. Docs.*, 35th Cong., 1st sess., No. 24.

7. Hubert Howe Bancroft, *History of Central America*, 3:364–65; *Dipl. Corr.*, 4:603–4.

8. *New York Herald*, Dec. 14, 15, 16, 21, 1857; *House Exec. Docs.*, 35th Cong., 2nd sess., No. 24.

9. *New York Tribune*, Dec. 28, 1857; *New York Herald*, Dec. 14, 15, 16, 21, 23, 1857; *House Exec. Docs.*, 35th Cong., 2nd sess., No. 24. Rebecca Paulding Meade, *Life of Hiram Paulding, Rear-Admiral, U.S.N.*, pp. 180–85; Louis N. Feipel, "The Navy and Filibustering in the Fifties."

10. *New York Tribune*, Jan. 15, 1858; *New York Herald*, Dec. 15, 1857, Jan. 15, 1858; Feipel, "The Navy and Filibustering in the Fifties."

11. Meade, *Life of Hiram Paulding*, pp. 186–200; *House Exec. Docs.*, 35th Cong., 2nd sess., No. 24; *New York Herald*, Dec. 28, 1857; *New York Tribune*, Dec. 28, 1857; Feipel, "The Navy and Filibustering in the Fifties."

12. *New York Herald*, Dec. 28, 29, 1857; *New York Tribune*, Dec. 29, 1857.

13. *New York Herald*, Jan. 28, Feb. 15, 1858; *Dipl. Corr.*, 4:619–20, 635, 640–41.

14. *Dipl. Corr.*, 4:586–87, 589–91, 596–600, 606–7, 607–8, 629–30, 631–35, 636–38; *New York Herald*, Mar. 27, Apr. 23, May 1, 31, 1858; *New York Times*, July 4, 27, Sept. 4, 1857.

15. *New York Herald*, Jan. 6, 7, 1858; *Congressional Globe*, 35th Cong., 1st sess., 1857–58: Senate, 174, 215–24, 264–72, 353–68, 377–78, 1538, 1583, House, 174–80, 254, 556, 1944, 1972, 1987; *Congressional Globe*, 35th Cong., 2nd sess., 1858–59: Senate, 655, 687–94, 711, House, 815–19.

16. *New York Herald*, Feb. 2, 1858.

17. *Dipl. Corr.*, 4:234–38, 929–36.

18. *New York Herald*, May 19, 1858; Walker to Fayssoux, Aug. 5, 1858, Callender I. Fayssoux Collection of William Walker Papers.

19. *New York Herald*, Nov. 22, 1858.

20. *New York Herald*, Jan 26, Feb. 1, Mar. 30, 1858; *New Orleans Picayune*, June 1, 2, 3, 1858.

21. *New York Herald*, Oct. 25, Nov. 22, 1857; *House Exec. Docs.*, 35th Cong., 2nd sess., No. 25, Fayssoux Collection.

22. *New York Herald*, Dec. 14, 1858, Jan. 11, 13, 1859; *House Exec. Docs.*, 35th Cong., 2nd sess., No. 25; Charles W. Doubleday, *Reminiscences of the "Filibuster" War in Nicaragua*, pp. 195–201.

23. Doubleday, *Reminiscences*, pp. 204–14; *New York Herald*, Jan. 11, 1859.

24. Doubleday, *Reminiscences*, p. 216; *New York Herald*, Jan. 11, 1859.

CHAPTER 19
The Last Expedition: Death in Honduras

1. *House Exec. Docs.*, 35th Cong., 2nd sess., No. 24.

2. W. R. Manning, ed., *Diplomatic Correspondence of the United States, Inter-American Affairs, 1831–1860* (hereafter cited as *Dipl. Corr.*), 4:132–34; *New York Herald*, Dec. 12, 13, 1858.

3. *Dipl. Corr.*, 4:104–8, 645, 659–61, 663–64, 672–74; *New York Herald*, Mar. 27, Apr. 28, May 1, 31, 1858.

4. *New York Herald*, Apr. 17, 28, May 1, June 5, 1858; Cyril Allen, "Felix Belly: Nicaraguan Canal Promoter."

5. *Dipl. Corr.*, 4:672–74, 676–78, 686, 692–93, 116–27, 696, 704–5, 709, 712.

6. James Buchanan, *The Works of James Buchanan*, 10:317.

7. *New York Herald*, May 31, 1858; *Dipl. Corr.*, 4:675–76.

8. Walker to Fayssoux, Jan. 13, 15, 20, 29, Mar. 4, 9, Apr. 19, May 4, 1859, Callender I. Fayssoux Collection of William Walker Papers; *New York Herald*, May 24, 27, June 24, 1859.

9. *New York Times*, Oct. 18, 1859.

10. *New York Times*, Oct. 4, 6, 7, 8, 10, 14, 18, 1859; *New York Herald*, Oct. 5, 1859; *New York Tribune*, Oct. 5, 1859.

11. Walker to Fayssoux, Feb. 17, 29, Mar. 5, 14, 26, 1860, Fayssoux Collection.

12. William Walker, *The War in Nicaragua*, p. 430.
13. Ibid., pp. 95, 99, 147, 171, 273.
14. Walker to Fayssoux, Feb. 17, 29, Mar. 17, 1860, Fayssoux Collection.
15. *New York Herald*, Feb. 6, 1859.
16. C. A. Bridges, "The Knights of the Golden Circle"; Ollinger Crenshaw, "The Knights of the Golden Circle"; Roy S. Dunn, "The KGC in Texas, 1860–1861"; Jimmie Hicks, "Some Letters Concerning the Knights of the Golden Circle in Texas, 1860–1861"; *New York Herald*, Feb. 6, Apr. 27, 1858, July 23, 1860.
17. Walker, *War in Nicaragua*, p. 280.
18. *New York Herald*, Sept. 1, 1860.
19. Walker to Fayssoux, June 5, 22, 23, July 14, Aug. 6, 1860, Fayssoux Collection; *New York Herald*, Aug. 18, Sept. 1, 1860; *New York Times*, Aug. 13, 1860.
20. Walker to Fayssoux, Aug. 11, 12, 16, 1860, Fayssoux Collection; *New York Herald*, Sept. 1, 1860.
21. *New York Herald*, Sept. 16, 18, 28, 1860; *New York Times*, Sept. 1, 6, 11, 1860; James Carson Jamison, *With Walker in Nicaragua*, pp. 169–75.
22. *New York Herald*, Sept. 28, 1860; *New York Times*, Sept. 18, 19, 21, 1860; *New York Tribune*, Oct. 4, 1860; *Harper's Weekly*, vol. 4, Oct. 13, 1860, p. 647.
23. Quoted in William O. Scroggs, *Filibusters and Financiers*, p. 394.
24. *New York Times*, Sept. 19, 1860; "The Late General Walker," *Harper's Weekly*, vol. 4, Oct. 13, 1860, p. 645.
25. *New York Herald*, Sept. 20, 1860.

EPILOGUE
The Later History of Filibusterism

1. Quoted in Albert K. Weinberg, *Manifest Destiny*, p. 201.
2. These theories, with copious quotations, are discussed in Weinberg.
3. Glyndon Van Deusen, *William Henry Seward*, pp. 488–548.
4. Joseph V. Fuller, "Hamilton Fish," in Samuel F. Bemis, ed., *The American Secretaries of State and Their Diplomacy*, 7:125–217.
5. David Healy, *U.S. Expansionism*, pp. 31, 38; Julius W. Pratt, *Expansionists of 1898*, pp. 4–5.
6. Marcus M. Wilkerson, *Public Opinion and the Spanish-American War*, p. 60.

Bibliography

Manuscript Sources

New Orleans, La.
Latin American Library, Tulane University.
Callender I. Fayssoux Collection of William Walker Papers.
Philadelphia, Pa.
Historical Society of Pennsylvania.
James Buchanan Papers.
San Francisco, Cal.
Sutro Library.
Theodore Henry Hittell Papers.
Washington, D. C.
Library of Congress.
John M. Clayton Papers.
Caleb Cushing Papers.
Jefferson Davis Papers.
Diary or Register of David Anderson Deaderick, 1797–1873.
William L. Marcy Papers.
Franklin Pierce Papers.
James K. Polk Papers.
William S. Thayer Papers.
Martin Van Buren Papers.
John H. Wheeler Scrapbooks, 5 vols.

Government Documents and Publications

Abridgment of the Debates of Congress, 1798 to 1856. 16 vols.
American State Papers. Documents, Legislative and Executive of the Congress of the United States. 38 vols.
Congressional Globe . . . 23rd Congress to the 42nd Congress, Dec. 2, 1833, to March 3, 1873.
House of Representatives. *Documents Relative to Central American Affairs and the Enlistment Question*. Washington, D.C., 1885.
———. Executive Documents:
31st Cong., 1st sess., 1849–50, Nos. 5, 57, and 75.
32nd Cong., 1st sess., 1851–52, Nos. 19 and 115.
32nd Cong., 2nd sess., 1852–53, Nos. 56 and 126.

33rd Cong., 1st sess., 1853–54, No. 126.
35th Cong., 2nd sess., 1857–58, Nos. 24, 25, and 64.
38th Cong., 2nd sess., 1865–66, No. 13.
39th Cong., 2nd sess., 1866–67, No. 17.
41st Cong., 2nd sess., 1869–70, No. 160.

———. Naval Affairs Committee. *Arrest of William Walker by Commodore Paulding*. Washington, D.C., 1858.

Senate. Executive Documents:
31st Cong., 2nd sess., 1850–51, No. 43.
32nd Cong., 1st sess., 1851–52, Nos. 1, 85, and 97.
32nd Cong., 2nd sess., 1852–53, No. 27.
33rd Cong., 2nd sess., 1854–55, Nos. 16 and 25.
34th Cong., 1st sess., 1855–56, Nos. 1, 25, and 68.

Contemporary Newspapers

Alta California, San Francisco, Cal.
El Nicaragüense, Granada, Nicaragua.
Los Angeles Star.
National Intelligencer, Washington, D.C.
New Orleans Crescent.
New Orleans Delta.
New Orleans Picayune.
New York Courier and Enquirer.
New York Evening Post.
New York Herald.
New York Times.
New York Tribune.
San Diego Herald.
San Francisco Herald.

Contemporary Magazines

Atlantic Monthly
De Bow's Review.
Harper's Monthly.
Harper's Weekly.
Leslie's Weekly.
Niles' Weekly Register.
Putnam's Monthly.
United States Magazine and Democratic Review (beginning in 1852, successively called *The Democratic Review, The United States Review, The United States Democratic Review*).

Books and Articles

Abdullah, Achmed. *Dreamers of Empire*. New York, 1929.

Abernethy, Thomas P. *The Burr Conspiracy*. New York, 1954.

Adams, John Quincy. *Memoirs of John Quincy Adams, Comprising Portions of His Diary from 1795 to 1848*. Edited by Charles Francis Adams. 12 vols. Philadelphia, 1874–77.

Ainsa, Joseph Y. *History of the Crabb Expedition into North Sonora*. Phoenix, 1951.
Alemán-Bolaños, Gustavo. *Centenario de la Guerra Nacional de Nicaragua contra Walker*. Guatemala, 1956.
Alfaro, Olmedo. *El Filibustero Walker en Nicaragua*. Panama, 1932.
Allen, Cyril. "Felix Belly: Nicaraguan Canal Promoter." *Hispanic American Historical Review* 37 (1957): 40–59.
———. *France in Central America: Felix Belly and the Nicaraguan Canal*. New York, 1966.
Allen, Merritt, P. *William Walker, Filibuster*. New York, 1932.
Ammen, Daniel. *The Certainty of the Nicaragua Canal Contrasted with the Uncertainty of the Eads Ship-Railway*. Washington, D.C., 1886.
Andrews, Wayne. *The Vanderbilt Legend: the Story of the Vanderbilt Family, 1794–1940*. New York, 1941.
"The Ashes of Greytown." *Democratic Review* 34 (Oct. 1854):281–312.
Atlantic and Pacific Ship Canal Company. *Terms of the Contract between the State of Nicaragua and the Company*. New York, 1849.
Bailey, Thomas A. "Interest in a Nicaraguan Canal." *Hispanic American Historical Review* 16 (1936): 2–28.
Baldwin, R. S. "Tarrying in Nicaragua; Pleasures and Perils of the California Trip in 1849." *Century* 42 (Oct. 1891): 911–31.
Bancroft, Hubert Howe. *California Inter Pocula*. San Francisco, 1888.
———. *History of California*. 7 vols. San Francisco, 1886–90.
———. *History of Central America*. 3 vols. San Francisco, 1886–87.
———. *History of Mexico*. 6 vols. San Francisco, 1886–88.
———. *History of the North Mexican States and Texas*. 2 vols. San Francisco, 1886–89.
"The Barrack and the Hospital in Nicaragua. A Personal Narrative." *Harper's Weekly* 1 (Mar. 14, 1857): 163–64.
Barrows, H. D. *Crabb's Filibusters*. Publications of the Historical Society of Southern California, vol. 8. Los Angeles, 1911.
Bartlett, John R. *Personal Narrative of Explorations and Incidents in Texas, New Mexico, California, Sonora, and Chihuahua Connected with the United States and Mexican Boundary Commission During the Years 1850, 1851, 1852, and 1853*. 2 vols. Chicago, 1965.
Bass, John M. *William Walker*. Nashville, 1898.
Bell, Horace. *Reminiscences of a Ranger, or Early Times in California*. Los Angeles, 1881.
Belly, Félix. *A Travers L'Amérique Centrale*. 2 vols. Paris, 1867.
Bemis, Samuel Flagg, ed. *The American Secretaries of State and Their Diplomacy*. 10 vols. New York, 1927–29.
———. *The Latin-American Policy of the United States. An Historical Interpretation*. New York, 1943.
Bigelow, John. *Retrospections of an Active Life*. 5 vols. New York, 1909.
Bill, Alfred H. *Rehearsal for Conflict. The War with Mexico, 1846–1848*. New York, 1947.
Bourne, Edward G. "The Proposed Absorption of Mexico in 1847–1848." *American Historical Association Annual Report for the Year 1899*. 1:155–69. Washington, D.C., 1900.
Boyle, Frederick. *A Ride across a Continent: A Personal Narrative of Wanderings through Nicaragua and Costa Rica*. 2 vols. London, 1868.

Bridges, C. A. "The Knights of the Golden Circle: A Filibustering Fantasy." *Southwestern Historical Quarterly* 44 (1941): 287–302.

Buchanan, James. *The Messages of President Buchanan with an Appendix Containing Sundry Letters from Members of His Cabinet*. Compiled by J. B. Henry. New York, 1888.

———. *The Works of James Buchanan*. Collected and edited by John B. Moore. 12 vols. Philadelphia, 1908–11.

Butler, Pierce. *Judah P. Benjamin*. Philadelphia, 1906.

Caldwell, Robert G. *The López Expeditions to Cuba, 1848–1851*. Princeton, N.J., 1915.

Calhoun, John C. "Correspondence of John C. Calhoun." Edited by J. Franklin Jameson. *Annual Report of the American Historical Association for the Year 1899*. Washington, D.C., 1900.

Callahan, James Morton. *American Foreign Policy in Mexican Relations*. New York, 1932.

Capron, Elisha S. *History of California . . . with a Journal of the Voyage from New York, Via Nicaragua, to San Francisco, and Back, Via Panama*. Boston, 1854.

"The Capture of General Walker and His Force." *Leslie's Weekly* V (Jan. 9, 1858): 81–82.

Carr, Albert Z. *The World and William Walker*. New York, 1963.

Cazneau, Mrs. William L. *Eagle Pass, or Life on the Border*. Austin, Tex., 1966.

"Central America." *United States Democratic Review* 38 (Nov. 1856): 298–303.

"Central America—The Late War in Nicaragua." *United States Democratic Review* 40 (July 1857): 9–23.

Chamorro, Pedro Joaquín. *Fruto Chamorro*. Managua, 1960.

———. *Máximo Jérez y Sus Contemporáneos*. Managua, 1948.

———. *El Último Filibustero*. Managua, 1933.

Choules, J. O. *The Cruise of the Yacht North Star*. New York, 1854.

Claiborne, John F. H. *Life and Correspondence of John A. Quitman*. 2 vols. New York, 1860.

Clark, Daniel. *Proofs of the Corruption of Gen. James Wilkinson, and His Connexion with Aaron Burr*. Facsimile edition of 1809 edition. Freeport, New York, 1970.

Clarke, James M. "Antonio Melendrez, Nemesis of William Walker in Baja California." *Quarterly of the California Historical Society* 12 (1933): 318–22.

Cleland, Robert G. "Bandini's Account of William Walker's Invasion of Lower California. *Huntington Library Quarterly* 7 (1944): 153–66.

Comisión de Investigación Histórica de la Campaña de 1856–1857. *Crónicas y Comentarios*. San José, Costa Rica, 1956.

———. *Documentos Relativos a la Guerra contra los Filibusteros*. San José, Costa Rica, 1956.

Cox, Isaac. J. "Hispanic-American Phases of the 'Burr Conspiracy.'" *Hispanic American Historical Review* 12 (1932): 145–75.

———. "Monroe and the Early Mexican Revolutionary Agents." *American Historical Association Annual Report for the Year 1911*. 1:197–215. Washington, D.C., 1913.

———. *The West Florida Controversy, 1798–1813. A Study in American Diplomacy*. Baltimore, 1918.

Craigie, Sir William, ed. *A Dictionary of American English on Historical Principles*. 4 vols. Chicago, 1938–44.

Crenshaw, Ollinger. "The Knights of the Golden Circle: The Career of George Bickley." *American Historical Review* 47 (1941): 25–50.

Crichfield, George W. *American Supremacy; the Rise and Progress of the Latin-American Republics and Their Relations to the United States Under the Monroe Doctrine*. New York, 1908.

"Cuba." *United States Magazine and Democratic Review* 25 (Sept. 1849): 193–203.

Curti, Merle E. "George N. Sanders: American Patriot of the Fifties." *South Atlantic Quarterly* 27 (1928): 79–87.

———. "Young America." *American Historical Review* 32 (1926): 34–55.

Davis, Charles H. *The Life of Charles Henry Davis, Rear Admiral, 1807–1877*. New York, 1899.

Davis, Charles Henry. *Report on Inter-Oceanic Canals and Railroads Between the Atlantic and Pacific Oceans*. Washington, D.C., 1867.

Davis, J. C. *History of the Late Expedition to Cuba, by O.D.D.O., One of the Participants, with an Appendix Containing the Last Speech of the Celebrated Orator, S. S. Prentis–"In Defence of General López."* New Orleans, 1850.

Davis, Mrs. Jefferson. *Jefferson Davis, a Memoir by His Wife*. 2 vols. New York, 1891.

Davis, Matthew L. *Memoirs of Aaron Burr. With Miscellaneous Selections from His Correspondence*. 2 vols. New York, 1837.

Davis, Richard Harding. *Real Soldiers of Fortune*. New York, 1906.

Davis, William H. *Seventy-Five Years in California*. San Francisco, 1967.

Deaderick, David, III. "The Experience of Samuel Absalom, Filibuster." *Atlantic Monthly* 4 (Dec. 1859): 653–65; 5 (Jan. 1860): 38–60.

de Armond, Louis. "Justo Sierra O'Reilly and Yucatán-United States Relations, 1847–1848." *Hispanic American Historical Review* 31 (1951): 420–36.

"The Destiny of Nicaragua." *Blackwood's Magazine* 79 (1856): 314–16.

The Destiny of Nicaragua, by "An Officer in the Service of Walker." Boston, 1856.

Diccionario Porrúa de Histórica, Biografía y Geográfica de México. Mexico City, 1964.

Dillon, Richard H. *Humbugs and Heroes, a Gallery of California Pioneers*. New York, 1970.

Dodd, William E. *Robert James Walker, Imperialist*. Chicago, 1914.

Doolittle, James R. *Justification of Commodore Paulding's Arrest of Walker and His Command at Punta Arenas. Speech of James R. Doolittle, of Wisconsin. Delivered in the United States Senate, January 21st, 1858*. Washington, D.C., 1858.

Doubleday, Charles W. *Reminiscences of the "Filibuster" War in Nicaragua*. New York, 1886.

Douglas, Stephen A. *The Letters of Stephen A. Douglas*. Edited by Robert W. Johannsen. Urbana, Ill., 1961.

Dueñas Van Sereren, J. Ricardo. *La Invasión Filibustera de Nicaragua y la Guerra Nacional*. San Salvador, El Salvador, 1962.

Dufour, Charles L. *Gentle Tiger. The Gallant Life of Roberdeau Wheat*. Baton Rouge, 1957.

Dunlop, Robert G. *Travels in Central America*. London, 1847.

Dunn, Roy S. "The KGC in Texas, 1860–1861." *Southwestern Historical Quarterly*. 70 (1967): 543–73.

Egan, Ferol. *The Eldorado Trail; the Story of the Gold Rush Routes across Mexico*. New York, 1970.

"Eighteen-Fifty-Two and the Presidency." *Democratic Review* 30 (Jan. 1852): 1–12.

Ettinger, Amos A. *The Mission to Spain of Pierre Soulé, 1853–1855*. New Haven, 1932.

Fabens, Joseph. *A Story of Life on the Isthmus*. New York, 1853.

Fehrenbach, T. R. *Lone Star, a History of Texas and the Texans*. New York, 1968.

Feipel, Louis N. "The Navy and Filibustering in the Fifties." *United States Naval Institute Proceedings* 44 (June 1918): 1220–40; (July 1918): 1527–45; (Aug. 1918): 1837–48; (Sept. 1918): 2063–85.

Fenwick, Charles G. *The Neutrality Laws of the United States*. Washington, D.C., 1913.

Field, Stephen J. *Personal Reminiscences of Early Days in California with Other Sketches*. Washington, D.C., 1893.

"Fillibustering." *Putnam's Monthly Magazine* 9 (Apr. 1857): 425–35.

Fisher, Lillian E. "American Influence upon the Movement for Mexican Independence." *Mississippi Valley Historical Review* 18 (1932): 463–78.

Floyd, Troy S. *The Anglo-Spanish Struggle for Mosquitia*. Albuquerque, N.M., 1967.

Foner, Philip S. *A History of Cuba and Its Relations with the United States*. 2 vols. New York, 1963.

Foote, Henry S. *Texas and the Texans; or, Advance of the Anglo-Americans to the Southwest*. 2 vols. Philadelphia, 1841.

Forbes, Robert H. *Crabb's Filibustering Expedition into Sonora, 1857*. Tucson, 1952.

"Foreign and Continental Policy of the United States." *Democratic Review* 32 (Jan. 1853): 10–11.

Fornell, Earl W. "Texans and Filibusters." *Southwestern Historical Quarterly* 59: 411–28.

Fredman, L. E. "Broderick: A Reassessment." *Pacific Historical Review* 30 (1961): 39–46.

Froebel, Julius. *Seven Years' Travel in Central America, Northern Mexico, and the Far West of the United States*. London, 1859.

Fuller, John D. P. *The Movement for the Acquisition of all Mexico*. Baltimore, 1936.

Gamez, José D. *Historia de Nicaragua*. Managua, 1889.

Garber, Paul N. *The Gadsden Treaty*. Philadelphia, 1923.

Garrett, Julia K. *Green Flag over Texas*. New York and Dallas, 1939.

Garrett, Lula May. "San Francisco in 1851 as Described by Eyewitnesses." *California Historical Society Quarterly* 22 (1943): 253–80.

Garrison, George P. *Westward Extension, 1841–1850*. New York, 1906.

"General López, the Cuban Patriot." *United States Magazine and Democratic Review*. 26 (Feb. 1850): 97–112.

"General Miranda's Expedition." *Atlantic Monthly* 31 (May 1860): 589–602.

Gessler, Clifford. *Tropic Landfall, the Port of Honolulu*. Garden City, N.Y., 1942.

González, Ambrosio José. *Manifesto on Cuban Affairs Addressed to the People of the United States*. New Orleans, 1853.

Graebner, Norman. *Empire on the Pacific: A Study in American Continental Expansion*. New York, 1955.

———. *Manifest Destiny*. The American Heritage Series. Indianapolis and New York, 1968.

Greene, Lawrence. *The Filibuster. The Career of William Walker*. Indianapolis, 1937.

Guier, Enrique. *William Walker*. San José, Costa Rica, 1971.

Hale, Edward E. "The Real Philip Nolan." *Publications of the Mississippi Historical Society* 4 (1901): 281–87.

Hanna, Alfred J., and Hanna, Kathryn A. *Confederate Exiles in Venezuela*. Confederate Centennial Studies No. 15. Tuscaloosa, 1960.

Hardy, Richardson. *The History and Adventures of the Cuban Expedition, from the First Movements Down to the Dispersion of the Army at Key West, and the Arrest of General Lopéz. Also: An Account of the Ten Deserters at Isla de Mugeres*. Cincinnati, 1850.

Harmon, George D. "Confederate Migrations to Mexico." *Hispanic American Historical Review* 17 (1937): 458–87.

Hart, Mrs. Alfred. *Via Nicaragua: A Sketch of Travel*. London, 1887.

Hasse, Adelaide. *Index to United States Documents Relating to Foreign Affairs, 1828–61*. 3 vols. Washington, D.C., 1914–21.

Hatcher, Mattie A. *The Opening of Texas to Foreign Settlement, 1801–1821*. University of Texas Bulletin No. 2714. Austin, 1927.

Hawthorne, Julian. *Hawthorne and His Wife*. 2 vols. Boston, 1885.

Healy, David. *U.S. Expansionism: The Imperialist Urge in the 1890s*. Madison, Wis., 1970.

Heiss, John P. "Papers of Major John P. Heiss of Nashville." Edited by William O. Scroggs. *Tennessee Historical Magazine* 1 (1915): 330–45 and 2 (1916): 137–49.

Henderson, Gavin B., ed. "Southern Designs on Cuba, 1854–1857, and Some European Opinions." *Journal of Southern History* 5 (1939): 371–85.

Hicks, Jimmie, ed. "Some Letters Concerning the Knights of the Golden Circle in Texas, 1860–1861." *Southwestern Historical Quarterly* 65 (1961): 80–86.

Hill, Lawrence F. "Confederate Exiles to Brazil." *Hispanic American Historical Review*. 7 (1927): 193–210.

———. "The Confederate Exodus to South America." *Southern Historical Quarterly* 39 (1935): 100–134, 161–99, 309–26.

Hitchcock, Ethan Allen. *Fifty Years in Camp and Field, Diary of Major-General Ethan Allen Hitchcock, U.S.A.* Freeport, N.Y., 1971.

Hittell, John S. *California*. 3 vols. San Francisco, 1878.

———. *A History of the City of San Francisco*. San Francisco, 1878.

Hoblitzell, H. S. *Early Historical Sketch of the City of Marysville and Yuba County*. Marysville, Cal., 1876.

Hudson, Randolph O. "The Filibuster Minister: The Career of John Hill Wheeler as U.S. Minister to Nicaragua, 1854–1856." *North Carolina Historical Review* 49 (1972): 280–97.

Hurtado Chamorro, Alejandro. *William Walker: Ideales y Propósitos; un Ensayo Biográphico*. Granada, Nicaragua, 1965.

Israel, Fred L., ed. *The State of the Union Messages of the Presidents, 1790–1966*. 3 vols. New York, 1966.

Jacobs, James R. *Tarnished Warrior, Major-General James Wilkinson*. New York, 1938.
Jamison, James Carson. *With Walker in Nicaragua, or Reminiscences of an Officer of the American Phalanx*. Columbia, Mo., 1909.
Jordan, H. Donaldson. "A Politician of Expansion: Robert J. Walker." *Mississippi Valley Historical Review* 19 (1932): 362–81.
Karnes, Thomas L. *The Failure of Union: Central America, 1824–1860*. Chapel Hill, N.C., 1961.
Katz, Irving. *August Belmont, a Political Biography*. New York, 1968.
Keasbey, Lindley M. *The Nicaragua Canal and the Monroe Doctrine*. New York, 1896.
Kemble, Edward. *A History of California Newspapers, 1846–1858*. Los Gatos, Cal., 1962.
Kemble, John H. *The Panama Route: 1848–1869*. University of California Publications in History, vol. 29. Berkeley, 1943.
______. "The Panama Route to the Pacific Coast, 1848–1869." *Pacific Historical Review* 7 (1938): 1–13.
King, Charles R., ed. *The Life and Correspondence of Rufus King, Comprising His Letters, Private and Official, His Public Documents, and His Speeches*. 6 vols. New York, 1894–1900.
Klein, Philip S. *President James Buchanan*. University Park, Pa., 1962.
Kuykendall, Ralph S. *The Hawaiian Kingdom, 1778–1854*. Honolulu, 1957.
Lambertie, Charles de. *Le Drama de la Sonora*. Paris, 1856.
Lane, Wheaton J. *Commodore Vanderbilt*. New York, 1942.
Latané, John H. "The Diplomacy of the United States in Regard to Cuba. *Annual Report of the American Historical Association for the Year 1897*. Washington, D.C., 1898.
______. *The Diplomatic Relations of the United States and Spanish America*. Baltimore, 1899.
______. *The United States and Latin America*. Garden City, N.Y., 1920.
"The Late Cuba State Trials." *Democratic Review* 30 (April 1852): 307–19.
"The Late General Walker." *Harper's Weekly* 4 (Oct. 13, 1860): 645.
Levy, Daniel. *Les Français en Californie*. San Francisco, 1884.
Lewis, Oscar. *Sea Routes to the Gold Fields. The Migration by Water to California in 1849–1852*. New York, 1949.
Lockey, Joseph B. "Diplomatic Futility." *Hispanic American Historical Review* 10 (1930): 265–94.
Lodge, Henry Cabot. "Our Blundering Foreign Policy." *Forum* 19 (Mar. 1895): 8–17.
Lossing, Benson J. "Three Weeks in Cuba." *Harper's New Monthly Magazine* 6 (Dec. 1852): 161–75.
Low, Garrett. *Gold Rush by Sea*. Philadelphia, 1941.
Lucas, Daniel B. *Nicaragua: War of the Filibusters*. Richmond, Va., 1896.
Lynch, Jeremiah. *Life of David C. Broderick*. New York, 1911.
McCaleb, Walter F. *The Aaron Burr Conspiracy and a New Light on Aaron Burr*. New York, 1966.
McCormac, Eugene I. *James K. Polk, a Political Biography*. Berkeley, 1922.
McLaughlin, Andrew C. *Lewis Cass*. New York, 1899.
McMaster, John B. *A History of the People of the United States from the Revolution to the Civil War*. 8 vols. New York, 1901–1914.

McPherson, Hallie M. "The Plan of William McKendree Gwin for a Colony in Mexico, 1863–1865." *Pacific Historical Review* 2 (1933): 357–86.
Mack, Gerstle. *The Land Divided; a History of the Panama Canal and Other Isthmian Canal Projects*. New York, 1944.
Malone, Dumas. *Jefferson and His Time*. 6 vols. Boston, 1948–74.
Manning, W. R., ed. *Diplomatic Correspondence of the United States, Inter-American Affairs, 1831–1860*. 12 vols. Washington, D.C., 1932–39.
Martin, Percy F. *Maximilian in Mexico; the Story of the French Intervention, 1861–1867*. New York, 1914.
Masis Rojas, Teresa. *Breve Introducción para el Estudio de la Guerra contra los Filibusteros, 1856–57*. San José, Costa Rica, 1956.
Mathews, Milford J., ed. *A Dictionary of Americanisms on Historical Principles*. Chicago, 1951.
Meade, Rebecca Paulding. *Life of Hiram Paulding, Rear-Admiral, U.S.N.* New York, 1910.
Meade, Robert D. *Judah P. Benjamin, Confederate Statesman*. New York, 1943.
Merk, Frederick. *Manifest Destiny and Mission in American History; a Reinterpretation*. New York, 1963.
———. *The Monroe Doctrine and American Expansionism, 1843–1849*. New York, 1966.
Metcalf, Helen B. "The California French Filibusters in Sonora." *California Historical Society Quarterly* 18 (1939): 3–21.
Miles, William. *Journal of the Sufferings and Hardships of Parker H. French's Overland Expedition*. Chambersburg, Pa., 1851.
Miller, Hugh G. *The Isthmian Highway. A Review of the Problems of the Caribbean*. New York, 1929.
Miller, Joaquin. "Night in Nicaragua." *Sunset Magazine* 16 (Apr. 1906): 553–64.
Milton, George F. *The Eve of Conflict: Stephen A. Douglas and the Needless War*. Boston and New York, 1934.
Mitford, M. Mathews, ed. *A Dictionary of Americanisms on Historical Principles*. Chicago, 1951.
Montgomery, Cora. See Cazneau, Mrs. William L.
Montúfar, Lorenzo. *Walker en Centro-America*. 2 vols. Guatemala, 1887.
Moore, J. Preston. "Pierre Soulé: Southern Expansionist and Promoter." *Journal of Southern History* 21 (1955): 202–23.
Morris, Richard B., ed. *Encyclopedia of American History*. New York, 1953.
Munro, Dana G. *The Five Republics of Central America*. New York, 1918.
Nasatir, A. P. "Guillaume Patrice Dillon." *California Historical Society Quarterly* 35 (1956): 309–23.
Nevins, Allan. *Ordeal of the Union*. 2 vols. New York, 1947.
Nicaise, Auguste. *Les Filibustiers Americains*. Paris, 1860.
Nichols, Roy F. *The Democratic Machine, 1850–1854*. New York, 1923.
———. *Franklin Pierce*. Philadelphia, 1958.
"The Nomination—the 'Old Fogies' and Fogy Conspiracies." *Democratic Review* 30 (Apr. 1852): 366–84.
North, Arthur W. *Camp and Camino in Lower California*. New York, 1910.
Obregón Loría, Rafael. *La Campaña del Tránsito, 1856–1857*. San José, Costa Rica, 1956.
Oliphant, Laurence. *Patriots and Filibusters, or Incidents of Political and Exploratory Travel*. London, 1860.
O'Meara, James. *Broderick and Gwin*. San Francisco, 1881.

Parmet, Herbert S., and Hecht, Marie B. *Aaron Burr, Portrait of an Ambitious Man*. New York, 1967.
Passos, John Dos. *The Shackles of Power: Three Jeffersonian Decades*. New York, 1966.
Peary, R. E. "Across Nicaragua with Transit and Machete." *National Geographic* 1 (Oct. 1889): 315–35.
Perez, Jerónimo. *Memorias para la Historia de la Revolución de Nicaragua, y de la Guerra Nacional contra los Filibusteros, 1854–1857*. Managua, 1865.
Perez, L. M., ed. "López's Expeditions to Cuba, 1850–51; Betrayal of the Cleopatra, 1851." *Publications of the Southern History Association* 10 (1906): 345–62.
Perkins, Dexter. *A History of the Monroe Doctrine*, rev. ed. Boston, 1955.
______. *The Monroe Doctrine, 1826–1867*. Baltimore, 1933.
Phillips, Ulrich. "The Correspondence of Robert Toombs, Alexander H. Stephens, and Howell Cobb." 2 vols. *Annual Report of the American Historical Association for the Year 1911*. Washington, D.C., 1913.
Pierson, William W., Jr. "The Political Influences of an Inter-Oceanic Canal, 1826–1926." *Hispanic American Historical Review* 6 (1926): 205–31.
Pinchon, Edgcumb. *Dan Sickles. Hero of Gettysburg and "Yankee King of Spain*." New York, 1945.
Polk, James K. *The Diary of James K. Polk During His Presidency, 1845 to 1849*. Edited by Milo M. Quaife. 4 vols. Chicago, 1910.
Pratt, Julius W. *Expansionists of 1812*. New York, 1925.
______. *Expansionists of 1898. The Acquisition of Hawaii and the Spanish Islands*. New York, 1951.
______. "John L. O'Sullivan and Manifest Destiny." *New York History* 14 (1933): 213–34.
______. "The Origin of 'Manifest Destiny.'" *American Historical Review* 32 (1927): 795–98.
Raddell, David R., and Parsons, James P. "Realejo: A Forgotten Colonial Port and Shipbuilding Center in Nicaragua." *Hispanic American Historical Review* 51 (1971): 295–312.
Rainwater, P. L. "Economic Benefits of Secession: Opinions in Mississippi in the 1850s." *Journal of Southern History* 1 (1935): 459–67.
"A Ranger's Life in Nicaragua." *Harper's Weekly* 1 (Apr. 18, 1857): 200–202; (Apr. 25, 1857): 248–51.
Ratterman, Elleanore. "With Walker in Nicaragua. The Reminiscences of Elleanore (Callighan) Ratterman." Edited by William O. Scroggs. *Tennessee Historical Magazine* 1 (1915): 315–30.
Rauch, Basil. *American Interest in Cuba, 1848–1855*. New York, 1948.
Reed, Nelson. *The Caste War of Yucatán*. Stanford, Cal., 1964.
Reeves, Jesse S. *American Diplomacy under Tyler and Polk*. Baltimore, 1907.
______. "The Napoleonic Exiles in America. A Study in American Diplomatic History, 1815–1819." John Hopkins Studies in Historical and Political Science, Series 23, Nos. 9 and 10 (1905): 523–656.
"Revolutions in Central America." *United States Review and Democratic Magazine* 40 (Oct. 1857): 315–29.
Richardson, James D., ed. *A Compilation of the Messages and Papers of the Presidents, 1789–1897*. 10 vols. Washington, D.C., 1896–99.
Rippy, J. Fred. "Anglo-American Filibusters and the Gadsden Treaty." *Hispanic American Historical Review* 5 (1922): 155–80.

———. "Diplomacy of the United States and Mexico Regarding the Isthmus of Tehuantepec, 1848–1860." *Mississippi Valley Historical Review* 6 (1920): 503–31.
———. *Rivalry of the United States and Great Britain over Latin America, 1808–1830*. Baltimore, 1929.
———. *The United States and Mexico*. New York, 1926.
Rister, Carl Coke. "Carlota, a Confederate Colony in Mexico." *Journal of Southern History* 11 (1945): 32–50.
"Rivers and Cities of Nicaragua." *Harper's Weekly* 1 (May 16, 1857): 312–14.
Rives, George L. *U.S. and Mexico, 1821–1848; a History of Relations from the Independence of Mexico to the Close of the War*. New York, 1913.
Robertson, William S. *The Life of Miranda*. 2 vols. Chapel Hill, N.C., 1929.
Roche, James J. *By-Ways of War: The Story of the Filibusters*. Boston, 1901.
Rodríguez, Mario. *A Palmerstonian Diplomat in Central America: Frederick Chatfield, Esq*. Tucson, 1964.
Rolle, Andrew F. "California Filibustering and the Hawaiian Kingdom." *Pacific Historical Review* 19 (1950): 251–63.
———. *The Lost Cause: The Confederate Exodus to Mexico*. Norman, Okla., 1965.
Rollins, Clinton. *William Walker. Traducción Directa del Inglés Guillermo con un Estudio Crítica: Dr. Carlos Cuadra Pasos, Director de la Academia Historia de Granada*. Managua, 1945.
Rosengarten, J. G. *French Colonists and Exiles in the United States*. Philadelphia and London, 1907.
Ruiz, Ramón Eduardo, ed. *The Mexican War. Was it Manifest Destiny*? American Problem Studies. New York, 1963.
Sanders, George N. *The Political Correspondence of the Late Hon. George N. Sanders*. New York, 1914.
Schachner, Nathan. *Aaron Burr. A Biography*. New York, 1937.
Scherer, James A. B. *The First Forty-Niner*. New York, 1925.
Scherzer, Carl. *Travels in the Free States of Central America; Nicaragua, Honduras, and San Salvador*. 2 vols. London, 1857.
Schlesinger, Louis. "Personal Narrative of Louis Schlesinger, of Adventures in Cuba and Cueta." *Democratic Review* 31 (Sept. 1852): 211–24; (Oct. 1852): 352–68; (Dec. 1852): 555–92.
Schurz, Carl. "Manifest Destiny." *Harper's New Monthly Magazine* 87 (Oct. 1893): 737–46.
Scroggs, William O. *Filibusters and Financiers. The Story of William Walker and His Associates*. New York, 1916.
———, ed. "Walker-Heiss Papers. Some Diplomatic Correspondence of the Walker Regime in Nicaragua." *Tennessee Historical Magazine* 4 (1915): 331–45.
———. "William Walker and the Steamship Corporation in Nicaragua." *American Historical Review* 10 (1905): 792–811.
———. "William Walker's Designs on Cuba." *Mississippi Valley Historical Review* 1 (1914): 198–211.
Sears, Louis M. *John Slidell*. Durham, N.C., 1925.
Shearer, Ernest C. "The Carvajal Disturbances." *Southwestern Historical Quarterly* 55 (1951): 201–30.
Shuck, Oscar T. *Bench and Bar in California*. San Francisco, 1889.
———. *Representative and Leading Men of the Pacific*. San Francisco, 1870.

Slidell, John. *The Arrest of William Walker. Speech of Hon. John Slidell, of Louisiana, on the Neutrality Laws. Delivered in the United States Senate, April 8, 1858*. Washington, D.C., 1858.
Smith, Henry Nash. *Virgin Land. The American West as Symbol and Myth*. Cambridge, Mass., 1950.
Smith, Joseph W. *Expedición Filibustera de William Walker en la Baja California*. Mexico City, 1944.
Smith, Justin H. "La República de Río Grande." *American Historical Review* 25 (1920): 660–75.
______. *The War with Mexico*. 2 vols. New York, 1919.
Soulé, Frank, Gihon, John H., and Nisbet, James. *The Annals of San Francisco*. Palo Alto, Cal., 1966.
Soulé, Pierre. "Correspondence of Pierre Soulé: The Louisiana Tehuantepec Company." Edited by John P. Moore. *Hispanic American Historical Review* 32 (1952): 59–72.
Soulie, Maurice. *The Wolf Cub. The Great Adventure of Count Gaston de Raousset-Boulbon in California and Sonora, 1850–1854*. Translated by Farrel Symons. Indianapolis, 1927.
"The Spaniards at Havana and the Whigs at Washington." *Democratic Review* 31 (Oct. 1852): 326–36.
Sparks, Edwin Erle, ed. "Diary and Letters of Henry Ingersoll, Prisoner at Carthegena, 1806–1809." *American Historical Review* 11 (1898): 674–702.
Spencer, Ivor D. *The Victor and the Spoils. A Life of William L. Marcy*. Providence, R.I., 1959.
Squier, Ephraim G. *Nicaragua, Its People, Scenery, Monuments, Resources, Condition, and Proposed Canal*. New York, 1860.
______. *Notes on Central America; Particularly the States of Honduras and San Salvador*. New York, 1855.
______. *Travels in Central America*. 2 vols. New York, 1853.
______. *Wakina, or Adventures on the Mosquito Shore*. Gainesville, Fla., 1965. (Facsimile copy of 1855 edition.)
Stephenson, George M. *The Political History of the Public Lands from 1840 to 1862*. Boston, 1917.
Stevens, Sylvester K. *American Expansion in Hawaii, 1842–1898*. Harrisburg, Pa., 1945.
Stewart, William Frank. *Last of the Fillibusters*. Sacramento, Cal., 1857.
Stout, Peter F. *Nicaragua: Past, Present and Future*. Philadelphia, 1859.
Strode, Hudson. *Jefferson Davis*. 2 vols. New York, 1955–59.
Swanberg, W. A. *Sickles the Incredible*. New York, 1956.
Tansill, Charles C. *The United States and Santo Domingo, 1798–1873*. Baltimore, 1938.
Tehuantepec Railway Co. *The Tehuantepec Railroad; Its Location, Features, and Advantages under the La Sere Grant of 1869*. New York, 1869.
Thomas, Hugh. *Cuba; the Pursuit of Freedom*. New York, 1971.
Thomas, Lately. *Between Two Empires. The Life Story of California's First Senator, William McKendree Gwin*. Boston, 1969.
Thompson, Edward H. "A Page of American History." *Proceedings of the American Antiquarian Society*, New Series 17 (1905): 245–51.
Thorning, Joseph F. *Miranda: World Citizen*. Gainesville, Fla., 1952.
Urban, Chester S. "New Orleans and the Cuban Question During the López

Expeditions of 1849–1851: A Local Study in 'Manifest Destiny.'" *Louisiana Historical Quarterly* 22 (1939): 1095–1167.
Van Alstyne, R. W., ed. "Anglo-American Relations, 1853–59." *American Historical Review*. 42 (1937): 491–500.
———. "The Central American Policy of Lord Palmerston." *Hispanic American Historical Review*. 16 (1936): 352–59.
Van Deusen, Glyndon. *William Henry Seward*. New York, 1967.
Van Evrie, John H. *White Supremacy and Negro Subordination; or, Negroes a Subordinate Race, and (So-called) Slavery Its Normal Condition*. New York, 1868.
Vijil, Francisco. *El Padre Vijil, Su Vida. Algunos Episodios de Neustra Historia Nacional*. Granada, Nicaragua, 1930.
Walker, Henry P., ed. "William McLane's Narrative of the Magee-Gutiérrez Expedition, 1812–1813." *Southwestern Historical Quarterly* 65 (1962): 234–51; (1963): 457–69, 569–88.
Walker, William. *The War in Nicaragua*. Mobile, 1860.
Wallace, Edward S. *Destiny and Glory*. New York, 1957.
———. *General William Jenkins Worth, Monterrey's Forgotten Hero*. Dallas, 1953.
Wandell, Samuel H., and Minnigerode, Meade. *Aaron Burr*. 2 vols. New York, 1927.
Ward, A. W., and Gooch, G. P., eds. *The Cambridge History of British Foreign Policy, 1783–1919*. 3 vols. New York, 1922–23.
Warren, Harris G. "Filibustering During the War of 1812." *Journal of Southern History* 8 (1942): 68.
———. "The Southern Career of Don Juan Mariano Picornell." *Journal of Southern History*. 8 (1942): 311–33.
———. *The Sword Was Their Passport. A History of American Filibustering in the Mexican Revolution*. Baton Rouge, La., 1943.
Warren, T. Robinson. *Dust and Foam; or, Three Oceans and Two Continents*. New York and London, 1859.
Webb, Walter Prescott, ed. *The Handbook of Texas*. 2 vols. Austin, Tex., 1922.
Webster, Sir Charles Kingsley. *Britain and the Independence of Latin America*. 2 vols. London, 1938.
Weinberg, Albert K. *Manifest Destiny: A Study of Nationalist Expansionism in American History*. Baltimore, 1935.
Wellman, Paul I. *The House Divides. The Age of Jackson and Lincoln, from the War of 1812 to the Civil War*. Garden City, N.Y., 1966.
Wells, William V. *Walker's Expedition to Nicaragua*. New York, 1856.
White, William W. *The Confederate Veteran*. Confederate Centennial Studies No. 22. Tuscaloosa, Ala., 1962.
Wilcox, Cadmus M. *History of the Mexican War*. Washington, D.C., 1892.
Williams, David A. *David C. Broderick, a Political Portrait*. San Marino, Cal., 1969.
Williams, John J. *The Isthmus of Tehuantepec: Being the Results of a Survey for a Railroad to Connect the Atlantic and Pacific Oceans, Made by the Scientific Commission under the Direction of Major J.G. Barnard*. New York, 1852.
Williams, Mary W. *Anglo-American Isthmian Diplomacy, 1815–1915*. Washington, D.C., 1916.
Wilson, Edmund. *Patriotic Gore*. New York, 1962.

Wilson, Howard L. "Buchanan's Proposed Intervention in Mexico." *American Historical Review* 5 (1900): 687–701.

Woodward, Arthur, ed. *The Republic of Lower California, 1853–1854. In the Words of Its State Papers, Eyewitnesses, and Contemporary Reporters*. Los Angeles, 1966.

Wyllys, Rufus K. *The French in Sonora, 1850–1854*. University of California Publications in History, vol. 21. Berkeley, 1932.

______. "The French of California and Sonora." *Pacific Historical Review* 1 (1932): 337–59.

______. "Henry A. Crabb—a Tragedy of the Sonora Frontier." *Pacific Historical Review* 9 (1940): 183–94.

______. "The Republic of Lower California, 1853–1854." *Pacific Historical Review* 2 (1933): 194–213.

Index

H

I

S